SELECTED PHYSICAL QUANTITIES AND MEASUREMENT UNITS

Physical quantity	Quantity symbol	Measurement unit	Unit symbol	Unit dimensions
Fundamental Units				
length	l	meter	m	m
mass	m	kilogram	kg	kg
time	t	second	sec	sec
electric charge	Q	coulomb	c	c
temperature	T	degree Kelvin	°K	°K
luminous intensity	I	candle	cd	cd
Derived Units				
acceleration	a	meter per second per second	m/sec^2	m/sec^2
area	A	square meter	m^2	m^2
capacitance	C	farad	f	$c^2\,sec^2/kg\,m^2$
density	D	kilogram per cubic meter	kg/m^3	kg/m^3
electric current	I	ampere	a	c/sec
electric field intensity	$\mathscr{E}$	newton per coulomb	n/c	$kg\,m/c\,sec^2$
electric resistance	R	ohm	Ω	$kg\,m^2/c^2\,sec$
emf	E	volt	v	$kg\,m^2/c\,sec^2$
energy	E	joule	j	$kg\,m^2/sec^2$
force	F	newton	n	$kg\,m/sec^2$
frequency	f	hertz	hz	sec^{-1}
heat	Q	joule	j	$kg\,m^2/sec^2$
illumination	E	lumen per square meter	lm/m^2	$cd\,sr/m^2$
inductance	L	henry	h	$kg\,m^2/c^2$
luminous flux	Φ	lumen	lm	$cd\,sr$
magnetic flux	Φ	weber	wb	$kg\,m^2/c\,sec$
magnetic flux density	B	weber per square meter	wb/m^2	$kg/c\,sec$
potential difference	V	volt	v	$kg\,m^2/c\,sec^2$
power	P	watt	w	$kg\,m^2/sec^3$
pressure	p	newton per square meter	n/m^2	$kg/m\,sec^2$
velocity	v	meter per second	m/sec	m/sec
volume	V	cubic meter	m^3	m^3
work	W	joule	j	$kg\,m^2/sec^2$

Modern Physics

The Holt Modern Physics Program
WILLIAMS, TRINKLEIN, METCALFE

Modern Physics (STUDENT TEXT)
Modern Physics (TEACHER'S GUIDE)
Exercises and Experiments in Physics
Test in Physics

Modern Physics

JOHN E. WILLIAMS
FREDERICK E. TRINKLEIN
H. CLARK METCALFE

Holt, Rinehart and Winston, Publishers
New York   Toronto   London   Sydney

JOHN E. WILLIAMS, 25702 Via Viento. Mission Viejo, CA 92675; formerly teacher of chemistry and physics at Newport Harbor High School, Newport Beach, California and Head of the Science Department, Broad Ripple High School, Indianapolis, Indiana.

FREDERICK E. TRINKLEIN, Dean of Faculty and Physics Instructor, Long Island Lutheran High School, Brookville, New York, and Adjunct Professor, Physical Science Department, Nassau Community College, Garden City, New York.

H. CLARK METCALFE, P.O. Box V2, Wickenburg, Arizona, 85358; formerly teacher of chemistry at Winchester-Thurston School, Pittsburgh, Pennsylvania and Head of the Science Department, Wilkinsburg Senior High School, Wilkinsburg, Pennsylvania.

The cover design of Modern Physics 1976 is a graphic representation of The Second Law of Thermodynamics, one of the most powerful of all concepts in physics, particularly in terms of its philosophical implications. The cover depicts the connection between the thermodynamic concept of entropy and the statistical concept of disorder. The cover design is by the firm of Pellegrini, Kaestle, and Gross, Inc.

Acknowledgment of source appears with each photograph in the text. The photos credited to Ken Chen and Alex Mulligan were taken for Holt, Rinehart and Winston at the Long Island Lutheran High School, Brookville, New York where these photographers are students.

Preface

MODERN PHYSICS 1976 is the latest revision of a textbook series that was first published more than 50 years ago. These many editions of MODERN PHYSICS have served more teachers and students than any other beginning physics text published in the United States. Many of today's scientists and technicians owe their careers to the interest and foundation in physics that a skillful teacher established using an edition of this book.

To achieve such success, each edition of MODERN PHYSICS had to be effective with a constantly changing population of teachers and students. With the 1976 edition, MODERN PHYSICS continues to evolve, appropriately guided by input from several sources:

1. *The authors are experienced classroom teachers.* They teach at the levels for which this beginning text is designed—the secondary and junior college levels. They are familiar with the needs, interests, and abilities of today's students. Questions, problems, exercises, experiments, and test items are continuously classroom tested for effectiveness.

2. *Each edition is reviewed by recognized authorities in the field.* For the 1976 edition, these reviewers were: Fernando B. Morinigo, Professor of Physics at California State University; James B. Rothschild, formerly a high school physics teacher and presently Visiting Lecturer in Mathematics at Rutgers University; Mario Iona, Professor of Physics and Astronomy at the University of Denver. Professor Iona is well-known as the editor of the "Would You Believe?" column on textbook errors in *The Physics Teacher* and has written numerous articles and conference papers on the subject. The authors are especially indebted to these critics who were kind enough to read the entire manuscript or special parts of it. Their many valuable suggestions and criticisms are greatly appreciated.

3. *Input from the classroom is encouraged.* Through interviews, questionnaires, and classroom visits, many useful suggestions were obtained from teachers and students. These suggestions were evaluated by the authors and the editor. Many changes have resulted from this input; but, proven methods have been retained. We urge all who use MODERN PHYSICS to submit any suggestions or criticism that will help to improve any part of this learning system.

MODERN PHYSICS 1976 strikes a realistic balance between physics theory and practical applications. This balance efficiently meets college requirements. At the same time, a wide variety of topics gives teachers great flexibility of selection for students with varied interests and abilities.

The *Table of Contents* is designed to serve as a study guide. Each topic listed there is developed in a separate section in the text. In addition, each section title in the text is printed in the margins in a second color for easy reference. Important terms, laws, and definitions are printed in *italic* and **bold faced type** for emphasis and rapid review. Example problems for all unfamiliar mathematical concepts are worked out, step by step, to ensure that students grasp the concepts involved.

A *Mathematics Refresher* section precedes the *Appendix*. This section presents a brief review of the mathematical skills required for successful problem solving. *Appendix A* presents a summary of all important equations in the text, given in the sequence in which they appear. Also, there is a notation for each equation indicating the chapter and section where it is first used. *Appendix B* provides twenty-four tables of useful data including a table of trigonometric functions and a table of logarithms.

Some of the changes from previous editions include an increase in historical material and more physics career information. Chapter 1 has been completely rewritten as an interesting and logical introduction to the course. Vectors are introduced in Chapter 2 before they are applied to force and velocity problems in Chapters 3 to 5. Simple navigational problems are used because this application of vectors is relatively easy to understand. Motion is completely developed in Chapter 3 before dynamics, the explanation of motion. This sequence more closely follows the historical development of these topics and is easier for most students to learn. For the same reason, addition of vectors precedes resolution of vectors. Similarly, many other sections of the text have been reorganized and rewritten to increase readability.

A new feature of the 1976 edition is the photo essays. These essays introduce physics-related topics in an informal way. They also add an historical flavor, provide visual variety, and emphasize the important role of women in physics.

The authors wish to acknowledge the efforts of Richard Gerfin who prepared the manuscript for the Teacher's Guide.

JOHN E. WILLIAMS, FREDERICK E. TRINKLEIN, H. CLARK METCALFE

Contents

DOING PHYSICS

Chien-Shiung Wu, an experimental physicist, works on a part of a particle accelerator in her laboratory at Columbia University. Dr. Wu is well-known for an experiment that disproved a basic principle of physics. She has many other achievements to her credit, mainly in the fields of subatomic particles.

Robert Kelly, TIME-LIFE Books

The photos on these pages show a few of the many people who have found satisfying careers in the field of physics. In addition to earning a living, many have made useful products and solved interesting problems. Some have achieved fame for their discoveries.

Cornell University

(Above) Hans Bethe is a theoretical physicist and Professor of Physics at Cornell University. He received a Nobel Prize in physics in 1967 for originating the theory (with Walter Heitler) of the source of the sun's energy: Matter is converted into energy by fusing lighter elements into heavier ones.

(Right) Marie Telkes, Adjunct Professor of Energy Conversion at the University of Delaware, has been a leader in solar energy research. Dr. Telkes has designed, constructed, and evaluated solar stills, dryers, ovens, thermoelectric generators, and water-heaters. Houses have been built using her solar energy conversion and thermal storage systems.

University of Delaware

(Left) Christine Kostek and David Anderson, graduate students in physics, discuss David's doctoral research at Columbia University. He is developing a sensitive X-ray detector for a rocket flight to observe a neutron star, a possible "black hole" candidate. After serving in the Navy on the atomic submarine *U.S.S. Abraham Lincoln,* David graduated from the University of Washington at Seattle with a Bachelor's degree in Physics and Astronomy. Christine graduated from Union Catholic High School and Mary Washington College of the University of Virginia. She has not yet decided upon her area of special interest in physics.

University of California, San Diego

(Above) Maria Goepert Mayer (1906-1972), a theoretical physicist, shared a Nobel Prize in 1963. She developed the shell theory of atomic nuclei. Dr. Mayer is one of two women to be awarded a Nobel Prize in physics. The other was Marie Curie.

Grumman, Bob Settles

(Above) Bob Schulte is using a data accumulation system at Grumman Aerospace. Dr. Schulte received a Bachelor of Science degree in Physics from Thomas More College, a Master of Science degree in Physics from the University of Kentucky, and a Ph.D. in Nuclear Physics from the University of Kentucky.

Joe Chang is working on a Van de Graaff accelerator at Grumman Aerospace. He received a Bachelor of Science degree in Engineering from Taiwan College, a Master of Science and a Ph.D. degree in Physical Chemistry from the University of Notre Dame.

Grumman, Bob Settles

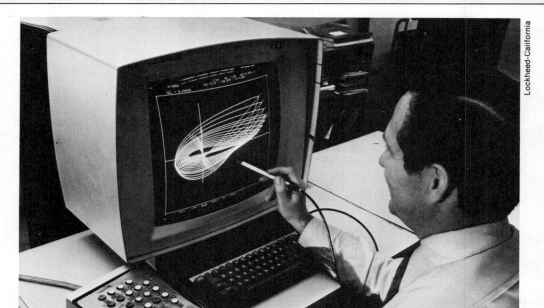

Donald Sherlock is using a computer to develop the surfaces and produce the "loft" and "isometric drawings" for the windmill airfoil pictured in construction and completed at the top of page 20. After graduating from Los Angeles Valley College, where he majored in chemistry and physics, he has continued his education by attending classes offered by the Scientific and Technical Training Group at Lockheed-California Company.

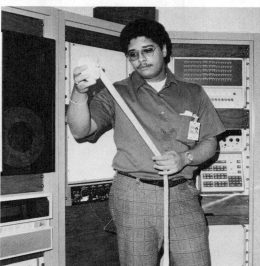

(Above) Alan Berry is a computer technician associated with the Research Department at Grumman Aerospace. He has an A.A. degree from Suffolk Community College.

(Left) Ed Kamykowski is working on a sputtering unit which is used to evaporate metals at Grumman Aerospace. Dr. Kamykowski received a Bachelor of Physics degree from Loyola University in Chicago and a Ph.D degree in Physics from the University of Notre Dame.

Chapter 1

Physics: The Science of Energy

PHYSICS IN TODAY'S WORLD

The use of energy is growing at an incredible rate. In the United States alone, energy demands have increased more than 250 percent since 1940. The increase may be even more rapid in the years ahead (Fig. 1-1). Many other countries are experiencing a similar growth in energy needs.

Figure 1-1 also shows that the energy demands of the United States are growing much more rapidly than is the population itself. In other words, the use of energy per person is also rising. This increase is largely a result of the improvement in the standard of living. The switch from human power to machine power has increased productivity and provided us with more goods and leisure time. Unfortunately, the use of labor-saving devices places serious demands on our available energy supplies.

The wise use of existing energy resources is one answer to this problem. By avoiding unnecessary uses of energy for heating, lighting, air conditioning, and transportation, serious energy shortages can be prevented.

Conservation of energy is only a partial answer, however. New energy sources must be found and developed in order to achieve and maintain a desirable living standard for the growing population of the world.

Actually, there is no shortage of energy at all. The sun floods the earth with enough radiant energy every day to supply the whole world's needs many times over. In fact, it has been calculated that present worldwide power demands could be met if we could completely convert into electrical power the solar energy falling on a plot of ground near the equator a mere 125 miles square. It has also been estimated that the Gulf Stream in the

1.1 Energy, more energy

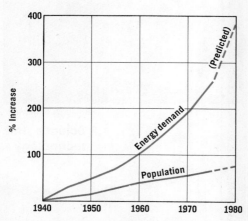

1-1 Energy demand and population growth in the U.S. since 1940.

3

1-2a This industrial-scale solar heating facility completed in 1975, is located on the roof of General Electric's Valley Forge Space Center. It will save about 12,000 gallons of fuel oil annually.

General Electric

1-2b Artist's conception of a microwave satellite. A device of this type may some day help to reduce the energy shortage by converting solar energy to microwaves and transmitting them to receiving stations on the earth.

Arthur D. Little, Inc.

1.2 Science and technology

Atlantic Ocean transports enough warm water to generate the electric energy needs of the United States many times over.

The shortage lies in our knowledge and our means to convert the ample energy supplies in and around our planet into usable forms. However, some very promising possibilities are beginning to emerge. For instance, the large-scale conversion of solar energy is being explored in the following ways:

— Heating and cooling of buildings by means of panels that use the sun's radiation (Fig. 1-2a)
— Generating electricity from solar heat
— Converting sunlight directly into electricity with solar cells
— Extracting solar heat from ocean water
— Converting solar energy into combustible fuels using bacteria
— Transmitting power from collecting panels on orbiting satellites (Fig. 1-2b)

The successful completion of these projects will require large expenditures of money as well as the close cooperation of government and private industry.

The discovery and utilization of new sources of energy is also a good example of the vital teamwork between scientists and technologists. Briefly stated, *science* is the search for relationships that explain and predict the behavior of the observable universe. *Technology* is the application of these relationships to our needs and goals.

The complementary work of scientists and technologists is also referred to, respectively, as *research* and *development* (sometimes called R and D). Both government and private industry allocate large sums of money to support the research and development activities of scientists and engineers. Without such support, there would be little improvement in the processes, products, and services that are derived from these activities.

So the struggle to keep pace with rising energy needs must first be won through research and development. For example, if the transmission of solar energy from earth satellites is to become practical, complex and difficult problems must first be solved by both science and technology. Research scientists must determine the principles that underlie the large-scale and long-distance transmission of energy through space. Then, technologists must develop pilot projects. And finally, they must build the full-scale equipment that will efficiently put the scientific principles into practice. A project such as this will require the invention of many completely new devices and procedures.

In science, *a **law** (or **principle**) is a statement that describes a natural phenomenon.* Unlike laws that *restrict* behavior (i.e., traffic laws), scientific laws *describe* behavior. For example, Jacques Charles (1746–1823) observed, under certain controlled conditions, a relationship between the temperature and the volume of most gases. This regular behavior of gases, which you will study in greater detail in Chapter 8, is now known as Charles' law. A scientific law, particularly in physics, may be stated in words but is usually expressed by a mathematical equation relating the natural phenomenon to the various factors that cause it.

*A **theory** is a reasonable explanation of a series of observed phenomena.* A theory often involves an imaginary *model* that helps scientists picture the way an observed phenomenon could be produced. A good example of this is our modern atomic theory which you will study in Chapters 7, 23, 24, and 25. Another example is the kinetic molecular theory. In this theory, gases are pictured as being made up of many small particles called molecules that are in constant motion (kinetic). You will study the kinetic molecular theory in Chapter 7.

A useful theory, in addition to explaining past observations, serves to predict behavior which has not as yet been observed. After a theory has been publicized, scientists design experiments to test the theory. For example, if matter is composed of small particles called atoms, it should behave in a certain way. If observations confirm the scientists' predictions, the theory is supported. If observations do not confirm the predictions, the scientists must search further. There may be a fault in the experiment. Or, the theory may have to be revised or rejected.

1.3 Scientific laws and theories

1.4 Scientific hypotheses

Albert Einstein (1879–1955) was one of the greatest theoretical scientists of all time. A theoretical scientist works mostly with ideas. He uses the results of other scientists' observations to develop his theories. Einstein's theories and predictions changed the course of modern science. Once he was asked to explain the way in which a scientist works. "If you want to know the essence of scientific method," he said, "don't listen to what a scientist may tell you. Watch what he does."

Science is a way of doing things, a way that involves imagination and creative thinking as well as collecting information and performing experiments. Facts (observations, principles, laws, and theories) by themselves are not science, but science deals with facts. The mathematician, Jules Henri Poincaré (1854–1912), said: "Science is built with facts just as a house is built with bricks, but a collection of facts cannot be called a science any more than a pile of bricks can be called a house."

Most scientists start an investigation by finding out what other scientists have learned about the problem. After the known facts have been gathered, the scientist comes to the part of the investigation that requires considerable imagination. Possible solutions to the problem are formulated. These possible solutions are called *hypotheses*.

For example, at the time of Johannes Kepler (1571–1630), most scientists believed that the planets move in circular orbits. But, the observed movements of the planets could not be satisfactorily explained by circular orbits. So Kepler formulated other hypotheses to explain planetary motion. The one that best fit the observations was: All the planets have elliptic orbits.

In a way, any hypothesis is a leap into the unknown. It extends the scientist's thinking beyond the known facts. The scientist plans experiments, calculations, and observations to test hypotheses. For, without hypotheses, further investigation lacks purpose and direction. In the case of Kepler, he continued his observations and calculations over a period of ten years after the announcement of his hypothesis about elliptic orbits. Eventually he was able to relate, in the form of an equation, the orbital speed of a planet and its distance from the sun.

When hypotheses are confirmed, they are incorporated into theories or laws. Thus, Kepler's hypotheses have become parts of what are now known as Kepler's laws of planetary motion.

Wherever a scientist must go to pursue an investigation becomes a laboratory. To an astronomer, the starry skies are a laboratory. The biologist may do experimental work in a swamp or an ocean. The physicist and chemist are often surrounded by a maze of apparatus housed in buildings designed specifically for their purposes (Fig. 1-3).

1-3 Thermonuclear fusion is a process occurring in the sun. Physicists at the Los Alamos Scientific Laboratory are trying to produce energy from a controlled thermonuclear fusion reaction by using a special light source. Here Dennis Gill and Clyde Reed adjust a part of the system that is used in these experiments.

Los Alamos Scientific Laboratory

1.5 Certainty in science

In a sense, there is no such thing as absolute truth in science. The validity of a scientific conclusion is always limited by the method of observation and, to a certain extent, by the person who made it. If a nurse took a patient's temperature with a thermometer that read 1° too high, the doctors might reach a wrong conclusion about the condition of the patient. Every scientist should keep in mind that the validity of his or her findings is limited by the precision of the apparatus used. Furthermore, not all limits are apparent to the experimenter. Galileo once tried to use lanterns to measure the speed of light between two distant points. It turned out that the time required to uncover and cover the lanterns was greater than the time required for light to travel the distance. His results were inconclusive.

This problem makes it doubly important to keep an open mind about the validity of scientific principles, theories, or hypotheses. A single crucial experiment can disprove any of them; but, no amount of experimentation can ever prove any one of them absolutely. When a scientist is unwilling to question a statement in science, no matter how well established it is, he or she has lost a very important attribute of a successful researcher. For this reason, the famous physicist, Niels Bohr (1885–1962), told his classes: "Every sentence I utter must be understood not as an affirmation but as a question."

The methods of science have been so successful in answering questions about the universe and in making life more pleasant and productive that it has been proposed that all areas of study should make use of the methods that scientists have found successful. This proposal suggests that the attitudes necessary for successful work in science could bear fruit in other areas as well. Among these attitudes are: imagination, a thirst for knowledge and understanding, a questioning mind, a regard for data and their meaning, the demand for proof, a respect for logical thinking, and the willingness to work with new ideas.

QUESTIONS

Group A
1. What is the relationship between a country's energy demand and its standard of living?
2. List two proposed solutions of the energy crisis.
3. Why is the heat of ocean water classified as a form of solar energy?
4. (a) Define the term "laboratory." (b) How does your school's physics laboratory fit this definition?
5. Distinguish between science and technology.

Group B
6. List areas and decisions in your life that cannot be dealt with according to scientific methods. See if your classmates agree with your list.
7. Edison once said: "Genius is 1% inspiration and 99% perspiration." Explain this remark in terms of the work of scientists and technologists.
8. How does a hypothesis become part of a law?
9. Define the term "truth" as it relates to science.
10. Name the Nobel prize winners in physics for the past five years and list the contribution for which each of them received the prize.

THE CONTENT OF PHYSICS

1.6 Matter
The best way to gain a concept of matter is to work with it and to describe its various forms. A description is not a definition in the real sense of the word, but it helps to bring an abstract idea down to familiar terms.

Matter can be described in terms of its measurable properties. In describing a person, you might refer to height, weight, eye color, hair color, etc. Similarly, all matter possesses properties. And just as a person can be identified by listing various properties, so a specimen of matter can be singled out by listing its properties.

The number of properties that can be measured for specimens of matter is very large. Special handbooks of chemistry and physics devote hundreds of pages to listings of the properties of various kinds of matter.

In the study of physics, it is important to recognize the fact that unless a property can be measured and compared with some kind of standard it is of no use to the scientist. Without measurement there can be no science. And the more precisely a specific property is measured, the more completely matter can be described.

A basic property of matter is its *mass*. The mass of an object is a measure of the quantity of matter it contains. Mass measurements are based on the standard kilogram mass, which is kept in a special vault by the International Bureau of Standards in Sèvres, France (near Paris). Duplicates of this standard are stored in various places around the world, including the National Bureau of Standards near Washington, D.C. (Fig. 1-4).

But how does one determine the mass of an object? Is a comparison of size with the standard mass sufficient? Two objects may have the same apparent size, yet one may contain hollow spaces. Even if no holes can be seen, an object might simply have more matter within a space of the same size. A piece of brass and a piece of gold may have the same size and appearance, but they differ in mass.

Instead of size, we must turn to another property of matter —*inertia*. **Inertia** *is the property of matter that opposes any change in its state of motion.* Inertia shows itself when objects are standing still as well as when they are moving. A baseball in flight will keep moving unless something stops it. This does not mean that there are two kinds of inertia—a stationary kind and a moving kind; the same property of matter is merely showing itself in different circumstances.

The inertia of matter can be used to measure mass with a device called an inertia balance (Fig. 1-5). One end of the balance

1.7 Mass

National Bureau of Standards

1-4 The national standard of mass, kept near Washington, D.C., is made of a non-corrosive alloy.

1.8 Inertia

1-5 An inertia balance. When this instrument is set in horizontal motion (right), the period of vibration can be used to compare the magnitudes of masses attached to it.

Alex Mulligan

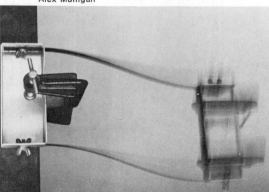

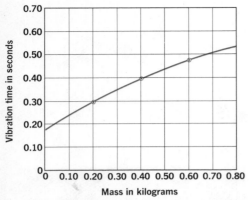

1-6 Graph of inertia balance data. If the vibration time of an object is measured, this graph can be used to find the mass of the object fastened to the pan.

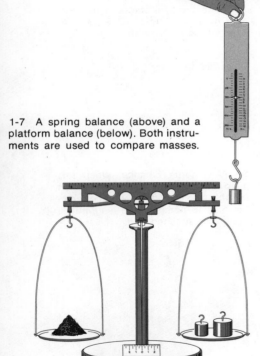

1-7 A spring balance (above) and a platform balance (below). Both instruments are used to compare masses.

is clamped to a table. The pan on the other end can be made to vibrate horizontally. The number of times this device vibrates in a second of time depends upon the length and stiffness of the two supporting metal blades and upon the total mass of the pan and any objects placed on it. Since the blades vibrate horizontally, the action of the inertia balance is entirely independent of gravity, which acts vertically. The more massive the pan and its contents, the slower will be the changes in their motion and the longer will be the time they will take to go through a complete vibration.

Unknown masses can be measured by comparing the amount of time required for each vibration with the time required by objects having known masses. First, several of the known objects are used and their vibration times are plotted as functions of their masses (Fig. 1-6). Then the vibration time of an unknown object is measured and its mass is read from the graph.

The graph in Fig. 1-6 is not a straight line. But by careful analysis of the data the relationship can be expressed by the following equation:

$$\frac{m_1}{m_2} = \frac{T_1{}^2}{T_2{}^2}$$

in which m_1 and m_2 are two masses (*including* the mass of the pan in each case) and T_1 and T_2 are their respective vibration times.

Masses can also be compared using either a spring balance or a beam balance (Fig. 1-7). These devices depend upon the pull of the earth's gravity for comparing masses. The stretch of a spring depends upon the amount of pull on the spring. The greater the pull, the greater is the amount of stretch. Since the pull of gravity is greater on a large mass than it is on a small mass, the spring in a spring balance stretches further for a large mass than it does for a small mass. The amount of stretch for standard masses can be marked on a scale. The stretch for an unknown mass can then be compared with the stretch produced by the standard mass.

In the case of a beam balance, a uniform beam is balanced at its center on a sharp blade. The blade acts as a pivot. If a mass is added to either side of the beam, the beam tips. Pans of equal masses are suspended from the beam at equal distances from the pivot. If an unknown mass is placed on one pan, known masses can be added to the other pan until the beam again balances. At that point, the known and the unknown masses are equal.

1.9 Mass density

A property of matter that is closely related to mass is *mass density*. **Mass density** refers to the amount of matter in a given amount of space and is defined as the *mass per unit volume of a* *substance.* Thus, if a substance occupies a space of 15 cm³ and has a mass of 45 g, its mass density is 3.0 g/cm³. The mathematical equation is:

$$\textit{mass density} = \frac{\textit{mass}}{\textit{volume}}$$

In giving the mass density of a substance, it is important to include the units (kilograms per cubic meter, grams per cubic centimeter, or some other unit of mass per unit of volume) in order that it may be compared with other values of mass densities. Mass density is an important quantity in describing the substance of which an object is composed.

Most properties of matter are not constant. They vary with the environment. Thus, water freezes when it gets cold enough and boils when it gets hot enough. In each case, the physical properties of the water have changed. Similarly, the mass density of a gas increases when it is placed under pressure and decreases when the pressure is reduced.

A quantity which is descriptive of the environment of an object, rather than of the object itself, is often referred to as a *condition.* Such quantities as temperature and pressure are conditions. Very often, a measurable property of an object will change if the conditions are changed.

There is a story that, when he was young, James Watt (1736-1819), became interested in steam power by watching water boil in a tea kettle over a fire. If the spout of the kettle was plugged, the lid rose. Perhaps this observation eventually led Watt to improvements of steam engines for which he is famous. In any case, this observation is a good example of how energy is related to work.

1.10 Energy

We say that work is done when a weight is lifted against the pull of the earth's gravity. Later, we will define work more carefully but, for now, this common use of the word will be adequate. We do work when we lift the lid of a tea kettle. When we plug the spout, the steam lifts the lid. Here, the work is done by the steam. So we reason that the steam in the kettle had the *capacity* for doing work before it lifted the lid. The steam had *energy.* **Energy**, then, *is a quantity that*, if the conditions are right, *has the capacity for doing work.* Since energy can often be transformed into mechanical work, the units we use for measuring energy are the same as the units of work.

Energy is sometimes quite noticeable because human beings are equipped with senses that are able to detect its presence in various forms. Our eyes respond to visible light. Our ears detect sound energy. Special nerves are sensitive to temperature, an indication of heat energy. Other nerves respond to electric energy.

Besides the forms of energy that can be directly detected by human senses, scientists have discovered other forms of energy. Special detecting and measuring instruments had to be developed to change these forms of energy into something that humans can sense. For example, humans cannot directly sense X rays, a form of energy similar to visible light. But X rays can affect a piece of photographic film. Under visible light, humans can look at a piece of exposed and developed X-ray film and tell where the X rays have affected the film. As another example, humans cannot directly sense small amounts of infrared radiation, an invisible form of energy similar to light. (We can feel large amounts of infrared radiation as heat.) However, a special thermometer exposed to infrared radiation registers an increase in temperature. Humans can observe the behavior of the thermometer and infer the presence of the invisible radiation. By means of devices such as these, scientists have extended the range and sensitivity of the human senses. Among the forms of energy that fall into this "extra-sensory" category are chemical energy, gravitational energy, nuclear energy, and forms of energy similar to light, like X rays and infrared rays, that humans cannot directly detect.

Energy is a concept that unifies physics. More specifically, it is the concern of physicists to follow and measure the course of energy from one form to another, for the forms of energy are mutually interchangeable. Take, for example, the energy you expend when you walk. Traced backwards, it came from the food you ate. The food got its energy from nutrients in the ground and radiations from the sun. The sun gets its energy from nuclear reactions in its interior, etc. Tracing your walking energy forward, the friction and motion of your feet on the ground heat the ground slightly, which radiates the heat into space and helps to evaporate water from the earth, which makes rain possible, etc.

1-8 An example of gravitational potential energy. The amount of energy of the books depends upon the zero level chosen for the experiment.

1.11 Potential energy

Two important forms of energy that an object may have are its energy of position and its energy of motion. The former is a form of *potential energy* while the latter is a form of *kinetic energy*. If a book is pushed off a desk top, it falls to the floor. While it is falling, it may strike some other object and give some of its energy to the other object. When the book is stopped by the floor, the rest of its kinetic energy is transformed into some other forms of energy such as sound and heat. The book acquired this energy when someone did the work of lifting it to the desk top. Thus, while it is on the desk top, the book has potential energy, or energy of position.

In a way, the floor is an arbitrary zero level for our example. If a hole were cut in the floor under the book, it would continue to fall and be able to do more work when its motion is stopped. For each problem in gravitational potential energy, an arbitrary zero level must be specified.

An object may also have potential energy which is not connected with gravitation in any way. For example, a compressed spring gets its energy from the push that is exerted on it to get it into a compressed position. This energy is called internal potential energy. Internal potential energy is not as easy to compute as the gravitational variety, since one must be familiar with the transformations of various forms of energy. Some of these forms of energy, especially those concerning the interior of the atom, can take the problem to the very frontiers of modern physics.

An interesting experiment in potential energy is to trace the energy in a compressed spring when it is dissolved by an acid while in the compressed position. Where will the potential energy go? What kind of control can you set up to verify your hypothesis? Discuss it with your classmates and see what you can propose. Then you might plan a laboratory experiment to test your ideas.

1.12 Kinetic energy

Every moving object has kinetic energy. This statement is the same as saying that everything has kinetic energy, because scientists believe that everything in the universe is moving in some way or other. Since the description of the motion of an object depends on another object in the universe designated as being "motionless," we are again faced with the necessity of choosing an arbitrary zero level or, in this case, an arbitrary stationary point. In ordinary, earthbound physics the surface of the earth is considered stationary. An object resting on the earth's surface is said to have zero kinetic energy even though the object rotates and revolves with the earth that moves in and among the galaxies.

There is a constant interplay between potential energy and kinetic energy in physics (Fig. 1-9). Consider the swinging of a pendulum. When the mass at the end of the string is at the top of its swing, it is momentarily stationary. At that point the energy of the mass is gravitational potential (except for internal energy). As the mass begins its downward swing, some of the gravitational potential energy changes into kinetic energy. At the bottom of the swing, which we will consider as the zero level for gravitational potential energy, the kinetic energy of the mass is at a maximum because it is moving at its maximum speed. As the mass swings up the other side of its arc, the energy interchange

Joel Gordon

1-9 Energy transformation. As the roller coaster and its occupants descend, their gravitational potential energy changes into kinetic energy.

is reversed. The total amount of energy is always the same — it is merely changing from one kind to another. This discussion demonstrates the *law of conservation of energy* — the total amount of energy of all kinds in a given situation is a constant.

1.13 Conservation of energy

The conservation of energy was demonstrated in a striking way by the classical experiments with heat energy conducted by Count Rumford and James Prescott Joule in the early part of the 19th century. At that time, most scientists thought of heat as a special kind of "fluid" called *caloric*, which was able to flow in and out of objects without affecting their weights. Count Rumford became interested in the caloric theory while supervising the boring of brass cylinders for the construction of cannon barrels (Fig. 1-10). Brass chips from these borings became so hot that cold water could be raised to the boiling point by throwing the chips into the water. Where did all this "caloric" come from?

According to the caloric theory, caloric is squeezed out of the brass during the boring. This meant that the chips did not have as much heat left in them as did hot brass pieces that had not been squeezed by the boring tool. But Count Rumford found that there was no difference in the heating ability of squeezed

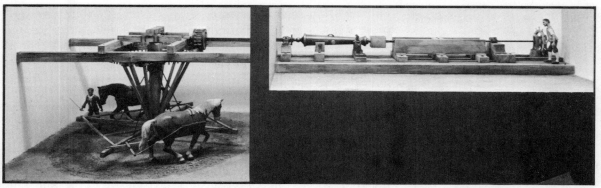

1-10 A model of Count Rumford's cannon-boring experiment. The cannon barrel was rotated against a stationary boring tool by a team of horses. Directly in front of the cannon is a small cubic container for the water used in the heat experiments.

or unsqueezed samples of brass. No "heating power" had been removed from the chips through the boring process.

Rumford then substituted a flat disc for the drill. Just by rubbing two pieces of metal together, he was able to show that the heat produced in the boring process did not depend on the amount of chips produced but only on how hard the horses pulled and the number of revolutions of the shaft. In other words, the heat was a result of the work done on the cannon barrel; it was not a substance (caloric) contained in the metal in a limited amount.

Joule continued the investigation of heat by establishing the exact relationship between heat and mechanical energy. He found that the amount of heat produced is determined by the amount of mechanical work done. This relationship will be discussed more fully in Chapter 9. The equivalence between heat and mechanical energy provided strong evidence that heat must be a form of energy. It also supported the theory that the total amount of energy remains constant when it is transformed from one kind to another.

1.14 Relation between matter and energy

So far we have been discussing matter and energy as though they were two entirely different entities. Yet, the two are usually inseparably related. Every object contains some kind of energy. Usually, the idea of energy is associated with some substance like a hot gas or an electrified object. In some cases it may even be necessary to associate energy with the empty space surrounding an electrified object.

In 1905, Einstein expressed the relationship between mass and energy with the following equation:

$$E = mc^2$$

in which E stands for units of energy (work units), m stands for mass, and c is the speed of light. Einstein developed this formula

Ernst Haas, Magnum

1-11 Albert Einstein developed the equations that show the relationship between matter and energy.

Table 1-1 RELATIVISTIC MASS

Speed of object (% of speed of light)	Relativistic mass (compared to rest mass)
0	1.00
25	1.03
50	1.15
75	1.51
80	1.67
85	1.88
90	2.30
95	3.16
99	7.07
99.9	22.4

entirely from theoretical considerations, and there was no way of verifying it in the laboratory at that time (Fig. 1-11). Recent experiments, however, have shown that such a relationship does exist.

Einstein's formula states that mass and energy are proportional to each other, that is, when one increases the other increases also; and when one decreases the other also decreases. The equation may also be interpreted to mean that a given amount of mass is equivalent to a certain amount of energy.

A simple example will serve to illustrate the relationship between mass and energy. When you throw a ball, you are imparting energy to it. Energy is transferred from you to the ball. The mass-energy equation says that while the ball is moving, its mass will be greater than it was while the ball was at rest. Both the energy and the mass of the ball have increased. The extra mass and energy of the ball both come from you.

When the object is at rest with respect to the observer and the observer's measuring instruments, the mass of the object is said to be the *rest mass*. When the object is moving, its mass increases. This new mass, which increases rapidly as the object approaches the speed of light, is called the *relativistic mass* because it is in keeping with Einstein's *theory of relativity*. In the mass-energy equation, m is the relativistic mass. Table 1-1 shows the relationship between the speed of an object and its relativistic mass.

Actually, what Einstein's equation means is that matter is merely one form of energy and that the two terms emphasize different aspects of the same quantity. This is one of the most important concepts of contemporary physics.

It should not be assumed, however, that Einstein's mass-energy equation is a proof of the conservation of matter and energy. The equation has value even if the matter and energy of the universe were constantly changing. The conservation laws rest on repeated measurements in the laboratory which show that mass and energy are not lost in chemical and physical changes. Some scientists think that the law of conservation may not hold for large energies and masses in outer space, but this hypothesis has not been verified. The deviations predicted by these scientists are too small for direct measurement with present instruments.

The relationship between matter and energy will become evident in the study of physics in still another way. We usually think of light energy in terms of waves and of matter in terms of particles. Actually, there are times when light acts as though it has granular properties. In other words, there are aspects of light that can be explained only by assuming that it is made up of discrete particles. Similarly, particles of matter exhibit wave properties. This wave-particle duality of nature is a key as well as a puzzle in physics, and scientists freely admit that they are far from understanding it completely. Perhaps you will play a role in unlocking this fundamental secret of nature.

The study of the physical universe is called *physical science*. *Chemistry* is a physical science. It deals with the composition of matter and reactions among various forms of matter. *Physics* is also a physical science. It is concerned with the relation between matter and energy. The ultimate goal of physics is to explain all processes and particles in terms of simple particles, processes, and interactions.

1.15 Subdivisions of physics

Since both chemistry and physics deal with matter, these two sciences overlap to some extent. But a distinguishing consideration in the study of physics always is the idea of energy: what it is, what form it takes, how it affects matter and how matter affects it, and how it can be changed from one form to another.

The study of physics can be subdivided in a number of ways. The sequence of topics followed in this book is one that has been used for many years because of its logical progression and because it leads from concepts that were developed many years ago to those at the very frontiers of physics.

The chapters in your text fall into four major categories: mechanics and heat, waves, electricity, and nuclear physics. The first category includes the study of motion, forces, work, power, and certain aspects of heat. These topics, and the ways in which they involve the transfer of energy, are considered in Chapters 3 through 9. (Chapter 2 describes measurement and problem solving, which are essential to the entire subject matter of physics.)

Waves are considered in Chapters 10 through 15. Sound energy and light energy are transmitted as waves. The nature of waves as a mechanism for energy transfer and the characteristics of sound and light comprise the subject matter of this section of your text.

Electricity involves a form of energy that is increasingly important to our way of life. In Chapters 16 to 22, the ways of generating and transmitting this vital commodity are explained. This section of the text also contains an introduction to the study of electronics, which is the basis for radio, television, and computers.

In the last three chapters of the book, the principles of *nuclear and particle physics* are introduced. It is here that the physicist tries to get to the very heart of the composition of matter and of the energy forms that bind the building blocks of the universe together. With topics ranging from "atom smashers" to the most

distant star systems, this part of the course is usually called
modern physics. Hopefully, as you reach this final section of the
course, you will have caught the excitement of physics, a subject
in which topics as well as possibilities are truly unlimited.

QUESTIONS

Group A
1. Distinguish between mass and inertia.
2. How does the mass of an object on the earth compare with the mass of the same object on the moon?
3. (a) Distinguish between properties and conditions. (b) Give examples of each.
4. What are the sources of energy, and how is the energy transformed, when you drive a car?
5. Classify the following as having mainly gravitational potential or mainly internal energy: (a) gasoline, (b) water behind a dam, (c) air in a tire, (d) a rocket in free flight, (e) gunpowder.
6. What limits the amount of heat energy that can be produced by the boring of a cannon barrel?
7. Define the law of conservation of energy.

Group B
8. How can Fig. 1-6 be used to find the mass of the balance pan used in the experiment?
9. Redraw Fig. 1-6 using values of T^2 instead of T. What is the shape of the resulting graph?
10. Why does it become increasingly difficult to increase the speed of an object as it approaches the speed of light?
11. In general, objects expand when they are heated. (a) How does this phenomenon show that heat is a form of energy? (b) How must your explanation be modified to fit objects which contract upon being heated?

MORE ENERGY

FOSSIL FUEL

Steel arms of a loading machine scoop up coal loosened by blasting. In the United States, the supply of coal is greater than oil. But, coal from many sources contains substances such as sulfur that pollute the atmosphere when the coal is burned. Economical processes for removing these substances would make coal a satisfactory substitute for low-sulfur oil as an energy source.

National Coal Association

Many sources of energy on the earth come directly or indirectly from energy radiated from the sun. Coal and oil, the fossil fuels, were formed from plants that captured energy from the sun millions of years ago. Hydroelectric power depends upon dammed-up rain water that was evaporated from the sea by solar energy. Winds and ocean currents, potential sources of additional energy, are caused by solar energy.

Some energy sources cannot be attributed to the sun. Nuclear energy comes from changing matter into energy. Geothermal energy (heat from the earth) uses heat locked in rocks since the earth was formed as a molten mass. The earth's rotation and the gravitational attraction between the earth and the moon moves large masses of water on the earth. These movements of water are called tides. In some places such as the Rance River in France, tides are usefully harnessed.

The amount of radiant energy we receive from the sun each day is limited. Also, the amount of fossil fuel is limited. Research efforts to supply more energy have aimed at increasing our supply of solar energy (see page 4), using our solar resources more efficiently, and increasing energy production from non-solar sources.

Centre National de la Recherche Scientifique, Font-Romeu Odeillo

Centre National de la Recherche Scientifique, Font-Romeu Odeillo

SOLAR FURNACE

(Above) Many moveable mirrors such as the one at the left, are mounted on a hillside facing south. These mirrors reflect the sun's rays into the large stationary parabolic mirror. (Left) High temperature experiments are conducted at the focus of the parabolic mirror.

WIND

Windmills first appeared in the 10th century and are still used today in localities with suitable weather. To improve efficiency, engineers have developed new windmill designs. (Left) This wind turbine generator has blades that are 62½ feet long. (Below right) This light-weight design has many blades mounted like the spokes in a bicycle wheel. Magnets for generating electricity are mounted in the outside rim. (Below left) Wind from any direction turns this windmill about a vertical axis.

Lockheed-California Co.

Lockheed-California Co.

20

NASA

Oklahoma State University

WATER

(Above left) This turbine, 33 feet in diameter is being lowered into place at Grand Coulee. (Above right) Aerial view of Glen Canyon Dam and powerplant. At the time this photograph was taken, a total of 53,400 cubic feet per second of water was going through the generating units. (Below left) Turbine with four variable shift blades at the Rance River Tidal Power Plant. The pitch of the blades and the guide-vane apparatus at the left are designed to be changed as the flow of the tide changes. (Below right) Four-lane highway, dam, and tidal power plant across the Rance River in France.

GEOTHERMAL

Natural steam occurs in a number of places around the world. It is formed when water runs over hot rock deep within the earth. This geothermal energy installation, The Geysers, is located in Sonoma County, California. It is the only geothermal power project in the United States and it is the world's largest. Wells bring the steam from the field to conventional steam turbines that drive the generators. Condensed steam is returned to the field for reheating by the rock.

PG&E News Bureau

KMS Fusion, Inc.

NUCLEAR

Many physicists are working to discover ways to control and harness the reaction that gives the sun its energy. High temperatures (about 50,000,000°C) are necessary. In this device (left below) high-energy light is fired at a small target in the center of the reaction chamber (left). Apparatus similar to that shown in Fig. 1-3, page 7, furnishes the light. Efforts to use a "magnetic bottle" to reach this temperature and contain the reaction are described on pages 613–614. (Below right) A nuclear reaction vessel being lowered into place in a power plant. Heat from the reaction contained in this vessel will produce steam to drive turbines and generators.

KMS Fusion, Inc.

Atomic Industrial Forum

Chapter 2

Measurement and Problem Solving

UNITS OF MEASUREMENT

Over the centuries, many different systems of measurement have been in use throughout the world, but the one that is best suited to modern measurements is the *metric system*. Developed in France near the end of the 18th century, the decimal basis of the metric system makes it as convenient to measure physical quantities as to make change with pennies, dimes, and dollars. Congress made the metric system legal for use in this country in 1866, and almost all the other countries of the world have adopted it as their official system of measurement. Legislation to convert to the metric system in the U.S. has not been passed by the Congress as of this writing. But, American auto makers went metric for the 1975 models in anticipation of the coming changeover.

In using a system of measurement, it is important to distinguish between *physical quantities* and *units of measurement*. Physical quantities are aspects of the universe. They can be measured by any desired units of measurement. For example, *length* is a physical quantity, while the metric unit that is used to measure length is the *meter*.

All units of measurement in a system are based on a few fundamental units. Other units are then derived from these basic units. For example, since length and time are such important physical quantities, some natural length and time period could be chosen as fundamental units. A unit based on a natural phenomenon is called a *conceptual unit*.

Another way to establish fundamental units is to choose arbitrary values for them. For example, a certain quantity of matter

2.1 Physical quantities and units

Ken Chen

These stamps are part of the Australian program of conversion from the English to the metric system of measurement.

23

can be selected as a unit of mass. A unit established in this way is called a *standard unit*. The disadvantage of the standard unit is that the arbitrary standard must be carefully preserved so that it can be used to keep the system accurate. If it is lost, the entire system is endangered. A conceptual unit, on the other hand, can be reestablished at any time.

Physicists have recognized that the physical quantities of mechanics can all be expressed in terms of the three fundamental quantities: *mass, length*, and *time*. The units by which these quantities are measured are established by international agreements. The definitions of other physical quantities provide the rules for expressing their values in terms of the fundamental quantities that can be measured.

For example, velocity can be defined in terms of length and time. To express a velocity, it is only necessary to know how to measure length and time. Similarly, momentum can be defined as the product of a mass and its velocity. To express momentum as a physical quantity, it is only necessary to know how to measure mass and velocity. Measuring these quantities is the same as measuring mass, length, and time.

When studying heat, it will be necessary to introduce a unit for *temperature*, another fundamental physical quantity. Later, during our study of light, we will introduce a fifth fundamental unit for measuring *luminous intensity*. Another fundamental unit we will use is the one for the measurement of *electric charge*. A seventh measures *molecular quantity*. The units for these seven fundamental quantities provide the base from which the units for the other physical quantities can be derived.

Since the exchange of scientific information is world-wide today, international committees have been set up to standardize the names and symbols for physical quantities. In 1960, an International System of Units (abbreviated SI for Système Internationale) was adopted by the 11th General Conference of Weights and Measures. The quantities, units, and symbols on the inside front cover of this book and in Appendix B are based on the International System of Units. It is not necessary to memorize these words and symbols at this time, but you should become accustomed to their use as they are introduced in this and later chapters. In a few cases, the symbols used in this text are different from the corresponding SI symbols. This has been done in order to simplify certain discussions for beginning physics students. For example, the SI abbreviation for "second" is s. Since *s* is also used to designate distance, however, this book uses the abbreviation sec for "second." For similar reasons, we will not always follow the SI rule that units named after people should be abbreviated with capital letters.

Table 2-1   METRIC SYSTEM PREFIXES

Prefix	Symbol	Factor
tera (*tair*-ah)	T	10^{12}
giga (*gig*-ah)	G	10^{9}
mega	M	10^{6}
kilo	k	10^{3}
hecto	h	10^{2}
deka	da	10^{1}
deci	d	10^{-1}
centi	c	10^{-2}
milli	m	10^{-3}
micro	μ	10^{-6}
nano (*nan*-oh)	n	10^{-9}
pico (*pea*-koh)	p	10^{-12}
femto (*fem*-toh)	f	10^{-15}
atto (*at*-toh)	a	10^{-18}

In the United States, the government agency that deals with standards of measurement is the National Bureau of Standards. It is a goal of the National Bureau of Standards, and its counterparts in other countries, to establish reproducible standard units. This has now been accomplished for all of the fundamental units except the unit of mass.

The International System of Units is also called the MKS system, because three of its fundamental units are the meter, the kilogram, and the second. The first of these, the *meter* (m), began as a conceptual unit. It was defined as 1/10,000,000th of the distance from the equator to the north pole along the meridian running through Paris. Soon a difficulty arose. Scientists found that they were able to measure the standard meter bar with a greater degree of precision than they were able to measure distances along the surface of the earth. This difficulty made it necessary to establish an arbitrary length for the meter as a standard. Accordingly, a special bar was marked and kept in a vault near Paris. Duplicate bars were made and placed in various capitals around the world.

2.2 Length

Scientific progress once again made the standard meter obsolete. Not only was it time-consuming to check meter bars against a single standard, but the original shortcoming of the meter cropped up again. Scientists were able to measure other distances more precisely than they could measure the distance between two marks on a standard meter bar. In 1960 the standard of length was changed once more, this time using a reproducible laboratory experiment. When an electric discharge is maintained in a sample of the gas krypton-86, the gas glows with a characteristic color somewhat similar to that of neon (Fig. 2-1). This color, produced by the atoms of krypton, consists of several different wavelengths of light. One wavelength is an orange-red light. *The standard of length is now based on the wavelength of the orange-red light emitted by krypton-86 atoms.*

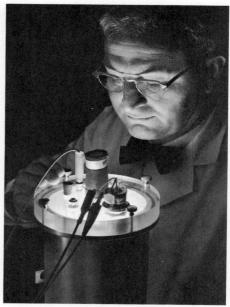

1 meter = 1,650,763.73 wavelengths in a vacuum of orange-red light of krypton-86

The number of wavelengths of light in a given distance can be counted by the use of an instrument known as an optical interferometer. This instrument is accurate to about two parts in one billion, or about one meter of uncertainty in measuring the distance between the earth and the moon.

Scientists are already at work on an even more accurate standard. One way of providing such a meter of the future is to use a laser beam. Accuracy of better than one part in a trillion is theoretically possible with this device.

2-1 The standard of length. Emissions from this lamp containing the gas krypton-86 are used to obtain a very precise value for the standard meter.

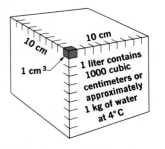

2-2 Relationship among metric units of length, volume, and mass.

The metric units for the measurement of area and volume are derived from the meter (Fig. 2-2). A rectangular floor 3 meters long and 2 meters wide has an area of 6 square meters. Similarly, a rectangular tank 2 meters long, 1 meter wide, and 3 meters deep has a volume of 6 cubic meters.

The liter is a special name for a cubic decimeter (1000 cm³). Since one milliliter (1 ml) is 1/1000th of a liter, it is equivalent to one cubic centimeter (1 cm³). In liquid measurements, it is helpful to remember that it takes about 15 to 20 drops of water (depending on the shape of the dropper) to make one milliliter and that a liter is slightly larger than a U.S. liquid quart.

2.3 Mass

The MKS standard of mass is the *kilogram* (kg). It was originally defined as the mass of 1000 cm³ (cubic centimeters) of water at its temperature of maximum density, 4° Celsius. Today the standard of mass is the mass of a certain cylinder designated as one kilogram. This standard is kept near Paris. Copies are located in other capitals of the world. The gram (g) is 1/1000th kilogram. One milliliter of water has a mass of approximately one gram. An American nickel coin has a mass of about 5 g.

It is interesting to note that mass units can be compared with each other and with the standard mass with a possible error of only a few parts in a billion. This difference corresponds to the mass of the ink in a single comma when compared to the mass of the ink in an entire book.

Scientists also use another mass unit suitable for comparing the masses of different atoms. This unit is needed in work with chemical and nuclear reactions. It is called an *atomic mass unit* and is defined as 1/12th of the mass of an atom of carbon-12, the most abundant form of that element. This unit can be related to the standard kilogram. You will work with atomic mass units in Chapters 7, 23, and 24.

The mass of an object should not be confused with its *weight.* Weight is the gravitational pull of the earth on an object. Weight varies at various locations around the earth, but the mass of an object does not depend on its position.

The unit of force in the MKS system is the newton (n). At New York City, a force of 9.803 n must be exerted to support a mass of one kilogram. For other locations in the United States, forces ranging from about 9.79 n to 9.82 n are needed to support one kilogram. The relation, 9.80 n per kilogram, is a useful approximation.

The above differences in the weight of a kilogram may give the impression that the newton is only loosely or approximately defined. That is not the case. A complete description of how the newton is determined will be given in Chapter 3. It will then become clear why the support of a given mass may require the exertion of different forces at different locations.

The unit of time is the *second* (sec). It was originally a conceptual unit based on the motion of the earth. The average time required for a single rotation of the earth in relation to the sun is called a mean solar day. The day is divided into 24 hours, the hour into 60 minutes, and the minute into 60 seconds. Hence, the second was defined as 1/86,400th of a mean solar day.

But again the progress of science made it necessary to set up a more precise standard. Careful measurements showed that the rotation of the earth varies not only from day to day but from year to year. In other words, a mean solar day was not the same in 1950 as it was in 1940, and scientists could not use it to check the accuracy of their time units. So in 1956 the standard second was changed to 1/31,556,925.9747th of the year 1900 at 12 hours ephemeris time, an astronomical term that specifies the exact starting time of the year.

Today we have a conceptual time unit that is reproducible in laboratories throughout the world. This new standard is based on the vibrations of cesium atoms. Radio waves of a certain frequency can cause cesium atoms to vibrate. Sensitive instruments can control the radio transmitter to·keep it in step with these vibrations. Outside influences such as changes in gravity do not affect these vibrations. Therefore, the vibrations of these atoms are used in a *cesium clock*. In 1964, this clock was adopted as providing the international standard of time.

1 second = 9,192,631,770 Cs-133 vibrations

2-3 The standard of time. The second is defined in terms of the vibrations of cesium-133 atoms. This instrument is a clock based on the cesium standard.

U.S. Department of Commerce

QUESTIONS

Group A
1. (a) Distinguish between a conceptual unit in physics and a standard unit. (b) Give an example of each.
2. (a) List the fundamental physical quantities. (b) List several derived quantities.
3. (a) Why has the standard meter bar become obsolete? (b) What is the present standard of length? (c) What units are derived from it?
4. What is the relationship between a cubic centimeter and milliliter?
5. Distinguish between mass and weight.
6. (a) What is the connection between the second and the meter? (b) between the second and the kilogram?
7. Define the present standard of time.

Group B
8. What is the connection between the metric system and the SI?
9. How is the standard of mass related to the standard of length?
10. What is the present status of American plans to switch to the metric system? Consult the *Reader's Guide to Periodical Literature* in the library in order to obtain the latest information on this question.
11. (a) Name two standards of mass. (b) List one way in which the two are related and one way in which they are different.

PROBLEMS

Group A
1. How many mm are there in (a) 2 cm? (b) 3 m? (c) 5 km?
2. Compute the number of ml in (a) 3 liters (b) 20 liters.
3. Find the number of liters in 10 m³.
4. How many g are there in (a) 0.7 kg? (b) 8 kg?
5. Express your height in meters and your mass in kilograms.
6. The top of a square table is 85 cm on one edge. What is its area?
7. A container is 0.80 m long, 25 cm wide, and 95 mm deep. What is the volume of the tank in liters?

Group B
8. A cubic container holds 1.00 kg of water. (a) What is the volume of the container in liters? (b) in m³? (c) What is the length of one side in meters?
9. The mass of 1.00 cm³ of sea water is 1.04 g. What is the mass of one liter of sea water?
10. A cable has a mass of 4.52 g per centimeter. What is the mass of 15 km of the cable?
11. Compute the number of seconds in a year of 365.24 days.

MAKING AND RECORDING MEASUREMENTS

The measurement of a physical quantity is always subject to some degree of uncertainty. There are several reasons for this: the limitations inherent in the construction of the measuring instrument or device, the conditions under which the measurement was made, and the different ways in which the person uses or reads the instrument. Consequently, in reporting the measurements made during a scientific experiment, it is necessary to indicate the degree of uncertainty so far as it is known.

One way to express the uncertainty of a measurement is in terms of *accuracy*. **Accuracy** *refers to the closeness of a measurement to the accepted value for a specific physical quantity*. It is expressed as either an *absolute* or *relative* error. Absolute error is the actual difference between the measured value and the accepted value. The equation for absolute error is

$$E_a = |O - A|$$

where E_a is the absolute error, O is the observed (measured) value, and A is the accepted value. (The vertical bars mean that only the absolute value is used, regardless of sign.)

Relative error is expressed as a percentage, and it is therefore often called the percentage error. It is calculated as follows:

$$E_r = \frac{E_a}{A} \times 100\%$$

where E_r is the relative error, E_a the absolute error, and A the accepted value.

In common usage, accuracy and *precision* are frequently synonymous terms. But in science it is important to make a distinction between them. You should learn to use them correctly and consistently (Fig. 2-4). In contrast with accuracy, **precision** *is the agreement among several measurements that have been made in the same way*. It tells how reproducible the measurements are and is expressed in terms of *deviation*. As in the case of accuracy, deviations in precision can be given as absolute or relative (percentage).

Absolute deviation *is the difference between a single measured value and the average of several measurements made in the same way*, or

$$D_a = |O - M|$$

where D_a is the absolute deviation, O is the observed or measured value, and M is the mean or average of several readings.

2.5 Accuracy and precision

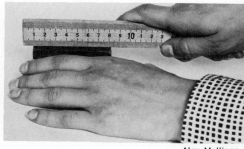

Alex Mulligan

The accuracy of a measurement depends upon the instrument used and the care with which the reading is made.

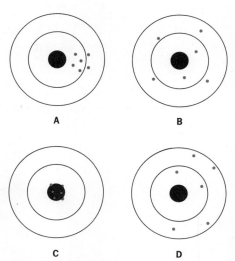

2-4 Distinction between accuracy and precision. Six shots were fired at each target. In A, the precision is good, but the accuracy is poor. In B, the average accuracy is good but the precision is poor. In C, both the accuracy and precision are good. In D, both the accuracy and the precision are poor.

Relative deviation is the percentage average deviation of a set of measurements and is calculated as follows:

$$D_r = \frac{D_a \text{ (average)}}{M} \times 100\%$$

where D_r is the relative deviation, D_a is the absolute deviation, and M is the mean or average of the set of readings.

Since relative deviation is based upon percent, it gives a more realistic description of precision than does the absolute deviation.

The precision of your laboratory measurements will be governed by the instruments at your disposal. In a measuring instrument, the degree of precision obtainable is called the *tolerance* of the device. Any figure for the tolerance of an instrument indicates only the limitations of the instrument. The instrument maker assumes that the instrument is used properly and that human errors are held to a minimum. The usual platform balance, for example, has a tolerance of ± 0.1 gram. Some modern research instruments are almost unbelievably precise (Fig. 2-5).

A third way of indicating the precision of a measurement is by means of *significant figures*. **Significant figures** *are those digits in a number that are known with certainty plus the first digit that is uncertain.* For example, if the length of a laboratory table was measured with a meter stick graduated in millimeters and found to be 1523.5 millimeters, the measurement has 5 significant figures. The 5 is the uncertain digit. It was an estimation of the value between two millimeter marks on the meter stick.

In working with significant figures, you can usually assume to know the last digit of a number, the uncertain digit, to within ± 1. For instance, when the value for π is given as 3.14 you can assume that the true value lies between 3.13 and 3.15.

The following rules will help you to understand how significant figures are used in physics problems. Even these rules do not cover all possible cases, however. Common sense will usually show how a specific case should be handled.

1. All nonzero digits are significant: $112.6°$ C has four significant figures.

2. All zeros between two nonzero digits are significant: 108.005 m has six significant figures.

3. Zeros to the right of a nonzero digit, but to the left of an understood decimal point, are not significant unless specifically indicated to be significant. In this book, the rightmost such zero which is significant is indicated by a *bar* placed above it: 109,000 km contains *three* significant figures; $109,0\overline{0}0$ km contains *five* significant figures.

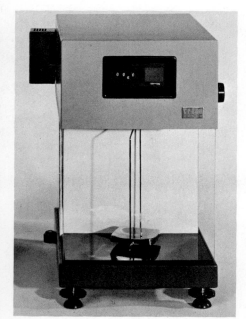

Cenco

2-5 A precision balance. With this instrument, differences of 10^{-8} kilogram can be measured.

4. All zeros to the right of a decimal point but to the left of a nonzero digit are not significant: 0.000647 kg has three significant figures. The single zero usually placed to the left of the decimal point in such an expression merely serves to call attention to the decimal point and is never significant.

5. All zeros to the right of a decimal point and following a nonzero digit are significant: 0.07080 cm and 20.00 cm each has four significant figures.

Further examples of these rules are given in Table 2-2.

Table 2-2 SIGNIFICANT FIGURES

Two Significant Figures	Three Significant Figures	Four Significant Figures
2300	$54\overline{2}0$	$152\overline{1}$
$4\overline{0}00$	$60\overline{0}0$	$504\overline{0}$
5.2	73.0	4.050
0.16	0.915	0.3780
0.0078	0.0467	0.01520

1. Rule for addition and subtraction. Remember that the rightmost significant figure in a measurement is uncertain. The rightmost significant figure in a sum or difference occurs in the leftmost place at which a doubtful figure occurs in any of the measurements being added or subtracted. The following example illustrates this rule.

$$
\begin{array}{ll}
13.05 \ \text{cm} & \left[\text{leftmost place of doubtful}\right. \\
309.2 \ \ \ \ \text{cm} & \left.\text{figure in measurements}\right. \\
\underline{3.785 \ \text{cm}} & \left[\text{being added}\right. \\
326.035 \ \text{cm} & \left[\text{rightmost significant figure} \atop \text{in the answer}\right.
\end{array}
$$

The answer should therefore be recorded as 326.0 cm.

2. Rule for multiplication and division. In multiplication and division, remember that when a doubtful figure is multiplied or divided by a number, the answer is likewise doubtful. Therefore, the product or quotient should not have more significant figures than the least precise factor. The following example will illustrate the rule for multiplication.

3.54 cm × 4.8 cm × 0.5421 cm = 9.2113632 cm³

least precise factor   **rightmost significant figure in the answer**

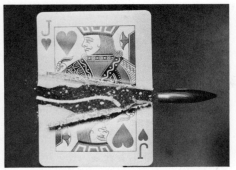

Dr. Harold E. Edgerton, Mass. Institute of Technology

A bullet cutting through a playing card. Split second timing was required to take this photograph.

Consequently, the answer should be recorded as 9.2 cm³. When more than one operation is involved in a calculation, the result may be rounded off to one figure more than the correct number of significant figures *after each operation*.

3. Rule for rounding. If the first digit to be dropped in rounding is 4 or less, the preceding digit is not changed; if it is 6 or more, the preceding digit is raised by 1. If the digits to be dropped in rounding are a 5 followed by digits other than zeros, the preceding digit is raised by 1. If the digits to be dropped in rounding are a 5 followed by zeros (or if the digit is exactly 5), the preceding digit is not changed if it is even; but if it is odd, it is raised by 1.

Example

Divide 8937.50 cm² by 13$\overline{0}$ cm.

Solution

Only three significant figures are required for the answer, so the quotient of 68.750 is rounded off to 68.8 cm because the fourth figure is a 5 followed by a zero and the 5 is preceded by an odd digit.

Many students doubt that an answer with two significant figures can be more acceptable than one with eight. This doubt may result from working problems with pure numbers. These numbers do not represent measurements of physical quantities. Each digit in such a computation involving pure numbers is of equal importance, and the last digit of a pure number is not an estimation. However, in the computation shown above, remember that the last digit of each number is uncertain and that the product of a certain digit and an uncertain digit is also uncertain. Working through such a multiplication, circling all the uncertain digits at each step, is good practice and a convincing exercise.

2.6 Exponential notation

Scientists frequently deal with very large and very small numbers. The velocity of light in air is about 300,000,000 meters per second. The mass of the earth is about 6,000,000,-000,000,000,000,000,000 kilograms. The mass of an electron is 0.000,000,000,000,000,000,000,000,000,000,910,953,4 kilogram. These numbers are inconvenient to write and difficult to read. Through the use of the mathematical laws of exponents, however, it is possible to express these numbers in a much simpler way. *Using powers of ten in writing a number is called **exponential notation**.* Such numbers have the form

$$M \times 10^n$$

where **M** is a number having a single nonzero digit to the left of the decimal point and **n** is a positive or negative exponent. To write a number in exponential notation:

1. Determine **M** by shifting the decimal point in the original number to the left or to the right until only one nonzero digit is to the left of it. Retain only significant figures in **M**.

2. Determine **n** by counting the number of places the decimal point has been shifted; if it has been moved to the left, **n** is positive; if to the right, **n** is negative.

By following these rules, we see that the velocity of light can be written as 3×10^8 m/sec, the mass of the earth as 6×10^{24} kg, and the mass of the electron as 9.109534×10^{-31} kg.

It is often helpful to know the magnitude of a number in terms of its powers of ten. In this form, it can be compared quickly with other numbers. An approximation to the nearest power of ten of a number is called its *order of magnitude*. The order of magnitude of the velocity of light in m/sec is 10^8. The order of magnitude of the mass of the earth in kg is 10^{25}, since its mass is nearer to 10^{25} kg than it is to 10^{24} kg. Similarly, the order of magnitude of the mass of the electron in kg is 10^{-30}. Orders of magnitude of length of a number of objects in the universe are shown in Fig. 2-7.

Hale Observatories

2-6 The order of magnitude of length of the Andromeda Galaxy is similar to that of our Milky Way Galaxy. It takes more than 100,000 years for light to cross its longest diameter.

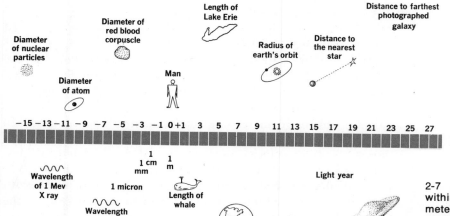

2-7 Orders of magnitude of length within the universe in terms of the meter. Notice that the earth is approximately half way between the smallest and largest objects known to exist. The numbers above the scale are the powers of ten.

SOLVING PROBLEMS

2.7 Data, equations and graphs

Scientists usually use the term "data" when referring to the numbers, units, and other information recorded in making measurements. Much of your homework in physics will consist of solving problems in which all the necessary data are already provided for you. The problems at the ends of the chapters in this book are like that. Your objective is to use the data properly in order to find the quantity that is called for. This usually means that all the given data will be used in the computations. But this is not always the case. Sometimes unnecessary data are included in the problem, just to make sure that you think the problem through instead of merely substituting numbers into an equation in a mechanical way. After all, in assigned problems of this sort, most of the scientific procedure has already been completed and all that is left is the mathematical part of the conclusion. By thinking about the necessary data in the problems, you will review the principles on which the problem is based.

The first step in solving an assigned problem of this kind is to list carefully all the data given in it. Be sure to include the correct symbol and unit for each physical quantity. If the symbol is not given in the problem, look it up inside the front cover of this book or in Table 3 of Appendix B. Record these symbols correctly at the start. As you continue working the problem, be sure you use only these symbols. Also check to make sure that you have copied the right numbers of significant figures in each case.

In the laboratory, most of the data needed must be obtained by direct measurement. In some experiments, you will be told what to measure, what instruments to use, and even how many significant figures to use. But in other experiments, you must make these decisions for yourself.

In recording and interpreting data in physics you will use mathematical skills that you have acquired in previous courses. The Mathematics Refresher, starting on page 653, contains a summary of knowledge and skills from arithmetic, elementary algebra, plane geometry, and trigonometry that are useful in the study of physics. At this time, you should review the information contained there and try some of the sample problems. Study carefully any topic with which you are not familiar.

The purpose of a scientific experiment is to discover any relationships between the quantities measured. (Of course, the experimenter tries to reduce or eliminate the effects of other conditons that might affect the measurements in an unpredictable way. Uncontrolled conditions might make the measurements so confusing that relationships would not be discovered.) As an example, suppose you wished to discover any relationships that might exist between the mass of a homogeneous substance (the same throughout) and its volume. You measure the volumes of several samples of different substances and determine the mass of each. Since temperature affects the volume of most substances, you control this condition by taking all of your measurements at a uniform temperature, such as 20°C. Your data for three substances, with the volume measured in cm³ at 20°C and the mass measured in grams, might look like Table 2-3 (in which the volumes have been simplified).

Table 2-3 VOLUME-MASS RELATIONSHIPS AT 20°C

Volume (cm³)	Mass (g) aluminum	water	maple wood	Volume (cm³)	Mass (g) aluminum	water	maple wood
$1\overline{0}$	27	$1\overline{0}$	6	$6\overline{0}$	162	$6\overline{0}$	36
$2\overline{0}$	54	$2\overline{0}$	12	$7\overline{0}$	189	$7\overline{0}$	42
$3\overline{0}$	81	$3\overline{0}$	18	$8\overline{0}$	216	$8\overline{0}$	48
$4\overline{0}$	108	$4\overline{0}$	24	$9\overline{0}$	243	$9\overline{0}$	54
$5\overline{0}$	135	$5\overline{0}$	30	$10\overline{0}$	270	$10\overline{0}$	60

Now, you look for mathematical relationships among these numbers. As the volume of each substance increases, the mass also increases. But, this statement would be true of many relationships. You are looking for a specific equation. The equation that expresses the relationship among the measurements is sometimes revealed by a graph, as you shall now see.

Figure 2-8 is a graph of the data in Table 2-3. Point **O** is the origin of the graph. The horizontal line through **O**, **Ox**, is called the X axis. On it are measured distances from the origin, or abscissas, equivalent to the various volumes. For convenience, use one small space to represent $1\overline{0}$ cm³. The vertical line through **O**, **Oy**, is called the Y axis. On it are measured distances from the origin, or ordinates, equivalent to the various masses. Use one small space to represent $1\overline{0}$ g.

When the data for aluminum, water, and maple wood are plotted on the graph, the data for each substance can be connected by a straight line. (Not all of the data for aluminum fit on the graph.) The mathematical relationship between the mass and the volume is called a *proportion*. The symbol that means "is proportional to" is ∝. Hence, the relationship between mass and volume is expressed mathematically as

$$mass\ (m) \propto volume\ (v)$$

*Plotting data that are **directly proportional** always results in the graph of a straight line.*

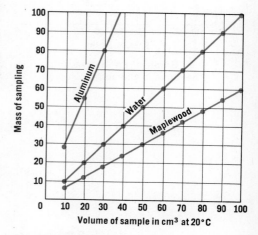

2-8 Graph of three direct proportions. Straight lines are typical of these relationships.

Table 2-4	SPEED-TIME RELATIONSHIPS
Speedometer reading (km/hr)	Time for 100-km trip (hr)
20.0	5.00
30.0	3.33
40.0	2.50
50.0	2.00
60.0	1.67
70.0	1.43
80.0	1.25
90.0	1.11
100.0	1.00

To illustrate another kind of graph, let us plot the data given in Table 2-4, which shows the time required to make a trip of $\overline{100}$ kilometers at various speeds. A line drawn through the plotted points (Fig. 2-9) is a **hyperbola**. Furthermore, the product of the speed and time is constant. *Two quantities whose product is a constant are in* **inverse proportion**.

A proportion can be changed into an equation by introducing a constant. The constant for each substance can be calculated from the data in Table 2-3. (For example, if each measurement in the volume column is multiplied by 2.7, the measured mass of aluminum results.) The equation for this relationship is $m = DV$ where D is a constant. Solving the equation for D,

$$D = \frac{m}{V}$$

This constant, D, *the ratio of the mass of a homogeneous substance to its volume, is called the* **mass density** *of the substance.* With this equation you can find any one of the three physical quantities (D, m, or V) if the measurements for the other two are given. (Mass density is given in g/cm³ rather than kg/m³ because the latter would involve more cumbersome numbers. This deviation from the MKS system is used in other places in this book when the deviation helps to simplify the calculations.)

The graphs we have just studied represent ideal situations. That is, a smooth line or curve could be drawn directly through the plotted points. In many problems and laboratory experiments, you will find that this is not the case. Errors in the experiment and in reading the instruments will result in data that deviate from the curve. Nevertheless, the curve you draw should be a smooth one. A look at the resulting graph will, as a rule, enable you to determine the precision of each reading.

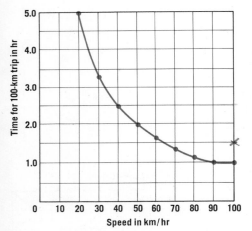

2-9 Graph of an inverse proportion. The curve is a hyperbola.

A carefully drawn graph provides you with another helpful tool. You can use it to estimate values between the plotted points (interpolation) and beyond the measurements made in the experiment (extrapolation).

Estimation of answers is not limited to interpolation and extrapolation. Whenever you solve a problem in physics, you should make an intelligent guess at the answer before doing the actual computation. Such a "check for reasonableness" will frequently disclose major errors in arithmetic or algebra. After going to all the effort of recording and interpreting data, this final check is well worthwhile.

2.8 Vectors

Physical quantities such as length, area, volume, capacity, mass, density, and time can be expressed as a single number with suitable units. For instance, the length of a table can be completely described as 1.5 m. The mass of a steel block is completely described as 54 kg. *Quantities*, such as these, *which can be expressed completely by a single number with appropriate units are called* **scalar quantities**, *or simply,* **scalars**. ("Scalar" is derived from the Latin word "scala," which means "ladder" or "steps" and implies magnitude.) Other examples of scalars in physics are energy and temperature.

Other physical quantities, such as force, velocity, acceleration, electric field strength, and magnetic induction, cannot be completely described in terms of magnitude alone. In addition to magnitude, these quantities always have a specific direction. *Quantities which require magnitude and direction for their description and whose behavior can be described by certain mathematical rules are called* **vector quantities**. *They can be represented by* **vectors**. ("Vector" is derived from a Latin word meaning "carrier," which implies displacement.) The ability to work with vectors is an important mathematical skill that is necessary in solving problems that deal with vector quantities.

A vector is usually represented by an arrow. The length of the arrow represents the magnitude of the vector, and the direction of the arrow shows the direction of the vector.

When both speed and direction are used to describe an object's motion, the term velocity is used. Also, velocities can be applied and they combine like other quantities that can be represented by vectors. A velocity is a vector quantity. As an example, imagine a plane flying north in quiet air at a speed of 120 km/hr (kilometers per hour). An arrow *ON* can be drawn to represent the plane's velocity (Fig. 2-10). The arrow starts at the plane's present position *O* and points to the north. (In vector diagrams, north is toward the top of the page, east is toward the right, south is toward the bottom and west is toward the left.) This arrow shows the plane's direction. The length of the arrow is proportional to the plane's speed.

Arrows representing vectors can be combined. And, many experiments have confirmed that their combination accurately represents the behavior of the objects. When two or more vectors have the same direction, the sum of the vectors is simply the arithmetic sum of the magnitudes of the separate vectors and acts in the same direction. The sum of two or more vectors is called the *resultant*.

As an example of the combination of two vectors, suppose an airplane flies through still air with a velocity of 485 km/hr eastward. There is a tail wind with a velocity of 28 km/hr eastward. What is the resultant velocity of the airplane? Since the plane is flying in moving air, the plane's velocity with respect to the ground is the vector sum of its velocity in still air and the wind's

2-10 Vector representation of a plane flying north with a velocity of 120 km/hr. Each mark on the arrow represents 10 km/hr.

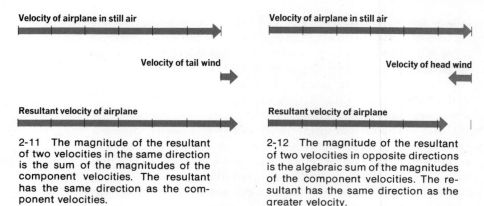

2-11 The magnitude of the resultant of two velocities in the same direction is the sum of the magnitudes of the component velocities. The resultant has the same direction as the component velocities.

2-12 The magnitude of the resultant of two velocities in opposite directions is the algebraic sum of the magnitudes of the component velocities. The resultant has the same direction as the greater velocity.

velocity. Therefore 485 km/hr eastward + 28 km/hr eastward = 513 km/hr eastward, the resultant velocity of the airplane with respect to the ground. It has the same direction as the velocities that were combined. The vector solution of this problem is shown in Fig. 2-11.

Now let us take another case. The airplane flies eastward, but the wind is a head wind having a velocity of 28 km/hr westward. What is the resultant velocity of the airplane? Again, the magnitude of the resultant is the algebraic sum of the magnitudes of the components. The head wind in the opposite direction can be taken into account by considering it as a negative velocity (with respect to the plane's eastward velocity which we took as positive). In this case, the resultant has the direction of the greater velocity. Therefore, 485 km/hr eastward + 28 km/hr westward = 457 km/hr eastward. The vector solution of this problem is shown in Fig. 2-12.

In a third case, the airplane still flies eastward with a velocity of 485 km/hr. But now the wind has a velocity of 42 km/hr southward. What is the resultant velocity of the airplane? In Fig. 2-13, v_E represents the velocity of the airplane, 485 km/hr east. The vector representing the velocity of the wind, 42 km/hr south is v_s. To find the resultant velocity, we construct the parallelogram of velocities, **OERS**. The diagonal of this parallelogram **OR** (also designated in the diagram as the vector v_R) is the resultant velocity. When we compute its magnitude we find it to

2-13 The resultant of two velocities that have an angle to each other is the diagonal of the parallelogram constructed by using the component velocity vectors as sides. The resultant velocity vector is the geometric sum of the component velocity vectors.

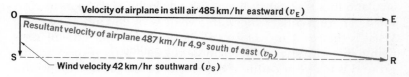

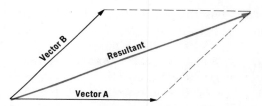

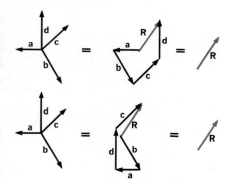

2-14 The parallelogram method can be used to find the resultant of two vectors even though they are not perpendicular.

2-15 Vector addition. The order in which the vectors are added does not affect the magnitude and direction of the resultant.

be 487 km/hr. Its direction is 4.9° south of east. (To understand this calculation, a review of page 657 of the *Mathematics Refresher*, **13. Triangles**, will be helpful.) The parallelogram method can also be used when vectors are at angles other than right angles (Fig. 2-14). But, the mathematical solution is more difficult as you will see in later chapters.

Vectors may also be added by placing arrows end to end as shown in Fig. 2-15. This method is particularly helpful when it is necessary to find the resultant of three or more vectors that start from the same point. With the parallelogram method, it would be necessary to find the resultant of two of the vectors first, then use this resultant with a third vector to find a second resultant, and so on until all the vectors have been applied. The final resultant then is the required answer. So the procedures shown in Fig. 2-15 are really a shortcut for the parallelogram method. In using this method, it does not matter in what sequence the arrows are drawn.

2.9 Thinking problems through

The problems in this text range from those that are quite simple and involve only a single computation to those that require several derivations and a number of separate mathematical steps. In general, problems of the first type will be found in Group A at the ends of the chapters and few examples of this type are given within the chapters themselves. Problems involving several steps and a more thorough understanding of the principles involved are included in Group B, and examples of these are shown in detail within the chapters.

The method used to solve physics problems consists of a number of logical steps. These steps are described below and they are illustrated in examples given throughout this book.

1. Read the problem carefully and make sure that you understand all the terms and symbols that are used in it. Write down all given data.
2. Write down the symbol for the physical quantity or quantities called for in the problem, together with the appropriate units.
3. Write down the equation relating the known and unknown quantities of the problem. This is called the *basic equation*. In this step you will have to draw upon your understanding

of the physical principles involved in the problem. It is helpful to draw a sketch of the problem and to label it with the given data.

4. Solve the basic equation for the unknown quantity in the problem, expressing this quantity in terms of those given in the problem. This is called the *working equation*.

5. Substitute the given data into the working equation. Be sure to use the proper units and carefully check the significant figures in this step.

6. Perform the indicated mathematical operations with the units alone to make sure that the answer will be given in the units called for in the problem.

7. Estimate the order of magnitude of the answer.

8. Perform the indicated mathematical operations with the numbers. Be sure to observe the rules of significant figures.

9. Review the entire solution and compare the answer with your estimate.

Solving a problem in physics is not merely a matter of "plugging" a set of numbers into the appropriate equations. Understanding the underlying principles of the problem is much more important than "getting the right answer."

Example

A rectangular metal block is 2.63 cm long, 2.15 cm wide and 1.52 cm thick. The mass of the block is 56.0 g. What is the mass density of the metal?

Solution

Given the length, width, thickness, and mass of a rectangular metal block, we are asked to calculate the mass density of the metal. Since this problem involves mass density, mass, and volume, the equation for mass density is the *basic equation*. Since the volume is not given directly, however, we must use a *working equation* in which the given data for length, width, and thickness are shown.

Basic equation: $D = \dfrac{m}{V}$

Working equation: $D = \dfrac{m}{(l)\ (w)\ (h)}$

Now we are ready to substitute the given data into the working equation and to compute the answer.

$$D = \frac{56.0 \text{ g}}{(2.63 \text{ cm})\ (2.15 \text{ cm})\ (1.52 \text{ cm})}$$
$$= 6.52 \text{ g/cm}^3$$

Notice that the rules of significant figures have been observed in calculating the answer and that the units for each quantity have been consistently used.

QUESTIONS

1. List three ways of expressing the precision of a measurement.
2. State the rule for the multiplication of significant figures.
3. (a) What is the shape of the graph of two quantities which are in direct proportion? (b) in inverse proportion?
4. (a) Should the curve pass through all the plotted points of a graph dealing with cause-and-effect relationships? (b) Explain.
5. What is the advantage of developing a working equation for a problem in physics before substituting the data given in the problem?
6. What is the value of estimating the order of magnitude of the answer in solving physics problems?

7. How can a graph be used to determine the precision of a series of measurements?
8. What is the purpose of checking a physics problem by using only the units of measurement?
9. Describe two ways in which the resultant of three or more vectors can be found.

PROBLEMS

1. How many significant figures are there in each of the following numbers? (a) 173.2; (b) 205; (c) 4000; (d) 0.025; (e) 700; (f) 0.09050.
2. Write each of the numbers in Problem 1 in exponential notation form.
3. Write each of the following numbers in exponential notation form:
   (a) 175,000,000
   (b) 602,300,000,000,000,000,000,000
   (c) 0.000047
   (d) 0.000,000,000,000,000,000,000,001,672,39
4. What is the order of magnitude of each of the numbers in Problem 3?
5. The time required for a 100-km trip is 1.5 hours. Determine the average speed from Fig. 2-9.
6. The mass density of mercury is 13.6 g/cm^3. (a) What is the mass of 12.2 cm^3 of mercury? (b) What volume would 472 g of mercury occupy?

7. Estimate the order of magnitude of the answer for each of the following calculations:

   (a) $(61. \times 10^8)$ (3.2×10^{-2}) (c) $65 \times 32 \times 10^{-5}$

   (b) $\dfrac{5.92 \times 10^{-2}}{5.37 \times 10^8}$ (d) $\dfrac{2.35 \times 0.45 \times 546}{379 \times 4.3 \times 10^4}$

8. An airplane is heading westward at a velocity of 950 km/hr. The wind is blowing northward with a velocity of 55 km/hr. What is the resultant speed and direction of the airplane relative to the ground?

9. A vector with a magnitude of 5.0 units is directed northward. Another vector with a magnitude of 3.0 units is directed northeastward from the same point. Draw these vectors to scale and measure the magnitude and direction of the resultant.

Group B 10. If the tension of a vibrating string is kept constant, the length of the string is related to the frequency of the tone it emits. Plot a graph of the following data for a typical vibrating string, using lengths as abscissas and frequencies as ordinates.

Length (m)	Frequency (sec^{-1})	Length (m)	Frequency (sec^{-1})
0.075	1024	0.60	128
0.15	512	0.80	96
0.20	384	1.20	64
0.30	256	2.40	32
0.40	192		

(a) What is the shape of the graph? (b) What relationship exists between the length of the vibrating string and the frequency of the tone it emits? (c) From the graph, interpolate the frequency the string would have if it were 0.75 m long. (d) How long must the string be to vibrate at the rate of $40\overline{0}$/sec?

11. In a laboratory experiment, a student obtained the following values for the acceleration of gravity by timing a swinging pendulum: 9.796 m/sec^2, 9.803 m/sec^2, 9.825 m/sec^2, and 9.801 m/sec^2. The accepted value for the location of the laboratory is 9.801 m/sec^2. (a) Give the absolute error of each reading. (b) Compute the relative error of each value. (c) What is the absolute deviation of each measurement? (d) Express the precision of the experiment in terms of relative deviation.

12. According to the laws of planetary motion, planetary orbits can be described by the following equation: $k = P^2/d^3$, where k is a constant that is the same for all of the sun's planets, P is the period of revolution for a specific planet, and d is its average distance from the sun. The average distance between the sun and the earth is 1.496×10^8 km. Find the value of k for the solar system.

13. Using the value of k found in the previous problem, find the average distance between the sun and Jupiter if the period of revolution of that planet is equal to 11.86 earth years.

Chapter 3

Nature and Cause of Motion

VELOCITY

3.1 The nature of motion

If you see a car in front of your house, then later you see it further along the street, you are correct in saying that the car has moved. To reach this conclusion, you observed two positions for the car and you also noted the passage of time. You might not know how the car got from one position to the other. For all you know, it might have moved at a steady rate or it might have speeded up and then slowed down before it got to its second position. It might also have been moving when you first noticed it and might still have been moving at its second location. But none of these possibilities change the truth of the statement that the car has moved.

Car and Driver

Every part of a modern racing car is designed to help attain the greatest possible velocity under the conditions prevailing on the track.

43

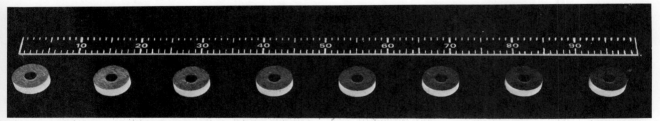

Project Physics

3-1 A study of motion. The disc was photographed every 0.1 sec as it moved from left to right along the meter stick. Note that the displacement of the disc is equal in equal time periods.

Usually, when we see something move, we do not just make two observations. We observe the moving object continuously. However, even a case of continuous observation can be thought of as a series of observations in which the interval of time between two successive observations is small.

Figure 3-1 shows several important things about the nature of motion. For one thing, it shows the changing positions of a moving object. Such *a change of position in a particular direction is called a* **displacement**. A displacement has magnitude, direction, and a point of application. Furthermore, displacements are vector quantities and can be manipulated like other vector quantities.

Figure 3-1 also shows that relative motion can be detected by comparing the displacement of one object with respect to another. The reference object is usually considered to be stationary. Thus, in the case of the moving car, the street and houses are the stationary references. So **motion** *may be defined as the displacement of an object in relation to objects that are considered to be at rest (stationary).*

This chapter deals with the simplest type of motion, the motion of an object along a straight line. More complicated types of motion will be discussed in Chapter 5.

3.2 Speed and velocity

The time rate of motion is called **speed**. This statement means that if you are walking at a speed of 3.0 m/sec, in one second you travel 3.0 meters. In 2.0 seconds, you travel 6.0 meters and in 3.0 seconds you travel 9.0 meters. A graph of this motion and of several other motions with constant speeds is shown in Fig. 3-2. Notice that the lines that represent greater speeds are more steeply inclined. The *slope* of a line indicates how steep the line is. The slope is defined as the ratio of the change in the quantity plotted vertically divided by the corresponding change in the quantity plotted horizontally. For example, the distance marked in color on line **A** represents a change of 3.0 units on the vertical axis. The same distance on line **A** represents a change of 1.0 unit on the horizontal axis. The slope of the line is $\frac{3.0}{1.0} = 3.0$.

This definition of the slope of a line on a graph may be used to represent a physical quantity such as speed. If the vertical axis represents path length and the horizontal axis represents time, then the ratio for the slope of the line represents speed. For each of the speeds graphed in Fig. 3-2, one computation of the slope of the line is indicated. This graph and the determination of speed from the slope of the graph is possible only if the speed is constant. *If the determination of speed over any randomly chosen interval gives the same value, the speed is constant.* The graph of constant speed is a straight line.

Average speed is found by dividing the total path length by the elapsed time. For example, if you run 112 m in 20.0 sec, you might not run at constant speed. You might speed up and slow down. But, as long as you move a total path length of 112 m in 20.0 sec, your average speed is $\frac{112 \text{ m}}{20.0 \text{ sec}} = 5.60$ m/sec.

Suppose you ride a bicycle 120 m in $2\overline{0}$ sec. Your average speed is $\frac{120 \text{ m}}{2\overline{0} \text{ sec}} = 6.0$ m/sec. A graph of your speed might look like Fig. 3-3. You start at a speed of 0.0 m/sec ($t = 0$) and increase your speed. Then from about $t = 3.0$ sec to $t = 15.0$ sec you travel at constant speed. Then at about $t = 15$ sec you begin to tire and slow down until, at $t = 2\overline{0}$ sec, you stop. On this graph, *instantaneous speed* can be defined as *the slope of the line that is tangent to the curve at a given point.* Without a speedometer, it is difficult to determine your instantaneous speed. It can be defined, however, as the speed that you would have if your speed did not change from that point on.

Instantaneous speed is measured approximately by timing the motion over a short path length. In Fig. 3-3, instantaneous speed is found approximately by dividing a small amount of time, measured on the graph, into the corresponding path length for that time. The region of the curve marked **A** represents your change in speed as you move faster. An interval of time of 2.3 sec is indicated on the horizontal axis. The corresponding path length for this time interval is 9.0 m. The slope of the colored line over the interval **A** is $\frac{9.0 \text{ m}}{2.3 \text{ sec}} = 3.9$ m/sec. This method gives only an approximation of the instantaneous speed because we found the *average speed* for the time interval indicated. This value for the average speed is the same as the instantaneous speed (the slope of the tangent line) at some point in the indicated region, but we can not precisely determine that point.

Since the graph of your motion is a straight line in the region **B**, it represents constant speed. The elapsed time in region **B** is 8.9 sec − 7.0 sec = 1.9 sec. The corresponding path length is

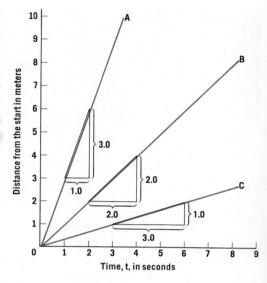

3-2 Three graphs of motion with different constant speeds. A is for 3 m/sec, B is for 1 m/sec, and C is for 1/3 m/sec. In each case, speed is represented by the slope of the line.

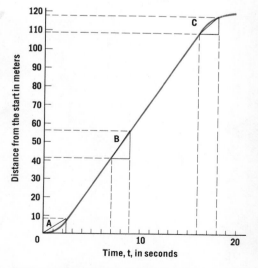

3-3 A graph of motion with changing speed.

56 m − 41 m = 15.0 m. The instantaneous speed in this case can be determined precisely because it is the same as the average speed. It is $\dfrac{15 \text{ m}}{1.9 \text{ sec}} = 7.9$ m/sec.

Region **C** on the graph is curved. The elapsed time is 18.0 sec − 16.0 sec = 2.0 sec. The corresponding path length is 118.0 m − 109.0 m = 9.0 m. The average speed over the interval **C** (as an approximation of the instantaneous speed) is $\dfrac{9.0 \text{ m}}{2.0 \text{ sec}} = 4.5$ m/sec.

Both instantaneous speed and average speed are completely described in terms of magnitude alone. Hence speed is a scalar quantity.

3.3 Velocity   When both speed and direction are specified by the motion, the term *velocity* is used. In other words, **velocity** *is speed in a particular direction.* A person walking eastward does not have the same velocity as a person walking northward, even though their speeds are the same. Two persons also have different velocities if they walk in the same direction at different speeds. As we described in Section 2.8, velocities are vector quantities. Both magnitude and direction are necessary to describe them and they behave like other quantities that can be represented by vectors.

For the simple cases of this chapter, in which the motion is along a straight line, the word velocity is often used without specifically mentioning the direction. In these cases the velocity may be either a positive or a negative number to indicate in which direction the object is moving. The speed is never a negative number; it always represents the magnitude of the velocity. So, the equations for velocity and speed appear the same.

Average velocity is defined as the total displacement divided by the total elapsed time.

$$v_{av} = \frac{s_f - s_i}{t_f - t_i}$$

where v_{av} is the average velocity, s_i is the initial position at time t_i and s_f is the final position at time t_f. This relationship may also be written

$$v_{av} = \frac{s}{t}$$

where s represents the change of position (displacement) during the time interval t.

Graphic representations of the velocity of motion along a straight line are shown in Fig. 3-4 and Fig. 3-5. These graphs

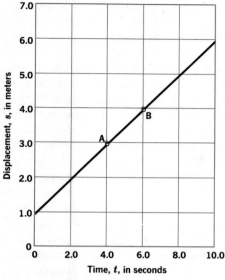

3-4 Graph of motion with uniform velocity.

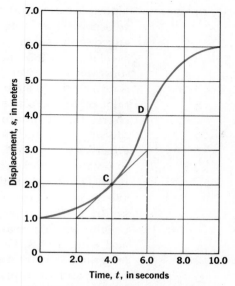

3-5 Graph of motion with variable velocity.

indicate that the direction of motion does not change in either case because displacement is continuously increasing. In Fig. 3-4, t for the entire range of the graph is $1\overline{0}$ sec and s is 5.0 m. Consequently, $v_{av} = \dfrac{5.0 \text{ m}}{1\overline{0} \text{ sec}}$ or 0.50 m/sec. The same value for v_{av} is obtained by choosing any other two points on the graph, such as **A** and **B**. In this case, t is 2.0 sec and s is 1.0 m, and v_{av} again equals 0.50 m/sec. The velocity, represented by the slope of the straight line, is constant, and the motion of the object is said to be *uniform*.

In Fig. 3-5, the motion is *variable*. The average velocity for the entire range of the graph is $\dfrac{5.0 \text{ m}}{1\overline{0} \text{ sec}}$ or 0.50 m/sec, as before. However, the average velocity between points **C** and **D** is $\dfrac{2.0 \text{ m}}{2.0 \text{ sec}}$ or 1.0 m/sec. To find the velocity at a specific time (such as point **C**), t is considered to be a very small interval. Consequently, s will also be very small. The ratio of $\dfrac{s}{t}$ at the point **C** is called the *instantaneous velocity*. It can be shown that the instantaneous velocity at point **C** in Fig. 3-5 is given by the slope of the line that is tangent to the curve at point **C**. The numerical value of this slope is found as in the case of the uniform motion in Fig. 3-4 by measuring s and t between two points on the tangent and calculating s/t.

3.4 Working velocity problems

Now let's expand on the parallelogram method for solving velocity vector problems that was illustrated in Section 2.8. In an example in that section, an airplane flies eastward (90.0°) with a velocity of 485 km/hr. The wind has a velocity of 42 km/hr southward. The resultant, found by the parallelogram method, is 487 km/hr in a direction 4.9° south of east. Now, suppose the pilot of the airplane does not want to go 42 km south of the course for each hour of flight. What change must be made in the velocity of the airplane so that it stays on course despite the effects of the wind blowing from the north? The velocity we wish to obtain is 485 km/hr, 90.0°. This situation is represented by v_R in Fig. 3-6. It is the diagonal of the velocity parallelogram. We know one component of this velocity; that of the wind, 42 km/hr, southward represented by v_S. To complete the parallelogram, we first draw **SR**. Then from **O**, **R** is drawn parallel and equal to **SR**. Connecting **V** with **OV** completes the parallelogram. The vector v_V represents the velocity the airplane must maintain, computed to be 487 km/hr with a direction of 4.9° north of east. By heading the airplane in this direction of 85.1° and increasing the air speed to 487 km/hr, the pilot actually travels with a speed of 485 km/hr with respect to the ground in an easterly direction.

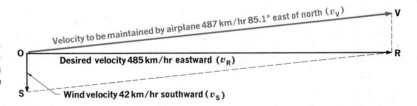

3-6 The vector representing the velocity which the airplane must maintain is a side of the parallelogram of which the desired velocity is the diagonal.

Example

A man can row a boat at the rate of 8.0 km/hr in still water. He heads the boat directly across a stream which flows at the rate of 6.0 km/hr. Find the resultant velocity (a) graphically and (b) trigonometrically.

Solution

(a) To solve this problem graphically, use a protractor and a ruler with a mm scale. Draw a force vector, **OB**, to represent the velocity of the boat in still water, v_S, using an appropriate scale such as $1\overline{0}$ mm = 1.0 km/hr. (See the accompanying figure, but bear in mind that the scale in the figure is smaller than the one suggested for your paper.) Draw the force vector, **OC**, to the same scale and at right angles to **OB** to represent the velocity of the stream, v_C.

Complete the parallelogram **OBRC** and draw in the diagonal, **OR**. Place an arrowhead at **R**. The vector **OR** represents the resultant velocity, v_R. Using the same scale that you used in drawing **OB** and **OC**, read the magnitude of **OR** as precisely as possible. It should be about $1\overline{0}$ km/hr. Use the protractor to measure the direction of **OR**. It should be about 37° downstream from **OB**.

(b) The graphic solution of vector problems is limited by the precision with which the angles and lines are drawn and measured. This limitation is avoided by using the trigonometric method. In this method, tables are used to determine the lengths of vectors. The precision of the tables is usually greater than that of the estimated answers in a graphic solution. Nevertheless, the graphic solution serves as an important check against errors in the trigonometric solution.

The trigonometric solution is found by using the relationship

$$\tan \theta = \frac{OC}{OB} = \frac{v_C}{v_B} = \frac{6.0 \text{ km/hr}}{8.0 \text{ km/hr}} = 0.75$$

$$\theta = 37°$$

$$\sin \theta = \frac{OC}{OR} = \frac{v_C}{v_R}$$

$$v_R = \frac{v_C}{\sin \theta} = \frac{6.0 \text{ km/hr}}{0.602} = 1\overline{0} \text{ km/hr}$$

Hence, $v_R = 1\overline{0}$ km/hr at an angle of 37° downstream.

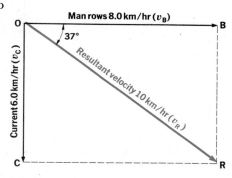

Example

Trigonometrically determine the resultant of the following two vectors, which are applied at the same point: 42 mm 55° east of north and 95 mm 64° south of east.

Solution

The accompanying diagram shows the angles that exist in this example. Carefully study the diagram to see how the value of each angle is obtained.

Since the vectors do not act at right angles, it is necessary to use the law of cosines and the law of sines in the solution. (Refer to page 658 of the *Mathematics Refresher*.) Designate the 42 mm vector as a, the 95 mm vector as b, and the resultant as c. Then apply the law of cosines, as follows:

$c = \sqrt{a^2 + b^2 - 2ab \cos C}$ $\cos C = \cos 81° = 0.156$

$c = \sqrt{(42 \text{ mm})^2 + (95 \text{ mm})^2 - 2 \, (42 \text{ mm})(95 \text{ mm})(0.156)}$

$c = 98$ mm, the magnitude of the resultant vector

$b/\sin B = c/\sin C$ $\sin C = \sin 81° = 0.988$

$\sin B = b \sin C/c = (95 \text{ mm})(0.988)/98 \text{ mm} = 0.958$

$B = 73°$ $73° - 35° = 38°$ south of east, direction of resultant vector

QUESTIONS

Group A   1. Define motion.
2. (a) Define speed. (b) Distinguish between average and instantaneous speed. (c) What are the units of speed in the MKS system?
3. (a) What is velocity? (b) Distinguish between speed and velocity.
4. (a) Describe the motion of an object which has constant speed. (b) Describe the motion of an object which has uniform velocity.

Group B   5. Why is speed a scalar quantity but velocity a vector quantity?
6. How can the magnitude and direction of the resultant of two velocities, which are directed at right angles to each other, be determined?
7. (a) Does a change in the speed of an object always produce a change in its velocity? (b) Does a change in the velocity of an object always indicate a change in its speed? Explain.

PROBLEMS

Note: Problems 2 through 9 should be solved (a) graphically and (b) trigonometrically.

Group A   1. The highway distance from Indianapolis to Denver is 1712 km. If the driving time is 29.25 hr, what is the average speed for the trip?
2. A motorboat travels 25 km/hr in still water. What will be the magnitude and direction of the velocity of the boat if it is directed upstream on a river which flows at the rate of 4 km/hr?
3. An airplane has a velocity, with respect to the air, of 825 km/hr northward. What is the velocity of the airplane with respect to the ground if the wind is blowing with a velocity of 35 km/hr southward?
4. A woman rows a boat at a speed of 5.0 km/hr in still water. She heads directly across a river which flows at a speed of 5.0 km/hr. Determine the magnitude and direction of the boat's resultant velocity.
5. An airplane flies westward at 650 km/hr. If the wind has a velocity of 40.0 km/hr northward, determine the magnitude and direction of the resultant velocity.
6. An airplane is to maintain a velocity of 475 km/hr in a northeasterly direction. If the wind velocity is 50.0 km/hr, southeast, what should be the magnitude and direction of the velocity of the airplane to offset the effect of the wind?

7. Determine the magnitude and direction of the resultant velocity of 75.0 m/sec, 25.0° east of north, and 100.0 m/sec, 25.0° east of south.

8. A boat is to cross a river on a course directed 20.0° upstream to a dock 815 m distance in 10.0 min. If the river flows at a speed of 3.0 km/hr, at what angle upstream must the boat be headed and what must be its speed in km/hr relative to the moving water?

9. An airplane must fly at a ground speed of 425 km/hr in a direction of 10.0° east of south to be on course and on schedule. If the wind velocity is 25.0 km/hr, 40.0° east of north, in what direction and at what speed relative to the speed of the air must the pilot fly?

Group B

ACCELERATION

The gas pedal of a car is sometimes called the accelerator. When you step on it, the speed of the car increases. The needle of the car's speedometer shows that for a certain amount of time, the car's speed is increasing. For the time that its speed is increasing, we say it is *accelerating*. When the driver of a moving car applies the brakes, the speedometer indicates that the car's speed is decreasing. We say that the car is *decelerating*.

3.5 The nature of acceleration

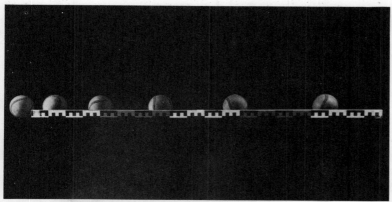

Educational Development Center

Accelerated motion. The baseball was photographed at equal time periods as it moved along a calibrated stick. Note that the displacement of the ball increases by a constant amount. This is an example of uniform acceleration.

Acceleration is defined as the rate of change of velocity. An automobile that goes from 0.0 km/hr to $6\overline{0}$ km/hr in $1\overline{0}$ seconds has greater acceleration than a car that goes from 0.0 km/hr to $6\overline{0}$ km/hr in 15 seconds. The first car has an average acceleration of $\frac{60 \text{ km/hr}}{10 \text{ sec}} = 6.0$ (km/hr)/sec. The second car has an average acceleration of 4.0 (km/hr)/sec.

Acceleration, like velocity, is a vector quantity. In the case of a car moving along a straight road, acceleration can be represented by a vector in the direction the car is moving. Deceleration occurs in the opposite direction. For the simple cases of this chapter, in which the motion is known to be along a straight line, the direction of the acceleration is specified by saying whether it is a positive or a negative number. In Section 3.3 we saw that the equations for speed and velocity appear the same. For the same reasons, the equations for "rate of change of speed" and acceleration appear the same. These equations involve only the magnitude and not the direction of motion or displacement.

Average acceleration is found by the relationship

$$a_{av} = \frac{v_f - v_i}{t_f - t_i}$$

where a_{av} is the average acceleration, v_i is the initial velocity at time t_i and v_f is the final velocity at time t_f. This relationship may also be stated

$$a_{av} = \frac{v}{t}$$

where v is the change in velocity during the time interval t.

Figures 3-7 and 3-8 are velocity-time graphs for accelerated motion. In Fig. 3-7 the velocity curve is a straight line. Hence, the acceleration is a constant. This is an illustration of *uniformly accelerated motion*.

The motion illustrated in Fig. 3-8 is an example of *variable acceleration*. As we mentioned in the case of finding instantaneous speed or instantaneous velocity, finding the average ac-

Rapid acceleration enables this jet airliner to take off on relatively short runways.

American Airlines

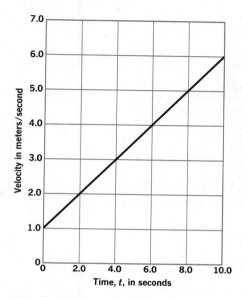

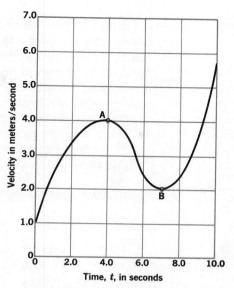

3-7 Graph of velocity versus time for uniformly accelerated motion.

3-8 Graph of velocity versus time for motion with variable acceleration.

celeration between two points on the curve only approximates the instantaneous acceleration. Instantaneous acceleration is equal to the slope of the line that is tangent to the curve at the given point.

Notice that the slope of the curve in Fig. 3-8 is not always positive. That is, the velocity does not increase during all time intervals. For the interval between points **A** and **B**, for example, t is 3.0 sec and v is -2.0 m/sec. Consequently,

$$a_{av} = \frac{-2.0 \text{ m/sec}}{3.0 \text{ sec}}$$

$$a_{av} = -0.67 \frac{\text{m/sec}}{\text{sec}}$$

This reduction in speed is deceleration.

The dimensions of acceleration should be carefully examined. Acceleration is the rate of change of the rate of displacement, or $(s/t)/t$. If s is in meters and t is in seconds, acceleration is given in m/sec/sec or m/sec². The commonly used metric units for speed are km/hr and for acceleration they are km/hr/sec.

Galileo Galilei was the first scientist to understand clearly the concept of acceleration. He found that the acceleration of a ball rolling down an inclined plane and the acceleration of a falling object were both part of the same natural phenomenon and were described by the same mathematical rules.

3.6 Uniformly accelerated motion

Let us consider one of Galileo's experiments. One end of a board is raised so that it is just steep enough to allow a ball to roll from rest to the 0.5-m position in the first second. The apparatus is shown in Fig. 3-9. As the ball rolls down the board, its position is determined at one-second intervals. The data obtained are shown in the first six columns of Table 3-1.

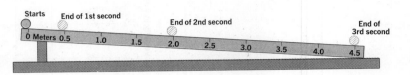

3-9 The ball rolls down the plane with uniformly accelerated motion.

The data in the next four columns show that the velocity at the end of each second is 1.0 m/sec greater than at the end of the previous second. Thus, the acceleration is 1.0 (m/sec)/sec or 1.0 m/sec². The motion of a ball rolling down an inclined plane is an example of uniformly accelerated motion.

The initial velocity of the ball is zero. Its acceleration, or rate of gain in velocity, is 1.0 m/sec². Therefore, its velocity at the end of the *first second* is 1.0 m/sec. (If, at that instant, the ball were no longer accelerated, it would continue to move with a constant velocity of 1.0 m/sec.) At the end of the next second, its velocity is 2.0 m/sec. (2.0 sec × 1.0 m/sec² = 2.0 m/sec.) Similarly, the ball's velocity at the end of the fifth second is 5.0 m/sec. These data show that *the final velocity of an object starting from rest and accelerating at a uniform rate equals the product of the acceleration and the elapsed time. If an object does not start from rest, its final velocity will equal the sum of its initial velocity and the increase in velocity produced by the acceleration.*

TABLE 3-1 UNIFORMLY ACCELERATED MOTION

Interval number	Time at start of interval (sec)	Time, t, at end of interval (sec)	Position at start of interval (m)	Position at end of interval (m)	Distance, s, travelled in interval (m)	Average velocity, v_{av}, during interval (m/sec)	Instantaneous velocity, v_i, at start of interval (m/sec)	Instantaneous velocity, v_f, at end of interval (m/sec)	Average acceleration, a_{av}, during interval (m/sec²)
1	0.0	1.0	0.0	0.5	0.5	0.5	0.0	1.0	1.0
2	1.0	2.0	0.5	2.0	1.5	1.5	1.0	2.0	1.0
3	2.0	3.0	2.0	4.5	2.5	2.5	2.0	3.0	1.0
4	3.0	4.0	4.5	8.0	3.5	3.5	3.0	4.0	1.0
5	4.0	5.0	8.0	12.5	4.5	4.5	4.0	5.0	1.0

a+ ⤳ if $\vec{v}$ & $\vec{a}$ are in same direction
a- ⤳ opp direction

freefall is negative

√ can't take square of neg no.

We may arrive at this same conclusion by mathematical reasoning. The equation defining acceleration is

$$a_{av} = \frac{v_f - v_i}{t_f - t_i}$$

For uniformly accelerated motion a_{av} becomes a. Then, assuming that v_i is the velocity in the direction of the acceleration when $t_i = 0$, and t_f is elapsed time t,

$$a = \frac{v_f - v_i}{t}$$

Multiplying both sides of the equation by t,

$$at = v_f - v_i$$

Isolating the term v_f yields

$$v_f = v_i + at \qquad \text{(Equation 1)}$$

If the object starts from rest, $v_i = 0$,

and $$v_f = at$$

In Section 3.2 we saw that

$$v_{av} = \frac{s}{t}$$

or $$s = v_{av}t \qquad \text{(Equation 2)}$$

When an object is uniformly accelerated, the average velocity for any given interval of time can be found by taking one-half the sum of the initial and final velocities.

$$v_{av} = \frac{v_i + v_f}{2} \qquad \text{(Equation 3)}$$

By substituting the value of v_f (obtained in Equation 1) in Equation 3,

$$v_{av} = \frac{v_i + (v_i + at)}{2} \qquad \text{(Equation 4)}$$

Now, substituting the value of v_{av} (obtained in Equation 4) in Equation 2, gives

$$s = v_i t + \tfrac{1}{2}at^2 \qquad \text{(Equation 5)}$$

If the object starts from rest,

$$v_i t = 0,$$

and $$s = \tfrac{1}{2}at^2$$

3-10 Galileo Galilei formulated the laws of accelerated motion and falling bodies.

From this equation we see that if an object starts from rest and travels with uniformly accelerated motion, the displacement of the object during the first second is numerically equal to one-half the acceleration.

Now let us solve Equation 1 for t, and substitute this value of t in Equation 5. From Equation 1,

$$t = \frac{v_f - v_i}{a}$$

Substituting in Equation 5,

$$s = v_i\left(\frac{v_f - v_i}{a}\right) + \tfrac{1}{2}a\left(\frac{v_f - v_i}{a}\right)^2$$

Multiplying by $2a$ and expanding terms,

$$2as = 2v_i v_f - 2v_i^2 + v_f^2 - 2v_f v_i + v_i^2$$

Combining terms,

$$2as = v_f^2 - v_i^2$$

Solving for v_f,

$$v_f = \sqrt{v_i^2 + 2as} \qquad \text{(Equation 6)}$$

With uniform acceleration, the final velocity equals the square root of the sum of the square of the initial velocity and twice the acceleration times the displacement.
If the object starts from rest,

$$v_i^2 = 0,$$

and

$$v_f = \sqrt{2as}$$

The equations just given apply whether the uniform acceleration is positive or negative, hence it is important to pay attention to the sign of the displacement. They may be used to calculate the distance an object will travel when its motion is uniformly decelerated and the time that elapses in bringing the object to a stop. The following examples show how the equations are used in problems dealing with both positively and negatively accelerated motion.

Example

A ball rolls down an inclined plane with a uniform acceleration of 1.00 m/sec². At a certain instant, its velocity is 0.50 m/sec. (a) What is the velocity of the ball 10.0 sec later? (b) How far has the ball travelled in that interval of 10.0 sec? (c) How far did the ball travel during the eighth second?

Solution

(a) Assuming that time is measured from the moment that the velocity of the ball is observed to be 0.50 m/sec,

$$v_f = v_i + at = 0.50 \text{ m/sec} + (1.00 \text{ m/sec}^2)(10.0 \text{ sec})$$
$$v_f = 10.5 \text{ m/sec}$$

(b) $s = v_i t + \frac{1}{2} a(t)^2$

$$s = (0.50 \text{ m/sec})(10.0 \text{ sec}) + \frac{1}{2}(1.00 \text{ m/sec}^2)(10.0 \text{ sec})^2$$
$$s = 55.0 \text{ m}$$

(c) The distance the ball travels during the eighth second equals the distance travelled in 8 sec minus the distance travelled in 7 sec.

$$s = v_i t_8 + \frac{1}{2} at^2 - (v_i t_7 + \frac{1}{2} at_7^2)$$
$$s = v_i (t_8 - t_7) + \frac{1}{2} a(t_8^2 - t_7^2)$$
$$s = (0.50 \text{ m/sec})(8.00 \text{ sec} - 7.00 \text{ sec}) +$$
$$\frac{1}{2}(1.00 \text{ m/sec}^2)(64.0 \text{ sec}^2 - 49.0 \text{ sec}^2)$$
$$s = 8.00 \text{ m}$$

Example

An automobile is traveling 65 km/hr. Its brakes decelerate it 6.0 m/sec². (a) How long will it take to stop the car? (b) How far will the car travel after the brakes are applied?

Solution

(a) $a = \dfrac{v_f - v_i}{t}$

$$t = \frac{v_f - v_i}{a} = \frac{(0 \text{ km/hr} - 65 \text{ km/hr})(1000 \text{ m/km})}{(-6.0 \text{ m/sec}^2)(3600 \text{ sec/hr})}$$
$$t = 3.0 \text{ sec}$$

(b) $s = v_i t + \frac{1}{2} at^2$

$$s = \frac{(65 \text{ km/hr})(3.0 \text{ sec})(1000 \text{ m/km})}{3600 \text{ sec/hr}} + \frac{1}{2}(-6.0 \text{ m/sec}^2)(3.0 \text{ sec})^2$$
$$s = 27 \text{ m}$$

(*Note:* Part B could also be solved by using the equation immediately preceding Equation 6.)

3.7 Freely falling bodies

If a body falls freely from rest somewhere in New York City, it reaches a velocity of 9.803 m/sec in one second of time. Since $a = v_f/t$, the acceleration equals 9.803 m/sec² at this location. We must consider the location since the value of the acceleration depends on the earth's gravity and varies from place to place.

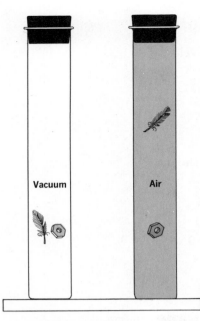

3-11 Objects fall at the same velocity in a vacuum (left) but at different velocities through air (right).

(The nature of gravity will be discussed more fully in Sections 3.10–3.12.) The "rounded-off" value of 9.80 m/sec² is approximately valid for locations in the United States.

The equations for accelerated motion apply to freely falling bodies. Since the acceleration due to gravity, g, is the same for all objects at a given location, we may substitute g for a in these equations. Thus

$$v_f = v_i + gt$$
$$s = v_i t + \tfrac{1}{2} g t^2$$
$$v_f = \sqrt{v_i^2 + 2gs}$$

When freely falling bodies start from rest, $v_i = 0$ and the motion is described by the following equations:

$$v_f = gt$$
$$s = \tfrac{1}{2} g t^2$$
$$v_f = \sqrt{2gs}$$

In the case of freely falling bodies, s is always a vertical distance. The vector quantities v and s in these equations are customarily assigned plus signs if they are directed downward and minus signs if they are directed upward. These equations apply only to objects that are falling freely in a vacuum because they do not take into consideration the resistance of air. These equations apply reasonably well to dense and compact objects such as baseballs or lead shot falling through air. Of course, they do not apply to objects whose air resistance is great compared to their mass such as leaves or feathers dropping through air.

A skydiver in free fall. Air resistance allows a skilled diver to control the orientation and direction of his body even before he opens his parachute.

Ebony-Tan-Jet-Hue

An object thrown upward is uniformly decelerated by the force of gravity until it finally stops rising. Then, as the object falls, it is uniformly accelerated by the force of gravity. The following example shows how a problem of this type is solved.

Example

An object is projected upward with a velocity of 125 m/sec. (a) To what height will it rise? (b) How long will it take to reach that height? (c) What will be the total time elapsed until it strikes the earth?

Solution

(a) $v_f = \sqrt{v_i^2 + 2gs}$

$$s = \frac{v_f^2 - v_i^2}{2g}$$

$s = \dfrac{0 - (-125 \text{ m/sec})^2}{2 \times 9.80 \text{ m/sec}^2}$ (The value for v_i is negative because the velocity is upward.)

$s = -797$ m (The negative value obtained for s indicates an upward displacement.)

(b) $v_f = v_i + gt$

$$t = \frac{v_f - v_i}{g} = \frac{0 - (-125 \text{ m/sec})}{9.80 \text{ m/sec}^2} = 12.8 \text{ sec}$$

(c) Neglecting the effect of the atmosphere, the same amount of time is required for the object to fall as for the object to rise. Thus, the total time elapsed will be 2×12.8 sec $= 25.6$ sec.

QUESTIONS

Group A

1. (a) What is acceleration? (b) Why is a unit of time used twice in a unit of acceleration?
2. How do the directions of an acceleration vector and its corresponding velocity vector compare for the uniformly accelerated linear motion of an object starting from rest?
3. Define the following: (a) uniformly accelerated motion; (b) variably accelerated motion; (c) uniformly decelerated motion; (d) variably decelerated motion.
4. What effect does the force of gravity have on a baseball thrown directly upward?
5. What is meant by instantaneous acceleration?

Group B

6. What equation relates final velocity to initial velocity, acceleration, and elapsed time?
7. How would you calculate displacement when the initial velocity, final velocity, and elapsed time are known?
8. Give an example of an object moving at high speed with zero acceleration.
9. Give an example of an object starting with zero speed and high acceleration.

X Wed

PROBLEMS

Note: Whenever necessary, use $g = 9.80$ m/sec^2. Disregard the effect of the atmosphere.

Group A
9.77m/s^2

1. If a ball is dropped and attains a velocity of 29.31 m/sec in 3.00 sec, what is the acceleration due to gravity?
2. An automobile can be accelerated from 95 km/hr to 142 km/hr in 8.1 sec. What is the acceleration?

A 17m/s
B 14m

3. A large rock is dropped from a bridge into the river below. (a) If the time required for it to drop is 1.7 sec, with what velocity, in m/sec, does it hit the water? (b) What is the height, in meters, of the bridge above the water?
4. (a) How many seconds does it take for a metal ball to drop 145 m from rest? (b) What velocity does it attain?

A 200cm
B 60 cm

5. An object with an initial velocity of 20.0 cm/sec is accelerated at 8.0 cm/sec^2 for 5.0 sec. (a) What is the total displacement? (b) What is the displacement during the fifth second?
6. What velocity is attained by an object which is accelerated at 0.30 m/sec^2 for a distance of 54 m, if its initial velocity is 0.50 m/sec?

A 3.26 S
B 179 m

7. (a) If the brakes of an automobile can decelerate it at 7.00 m/sec^2, what time is required to reduce the velocity of the automobile from 157.0 km/hr to 75.0 km/hr? (b) How many meters does the car travel during this deceleration?

Group B
20m

8. A girl throws a ball from the ground to the top of the school flagpole. If it returns to the ground after 4.0 sec, what is the height of the flagpole in meters?
9. A stone is released from a balloon while the balloon is ascending at the rate of 5.0 m/sec when the balloon is 353 m above the ground. What time is required for the stone to reach the ground?

A 61m/s
B 3.7S

10. A baseball is thrown vertically downward from the top of a 155-m tower with an initial velocity of 25 m/sec. (a) With what velocity does it reach the ground? (b) What time is required?

NEWTON'S LAWS OF MOTION

Thus far in Chapter 3 we have largely discussed motion apart from other physical quantities. Now we shall study the relationship between forces and the motion of bodies. A push or a pull is a force. A force is a vector quantity. It requires magnitude, direction, and a point of application for its description. Also, forces behave like other quantities that can be represented by vectors.

In the MKS system of measurement, forces are measured in *newtons* (n). In terms of fundamental units, a newton is a kg m/sec². Why the newton is measured in these units will be explained later in this chapter. Right now, it is important to remember that *a **force** is a physical quantity that can affect the motion of an object.*

The relationships among force, mass, and motion were described clearly for the first time by Sir Isaac Newton in three laws of motion that bear his name. While some aspects of Newton's laws of motion can be tested only under carefully controlled conditions, repeated experiments and observations have led scientists to believe that they are universally true. That is, the laws apply not only to objects on or near the earth, but to objects throughout the universe.

Newton's first law of motion deals with the motion of a body on which no net force is acting. That is, either there is no force at all acting on the body, or the *vector sum* of all forces acting on the body is zero. The word "net" refers to the second situation. Even though a body may have many forces acting on it, these forces may act against each other. They may balance each other in such a way that the body does not move. If such a body is at rest, it will remain at rest. If it is in motion, it will continue in its motion *in a straight line with uniform velocity.* **Newton's first law of motion** may therefore be summarized as follows: *If there is no net force acting on a body, it will continue in its state of rest or will continue moving along a straight line with uniform velocity.*

At first glance, this law seems to contradict our everyday experiences. If we want to keep a car moving with a constant velocity, the car's engine must apply a constant force to it. If the engine stops applying this force, the car comes to a stop. Only then does the car seem to obey the part of Newton's law that states that objects at rest will remain at rest unless acted upon by an unbalanced force.

Close study of a moving car shows, however, that it is the force of friction that brings the car to a stop, and not the absence of the force provided by the engine. If it were possible to remove

3.8 Inertia

The Bettman Archive

3-12 An artist's conception of Sir Isaac Newton contemplating the fall of an apple. Newton formulated the law of gravitation and three laws of motion that describe how forces act on matter.

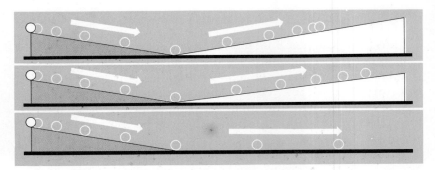

3-13 Diagram of Galileo's thought experiment. In the upper and middle drawings, the ball reaches the same height at which it started. In the lower drawing, the ball continues to move indefinitely at constant speed. In each drawing, the successive images show the positions of the ball after equal time intervals.

this friction, it would be reasonable to assume that the car would keep rolling without applying a constant force.

The study of the motion of a car in the absence of friction is an example of a *thought experiment*, since it cannot be performed under actual conditions. It was a thought experiment of this kind that led Galileo to an understanding of inertia even before Newton described it. Galileo noticed that if a ball rolls down one incline and up a second one (as shown in Fig. 3-13), the ball will reach almost the same height on the second incline as the height from which it started on the first incline. Galileo concluded that the difference in height is caused by friction, and that if friction could be eliminated the heights would be exactly alike. Then he reasoned that the ball would reach the same height no matter how shallow the slope of the second incline. Finally, if the second slope were eliminated altogether, the ball would keep rolling indefinitely with constant velocity. This is the same idea as the one expressed in Newton's first law of motion which deals with the property of inertia. Inertia keeps a stationary object stationary and it keeps a moving object moving.

The greater the inertia of an object, the greater is the force required to produce a given acceleration. A pencil lying on the floor has relatively little mass and therefore little inertia, and you can produce acceleration easily by kicking it with your foot. A brick has much more inertia. You can easily tell its difference from the pencil if you try to kick it. Newton's first law specifies which aspects of motion have a *cause*, and which aspects do not. Uniform motion in a straight line is the only motion possible for an isolated object, far removed from other objects. Non-uniform motion of an object is always *caused* by the presence of some other object.

3.9 Law of acceleration

Newton's first law of motion tells us how a body acts when there is no net applied force. Now let us consider what happens when there *is* either a single applied force or there are two or more applied forces whose *vector sum* is not zero. In the following discussion, we shall use "applied force" or just "force" to mean the vector sum of all forces applied to the body.

Newton's second law of motion may be stated: *the effect of an applied force is to cause the body to accelerate in the direction of the force. The acceleration is in direct proportion to the force and in inverse proportion to the mass of the body.*

If the body is at rest when the force is applied, it will begin to move in the direction of the force and will move faster and faster so long as the force continues.

If the body is moving in a straight line and a force is applied in the direction of its motion, it will increase in speed and continue to do so as long as the force continues. If the force is applied in the direction opposite to the motion, the acceleration will again be in the direction of the force, causing the body to slow down. If such a force continues long enough, the body will slow down to a stop and then begin to move with increasing speed in the opposite direction.

If the force applied to a moving object is not along the line of its motion, the acceleration will still be in the direction of the force. The effect in general will be to change both the direction and the speed of the motion. We shall postpone detailed consideration of this more complex case until Chapter 5. For the present, we shall consider only the velocity of an object initially at rest or one that is moving in a straight line, changed only by a force acting along that line.

It should be emphasized again that a body to which no force is applied has zero acceleration. If such a body is in motion, its velocity does not change. If it is at rest, its velocity also remains unchanged, that is, it stays at zero. And when there is no change in velocity, the acceleration is zero. When a force is applied to a body, the acceleration is not zero and the acceleration is in the direction of the applied force.

This statement about the direction of acceleration is the first of the three parts of Newton's second law of motion. The second and third parts deal with the *magnitude* of the acceleration caused by an applied force. If different forces are applied to the same body, the magnitude of the acceleration is directly proportional to the amount of the force. That is, doubling the force causes the acceleration to double, and so on.

We can express such a direct proportion as an equation by saying that one of the quantities equals the other one times a constant, or

$$F = ka$$

in which F is the applied force, a is the resulting acceleration,

Northrop Corporation

3-14 A demonstration of inertia. Just before this picture was taken, the dishes were sitting on a table. Then the table and the platform on which it was standing were pushed quickly toward the right.

and k is the constant of proportionality. Since F and a are both vectors, this equation also says that the applied force and the resulting acceleration are in the same direction (which is a restatement of the first part of Newton's second law of motion).

What happens when forces are applied to *different* objects? This question brings us to the third part of Newton's second law. It turns out that the equation, $F = ka$, is always true, but that the value of k is different for different objects. In fact, we find that if we properly define the units of force and mass, the value of k for any object is identical with the mass, m, of that object. The equation may be written

$$F = ma$$

In the MKS system, the unit of mass is the kilogram, and acceleration has the units of meters per second^2. (See Section 3.5.) The force required to accelerate 1 kilogram of mass at 1 meter per second^2 is 1 kg m/sec^2. As we defined it previously, this force is called a *newton* (n).

$$1 \text{ n} = 1 \text{ kg m/sec}^2$$

Since the acceleration acquired by a particular object is directly proportional to the amount of force applied, this law of acceleration can be expressed as the proportion:

$$\frac{F}{F'} = \frac{a}{a'}$$

In the case of a freely falling object, one of the forces is known. It equals the weight, F_w, of the object. The acceleration g is also known. It is the acceleration due to gravitational attraction, 9.80 m/sec^2. Making these substitutions, the proportion becomes

$$\frac{F}{F_w} = \frac{a}{g}$$

and

$$F = \frac{F_w a}{g}$$

Using this equation, we can calculate the force needed to give any desired acceleration to an object of known weight.

Since $F = ma$, we can substitute this value for F in the above equation and get

$$ma = \frac{F_w a}{g}$$

Dividing both sides of the equation by *a*, we have

$$m = \frac{F_w}{g} \quad \text{and} \quad F_w = mg$$

See the following example.

Example

What force is required to accelerate a car weighing 2.00×10^4 n from 30.0 km/hr to 70.0 km/hr in 10.0 sec?

Solution

Basic equation: $F = ma$

but $m = \dfrac{F_w}{g}$

and $a = \dfrac{\Delta v}{\Delta t} = \dfrac{v_f - v_i}{\Delta t}$

Substituting for *m* and *a* we get
Working equation:

$$F = \frac{F_w(v_f - v_i)}{gt}$$

$$F = \frac{2.00 \times 10^4 \text{ n } (70.0 \text{ km/hr} - 30.0 \text{ km/hr})(1000 \text{ m/km})}{(9.80 \text{ m/sec}^2)(10.0 \text{ sec})(3600 \text{ sec/hr})}$$

$$F = 2.28 \times 10^3 \text{ n}$$

3.10 Law of interaction

Newton's third law of motion states: *Whenever one body exerts a force on another, the second body exerts on the first a force of equal magnitude in the opposite direction.* To illustrate this law, consider some of the forces which are exerted when a book is resting on the top of a level table. The book exerts a downward force against the table. The table top exerts an upward force on the book. These forces are equal in magnitude and opposite in direction. In order to walk forward on a level floor you exert a horizontal force against the floor with your feet, while the floor pushes against your feet with a force, in the opposite direction, of equal magnitude.

In each of these situations we have two objects. In the first instance, the objects are the book and the table. In the second instance, they are the foot and the floor. Two forces are involved in each situation. In the first, they are the force of the book against the table and the force of the table against the book. In the second, they are the force of the foot against the floor and the force of the floor against the foot. In cases such as these, one force may be called the *action*, while the second force may be called the *reaction*.

The law of reaction holds true for all objects at all times, whether they are stationary or moving. Let us consider another example. A boy rows a boat toward the shore of a lake and when he is a meter or so from shore, he attempts to leap ashore. He exerts a force against the boat and the boat exerts an equal but opposite force against him. The boy's force against the boat accelerates him in the opposite direction. If we assume the resistance to the motion of the boat by the water to be negligible, the amount of acceleration of each object is inversely proportional to its mass. The boy might judge the force he must exert to reach shore on the basis of his experience in jumping the same distance from an object fixed to the earth. If so, when he jumps from the boat, he might not reach shore, but instead fall into the water.

Suppose we fasten one spring balance to a rigid support and hook another spring balance to it. If we pull on one balance, we find that both balance readings are the same. The pull of the first balance on the second equals the pull of the second on the first. The action is equal but opposite to the reaction.

3-15 An example of action-reaction. The readings on the two spring balances are equal because the force exerted by the person pulling on one balance is accompanied by an equal and opposite resisting force of the table.

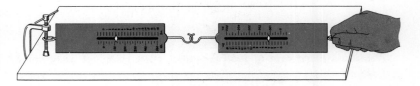

You may argue that motion cannot occur if action and reaction are equal. If two people pull upon a lightweight wagon, with equal force in the opposite directions, the wagon will not move. But this is not an example of action and reaction. There are two forces, it is true, *but they are both exerted on the same object.* Action and reaction are shown in the force which each one's feet exert against the ground and the equal but opposite force the ground exerts against the feet.

QUESTIONS

1. If a steel ball is placed on the top of a level table, it will remain there. (a) What forces are acting on the ball in this situation? (b) Are there any unbalanced forces acting on the ball?

2. (a) If the steel ball of Question 1 is given a slight push, what happens to the ball? (b) What forces act on the ball after it has been pushed? (c) Are any of these unbalanced forces? (d) What is the effect of the various forces on the motion of the ball?

3. (a) State Newton's first law of motion. (b) Describe the motion of a body in equilibrium.

4. (a) If other conditions are constant, how does the acceleration of an object vary with the amount of force applied? (b) How does the direction of the acceleration compare with the direction of the applied force?

5. How does the acceleration produced on different objects by identical forces vary with the mass of the object?

6. (a) State Newton's second law of motion. (b) What equation expresses the relationship of force to mass and acceleration?

7. How can the amount of force required to produce a certain acceleration of an object of known weight be calculated?

8. Suppose a brick is suspended from a rigid support by a suitable length of cord. (a) What downward force acts on the brick? (b) If this force is the action force, what force is the reaction force?

9. (a) What upward force acts on the suspended brick in Question 8? (b) If this force is the action force, what is the corresponding reaction force?

10. (a) What is meant by a thought experiment? (b) Give an example.

11. Why does a falling object in a vacuum undergo constant acceleration?

12. (a) Does Newton's second law hold only when frictional forces are absent? (b) Explain.

13. A fishline will break when a force of more than 600 n is exerted on it. Two people pull on the line in opposite directions with a force of 400 n each. (a) Will the fish line break? (b) Explain.

14. Explain the thought experiment you could devise to determine the mass of an object if you had only the following objects: A frictionless horizontal plane, a 1-kilogram standard, a meter stick, a spring balance in which the scale is marked in units unknown to you, and a stopwatch.

15. A tractor is pulling a heavy load. (a) If, according to Newton's third law, the load is pulling back as hard as the tractor is pulling forward, then why does the tractor move? (b) Make a drawing of the situation and show the appropriate force vectors.

PROBLEMS

Note: Use $g = 9.80$ m/sec^2. All forces are net forces.

Group A
1. What force is required to accelerate a 3.0-kg object (which is free to move) at 5.0 m/sec^2?
2. What is the mass of an object which is accelerated 3.00 m/sec^2 by a force of 125 n?
3. What acceleration does an object, mass 15 kg, undergo when a force of 25 n acts on it?
4. What is the weight of a 24-kg block of stone at sea level?

Group B
5. What is the mass of a bag of cement that weighs 485 n at sea level?
6. What force is required to give a projectile weighing 475 n an acceleration of 3.00×10^3 m/sec^2?
7. A truck weighs 1.0×10^5 n. What force will give it an acceleration of 1.5 m/sec^2?

GRAVITATION

3.11 Newton's Law of Universal Gravitation

In addition to formulating his three laws of motion, Newton described the force that makes falling bodies accelerate toward the earth. In doing so, he made use of the laws of planetary motion that were developed by Johannes Kepler almost a century before Newton's time. In Newton's own account of his study of falling bodies, he states that he wondered whether the force that makes an apple fall to the ground was related to the force that keeps the planets in their orbits. If so, a single law could be used to describe the attraction between objects in all parts of the universe.

From Kepler's laws, Newton deduced the fact that the *force of attraction between two objects is directly proportional to the product of the masses of the objects and inversely proportional to the square of the distance between their centers of mass.* (The center of mass of an object is that point at which all of its mass can be considered to be concentrated. This concept is similar to that of "center of gravity," which will be discussed in Chapter 4.) Newton called this attractive force the force of *gravitation*, hence the statement is known as Newton's **law of universal gravitation**. In equation form the law is

$$F = G\frac{m_1 m_2}{s^2}$$
(Equation 1)

where F is the force of gravitational attraction, m_1 and m_2 are the masses of the attracting objects, s is the distance between their centers of mass, and G is a proportionality constant called the *universal gravitational constant*.

Newton was only able to confirm his theory with astronomical observations. He was unable to confirm his theory in the laboratory and to measure *G* with the instruments available to him at his time. The first determination of *G* was made in 1797 by the English scientist Henry Cavendish (1731–1810). A schematic diagram of his apparatus is shown in Fig. 3-16. Two small lead balls are attached to the end of a lightweight rod that has a mirror attached to it. The rod is suspended by a thin quartz fiber. Two large lead balls are placed in fixed positions near the small balls. The gravitational force between the fixed and movable balls draws the movable balls toward the fixed ones. This motion causes the suspending fiber to twist. The fiber offers a slight resistance to twisting. The resistance increases as the twisting increases and the angle of twist is proportional to the force of gravitation between the fixed and the movable balls. The angle of twist could be measured directly from the rod's movement, but the sensitivity of the instrument can be increased by shining a light into the mirror. The light is reflected onto a distant scale and small movements of the mirror result in large movements of the reflected light across the scale. Such an arrangement is called an optical lever. Since *G* has a very small value, extreme care must be used to isolate the Cavendish apparatus from outside forces such as those produced by air currents and electric charges.

The value of *G* has been found to be 6.67×10^{-11} n m^2/kg^2. But recent studies of bodies in the solar system, especially the moon, indicate that *G* may not be constant. Gravitational attraction between the earth and the moon moves large masses of water on the earth. (These movements of water are called tides.) Moving this mass on the earth causes the moon's rotation to slow down. However, the moon is slowing down at twice the rate that can be attributed to the tides. The extra decrease can be explained by a decrease in *G* of about 1 part in 10 billion per year. Similar evidence is seen in the orbits of binary stars (stars that revolve around each other). The rate of revolution of binary stars, as well as the sizes of their orbits, depend upon the value of *G*. The large number of binary stars having large orbits supports the idea that the value of *G* is gradually decreasing.

Once *G* has been measured, the equation for Newton's law of universal gravitation (Equation 1 in the previous section) can be used to find the force of gravitation between any two objects of known mass with a known distance between their centers of mass. Or, if the force of gravitation, the distance, and one of the masses are known, the equation can be used to

3-16 Schematic diagram of the Cavendish experiment. The gravitational attraction between the balls can be measured by observing, with the help of a light beam, the deflection of the rod carrying the small balls.

NASA

The earth as seen from lunar orbit by the Apollo 8 astronauts. Separated by 380,000 kilometers of space, the earth and moon are held by gravitation in a mutually revolving system.

3.12 The mass of the earth

$$F_g = G \frac{M_1 M_2}{R^2}$$

[handwritten annotations:]

$w = 980N$

$w = mg$

$980N = m (9.80 m/s^2)$

$\dfrac{}{9.80} \qquad \dfrac{}{9.80}$

$m = 100 kg$

$F = 2000 N$

$F = ma$

$2000N = 100 kg \cdot \vec{a}$

$\vec{a} = 20 m/s^2$

find the value of the other mass. For example, Equation 1 can be used to find the mass of the earth. In the equation, use m_e, the mass of the earth, for m_1. For m_2, use m_p, the mass of a particle on the earth's surface. In this case s will be the radius of the earth. The force of attraction, F, will be the weight of the particle, so we shall replace F by F_w.

$$F_w = G\frac{m_e m_p}{s^2} \qquad \text{(Equation 2)}$$

Dividing both sides of the equation by m_p,

$$\frac{F_w}{m_p} = \frac{Gm_e}{s^2} \qquad \text{(Equation 3)}$$

But

$$F_w = m_p g \qquad \text{(Equation 4)}$$

Or

$$\frac{F_w}{m_p} = g \qquad \text{(Equation 5)}$$

Substituting Equation 5 in Equation 3,

$$g = \frac{Gm_e}{s^2} \qquad \text{(Equation 6)}$$

Since both G and m_e are constants, Equation 6 shows that the acceleration due to gravity in a given location depends only on the square of the distance from the center of the earth.

Equation 6 may be used to determine the mass of the earth. Solving this equation for m_e

$$m_e = \frac{gs^2}{G}$$

Substituting 9.80 m/sec² for g, 6.37×10^6 m for s, and 6.67×10^{-11} n m²/kg² for G, $m_e = 5.96 \times 10^{24}$ kg, the mass of the earth.

3.13 Relation of gravity and weight

*The term **force of gravity** is used to describe the force of gravitational attraction on or near the surface of a celestial body, such as the earth.* Thus we say that the moon has less gravity than the earth because the force of gravitational attraction near the moon's surface is smaller than the force of gravitational attraction near the earth's surface. A calculation of the force of gravity of a celestial body must also take into consideration the size of the body, since the force of gravitational attraction also varies inversely with the square of the distance to the center of mass of the body.

The value for the mass of the earth can be used to determine the theoretical value of the force of gravity at any given location on or above the earth's surface. Such factors as local variations in the composition of the earth's crust and the effect of the earth's rotation must be considered to obtain the actual value of the force of gravity at a particular location.

Equation 2, Section 3.11 shows that the weight of an object is the measure of the force of attraction between the object and the earth. When we say that a man weighs $90\overline{0}$n, we mean that the force exerted on him by the earth is $90\overline{0}$ n. The man also exerts a force of $90\overline{0}$ n on the earth. Equation 4 tells us that the weight of an object equals the product of its mass and the acceleration due to the force of gravity. The mass of an object is constant. But Equation 6 indicates that the acceleration due to the force of gravity is inversely proportional to the square of the distance from the center of the body to the center of the earth. All parts of the earth's surface are not the same distance from its center, the variations ranging from 393 m below sea level at the shore of the Dead Sea to 8848 m above sea level at the top of Mount Everest. An object at the top of a mountain, where the force of gravity is less, will weigh less there than it does at sea level. Also, since the earth is slightly flattened at the poles and since the earth's rotation counteracts the force of gravitation, an object weighs a little more at the North Pole than it does at the equator.

The value of g, the acceleration due to gravity, at a particular point is sometimes called the *gravitational field strength* at that point. The effect of rotation, if any, is usually included in determining g. *A region of space in which each point is associated with the value of g at that point is called a* **gravitational field**. Since g is an acceleration, it is a vector. Hence, a gravitational field is a region of space in which each point has associated with it a vector equal to the value of g at that point and which is called the gravitational field strength.

If an object of mass m is located at any point in a gravitational field, the gravitational force on the object can be calculated by the equation in Section 3.8

$$F_W = mg$$

If the mass of the object is 1 kg, then F_w is numerically equal to g. Therefore, another way to think of the gravitational field strength at a point is that it equals the gravitational force that

Table 3-2 SURFACE GRAVITIES OF THE MOON AND PLANETS

Body	Relative gravity (Earth = 1.00)
Jupiter	2.64
Neptune	1.41
Saturn	1.13
Uranus	1.07
Earth	1.00
Venus	0.91
Mercury	0.39
Mars	0.38
Pluto	uncertain
Moon	0.16

3.14 Gravitational fields

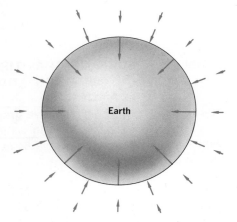

3-17 Simplified diagram of the earth's gravitational field. The inner circle of vectors represents the magnitude and direction of the field at various places on the earth's surface. The other vectors represent the field at different altitudes.

would be exerted on a mass of one kilogram if the mass were located at that point, or

$$g = \frac{F_W}{m}$$

The value of g for the earth varies with the distance from the center of the earth and with certain other aspects of the earth's motion and composition. In Fig. 3-17, vectors are used to represent the gravitational field strength at various altitudes. Table 3-3 lists the values of gravitational field strength for various locations on the earth's surface, as determined by careful measurements.

The concept of a field is more subtle and more complicated than the idea of direct forces acting between objects. Yet the field concept can explain more physical phenomena (such as electromagnetic waves) than the simpler concept of action at a distance. The field idea pictures objects as having associated regions such that a mass would be acted on by a force if it were placed in the region. Thus a ball falls to the earth because of the interaction between the gravitational field of the earth and the ball.

A gravitational field may be thought of as resulting from the fact that an object changes the properties of the space in its vicinity. It should not be supposed, however, that the field concept is an explanation of the cause of gravitation any more than the idea of acceleration is. Even though scientists are able to

NASA

On the earth, this astronaut's gear would be much too heavy for him to carry. On the moon, it weighs only about 1/6 as much.

Table 3-3 GRAVITATIONAL FIELD STRENGTH OF THE EARTH

Location	Latitude	Altitude (m)	Field Strength (n/kg)
North Pole	90°N	0	9.832
Greenland	70°N	20	9.825
Stockholm	59°N	45	9.818
Brussels	51°N	102	9.811
Banff	51°N	1376	9.808
Chicago	42°N	182	9.803
New York	41°N	38	9.803
Denver	40°N	1638	9.796
San Francisco	38°N	114	9.800
Canal Zone	9°N	6	9.782
Java	6°S	7	9.782
New Zealand	37°S	3	9.800

express certain aspects of gravitation in terms of acceleration and force fields, the real nature and origin of the force of gravitation are still unknown.

The concept of fields is not restricted to gravitation. The concept is useful whenever effects extend into the region surrounding their source. We will have occasion to use the idea of fields again in the discussion of magnetism, electricity, and nuclear structure.

wt in N

m in Kg

QUESTIONS

Group A

1. (a) What force acts on an artificial satellite in orbit around the earth? (b) What force is the satellite exerting?
2. (a) On what factors does the magnitude of the force of gravitational attraction depend? (b) How is the force of gravitational attraction related to these factors?
3. Why must we exert five times as much force to lift a mass of 5 kg as we must to lift a mass of 1 kg?
4. Assuming your mass remains constant, how will your weight vary as you go from Colorado Springs, elevation 1800 m, to the top of Pikes Peak, elevation 4300 m?
5. Even though your mass remains constant, what happens to your weight as you drive from the entrance to Death Valley National Monument, elevation 1600 m, down to the lowest spot in Death Valley, 85 m below sea level?
6. Describe the method used by Cavendish to measure the universal gravitational constant.

Group B

7. (a) How would the weight of an object vary as it is transported from the earth to the moon? (b) How would its weight vary if it were transported to the center of the earth?
8. Why does the equation $g = Gm_e/s^2$ give a theoretical and not an actual value for the acceleration due to gravity at a given location?
9. (a) What is meant by a gravitational field? (b) How is gravitational field strength defined?

PROBLEMS

Group A

1. The acceleration due to gravity on the moon has been calculated to be 1.98 m/sec². If a person weighs 795 n on the earth, what will be the weight on the moon?
2. The instrument-carrying payload of a rocket weighs 1058 n on the surface of the earth. What does it weigh 2.560 × 10⁴ km above the earth?

3. The acceleration due to gravity at Hartford, Connecticut, is 9.80336 m/sec². What is the force of gravitational attraction in newtons on a mass of 0.250000 kg at this location?

Group B 4. What is the force of gravitational attraction between two spherical $10\bar{0}$-kg masses whose centers are 2.00 m apart?

5. Two spheres with masses of 5.00 kg and 10.0 kg respectively are 0.300 m apart. Calculate the force of gravitational attraction between them.

6. Calculate the theoretical value for the acceleration due to gravity at a point 1.00×10^7 m from the center of the earth.

7. Show that the dimensions of g in the equation $g = F_w/m$ are m/sec².

Chapter 4

Resolution and Composition of Forces

We saw in the last chapter that a force is a physical quantity that is required to change the motion of an object. Now we shall take a look at some other characteristics of forces and see how these characteristics are used in solving force problems.

When you push a door shut with your hand, your hand exerts a force on the door. The door also exerts a force on your hand. When you sit in a chair, you push on the chair and the chair pushes on you. In both of these cases, there is physical contact between the objects that are exerting forces on each other.

Forces can also be exerted without such physical contact. While an object is falling toward the earth, the earth exerts a force on the object and the object exerts a force on the earth. Yet there is no physical contact between the earth and the falling object. These examples illustrate several important characteristics of forces:

1. A net force will change the state of motion of an object. The door moved because the force exerted by your hand was sufficient to overcome friction and other forces acting on the door. The falling object moved as it did because a force pulled it toward the earth. As we saw in Chapter 3, the application of a net force to an object always produces an acceleration.

2. Forces can be exerted through long distances. Gravitational forces and magnetic forces are examples of this characteristic.

3. Forces always occur in pairs. Whenever one object pushes or pulls on another object, there is a force on *each* of the two objects. In the given examples, the two objects were your hand and the door, you and the chair, the falling object and the earth.

4.1 Defining forces

Wrecking Corp. of America, Washington, D.C. and Controlled Demolition, Inc., Towson, Md., Courtesy, WRECKING & SALVAGE JOURNAL Hingham, Ma.

Large forces are needed in construction projects. Here dynamite is used to demolish a building in preparation for new construction.

4-1 The spring balance shows that the one-kilogram mass hanging from it weighs about 9.8 newtons at the location where the photograph was taken.

4.2 Using vectors to represent forces

4-2 Vector diagram of a force of 10,000 n applied by a tugboat to a barge through a towline. In such a diagram, the direction and point of application of the vector represents the line of action and point of application of the force. These may be reasoned from the direction and point of attachment of the towline.

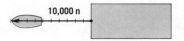

10,000 n

4. In each pair of forces, the two forces act in exactly opposite directions. You pushed on the door and the door pushed back. You pushed down and the chair pushed up. The earth pulled the falling object toward the earth's center and the object pulled the earth toward the object's center.

Now let us see how the magnitudes of forces are measured. (You will remember from Chapter 3 that forces are vector quantities and have both magnitudes and directions.) When an object is suspended from a spring, it is pulled toward the earth by the force of gravitation. The spring stretches until the restoring force of the spring is equal to the force of gravitation on the object. Another object having the same weight stretches the spring by the same amount. Both objects together stretch the spring twice as far, and an object with three times the weight stretches it three times as far, etc. This characteristic of coiled springs, that the amount of stretch is proportional to the force pulling on the spring, means that we may use the amount of stretch to measure the size of a force. A device that measures forces in this way is called a *spring balance.* (Fig. 4-1)

In physics, spring balances are often calibrated directly in newtons. Forces may also be measured with devices other than spring balances. But the results of such measurements can always be expressed in terms of a number of newtons.

In Section 2.8, vectors were introduced and used to solve velocity problems. Now vectors will be used to represent forces and to solve force problems. Vector quantities, such as forces, require a magnitude and a direction for their description. The magnitude of the force is represented by the length of the arrow. The line of action of the force, its direction, may be deduced from the physical situation. For example, suppose a barge is being towed through still water by a tugboat. The tugboat applies a force of 10,000 n (newtons) to the barge through the towline. The length of the arrow representing the force is proportional to the magnitude of the force, 10,000 n (Fig. 4-2). The point of application of the force is the point at which the rope is attached to the barge. A long rope can transmit only a pull in a direction along its length. It cannot transmit a push or a sideways force. The rope is in the direction of the force. The arrow should represent this direction.

Force vectors are manipulated like velocity vectors. For example, suppose two tugboats are attached to the same barge. Tugboat **A** is pulling with a force of 10,000 n and tugboat **B** is pulling with a force of 7,500 n in the same direction. Figure 4-3 represents this situation with vectors. The resultant force vector is 17,500 n in the direction of the towline. (Remember

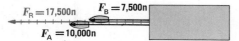

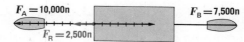

4-3 Vector diagram of two tugboats applying forces at point 0_1 and 0_2 to a barge. Tugboat A exerts a force of 10,000 n and tugboat B exerts a force of 7,500 n. The resultant force vector is 17,500 n in the direction both tugs are pulling.

4-4 Vector diagram of two tugboats applying forces to a barge in opposite directions. In many cases, even though the forces act on extended objects such as opposite ends of the barge as in our example, vectors may be considered as acting at the same point 0. Tugboat A pulling west exerts a force of 10,000 n. Tugboat B pulling east exerts a force of 7,500 n. The resultant force vector is 2,500 n in the direction of tugboat A.

that the sum of two or more vectors is called the *resultant*.) Figure 4-4 shows a vector diagram representing two tugboats pulling in opposite directions on a barge. In many cases, even though the forces act on extended objects such as opposite ends of the barge, vectors may be considered as acting at the same point, **O**. The resultant force vector is 2,500 n in the direction of tugboat **A**.

Example

Two tugboats are attached by separate towlines to the same point, **O**, on a barge. Tugboat **A** is pulling north with a force of $10,\overline{0}00$ n. Tugboat **B** is pulling east with a force of 7,500 n. What is the magnitude and direction of the resultant force vector?

Solution

Figure 4-5 represents this situation. In the figure, the resultant force is represented by F_R. Since **AOB** is a right angle, the parallelogram is a rectangle and **OAR** is also a right angle. **AR** is equal in length to **OB**.

$$\tan \theta = \frac{\mathbf{AR}}{\mathbf{OA}} = \frac{F_B}{F_A} = \frac{7,500 \text{ n}}{10,000 \text{ n}} = 0.75$$

$$\theta = 37°$$

$$\cos \theta = \frac{\mathbf{OA}}{\mathbf{OR}} = \frac{F_A}{F_R}$$

$$F_R = \frac{F_A}{\cos \theta} = \frac{10,000 \text{ n}}{0.799} = 12,500 \text{ n}$$

Hence, F_R = 12,500 n at an angle of 37° east of north.

4-5 Vector diagram of two tugboats applying forces to a barge. Tugboat A exerts a force of 10,000 n north. Tugboat B exerts a force of 7,500 n east. The resultant force vector is 12,500 n at an angle 37° east of north.

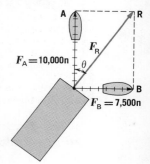

RESOLUTION OF FORCES

4.3 Components of force vectors

Frequently a force acts on a body in a direction in which the body cannot move. For example, gravitational force pulls vertically downward on a wagon on an incline, but the wagon can move only along the incline. Finding the magnitude of the force that is pulling the wagon along the incline is an example of a problem of *resolution of forces*. Instead of a single force, we can imagine two forces which, acting together, would have the same effect as the original single force. The advantage of this method is that we can choose the directions of the two single forces to be at any angle to each other and we can also choose the direction of any one of the two forces. In the case of the wagon one of the forces we can imagine, parallel to the surface of the incline, pulls the wagon along the incline. The other is perpendicular to the surface of the incline. This force was chosen because it does not contribute to the force along the incline. These forces are at right angles to each other. The two forces that have the same effect as the single force are called the *components* of the original force. *This procedure of finding component forces is called* **resolution of forces**. Most of the examples we shall consider involve resolving a force into components that are at right angles to each other.

4-6   Diagram for the determination of the eastward and southward components of a 10.0-n force acting at an angle of 53.0° south of east. (See the Example below.)

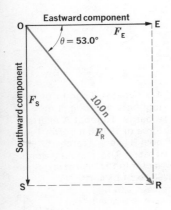

Example

A force of 10.0 n acts on point **O** at an angle of 53.0° south of east. Find the magnitudes of the southward and eastward components of its force vectors graphically and trigonometrically.

Solution

$F_S = F_R \sin \theta$
$\sin \theta = \sin 53.0° = 0.799$
$F_S = (10.0 \text{ n})(0.799) = 7.99 \text{ n}$, the southward component

$\cos \theta = \dfrac{\mathbf{OE}}{\mathbf{OR}} = \dfrac{F_E}{F_R}$ (F_E is the eastward force vector)

$F_E = F_R \cos \theta$
$\cos \theta = \cos 53.0° = 0.602$
$F_E = (10.0 \text{ n})(0.602) = 6.02 \text{ n}$, the eastward component

4.4 Resolving the force vector of gravitational attraction

An object placed on an inclined plane is attracted by the earth. The force of attraction is the weight of the object. See Fig. 4-7. The plane prevents the motion of the object in the direction of

F_W, the direction in which the earth's attraction acts. The vector representing the force of attraction may, however, be resolved into two components. One component acts in a direction perpendicular to the surface of the plane. (In physics, the term *normal* is often used to mean perpendicular. Hence we label the normal component F_N.) The other component, F_P, acts parallel to the plane. We choose these two components because they have physical significance. The vector F_N represents the force exerted by the object perpendicular to the incline or the amount of the object's weight supported by the incline. The vector F_P represents the component that tends to move the object down the incline. (The plane is assumed to be frictionless.)

Using F_W as the diagonal, we can construct the parallelogram **ODEF** and find the relative values of the sides F_P and F_N by plotting to scale. We can also express these values trigonometrically. Since triangles **ABC** and **OED** have mutually perpendicular or parallel sides, the triangles are similar and $\angle$ EOD $= \theta$. Hence $\sin \theta$ can be expressed either as $\dfrac{BC}{AB}$ or $\dfrac{F_P}{F_W}$. This equation means that the force vector parallel to the plane, F_P, is smaller in magnitude than the weight vector, F_W, in the same ratio as the height of the plane, **BC**, is smaller than its length, **AB**.

By using $\cos \theta$, it may be similarly shown that the magnitude of the force vector perpendicular to the plane, F_N, is related to the weight vector of the object in the same way that the base of the plane is related to its height.

If θ and F_W are known,
$$F_P = F_W \sin \theta$$
and $F_N = F_W \cos \theta$

Making the plane steeper increases the component F_P and decreases the component F_N. This steeper inclined plane is shown in Fig. 4-8. The vector F_a which is equal and opposite to F_P represents the applied force needed to keep the object from sliding down the plane. The steeper the plane, the greater this force becomes.

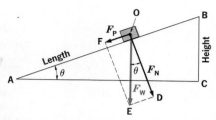

4-7   Resolution of gravitational force. One component acts parallel to the plane while the other component acts normal (perpendicular) to the plane.

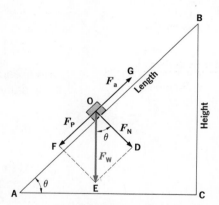

4-8   When the angle of the incline increases, the component of the weight acting parallel to the plane increases, while the component that acts normal (perpendicular) to the plane decreases.

QUESTIONS

1. (a) Define force. (b) Give examples of forces exerted by bodies in contact with each other. (c) What types of forces do not require such contact?
2. (a) What is the MKS unit of force? (b) From what fundamental units can it be derived?

Group A

3. How does a spring balance measure forces?
4. (a) What is the relationship between force and mass? (b) Between force and weight?
5. What properties of a force are represented by a force vector?

Constant Velocity

Group B 6. What type of motion is *not* the result of a net force?
7. List some possible sources of error in the use of the spring balance.
8. (a) Describe two convenient components of the weight of an object lying on an inclined plane. (b) How are the magnitudes of these components related to the angle of the incline?

Vertical and Horizontal
x + y

9. The transmitting tower of a TV station is held upright by guy wires which extend from the top of the tower to the ground. The wires make a 30.0° angle with the tower. Into what two convenient components can the force which the tower exerts on each guy wire be resolved?
10. An automobile is parked on a hill. (a) Into what two convenient components can the weight of the automobile be resolved? (b) Which component is counteracted by the brakes of the automobile?

PROBLEMS

Solve each of the following problems (a) graphically and (b) trigonometrically.

245 N

Group A 1. What single force is needed to support a stationary mass of 25.0 kg near the earth's surface?

160 N
160 N

2. A person pushes with 150.0 n of force along the handle of a lawn roller. The angle between the handle and the ground is 45.0°. Determine the magnitudes of the horizontal and vertical components of this force.

2.97 × 10³ N

3. A truck weighing 1.00×10^5 n is parked on a hill which rises 3.00 m in each 100 m of road. What is the magnitude of the component of its weight that tends to make the truck roll down the hill?

4. A rectangular picture frame weighing 4.00 n is supported by a wire attached to its two top corners and passed over a nail in the wall. The top edge of the picture frame is horizontal. What force is exerted by each half of the wire if the angle between them is (a) 60.0°; (b) 90.0°; (c) 120.0°?

2.3 N

Group B 5. A force of 25.0 n acts on point C at an angle of 35.0° west of north. What are the magnitudes of the northward and westward components of this force?

6. The rafters of a roof meet at an angle of 120.0°. What force is exerted along the rafters by an object weighing 6.00 × 10³ n suspended from the peak?

7. A boy pulls a sled along level ground. The rope with which he pulls the sled makes an angle of 20.0° with the ground as the boy pulls with a force of 78.0 n. What are the horizontal and vertical components of the force?

8. A crate having a mass of 114 kg rests on an inclined plane which makes an angle of 5.00° with the horizontal. (a) What force does the crate exert perpendicular to the plane? (b) What force tends to make the crate slide down the plane?

COMPOSITION OF FORCES

Just as it is possible to resolve a force into components, it is possible to combine several forces into a single force that produces the same effect. *When two or more forces have lines of action that pass through the same point, they are called* **concurrent forces** *and are said to act concurrently.* (Forces that have the same point of application act concurrently because their lines of action pass through the same point.) *A* **resultant force** *is a single force that produces the same effect as several forces acting concurrently.*

The resultant of two or more concurrent forces may be used as a substitute for those forces. The simplest example of such a resultant is that of two concurrent forces acting in the same direction. Suppose one boy pulls eastward with a force of $20\overline{0}$ n and another boy joins him and pulls in the same direction with a force of $30\overline{0}$ n. Refer to the vector diagram shown in Fig. 4-9. The resultant is the sum of the two forces, or $50\overline{0}$ n, acting eastward. One man, taking the place of the two boys, could produce the same effect with a force of $50\overline{0}$ n.

Now suppose one boy pulls eastward with a force of $40\overline{0}$ n and another boy pulls westward on the same point with a force of $60\overline{0}$ n. This time the resultant force is $20\overline{0}$ n westward, as shown in Fig. 4-10. *The resultant of two forces acting in the same or in opposite directions upon the same point has a magnitude equal to the algebraic sum of the forces, and acts in the direction of the greater force.*

Suppose one force of 10.0 n F_E, acts eastward upon an object at a point **O**. Another force of 15.0 n, F_S, acts southward upon the same point. Since these forces act concurrently upon point **O**, the vector diagram is constructed with the tails of both vectors at **O**. See Fig. 4-11. F_E tends to move the object eastward. The second force F_S tends to move the object southward.

4.5 Resultant force of concurrent forces

4-9 The resultant of two forces acting in the same direction has a magnitude equal to the sum of the forces and acts in the same direction.

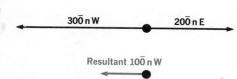

4-10 The resultant of two forces acting in opposite directions has a magnitude equal to the difference between the forces and acts in the direction of the greater force.

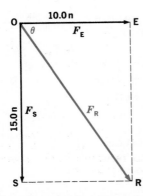

4-11 Diagram for the graphic and trigonometric determination of the resultant force vector of two force vectors acting at right angles.

When the forces act simultaneously, the object tends to move along the diagonal of the parallelogram of which the two forces are sides, or in the direction of F_R. *The resultant force vector of two forces acting at an angle upon a given point is equal to the diagonal of a parallelogram of which the two force vectors are sides.*

A graphic determination of the magnitude and direction of a resultant force can be made from a diagram constructed to scale. As in the problems of the resolution of forces in Section 4.4, the trigonometric solution makes use of the facts that the opposite sides of a parallelogram are equal and that the diagonal of a parallelogram divides it into two congruent triangles. If the two forces act at right angles, the magnitude and direction of the resultant F_R can now be determined as shown in the following example.

Example

Calculate the magnitude and direction of the resultant of the two forces acting on point **O** as shown in Fig. 4-7.

Solution

Triangle **OER** is a right triangle.

$$F_E = 10.0 \text{ n}$$
$$F_S = 15.0 \text{ n}$$
$$\tan \theta = \frac{F_S}{F_E} = \frac{15.0 \text{ n}}{10.0 \text{ n}} = 1.50$$
$$\theta = 56.3°$$
$$F_R = \frac{F_S}{\sin \theta} = \frac{15.0 \text{ n}}{0.833} = 18.0 \text{ n}$$

So $F_R = 18.0$ n 56.3° south of east

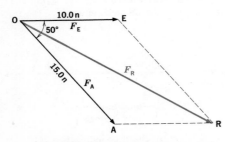

4-12 Diagram for the graphic and trigonometric determination of the resultant of two force vectors acting at an acute angle.

The angle between two forces acting on the same point is generally not a right angle. Figure 4-12 represents the vectors for two forces, 10.0 n east, and 15.0 n 50.0° south of east, acting on point **O**. The parallelogram is completed as shown. Observe that the diagonal vector representing the resultant *is drawn from the point on which the two original forces are acting, since the resultant will also act on this point.* (The other diagonal of the parallelogram does not represent the resultant of the two forces.) The magnitude of F_R is found graphically to be 23 n. The direction is 30° south of east.

The resultant is very different if the angle between the same two forces is 140.0°. The parallelogram is constructed to scale in the same manner, using the force vectors as sides, and making the angle between them 140.0°. This parallelogram is shown in Fig. 4-13. The diagonal must be drawn from **O**, the point at which the two forces act. The graphic solution for F_R yields $\overline{10}$ n 8° west of south.

The resultant of two forces acting at an acute or obtuse angle may be found trigonometrically by means of special formulas called the *law of sines* and *law of cosines*. Use of these formulas is shown in the following examples.

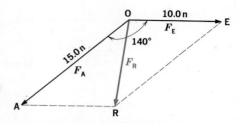

4-13 Diagram for the graphic and trigonometric determination of the resultant of two force vectors acting at an obtuse angle.

Example

Determine the magnitude and direction of the resultant of the forces shown in Fig. 4-14.

Solution

The magnitude and direction of F_R can be found by the application of the law of cosines and law of sines.

$\angle \textbf{EOA} = 50.0°$

$\angle \textbf{OER} = 130.0°$

By the cosine law,

$$F_R = \sqrt{F_E^2 + F_A^2 - 2\,F_E F_A \cos \angle \textbf{OER}}$$

where $\cos \angle \textbf{OER} = \cos 130.0° = -\cos(180.0° - 130.0°)$

$\qquad\qquad\qquad = -\cos 50.0° = -0.643$

$F_R = \sqrt{(10.0\text{ n})^2 + (15.0\text{ n})^2 - 2(10.0\text{ n})(15.0\text{ n})(-0.643)} = 22.8$ n

By the sine law,

$$\frac{\textbf{ER}}{\sin \angle \textbf{EOR}} = \frac{\textbf{OR}}{\sin \angle \textbf{OER}}$$

$$\sin \angle \textbf{EOR} = \frac{(\textbf{ER})(\sin \angle \textbf{OER})}{\textbf{OR}}$$

$\sin \angle \textbf{OER} = \sin 130.0° = \sin(180.0° - 130.0°) = \sin 50.0° = 0.766$

$$\sin \angle \textbf{EOR} = \frac{(15.0\text{ n})(0.766)}{22.8\text{ n}} = 0.504$$

$\angle \textbf{EOR} = 30.3°$

The direction of F_R is 30.3° south of east.

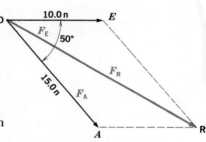

4-14 Diagram for a simplified trigonometric determination of the resultant of two force vectors acting at an acute angle.

4.6 The equilibrant force

Equilibrium is the state of a body in which there is no change in its motion. A body in equilibrium is either at rest or moving at constant speed in a straight line. In this section we shall discuss the conditions for equilibrium of bodies at rest. The same conditions hold for the equilibrium of bodies which are in motion. Examples of these conditions will be discussed in Chapter 5.

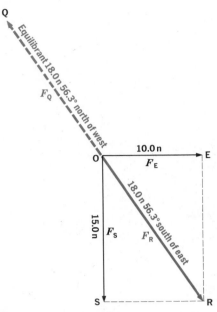

4-15 The equilibrant of two forces acting at a point is applied at the same point. It equals the magnitude of their resultant, but acts in the opposite direction.

A body at rest must be in both translational and rotational equilibrium. Translational equilibrium means that there is no linear motion of the body. It requires that no unbalanced (net) forces are acting on the body. This statement is called the *first condition of equilibrium*. (The second condition of equilibrium deals with rotation. It will be discussed in Section 4.13.)

When there are no unbalanced forces acting on a body, the vector sum of all the forces acting on the body is zero. For example, if a girl pulls on a rope with a force of $\overline{80}$ n and another girl pulls on the same rope in the opposite direction with a force of $\overline{80}$ n, the vector sum of the two forces is zero and the system is in equilibrium. We can say also that each force is the *equilibrant* of the other.

To find the equilibrant of two forces, we first find their resultant. Then, since the equilibrant must balance the effect of this resultant, the equilibrant must have the same magnitude but act in the opposite direction. Figure 4-15 shows the equilibrant for the same force vectors that were used in the explanation of the resultant shown in Fig. 4-11.

Similarly, the equilibrant of three or more concurrent forces can be found, first, by vector addition of their force vectors to obtain the resultant. The equilibrant is then drawn from the origin of the resultant so that it is equal in magnitude to the resultant but extends in the opposite direction. *When two or more forces act concurrently at a point, the* **equilibrant force** *is that single force which, if applied at the same point, would produce equilibrium.*

QUESTIONS

Group A   1. (a) What is a resultant force? (b) How is the resultant found when two forces act on the same point at the same time?
2. How can we determine mathematically the magnitude and direction of the resultant of two forces which act at right angles to each other on the same point?
3. (a) What is equilibrium? (b) What condition must be met for a body to be in equilibrium?
4. (a) What is an equilibrant force? (b) At what point must it be applied? (c) How does it compare with the resultant force?

Group B   5. How can we determine mathematically the magnitude and direction of the resultant of two forces which act at any angle to each other on the same point?

6. What method can be used to find the magnitude of the resultant of three or more forces which act simultaneously on the same point?

7. How is the resultant affected when force vectors are added in different order?

PROBLEMS

1. Two forces act simultaneously on point **A**. One force is 5.0 n south; the other is 15.0 n south. Determine the magnitude and direction of the resultant force vector.

Group A

2. Two forces act on point **E**. One is 20.0 n north; the other is 20.0 n 30.0° south of east. Determine the magnitude and direction of (a) the resultant, (b) the equilibrant.

(a) 20 n @ 30°

(b) 20 n @ 210°

3. A girl weighs 612 n. If she sits in the middle of a hammock which is 3.0 m long and sags 1.0 m below the points of support, what force would be exerted by each of the two hammock ropes?

460 n

4. Trigonometrically determine the magnitude and direction of the resultant of the two force vectors shown in Fig. 4-13.

Group B

9.8 n @ 261° or -99°

5. Two forces of 10.0 n east and 30.0 n 30.0° south of west respectively, act on the same point. Determine the magnitude and direction of (a) the resultant, (b) the equilibrant.

21.9 n @ 223° or -137°

6. Three forces act simultaneously on point **J**. One force is 10.0 n north; the second is 15.0 n west; the third is 15.0 n 30.0° east of north. Determine the magnitude and direction of the resultant.

24.2 n @ 108°

7. A sign weighing 495 n is supported as shown in the diagram at the right. Determine the magnitudes and directions of the forces exerted by the chain and by the bracket. Assume that the horizontal rod cannot support vertical forces.

chain 862 n

Bracket 706 n

8. A block of stone having a mass of 2.00 × 10³ kg is to be raised by a crane. The angle between the load cable and the crane boom is 30.0°. The hinged boom is held in place by a tie cable which forms an angle of 20.0° with the boom. See the diagram at the right. Determine the magnitude of the thrust force (push) of the boom and of the tie force (pull) of the cable.

$F_T = 2.90 \times 10^4$ n

$F_B = 4.44 \times 10^4$ n

FRICTION

4.7 The nature of friction

In Section 4.4 we discussed the resolution of the weight of an object resting on an incline. One of the components of the weight tends to pull the object down the incline. As the angle of the incline increases, this component also increases. If there is no restraining force on the object, the slightest angle of incline produces this component that causes the object to slide.

In performing experiments of this type, however, we find that the object does not begin to slide until the component parallel to the incline reaches a certain value. Forces must exist between the object and the incline that prevent the object from sliding. These forces are called *forces of friction*, or simply *friction*. **Friction** *is a force that resists motion. It involves objects that are in contact with each other and are sliding or rolling over each other.*

The cause of friction is not simple. Some scientists believe that friction is caused mainly by the uneven surfaces of the touching objects. As the surfaces are rubbed together, they tend to interlock and thus offer resistance to being moved over each other. It has been shown that tiny particles are actually torn from one surface and become imbedded in the other.

One would expect from this theory of friction that if the two surfaces are carefully polished, sliding friction between them would be lessened. Experiments have shown, however, that there is a limit to the amount by which friction may be reduced by polishing the surfaces. If they are made very smooth, the friction between them actually increases. This observation has led to the theory that some cases of sliding friction may actually be caused by the same forces that hold atoms and molecules together.

In many instances, friction is very desirable. We would be unable to walk if there were no friction between the soles of our shoes and the ground. There must be friction between the tires of an automobile and the road before the automobile can move. When we apply the brakes on the automobile, the friction between the brake linings and brake drums or discs slows down the wheels. Friction between the tires and the road brings the car to a stop. In a less obvious way, friction holds screws and nails in place and, if the table is not perfectly level, it keeps dishes from sliding off the table. On the other hand, friction can also be a disadvantage, as is the case when we try to move a heavy piece of furniture by sliding it across the floor.

4.8 Principles of friction   Friction experiments are not difficult to perform but the results are not always easy to express as equations or laws. The following statements, therefore, should be understood as approximate descriptions only. Furthermore, they deal only with solid objects. Frictional forces involving liquids and gases are beyond the scope of this book. Also, our discussion is restricted to starting and sliding friction. Rolling friction is not considered in this introductory treatment.

1. Friction acts parallel to the surfaces that are in contact and in the direction opposite to the motion of the object or to the net force tending to produce such motion. Figure 4-16 illustrates this principle. The weight of the block F_W is balanced by the upward force of the table $F_W{}'$. The force F_a is sliding the block along the table top. In this case, F_a is parallel to the table top. The frictional force F_f resists the motion and is exerted in a direction opposite to that of F_a.

2. Friction depends on the nature of the materials in contact and the smoothness of their surfaces. The friction between two pieces of wood is different from the friction between wood and metal.

3. Sliding friction is usually less than starting friction. Starting friction prevents motion until the surfaces begin to slide.

4. Sliding friction is practically independent of speed. This statement is approximately true for sliding speeds that are neither very small nor very great. At very small speeds, the sliding motion of two objects tends to be jerky, as though the two surfaces stick and then slip. There is starting friction and then sliding friction between them. At very high speeds, the points of contact between the two objects may become very hot (to the point of melting) and this effect tends to reduce the friction.

We do not notice much difference in the friction between sled runners and snow when we change the speed of the sled. However, when a steady pressure is applied to the brake pedal of a car, the car slows down and comes to a jolting halt. In this case, friction is apparently greatest just before the car stops. Objects moving at very high speeds, such as a bullet moving through a gun barrel, experience less friction than slower-moving objects. Nevertheless, beyond certain speeds there seems to be no change in friction. These differences are probably due to the changing nature of the rubbing surfaces as they get warm. So it is best to restrict the fourth statement about friction to "medium" speeds.

5. Friction is practically independent of the area of contact. The force needed to slide a block along a table is almost the same whether the block lies on a side or on end (Fig. 4-17). The surfaces are in contact in more places when the area of contact is large, but the pressure is greater when the area is small.

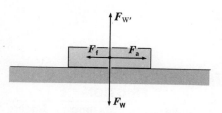

4-16 Forces on a block being pulled along a surface. The block does not move until F_a exceeds the force of friction, F_f.

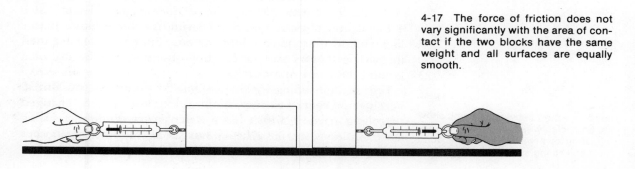

4-17 The force of friction does not vary significantly with the area of contact if the two blocks have the same weight and all surfaces are equally smooth.

6. Friction is directly proportional to the force pressing the two surfaces together. It does not require as much force to slide an empty chair across the floor as it does to slide the same chair when a person is sitting on it. The reason for this is that the extra force actually deforms the surfaces to some extent so that there are more areas of contact between them.

A simple way to measure starting and sliding friction is with a spring balance, as shown in Fig. 4-17. By sliding blocks of different sizes but of the same material and with equally smooth surfaces across the same surface, we can easily find the ratio between friction and the weight of the block. This ratio is called the *coefficient of friction*. It may be defined as *the ratio of the force of friction to the normal (perpendicular) force, F_N, pressing the surfaces together.* As an equation, it can be written as

$$\mu = \frac{F_f}{F_N}$$

where F_f is the force of friction, μ is the coefficient of friction, and F_N is the normal (perpendicular) force between the surfaces. (Within certain limits, this equation is an approximate summary of friction measurements.) The approximate values for the coefficients of friction of various surfaces in contact with each other are given in Table 4-1.

Table 4-1   COEFFICIENTS OF FRICTION

Surfaces	Starting friction	Sliding friction
steel on steel	0.74	0.57
glass on glass	0.94	0.40
wood on wood	0.50	0.30
rubber tire on dry road		0.70
rubber tire on wet road		0.50
Teflon on Teflon	0.04	0.04

4.9 Changing friction

In winter, we sand icy sidewalks and streets in order to increase friction. Tire chains and snow tires are used for the same reason. In baseball, a pitcher often uses a rosin bag in order to get more friction between his fingers and the ball. Many more examples could be given where friction is purposely increased.

The most common method of reducing sliding friction is by lubrication. A thin film of oil between rubbing surfaces reduces friction. The slight friction between a liquid and a solid is substituted for the greater friction between two solids. Alloys have also been developed which are, in effect, self lubricating. For example, when steel slides over an alloy of lead and antimony, the coefficient of friction is less than when steel slides on steel. Bearings lined with such an alloy reduce friction. From Table 4-1 it is also obvious that if a bearing is coated with a plastic like Teflon, there is very little friction. Such bearings are used in electric motors and other applications where the use of a liquid lubricant is undesirable.

Friction may also be greatly reduced through the use of ball bearings or roller bearings. Sliding friction is thereby changed to rolling friction, which has a much lower coefficient. Using steel cylinders to roll a heavy box along the floor is another example of changing sliding to rolling friction.

Ebony Magazine

4-18 Friction between skis and snow is appreciably reduced with the application of a wax layer on the wood or metal skiing surface.

The force required to slide an object along a level surface can be computed easily from the weight of the object and the coefficient of friction between the two surfaces. However, when the force applied to the object is not applied in the direction of the motion, it is necessary to resolve forces in the calculation. This resolution of forces is illustrated in the following example.

In the case of an object resting on an incline, the force of friction will determine whether the object remains at rest, slides down the incline with constant speed, or accelerates as it descends. How the angle of the incline and coefficient of friction are used in such a problem is illustrated in another example.

4.10 Solving friction problems

Example

A box weighing 450 n is pulled along a level floor at constant speed by a rope which makes an angle of 30.0° with the floor. If the force on the rope is 260 n, what is the coefficient of sliding friction?

Solution

Basic equation: $\mu = \dfrac{F_f}{F_N}$

Before we can use this equation, we must calculate the component of the applied force that acts parallel to the floor. Also, we must calculate the net normal force acting on the floor while the box is being pulled. This is done by finding the appropriate vector components.

The force F_a has a horizontal component F_h tending to speed up the object. The force of friction F_f acts opposite to F_h. Since the speed is constant, $F_f = F_h$

$$F_f = F_h = F_a \cos 30.0°$$

The force between the surfaces, F_N, is due to the downward action of the weight which is decreased by the vertical upward component, F_v, of the force F_a.

$$F_N = F_W - F_v$$
$$F_v = F_a \sin 30.0°$$
$$F_N = F_W - F_a \sin 30.0°$$

Since $\mu = \dfrac{F_f}{F_N}$ while $F_f = F_a \cos 30.0°$ and $F_N = F_W - F_a \sin 30.0°$, substitution gives the

Working equation: $\mu = \dfrac{F_a \cos 30.0°}{F_W - F_a \sin 30.0°}$

$$\mu = \frac{(260\ \text{n})(0.866)}{450\ \text{n} - (260\ \text{n})(0.500)} = \frac{225\ \text{n}}{320\ \text{n}} = 0.703$$

Example

A wood block weighing $13\overline{0}$ n rests on an inclined plane. The coefficient of sliding friction between the block and the plane is 0.620. Find the angle of the inclined plane at which the block should slide down the plane at constant speed once it has started moving.

Solution

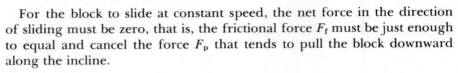

For the block to slide at constant speed, the net force in the direction of sliding must be zero, that is, the frictional force F_f must be just enough to equal and cancel the force F_p that tends to pull the block downward along the incline.

Basic equation: $F_p = F_f$

But we know that the frictional force equals the coefficient of friction times the normal force, or $F_f = \mu F_N$. Substituting in the basic equation, we have

$$F_p = \mu F_N \qquad \text{or} \qquad \frac{F_p}{F_N} = \mu$$

From the diagram, we see that $\frac{F_p}{F_N} = \tan \theta$. Substituting in the previous equation, we now have, $\tan \theta = \mu$. This is a useful result that holds for similar problems.

Since $\tan \theta = \mu$, then

Working equation: $\theta = \arctan \mu$ (this expression is read as θ is the angle whose tangent has a value of μ). Substituting the given value of μ in the equation,

$$\theta = \arctan 0.620$$

Looking up the angle whose tangent is 0.620 in Table 6, page 674, gives

$$\theta = 31.8°$$

In other words, the block should slide uniformly when the angle of the incline is 31.8°, no matter what the block weighs. (The weight of the block cancels out.) The angle at which the block slides depends only on the coefficient of friction.

QUESTIONS

Group A   1. (a) What is friction? (b) What ideas have physicists presented to explain friction?
2. Give several examples of ways in which friction is helpful.
3. What methods are used to reduce friction?

4. How does sliding friction compare with starting friction?
5. (a) On what does the amount of sliding friction usually depend? (b) Of what is it independent?
6. What is meant by the coefficient of friction?

7. What is the orientation of the force of friction to two surfaces which are moving over one another?   **Group B**
8. Name as many devices as you can which are used to increase friction between the tires of an automobile and the pavement.
9. Why does a lubricant reduce friction in a bearing?
10. (a) Under what conditions is the weight of an object the normal force pressing it to the surface over which it is moving? (b) How is the normal force component of the weight of an object determined under other conditions?

PROBLEMS

Note: For each problem, draw a force diagram using a suitable scale, and then perform the necessary calculations.   **Group A**

1. A block weighs 2.00×10^3 n. If a horizontal force of 1.00×10^2 n is required to keep it in motion with constant speed on a horizontal surface, what is the coefficient of sliding friction? $\mu = .05$

2. In a coefficient of friction experiment, a horizontal force of 45 n was needed to keep an object weighing 125 n sliding at constant speed over a horizontal surface. Calculate the coefficient of sliding friction. $\mu = .36$

3. A crate weighing 1.25×10^3 n slides down an inclined plane at constant speed. The plane is 6.0 m long. Its height is 3.0 m. What is the coefficient of sliding friction between the crate and the inclined plane? $\mu k = .45$

4. The coefficient of sliding friction between a metal block and the inclined surface over which it will slide is 0.200. If the surface makes an angle at 20.0° with the horizontal and the block has a mass of 80.0 kg, what force is required to slide the block at constant speed up the plane?   **Group B**

    $637 N$ required

5. A crate weighing 200.0 n is pulled along a horizontal sidewalk at constant speed by a rope which makes an angle of 45.0° with the sidewalk. If a force of $15\overline{0}$ is applied to the rope, what is the coefficient of sliding friction? $\mu k = 1.13$

6. A box having a mass of 50.0 kg is dragged across a horizontal floor by means of a rope tied on the front of it. The coefficient of friction between the box and the floor is 0.300. If the angle between the rope and the floor is 30.0°, what force must be exerted on the rope to move the box at constant speed?

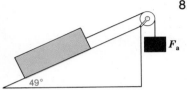

$\mu = \dfrac{EF}{FN} = Tan\,\Theta$

a. 84.3

b. 87.1

c.

7. (a) If a crate slides down a 10.0° incline at constant speed, what is the coefficient of sliding friction between the crate and the incline? (b) What is the coefficient of sliding friction when a crate slides down a 20.0° incline at constant speed? (c) What is the coefficient of sliding friction for a crate moving at constant speed down an incline of n°?

8. A block weighing 130 n is on an incline. It is held back by a weight of 45.0 n hanging from a cord that passes over a frictionless pulley and is attached to the block as shown in the accompanying diagram. Find the angle at which the block will slide down the plane at constant speed if the coefficient of friction is 0.620.

PARALLEL FORCES

4.11 Center of gravity

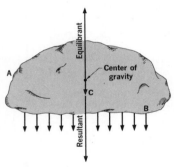

4-19 All the weight of the stone appears to be concentrated at the point called its center of gravity.

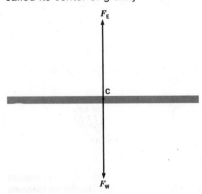

4-20 The weight of the bar, F_w, is apparently concentrated at the center of gravity, **C**, and can be balanced by an equal and opposite force, F_E, applied at **C**.

Thus far in our study of forces, we have been treating all the forces on each body as if these forces were acting at a single point. In general, however, there may be many forces, each acting at a different point on the object. For example, Fig. 4-19 represents a stone lying on the ground. Since every part of the stone has mass, every part is attracted to the earth. All the downward forces exerted on the stone are parallel. The weight of the stone can be thought of as a force vector that is the vector sum, or resultant, of all these parallel force vectors.

But where in the stone is this resultant force acting? Experiments show that, if the proper point of application is chosen, the stone can be lifted without producing rotation. As shown in Fig 4-19, the equilibrant lifting force vector is then in line with the resultant (weight) vector of the stone. In other words, the stone acts as if all its weight were located at one point, which is called the *center of gravity*. **The center of gravity** *of any object is that point at which all of its weight can be considered to be concentrated.*

In Fig. 4-20, the center of gravity of the bar is at **C**. In a bar of uniform construction, **C** is at the geometric center. But if the density or shape of the bar is not uniform, **C** is not at the geometric center.

Since the weight of the bar, F_w, can be considered to be acting at **C**, the bar can be suspended without changing its rotation by an equilibrant force, F_E, applied at **C**. Since F_w and F_E are equal but opposite vectors, they counterbalance each other. In this condition the bar is both in *translational and rotational equilibrium.* This expression means that the bar is not accelerating and that its rotation (if any) is uniform.

Suppose, however, that the suspending force is not applied at **C**, but rather at some other point along the bar, **P** (Fig. 4-21).

In this condition a clockwise rotating effect is produced on the bar. This rotating effect is produced by *torque*.

The two forces represented in Fig. 4-21 by the vectors F_S and F_W, are parallel. They do not act on the same point, as did the concurrent forces we studied earlier in this chapter. To measure the rotating effect of such parallel forces in a given plane, it is first necessary to choose a reference point for the measurements. We shall refer to this reference point as the *pivot point*.

Sometimes, as in the case of a seesaw, there is a "natural" point about which the rotating effects can be measured. However, such a pivot point is "natural" only when the seesaw is in motion. When it is motionless there is no "natural" pivot point. Any point on the seesaw, or even beyond it, may be chosen.

Once a suitable pivot point is chosen, a perpendicular line is drawn on the vector diagram from it to each of the force vectors acting on the object. Each such line is called a *torque arm*. **Torque** *(T) is the product of a force and the length of its torque arm.* The unit of torque is the meter-newton.

To illustrate the concept of torque, consider the bar in Fig. 4-21 with the application of an additional force F_a (Fig. 4-22). Choosing **P** as the pivot point, **CP** is the torque arm of F_W and **AP** is the torque arm of the additional upward force, F_a. The clockwise torque around **P** is the product of F_W and **CP**. The counterclockwise torque is the product of F_a and **AP**. Since F_S has a torque arm of zero, it produces no torque and does not enter into the calculations.

In Section 4.6 we discussed the conditions necessary for the translational equilibrium of an object. These conditions, however, do not prevent the *rotary motion* of an object that is subjected to torques. To prevent rotation in a given plane a second condition of equilibrium must be met. *The second condition of equilibrium in a given plane is that the sum of all the clockwise torques equals the sum of all the counterclockwise torques about a pivot point.*

Both conditions of equilibrium are illustrated in Fig. 4-23. The sum of the force vectors is zero ($\overline{30}$ n upward against $\overline{20}$ n + $\overline{10}$ n downward). The sum of the clockwise torques is equal to the sum of the counterclockwise torques. Two methods of computing the torques are shown. In the upper drawing, the left end of the bar is chosen as a pivot point. In the lower drawing, the point of application of the upward force is used as the pivot point. This simplifies the computation.

When a force is applied to a bar at an angle other than perpendicular, the distances along the bar measured from the points of application of the forces cannot be used to measure

4.12 The nature of torque

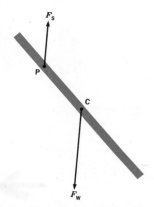

4-21 The two forces acting on the bar, F_W and F_S, are parallel but are not applied at the same point. A tendency to rotate results.

4.13 The second condition of equilibrium

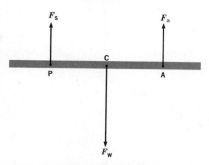

4-22 Rotational equilibrium results when the sum of the clockwise torques is equal to the sum of the counterclockwise torques. Any point may be chosen as the pivot point in making the computation provided the vector sum of the forces is zero.

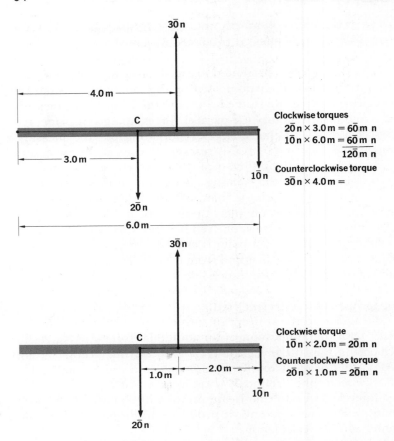

Clockwise torques
$2\bar{0}$ n × 3.0 m = $6\bar{0}$ m n
$1\bar{0}$ n × 6.0 m = $6\bar{0}$ m n
$12\bar{0}$ m n

Counterclockwise torque
$3\bar{0}$ n × 4.0 m =

Clockwise torque
$1\bar{0}$ n × 2.0 m = $2\bar{0}$ m n

Counterclockwise torque
$2\bar{0}$ n × 1.0 m = $2\bar{0}$ m n

4-23 The computation of torques can be simplified by setting one of the torque arms equal to zero.

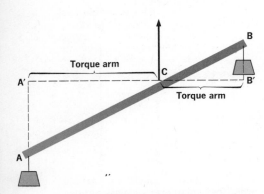

4-24 The torque arm is measured from the center of rotation to the perpendicular intersection with the line indicating the direction of the applied force.

the torque arms. The torque arms must always be measured perpendicular to the directions of the forces. Figure 4-24 shows such a situation. A meter stick is under the influence of three parallel forces. To find the torque arms it is necessary to draw a horizontal line through the pivot point. Since the weights hang vertically, a horizontal line is perpendicular to the force vectors of the weights. The problem is simplified by locating the pivot point at the center of gravity. If the bar is not homogeneous, this center of gravity may not be located at the geometrical center of the bar. (But the center of gravity can be approximately located experimentally by finding the point where the bar balances.) Locating the pivot point at the center of gravity eliminates one torque in the equation. It eliminates the torque produced by the weight of the bar located at some distance from the geometrical center of the bar. The required torque arms, **CA'** and **CB'**, are then found by multiplying the distances **CA** and **CB** by the cosine of the angle **ACA'** or **BCB'** (which are equal).

In Fig. 4-25, F_a is applied to the right end of the bar'at an angle other than perpendicular. In order to find the counterclockwise torque produced by F_a, we use the left end of the bar as the pivot point. Then we find the vertical component, F_N, of F_a. Then, by trigonometry,

$$F_N = F_a \sin \theta$$

Since F_N is perpendicular to the bar, the required torque is

$$T = F_n l$$

Substituting, $$T = F_a l \sin \theta$$

Hence, $l \sin \theta$ is the torque arm of F_a. This result is further verified in Fig. 4-25, where $l \sin \theta$ is the length of the perpendicular from the pivot point to the extended line of direction of F_a. This approach is in accord with the definition of torque arm in Section 4.12.

The conditions of equilibrium hold true no matter how many forces are involved. An interesting example is one in which *two forces of equal magnitude act in opposite directions in the same plane, but not along the same line.* Such a pair of forces is called a **couple**. See Fig. 4-26. The torque is equal to the product of one of the forces and the perpendicular distance between them. (This can be proved by computing the sum of the torques produced by the action of the separate forces about any desired pivot point.) A good example of a couple is the pair of forces acting on the opposite poles of a compass needle when the needle is not pointing north and south.

A couple cannot be balanced by a single force, since this force would be unbalanced and would thus produce linear motion, no matter where it is applied. The only way to balance a couple is with another couple; the torques of the two couples must have equal magnitudes but opposite directions.

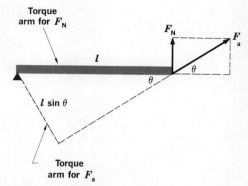

4-25   The resolution of forces is used to find the torque produced by a force acting on the bar at an angle other than perpendicular.

4.14 Two forces acting as a couple

4-26   A pair of parallel forces of equal magnitude acting in opposite directions but not in the same line is called a couple. (The weight of the bar is not considered in this example.)

Example

A horizontal rod, **AB**, is 10.0 m long. It weighs $50\overline{0}$ n and its center of gravity, **C**, is 3.00 m from **A**. At **A** a force of $100\overline{0}$ n acts downward. At **B** a force of 750 n acts downward. At **D**, 2.00 m from **B**, a force of 400 n acts upward. At **E**, 1.00 m from **A**, a force of $75\overline{0}$ n acts upward. (a) What is the magnitude and direction of the force that must be used to produce equilibrium? (b) Where must it be applied?

Solution

Construct a diagram as shown below.

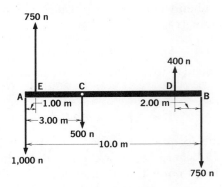

(a) Consider the known upward force vectors as being positive and the known downward force vectors as being negative. The algebraic sum of these force vectors will then be the resultant force vector that must be counterbalanced to establish translational equilibrium.

$$750\ \mathrm{n} + 40\overline{0}\ \mathrm{n} - 100\overline{0}\ \mathrm{n} - 50\overline{0}\ \mathrm{n} - 75\overline{0}\ \mathrm{n} = 110\overline{0}\ \mathrm{n}$$

Therefore, $110\overline{0}$ n must be applied upward to establish translational equilibrium.

(b) Use **A** as the pivot point, and let x be the distance from **A** to the point where the $110\overline{0}$-n force must be applied. To prevent rotary motion,

clockwise torque = counterclockwise torque
$$(50\overline{0}\ \mathrm{n})(3.00\ \mathrm{m}) + (75\overline{0}\ \mathrm{n})(10.0\ \mathrm{m}) =$$
$$(75\overline{0}\ \mathrm{n})(1.00\ \mathrm{m}) + (40\overline{0}\ \mathrm{n})(8.0\ \mathrm{m}) + (110\overline{0}\ \mathrm{n})x$$
$$x = 4.60\ \mathrm{m},$$

the distance from **A** to the point where the $110\overline{0}$-n force must be applied.

QUESTIONS

Group A
1. Define center of gravity.
2. (a) What are parallel forces? (b) How is the resultant of two parallel forces which act in the same direction calculated? (c) How is the resultant of parallel forces which act in opposite directions calculated?
3. Explain two possible adjustments that can be made so two children of unequal weight can balance on a seesaw.
4. (a) A force acts at right angles to a pivoted bar. How is the force produced by this force calculated? (b) What is the unit of torque in the MKS system?

5. If a bar on which parallel forces act is to be in equilibrium, what conditions must be met?

6. How can the choice of the pivot point simplify the calculations of the torques in a problem?

Group B

7. Distinguish between center of gravity and the pivot point.
8. Give an example of an object with a center of gravity that is not within the object.
9. A certain force does not act at right angles to a pivoted bar. How is the torque produced by this force calculated?
10. (a) What is a couple? (b) How is the torque of a couple calculated?

PROBLEMS

Note: For each problem, draw a force diagram using a suitable scale and perform the necessary calculations. Unless otherwise noted, the center of gravity is at the geometric center of the object.

1. A steel beam of uniform cross section weighs 2.5×10^5 n. If it is 5.00 m long, what force is needed to lift one end of it?

Group A

2. A bar 4.0 m long weighs $40\overline{0}$ n. Its center of gravity is 1.5 m from one end. A weight of $30\overline{0}$ n is attached at the heavy end and a weight of $50\overline{0}$ n is attached at the light end. What are the magnitude, direction, and point of application of the force needed so that the bar will be in translational and rotational equilibrium?

$-40 0 N (1.5) - 50 0 N (4) + 1200 N x = 0$

3. A painter weighing 875 n stands on a plank 3.00 m long, which is supported at each end by a stepladder. The plank weighs 223 n. If she stands 1.00 m from one end of the plank, what force is exerted by each stepladder?

4. A bricklayer weighing 8.00×10^2 n stands 1.00 m from one end of a scaffold 3.00 m long. The scaffold weighs $75\overline{0}$ n. A pile of bricks weighing 3.20×10^2 n is 1.50 m from the other end of the scaffold. What force must be exerted on each end of the scaffold in order to support it?

5. A bench is 2.40 m long and weighs 3.20×10^2 n. The legs are attached 0.30 m from each end and weigh 15.0 n each. If three persons, weighing, in order 5.00×10^2 n, 7.50×10^2 n, and 1.000×10^3 n, sit 0.40 m, 1.20 m, and 2.00 m respectively from one end of the bench, what downward force must each set of legs exert on the floor?

6. Give an example showing the correctness of the rule for finding the torque of a couple by placing the pivot point somewhere between the two force vectors.

7. The bridge **AB** in the accompanying figure is 36.5 m long. It weighs 2.56×10^5 n. A truck weighing 5.25×10^4 n is 10.2 m from one end of the bridge. Calculate the upward force that must be exerted by each pier to support this weight.

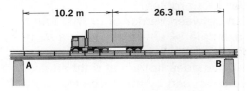

Group B

8. A bar 5.0 m long has its center of gravity 1.5 m from the heavy end. If it is placed on the edge of a block 1.5 m from the light end and a weight of 750 n is placed on the bar at the light end, it will be balanced. What is the weight of the bar?

9. A uniform bar 25.0 m long weighs 1.000×10^4 n. From end **A** a weight of 2.50×10^3 n is hung. At **B**, the other end of the bar, there is a weight of 3.50×10^3 n. An upward force of 3.00×10^3 n is exerted 4.0 m from **B**, while an upward force of 4.00×10^3 n is exerted 8.0 m from **A**. Determine the magnitude, direction, and point of application of the force needed for translational and rotational equilibrium.

10. A door is 2.50 m high and 1.00 m wide. It weighs 204 n and its center of gravity is at its geometric center. The door is supported by hinges located 0.30 m from the top and bottom. If each hinge supports half the weight of the door, find the horizontal component of the force exerted by each hinge.

11. (a) Find the torques exerted on the rod in the accompanying drawing. (b) Find the magnitude and direction of the additional force that must be exerted at the right end, perpendicular to the rod, in order to produce rotational equilibrium. Horizontal components are not taken into consideration in this problem.

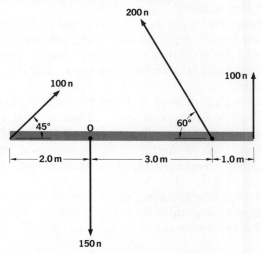

Chapter 5

Curvilinear and Harmonic Motion

Circular Motion

In Section 3.2 we described the motion of an object having uniform velocity. Such an object moves equal distances along a straight path in equal time intervals as shown photographically in Fig. 3-1. This photograph was taken using a light flashing at regular time intervals. Notice that the distances between adjacent images are equal.

In Section 3.5 we described the motion of an object having uniform acceleration. Such an object moves an increasing distance along a straight path in equal time intervals as shown photographically by the ball at the left in Fig. 5-1. This photograph was taken by flashing a light at regular time intervals. The ball on the left was accelerated downward from rest by the force of gravity. There is an increase in the vertical distance the ball travels in equal amounts of time.

Now let us examine what happens to the motion of an object which moves horizontally with uniform velocity but is also accelerated vertically. That is, there is a right angle between the direction of the uniform velocity and the direction of the acceleration. What will be the path of such an object? The ball at the right of Fig. 5-1 illustrates such motion. It was released at the same time as the ball on the left, but had a uniform horizontal velocity. The horizontal distances between adjacent images of the right-hand ball are equal. This fact indicates that the ball is still traveling horizontally with uniform velocity. At the same time, the ball on the right covered the same vertical distance between each image as does the ball on the left which had no horizontal velocity. Each position of the ball on the right

5.1 Motion in a curved path

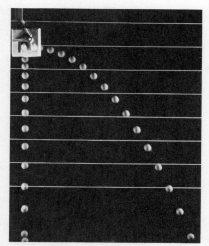

From PSSC Physics, Second Edition, D. C. Heath and Co.

5-1 Even though the ball at the right has a horizontal velocity, the force of gravity acts in the same way on both balls, causing them to move vertically with the same acceleration.

99

is the resultant of motion with uniform velocity in one direction and motion with uniform acceleration in the other. This combination produces motion along a curved path. *Motion along a curved path is called **curvilinear motion**.*

Suppose a rifle bullet is fired horizontally with a velocity of 1250 m/sec. Neglecting air resistance, the bullet travels 1250 m by the end of the first second. Immediately after it leaves the muzzle of the gun, the force of gravity begins to accelerate the bullet toward the earth's center of gravity. This force is vertical. During the first second, a freely falling body drops 4.90 m. The bullet drops 4.90 m while traveling the first 1250 m horizontally. In two seconds the bullet travels 2500 m, but it also drops 19.6 m. Over short distances the path of a high-velocity projectile approximates a straight line, but over greater distances, the path of a high-velocity projectile is noticeably curved. The fact that the path of a slow-moving projectile is curved is more evident over shorter distances. Figure 5-2 compares the paths of high- and low-velocity projectiles.

A rifle aimed horizontally at a target is generally fired at a small upward angle in order to hit the target. This angle compensates for the downward acceleration due to the force of gravity on the bullet. Provided the same ammunition is used the size of this angle depends upon the gun's distance from the target. The front sight of most rifles is fixed at the end of the barrel while the rear sight is moveable. Since the line of sight is a straight line to the target, the angle the barrel makes with this line is increased by raising the rear sight. When the rifle is aimed, its muzzle is directed upward at the predetermined angle. When the gun is fired, this angle gives the bullet the

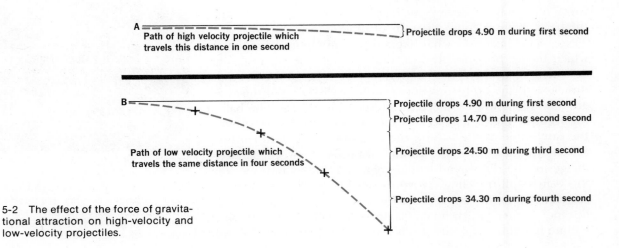

5-2   The effect of the force of gravitational attraction on high-velocity and low-velocity projectiles.

upward velocity component necessary to compensate for the bullet's drop on its way to the distant target.

The path a projectile fired from a long-range field gun might take is shown in Fig. 5-3. The horizontal and vertical components of the muzzle velocity v_m are v_h and v_v; **AC** is the range. The path of the projectile, **ABC**, is the trajectory.

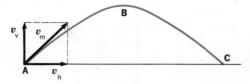

5-3 Neglecting air resistance, the path of a projectile fired from a long-range field gun is a parabola.

5.2 Motion in a circular path

An important type of curvilinear motion is motion in a circular path. Figure 5-4 shows motion of this kind. Ball **A** is attached to the end of a string **CA**. The string is fastened at **C**. If the speed of the ball in the circular path is constant, the ball is said to describe *uniform circular motion*. If the speed of the ball in the circular path varies, its motion is *variable circular motion*.

Imagine that you are at a location where there is no force of gravity. You attach a ball to a string as shown in Fig. 5-4, and hold the string at **C**. Then you give the ball an initial velocity in the direction of **B**, tangent to the circumference of the circle. The ball whirls in a circular path around **C**. You can feel yourself pulling continuously on the string to keep the ball in the circular path.

Let's analyze what you would observe in this situation. We know that the radius of a circle (**AC**, for example) is perpendicular to the tangent drawn through the end of the radius. So if the string is in the direction of the radius, and the velocity is always directed along a tangent, your pull on the string is always directed perpendicularly to the velocity. Your pull accelerates the ball into a circular path, but the ball does not speed up or slow down. Your pull changes only the direction and not the magnitude of the velocity. If your pull were not perpendicular to the velocity, a component of the acceleration would change the ball's speed.

In this example, the acceleration is directed toward the center of a circle. *Acceleration directed toward a central point is called* **centripetal acceleration**. (The word centripetal means "directed toward a center.")

This example can also be analyzed by means of velocity vectors. Even though the *speed* of the ball in its circular path is uni-

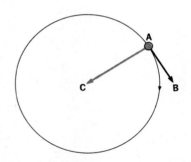

5-4 Uniform circular motion. When the force along **AC** stops acting, the ball moves in a direction which is indicated by the tangent **AB**.

$$F_c = ma_c = m\frac{v^2}{R}$$

$$F_c = m\,4\pi^2 R f^2$$

$$F_c = m\,\frac{4\pi^2 R}{T^2}$$

$$v = 2\pi R f$$

$$v = \frac{2\pi R}{T}$$

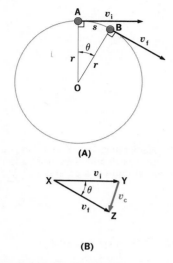

(A)

(B)

5-5 Diagrams for deriving the centripetal acceleration formula.

$T = \dfrac{s}{R \varphi u}$

$f = \dfrac{R e u}{s}$

form, the *velocity* is constantly changing. In Figure 5-5(A), **A** and **B** represent two successive positions of an object moving with uniform circular motion about point **O**. The velocity vector v_i indicates the velocity of the object when at point **A**, and the velocity vector v_f indicates its velocity at point **B**. The velocity vectors are tangent to the circle respectively at **A** and **B**, and are thus perpendicular to the respective radii **OA** and **OB**.

In order to study the change of velocity between v_i and v_f, a separate vector diagram, Fig. 5-5(B), may be drawn in which v_i and v_f originate at point **X**. If v_f is considered as the resultant and v_i one of its components, then v_c is the other component. It represents the change in velocity between v_i and v_f. Because the vectors v_i and v_f are equal in magnitude and are perpendicular to their respective radii, $\angle \theta$ in Fig. 5-5(A) equals $\angle \theta$ in Fig. 5-5(B) and triangle **ABO** is similar to triangle **XYZ**. Then

$$\frac{v_c}{v_i} = \frac{\text{chord } \mathbf{AB}}{r}$$

If angle θ is made smaller, arc s becomes more nearly equal to chord **AB** and can be substituted for it.

$$\frac{v_c}{v_i} = \frac{s}{r}$$

But v_i and v_f are equal in magnitude and can be represented by v. If we let t represent the time between v_i and v_f and use the equation $s = vt$ (Section 3.2) we can write

$$\frac{v_c}{v} = \frac{vt}{r}$$

And, transposing terms

$$\frac{v_c}{t} = \frac{v^2}{r}$$

But v_c/t is the acceleration directed along a radius of the circle (the centripetal acceleration) and can be represented by a. Then

$$a = \frac{v^2}{r}$$

in which a is the centripetal acceleration of the object, v is its speed along the circular path, and r is the radius of its circular path.

By Newton's second law of motion, $F = ma$. Thus the force producing centripetal acceleration can be written

$$F_c = \frac{mv^2}{r}$$

and is called the *centripetal force*. Like the centripetal acceleration, it is also directed toward the center of the circle. The equation for centripetal force indicates that it is directly proportional to the mass of the object, directly proportional to the square of its speed along the circular path, and inversely proportional to the radius of its circular path.

Since matter has inertia, a centripetal force is required to produce the centripetal acceleration which changes the direction of a moving object. If the centripetal force applied by the string on the ball ceases to act (for example, if the string breaks), the ball will move in a straight line tangent to the curved path at the point where the string breaks. This behavior is in accordance with Newton's first law of motion, because when the string is broken the centripetal force no longer acts on the ball. The ball has no unbalanced forces acting on it and moves in a straight line with constant speed.

NASA

The first American "space walk." Astronaut Edward White appears to be floating in space, but actually he is undergoing centripetal acceleration as he orbits the earth. The centripetal force is that of gravitational attraction between the earth and the astronaut.

5.3 Motion in a vertical circle

In describing the motion of an object in a horizontal circle, we neglected the effect of the force of gravitational attraction. We did this because the force of gravity is constant and acts at a 90° angle to the centripetal force. Consequently, no component of the force of gravity affects the magnitude of the centripetal force. However, if the body moves in a vertical circle, the situation is not so simple.

Suppose a ball on the end of a string moves along a circular path. The plane of the circle is vertical. Figure 5-6 is a diagram of the ball's motion. Because of the force of gravity, the speed of the ball in the circular path is not uniform. It accelerates on the downward part of its path and decelerates on the upward part. The speed of the ball is a minimum at the top of the circle and a maximum at the bottom. Consequently, the centripetal force is a minimum at the top of the circle and a maximum at the bottom. Let us see what forces comprise the centripetal force to make this so.

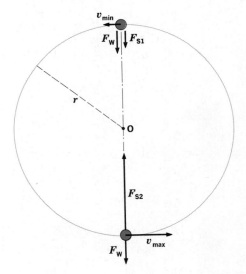

5-6 Motion in a vertical circle. When the ball is at its highest point, the centripetal force on the ball equals the tension of the string plus the weight of the ball. At its lowest point, the weight of the ball must be subtracted from the tension to find the centripetal force.

At the top of the circle the ball has velocity v_{min}. The centripetal force, F_{c1}, is the sum of the force the string exerts on the ball, F_{s1}, and the weight of the ball, F_W, since these both act toward the center of the circle.

$$F_{c1} = \frac{mv_{min}^2}{r} = F_{s1} + F_w \qquad \text{(Equation 1)}$$

At the bottom of the circle, the ball has velocity v_{max}. The centripetal force, F_{c2}, is the difference between the force the string exerts on the ball, F_{s2}, and the weight of the ball, F_W, since these forces now act in opposite directions. The force the string exerts is inward and the weight of the ball acts outward.

$$F_{c2} = \frac{mv_{max}{}^2}{r} = F_{s2} - F_w \qquad \text{(Equation 2)}$$

Observe that since v_{max} is greater than v_{min}, F_{c2} is greater than F_{c1}. Further, since the weight of the ball is added in Equation 1, but subtracted in Equation 2, F_{s2} is greater than F_{s1} by a ratio greater than the ratio F_{c2}/F_{c1}.

When a ball on a string moves in a vertical circle, there is a certain velocity below which the ball will not describe a circular path—the string slackens as the ball approaches its highest point. To find this minimum value of the velocity we shall use Equation 1. When the string begins to slacken, $F_{s1} = 0$ and

$$\frac{mv_{min}{}^2}{r} = F_w$$

But

$$F_w = mg$$

So

$$\frac{mv_{min}{}^2}{r} = mg$$

Solving for v_{min}

$$v_{min} = \sqrt{rg}$$

This value of v_{min} is called the *critical velocity*. As the equation indicates, critical velocity depends only on the acceleration due to gravity and the radius of the vertical circle. The critical velocity does not depend on the mass of the object describing the motion. This is due to the fact that the forces of gravity and the centripetal forces required are both proportional to the mass of the object.

A similar statement can be made about projectiles. Irrespective of their masses, all projectiles with the same initial velocity follow the same path.

Figure 5-7 shows a chamber attached to the end of a long boom. The boom is designed to rotate around a central point under the observation booth at the top of the picture. In operation, the chamber revolves at constant speed in a large circle around the central point.

5.4 Frames of reference

Suppose you were an observer in the chamber conducting experiments while the chamber is revolving. You would still feel the pull of gravity. In addition, you would feel your body being pressed against the outside wall of the chamber. You would observe that a ball placed on the floor would move across

U.S. Navy

5-7 This centrifuge is used to study the effects of angular acceleration on the human body. A volunteer is entering the test chamber of the centrifuge at the left.

the floor toward the outside wall of the chamber. If you dropped an object in the chamber, you would see it fall to the floor in a curved path.

It would seem, from these strange observations, that Newton's laws of motion do not all hold true in the revolving chamber. These observations can be explained, however, by attributing them to a force that tends to move all particles toward the outside wall of the chamber. This force moves the ball across the floor and accelerates the falling object so its path is curvilinear. When described by an observer in a rotating system who is considered to be stationary, *a force that tends to move the particles of a rotating object away from the center of rotation is called **centrifugal force***.

An observer in the booth above the revolving chamber in Fig. 5-7 interprets the situation quite differently, however. To this observer, the chamber and its occupant tend to continue their motion in a straight line because of their inertia. A force in the boom, a centripetal force, causes the chamber to follow a circular path. And a force exerted by the chamber on its occupant causes the occupant also to follow a circular path. The observer in the booth can explain the behavior of objects in the chamber in terms of inertia and centripetal force. To the observer, centrifugal force is a fiction.

To resolve this seeming contradiction, it is helpful to discuss this situation in terms of *frames of reference*. Each observer assumes that some surrounding objects are stationary because they don't move with respect to each other. To the observer in the revolving chamber, the walls and floor of the chamber are stationary and are used as the basis of measurements. Other objects, such as the ball on the floor, move with respect to these stationary objects. The walls and floor of the chamber are the basis for this observer's *frame of reference.*

*A **frame of reference** is a system for specifying precisely the location of objects.* It is used to describe the positions and relative motions of objects. A frame of reference in which Newton's first law holds true is called an *inertial frame.* An accelerating frame of reference is *noninertial* because Newton's first law does not hold true.

The observer in the booth in Fig. 5-7 is stationary with respect to the earth. Strictly speaking, however, a frame of reference based upon the earth is not an inertial frame. The earth rotates and revolves around the sun and experiences continuous acceleration in order to do so. However, the earth is so close to being an inertial frame that we can consider a frame of reference based upon the booth as an inertial frame. (For practical purposes, we often neglect the accelerations of frames of reference that are stationary with respect to the earth).

The direction of motion of the revolving chamber is continually changing. With respect to the observer in the booth, the revolving chamber is accelerating. It is, therefore, a noninertial frame. Using such a frame, one can observe acceleration which cannot be attributed to friction or gravitational attraction or any other well-known sources of forces. Centrifugal force is sometimes called fictitious because it disappears once we decide to use an inertial frame to describe motion.

Daytona International Speedway

The turns of the Daytona International Speedway are sharply banked in order to provide sufficient centripetal force to keep the speeding cars from leaving the roadway.

QUESTIONS

Group A
1. (a) What is curvilinear motion? (b) Describe how it can be produced.
2. (a) A projectile is fired horizontally. As the result of what motions may its path be described? (b) What effect does each of these motions have on the path of the projectile?
3. (a) What is uniform circular motion? (b) What force causes circular motion? (c) Why must a force be used to produce circular motion?
4. What factors determine the magnitude of a centripetal force?
5. (a) How does motion in a vertical circle differ from uniform circular motion? (b) What causes this difference?
6. (a) What is meant by critical velocity? (b) What happens to an object that does not have critical velocity?
7. (a) What is meant by a frame of reference? (b) List four frames of reference that could be used to describe the motion of an earth satellite.

Group B
8. (a) What adjustment is made on the rear sight of a rifle when the distance to the target is increased? (b) How would the use of a higher velocity bullet affect the adjustment?
9. Why does an astronaut experience unusual forces (a) During the launching of a space vehicle? (b) During the reentry of the vehicle?
10. (a) In what way is the motion of a satellite in a circular orbit similar to motion in a vertical circle? (b) How are the two motions different?
11. Evaluate the statements: (a) "An earth satellite is weightless." (b) "An earth satellite is continuously falling around the earth."
12. Describe the motion of a car rounding a turn in the road in terms of two different frames of reference.

PROBLEMS

Group A
1. What is the centripetal acceleration of an object moving along a horizontal circular path of 16.0-m radius with a speed of 40.0 m/sec?
2. If the mass of the object in Problem 1 is 2.00 metric tons, what centripetal force is required to maintain it in a circular path?
3. A ball, mass 2.5×10^{-2} kg, is swung at the end of a string in a horizontal circular path at a speed of 5.0 m/sec. If the length of the string is 2.0 m, what centripetal force does the string exert on the ball?
4. Calculate the centripetal force exerted on a 5.0-kg mass that is moving at a speed of 3.0 m/sec in a horizontal circular motion if the radius of the circle is (a) 1.0 m; (b) 3.0 m.
5. Find the critical velocity of the mass in Problem 4 for both radii if the mass is moving (a) in a vertical circle at the earth's surface; (b) in a vertical circle 6.0×10^2 km above the earth's surface.

6. An automobile weighs 6.0×10^4 n. If it is driven around a horizontal curve which has a radius of 250 m at the rate of 22 m/sec, what is the centripetal force of the road on the automobile?

7. What is the orbiting speed of a satellite moving uniformly in a circular path 1.00×10^3 km above the earth?

8. A man has a mass of 75 kg. If he is standing on the equator, how much of his weight is offset by the earth's rotation?

9. A baseball player hits a fly ball to a height of 50.0 m. After the bat strikes the ball, how much time does a fielder have to get into position to make the catch?

10. A person throws a ball from the roof of a building. The ball has a velocity of 25 m/sec horizontally when it leaves the person's hand, and the ball hits the ground 3.0 sec later. (a) How far does the ball fall during each second? (b) How far does the ball move horizontally during each second?

Group B

ROTARY MOTION

5.5 Motion about an axis

Rotary motion is the motion of a body turning about an axis. Rotary motion occurs in a turning bicycle wheel, the rotating crankshaft of an automobile engine, and a pulley wheel attached to the spinning shaft of an electric motor. Note the difference between circular motion and rotary motion. In circular motion the center of gravity of the object travels along a circular path. In rotary motion, the object spins about an axis. While a bicycle wheel spinning on a stationary axle is in rotary motion, a part of the wheel, say the valve stem of the tire, undergoes circular motion.

For rotary motion to be *uniform*, the object must spin about a fixed axis at a constant rate. The movements of the hands of an electric clock are examples of uniform rotary motion. If either the direction of the axis or the rate of spin varies, the rotary motion is *variable*. The movements of automobile wheels as a car is driven at different speeds, and the movements of a spinning top as it slows down, are examples of variable rotary motion.

5.6 Angular velocity

For uniform linear motion, velocity is defined as the rate of displacement (Section 3.2). Similarly, for uniform rotary motion, *angular velocity* is defined *as the rate of angular displacement.* Angular displacement is the angle about the axis of rotation through which the object turns. The equation for angular velocity, ω (omega), is

$$\omega = \frac{\theta}{t}$$

$w = a \times t$

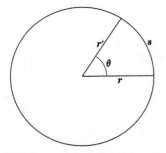

5-8 Since arc *s* equals radius *r*, angle *θ* is 1 radian. There are 2*π* radians in one revolution.

where *θ* is an angular displacement, and *t* is the time interval in which the angular displacement occurs. The units of angular velocity are revolutions per second or degrees per second or *radians per second*.

An angle of one radian is that angle which, when placed with its vertex at the center of a circle, subtends on the circumference an arc equal in length to the radius of the circle. Thus in Fig. 5-8, if radius *r'* is rotated from radius *r* until arc *s* = radius *r*, the angle *θ* is 1 radian. Since the circumference of a circle is 2*π* times the radius

$$1 \text{ revolution} = 360° = 2\pi \text{ radians}$$

and

$$1 \text{ radian} = \frac{360°}{2\pi} = \frac{180°}{\pi}$$

$$1 \text{ radian} = 57.3°$$

Since an angle measured in radians equals the ratio of the length of the subtended arc to the length of the radius, the units cancel. An angle in radians is a pure number without dimensions.

The concept of angular velocity includes both the rate of rotation and the direction of the axis of rotation. Angular velocity is a vector quantity represented by a vector parallel to the axis of rotation. The length of the vector indicates the magnitude of the angular velocity. The direction of the vector is the direction in which the thumb of the right hand points if the fingers of the right hand encircle the vector in the direction in which the body is rotating. See Fig. 5-9.

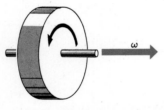

5-9 Angular velocity is represented by a vector parallel to the axis of rotation.

5.7 Angular acceleration

We have already recognized from the study of linear motion that a change of velocity defines acceleration. The same principle is true for rotary motion. Changing either the rate of rotation or the direction of the axis involves a change of angular velocity and defines angular acceleration. The uniform rate of change of linear velocity is called linear acceleration (Section 3.7). Similarly, the uniform rate of change of angular velocity is called angular acceleration. It is designated by the symbol *α* (alpha).

$$w = a \times t \qquad\qquad \alpha = \frac{\omega}{t} \qquad t = \frac{w}{a}$$

The equations for uniformly accelerated linear motion can be transformed easily into corresponding equations for uniformly accelerated rotary motion by substituting *θ* for *s*, *ω* for *v* and *α* for *a*. These equations are shown in Table 5-1.

$$t = \frac{w}{a}$$

Table 5-1 EQUATIONS FOR UNIFORMLY ACCELERATED MOTION

Linear	Rotary
$v_f = v_i + at$	$\omega_f = \omega_i + \alpha t$
$s = v_i t + \frac{1}{2}at^2$	$\theta = \omega_i t + \frac{1}{2}\alpha t^2$
$v_f = \sqrt{v_i^2 + 2as}$	$\omega_f = \sqrt{\omega_i^2 + 2\alpha\theta}$

Example

Find the angular displacement in radians during the second 20.0-sec interval of a wheel that accelerates from rest to 725 revolutions per minute in 1.50 min.

Solution

The angular displacement θ required for the second 20.0-sec interval is equal to the difference between the angular displacement θ_2 achieved during the first 40.0 sec (t_2) and the angular displacement θ_1 achieved during the first 20.0 sec (t_1).

Basic Equation: $\theta = \theta_2 - \theta_1$

Since $\omega_1 = 0$ for each time interval,

$$\theta_2 = \tfrac{1}{2}\alpha t_2^2 \quad \text{and} \quad \theta_1 = \tfrac{1}{2}\alpha t_1^2$$

$$\theta = \tfrac{1}{2}\alpha t_2^2 - \tfrac{1}{2}\alpha t_1^2$$

Working Equation: $\theta = \tfrac{1}{2}\alpha(t_2^2 - t_1^2)$

$$\theta = \frac{725/\text{min} \times 2\pi \text{ rad}}{2 \times 1.50 \text{ min}} \times \left(\frac{\text{min}}{60 \text{ sec}}\right)^2 \times [(40.0 \text{ sec})^2 - (20.0 \text{ sec})^2]$$

$$\theta = 505 \text{ rad}$$

5.8 Rotational inertia

A wheel mounted on an axle will not start to rotate unless a torque is applied to the wheel. A wheel which is spinning will continue to spin at constant angular velocity unless a torque acts on it. In both cases the wheel is in equilibrium. Thus if we replace "force" with "torque," Newton's first law of motion also applies to rotary motion.

If we wish to change the rate of rotation of an object about an axis, that is, change its angular velocity, we must apply a torque about the axis. The angular acceleration which this torque produces depends on the mass of the rotating object and upon the distribution of its mass with respect to the axis of rotation.

In Fig. 5-10 two masses m_1 and m_2 are mounted on a bar which is fastened to an axle. The masses can be placed on the bar at varying distances from the axle. If a cord is wrapped around

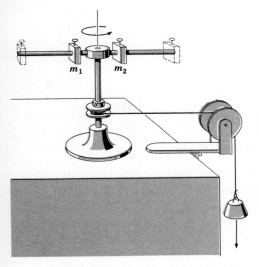

5-10 Apparatus for demonstrating rotational inertia.

the axle and attached to a weight which falls under the influence of gravity, a constant torque is applied to the axle. If different weights are attached to the cord, different torques are applied. If the masses mounted on the bar are not shifted, the greater the torque, the greater the angular acceleration. If the masses are placed near the axis of rotation, the acceleration produced by a given torque is greater than if they are placed at the ends of the bar. Note that moving the masses farther apart does not change the amount of mass which is rotated. It does, however, change the distribution of mass, and in this case we say that it increases the *rotational inertia*. The angular acceleration, α, is directly proportional to the torque, T, but inversely proportional to the rotational inertia, I,

$$\alpha = \frac{T}{I}$$

Transposing,

$$T = I\alpha$$

which, for rotary motion, is analogous to $F = ma$ for linear motion. The torque T is computed by

$$T = Fr$$

where F is the force applied tangentially at distance r from the axis of rotation. Like a force, a torque has magnitude and direction. Torques behave like other quantities that can be represented by vectors.

(α) angular acceleration rads/s

(T) torque Nm

(I) rotational inertia Kg m²

(W) angular velocity

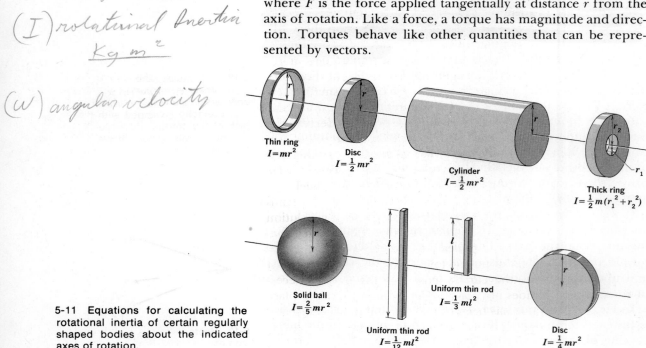

Thin ring
$I = mr^2$

Disc
$I = \frac{1}{2} mr^2$

Cylinder
$I = \frac{1}{2} mr^2$

Thick ring
$I = \frac{1}{2} m(r_1^2 + r_2^2)$

Solid ball
$I = \frac{2}{5} mr^2$

Uniform thin rod
$I = \frac{1}{3} ml^2$

Uniform thin rod
$I = \frac{1}{12} ml^2$

Disc
$I = \frac{1}{4} mr^2$

5-11 Equations for calculating the rotational inertia of certain regularly shaped bodies about the indicated axes of rotation.

The rotational inertia in rotary motion takes into account both the shape and the mass of the rotating object. Equations for the rotational inertia of certain regularly shaped bodies are given in Fig. 5-11. Rotational inertia has the unit dimensions kg m². The following analysis illustrates this.

$$I = \frac{T}{\alpha} = \frac{m\ n}{1/sec^2} = \frac{kg\ m^2/sec^2}{1/sec^2} = kg\ m^2$$

Figure 5-12 shows a spinning bicycle wheel that seems to be defying gravity. The only means of support of the wheel is the cord that is holding up the left end of the axle. Yet, if the wheel is spinning fast enough, its axle will remain almost horizontal in space. Instead of falling, the axle will slowly rotate counterclockwise (as seen from above) around the axis marked by the cord. This horizontal rotation of the axle is called *precession*.

To understand the behavior of a wheel that is spinning, and in particular its precession, refer to Fig. 5-12: **OA** is the axle of a wheel spinning counterclockwise as seen from **A**. **OC** is the cord from which the wheel is suspended. ω_S is the vector representing the angular velocity of the spinning wheel.

The weight of the wheel produces a clockwise torque about **O** (as seen from the front). In the diagram α_i describes the angular acceleration due to this torque. (α_1 is horizontal and directed into the paper.) Because of this angular acceleration there will be a change in the angular velocity during the short time t: $\Delta\omega_a = \alpha_1 t$. This, added vectorially to ω_S results in a new angular velocity ω_S' of the same magnitude but different direction. (Remember that the change in angular velocity is small and it is therefore at right angles to both the initial and new angular velocities just as was the case with v_c in the previous derivation.) Because of the mounting of the device at **O**, if the new axis is along this new ω_S the whole object has to turn toward this new position. The analysis has to be repeated for successive time intervals resulting in the precessional motion of the wheel.

A good example of precession is the earth itself, since it spins about an axis that is tilted with respect to its plane of revolution around the sun. The rotation of the earth produces an equatorial bulge. This bulge is pulled toward the sun just as the spinning bicycle wheel is pulled toward the earth. Because of the resulting torque, the earth's axis goes through a precessional motion and does not continually point at the same place in space (Fig. 5-14). It has been calculated that it takes a period of about 26,000 years for the earth's axis to complete a single precessional cycle.

5.9 Precession

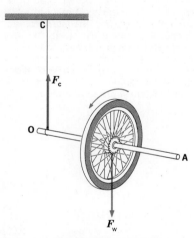

5-12 Precession. The axle of the bicycle wheel is supported at one end only. When the wheel rotates, the angular velocity combined with the effect of the torque produced by the weight of the wheel causes a precession.

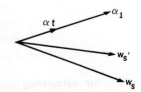

5-13 Vector analysis of the precession of a gyroscope.

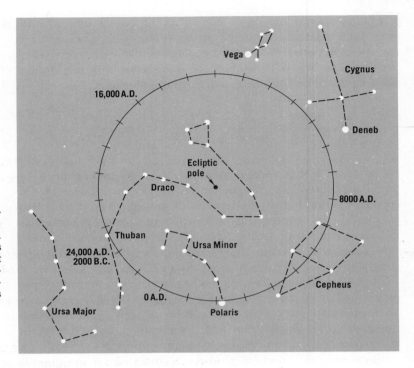

5-14 At the present time, the northern end of the earth's axis points approximately toward the star Polaris. Hence, it is called the North Star. As the earth's axis precesses, however, it points successively toward other regions of the sky. This precessional circle has a radius of 23½° and takes about 26,000 years to complete.

QUESTIONS

Group A

1. (a) What is rotary motion? (b) Give examples of uniform and variable rotary motion.
2. How is a 1-radian angle defined?
3. (a) What is angular velocity? (b) What is angular acceleration?
4. (a) Explain why we say that angular velocity is a vector quantity. (b) How is a vector representing an angular velocity drawn?
5. How do equations for uniformly accelerated rotary motions compare with those for uniformly accelerated linear motions?

Group B

6. Explain how a revolving flywheel tends to maintain the axle on which it is mounted at a constant angular velocity.
7. What is the result of the addition of two angular velocities about different axes?
8. How do the directions of an acceleration vector and its corresponding velocity vector compare in the case of precession?
9. How do the direction of an acceleration vector and its corresponding velocity vector compare for uniformly accelerated rotary motion?
10. (a) What causes precession? (b) How does precession affect the apparent location of the present day North Star?

PROBLEMS

1. What is the angular velocity in radians per second of a flywheel which turns 4820 revolutions per minute?

2. If a wheel turns 625 rad/sec, what is its angular velocity in revolutions per minute?

3. A net force of 10.0 n is applied tangentially to the rim of a wheel having a 0.25-m radius. If the rotational inertia of the wheel is 0.500 kg m², what is its angular acceleration?

4. Calculate the rotational inertia of a thin ring, mass 5.7 kg, radius 0.15 m, rotating about an axis through the center perpendicular to the plane of the ring.

5. What is the rotational inertia of a solid ball 0.100 m in diameter which weighs 80.0 n, if it is rotated about a diameter?

6. Calculate the angular acceleration in radians per second² of a wheel which starts from rest and attains an angular velocity of 545 revolutions per minute in 1.00 minute.

Group B

$\alpha = \dfrac{\omega}{t}$ 545 rev/min

7. (a) What is the angular displacement in radians of the wheel of Problem 6 during the first 0.500 min? (b) During the second 0.500 min?

8. (a) If a force of 25.0 n is applied tangentially to the rim of a uniform disc 0.200 m in radius, mass 30.0 kg, what angular velocity will the disc attain in 0.200 min? (b) What is the angular displacement during this acceleration?

9. A disc-shaped flywheel 1.00 m in radius weighs 2.00×10^3 n. If a force of 50.0 n is applied tangentially to the rim, how many seconds will be required for it to attain an angular velocity of 1200 rev/min?

$\omega = \dfrac{\theta}{t}$

$t = \dfrac{\omega}{\alpha}$

SIMPLE HARMONIC MOTION

5.10 Periodic motion

When a body continually moves back and forth over a definite path in equal intervals of time it is said to undergo **periodic motion**. In Fig. 5-15 a mass is shown attached to a spring supported from a horizontal beam. If we pull down on the mass and then let it go, it will vibrate up and down in periodic motion. Let us investigate quantitatively the periodic motion of this mass.

If we exert a force *F* acting downward on mass *m* we displace it from its equilibrium position by a distance *s*. We also find by experiment that if we exert force 2*F* we displace the mass a distance 2*s*. Thus the downward force we exert is directly proportional to the downward displacement from the equilibrium position.

$\omega = \omega i + \alpha t$
no initial vel.

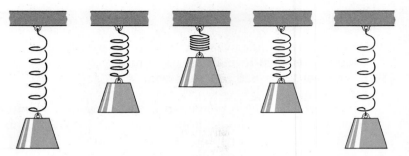

5-15 Simple harmonic motion. The frequency of vibration of the mass depends on the stiffness of the spring and the magnitude of the mass.

In exerting this force downward we pull against the spring, and the spring also pulls against our hand with a force $-F$ (law of interaction). When we release the mass, the upward force of the spring exceeds the downward pull of gravity on the mass and produces an upward acceleration which is directly proportional to the excess force (law of acceleration).

As the mass m returns to its equilibrium position, less and less force is exerted on it by the spring. Consequently the acceleration becomes less. The net force is zero when the mass is at its equilibrium position. The acceleration is also zero. The mass m has acquired its maximum velocity at this point. It moves past its equilibrium position because of its inertia. As this overshoot occurs, the upward pull of the spring becomes less than the downward force on the mass. There is a net downward force on the mass. This downward force decelerates it. The mass stops. (During the upward movement of the mass, the spring's pull may even change to a downward force due to compression.) The downward force then accelerates it again. As a consequence of the upward force exerted by the spring and the downward force due to gravity, the mass describes an up-and-down motion.

Assuming the ideal conditions of a frictionless spring, the mass goes up above the equilibrium position as far as it goes down, and it completes each up-and-down cycle in the same amount of time. At each point in the up-and-down cycle, the force exerted on the mass, and therefore the resulting acceleration, are directly proportional to the displacement of the mass from the equilibrium position. Both the force and the acceleration are directed toward the equilibrium position. The type of periodic motion which has these particular characteristics is known as *simple harmonic motion.*

Simple harmonic motion *is a type of linear motion of a particle in which the acceleration is proportional to the displacement of the particle from its equilibrium position and is always directed toward the equilibrium position.*

Obviously not all back-and-forth or up-and-down motion is simple harmonic motion. The motion of a mass vibrating up-and-down on a spring, the motion of the prongs of a vibrating tuning fork, and the motion of a swinging pendulum bob are familiar examples of motion that is simple harmonic motion or very nearly so.

5.11 The relationship between circular motion and simple harmonic motion

It is sometimes quite helpful to analyze simple harmonic motion in terms of circular motion. Let us see how this analysis is made. We shall also be interested in certain definitions relating to simple harmonic motion.

In Fig. 5-16 **P** is moving with uniform speed in a circular path around point **O**. **P'** is the perpendicular projection of **P** along line **MN**. When **P** is at **a**, its projection is at **a'**; when it is at **b**, its projection is at **b'**, and so on. As **P** makes a complete revolution on the reference circle, **P'** describes a *complete vibration*. It can be shown that **P'** moves with an acceleration proportional to **O'P** and the acceleration is always directed toward **O'**. Thus the motion of **P'** along **MN** is simple harmonic. When **P'** is at **b'**, the *displacement* of **P'** is the distance **b'O'** — its distance from the midpoint of its vibration at that particular instant. The *amplitude* of the vibration is the maximum displacement **O'M** or **O'N** — it equals the radius of the reference circle. The *period* is the time of one complete vibration — the time required for the point to make one revolution on the reference circle. The *frequency* of a vibratory motion is the number of vibrations per second — the number of revolutions per second of a point on the reference circle. *The frequency is the reciprocal of the period.* The *equilibrium position* of an object which is executing simple harmonic motion is the midpoint of its path, **O'**.

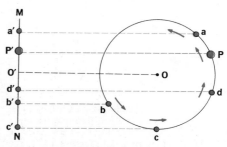

5-16 Simple harmonic motion can be analyzed in terms of circular motion.

5.12 The pendulum

*An object mounted so that it can swing back and forth about an axis is called a **pendulum**.* Figure 5-17 shows a simple pendulum, in which a small dense mass (called the bob) is suspended by a cord. The mass of the cord is small when compared to the mass of the bob, hence the mass of the cord can be neglected in working simple pendulum problems. If the displacement is small compared to the length of the pendulum, the motion of a pendulum is a very close approximation to simple harmonic motion.

As the pendulum bob moves from **A** to **B** and back again to **A**, it makes a complete vibration. The time required for a complete vibration is the period of the pendulum. The number of complete vibrations per second is the frequency. The displacement is the distance of the bob at any instant from the

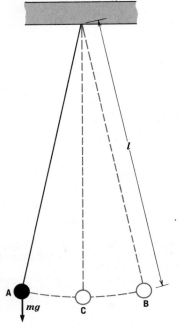

5-17 The simple pendulum. The frequency of vibration depends only on the values of *l* and *g*, provided that the displacement is small compared to the length of the pendulum and air resistance is negligible.

equilibrium position **C**. The amplitude is the maximum displacement.

Galileo was probably first to make quantitative studies of the motion of a pendulum. It is said that he observed the gentle swaying of a sanctuary lamp in the cathedral at Pisa. Using his pulse as a timer, he found that successive vibrations were made in equal lengths of time, regardless of the amplitude of the vibrations of the lamp. He later verified his observations by experiment and then suggested that a pendulum be used to time the pulse rates of medical patients.

In the simple pendulum shown in Fig. 5-17, all the mass may be considered to be concentrated in the bob. For an ideal pendulum of this type, the following statements hold true.

1. The period of a pendulum is independent of the mass or material of the pendulum. This statement is strictly true only if the pendulum vibrates in a vacuum. Air resistance has more effect on a ball of cotton used as a pendulum bob than it does on a ball of lead.

2. The period of a pendulum is independent of the amplitude if the arc is small. The arc is considered small if it is a small fraction of one radian, say 10° or less.

3. The period of a pendulum is directly proportional to the square root of its length. We may express this in algebraic notation as

$$T : T' = \sqrt{l} : \sqrt{l'}$$

If we have two pendulums, one 25 cm long and the other 100 cm long, the period of the longer one will be twice that of the shorter one. Since the squre roots of 25 and 100 are 5 and 10 respectively, the periods are in the ratio of 5 to 10, or 1 to 2.

4. The period of a pendulum is inversely proportional to the square root of the acceleration of free fall. A pendulum vibrates slightly faster at the north pole than at the equator. If we use the letter *l* to denote the length of a pendulum and *g* to denote the acceleration due to gravity, the period *T* is

$$T = 2\pi \sqrt{\frac{l}{g}}$$

Any real object that can vibrate like a pendulum is called a *physical pendulum* (as distinguished from the ideal *simple pendulum*). For example, a baseball bat can be a physical pendulum (Fig. 5-18). When the bat is suspended from point **O** and set in vibration, its period will be the same as that of a simple pendulum with a length equal to the distance between **O** and **C**. Consequently, point **C** is called the *center of oscillation*. The interesting thing is that **O** and **C** are interchangeable, so that if the bat is suspended from **C**, the center of oscillation will be at **O**.

Point **C** also has the property of being the *center of percussion* of the bat. There is no sting to the hands if a ball strikes a bat at the center of percussion and the hands are turning the bat about the center of oscillation. If the ball and bat meet at any other point, the bat rotates about some point other than **O** so that **O** or the hand is quickly pushed to one side, which accounts for the "sting."

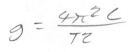

$$g = \frac{4\pi^2 C}{T^2}$$

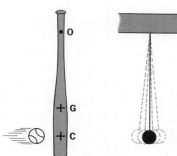

5-18 A physical pendulum and simple pendulum with the same period of vibration. O is the point of suspension of the bat, G is the center of gravity, and C is the center of oscillation and precession.

QUESTIONS

Group A

1. How is periodic motion related to simple harmonic motion?
2. Define the following terms as they are used in describing simple harmonic motion: (a) complete vibration; (b) displacement; (c) period; (d) frequency.
3. What factors determine the period of motion of a pendulum?
4. (a) What is a physical pendulum? (b) How is it related to a simple pendulum?
5. List two ways of finding the center of percussion of a baseball bat.

Group B

6. If a pendulum clock loses time, how should the pendulum be adjusted?
7. Describe a method of using the simple pendulum to find the value of *g* for a given location.
8. Explain why less force is exerted on the mass in Fig. 5-16 as the mass returns to its equilibrium position.
9. In what sense may the balance wheel of a wrist watch be compared with a simple pendulum?

PROBLEMS

Group A

1. A pendulum 0.25 m long has a period of 1.1 sec. What is the period of a pendulum in the same location if it has a length of 0.10 m?
2. What is the period of a pendulum 1.5 m long at sea level?

Group B   3. What is the value of g for a location where a pendulum 1.08 m long
               has a period of 2.05 sec?
            4. A seconds pendulum is one with a period of exactly two seconds.
               Find the length of a seconds pendulum at Denver, Colorado ($g =$
               9.79609 m/sec^2).

Chapter # 6

Conservation of Energy and Momentum

WORK AND POWER

The word *work* has a very special meaning in physics. ***Work is done when a force affects the motion of an object moving in the direction of a component of the applied force.*** No matter how long you hold a heavy load on your shoulder, in a scientific sense, you are not doing any work on the load. You are merely exerting an upward force which counteracts the downward force of gravity on the load. You do work, in a scientific sense, when you raise the load to your shoulder, when you carry it up a flight of stairs, or when you pull it across the floor. In these cases, *you exert a force which has a component in the direction in which the object moves.*

Two factors must be considered in measuring work: the displacement of the object, and the magnitude of the force in the direction of displacement. *The amount of work, W, equals the product of the force, F, and the displacement of the object, s.*

$$W = Fs$$

When the force is measured in newtons and the distance through which it acts is measured in meters, the work is expressed in *joules* (j). *A force of one newton, acting through a distance of one meter, does **one joule** (jool) of work.* This unit of work was named for the English physicist, James Prescott Joule. Note that *a joule is a newton meter.*

For example, let us compute the work required to lift a 1.0-kg mass to a height of 5.0 m. From the relationship between mass and weight discussed in previous chapters, we know that a force of about 9.8 n must be exerted to lift a mass of 1.0 kg

6.1 Scientific definition of work

Chesapeake Bay Bridge-Tunnel Authority

A large pile driver. Many joules of work are performed during each blow struck by this powerful machine, which was specially built for the construction of the 17 1/2-mile Chesapeake Bay Bridge-Tunnel in Virginia.

at sea level. Thus, the amount of work involved is

$$W = Fs$$
$$W = (9.8 \text{ n})(5.0 \text{ m})$$
$$W = 49 \text{ j}$$

If we merely slide the 1.0-kg mass for a distance of 5.0 m along a horizontal surface with a coefficient of sliding friction, μ, of 0.30, the work required is

$$W = F_f s$$
$$W = \mu F_N s \quad \textbf{(see Section 7.9)}$$
$$W = (0.30)(9.8 \text{ n})(5.0 \text{ m})$$
$$W = 15 \text{ j}$$

In both instances, the force is applied in the direction in which the object moves.

Suppose, however, that the force is applied to the object in a direction other than that in which it moves. Then, only that component of the applied force which acts in the direction the object moves is used in computing the work done on the object. Thus, in Fig. 6-1 the relationship between the applied force, F_a, and the component in the direction of motion, F, is

$$F = F_a \cos \theta$$

This relationship is applied in the following example.

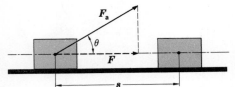

6-1 Definition of work. The work done by the applied force, F_a, is equal to the product of F, the component of F_a in the direction of the displacement, and s, the distance through which the mass moves.

Example

A box with a mass of 115 kg is pushed up an inclined plane 10.0 m long. The push is applied parallel to the plane, which makes an angle of 15.0° with the horizontal. How much work is done if the coefficient of sliding friction between the box and plane is 0.30? (It is assumed that the box is moving with constant speed.)

Solution

Basic equation: $W = Fs$

In this case, F is the sum of the force of friction, F_f, and the component of the weight of the box parallel to the plane, F_p, or $F = F_f + F_p$.

The weight of the box, $F_w = mg$.

The force of friction, $F_f = \mu F_N$

F_N is the component of the weight of the box normal to the plane, or
$F_N = F_w \cos \theta = mg \cos \theta$. Thus, $F_f = \mu mg \cos \theta$.
The component of the weight of the box parallel to the plane,
$F_p = F_w \sin \theta = mg \sin \theta$.
Substituting these values in the basic equation, we get the
Working equation:

$$W = (\mu mg \cos \theta + mg \sin \theta)s, \text{ or}$$
$$W = mgs \, (\mu \cos \theta + \sin \theta)$$
$$W = [(115 \text{ kg})(9.80 \text{ n/kg})(10.0 \text{ m})][(0.30)(0.966) + 0.259]$$
$$W = 6.20 \times 10^3 \text{ j}$$

In the examples of work in Section 6.1, the forces involved did not vary. In many problems involving work, however, the forces may vary either in direction or in magnitude (or both) during the time that they are acting on an object. For example, when a force is used to stretch a spring, the magnitude of the force increases as the spring gets longer.

An easy way to find the amount of work done by a varying force is by means of a graph. In Fig. 6-2, the area under the curved line represents the work done by a force that varies in magnitude and direction. The horizontal axis denotes the distance, *s*, and the vertical axis the force that acts in the direction of motion, *F*. The amount of work required to provide the displacement indicated by the curve up to point **A,** for example, is equal to the area bounded by the curve at the top, at the right by a vertical line from **A** to the horizontal axis, and at the left and bottom by the two coordinate axes.

To calculate the area of a geometric figure that is bounded by one or more curved lines requires special mathematical techniques. A good approximation is obtained, however, by the use of suitable rectangles. For example, the work indicated by the curve between points **B** and **C** is approximately equal to the area of the colored rectangle in the figure. Thus, if *s* is in meters and *F* is in newtons, the approximation is equal to 2.0 m times 6.5 n, or 13 j.

The total amount of work which may be represented by the area under the curve can be found by adding the areas of many rectangles formed in the same way as the one in the figure. If the rectangles are made very narrow, the answer will be more accurate, (Calculus, a branch of mathematics, gives a method of finding the area under specific curves without using rectangles.) An interesting way to measure the area under a curve is to cut it out of a piece of paper, weigh it, and compare it with the weight of a known area.

6.2 Work done by varying forces

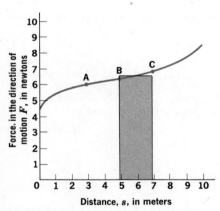

6-2 Work done by a variable force. The area under the curve represents the total work.

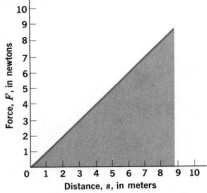

6-3 Work done by a constantly increasing force. The total work is represented by the colored triangle.

6.3 Work done in rotary motion

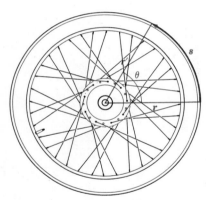

6-4 Work done in rotary motion. A torque is required to increase the kinetic energy of the wheel.

MODERN PHYSICS

The problem of finding the total work done by a varying force is somewhat simpler in the case of the stretching spring, as long as the force is constantly applied in the direction of the stretching. The force required to stretch a spring depends on its stiffness, but the force is directly proportional to the amount of stretching. (The limits within which this relationship is true will be more fully discussed in Section 7.8.) Consequently, a graph of the work done in stretching the spring looks like Fig. 6-3. No approximations are required in computing the total work, since the area of the triangle under the curve is exactly equal to one-half the product of its base and height.

To compute the work done in rotary motion, we make use of the principles of radian measure (Section 5.6). In Fig. 6-4, the displacement of the rim of the wheel is designated by the arc s. If the angle θ is expressed in radians, then $s = r\theta$. Substituting this expression for s in the work equation, we get

$$W = Fr\theta$$

Furthermore, in Section 4.11, we saw that a torque, T, is equal to the product of a force and the length of its torque arm. In Fig. 6-4, the torque arm is the radius of the circle, so that $T = Fr$. The work equation can now be written

$$W = T\theta$$

which means that the work done in rotary motion can be computed by finding the product of the torque producing the motion and the angular displacement in radians.

For example, if the radius of the wheel in Fig. 6-4 is 2.0 m and a force of 12 n is applied tangentially to it, the work done in a single revolution is

$$W = T\theta$$
$$W = Fr\theta$$
$$W = 2\pi Fr$$
$$W = 2(3.14)(12 \text{ n})(2.0 \text{ m})$$
$$W = 150 \text{ j}$$

6.4 The scientific meaning of power

Like the term *work*, the term *power* has a scientific meaning that differs somewhat from its everyday meaning. When we say a person has great power, we usually mean he has great strength, or he wields great authority. In physics, the term *power* means *the time rate of doing work.*

You do the same amount of work whether you climb a flight of stairs in one minute or in five minutes, but your power output

6-5 A power comparison. In each case, the boy will do the same amount of work in climbing the stairs. However, on the right his output of power is greater and he accomplishes the climb in a shorter time. (Kinetic energy is disregarded by assuming that both boys start from rest and come to a stop at the top of the stairs.)

is not the same (Fig. 6-5). Power depends upon three factors: the displacement of the object, the force in the direction of the displacement, and the time required.

Since power is the time rate of doing work,

$$P = \frac{W}{t}$$

in which P represents power, W is work, and t is time. Or, because $W = Fs$,

$$P = \frac{Fs}{t}$$

When work is measured in joules and time is measured in seconds, power is expressed in *watts* (w). *A **watt** is a joule per second.* This unit is named in honor of James Watt (1736–1819)

$t = \frac{w}{p}$

$t =$

$t = \underline{10000 \ \text{N/m/sec}}$

New York Public Library

James Watt, the Scottish inventor for whom the metric unit of power is named, in his workshop.

who designed the first practical steam engine. Since the watt is an inconveniently small unit, power is more commonly measured in units of 1000 watts, called kilowatts (kw).

The terms watt and kilowatt, used frequently in connection with electricity, apply to situations other than electric power. The watt is the basic unit of power in the MKS system and may be used to express quantities of mechanical as well as electric power. (The familiar unit called the "horsepower" is equal to 746 watts.)

6.5 Power in rotary motion   Just as in the computation of work done in rotary motion (Section 6.3), radian measure is used in finding the power involved. Substituting the expression for work, $T\theta$, in rotary motion, the power equation becomes

$$P = \frac{T\theta}{t}$$

Furthermore, we saw in Section 5.6, that the time rate of angular displacement, θ/t, is called the angular velocity, ω. If θ is measured in radians, then ω is in radians per second.

For rotary motion, the expression for power can now be written

$$P = T\omega$$

which means that the power required to maintain rotary motion against an opposing torque is equal to the product of the torque maintaining the rotary motion and the constant angular velocity.

Example

A boy's mass is 75.2 kg. If he walks up a flight of stairs 12.6 m high in 28.0 sec, what is his power output? Assume that the kinetic energy of the boy is the same at the bottom and top of the stairs.

Solution

Basic equation: $P = \dfrac{Fs}{t}$

In this case, F is the weight of the boy, F_w, which is found from his mass by the relationship

$F_w = mg$

The distance s is not given, but the vertical height of the staircase is. This is the value of s in this problem.

Working equation: $P = \dfrac{mgs}{t}$

$$P = \frac{(75.2 \text{ kg})(9.80 \text{ m/sec}^2)(12.6 \text{ m})}{28.0 \text{ sec}}$$

$$P = 332 \text{ w}$$

Example

A flywheel, mass 75.2 kg, is accelerated uniformly from rest to a rotational speed of $95\bar{0}$ revolutions per minute in one minute. The wheel is a uniform disc with radius of 0.500 m. What power is required to produce this motion?

Solution

Basic equation: $P = W/t$

For a uniform disc, $I = 1/2\ mr^2$ (See Fig. 5-11), and since

$W = E_k = 1/2\ I\omega^2$, we get the

Working equation: $P = 1/4\ mr^2\omega^2/t$

$$P = \frac{(75.2\text{ kg})(0.500\text{ m})^2[(95\bar{0}/\text{min})(2\pi)(1\text{ min}/60\text{ sec})]^2}{4(60\text{ sec})}$$

$$P = 780\text{ w}$$

QUESTIONS

1. (a) Give the scientific definition of "work." (b) Is work done when   **Group A**
   you walk down a flight of stairs? Explain.
2. Does a baseball catcher do work in catching a ball? Explain.
3. (a) How is a graph used to find the work done by a varying force?
   (b) What method can easily be applied if the force varies constantly?
4. Is work done by the centripetal force that produces circular motion?
   Explain.
5. (a) Give the scientific definition of "power". (b) What is the MKS
   unit of power?

6. How are the coordinates of a graph used to find the area under a   **Group B**
   given curve?
7. (a) What physical quantity is expressed in kilowatt-hours? (b) Use
   dimensional analysis to verify your answer.
8. Show how the formula for power in rotary motion is derived.

PROBLEMS

1. A man weighing 750 n climbs a flight of stairs that is 5.0 m high.   **Group A**
   What work does he do?
2. What work is done when a girl lifts a 2.5-kg package and places
   it on a shelf 2.2 m high?
3. How much work must be done to roll a metal safe, mass 116 kg, a
   distance of 15.0 m across a level floor? The coefficient of friction
   is 0.050.
4. A sled is pulled over level snow a distance of 0.500 km by a force of
   124 n applied to a rope which makes an angle of 35.0° with the snow.
   How much work is done?

$F = \frac{w}{d}$

5. A force of 18 n is required to stretch a spring 0.25 m from its neutral position. (a) Compute the amount of work done on the spring. (b) How much force is required to stretch the spring 0.50 m (assuming that the elastic limit of the spring is not exceeded)? (c) Compute the amount of work done.

6. What power is required to raise a mass of 47 kg to a height of 12 m in 15 sec?

7. A loaded elevator has a mass of 2.50×10^3 kg. If it is raised in 10.0 sec to a height of 50.0 m, how many kilowatts are required?

8. The mass of a large steel ball is 1500 kg. What power is used in raising it to a height of 33 m if the work is performed in 30.0 sec?

$W = Fd$

Group B

9. A loaded trunk has a mass of 35 kg. The coefficient of friction between the trunk and the floor is 0.20. How much work is done in moving the trunk 8.0 m across a level floor and then lifting it into a truck 1.3 m above the floor?

10. A crate, mass 75.0 kg, is to be pushed up an inclined plane 3.00 m long, which makes an angle of 20.0° with the horizontal. If the coefficient of friction between the crate and the inclined plane is 0.150, how much work must be done?

$F = ma$

11. A tangential force of 7.5 n is applied to a wheel 0.25 m in radius to maintain it at a constant speed of 240 revolutions per minute. How much work is done per minute?

$F = mg$

12. An unbalanced force of 5.0 n acts on a mass of 2.0 kg which is initially at rest. How much work is done (a) during the first two seconds; (b) during the tenth second?

13. A flywheel, mass 203 kg, is a uniform disc 1.00 m in radius, (a) What constant torque must be applied to bring the flywheel from rest to an angular velocity of 195 revolutions per minute in 60.0 sec? (b) How much work is done during this time?

14. A girl pulls a loaded sled by means of a rope which makes an angle of 45.0° with the horizontal. If the mass of the sled is 60.0 kg and the coefficient of friction is 0.020, how much work is done in pulling the sled along a level road for a distance of 1.000 km?

15. A pump can deliver 20.0 liters of gasoline per minute. What power, in kilowatts, is expended by the pump in raising gasoline a distance of 6.00 m? One liter of gasoline has a mass of 0.700 kg. (The kinetic energy acquired by the gasoline may be disregarded.)

16. A motor is rated to deliver 10.0 kw. At what speed in m/min can this motor raise a mass of 2.75×10^4 kg?

17. What power will be required to move a locomotive weighing 1.00×10^6 n up a grade which rises 1.50 m for each $10\bar{0}$ m of track, at 40.0 km/hr, if the frictional force opposing the motion is 2.00×10^3 n?

18. A torque of 2.97 n m is supplied by a motor running at the angular speed of $120\bar{0}$ revolutions per minute. What is the power output?

ENERGY

In Chapter 1 we saw that there are two kinds of energy, potential and kinetic. In the following sections, we will deal quantitatively with these concepts and see how the various forms of energy are expressed in terms of work units.

The potential energy acquired by an object equals the work done against gravity or other forces to place it in position (Fig. 6-6). The equation for calculating work, when the force acts in the same direction as the displacement, is

$$W = Fs$$

Therefore

$$E_p = Fs$$

In lifting an object, F is its weight, which from Newton's second law of motion equals mg, and s is the vertical distance h through which it is lifted, so

$$E_p = mgh$$

The gravitational potential energy defined by this equation is expressed in relation to an arbitrary reference level where $h = 0$. It makes no difference what level is chosen. Sea level, street level, ground level, or floor level are useful reference levels.

When the mass of an object is given in kilograms, the height in meters, and the acceleration due to gravity in m/sec², the gravitational potential energy is expressed in joules. Thus, if a 50-kg mass of steel is raised 5.0 m, its gravitational potential energy is

$$E_p = mgh$$
$$E_p = 50 \text{ kg} \times 9.8 \text{ m/sec}^2 \times 5.0 \text{ m}$$
$$E_p = 2.5 \times 10^3 \text{ j}$$

At any particular instant, the velocity of a freely falling object starting from rest, in terms of the acceleration of gravity and the distance traveled, is given by the equation

$$v = \sqrt{2gs}$$

Solving for s, we obtain

$$s = \frac{v^2}{2g}$$

Since s in this equation means the same quantity as h in the equation $E_p = mgh$, let us substitute for h the expression we

6.6 Gravitational potential energy

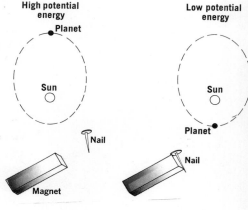

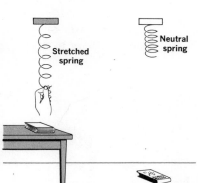

6-6 Examples of potential energy. Can you give the reason for the difference in energy for each pair of situations?

6.7 Measurement of kinetic energy

θ angular displacement
I rotational inertia
ω angular velocity
α angular acceleration

$$\omega = \frac{\theta}{t}$$

$$\alpha = \frac{\omega}{t} \qquad \alpha = \frac{T}{I} \quad (rad/s)$$

$$I = \frac{T}{\alpha} \quad (kg\,m^2)$$

$$T = Fr \quad (Nm)$$

$$T = I\alpha \quad (Nm)$$

have just derived for *s*. Since this object is moving with velocity *v*, it possesses kinetic energy. We then obtain

$$E_k = mg \times \frac{v^2}{2g}$$

$$E_k = \tfrac{1}{2}mv^2$$

Although this equation for kinetic energy was derived from the motion of a falling body, it can be shown that it applies to motion in any direction or from any cause (Fig. 6-7).

As in the case of gravitational potential energy, kinetic energy is expressed in joules if the mass is given in kilograms and the velocity in meters per second. Thus, if a baseball has a mass of 0.14 kg and is thrown with a velocity of 7.5 m/sec, its kinetic energy is

$$E_k = \tfrac{1}{2}mv^2$$

$$E_k = \frac{0.14 \text{ kg}(7.5\text{m/sec})^2}{2}$$

$$E_k = 3.9 \text{ j}$$

6.8 Kinetic energy in rotary motion

If a rotating object starts from rest, the angular velocity in terms of the angular acceleration and angular displacement is

$$\omega = \sqrt{2\alpha\theta}$$

For this same rotating object, the relationship between torque, rotational inertia, and angular acceleration is

$$T = I\alpha$$

Solving both of these expressions for angular acceleration,

$$\alpha = \frac{\omega^2}{2\theta} \text{ and } \alpha = \frac{T}{I}$$

Setting these two expressions equal

$$\frac{T}{I} = \frac{\omega^2}{2\theta}$$

Solving for $T\theta$,

$$T\theta = \frac{I\omega^2}{2}$$

When only the net force and torque are considered in these equations, all of the work done to produce rotation appears as kinetic energy. Since, for rotary motion $W = T\theta$,

$$E_k = \tfrac{1}{2}I\omega^2$$

The wheel of a moving automobile has both linear motion and rotary motion. The wheel turns on its axle as the axle

6-7 Examples of kinetic energy. In each case, the energy is dependent upon the mass of the moving particle and its speed.

moves along parallel to the road. The kinetic energy of such an object is the sum of the kinetic energy due to linear motion plus the kinetic energy due to rotary motion.

$$E_k = \tfrac{1}{2}mv^2 + \tfrac{1}{2}I\omega^2$$

(See the Example below.)

Example

A metal ring, mass 2.50 kg, rolls along a horizontal surface with a velocity of 5.25 m/sec. What is the total kinetic energy of the moving ring?

Solution

Basic equation: $E_k = \tfrac{1}{2}mv^2 + \tfrac{1}{2}I\omega^2$

The rotational inertia of a ring, $I = mr^2$ (See Fig. 5-13)

By definition, $\omega = \dfrac{\theta}{t}$ and $\theta = \dfrac{s}{r}$ and $v = \dfrac{s}{t}$

Consequently, $\omega = \dfrac{s/r}{t} = \dfrac{s}{rt} = \dfrac{v}{r}$

Substituting, $\tfrac{1}{2}I\omega^2 = \tfrac{1}{2}mr^2(v/r)^2 = \tfrac{1}{2}mv^2$

Working equation: $E_k = \tfrac{1}{2}mv^2 + \tfrac{1}{2}mv^2 = mv^2$

$$E_k = (2.50 \text{ kg})(5.25 \text{ m/sec})^2$$

$$E_k = 68.9 \text{ j}$$

When energy is supplied to an object and simultaneously gives it both linear and rotary motion, the energy division depends on the rotational inertia of the object. If a ring and a solid disc of equal mass and diameter roll down the same incline, the disc will accelerate more. Its rotational inertia is less, and thus its rotational kinetic energy is less than that of the ring. Its linear kinetic energy is therefore greater than that of the ring; the disc acquires a higher linear velocity and reaches the bottom of the incline first. However, the total kinetic energy of the ring at the bottom of the incline will be the same as that of the disc, since they have the same gravitational potential energy at the top.

When a spring is compressed, energy is stored in the spring. At any instant during the compression, the elastic potential energy in the spring is equal to the work that was done on the spring. The potential energy in a stretched or compressed elastic object is called *elastic potential energy*.

6.9 Elastic potential energy

The work required to stretch or compress a spring does not depend on the weight of the spring. Consequently, gravity is not involved in the measurement of elastic potential energy. Instead, the work required for the stretching or compressing is dependent upon a property of the spring known as the *force constant*, which does not change for a specific spring so long as the spring is not permanently distorted.

The force required to stretch a spring is given by the equation

Spring → $$F = ks$$ (Equation 1)

where k is the force constant of the spring and s is the distance over which F is applied. We noted in Section 6.2 that the force is directly proportional to the length of the stretch (within definite limits). Consequently, the work done on the spring also varies directly with the amount of stretching. The total amount of work, therefore, is given by the equation

$$W = \tfrac{1}{2}Fs$$ (Equation 2)

where F is the force exerted on the spring at the end of the stretch through distance s. (The force varies from zero to F, and the equation uses the average of these two values, or $\tfrac{1}{2}F$.)

Substituting the expression for F from Equation 1 in Equation 2, we get

$$W = \tfrac{1}{2}ks^2$$ (Equation 3)

This equation applies to the compression of a spring as well as to the stretching that was used to illustrate it in this section. Also, since the potential energy of an object is equal to the work done on the object, Equation 3 can be rewritten as an elastic potential energy equation

$$E_p = \tfrac{1}{2}ks^2$$ (Equation 4)

This equation represents ideal conditions. In actual practice, a small fraction of the work of stretching or compression is converted into heat energy in the spring and does not show up as elastic potential energy.

6.10 Conservation of mechanical energy

The exchange of energy in a pendulum is similar to that in the vertical motion of a mass on a spring. (See Section 5.10.) Both are examples of simple harmonic motion. They illustrate an important principle of physics called the **law of conservation of mechanical energy,** which states that *the sum of the potential and kinetic energy of an ideal energy system remains constant.*

Forces involved in the conservation of mechanical energy are called *conservative forces.* Thus, gravitational forces and elastic forces are conservative forces since they are responsible for the exchange between potential and kinetic energy in simple harmonic motion. However, there are forces that produce deviations from the law of conservation of mechanical energy, such as the force of friction. Forces of this type are called nonconservative, or *dissipative forces*.

The reason that friction is a dissipative force is that it produces a form of energy (heat) that is not mechanical. In the larger frame of reference of the law of conservation of total energy, of course, there is no "lost" energy. The calculation of heat energy and its role in energy transformations will be discussed in Chapter 8.

Another way to distinguish between conservative and dissipative forces is to observe the relationship between the force and the path over which it acts. In the case of a conservative force, the work done (and energy involved) is completely independent of the length of the path. For example, in the illustration of gravitational potential energy in Fig. 6-8, the gravitational potential energy of both men is the same (provided they have equal masses) even though one of them travelled much farther than the other one. The only thing that matters is the mass of the men and the height above the reference level.

The amount of heat energy lost through friction can be quite different for two objects descending from the same height, however. The longer the path, the greater is the amount of mechanical energy that is converted to heat energy even if the frictional forces would remain constant. Thus, the work done by a given dissipative force varies directly with the length of the path followed by an object.

6-8 The work done by conservative forces is independent of the path. The potential energy of the man is, in each case, dependent only on his mass and the height above the reference level.

QUESTIONS

Group A

1. (a) Differentiate between potential and kinetic energy. (b) Between gravitational potential energy and elastic potential energy.
2. Show how the formula for gravitational potential energy is derived from the work formula.
3. (a) Describe the kinetic energy of the wheel of a moving automobile. (b) Give the equations that can be used to calculate this energy.
4. (a) What determines the force required to stretch or compress a spring? (b) In what units is this factor expressed?
5. (a) Define mechanical energy. (b) How is it conserved in the motion of a pendulum?

Group B   6. (a) Show how the equation for kinetic energy is derived. (b) Use dimensional analysis to show that kinetic energy is expressed in work units.
7. Explain the similarity between a swinging pendulum and the motion of a mass on the end of a horizontally compressed spring on a frictionless table.
8. (a) Distinguish between conservative and dissipative forces. (b) Why is the force of friction a dissipative force?

PROBLEMS

Group A   1. A woman lifts a mass of 2.00 kg from the floor to a table 0.80 m high. What potential energy does the mass have because of this change of position using the floor as a reference?
2. A large rock with a weight of 1470 n rests at the top of a cliff 40.0 m high. What potential energy does it have using the bottom of the cliff as a reference?
3. What is the kinetic energy of a baseball, mass 0.14 kg, thrown with a speed of 18 m/sec?
4. A meteorite weighing 1860 n strikes the earth with a velocity of 45.2 m/sec. What is its kinetic energy?
5. A spring scale is calibrated from zero to $2\bar{0}$ n. The calibrations extend over a length of 0.10 m. (a) What is the elastic potential energy of the spring in the scale when a weight of 5.0 n hangs from it? (b) when the spring is fully stretched?
6. The force constant of a spring is 150 n/m. (a) How much force is required to stretch the spring 0.25 m? (b) How much work is done on the spring in that case?

R^2 cancell

Group B   7. A stone, mass 50.0 kg, is dropped from a height of 197 m. What is the potential energy and the kinetic energy of the stone (a) at $t = 0$ sec; (b) at $t = 1.00$ sec; (c) at $t = 5.00$ sec; (d) when the stone strikes the ground?
8. An automobile weighing 2.00×10^5 n is accelerated on a level road from 45 km/hr to 75 km/hr in 11.0 sec. (a) What is its increase in kinetic energy? (b) What force produces the acceleration? (c) What power is required?
9. What is the kinetic energy, in joules, of an electron, mass 9.1×10^{-31} kg, moving at a speed of 1.0×10^7 m/sec?
10. The rotor of an electric motor has a rotational inertia of 45 kg m^2. What is its kinetic energy if it turns at 1500 revolutions per minute?
11. A bowling ball has a mass of 8.00 kg. If it rolls down the alley, without slipping, at 7.00 m/sec, calculate (a) the linear kinetic energy; (b) the rotational kinetic energy; (c) the total kinetic energy.

$W = \dfrac{V}{R}$

12. A solid ball, mass 10.0 kg, is at the top of an incline 2.00 m high and 10.00 m long. If it rolls down a frictionless incline, what is its linear speed as it reaches the bottom?

13. A 1.00-kg mass is placed at the free end of a compressed spring. The force constant of the spring is 115 n/m and it has been compressed 0.200 m from its neutral position. The spring is now released. Neglecting the mass of the spring and assuming that the mass is sliding on a frictionless surface, how fast will the mass move as it passes the neutral position of the spring?

EFFICIENCY OF MACHINES

In everyday language, the term "machine" is used to refer to any mechanical device, usually with several moving parts, that is used to accomplish a task faster or more conveniently than it could be done without the machine. In science, it is important to define a machine more exactly, so that its operation can be studied quantitatively.

One type of machine is used to *transform energy*. For example, a generator transforms mechanical energy into electric energy. A steam turbine or gas turbine transforms heat energy into mechanical energy.

Another type of machine is used to *transfer energy* from one place to another. The connecting rods, crankshaft, drive shaft, and rear axle transfer energy from the combustion in the cylinders of an automobile to the rear wheels.

Some machines may also be used to *multiply force*. If a garage mechanic wishes to lift the engine out of an automobile, he may use a system of pulleys. The pulley system enables him to raise the engine by exerting a force which is smaller than the weight of the engine.

Still other machines may be used to *multiply speed*. For example, the rim of a bicycle wheel moves faster than do the sprockets that are used to propel it.

Finally, machines may be used to *change the direction of a force*. The single pulley at the top of a flagpole enables one end of the rope to exert an upward force on the flag as a downward force is exerted on the other end.

Six types of simple machines are shown in Fig. 6-9. Each of them can be used to multiply force. Other machines are either modifications of these simple machines or combinations of two or more of them. Actually, the six machines shown are variations of two basic types: the pulley and the wheel and axle are forms of the lever, while the wedge and screw are modified inclined planes.

6.11 Scientific definition of a machine

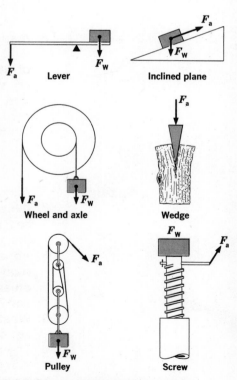

6-9 The six simple machines. Each machine multiplies force at the expense of distance.

6.12 Efficiency of machines

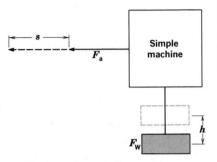

6-10 Principle of the simple machine. The efficiency of the machine is the ratio of the work output, $F_w h$, to the work input $F_a s$.

A machine can be used to multiply force, but this statement does not mean that the machine also multiplies work. Energy conservation laws hold true for machines just as they do for other applications of physics. Therefore the work output of a machine cannot exceed the work input. In a frictionless machine (where no dissipative forces are acting), work output and work input would be exactly equal. This equality means that, in a machine that multiples force, the distance over which the input force moves is always greater than the distance over which the load moves. (See Fig. 6-10.)

The ratio of the useful work output of a machine to total work input is called the *efficiency*, or

$$\text{Efficiency} = \frac{W_{\text{output}}}{W_{\text{input}}}$$

The efficiency of all machines is less than 100%, because of the presence of dissipative forces.

Thus, in using a machine to lift an object, the efficiency equation becomes

$$\text{Efficiency} = \frac{F_w h}{F_a s}$$

where F_w is the weight of the object, h is the height through which it is lifted, F_a is the input force applied to the machine, and s is the distance through which F_a acts in the direction of the input motion.

The following example illustrates the use of the efficiency equation in solving problems dealing with simple machines.

If all the dissipative forces in a machine could be eliminated, it would still not be a "perpetual motion" machine. In order to operate without an input of energy and do useful work besides, the efficiency of a machine would have to be greater than 100%. This condition would contradict the law of conservation of energy. Still, plans for supposed perpetual motion machines are frequently submitted to the U.S. Patent Office. All patent applications for such machines must be accompanied by working models. Obviously, no such models have ever been submitted.

Example

An inclined plane is 6.00 m long and 1.00 m high. The coefficient of friction is 0.050. (a) What force is required to pull a weight of 1.00×10^4 n up the plane? (b) What is the efficiency of the plane?

Solution

(a) The required force is the sum of the useful input force and the force required to overcome the dissipative force of friction.

Basic equation:
$$F = F_u + F_f$$
$$W_{input} \text{ (useful)} = W_{output} \text{ (useful)}$$
$$F_u s = F_w h$$
$$F_u = \frac{F_w h}{s}$$
$$F_f = \mu F_N$$

Working equation:
$$F = \frac{F_w h}{s} + \mu F_N$$

F_N is found by the method outlined in Section 4.5.
$$F_N = 9860 \text{ n}$$
$$F = \frac{(1.00 \times 10^4 \text{ n})(1.00 \text{ m})}{(6.00 \text{ m})} + (0.050)(9860 \text{ n})$$
$$F = 2160 \text{ n}$$

(b) *Working equation:*
$$\text{Efficiency} = \frac{F_w h}{F_a s}$$
$$\text{Efficiency} = \frac{(1.00 \times 10^4 \text{ n})(1.00 \text{ m})}{(2160 \text{ n})(6.00 \text{ m})}$$
$$\text{Efficiency} = 0.772, \text{ or } 77.2\%$$

QUESTIONS

Group A

1. Explain which of the following machines transform energy from one form to another, and which merely transfer energy from one place to another: (a) electric motor; (b) gear wheels in a watch; (c) fan belt and pulleys in an automobile engine; (d) gasoline engine on a lawnmower; (e) the drive shaft, differential gears, and rear axle of an automobile.
2. (a) List the six simple machines. (b) Into what two basic types can they be divided?
3. (a) Define efficiency for a machine. (b) How is it computed?
4. Why is it impossible for the efficiency of a machine to reach 100%?
5. (a) What are the requirements of a perpetual motion machine? (b) Why are these requirements impossible to achieve?
6. List the advantages and disadvantages of friction in the use of a screw.

Group B

7. Suppose that you have two simple machines, each of which multiplies a force by a factor of three. By what factor will the force be multiplied if the two machines are used in series? Explain.

8. If you were handed a model of a supposed perpetual motion machine, how would you proceed to check it out?

PROBLEMS

Group A

1. A plank 5.0 m long is used as a lever with the fulcrum placed between the effort force and the resistance force. The fulcrum is 2.0 m from the resistance force. What force is needed to counterbalance a 12-kg mass?

2. A force of 250 n must be used in order to lift the handles of a loaded wheelbarrow. The distance from the wheel to the handles is 1.3 m and the loaded wheelbarrow weighs 750 n. How far is the center of gravity of the wheelbarrow from the wheel?

3. A force of 545 n is exerted on the rope of a pully system, and the rope is pulled in 10.0 m. This work causes an object weighing 2520 n to be raised 1.50 m. What is the efficiency of this machine?

4. Two boys use a wheel and axle to raise a mass of 750 kg. The radius of the wheel is 0.50 m and the radius of the axle is 0.040 m. If the efficiency of the machine is 62% and each boy exerts an equal force, how much force must each apply?

5. The raised end of an inclined plane 4.0 m long is 0.90 m high. Neglecting friction, what force is required to push a steel box weighing 750 n up this plane?

6. A jackscrew has a level arm 0.75 m long. The screw has 1.5 threads to the centimeter. If 320 n of force must be exerted in order to raise a load of 6.0×10^3 kg, calculate the efficiency.

7. A jackscrew, exerting a force of 11×10^3 kg on a house, can raise one corner 0.17 m in 14 min. If the efficiency of the jackscrew is 38%, what is the power input?

MOMENTUM

6.13 The nature of momentum

It is much harder to stop a train than it is to stop a car, even though both are moving with the same velocity. A bullet fired from a gun has more penetrating power than a bullet that is thrown by hand, even though both bullets may have the same mass. The physical quantity that describes this aspect of the motion of an object is called *momentum*. **Momentum** *is the product of the mass of a moving body and its velocity.* Written as an equation,

$$p = mv,$$

where p is the momentum, m the mass, and v the velocity of an object.

In the first example above, the greater mass of the train gives it more momentum than the car. Consequently, a greater change of momentum is involved in stopping the train than in stopping the car. In the second case, the greater momentum of the fired bullet is due to its greater velocity, and a large change of momentum takes place when the speeding bullet is stopped.

From Newton's second law of motion (Section 3.9), we can derive an important relationship involving momentum. We know that, over a short time interval, $a_{av} = v/t$ (Section 3.4). If we substitute this value of acceleration for a in $F = ma$, we get

$$F = \frac{mv}{t} \quad \text{or} \quad Ft = mv$$

The product of a force and the time interval during which it acts (Ft) is called **impulse**. Hence, from Newton's second law of motion we have established that impulse equals change in momentum. Also, the first of the above equations tells us that when a force is applied to a body, the body's rate of change of momentum is equal to the force (and in the direction of the force, since the equation is a vector equation).

A good example of the relationship between impulse and change in momentum is that of a golf club hitting a golf ball. The impulse imparted to the ball depends on the force with which the ball is hit and the length of time during which the ball and club are in contact. On leaving the club, the ball has acquired a momentum equal to the product of its mass and velocity. In a sense, the impulse produced the momentum; hence, the two are equal.

In Fig. 6-11, a boy with a mass of $4\overline{0}$ kg and a man with a mass of $8\overline{0}$ kg are standing on a frictionless surface. When the man pushes on the boy from the back, the boy moves forward and the man moves backward.

The velocities with which the boy and the man move are specified by one of the most important principles of physics, called the *law of conservation of momentum*. This law states

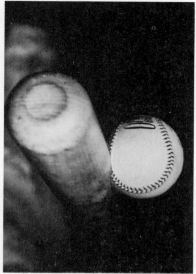

Harold E. Edgerton

During the moment of contact, much of the momentum of the bat is transferred to the baseball.

6.14 The conservation of momentum

.50 m/sec   .25 m/sec

6-11 Momentum experiment. On a frictionless surface, the momentum of the boy toward the left would equal the momentum of the man toward the right.

that *when no outside forces are acting on a system of objects, the total vector momentum of the system remains constant.*

Let us apply this law to the situation in Fig. 6-11. Initially the man and the boy are at rest. The system, therefore, has zero momentum. When the man and the boy move apart, the law of conservation of momentum requires that the vector momentum must remain zero. Hence the momentum of the boy in one direction must equal that of the man in the other direction.

If the boy moves with a velocity of 0.50 m/sec, the man will move with a velocity of 0.25 m/sec, since the mass of the man is twice as great as that of the boy. The momentum of the boy toward the left ($4\overline{0}$ kg × 0.50 m/sec) must equal the momentum of the man toward the right ($8\overline{0}$ kg × 0.25 m/sec).

An important application of the law of conservation of momentum is the *reaction principle*. When a rocket engine fires,

6-12 The unbalanced force of the expanding gases inside the rocket engine pushes this model rocket upward.

Ken Chen

for example, hot exhaust gases are expelled through the rocket nozzle. The gas particles have a momentum equal to the mass of the particles times their exhaust velocity. Momentum equal in magnitude is therefore imparted to the rocket engine in the opposite direction. Actually, Newton's third law of motion (Section 3.10) is a special case of the law of conservation of momentum. The law of conservation of momentum is more fundamental, since it applies also to forces exerted by gravitation and by electromagnetism.

The law of conservation of momentum is very helpful in studying the motions of colliding objects. Such collisions can take place in various ways, and we shall now see how the momentum conservation principles of the previous section apply in several such cases.

6.15 Inelastic and elastic collisions

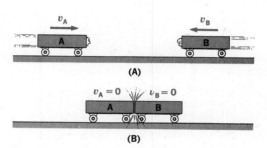

(A)

(B)

6-13 An inelastic collision. The carts have equal masses and approach each other with velocities of equal magnitude along the same straight line. The total momentum of the system is the same before and after the collision.

In Fig. 6-13A, two carts of equal mass approach each other with velocities of equal magnitude. A lump of putty is attached to the front of each cart, so that the two carts will stick together after the impact. This situation is an example of *inelastic collision*. Since the carts are traveling along the same straight line, it is also an example of a *collision in one dimension*.

The momentum of cart **A** is $m_A v_A$. It is equal in magnitude to the momentum of cart **B**, $m_B v_B$. However, the direction of v_A is opposite to the direction of v_B, so

$$v_A = -v_B$$

Consequently,

$$m_A v_A = -m_B v_B$$

and

$$m_A v_A + m_B v_B = 0$$

This means that the total vector momentum of the system of two moving carts is zero. (We assume that the system is *isolated*, that is, that there are no net external forces acting on it. In

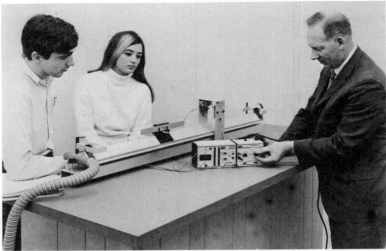

6-14 An air track designed for collision experiments. Air jets minimize
the friction between the track and the
masses placed on it.

actual collision studies, the external force of friction is usually
minimized by the use of rolling carts or air tracks, such as the
one shown in Fig. 6-14.)

After the carts in Fig. 6-13 collide, both of them come to
rest. The cart velocities, v_A and v_B, are now both zero; the sum
of the momentums of the two carts is zero, just as it was when
the carts were in motion in opposite directions. Thus, the total
vector momentum of the system is unchanged by the collision.

If one of the carts has a greater mass than the other, but their
velocities are still of equal magnitude but opposite sign, after
impact the combined carts will move in the direction of the cart
with the larger mass. The velocity of the combined carts will be
such that the total momentum of the system remains unchanged.

For example, suppose

$$m_A = 2m_B$$

and $v_A = -v_B$, as before.

Then, $m_A v_A + m_B v_B \neq 0$

Rather, by substitution, since $m_B = \dfrac{m_A}{2}$,

$$m_A v_A - 1/2 \; m_A v_A = 1/2 \; m_A v_A$$

That is, the total momentum of the system, before and after
the collision, is $1/2 \; m_A v_A$; the combined carts will move with
this momentum in the direction of the original velocity of cart **A**.

The velocity after the collision can be found by dividing the total momentum by the total mass:

$$\frac{1/2 \ m_A v_A}{3/2 \ m_A} = \tfrac{1}{3} v_A$$

When carts of equal and opposite momentums collide inelastically, they come to rest. Before the collision, they have kinetic energy. After the collision, they have none. When colliding objects rebound from each other without a loss of kinetic energy, it is an example of a perfectly *elastic collision.* Perfectly elastic collisions do not occur except between atomic and subatomic particles, but the situation can be approximated by the use of hard steel balls or with springs on an air track. The momentum conservation law holds for elastic collisions as well as inelastic ones and for collisions that are partly elastic and partly inelastic.

The law also holds for *collisions in two dimensions,* that is, when the colliding objects meet at an angle other than head-on. Fig. 6-15 shows a vector diagram that depicts the momentums of two balls with equal masses before and after an elastic, two-dimensional collision in which one of the balls is initially at rest.

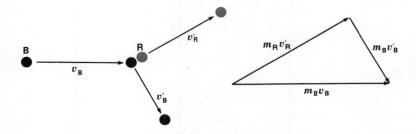

6-15 A vector diagram can be used to show that the total momentum of a system remains constant in a collision.

In the diagram, $m_B v_B$ is the momentum of the black ball before the collision. Since the colored ball is stationary before the collision, its momentum is zero and is not represented by a vector. The total momentum of the system before collision is

$$m_B v_B + 0 = m_B v_B$$

After the collision, the measured velocities of the black and colored balls are v_B' and v_R', respectively in the directions indicated. The total momentum now is the vector sum $m_B v_B' + m_R v_R'$. Since the momentum is conserved the vector $m_B v_B$ must equal the vector sum of $m_B v_B'$ and $m_R v_R'$. The vector diagram should therefore appear as a closed triangle (Fig. 6-15).

The examples that follow show how collision problems can be solved by the principles just discussed.

Example

A ball having a mass of 0.25 kg and a velocity of 0.20 m/sec eastward collides with another ball having a mass of 0.10 kg and a velocity of 0.10 m/sec, also eastward and along the same straight line. Suppose that, after the collision, the more massive ball has a velocity of 0.15 m/sec eastward. What is the velocity of the less massive ball?

Solution

Let m = the mass of the more massive ball

            m' = the mass of the less massive ball

v_i and v_f = the initial and final velocities of the more massive ball

v_i' and v_f' = the initial and final velocities of the less massive ball

The total vector momentum is the same after the collision as before the collision, or

$$mv_i + m'v_i' = mv_f + m'v_f'$$

$$v_f' = \frac{mv_i + m'v_f' - mv_f}{m'}$$

$$v_f' = \frac{(0.25 \text{ kg})(0.20 \text{ m/sec}) + (0.10 \text{ kg})(0.10 \text{ m/sec}) - (0.25 \text{ kg})(0.15 \text{ m/sec})}{0.10 \text{ kg}}$$

$$v_f' = 0.22 \text{ m/sec eastward}$$

Example

Two balls with equal masses collide in the way shown in Fig. 6-15. Before the collision, the black ball moves with a speed of 0.80 m/sec. After the collision, the balls are observed to move along paths that are perpendicular to each other. If the angle between $m_R v_R'$ and $m_B v_B$ is $40°$, calculate the speed of each ball after the collision.

Solution

Since the balls have equal masses, we can ascribe any convenient mass to them for the purposes of the problem. If we choose 1.00 kg, then the numerical value of the momentum for each ball will equal the numerical value of the velocity. The vector diagram will then yield the velocities directly.

$v_B = 0.80$ m/sec (the speed of the black ball before the collision)

$v_R' = v_B \times \cos 4\overline{0}° = (0.80 \text{ m/sec})(0.77)$

    $= 0.62$ m/sec (the speed of the white ball after the collision)

$v_B' = v_B \times \sin 4\overline{0}° = (0.80 \text{ m/sec})(0.64)$

    $= 0.51$ m/sec (speed of the black ball after the collision)

The conservation of momentum also holds for collisions among more than two bodies and in three-dimensional situations.

For rotary motion, the relationship between impulse and the change of momentum is similar to that for linear motion (Section 6.13). Using the symbols for rotary motion, the equation becomes

$$Tt = I\omega_f - I\omega_i$$

Tt is the *angular impulse,* while $I\omega_f - I\omega_i$ is the change in *angular momentum.*

The dimensions of both angular impulse and angular momentum are kg m²/sec.

Just as the linear momentum of an object is unchanged unless an external force acts on it, *the angular momentum of an object is unchanged unless an external torque acts on it.* This is a statement of the *law of conservation of angular momentum.* A rotating flywheel, which helps maintain a constant angular velocity of the crankshaft of an automobile engine, is an illustration. The rotational inertia of a flywheel is large. Consequently torques acting on it do not produce rapid changes in its angular momentum. As the torque produced by the combustion in each

6.16 Angular momentum

Angular momentum of a boy on a turntable. By lowering his arms the angular velocity increases in keeping with the law of conservation of angular momentum.

Ken Chen

cylinder tends to accelerate the crankshaft, the flywheel provides a torque which resists this action. Similarly, as the torques produced in the cylinders where compression is occurring tend to decelerate the crankshaft, the flywheel provides a torque which resists this action also. Consequently the flywheel tends to maintain a uniform rate of crankshaft rotation.

If the distribution of mass of a rotating object is changed, its angular velocity changes so that the angular momentum remains constant.

A skater, spinning on the ice with arms folded (Fig. 6-16) turns with a relatively constant angular velocity. If she extends her arms, her rotational inertia increases. Her angular velocity decreases thereby conserving angular momentum.

6-16 Angular momentum of a skater on ice. By extending her arms, the skater increases her rotational inertia and decreases her angular velocity. These changes are in keeping with the law of the conservation of angular momentum.

QUESTIONS

Group A

1. (a) What is impulse? (b) What is momentum? (c) How are impulse and change of momentum related?
2. Why do both a slowly docking ferryboat and a speeding rifle bullet have a large amount of momentum?
3. Are impulse and momentum scalar or vector quantities?
4. What is the law of conservation of momentum?
5. How does an aerial display of fireworks illustrate conservation of momentum?
6. Distinguish between elastic and inelastic collisions.
7. What is meant by an isolated system?
8. Give examples of one-dimensional and two-dimensional collisions.
9. Explain why it is impossible for a moving ocean liner or a speeding airplane to make an abrupt turn.
10. What happens to the momentum of a car when it stops?

11. What part does angular momentum play in a spinning gyroscope (Section 5.9)?
12. (a) What other external forces, besides friction, are acting on the moving carts in Fig. 6-13? (b) Why can they be ignored in the experiment?

PROBLEMS

1. A 50$\bar{0}$-kg mass is at rest and is free to move. At a certain time, (25.0 sec) after a force acts on it, the mass has a velocity in the direction of the force of 15$\bar{0}$ m/sec. What is the magnitude of the force?

   Group A

2. A bullet, mass 60.0 g, is fired from a gun that is suspended by wires and is free to move, mass 5.00 kg, with a speed of 615 m/sec. What is the speed of recoil of the gun?

3. A 1.50-kg ball, velocity, 8.00 m/sec southward, collides with a 2.00-kg ball traveling along the same path with a velocity of 3.00 m/sec southward. If the velocity of the 2.00-kg ball after impact is 4.50 m/sec southward, what is the velocity of the 1.00-kg ball?

4. A proton (mass $= 1.67 \times 10^{-27}$ kg) moves with a velocity of 6.00×10^6 m/sec. Upon colliding with a stationary particle of unknown mass, the proton rebounds upon its own path with a velocity of 4.00×10^6 m/sec. The collision sends the unknown particle forward with a velocity of 2.50×10^6 m/sec. What is the mass of the unknown particle?

5. An object with a mass of 15.0 kg and a velocity of 2.00 m/sec collides with a stationary object having the same mass. After the collision the first object moves along a line that makes an angle of 4$\bar{0}$° to the right of its original path. The second object moves at an angle of 10$\bar{0}$° to the left of the path of the first object after the collision. (a) Graphically determine the momentum of each object after the collision. (b) Calculate the speed of each object after the collision.

6. A freight car with a mass of 3.0×10^5 kg travels at a velocity of 2.5 m/sec. It collides with a stationary car with a mass of 1.5×10^5 kg on a horizontal track. The cars connect and roll together after impact. What is the velocity of the connected cars?

   Group B

7. Benjamin Franklin once said that light could not consist of particles because, if a particle would travel at such tremendous speeds (3×10^8 m/sec), it would have the impact of a 10-kg cannon ball fired from a cannon with a velocity of 100 m/sec. According to this comparison, what is the mass of Franklin's particle of light?

8. A girl is skiing down a hill. Her mass, including skis, is 65 kg. When she reaches the bottom of the hill her speed is 15 m/sec. She hits a snowdrift and stops in 0.30 sec with uniform deceleration. (a) How far does she penetrate the snowdrift? (b) With what average force does she hit the drift?

9. Show that angular momentum has the unit dimensions kg m²/sec.

10. Two balls collide head-on with equal velocity. One ball has three times the mass of the other. After the elastic collision, the more massive ball stops and the less massive one moves back along its original path with twice its original velocity. Show that momentum is conserved in the collision.

11. In the multiple-exposure photograph below, a large ball approaches from the top and a smaller one from the bottom. The mass of the large ball is 15̄0 g. The photo shows the balls at equal time intervals. By means of an appropriate vector diagram, find the mass of the smaller ball.

Chapter 7

Phases of Matter

MOLECULES AND ATOMS

When a sample of matter such as a lump of sugar is crushed into smaller particles, each of these particles is still a particle of sugar. Only the size of the particle of the sugar is changed. If the subdividing process is continued by grinding the material into a fine powder, the results are the same. Even when the sugar is dissolved in water, identifying properties of the substance are retained even though the particles are now too small to be seen even with a microscope. Evaporation of the water returns the sugar's identifying properties. These observations suggest these conclusions about the nature of matter: (1) that matter is composed of particles and (2) that the *ultimate particles* of matter are extremely small.

As early as 400 B.C., some Greek philosophers formulated ideas about the ultimate composition of matter. Democritus (460–370 B.C.) believed that matter was indestructible and that the subdividing process mentioned above would reach a limit beyond which no further separation was possible. He called these ultimate particles *atoms*, after a Greek word meaning indivisible. This idea was largely the result of rational thinking. Democritus had no direct evidence with which to back up his concept of atoms.

Another Greek philosopher, Aristotle (384–322 B.C.), suggested that all matter eventually can be reduced to four basic *elements*: air, earth, fire, and water. The reasoning that was used to support this idea frequently became quite complex, but it was a beginning in the attempt to list the ultimate particles of the universe.

7.1 The structure of matter

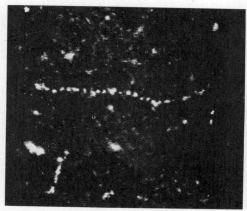

Albert V. Crewe, University of Chicago
Division of Physical Sciences

The bright spots in a line across the center of this photograph are the images of single atoms of the element thorium. These images have been enlarged more than a million times. Albert V. Crewe of the University of Chicago designed and built the scanning electron microscope that resolves images of objects this small.

149

It was a long time in the history of science before the idea of atoms and of ultimate particles was actively studied again. Near the beginning of the 19th century, the English scientist John Dalton (1766–1844) conducted a series of experiments that added greatly to our knowledge of the nature of atoms. Dalton's *atomic theory* explained the known reactions between substances and made it possible to extend the list of known elements.

The atomic theory has been modified and expanded many times since Dalton's day. A century and a half of investigation has added much information about the makeup and properties of atoms, the way in which they interact, and the nature of the compounds they form. Modern theory includes data concerning the mass, size, and energy relationships among atoms. Experiments have also revealed the fact that atoms are not ultimate particles of matter after all. A whole array of subatomic particles is presently being studied by scientists.

7.2 Molecules

A *molecule is the smallest particle of a substance that is capable of stable existence by itself.* Thus, in the example in the previous section, the smallest particle of sugar that retains the identifying properties of sugar is a molecule of sugar. (Not all substances, however, are composed of molecules. Some substances are composed of electrically charged particles called ions. These particles are discussed in Chapter 25.)

A molecule of sugar is so small that it has never been seen, even with the help of the most powerful microscope. To get an idea of the extremely small size of molecules, imagine a drop of water magnified until it is as large as the earth. With this tremendous increase in size, a single molecule of water would be about one meter in diameter. A simple molecule, like that of water, is about 3 Å across.

Molecules of more complex substances, however, may have sizes of more than 200 Å. The electron microscope, which is capable of magnifications of several million times, can be used to photograph some of these "giant" molecules. Such photographs serve as convincing evidence that matter is indeed composed of these tiny particles.

7.3 Atoms

If a molecule of sugar is analyzed, it is found to consist of particles of three simpler kinds of matter: carbon, hydrogen, and oxygen. These simpler forms of matter are called *elements*. *An atom is the smallest particle of an element that can exist either alone or in combination with other atoms of the same or of other elements.* A molecule of sugar, therefore, is made up of atoms of carbon, atoms of hydrogen, and atoms of oxygen.

Since atoms make up molecules, atoms are usually smaller than molecules. The smallest atom, an atom of hydrogen, has a diameter of about 0.6 Å. The largest atoms are a little more than 5 Å in size. The hydrogen atom is also the lightest atom. It has a mass of 1.67343×10^{-27} kg. The most common uranium atom, which is one of the heaviest atoms, has a mass of 3.95268×10^{-25} kg. There is about a tenfold range in the sizes of atoms and about a 250-fold range in their masses.

Even with the use of exponential notation, it is difficult to express the masses of individual atoms conveniently. Consequently, scientists usually express the *atomic mass* of an atom in **atomic mass units** (u). One u is equal to 1.660×10^{-27} kg, which is $\frac{1}{12}$th of the mass of a carbon-12 atom, the most abundant form of carbon atoms. In other words, scientists use carbon-12 as the standard of mass for atoms, a fact that was noted in the discussion of standard units in Chapter 2.

In atomic mass units, the atomic mass of the most abundant form of hydrogen is 1.007825 while that of the most abundant form of uranium is 238.0508. You will notice that atomic masses are known very accurately. *The integer nearest to the atomic mass is called the **mass number** of an atom.* The mass number is represented by the symbol A. Thus, for the common hydrogen atom, $A = 1$, while for the common uranium atom, $A = 238$.

Even though direct photographs of atoms have not been taken, a special instrument called the field ion microscope has made it possible to photograph the arrangement of atoms in metals. In addition to such evidence, the existence of atoms has been a useful concept in the study of chemical reactions. When substances interact chemically, atoms are rearranged (to form new molecules) but the number of the various kinds of atoms does not change during the reaction.

So far in our study of physics, we have been concerned almost entirely with the behavior of solid particles of matter. A solid is one of the three *phases* (or states) of matter—the solid phase, the liquid phase, or the gas phase. In the description of matter, **phase** means the way in which particles group together and form a substance. This structure of a substance can vary from compactly arranged particles to highly dispersed ones.

In a *solid*, the particles are close together in a fixed pattern. In a *liquid*, the particles are not usually as close together as in a solid and are not held in any fixed pattern. In a *gas*, the average separation of the particles is relatively large; and, as in a liquid, the particles are not held in any fixed pattern. (Frequently, the term *vapor* is used to describe a gas that is in the liquid phase under ordinary conditions of temperature and pressure.)

7.4 Kinetic theory of matter

To explain the motions of molecules and the energy they possess, particularly in the gaseous phase, scientists have developed the **kinetic theory of matter**. Two basic aspects of this theory are:

a. The molecules of a substance are in constant motion. The amount of motion depends upon the average kinetic energy of the molecules and this energy depends upon the temperature.

b. Collisions between molecules are perfectly elastic (except when chemical changes or molecular excitations occur).

7.5 Forces acting between molecules

The forces required to pull a solid apart are generally much greater than the forces required to separate a similar amount of liquid. Liquids separate into drops, indicating that the forces of attraction between the molecules of liquids are not as great as those of solids. Even though the size of a molecule of a substance does not change appreciably with the phase of the substance, most liquids occupy a larger volume than the same mass of solid. Thus, molecules of liquids must be farther apart than those of solids. In a gas, which occupies a volume of the order of 10^3 times that of an equal mass of liquid, molecules separate from each other spontaneously, indicating that the kinetic energy of the motion of the molecules is great enough to keep them separated. We may conclude then, that forces between molecules decrease as the distance between them increases.

Solids and liquids are not easily compressed. Apparently, when molecules are closer together than their normal spacing in solids and liquids, they repel each other. The closer molecules are pushed together, the greater the repulsive forces become.

Intermolecular forces are predominantly electric. If we compare the strength of intermolecular forces with the gravitational forces of attraction between molecules at the typical distances found in solids and liquids, we find that the intermolecular forces are of the order of 10^{29} times as strong. Thus gravitational forces between molecules are negligible in comparison with intermolecular forces. Intermolecular forces are small compared to the weight of objects we can see and handle; but the masses they act on—the masses of molecules—are small, too. These forces can impart instantaneous accelerations 10^{14} times the acceleration of gravity. Such accelerations last only a very short time, since one molecule, so accelerated, moves very quickly out of the range of another.

Intermolecular forces can be described graphically. Figure 7-1 shows the variation of the force of interaction between molecules with the distance between their centers. If we imagine one molecule to be fixed at the intersection of the axes, the other

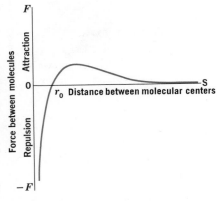

7-1 The force between molecules varies with the distance between molecular centers.

molecules will be repelled until the distance of separation is such that their outer charges do not overlap. This condition occurs at r_0 where no net force acts between the molecules. The distance to r_0 is often called the equilibrium distance. This distance (about 2.5×10^{-10} meter) is, therefore, the distance between the centers of two "touching" molecules and the diameter of a single molecule. As the separation between the molecules increases, the force of attraction between opposite charges first increases and then approaches zero at a distance of about four molecular diameters. Different molecules have different sizes and charge configurations but they always show the qualitative behavior indicated by Fig. 7-1.

In the solid phase molecules vibrate about the equilibrium position r_0. They do not have enough energy to overcome the attractive force. The equilibrium positions are fixed. In a liquid the molecules have greater vibrational energy about centers which are free to move, although the average distance between the centers of the molecules remains nearly the same. The average distance of separation between gas molecules is considerably greater than the range of intermolecular forces and the molecules move in straight lines between collisions.

AMF—Voit

The kinetic theory helps to explain why gas, released from the high-pressure tank on the diver's back, expands as it rises to the surface.

SOLIDS

Solids have definite shape and definite volume. Scientists usually describe solids as either *crystalline or amorphous.* Crystalline solids have a regular arrangement of particles, while amorphous solids have a random particle arrangement.

In addition to the forces which bind particles of a solid together, the motion of particles of a solid must also be considered. Particles of a solid are held in relatively fixed positions by the forces which bind them together. However, they do have a vibratory motion about their fixed positions. The amplitude of their vibration, and therefore their vibratory energy, is related to the temperature of the solid. At low temperatures the kinetic energy is small, while at higher temperatures it is larger.

Diffusion *is the penetration of one type of particle into a mass consisting of a second type of particle.* If a lead plate and a gold plate are in close contact for several months, particles of gold may be detected in the lead and vice versa, showing that even solids may diffuse. Diffusion is slow in solids because of the limited motion of the particles and of their close-packed, orderly arrangement.

7.6 The nature of solids

7.7 Cohesion and adhesion

The general term for the force of attraction between molecules of the same kind is **cohesion**. Cohesion, which holds the closely packed molecules of a solid together, is a short-range force. If a solid is broken, layers of gas molecules from the air cling to the broken surfaces. These gas molecules prevent rejoining of the surfaces. The molecules on the broken surfaces are not close enough together to have sufficient attraction to hold. However, if the surfaces of two like solids are polished and then slid together, the cohesive forces cause the solids to cohere. This cohesion can be demonstrated by sliding carefully ground and polished glass or metal plates over each other. Cohesion will make the plates stick together.

Molecules of different kinds sometimes attract each other strongly. Water wets clean glass and other materials. Glue sticks to wood. *The force of attraction between molecules of different kinds is called* **adhesion**. The forces of cohesion or adhesion are characteristic for specific molecules.

7.8 Tensile strength

Several properties of solids depend on cohesion; one of these is tensile strength. Suppose two wires of the same diameter, one copper and one steel, are put in a machine which pulls the wires until they break. When tested in this manner, steel wire proves stronger than copper wire of the same diameter. Therefore we say that steel has a higher *tensile strength* than copper. *The* **tensile strength** *of a material is the force required to break a rod or wire of that material having a unit cross-sectional area.* (See Fig. 7-2 and Table 7, Appendix B.) Tensile strength is a measure of cohesion between adjacent molecules over the entire cross-sectional area.

United States Steel

7-2 Tensile test of steel exhibiting high ductility in a half-inch-diameter sample. Note localized reduction of area in center of specimen.

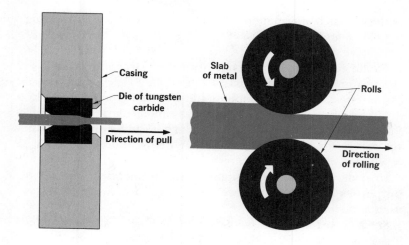

7-3 During the process of drawing (left) and of rolling (right), the atoms of a metal are forced to move over each other from one position in the crystal pattern to another.

If a metal rod can be drawn through a die to produce a wire, the metal is said to be *ductile* (*duk*-til), or to possess *ductility*. As the metal is pulled through the die, its diameter is decreased but its length is increased, and the rod becomes a wire. See Fig. 7-3 (left). In one industrial application of ductility, more than 1000 meters of wire per minute are extruded continuously from a device in which the necessary pressure is exerted by a fluid and the extruded wire does not even touch the solid die.

Metals which can be hammered or rolled into sheets are said to be *malleable* (*mal*-ee-uh-bul) or to have *malleability*. During the hammering or rolling, the shape or thickness of the metal is greatly changed. See Fig. 7-3 (right).

During hammering, rolling, or drawing, layers of atoms of a metal are forced to slide over each other from one position in the crystal pattern to another. Since the cohesive forces are strong, and the atoms do not become widely separated from each other during their rearrangement, the metal holds together while its shape is being changed. Silver, gold, platinum, copper, aluminum, and iron are all highly malleable and ductile.

When opposing forces are applied to an object, it becomes deformed. The deformation can be a change in its dimensions or shape. *The ability of an object to return to its original size or shape, when the external forces are removed*, is described as its **elasticity**. In the deformed configuration the intermolecular forces are not in equilibrium, while in the original configuration they are. There exists a limit beyond which the deformation produced by the applied forces does not disappear when the forces are removed. The object is then said to be permanently deformed. Ductility and malleability are properties of substances that can

7.9 Ductility and malleability

Bethlehem Steel

The ductility of hot steel is utilized in this steel mill.

7.10 Elasticity

undergo such permanent deformations without fracturing. *When a substance is just on the verge of becoming permanently deformed*, we say it has reached the **elastic limit**.

At the elastic limit, molecular forces are overcome to such an extent that particles slide past each other. Particles shift places in the crystal and the shape of the material is altered. Such a drastic change cannot be restored by molecular forces. Every solid has a certain range through which it can be deformed and yet return to its original condition before its elastic limit is reached.

In order to make quantitative measurements of the elastic properties of a substance we shall introduce two new terms: *stress* and *strain*.

Stress *is the ratio of the internal force* **F**, *that occurs when a substance is deformed in any way, to the area* **A** *over which the force acts.*

$$stress = \frac{F}{A}$$

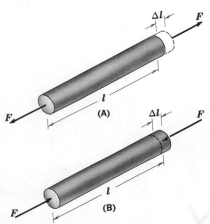

7-4 Strain may be a change in the length of a rod resulting from applied forces. (A) Elongation equals $\Delta l/l$. (B) Linear compression equals $\Delta l/l$.

Stress represents the tendency of a substance to recover its normal configuration. The deforming force changes the distance between molecules, either pulling them farther apart or pushing them closer together. When the deforming force is removed, molecular forces restore the molecules to their normal spacing.

The *relative amount of deformation produced in a body under stress is called* **strain**. There are various kinds of deformation or strain but its measure is always an absolute ratio—a number without units. When a rod is placed under tension or stretched, it elongates. *The ratio of the increase in length to the unstretched length is called the* **elongation strain** *and can be expressed as* $\Delta l/l$. (The Greek letter, Δ, is used to designate "a small increase of.") Linear compression is the reverse of elongation (Fig. 7-4). Both processes are accompanied by small changes in the cross-sectional area. We will not consider these changes further because of their small effect in situations where elastic limits are not exceeded.

In an *elongation strain*, the particles have been moved in a direction perpendicular to the area over which the forces act. In a *shear strain*, the particles move in a direction parallel to the area over which the forces act. An imaginary cube of unstrained material will take the shape of a rhombic prism when shear forces are applied to it. The measure of shear is the ratio of the amount the top of the imaginary cube is moved to the side, to the dimension of one side of the cube. This is expressed as the tangent of the angle through which the oblique edges of the imaginary cube have been rotated from their original direction (Fig. 7-5).

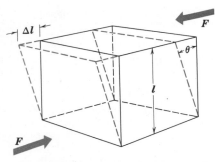

7-5 Consider this as an imaginary cube of substance within a larger body of material to which the shear forces are applied. Shear = $\tan \theta = \Delta l/l$.

Volume strain is the ratio of the decrease in volume to the volume before the stress was applied.

Flexure (bending) and torsion (twisting) are combinations of the strains just described. A straight beam bent into a plane curve undergoes compression on the concave side and elongation on the convex side. The layer of material down the center of the beam undergoes neither compression nor elongation.

Beams and girders of buildings and bridges are often acted on by varying forces or stresses. It is important for engineers to know what deformation or strain these forces will produce. In order to do this, they must have some way to measure the elasticity of materials.

If a coiled spring is stretched by a weight as shown in Fig. 7-6(A), it probably will return exactly to its original form after the stretching force is removed. If it does, it is said to be *perfectly elastic*. If the spring is stretched too far, it remains permanently distorted or deformed; its elastic limit has been exceeded.

Suppose we fasten one end of a steel wire to a beam, as in Fig. 7-6(B). Now let us add weights to the hanger attached to the lower end. The wire is stretched gradually as weights are added one by one. We find that the wire elongates by an amount which is exactly proportional to the weight pulling on it, and that it returns to its original length when the weight is removed. If we continue to apply more weights, eventually we reach the elastic limit. Then when we remove the weights, the wire remains deformed; it does not return to its original length.

By making such measurements, Robert Hooke (1635–1703) found that the amount of elongation in elastic solids is directly proportional to the deforming force, provided the elastic limit is not exceeded. The elongation also depends on the length and cross-sectional area of the wire or rod. Yet it is possible to combine all these factors in one simple law given by Hooke. **Hooke's law** states that *within certain limits strain is directly proportional to stress.*

The value of the ratio, stress/strain, is different for different solids. However, the proportionate elongation is approximately the same for a given substance, even when the material is fashioned into different shapes and sizes. This ratio gives us a means of comparing the elasticity of various solids. It is called *Young's modulus*, represented by *Y*, and is defined by the equation

$$Y = \frac{\text{stress}}{\text{strain}}$$

7.11 Hooke's law and elastic modulus

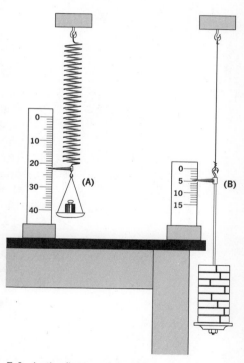

7-6 In the figures above, the pointers stood at zero before weights were applied. (A) If the pointer returns to the zero mark after the weight is removed, the spring is perfectly elastic. (B) If the weights stretch the wire beyond its elastic limit, the pointer will not return to zero when the weights are removed.

From the definitions of stress and strain we get

$$Y = \frac{F/A}{\Delta l/l}$$

and transposing terms,

$$Y = \frac{Fl}{\Delta lA}$$

As an example, the steel "A" string of a piano is 43.0 cm long. It has a cross-sectional area of $6.5 \times 10^{-7} m^2$. How much will it elongate when a force of 710 n is applied to it by the piano tuner to bring it up about to pitch?

$$\Delta l = \frac{Fl}{YA} = \frac{7.1 \times 10^2 \, n \times 4.3 \times 10^{-1} \, m}{20.0 \times 10^{10} \, n/m^2 \times 6.5 \times 10^{-7} \, m^2}$$

$$= \frac{3.1 \times 10^2 \, nm}{1.30 \times 10^5 \, n} = 2.38 \times 10^{-3} \, m$$

676

QUESTIONS

Group A

1. What are the main aspects of the kinetic theory?
2. (a) What is meant by the phase of matter? (b) Describe the three phases of matter.
3. Why are molecular collisons said to be elastic?
4. Under what circumstances are the forces between molecules in a solid (a) attractive, (b) repulsive?
5. (a) What are the two classes of solids? (b) What is the particle arrangement in each?
6. (a) Describe the motion of the particles of a solid. (b) What experimental evidence supports this description?
7. What name is given to the force of attraction between (a) like molecules, (b) unlike molecules?
8. (a) What is tensile strength? (b) In what units is the value for tensile strength usually expressed?
9. Define elasticity.
10. Distinguish between stress and strain.
11. What is meant by the elastic limit?
12. State Hooke's law.
13. (a) What is Young's modulus? (b) What is the equation by which it is defined? (c) Identify each term in the equation.

Group B

14. In a given mass of matter as a solid, liquid, and gas, what does the volume indicate about the spacing between molecules in these three phases?

15. (a) What is the magnitude of an atomic mass unit? (b) How is this value established?
16. What direct evidence do we have that matter is composed of molecules?
17. Distinguish between a molecule and an atom.
18. What happens to the crystal pattern of an elastic material when its elastic limit is exceeded?

PROBLEMS

Group A

1. A coiled spring is stretched 0.050 m by a mass weighing 0.500 n hung from one end. How far will it be stretched by a mass weighing 1.000 n?
2. The hook of a spring balance is pulled down 5.00 cm by a mass weighing 40.0 n. (a) If a mass weighing 125.0 n is substituted for the previous mass, how far is the hook pulled down? (b) How far apart are the 5.00-n graduations?
3. Two identical wires are respectively 125.0 cm and 375.0 cm long. The first wire is broken by a force of 489.0 n. What force is needed to break the other?
4. A copper wire 100.0 cm long and 0.200 cm in diameter is suspended from a solid support. A 10.00-kg mass is hung from the lower end of the wire. (a) Determine the stress in the wire. (b) Determine the strain in the wire.
5. The cross-sectional area of an aluminum wire is 2.50×10^{-3} cm^2. What force will break it?
6. A brass wire 2.57 m long and 2.00 mm in diameter is suspended from a fixed support. A mass of 8.25 kg is hung from the lower end. Determine the increase in the length of the brass wire.
7. A brass wire 215 cm long and 5.00×10^{-2} cm^2 in cross-sectional area supports a mass weighing 1.25 n. How much is the wire stretched?

Group B

8. An aluminum wire 2.00 m long and 0.400 mm in diameter is attached to a firm support. Masses weighing 1.00 n are hung from it in succession. The measured changes in the length of the wire as determined by a microscope and scale are 0.0224 cm, 0.0464 cm, 0.0681 cm, 0.0897 cm, and 0.1128 cm respectively. Plot a graph with the stresses as ordinates and the strains as abscissas. From the information given above, and using the graph, determine the elastic modulus. How is the graph used to determine the elastic modulus?
9. A rod 6.00 mm in diameter is composed of a material having an elastic modulus of 9.00×10^{10} n/m^2. What force will stretch it by 0.02% of its length?

LIQUIDS

7.12 The nature of liquids

In 1827 an English botanist, Robert Brown (1773–1858), placed some pollen grains in water. He dropped a bit of this suspension on a small glass slide. When he examined the suspension through a microscope, he found that the pollen grains moved in a very haphazard way. The path of one particle resembled that shown in Fig. 7-7. This *Brownian movement* is caused by the ceaseless bombardment of the suspended particles by molecules of the suspending liquid. It indicates that molecules of a liquid are in continuous, rapid, random motion.

7-7 The haphazard movement of the large particle is the result of its bombardment by the molecules of the liquid (black dots) in which it is suspended. The black arrows indicate the directions of the liquid molecules after the collisions. (The relative distances between collisions have been exaggerated for clarity.)

Liquids diffuse. To demonstrate this effect, pour enough concentrated copper (II) sulfate solution into a tall cylinder to form a layer of blue liquid several centimeters deep. Next, float a flat cork on the surface of the solution. Pour water carefully through a funnel tube onto the top of the cork, as shown in Fig. 7-8. The water flows around the edge of the cork and spreads out over the surface of the blue liquid, producing two distinct layers. The water "floats" on the copper(II) sulfate solution because the water has a lower density than the copper(II) sulfate solution. After the cylinder stands for a few days, the boundary between the layers is less distinct. Some of the blue solution diffuses into the water above, while some of the water molecules diffuse into the copper(II) sulfate solution below. Even though weeks may pass before the diffusion is complete, we can see that diffusion does occur in liquids in spite of the force of gravity. The rate of diffusion of liquids is considerably faster than that of solids because of the slightly more open molecular arrangement and greater molecular mobility of liquids.

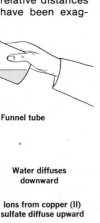

7-8 The figure illustrates the method of preparation of an experiment to visually demonstrate the diffusion of ions from one layer of liquid into another.

7.13 Cohesion and adhesion in liquids

If you thrust a spoon into a jar of honey and then pull it out, you discover that a certain amount of force is needed to pull apart the molecules that make up the honey. If you lick the honey from the spoon you realize that force is required to pull the molecules of the honey away from the molecules of the spoon. This observation demonstrates cohesion within a liquid and adhesion between a liquid and a solid. The relative strength of these forces determines what occurs at the surface of a liquid and a solid.

If a clean glass rod is dipped into water and then removed, some of the water clings to the glass rod. We say that the water wets the glass. The adhesion of water molecules to glass must therefore be greater than the cohesion between water molecules.

If the glass rod is dipped into mercury and then removed, the mercury does not cling to the glass. The cohesion of mercury molecules is greater than their adhesion to glass. Cohesive forces vary in different liquids. They are usually smaller in liquids than in solids.

Have you ever supported a sewing needle or a safety-razor blade on the surface of water? If you place them carefully on the surface they remain there, even though they are about seven times as dense as water. A close look at the water surface shows that the needle or razor blade is supported in a hollow in the water surface. *The water acts as though it has a thin, flexible surface film.* The weight of the needle or razor blade is counterbalanced by the upward force which is exerted by the surface film. This property of liquids is due to *surface tension.*

All liquids show surface tension. Mercury has a very high surface tension. However, in many liquids the surface film is not as strong as that of water or mercury. Part of the cleaning action of detergents is due to their ability to lower the surface tension of water, making it possible for the water and detergent to penetrate more readily between the fibers of the substances being cleaned and the dirt particles.

Since particles in a liquid attract other nearby liquid particles, they tend to arrange themselves so that they are as close together as possible. Hence the surface will tend to have a minimum area.

7.14 Surface tension

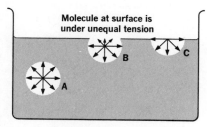

7-9 The unbalanced downward force on molecules near the surface of a liquid causes surface tension.

Ken Chen

7-10 Surface tension keeps this razor blade afloat even though its mass density is much greater than that of water.

The effect of this attraction is to make the liquid behave as though it were contained in a stretched elastic skin. The *tension* in this "skin" is the *surface tension*. When a force acts on a liquid surface film and distorts that film, the cohesion of the liquid molecules exerts an equal and opposite force tending to restore the horizontal surface. Thus the weight of a supported needle produces a depression in the water surface film which increases the area of the film. The cohesion of the water molecules exerts a counterbalancing upward force on the needle by tending to restore the surface of the liquid to its original horizontal condition.

Surface tension produces contraction forces in liquid films. A liquid film has two free surfaces on which molecules are subject to an unbalanced force toward the inside of the film. Thus both free surfaces tend to assume a minimum area. The contraction of the film can be demonstrated by the device shown in Fig. 7-11. If a wire ring containing a loop of thread, Fig. 7-11(A), is dipped into a soap solution, a film is formed across the ring. If the film inside the loop of thread is broken with a hot wire, the unbroken film outside the loop contracts and pulls the thread equally on all sides to form a circle, as shown in Fig. 7-11(B).

Surface tension causes a free liquid to assume a spherical shape. A free liquid is one which is not acted upon by any force. This is an ideal condition, but is approximated by small drops of mercury on a table top (Fig. 7-12). In geometry you learned that a sphere has the smallest surface area for a given volume. The unbalanced force acting on liquid surface molecules tends to pull them toward the center of the liquid, reducing the surface area and causing the liquid to assume a spherical shape. Since the cohesive force between mercury molecules is great and mercury has a very high surface tension, small drops of mercury are almost spherical. Larger drops of mercury, on which the effect of the force of gravity is greater, are noticeably flattened.

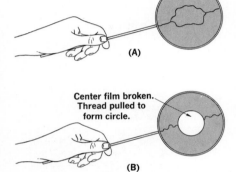

7-11   (A) A soapy-water film is formed across the ring. (B) When the center of the film is broken, the outer portion of the film contracts and pulls the loop of thread into a circle. This shows that surface tension causes liquid films to stretch.

7-12   Small drops of mercury assume a spherical shape because of surface tension. Large drops are flattened because the downward force of gravitational attraction is greater than the upward force produced by surface tension.

Ken Chen

If you examine the surface of water in a glass container, you will find that it is not exactly level. It is very *slightly concave* when viewed from above. The edge of the surface where water comes in contact with the glass is lifted a little above the general level, as shown in Fig. 7-13(A). *The crescent-shaped surface of a liquid column is called the* **meniscus** (meh-*niss*-kus). The water at the edge is lifted above the normal level because adhesion of water to glass is greater than cohesion between water molecules.

If the container is filled with mercury instead of water, the edges of the liquid are depressed and the surface is *slightly convex*. See Fig. 7-13(B). In this case cohesion between mercury molecules is greater than their adhesion to glass.

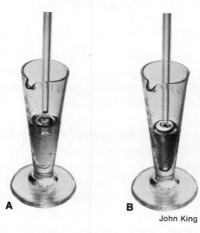

A   B

John King

7.15 The shape of liquid surfaces

7-13   (A) Liquids which wet the surfaces of their containers have surfaces with concave edges. (B) Liquids which do not wet the surfaces of their containers have surfaces with convex edges.

7.16 Capillarity

Liquids stand at the same level in tubes with their lower ends immersed only if the tubes have large enough diameters so that the centers of the liquid surfaces are relatively flat. *Water does not stand at the same level in tubes of varying small diameters.* The height to which it rises increases as the diameter of the tube decreases. See Fig. 7-14(A). When mercury is used, the depression of the surface is greater as the diameter of the tube is reduced. See Fig. 7-14(B). *This elevation or depression of liquids in small diameter or capillary (hair-like) tubes is called* **capillarity**.

Capillarity depends on both adhesion and surface tension. Adhesion of water to glass causes water to creep up the glass walls and produce a concave surface; surface tension tends to flatten this surface by contraction. The combined action of these two forces raises the water above its surrounding level. The water level rises until the upward force is counterbalanced by the weight of the elevated liquid.

Several conclusions about capillarity have been verified by experiment. *(1) Liquids rise in capillary tubes they wet and are*

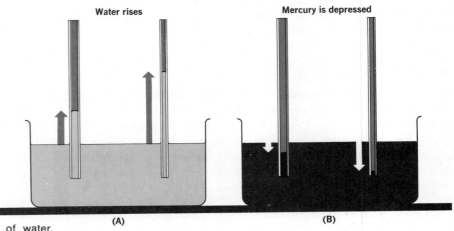

Water rises   **Mercury is depressed**

(A)   (B)

7-14 (A) Capillary action of water. (B) Capillary action of mercury. The elevation or depression is inversely proportional to the diameter of the tube. (The tube diameters and amounts of capillarity are exaggerated for clarity.)

depressed in tubes they do not wet. (2) Elevation or depression is inversely proportional to the diameter of the tube. (3) The elevation or depression decreases as the temperature increases. (4) The elevation or depression depends on the surface tension of the liquid.

7.17 Melting   *The change of phase from a solid to a liquid is called* **melting***.* The temperature at which this change occurs is called the *melting point.* Pure *crystalline* solids have definite melting points and different solids have different melting points.

When a substance changes from a liquid to a solid, it is said to *freeze.* The temperature at which freezing occurs is known as the *freezing point.* For pure crystalline substances, the melting point and the freezing point are the same temperature at any given pressure.

Noncrystalline solids like paraffin have no definite melting point. When they are heated, they soften gradually. The temperature at which noncrystalline solids first soften and the temperature at which they flow freely are often greatly different.

Energy must be supplied to a solid that is melting. This energy increases the energy of the particles of the solid, and gives them the freedom of motion characteristic of the particles of a liquid. As the temperature of a solid increases, the vibrations of its particles increase in amplitude and more and more potential energy is stored in the average stretching of the bonds between the particles. Finally a point is reached where the bonds between the particles cannot absorb any more energy without breaking. Thus crystalline solids have a definite melting point. When the liquid formed by melting a crystalline solid cools to a certain temperature, the energy of the liquid particles is reduced to such an extent that the forces between them draw them into fixed positions in a crystal. Thus a liquid which forms a crystalline solid freezes at a definite temperature.

All the energy supplied to a substance during melting appears as work done by the particles in changing from solid crystal structure to liquid "structure." The kinetic energy of the particles does not change. Since average kinetic energy depends on temperature, melting is a constant temperature process.

The particles of noncrystalline solids are commonly held by forces of attraction, and by the physical entanglement of long-chain molecules. The bonding combination is not of such definite strength that the bonds are broken when the particles acquire a fixed amount of energy. The energy required to overcome these bonds varies with the extent of the bonding and entanglement of each molecule. Consequently, as they are heated, such substances soften at a lower temperature than that at which they flow freely. Similarly, as they are cooled, the molecules become bonded at various kinetic energies and the liquid does not solidify at a definite temperature.

The separation of particles of a substance is different in the solid and liquid phases because of the difference in the potential energy of the particles. If melted paraffin is poured into a vessel and allowed to harden, the center becomes indented, or depressed, as shown in Fig. 7-15. The paraffin cools and contracts as it solidifies. Both kinetic and potential energy are lost in the process. The loss of kinetic energy is indicated by the lower temperature. Loss of potential energy permits the particles to move closer together and take up less space. Almost all substances behave in this manner, for the particles of most substances are closer in the solid than in the liquid phase.

Water is the most important exception to the rule that a substance contracts when it changes from a liquid to a solid. The level of the water in the sections of an ice cube tray is uniform when the tray is placed in the freezing compartment, but when the ice cubes are formed, each one has a slightly raised spot in the center as shown in Fig. 7-15(B). The volume occupied by ice is about 1.1 times that occupied by the water from which it was formed. The force of expansion when water freezes is enormous. Antifreeze is used in the cooling system of cars which are driven in areas where the atmospheric temperature drops below the freezing point of water. Such a mixture of antifreeze and water freezes at a lower temperature and, when sufficiently concentrated, does not expand significantly in freezing.

Bismuth and antimony are two metals which expand rather than contract when they solidify. Antimony is used as a compo-

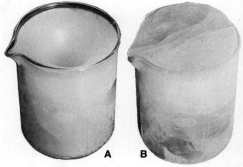

A B

John King

7-15 (A) Most substances, like paraffin, contract when they solidify. (B) Water is one of the few substances which expands on solidification.

nent of type metal because it expands when the molten metal is poured into a mold, producing type that is sharp and clear-cut.

Substances like ice, bismuth, and antimony have open crystal structures in which the particles are more widely separated, on the average, than they are in the liquid phase. That is why the solid occupies a larger volume than the liquid.

7.18 Effect of pressure on the freezing point

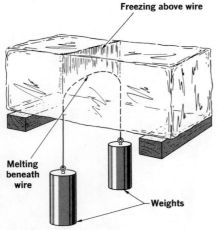

Freezing above wire

Melting beneath wire

Weights

7-16 Melting under pressure and freezing again after the pressure is released is called regelation.

In substances that contract when they solidify, like the paraffin in Fig. 7-15(A), the molecules of the solid are closer together than the molecules of the liquid. If additional pressure is exerted, such a liquid can be made to solidify at a higher temperature than its normal freezing point under atmospheric pressure. An increase in pressure raises the freezing point of most substances.

Some of the rock in the interior of the earth is hot enough to melt at normal pressure, but most of it remains solid because of the tremendous pressure. If the pressure is released, as when a volcano erupts, more of the rock melts, forming lava.

An increase in pressure has the opposite effect on the freezing point of a substance like water which expands as it freezes. In such a substance the molecules are farther apart in the solid than they are in the liquid. Since an increase in pressure makes formation of the solid more difficult, the freezing point is lowered if the pressure is raised.

We can illustrate this effect by suspending two weights by means of a strong wire over the surface of a large cake of ice, as shown in Fig. 7-16. The pressure of the wire on the ice lowers the melting point of the ice immediately below the wire. If the temperature of the surroundings is high enough, this part of the ice melts, and the molecules of water are forced upward around the wire. When they reach a spot above the wire, the pressure returns to normal, the melting point rises, and the water freezes again. When the wire is embedded in the ice, the extra heat needed to melt the ice below the wire is supplied by the freezing of the water above the wire. In this way, the wire may cut its way through the cake of ice, and yet leave the ice in one piece. This melting under pressure and freezing again after the pressure is released is called *regelation* (ree-jeh-lay-shun).

When the pressure of ice skate blades on ice is sufficient to melt the ice at its existing temperature, the blades slide along with very little friction on a thin layer of water. However, if the ice is so cold that the pressure of the skate blades cannot melt it, the blades are retarded by the higher friction of steel on ice, and skating is difficult.

Dick Saunders, Ebony-Tan-Jet-Hue

7-17 Mobile regelation. A thin film of water forms as the skates press on the ice. As the skates pass, the water film freezes again.

The freezing point of a liquid is lowered when another substance is dissolved in it. The extent of the lowering depends on the nature of the liquid and of the dissolved substance, as well as on the relative amounts of each. The greater the amount of the substance dissolved in a fixed amount of liquid, the lower the freezing point of the liquid. We apply this principle when we use rock salt to prevent the formation of ice on roads and sidewalks and to melt the ice that has formed. The dissolved substance interferes with crystal formation as the liquid cools. Thus the kinetic energy of the liquid particles must be reduced to a level below that at which they normally go into a crystal pattern before crystals form.

GASES

Gas molecules are mostly independent particles traveling at high speed. Evidence for this concept comes from observing three properties of gases:

a. Expansion. A gas does not have a definite shape or a definite volume, but expands and completely fills any container. This observation indicates that gas molecules are independent particles.

b. Pressure. A toy balloon may burst from the force which the air inside it exerts on its inside surface. This force is caused by the continual bombardment of the inside surface by many billions of moving molecules. If we increase the number of molecules within the balloon by blowing more air into it, the number of collisions against the inside surface and therefore the pressure on the inside surface increases and the balloon expands.

c. Diffusion. Hydrochloric acid is a water solution of a dense gas, hydrogen chloride; ammonia water is a water solution of a low density gas, ammonia. When these gases react chemically, they form a cloud of fine, white particles of solid ammonium chloride. Suppose we put a few drops of hydrochloric acid in a warm bottle, and an equal amount of ammonia water in a second warm bottle. Then the mouth of each bottle is covered with a glass plate, and the bottle containing ammonia inverted over the one containing hydrogen chloride, as shown in Fig. 7-18(A). After letting the bottles stand for a minute or two, the glass plates are removed leaving the bottles mouth-to-mouth. The formation of white smoke indicates that the less dense ammonia descends and mixes with the more dense hydrogen chloride. The hydrogen chloride also rises and mixes with the ammonia in the upper bottle. The movement of each of these

7.19 Effect of dissolved materials on the freezing point

7.20 The nature of gases

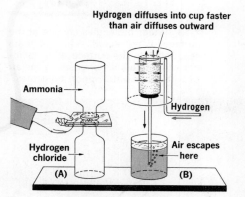

7-18 (A) When the glass plates are removed, the gases mix by diffusion. (B) Hydrogen diffuses into the cup more rapidly than air diffuses out. This diffusion difference increases the pressure within the cup. As a result, some of the air is forced down the tube and bubbles through the liquid.

gases is opposite to that which would be caused by the density of the gases, and must be due to molecular motion. Thus diffusion of gases is evidence of the rapid movement of gas molecules.

Gases diffuse through porous solids. In the apparatus shown in Fig. 7-18(B), an unglazed earthenware cup is closed with a rubber stopper through which passes a glass tube which dips into a colored liquid. When a low-density gas, such as hydrogen, is led into a beaker placed over the cup, air immediately begins to bubble through the colored liquid. Evidently the lighter molecules of hydrogen move in through the porous walls of the cup faster than the heavier molecules in the air move out. Thus there is an accumulation of hydrogen molecules inside the cup which increases the pressure there and pushes the liquid down the tube, forcing some of the air and hydrogen mixture in the tube to escape. Now let us surround the porous cup with a dense gas like carbon dioxide. Since carbon dioxide is denser than air, we must change the apparatus. The vessel surrounding the porous cup must be closed at the bottom and open at the top. When this vessel is filled with carbon dioxide, molecules from the air flow out through the porous cup faster than carbon dioxide molecules enter. This difference reduces the pressure inside the cup and the colored liquid rises in the tube. Thus we see that there is an inverse relation between the rate of diffusion of a gas and its density.

Diffusion of gases through porous solids is an important process. Such diffusion occurs through the membranes of plants, animals, and humans, allowing oxygen to reach living cells and carbon dioxide to escape. Uranium isotopes are separated by means of the different rates of diffusion of $^{235}_{92}UF_6$ and $^{238}_{92}UF_6$, two gaseous hexafluorides of uranium, through a suitable porous barrier.

7-19 Water molecules escape at the surface of the liquid. Some of them rebound into the surface after colliding with molecules of gases in the air or with other water vapor molecules.

7.21 Vaporization

If some ether is placed in a shallow dish, in a short time the quantity of liquid decreases, while the odor of ether becomes quite strong near the dish. Apparently molecules of ether liquid become molecules of ether vapor, and mix with molecules of the gases in the air that surrounds the dish. Similarly, though much more slowly, moth balls left out in the air become smaller and smaller and eventually disappear, while their characteristic odor is noticed in the air nearby. In this case, molecules of the solid moth balls turn into vapor and diffuse into the surrounding air. These are two examples of *vaporization*, which is *the production of a vapor or gas from matter in another phase.* See the diagram, Fig. 7-19.

The particles of all liquids and solids have an average kinetic energy that depends on the temperature of the liquid or solid. However, because of random collisions or vibratory motion, some particles have energies higher than average and others have energies lower than average. When the particle on the surface of a liquid or solid acquires enough energy to overcome the forces that hold it as part of the substance, the particle escapes and becomes a particle in the vapor phase. When vaporization occurs from liquids, it is known as *evaporation*; when it occurs from solids, it is called *sublimation*. Sublimation is a direct change from solid to vapor without passing through the liquid phase.

Since the rate of evaporation or sublimation depends on the energy of the particles undergoing the change, and since their energy depends upon their temperature, evaporation and sublimation occur more rapidly at higher temperatures and more slowly at lower temperatures.

The tendency of liquids to evaporate and of solids to sublime is determined by a property called *equilibrium vapor pressure*. A bell jar covering a container of water is shown in Fig. 7-20. There are as many molecules of the gases of the air within the bell jar as there are in an equal volume of air outside it. The pressure (force per unit area) exerted by the gas molecules on the inside walls of the bell jar is the same as the pressure that such molecules exert on the outside walls.

When a molecule at the surface of the water within the bell jar acquires sufficient kinetic energy, it escapes and becomes a water vapor molecule. As the water evaporates, water vapor molecules mix with the gas molecules in the bell jar. These water vapor molecules collide with gas molecules, the walls of the bell jar, the outside surface of the container of water, and the surface on which the bell jar rests. They can also touch the water surface, be held by it, and become molecules of liquid again. The conversion of molecules of vapor to molecules of liquid is called *condensation*. Eventually the rate of evaporation equals the rate of condensation, and a condition of equilibrium prevails. At equilibrium, evaporation and condensation do not cease; they occur at the same rate. The number of water vapor molecules in the air in the bell jar remains constant. At equilibrium, the space above the water in the vessel is said to be *saturated* with water vapor.

The collision of water vapor molecules against the walls of the bell jar increases the pressure on it beyond that exerted by the gases of the air. *Added pressure exerted by vapor molecules in equilibrium with liquid* is called *equilibrium vapor pressure*.

7.22 Evaporation and sublimation

7.23 Equilibrium vapor pressure

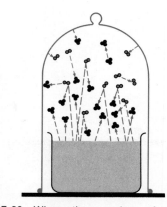

7-20 When the number of water molecules evaporating from the liquid equals the number of water vapor molecules returning to the liquid, the pressure exerted by the water vapor molecules against the walls of the bell jar is the equilibrium vapor pressure.

Since the kinetic energy of the particles of the liquid depends on both the temperature and mass of the particles, the equilibrium vapor pressure of a liquid depends on the composition as well as the temperature of the liquid. As the kinetic energy of the particles increases, so does the vapor pressure.

7.24 Boiling   When water is heated sufficiently, its vapor pressure will eventually equal the combined pressure of the atmosphere and the liquid pressure of the water. Vaporization then occurs at such a rapid rate throughout the water that the water becomes agitated. *This rapid vaporization which disturbs the liquid, and which occurs when the vapor pressure of the liquid equals the pressure on its surface, is called* **boiling**. If the pressure on the liquid surface is one atmosphere, the temperature at which boiling occurs is called the *normal boiling point*. If the pressure on the liquid sur-

M. Woodbridge Williams, National Park Service

7-21 Castle Geyser in Yellowstone National Park.

face is greater than one atmosphere, boiling occurs at a higher temperature than the normal boiling point; if the pressure on the liquid surface is less than one atmosphere, boiling occurs at a lower temperature than the normal boiling point. Greater pressure is largely the result of the greater number of collisions of the particles against the surface of the liquid. Consequently, the kinetic energy of the liquid (and thus its temperature) must be raised to make boiling possible. The opposite is true when the pressure on a liquid is decreased.

Water, or any other liquid that is boiling rapidly, does not get hotter than when it is simmering. While a liquid is boiling away, the boiling temperature remains constant until all of the liquid has been vaporized.

Solids or gases dissolved in a liquid change its boiling temperature. For example, salt water boils at a higher temperature than pure water. In general, solids dissolved in liquids raise the boiling temperature, while gases dissolved in liquids usually lower the boiling temperature.

QUESTIONS

1. What characteristic of liquid molecules did Brown's experiment reveal? *molecules are in constant motion*   **Group A**
2. Describe a demonstration which shows that molecules of liquids diffuse.
3. In terms of adhesion and cohesion, explain why alcohol clings to a glass rod while mercury does not. *mercury has higher cohesion*
4. What is the effect of adding a detergent to the water on which a needle is supported? *the needle will sink, deter. lowers surface tension*
5. Why is a soap bubble floating through the air spherical in shape? *surface tension*
6. What determines whether a meniscus is concave or convex when viewed from above? *the adhesion and cohesion characteristics of the liquid*
7. Water rises to a certain height in a capillary tube of given diameter. What is the effect on the amount of rise if (a) the tube is lengthened, *none* (b) the diameter of the tube is decreased, (c) the temperature of *go higher* the water is raised? *go lower*
8. (a) Which change of phase is called melting? (b) What name is *a. solid to liquid* given to the temperature at which melting occurs? (c) What is *b. melting point* freezing? (d) What name is given to the temperature at which *c. liquid to solid* freezing occurs? *d. freezing point*
9. (a) Which has a greater density, water or ice? (b) Explain in terms *water* of molecular configuration. *molecules are closer together*
10. What is the meaning of the term "regelation"? *melting under pressure + freezing again*
11. In terms of the kinetic theory, explain why gases (a) expand when heated, (b) exert pressure, (c) diffuse through porous substances.
a. temperature increases molecule movement
b. bombardment of molecules
c.

Group B   12. Describe the characteristics of the particles of a substance which is liquid at room temperature.

13. (a) What is the nature of the action force when a safety-razor blade is supported on water? (b) What is the nature of the reaction force?

14. Why is lead shot made by allowing melted lead to fall through cool air?

15. In terms of adhesion and cohesion, explain why mercury is depressed in capillary tubes.

16. (a) What are the action forces which cause water to rise in a capillary tube? (b) What is the reaction force?

17. Why do crystalline solids have a definite melting point, while noncrystalline solids do not?

18. What is the effect of increased pressure on the freezing point of (a) substances which contract as they freeze, (b) substances which expand as they freeze?

19. Why do sharp ice skates melt the ice better than dull ones?

20. What would happen if the gas introduced into the large beaker of the apparatus shown in Fig. 7-18(B) were (a) helium, (b) argon?

Chapter 8

Thermal Effects

TEMPERATURE AND HEAT MEASUREMENT

We know from experience that heat and temperature are related. They are not the same, however. A burning match has a much higher temperature than a steam radiator, but the heat given out by the match is not enough to warm a room. Suppose we have a kettle full of boiling water. If we pour some of the water into a cup, the temperature of the water in the cup will be about the same as that in the kettle (Fig. 8-1). However, we could melt more ice with the water in the kettle than we could with the water in the cup because the water in the kettle can give out more heat. It is possible for a material to be at a high temperature and give out little heat; to be at a high temperature and give out a large quantity of heat; to be at a low temperature and give out little heat; or to be at a low temperature and give out a large quantity of heat.

When a material is hot, it has more *thermal energy* than when it is cold. We do not know the exact relationship between thermal energy and the structure of matter, but we define *the **thermal energy** of a material as the total potential and kinetic energy associated with the random motion and arrangements of its particles.*

What we call temperature is simply the "hotness" or "coldness" of a material. The quantity of thermal energy possessed by a body determines its temperature. The same quantity of thermal energy possessed by different bodies, however, does not give each the same temperature. The ratio between temperature and thermal energy is different for different materials.

8.1 Difference between heat and temperature

8-1 The water in the kettle and the water in the cup are at the same temperature, but the water in the kettle can give out more heat.

173

We saw in Chapter 7 that the temperature of a substance will rise if the average kinetic energy of its particles is increased. If the average kinetic energy is decreased, the temperature goes down. On the other hand, when the potential energy of the particles is increased or decreased without a change in the average kinetic energy, a change of phase takes place without a change in temperature. (See Section 7.16 and 7.21.)

Thermal energy which is absorbed, given up, or transferred from one material to another is heat. The temperature of a body is a measure of its ability to give up heat to, or absorb heat from, another body. Thus, the temperature of a body determines whether or not heat will be transferred to or from any nearby body.

The classical experiments of Count Rumford and James Prescott Joule (Section 1.11) showed that mechanical energy and heat are equivalent and that *heat must be a form of energy*.

Since thermal energy has also been defined as a form of energy, you may wonder why two different terms are used. The distinction is not essential, but an example will serve to illustrate the usage of these terms. The air in a bicycle tire will rise in temperature when the tire is being pumped up. It will also rise in temperature when the tire is out in the sun. In both cases the thermal energy of the air (and its temperature) is increased. In the first case the work done in pumping was converted to thermal energy. In the second case the rise in temperature was due to energy transferred from the sun to the tire. *The term* **heat** *is used when it involves the transfer of thermal energy from one body at higher temperature to another at lower temperature.*

8.2 The unit of temperature

To measure temperature it is necessary to introduce a fourth fundamental unit. The unit of temperature difference, the degree, cannot be derived from length, mass, and time; a measurable physical property which changes with temperature is used.

There are many physical properties which change with temperature. Examples are the linear dimension of a solid, the volume of a liquid, the pressure of a gas held at constant volume, the volume of a gas held at constant pressure, the resistance of an electric conductor, and the color of a solid heated to a high temperature. These are some of the properties of matter which can be used in developing a temperature scale and thus in the construction of a thermometer.

To establish a temperature scale it is necessary to identify a process that occurs without a change in temperature. The temperature at which such a process takes place can be used then as a fixed point on a temperature scale. A change of phase of a substance, such as melting, can be used. The temperature at which a substance exists with its solid phase in thermal equilibrium with its liquid phase is a fixed value at a given pressure. The same is true if the substance is boiling. At this point the liquid is in thermal equilibrium with its vapor. The boiling temperature of the substance is always higher than the melting temperature.

There is only one pressure at which the solid, liquid, and vapor phases of a substance can be in thermal contact and in thermal equilibrium. This occurs at only one temperature, which is known as the *triple-point temperature* (Fig. 8-2). For example, there is only one pressure and temperature condition at which ice, liquid water, and water vapor can exist in a vessel in thermal equilibrium. The ice, liquid water, and vapor are all at the same temperature and can continue to exist indefinitely in the constant volume of the sealed vessel.

The temperature of the triple point of water is of particular significance because in 1954 the Tenth Conference on Weights and Measures adopted this temperature as the single fixed point for defining temperature. This conference arbitrarily assigned the numerical value of 273.16°K (Kelvin) to this temperature.

Although temperature is actually defined in terms of measurements made by idealized thermometers, the known relationships among temperature, the structure of matter, and energy are consistent with the following definition of temperature: ***Temperature*** *is a physical quantity which is proportional to the average kinetic energy of translation of particles in matter.*

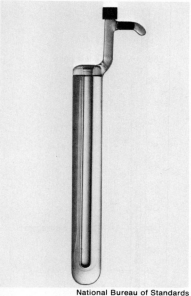

National Bureau of Standards

8-2 The National Bureau of Standards triple-point cell. Pure water with air removed is sealed permanently in the cell which is then immersed in a water-ice bath. The system is at the triple point when ice, water, and vapor are all present within the cell. A central well is provided for the immersion of the thermometer to be calibrated.

8.3 Temperature scales

Before 1954 two fixed points were used to define the standard temperature interval. These were the temperatures of the boiling point of water at standard atmospheric pressure (*steam point*), and the melting point of ice when in equilibrium with water saturated with air at standard atmospheric pressure (*ice point*). The Celsius scale (formerly called the centigrade scale) devised by the Swedish astronomer, Anders Celsius (1701–1744), assigned the value 0°C to the ice point and 100°C to the steam point. Thus the interval between the two fixed points was 100C°. (Fig. 8-3.) Note that specific temperatures on the Celsius scale are expressed in the unit °C. Temperature differences or intervals on the Celsius scale are expressed in the unit C°. Kelvin scale temperatures have the unit °K; while Kelvin scale temperature differences are expressed in K°.

In the temperature scale adopted in 1954, the magnitude of the Kelvin degree (K°) is the same as that of the Celsius degree (C°). These are arbitrarily established units for the measurement

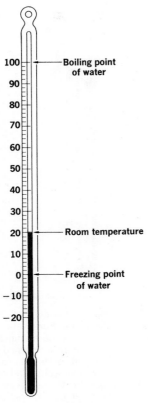

8-3 The Celsius thermometer shown is one type used in laboratory work.

of temperature difference. A second fixed point on the Kelvin scale ($0°$ K) is implied but cannot be defined at this stage in your study of physics. It should be noted, however, that it is possible to define the *absolute zero of temperature* ($0°$ K) in a way that is not dependent on any physical property of any material. Absolute zero should not be thought of as a condition of matter with zero energy and no molecular motion. Molecular action does not cease at absolute zero. The molecules of a substance at absolute zero have a minimum amount of kinetic energy, the zero-point energy. Molecular energy is a minimum (but not zero) at absolute zero.

Now consider the results obtained when a temperature is measured using any of the thermometers in common use. To assign numbers on the temperature scale, it is assumed that a measurable physical property of a substance that changes with temperature X, is proportional to the Kelvin temperature T; thus $X \propto T$. If X_t is the measurement of the physical property at the standard fixed temperature T_t, the triple point of water, and X is the measure of the same property of the same substance at temperature T (to be determined), then we can write the proportion

$$\frac{X}{X_t} = \frac{T}{T_t}$$

Since T_t is $273.16°$ K, we can rewrite the proportion as

$$T = 273.16° \text{K} \frac{X}{X_t}$$

Equation 1

Because X and X_t are measurable quantities, we can use this expression to compute the value of the temperature T.

When a temperature is measured by different thermometers using different thermometric properties, the results may vary considerably. The most consistent results are obtained by using thermometers which measure the pressure p of a definite volume of gas. When a constant-volume gas thermometer is used, Equation 1 becomes

$$T = 273.16° \text{K} \frac{p}{p_t}$$

where p is the pressure of the gas at the temperature T being measured, and p_t is the pressure of the gas at the temperature of the triple point of water.

Even with constant-volume gas thermometers there is some variation in the measured value of the temperature of a substance depending on the gas used and its pressure at the triple-point temperature of water. Different gases have slightly different rates of expansion with increased temperature and reduced pressure because of intermolecular attraction. By decreasing the quantity of gas used in the thermometer, we reduce the pressure p_t at the temperature of the triple point, separate the gas molecules further, and partially eliminate the differences observed with different gases. Thus, the measured values of the temperature of a substance, obtained by different constant-volume gas thermometers as their internal gas pressure is reduced, approach the same value.

A set of readings of the temperature of a substance, taken by a constant-volume gas thermometer as the gas pressure p_t is reduced toward zero by the withdrawal of gas from the thermometer between readings, may be extrapolated to give the reading of T when p_t is theoretically equal to zero. This procedure gives the temperature of the ice-point on the Kelvin scale as 273.15°K. (Note that the difference in temperature between the ice-point and the triple-point of water is 0.01 K°.) When determined by this same method, the temperature of the steam-point of water is 373.15°K. The temperature difference between the ice-point and the steam-point of water is 100.00 K°. This is numerically equal to the difference in temperature as measured on the Celsius scale, thus, 1 K° = 1 C°.

The Celsius scale is commonly used in almost all foreign countries and for scientific work in the United States. The degrees between the ice and steam points are numbered from zero degrees Celsius, 0°C, to one hundred degrees Celsius, 100°C. From one degree to the next is a temperature interval of one Celsius degree, 1 C°. Temperatures below 0°C and above 100°C are measured by extending the scale in 1 C° intervals. Temperatures below 0°C are represented by negative values.

The relationship between the Celsius and Kelvin temperature scales is given by

$$\text{°K} = \text{°C} + 273.15°$$

Since we normally use three significant figures in our work, we can use 0°C = 273°K and write the conversion equation as

$$\text{°K} = \text{°C} + 273°$$

The most commonly used thermometers contain either mercury or alcohol. In both cases, the liquid volume increases rather uniformly with temperature over the useful range of the instruments.

The expansion of mercury in a thermometer provides a convenient and accurate method of measuring temperature. The measurement of heat is not so simple, for there is no instrument that will tell directly the amount of thermal energy a

8.4 The measurement of heat

body gives out or absorbs. Therefore, *quantities of heat must be measured by the effects they produce*. For example, the amount of heat given out when a fuel burns can be measured by the temperature change that its burning produces in a known quantity of water. If one sample of coal warms 1.0 kg of water 1.0 C°, and another sample warms 1.0 kg of water 2.0 C°, then twice as much heat is given out by the second sample.

In the past, water was the standard substance for defining heat units. In the MKS system of units, the *kilocalorie* (kcal) was defined as the quantity of heat needed to raise the temperature of one kilogram of water one Celsius degree. The *calorie* (cal) was defined as the quantity of heat needed to raise the temperature of one gram of water one Celsius degree. Observe that a unit mass of water was used for defining each heat unit and that the kilocalorie is one thousand times larger than the calorie. The kilocalorie is the "Calorie" used by biologists and dieticians to measure the fuel value of foods.

As thermal measurements increased in precision, the older definitions given above became inadequate. Physicists are now sure that heat is a form of energy. Consequently there is no need to define an arbitrary heat unit which then must be related to the joule experimentally. Also it has been found that the quantity of heat required to raise the temperature of 1 gram of water through 1 Celsius degree varies slightly for different water temperatures.

Today, by international agreement, *the calorie is defined as a specific number of joules.*

$$1 \text{ calorie} = 4.18605 \text{ joules}$$

Since the kilocalorie equals 10^3 calories, it follows that

$$1 \text{ kilocalorie} = 4.18605 \times 10^3 \text{ joules}$$

The size of the calorie defined in this way is very nearly the same as the original calorie. When taken to three significant figures (4.19 joules) for ordinary computation purposes this slight difference disappears. Thus the relationships stated in the original definition, while no longer valid for defining purposes, are still useful in the measurement of thermal properties.

The MKS units, the kilocalorie and the kilogram, are consistent with the units of measurement we have stressed throughout this book. They are often inconveniently large for laboratory and discussion purposes, however. We shall use the calorie and gram units of heat and mass generally in our considerations of the thermal properties of matter because of their more practical size.

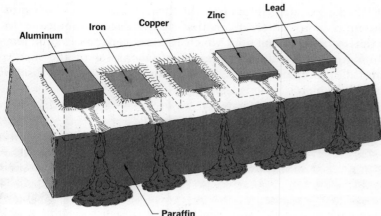

Aluminum Iron Copper Zinc Lead

Paraffin

8-4 Because metals have different heat capacities, these blocks, all of equal mass and heated to the same temperature, melt the paraffin to different depths.

8.5 Heat capacity

Blocks of five different metals, aluminum, iron, copper, zinc, and lead, are shown in Fig. 8-4. They all have the same mass and the same cross-sectional area, but because these metals have different densities, the pieces have different heights. We first put them in a pan of boiling water to heat them all to the same temperature. Then we transfer them to a block of paraffin. The diagram shows the relative depths to which they melt the paraffin. The aluminum block melts the most paraffin, iron follows as a poor second, copper and zinc are tied for third, and lead melts the least paraffin. This demonstration shows that different materials absorb or give out different amounts of heat, even though the materials have the same mass and undergo the same temperature change. Similarly, different amounts of heat are absorbed by blocks of the same material if their mass is different and their temperature change the same, if their mass is the same and their temperature change is different, or if they have different masses and undergo different temperature changes. Such objects are then said to differ in *heat capacity*. Those with a high heat capacity warm more slowly because they must absorb a greater quantity of heat; they also cool more slowly because they must give out more heat. *The **heat capacity** of a body is the quantity of heat needed to raise its temperature 1°.*

$$\text{heat capacity} = \frac{Q}{\Delta T}$$

where Q is the quantity of heat needed to produce a change in the temperature of the body, ΔT. The units we shall use for heat capacity are cal/C°.

8.6 Specific heat

The heat capacity of an object does not indicate much about the thermal properties of the material of which it is made. For example, the heat capacity of 1.0 kg of copper differs from that of 1.0 kg of aluminum, but the heat capacity of 1.0 kg of aluminum also differs from that of 2.0 kg of aluminum. In order to obtain a quantity which is characteristic of copper or aluminum, the heat capacities of equal masses of the metals must be compared. This comparison yields a more useful quantity which is called *specific heat*.

The specific heat of a body is characteristic of the material of which the body is composed. **Specific heat** *is the heat capacity of a material per unit mass*. It is numerically equal to the quantity of heat that must be supplied to a unit mass of a material to raise its temperature one degree. If Q represents the quantity of heat needed to produce a temperature change ΔT, in a quantity of material of mass m, the specific heat c is given by

$$c = \frac{Q/\Delta T}{m}$$

which, on being simplified, yields

$$c = \frac{Q}{m\Delta T}$$

Since 1 calorie of heat raises the temperature of 1 g of water 1 C°, the specific heat of water is 1 cal/g C°. In MKS units the specific heat of water is 1 kcal/kg C°. Table 13, Appendix B, shows that the specific heat of most substances is less than that of water.

Let us solve the specific heat equation for Q.

$$Q = mc\Delta T$$

Thus the quantity of heat needed to produce a certain temperature change in a body equals the product of the mass of the material, its specific heat, and its temperature change. If m is in g, c in cal/g C°, and ΔT in C°, Q will be expressed in calories.

8.7 The law of heat exchange

If water is too hot for washing, you may cool it quickly by adding cold water. As the two mix, the temperature of the hot water is lowered while the temperature of the added cold water is raised. The final temperature of the mixture lies between the original temperatures of the hot and cold water. Each time two substances of unequal temperature are mixed, the warmer one loses heat and the cooler one gains heat until both finally reach the same temperature. No heat is lost when substances of unequal temperatures are mixed. *In any heat-transfer system, the heat given off by hot substances equals the heat received by cold substances.* This is known as the **law of heat exchange**. The total number of heat units given off by warmer substances equals the total number of heat units received by cooler substances. This can be expressed as

$$Q_{\text{lost}} = Q_{\text{gained}}$$

This equality provides the basis for a simple technique for measuring a quantity of heat in transit from one substance to another known as the *method of mixtures*. The method of mixtures and the law of heat exchange can be used to determine the specific heat of a solid (Fig. 8-5). The hot solid of unknown specific heat, but of known mass and temperature, is "mixed" with water of known mass and temperature in a *calorimeter* (usually nested metal cups separated by an insulating air space) of known mass and temperature. The final temperature of the mixture is measured. Thus, all of the data for the law of heat exchange equation are known except the specific heat of the solid, which then can be calculated as in the example below.

In practical situations, some heat is usually lost to the surroundings. This loss affects the accuracy of most heat experiments in the high school laboratory.

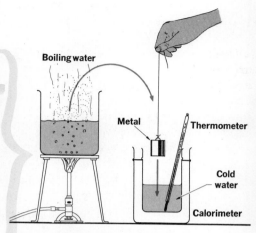

8-5 Apparatus for measuring the specific heat of a metal by the method of mixtures.

Example

A laboratory experiment to determine the specific heat of a sample of brass yielded the following data:

Mass of calorimeter	160.0 g
Specific heat of calorimeter	0.0930 cal/g C°
Mass of water	225.0 g
Specific heat of water	1.00 cal/g C°
Mass of brass	184.7 g
Initial temperature of water and calorimeter	18.0°C
Initial temperature of brass	99.5°C
Final temperature of water, calorimeter, and brass	23.5°C

Solution

To calculate the specific heat of the brass from these data, first identify the substances losing and gaining heat. The brass cylinder lost heat while the water and the calorimeter gained heat. It is assumed that the inner cup of the calorimeter which has a mass of 160.0 g and which is in direct contact with the water will always be at the temperature of the water. Since this cup is thermally insulated from the outer cup by a fiber ring and an air space, we can disregard, at this level of accuracy, any heat transfer to or from the inner cup system.

Now apply the basic idea that heat lost by the brass in cooling, Q_b, will equal heat gained by the water, Q_w, and the calorimeter, Q_c, in warming.

Basic Equation: $\quad Q_b = Q_w + Q_c$

Since $Q = mc\,\Delta T$ in each case, we can substitute for Q_b, Q_w, and Q_c,

$$m_b c_b\,\Delta T_b = m_w c_w\,\Delta T_w + m_c c_c\,\Delta T_c$$

Solving for c_b

Working Equation: $\quad c_b = \dfrac{m_w c_w\,\Delta T_w + m_c c_c\,\Delta T_c}{m_b\,\Delta T_b}$

Substituting the given data and solving

$$c_b = \frac{[225.0\text{ g} \times 1.00\text{ cal/g C}^\circ \times (23.5-18.0)\text{ C}^\circ] + [160.0\text{ g} \times 0.093\text{ cal/g C}^\circ \times (23.5-18.0)\text{ C}^\circ]}{184.7\text{ g} \times (99.5-23.5)\text{ C}^\circ}$$

$$c_b = \frac{1240\text{ cal} + 82\text{ cal}}{14,\overline{0}00\text{ g C}^\circ} = \frac{1320\text{ cal}}{14,\overline{0}00\text{ g C}^\circ}$$

$$c_b = 0.0943\text{ cal/g C}^\circ$$

Example

In a laboratory experiment, 100.0 g of iron at 80.0°C was added to 53.5 g of water at 20.0°C. What is the final temperature of the mixture?

Solution

From Table 13, Appendix B, we learn that the specific heat of iron is 0.108 cal/g C°, and the specific heat of water is 1.00 cal/g C°. Using T_f as the final temperature of the mixture, the heat lost by the iron is

$$Q_i = m_i c_i\,\Delta T_i = m_i c_i (T_i - T_f)$$

and the heat gained by the water is

$$Q_w = m_w c_w\,\Delta T_w = m_w c_w (T_f - T_w)$$

These expressions are equal. Therefore

$$m_i c_i (T_i - T_f) = m_w c_w (T_f - T_w)$$

Solving for T_f

$$T_f = \frac{m_i c_i T_i + m_w c_w T_w}{m_i c_i + m_w c_w}$$

$$T_f = \frac{100.0\text{ g} \times 0.108\text{ cal/g C}^\circ \times 80.0^\circ\text{ C} + 53.5\text{ g} \times 1.00\text{ cal/g C}^\circ \times 20.0^\circ\text{ C}}{100.0\text{ g} \times 0.108\text{ cal/g C}^\circ + 53.5\text{ g} \times 1.00\text{ cal/g C}^\circ}$$

$$T_f = 30.0^\circ\text{C}$$

QUESTIONS

Group A
1. Define heat.
2. How do heat and temperature differ?
3. Why were the temperature of the melting point of ice and the tem-

Exam →

perature of the boiling point of water called "fixed points" in defining a temperature scale?

4. What single fixed point is now established for the definition of temperature scales?
5. Compare the magnitude of a Celsius degree with that of a Kelvin degree.
6. (a) What is the Celsius temperature at absolute zero? (b) What would be the thermal energy of a material at absolute zero?
7. Compare the amount of thermal energy possessed by each of the following: (a) a soldering iron and a needle, both at $15\bar{0}°C$, (b) a 4-section radiator and a 10-section radiator, (c) a kettle of boiling water and cup of boiling water, (d) 20.0 kg of ice at $-10.0°C$ and 10.0 kg of ice at $-10.0°C$, (e) a liter of liquid air and a milliliter of liquid air, both at $-189°C$.
8. How are quantities of heat measured?
9. What is a kilocalorie?
10. What is the heat capacity of a body?
11. (a) Give a word definition for specific heat. (b) What is the formula which defines specific heat?
12. How do the specific heats of most common substances compare with the specific heat of water?
13. How is the amount of thermal energy required to produce a given temperature change in a substance calculated?

← Fri. 29 Feb

14. What is the law of heat exchange?
15. What data are required for the determination of specific heat by the method of mixtures?

16. How does the thermal energy of a material determine its temperature?   **Group B**
17. Describe a triple-point scale.
18. How can the boiling points of substances be determined from the triple point of water?
19. If you examine several similar laboratory thermometers, you may find that the distance between 0°C and 100°C is not exactly the same on all of them. Why is there such a difference when they are all the same make and model?

$T_F - T_i$

20. On what basic law are experiments with calorimeters based?

PROBLEMS

1. The temperature in a classroom is 24.0°C. What is the Kelvin reading?   **Group A**
2. Liquid nitrogen boils at 77.0°K. What is the reading on the Celsius scale?
3. The boiling point of liquid oxygen is $-183°C$. What is this temperature in °K?

4. What is the boiling point of helium on the Celsius scale if its boiling point is 4.1°K?

5. How many calories will be needed to change the temperature of $50\overline{0}$ g of water from $2\overline{0}$°C to $10\overline{0}$°C?

6. How much heat is given out when 85 g of lead cools from $20\overline{0}$°C to $1\overline{0}$°C?

20°c 7. If 10.0 g of water at 0.0°C is mixed with 20.0 g of water at 30.0°C, what is the final temperature of the mixture?

27°c 8. What is the final temperature of a mixture of 135 g of water at 21.0°C in a 45.0-g brass calorimeter, and 200 g of silver at 100.0°C?

9. An aluminum calorimeter has a mass of 60.0 g. Its temperature is 25.0°C. What is the final temperature attained when 75.0 g of water at 95.0°C is poured into it?

10. A piece of tin weighing 225 g and having a temperature of 100.0°C is dropped into $10\overline{0}$ g of water at a temperature of 10.0°C. If the final temperature of the mixture is 20.0°C, what is the specific heat of the sample of tin?

Group B 11. The stem of a thermometer is marked off in 150 equal scale divisions. When the bulb of this thermometer is placed in melting ice, the mercury stands at 30.0. When the bulb is suspended in the steam from water boiling at standard pressure, the mercury stands at 80.0. To what Celsius temperature does a reading of 125 on this thermometer correspond?

.0335 cal/gram C° 12. A block of metal has a mass of $100\overline{0}$ g. It is heated to 300.0°C and then put in 100.0 g of water at 0.0°C in a calorimeter. The mass of the calorimeter is 50.0 g; its specific heat is 0.200 cal/g C°. If the final temperature is 70.0°C, calculate the specific heat of the metal.

13. A block of brass, mass 500.0 g, temperature 100.0°C, is put in 300.0 g of water, temperature 20.0°C, in an aluminum calorimeter, mass 75.0 g. If the final temperature is 30.0°C, what is the specific heat of the brass?

,427 cal/gram C° 14. A cylinder of copper has a mass of 95.3 g and a specific heat of 0.092 cal/g C°. It is heated to 90.5°C and then put in 75.2 g of turpentine, temperature 20.5°C. The temperature of the mixture after stirring is 35.5°C. What is the specific heat of the turpentine?

15. A metal cylinder, mass 450.0 g, temperature 100.0°C, is dropped into a 150.0-g iron calorimeter, specific heat 0.100 cal/g C°, which contains 300.0 g of water at 21.5°C. If the resulting temperature of the mixture is 30.5°C, what is the specific heat of the metal cylinder?

THERMAL EXPANSION

8.8 Thermal expansion of solids *With few exceptions, solids expand when heated and contract when cooled.* They not only increase in length, but also in width and thickness.

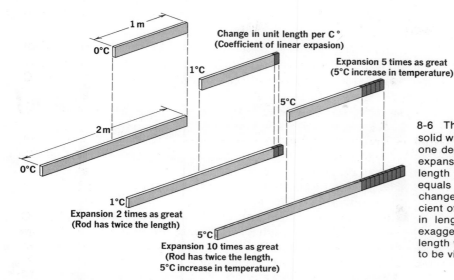

8-6 The change per unit length of a solid when its temperature is changed one degree is the coefficient of linear expansion. The total increase in the length of a solid when it is heated equals the product of its length, its change in temperature, and its coefficient of linear expansion. The change in length illustrated here is greatly exaggerated. The actual change in length which would occur is too small to be visible in this drawing.

The atoms and molecules of a crystalline solid are constantly vibrating. They are held in place by electric forces. When a solid is heated, it expands because the increase in thermal energy increases the average distance between the atoms and molecules of the solid.

The expansion of solids can be measured experimentally. A metal rod is heated in an apparatus which has a precise measuring device. If the temperature of an aluminum rod 1.0 m long is raised 1.0 C°, the increase in length is 2.3×10^{-5} m. An iron rod of the same length expands only 1.1×10^{-5} m when its temperature is raised 1.0 C°. Different materials of the same length expand different amounts for the same increase in temperature. *The change in length per unit length of a solid when its temperature is changed one degree is called its* **coefficient of linear expansion.** See Fig. 8-6. While the coefficient of linear expansion of most solids varies with temperature, the change is slight and we shall neglect it in our discussion.

As we said above, 1.0 m of aluminum expands 2.3×10^{-5} m when its temperature is raised 1.0 C°. The coefficient of linear expansion of aluminum is therefore said to be $2.3 \times 10^{-5}/$C°. Likewise the coefficient of linear expansion of iron is $1.1 \times 10^{-5}/$C°. Since the coefficient of linear expansion is defined as *the change in length per unit length,* its value does not depend upon any particular length unit. Table 14, Appendix B, gives the value of the coefficient of linear expansion of several solids per Celsius degree.

So far, we have been discussing 1.0-m lengths of aluminum and iron, and a rise in temperature of only 1.0 C°. If the tem-

Alex Mulligan

Expansion and contraction of the roadway is compensated for by this special joint.

perature of 10.0 m of aluminum rod is raised 1.0 C°, the expansion is $1\overline{0}$ times as much as the expansion of the 1.0-m length: $1\overline{0} \times 2.3 \times 10^{-5}$ m = 2.3×10^{-4} m. If the temperature of this 10.0 m of aluminum is raised 10.0 C°, the increase is $1\overline{0}$ times as great as for 1.0 C°; $1\overline{0} \times 2.3 \times 10^{-4} = 2.3 \times 10^{-3}$ m. We can conclude from these observations that *the change in length of a solid equals the product of its original length, its change in temperature, and its coefficient of linear expansion.*

This can be given by the equation

$$\Delta l = \alpha l \, \Delta T$$

where Δl is the change in length, α is the coefficient of linear expansion, l is the original length, ΔT is the difference between the final temperature T_f and the initial temperature T_i.

In most practical situations, we are interested in the amount of linear expansion of solids. We must bear in mind however, that when solids are heated they increase in all dimensions. The **coefficient of area expansion**, or *the change in length per unit area per degree change in temperature,* is defined to be *twice* the coefficient of linear expansion. The **coefficient of cubic expansion**, or *the change in volume per unit volume per degree change in temperature,* is defined to be *three times* the coefficient of linear expansion.

Expansion of solids is considered in designing and building any structure that will undergo temperature changes. When a contractor lays a concrete road, he provides for expansion by pouring the concrete in sections that are separated by small spaces. Steel rails for railroads can be laid with small spaces between the ends of the rails for the same reason. Bridges are also built so that the parts can expand and contract without distorting the entire structure.

Suitable allowance must be made not only for changes in size due to expansion and contraction, but also for the different rates of expansion and contraction of different materials. For a tight seal, the wires that lead into the filament of an incandescent lamp must have the same coefficient of expansion as the glass of which the lamp is made. The principle of the expansion of solids is also applied in metallic thermometers, thermostats, and the compensated balance wheels of watches.

8.9 Thermal expansion of liquids

If the gasoline tank of an automobile is filled on a cool morning and the car is then parked in the sun, some of the gasoline may overflow the tank. Heat causes the gasoline to expand. Here again the increased thermal energy of the molecules and their resultant increase in amplitude of vibration cause them to move away from each other slightly. The principle of expansion of liquids has many useful applications. Thermometers contain either mercury or colored alcohol because these liquids expand and contract quite uniformly as the temperature changes.

Since liquids do not have a definite shape, but take the shape of their container, we are concerned only with their volume expansion. An apparatus like that shown in Fig. 8-7 can be used to measure the volume expansion of a liquid.

Liquids expand more than solids, consequently they have higher coefficients of volume expansion. Otherwise the liquid in a thermometer would not rise. The coefficients of volume expansion for some common liquids are given in Table 15, Appendix B.

The change in volume of a liquid can be given by the formula

$$\Delta V = \beta V \, \Delta T$$

where ΔV is the change in the volume, β is the coefficient of volume expansion, and ΔT is the difference between the final and initial temperatures.

Suppose an expansion bulb, like that shown in Fig. 8-7, is filled with pure water at 0°C. As the bulb and water are warmed, the water gradually *contracts* until a temperature of 4°C is reached. As the temperature of the water is raised above 4°C, the water *expands*. Because the volume of water decreases as the temperature is raised from 0°C to 4°C, the mass density of the water increases. (The mass of the water is constant.) Above 4°C, the volume of water increases as the temperature is raised. Therefore, water has its maximum mass density, 1.0000 g/cm³, at 4°C. The variation of the density of water with the temperature is shown in Fig. 8-8. The temperature range of the graph was chosen to include the temperature at which the density of water is a maximum.

This unusual variation of the density of water with the temperature can be explained as follows. When ice melts to water at 0°C, the water still contains groups of molecules bonded in the open crystal structure of ice. These flow over one another and give the water fluidity. As the temperature of water is raised from 0°C to 4°C, these open crystal fragments begin to collapse, and the molecules move closer together. The molecular speeds of the molecules also increase during the 0°C to 4°C interval, but the effect of the collapsing crystal structure predominates, and the density increases. Above 4°C the effect of increasing molecular speed exceeds the effect of collapsing crystal structure, and the volume increases (Fig. 8-9).

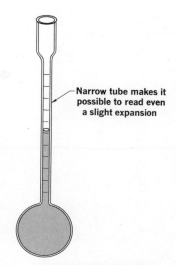

Narrow tube makes it possible to read even a slight expansion

8-7   A tube for measuring the volume expansion of liquids. The scale takes into account the expansion of the container.

8.10 The abnormal expansion of water

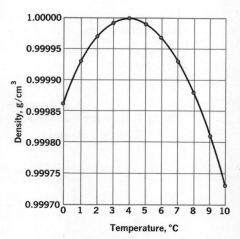

8-8   The density of water is greatest at 4°C.

Canadian Consulate General

Ice floes on the Hudson River.

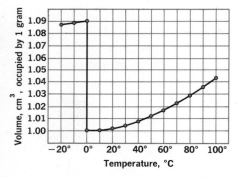

8-9   A graph showing the variation in the volume of one gram of water as it is cooled from 100°C on the right to 0°C, frozen to ice and further cooled from 0°C to −20°C.

If water did not expand slightly as it is cooled below 4°C and expand much more as it freezes, the ice which forms on the surface of a lake would sink to the bottom. During the cold winter months, ice would continue to form until the lake was frozen solid. In the summer months only a few feet of ice at the top of the lake would melt. However, because of the unusual properties of ice and water, no ice forms at the surface of a pond until all the water in it is cooled to 4°C. At 4°C water is more dense than at any other temperature. As the surface water cools below 4°C, it expands slightly and floats on the 4°C water. Upon freezing at 0°C, further expansion takes place and the ice floats on the 0°C water.

The graph in Fig. 8-9 shows, from right to left, the gradual contraction of a given mass of water as it is cooled. The sharp expansion on freezing, and the slight contraction as ice is cooled below 0°C is evident.

8.11 Expansion of gases: Charles' Law

The expansion of gases when heated is due to increased kinetic energy of the molecules of the gas because their thermal energy has been increased.

Different solids and liquids have different coefficients of expansion, but *all gases have approximately the same coefficient of expansion*. Also, *the coefficient of expansion of gases is nearly constant at all temperatures*, except for those near the liquefying temperature of the gas.

In 1787, the French scientist Jacques Charles (1746–1823) performed experiments which showed that all gases expand the same amount when heated one Celsius degree if the pressure is kept constant.

In order to determine the rate at which gases expand, a capillary tube sealed at one end, as shown in Fig. 8-10, can be used. A mass of air is trapped in this capillary tube by a globule of mercury. First, the length of the air column is measured when the tube is immersed in a mixture of ice and water. Then, the length of the air column is measured when the tube is surrounded by steam. Comparing these two readings, we find that the air column increases by $\frac{100}{273}$ of its original length when heated from 0°C to 100°C. For each degree of temperature change, the expansion is $\frac{1}{273}$ of the volume at 0°C. When gases other than air are used, similar results are obtained. The same fractional contraction occurs when gases are cooled below 0°C.

The coefficient of volume expansion for gases is $\frac{1}{273}$ of the volume at 0°C or $3.663 \times 10^{-3}/C°$. This is about 20 times the volume expansion of mercury, and almost 60 times that of aluminum. All gases have approximately the same coefficient of expansion because they all consist of widely separated, exceedingly small molecules that are, in effect, independent particles. Gas molecules are separated by distances much greater than their molecular diameters. Consequently, the forces acting between them, and their volume in relation to the total gas volume, are negligible. For these reasons, except at temperatures and pressures near those at which they liquefy, all gases have similar physical properties.

If a gas is confined so that it cannot expand when it is heated, it exerts a greater pressure. An increase in the pressure of the air in an automobile tire accompanies an increase in temperature. The temperature increase may result from exposure to the sun or from the flexing of the tire as it is driven over the highway. When a gas is heated, the speed of the molecules becomes greater. The molecules bombard the inner walls of the tire more vigorously, thus producing a higher pressure.

Table 8-1 gives the volume occupied by a certain mass of gas at various Celsius and Kelvin temperatures. From the table we see that the volume of a gas varies directly with the Kelvin temperature. *Charles' law* states: *The volume of a dry gas is directly proportional to its Kelvin temperature, provided the pressure is held constant.* In equation form, Charles' law becomes

$$\frac{V}{T_K} = \frac{V'}{T_K'}$$

where V is the original volume, T_K the original Kelvin temperature, V' the new volume, and T_K' the new Kelvin temperature.

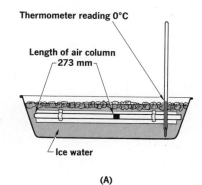

Thermometer reading 0°C

Length of air column
273 mm

Ice water

(A)

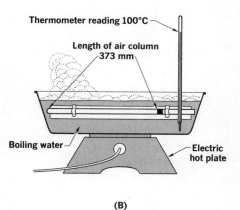

Thermometer reading 100°C

Length of air column
373 mm

Boiling water

Electric hot plate

(B)

8-10 For each degree rise in temperature a gas expands 1/273rd of its volume at 0°C.

Table 8-1 THE VOLUME-TEMPERATURE RELATIONSHIP OF A GAS

Volume	Temperature	
(cm³)	(°C)	(°K)
373	10$\overline{0}$	373
323	5$\overline{0}$	323
273	$\overline{0}$	273
223	−5$\overline{0}$	223
173	−10$\overline{0}$	173

Plotting the gas volumes given in the table as a function of the Kelvin temperatures gives the curve shown in Fig. 8-11. This linear relationship between the volume of a gas and its Kelvin temperature shows that these two quantities are directly proportional. Since 0°C (273°K) is frequently used as a reference point in calculations that involve temperature, this value is called *standard temperature*.

8.12 Compressibility of gases: Boyle's Law

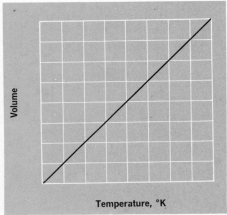

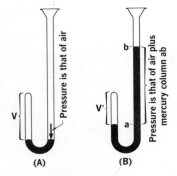

8-11 At constant pressure, the volume of a dry gas varies directly with the Kelvin temperature.

8-12 J-tube apparatus used to demonstrate Boyle's law. This is similar to the apparatus actually used by Boyle.

An English scientist, Robert Boyle (1627–1691), was the first person to investigate what he called the "spring [elasticity] of the air." Other scientists at that time knew about compressed air, but none of them had performed experiments to learn how the volume of a gas is affected by the pressure exerted on it.

In his experiments, Boyle used a large J-shaped glass tube similar to that shown in Fig. 8-12. The straight portion of the shorter arm was about one foot in length, while the longer arm had a length of about eight feet. He set up the apparatus in the stairwell of his laboratory at Oxford. Enough mercury was poured into the tube to fill the bent portion. The mercury levels were then adjusted by tipping the tube to allow air to escape from the small arm so that the mercury would stand at the same height in both arms. In this way Boyle trapped a column of air in the short arm of the tube. Next he measured the height of this air column. By assuming that the bore of the tube was uniform, Boyle used the height of the air column as a measure of the volume of air. The air must have been under atmospheric pressure because the mercury levels were the same in both arms of the tube. See Fig. 8-12(A). By reading the height of the mercury in a Torricellian apparatus, (an early-style mercurial barometer) Boyle found the pressure exerted by the atmosphere on the volume of air.

In successive steps, Boyle added more mercury to the long arm of the tube, as shown in Fig. 8-12(B). By measuring the height of the column of air in the short arm, he could determine each new volume. He found the corresponding pressure on this volume of air by measuring the height of the mercury column **ab**, and adding that height to that of the mercury in the Torricellian apparatus.

Boyle cooled the trapped, compressed air with a wet cloth, and warmed it with a candle flame, noticing small changes in volume as a result. However, these changes were so slight that, while it was obvious to Boyle that the temperature of the air during the experiment should be kept constant, he recognized that small changes in temperature would not seriously affect the experimental results. Boyle's data, while not exceedingly accurate, convinced him and other scientists of his time that "the pressures and expansions . . . [are] in reciprocal proportion." Increasing the pressure on a column of confined air reduces its volume correspondingly. To reduce the volume to one-half, the pressure must be doubled; to reduce the volume to one-third, the pressure must be tripled. Today we state **Boyle's law** as follows: *The volume of a dry gas varies inversely with the pressure exerted on it, provided the temperature remains constant.*

Boyle's original data are plotted in the graph of Fig. 8-13, using the total pressures as abscissas, and the heights of the air columns (volumes) as ordinates. You will recall from Chapter 2 that a graph of this shape (a hyperbola) suggests an inverse proportion.

When two quantities are in inverse proportion, their product is a constant. At any given temperature, *the product of pressure and volume is always a constant:*

$$pV = k$$

In all cases, except under very high pressures, or very low temperatures, or both,

$$pV = p'V'$$

and

$$V' = V\frac{p}{p'}$$

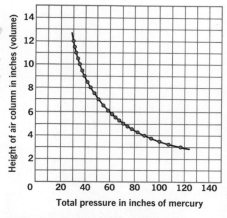

8-13 Graph of Boyle's original pressure-volume data. This is the graph of two quantities which are inversely proportional.

Here p is the former pressure, V is the former volume; p' represents the new pressure, and V' the new volume.

The pressure of a column of mercury exactly 760 mm high is called *standard pressure*. It is approximately equal to the average pressure of the atmosphere at sea level. Standard temperature (0°C) and standard pressure are frequently designated as S.T.P.

There is no change in the mass of a gas when its volume is changed by a difference in the pressure exerted upon it. Since an increase in pressure produces a decrease in the volume of a gas, it must also increase the density of the gas. *The density of a gas varies directly with the pressure exerted on it.*

$$\frac{D}{D'} = \frac{p}{p'}$$

A cubic meter of air has a mass of 1.29 kg at a pressure of one atmosphere. A container having a volume of one cubic meter can hold four times 1.29 kg or 5.16 kg of air under a pressure of four atmospheres, because the air is four times as dense.

It frequently happens that temperature and pressure conditions affecting a gas both change. To find the new volume that

8.13 The general gas law

a gas will occupy in such a case, we must consider the effects of both Boyle's and Charles' laws. This calculation can be made in separate steps by first correcting the original volume to the new pressure conditions and then correcting this volume for the temperature change. Usually, however, these two steps are carried out simultaneously.

We can derive an equation which combines Boyle's and Charles' laws. At constant Kelvin temperature T_{K1}, a certain mass of gas occupying volume V_1 is subject to a change in pressure from p_1 to p_2. The new volume V_2, from Boyle's law, is

$$V_2 = \frac{p_1 V_1}{p_2} \qquad \text{(Equation 1)}$$

Now if V_2 is subject to an increase in temperature from T_{K1} to T_{K2} at constant pressure p_2, the new volume V_3, from Charles' law, is

$$V_3 = \frac{V_2 T_{K2}}{T_{K1}} \qquad \text{(Equation 2)}$$

Substituting the value of V_2 in Equation 1 into Equation 2, V_3 becomes

$$V_3 = \frac{p_1 V_1 T_{K2}}{p_2 T_{K1}}$$

and rearranging the terms, this expression becomes

$$\frac{p_1 V_1}{T_{K1}} = \frac{p_2 V_3}{T_{K2}}$$

But V_3 is the volume at pressure p_2 and temperature T_{K2}, and therefore we can write

$$\frac{pV}{T_K} = \frac{p'V'}{T_K'}$$

where p, V, and T_K are former pressure, volume, and Kelvin temperature; and p', V', and T_K' are the new pressure, volume, and Kelvin temperature of a given mass of gas. This last equation is one form of the general gas law.

8.14 Ideal gases   The gas laws we have just discussed are true for *ideal gases*. An ideal gas is imagined to consist of infinitely small, perfectly elastic molecules which exert only short-range attractive or repulsive forces. Real gases within the usual experimental ranges of temperature and pressure conform closely to the theoretical behavior of an ideal gas, even though they consist of molecules of finite size which do exert forces on each other. Under usual temperatures and pressures, the space between molecules of a gas is large enough so that the actual size of the molecules and the attractive or repulsive forces between them have little effect on the volume of the gas. However, when the pressure and temperature are such that condensation is about to take place, there are significant deviations from the ideal gas laws.

QUESTIONS

Group A

1. What is meant by the coefficient of linear expansion?
2. What provision is made to allow for the expansion of (a) concrete highways, (b) bridges, (c) piston rings?
3. A hole 1.00 cm in diameter is drilled through a piece of steel at 20.0°C. What happens to the diameter of the hole as the steel is heated to 100.0°C?
4. A platinum wire can be easily sealed into a glass tube, but a copper wire does not form a tight seal with glass. Explain.
5. How does the coefficient of volume expansion of mercury compare with the coefficient of volume expansion of glass?
6. Why are mercury and alcohol used in making thermometers?
7. Why does the pressure of a confined gas increase as its temperature is raised?
8. What is the meaning of S.T.P.?
9. State Boyle's law.
10. How does the density of a gas vary with the pressure exerted on it?

Group B

11. Does the coefficient of linear expansion depend on the unit of length used? Explain.
12. Why do solids expand when their temperature is raised?
13. (a) Why does water contract as its temperature is raised from 0°C to 4°C? (b) Why does it expand when heated above 4°C?
14. Why does the measurement of the expansion of a liquid contained in a bulb or tube fail to give a true value for the expansion of the liquid?
15. A brass disc fits a hole in a steel plate snugly at 20.0°C. In order to make the disc drop out of the plate, should the disc and plate combination be heated or cooled?
16. Why are the coefficients of volume expansion very nearly the same for all gases?
17. (a) What is an ideal gas? (b) Why do real gases within the usual experimental ranges of temperature and pressure conform to the behavior of an ideal gas?

14.8×10^{-6} copper

PROBLEMS

2×10^{-3} m

Group A

1. A piece of copper pipe is 5.00 m long at 20.0°C. If it is heated to 70.0°C, what is the increase in its length?
2. A rod of silver is 100.0 cm long at 0.0°C. What is its increase in length when heated to 100.0°C?

3. A steel pipeline is $150\bar{0}$ m long at 30.0°C. What is its length when the temperature is 10.0°C?

4. The diameter of a hole drilled through a piece of brass is 1.500 cm when the temperature is $2\bar{0}$°C. What is its diameter when the brass is heated to $15\bar{0}$°C?

5. What is the increase in volume of 15.0 liters of ethyl alcohol when it is heated from 15.0°C to 25.0°C?

6. A quantity of carbon tetrachloride occupies a volume of 500.00 ml at 20.0°C. What is its volume at 45.0°C?

7. Some oxygen occupies a volume of 5.00 liters at 27°C. If the pressure is unchanged, what volume does it occupy at 77°C?

8. A gas occupies a volume of 250.0 cm³ at 37°C. What is its volume at 67°C if the pressure is not changed?

9. A gas occupies 2.00 liters at 73.5 mm pressure. What is the volume at standard pressure if the temperature is unchanged?

10. A gas occupies 625 ml at 745 mm pressure. What is the volume at 815 mm pressure? The temperature remains constant.

11. We measure 465 cm³ of a gas at a pressure of 725 mm of mercury. What volume will the gas occupy if the pressure is increased to 825 mm?

12. A certain gas has a density of 1.55 g/liter at a pressure of $76\bar{0}$ mm. What is the density if the pressure is decreased to 725 mm?

Group B

13. The spaces between 12.0-m steel rails are 0.0075 m at −18.0°C. If the rails close up at 32.0°C, what is their coefficient of linear expansion?

14. Mercury has a mass density of 13.6 g/cm³ at 20.0°C. Find its mass density at 100.0°C.

15. What must be the length of a steel rod if its length increases by 0.00102 m as a result of a 20.0-C° change in temperature?

16. A steel steam pipe is 100.0 m long. How much room must be provided for expansion if its temperature change varies from $-1\bar{0}$°C to 105°C?

17. A steel tape is correctly calibrated in metric units at 0.00°C. It is used at a temperature of 25.00°C to measure the distance between two lines on a cement floor. The reading obtained is 25.000 m. (a) What is the actual distance between the lines? (b) What would the reading of the tape have been if its temperature had been 0.00°C?

18. A copper ring has an inside diameter of 3.980 cm at 20.0°C. To what temperature must it be heated to fit exactly on a shaft 4.000 cm in diameter?

19. A Pyrex glass vessel has a volume of 1.0000 liter at 20.0°C. What volume will it have at 50.0°C?

20. The pressure exerted on a volume of gas at 0°C is $60\bar{0}$ mm of mercury. The temperature of the gas is increased to $3\bar{0}$°C, while the volume is held constant. What will the new pressure be?

21. A constant-pressure air thermometer contains a mass of air whose volume is 60$\bar{0}$ cm³ at 0°C. What will be its volume at 8$\bar{0}$°C?

22. A calibrated Pyrex glass flask is filled to the 1000.0 cm³ level with water. Both flask and water are at a temperature of 20.0°C. The system is heated to 80.0°C. Determine what the volume reading will be at this new temperature. (Bear in mind that both the water and the flask will expand.)

23. A certain mass of gas has a volume of 1.25 liters at a pressure of 76.0 cm of mercury, and a temperature of 27.0°C. The gas expands to a volume of 1.55 liters at which time its pressure is 80.0 cm of mercury. What is the final temperature?

CHANGE OF PHASE

The phase and density of any pure substance are determined by its temperature and pressure. When temperature and pressure are completely controlled, it is possible to cause a pure substance to pass from any one phase to either of the other two phases. This can be done either directly by a single transition, or by passing through the third phase with two transitions.

The diagram (Fig. 8-14) represents the temperature-pressure equilibrium curves for a *pure, water-like* substance. At the pressure and temperature of the triple point **T**, the three phases of the substance, solid, liquid, and vapor, may exist in equilibrium. This substance exists as a solid for temperature-pressure values lying in the area between the curves **TC** and **TB**. It is a liquid when these values lie in the area between **TB** and **TA**. In the area below the **ATC** curve it is a vapor. If the temperature-pressure values fall anywhere on the curve **TA** the substance can exist with its vapor and liquid phases in equilibrium. Similarly, if these values fall on the curve **TB** the solid and liquid phases can exist in equilibrium. For values on the curve **TC** the solid and vapor phases can exist in equilibrium. When there are two or more phases of a substance in equilibrium at any given temperature and pressure, there will always be interfaces separating the phases.

Figure 8-14 with the solid-liquid curve **TB**, the liquid-vapor curve **TA**, and the solid-vapor curve **TC** plotted on a single graph is typical of pure crystalline materials. However, each substance has definite temperatures at which changes of phase occur at any given pressure, and thus will have its own characteristic set of curves.

Figure 8-15 is like Fig. 8-14 except that it is for a particular substance, water, having a triple point at a temperature of 0.01°C and a pressure of 4.58 mm of mercury. A point on any

8.15 Phase equilibrium

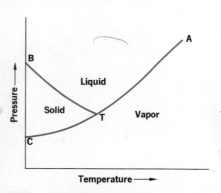

8-14 Temperature-pressure curve for a substance like water. **T** is the triple point. At this point all three phases of the substance are in equilibrium.

8.16 Temperature-pressure values of water

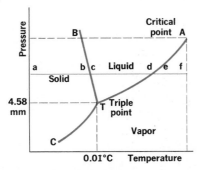

8-15 Temperature-pressure curves for pure water, also known as the triple-point diagram for water.

8.17 Heat of fusion of ice

curve represents a condition of equilibrium between two phases at a definite temperature and pressure. At the triple point **T**, ice, water, and water vapor can coexist in a sealed vessel that contains only these three substances. If the system varies in either temperature or pressure from the triple point value, at least one of the three phases disappears. For example, if the temperature is raised and the pressure reduced from their triple point values, the ice and water will change to vapor.

For most pure substances the triple point diagram differs slightly from that of water since the temperature of the melting point usually increases with an increase in pressure. Thus for most crystalline substances the solid-liquid curve **TB** would have an upward rather than a downward slope.

Figure 8-15 is the temperature-pressure curve for water. At the temperature and pressure indicated by point **a** on line **af**, water exists as ice, a solid. Let us assume that we keep the pressure constant as we apply heat at a uniform rate. The ice will be warmed from its initial temperature to the temperature at point **b** where the **af** line intersects the **TB** (fusion) curve. At this temperature the ice will begin to melt. The application of more heat will melt more ice, but the temperature will not rise until all the ice is melted.

Following this change in phase, the temperature of the liquid water will rise. The horizontal line **abcdef** shows the temperature values as heat is applied first to the ice, then to the water, and finally to the vapor while the pressure on the system is held constant. This information can be shown more strikingly in another way. Assume that we start with a block of ice at $-2\overline{0}°C$ and add heat at a constant rate while holding the pressure con-

8-16 Temperature vs. time of heating for a constant input of heat of $10\overline{0}$ cal per minute, starting with $10\overline{0}$ g of ice at $-2\overline{0}°C$.

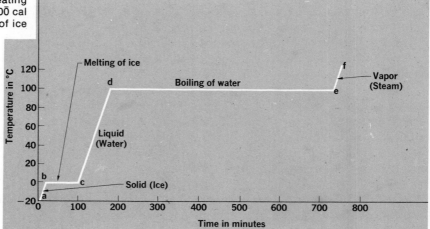

stant at a value indicated by the line **af**. A plot of temperature readings against time while heat is being applied at a uniform rate gives us Fig. 8-16. The line **ab** in each figure represents the warming of the ice without change of state; **bc** (Fig. 8-16) represents the heat required to change the solid to a liquid without a change of temperature (note that **b** and **c** on Fig. 8-15 are one and the same point); **cd** represents the warming of the water. We will continue the interpretation of Figs. 8-15 and 8-16 in Section 8.19. As noted in Section 7.16, the addition of heat to a solid at its melting point produces a change of phase instead of a rise in temperature. All the energy goes to increase the potential energy of the particles. The average kinetic energy is unchanged. Thus, the addition of heat to ice at a pressure of one atmosphere and a temperature of 0°C causes it to change into water at 0°C.

*The amount of heat needed to melt a unit mass of a substance at its melting point is called its **heat of fusion**.* The symbol for heat of fusion is L_f. L_f for ice is approximately 80 cal/g at 0°C, meaning that this quantity of heat must be added to each gram of ice at 0°C to convert it to water at 0°C. Heats of fusion of various substances are given in Table 13, Appendix B.

The method of mixtures can be used to determine the heat of fusion of a solid. Suppose we wish to determine experimentally the heat of fusion of ice. Since hot water melts ice, we find the mass of ice at a known temperature that can be melted by a known mass of water at a known temperature. The example below illustrates these calculations.

Example

A calorimeter has a mass of 100.0 g and a specific heat of 0.0900 cal/g C°. It contains 400.0 g of water at 40.0°C. When 91.0 g of ice at 0.0°C is added and completely melted, the temperature of the water is 18.2°C. What is the heat of fusion of ice?

Solution

Basic Equation: $Q_1 = Q_g$

Heat lost by water + heat lost by calorimeter = heat gained by melting ice + heat gained by ice water.

$$(mc\,\Delta T)_w + (mc\,\Delta T)_c = (mL_f)_i + (mc\,\Delta T)_{iw}$$

Working Equation: $\quad L_f = \dfrac{(mc\,\Delta T)_w + (mc\,\Delta T)_c - (mc\,\Delta T)_{iw}}{m_i}$

$$(mc\,\Delta T)_w = [400.0\text{ g} \times 1.00\text{ cal/gC}° \times (40.0 - 18.2)\text{C}°] = 8720\text{ cal}$$
$$(mc\,\Delta T)_c = [100.0\text{ g} \times 0.0900\text{ cal/gC}° \times (40.0 - 18.2)\text{C}°] = 196\text{ cal}$$
$$(mc\,\Delta T)_{iw} = [91.0\text{ g} \times 1.00\text{ cal/gC}° \times (18.2 - 0.0)\text{C}°] = 1660\text{ cal}$$
$$m_i = 91.0\text{ g}$$

Then $\quad L_f = \dfrac{8720\text{ cal} + 196\text{ cal} - 1660\text{ cal}}{91.0\text{ g}} = \dfrac{7260\text{ cal}}{91.0\text{ g}}$

$$L_f = 79.8\text{ cal/g}$$

8.18 Water gives up heat as it freezes

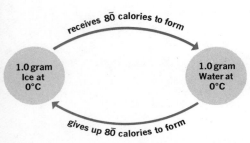

8-17 The reversible energy change between 1.0 g of ice and 1.0 g of water at 0°C.

The heat added to ice to make it melt increases the thermal energy of its molecules and changes it into water. This same amount of heat is evolved when water freezes because this is a reversible energy change. Each gram of water at 0°C that forms ice at 0°C gives off approximately 80 calories of heat. When the molecules of water return to their fixed positions in ice, they give up, in the form of heat, the energy which enabled them to slide over one another. The reversible energy change between 1 g of ice and 1 g of water at 0°C is shown in Fig. 8-17. To change the ice to water, $8\overline{0}$ cal must be added; to change the water to ice, $8\overline{0}$ cal must be taken away. A more precise value for the heat of fusion of ice to use in computation is 79.7 cal/g.

If pure water is very carefully cooled without being disturbed, it can reach temperatures as low as −20°C without freezing. Water that is cooled below the normal freezing point is said to be *supercooled*. If a piece of ice or a speck of dust is added to such water, freezing takes place rapidly and the temperature rises to 0°C, the normal freezing point. The formation of ice takes place readily at 0°C if there is some dust or other foreign matter on which the first crystals of ice can form. Supercooling occurs when no such foreign matter is present. Supercooling is of particular interest in meteorology, since the process of supercooling takes place in the formation of some clouds and when "freezing rain" turns to ice as it hits trees, telephone wires, and other surfaces.

8.19 Temperature and vapor pressure

If the temperature of water is raised, its molecules acquire more kinetic energy, and the water evaporates more rapidly. More water vapor molecules become mixed with gas molecules before the rate of condensation once again equals the rate of evaporation. Thus, when the water temperature is raised, the water vapor molecules exert a greater pressure against the walls of the bell jar, and the equilibrium vapor pressure is greater. (See Section 7.22.) This point will lie somewhat farther to the right and higher on the **TA** curve in Fig. 8-15. Of course, if the temperature is lowered, the equilibrium vapor pressure decreases; the point still lies on the **TA** curve (Fig. 8-15) but nearer the triple point **T**.

The equilibrium vapor pressure of a liquid is a characteristic of the liquid which depends only on the temperature. Table 12, Appendix B, gives the equilibrium vapor pressure of water at various temperatures. The vapor pressure curve for water is graphed in Fig. 8-18. This curve shows the relationship between the pressure and temperature of water and its saturated vapor. Any point on the curve (Fig. 8-18) or on **TA** (Fig. 8-15) represents a definite temperature and pressure at which water is in equilibrium with its saturated vapor. Figure 8-18 is, of course, simply a portion of the curve **TA** in Fig. 8-15 drawn to specific temperature and pressure scales. Other liquids show vapor pressure curves which are similar.

Solids, like liquids, exert a vapor pressure. The equilibrium vapor pressure of ice at 0°C equals about 4.5 mm of mercury.

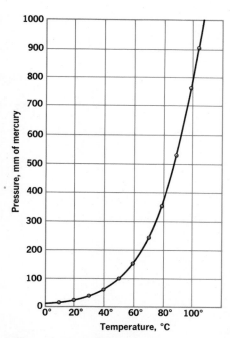

8-18 The equilibrium vapor pressure of water increases rapidly as the temperature is raised.

U.S. Govt. Office of Saline Water

This water plant at Roswell, New Mexico, uses a forced circulation, vapor-compression distillation process to make one million gallons of fresh water a day from brackish water.

The vapor pressure of solids is much less than that of liquids, since they sublime more slowly, or practically not at all, at normal temperatures. Evaporation of both solids and liquids can occur at temperatures and pressures other than the equilibrium values which fall on the curves **TC** and **TA** of Fig. 8-15. A solid at any temperature and pressure to the left of the curve **TC**, or a liquid at a temperature and pressure to the left of the curve **TA** may be evaporating to some degree depending upon the nature of the substance. The vapor pressure of the substance under these conditions will, however, be less than the pressure at saturation.

Since the vapor pressure of water is 760 mm of mercury, or one atmosphere pressure, at 100.0°C this is the *normal boiling point* of water. If the air pressure is reduced to 525.8 mm of mercury, water boils at 90.0°C, because at this temperature the vapor pressure of water is 525.8 mm of mercury. (See Section 7.23.) In order to make water boil at 50.0°C, the pressure must be reduced to 92.5 mm. If the pressure is increased to 787.5 mm of mercury, water will not boil until its temperature reaches 101°C.

Strong-walled pressure cookers, in which water is boiled at pressures up to about 2 atmospheres, and at temperatures up to about 120°C, are useful for rapid cooking of foods. Special pans, in which water is boiled at room temperature or slightly above, are used in the production of sugar crystals.

If a mixture of ethyl alcohol and water is boiled, its boiling temperature is not the same as the boiling point of either liquid by itself. Alcohol boils at 78°C and water at 100°C; the boiling temperature of the mixture is between 78° and 100°C, depending on the proportions of alcohol and water in the mixture. A mixture of two or more liquids having different boiling points usually has a boiling temperature different from that of any of the liquids used.

A liquid can be separated from a nonvaporizing dissolved solid by *distillation*. Distillation includes evaporation followed by condensation of the vapors in a separate vessel. Liquids which have different boiling points can be separated by *fractional distillation*. As the mixture boils, more of the low-boiling component vaporizes, and the boiling point of the resulting mixture rises. Samples collected at different temperatures are then re-distilled.

8.20 Heat of vaporization of water

Suppose a liter of water at 0°C is heated. During the time the water is heating from 0°C to $10\bar{0}$°C, each gram of water absorbs $10\bar{0}$ cal. If heat is supplied at a constant rate, it takes more than five times as long to boil the water away as was required to heat it from 0°C to $10\overline{0}$°C. (See Fig. 8-16.) Each gram of water absorbs more than 500 calories of heat as it is changed into steam. The temperature of the water remains constant during boiling, and the steam produced has the same temperature as the boiling water. *The heat required per unit mass to vaporize a liquid at its boiling point is called its* **heat of vaporization**. The symbol for heat of vaporization is L_v.

The heat required for vaporization gives the particles of liquid sufficient thermal energy to overcome the energy binding them to the liquid, and enables them to separate from one another and move among the molecules of the gases above the liquid. As noted in Section 7.21, all the energy goes to increase the potential energy of the particles. Their average kinetic energy is not changed. Since the energy required for these changes varies with temperature, the heat of vaporization varies with temperature. The heat of vaporization for water is about 540 cal/g at 100°C. For calculation purposes the more precise value of 539 cal/g should be used. Water boiling under reduced pressure at a lower temperature has a heat of vaporization that is somewhat higher; at boiling temperatures above the normal boiling point, the heat of vaporization is lower.

The method of mixtures is used to determine the heat of vaporization of water. As shown in Fig. 8-19, a known mass of steam is passed into a known mass of cold water at a known temperature and the increase in temperature is measured. To insure that only steam enters the water in the calorimeter, a trap is used to catch any condensed water from the steam generator. The calculations for this method are given in the following example.

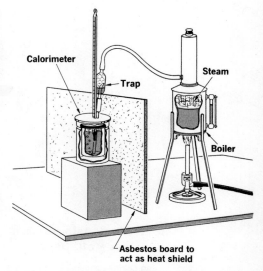

8-19 Laboratory apparatus which may be used for finding the heat of vaporization of water by the method of mixtures.

Example

Given the following data:

Mass of calorimeter	120.0 g
Specific heat of calorimeter	0.100 cal/gC°
Mass of water	402.0 g
Mass of steam	23.5 g
Initial temperature of cold water	6.0°C
Temperature of steam	100.0°C
Final temperature of water	40.0°C

Calculate the heat of vaporization of water.

Solution

Basic Equation: $Q_1 = Q_g$

Heat lost by steam in condensing + heat lost by resulting water = heat gained by calorimeter + heat gained by water.

$$(mL_v)_s + (mc\,\Delta T)_{sw} = (mc\,\Delta T)_c + (mc\,\Delta T)_w$$

Working Equation: $L_v = \dfrac{(mc\,\Delta T)_c + (mc\,\Delta T)_w - (mc\,\Delta T)_{sw}}{m_s}$

$(mc\,\Delta T)_c = [120.0\text{ g} \times 0.100\text{ cal/gC}° \times (40.0 - 6.0)\text{C}°] = 408\text{ cal}$
$(mc\,\Delta T)_w = [402.0\text{ g} \times 1.00\text{ cal/gC}° \times (40.0 - 6.0)\text{C}°] = 13{,}700\text{ cal}$
$(mc\,\Delta T)_{sw} = [23.5\text{ g} \times 1.00\text{ cal/gC}° \times (100.0 - 40.0)\text{C}°] = 1410\text{ cal}$
$m_s = 23.5\text{ g}$

Then

$$L_v = \frac{408\text{ cal} + 13{,}700\text{ cal} - 1410\text{ cal}}{23.5\text{ g}} = \frac{12{,}700\text{ cal}}{23.5\text{ g}}$$
$$L_v = 54\overline{0}\text{ cal/g}$$

8.21 Condensing steam gives out heat

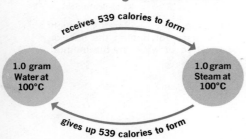

receives 539 calories to form

1.0 gram Water at 100°C

1.0 gram Steam at 100°C

gives up 539 calories to form

8-20 It takes 539 calories to change 1.0 g of water at $10\overline{0}$°C into steam. Steam at $10\overline{0}$°C sets free this much heat in condensing to water.

Heat is absorbed during vaporization. This increase in the thermal energy of the molecules of a liquid enables them to break away from the liquid and become molecules of vapor. When the vapor condenses to a liquid, this thermal energy is evolved as heat. This reversible energy change, shown in graphic form in Fig. 8-20, is useful in a steam heating system. The heat of vaporization changes water to steam in the boiler. The steam passes into radiators, where it gives up its heat of vaporization and condenses to a liquid.

Even though steam and boiling water are at the same temperature, steam can produce a more severe burn. One reason is that steam at 100°C has acquired about 540 more calories of heat per gram than water at 100°C. When steam condenses, this heat of vaporization is given out. Then the water which is formed gives out the same amount of heat that water at 100°C does as it cools.

8.22 A further look at the triple point diagram

Let us return now to Figs. 8-15 and 8-16 and continue the discussion begun in Section 8.15 concerning fusion. As heat is applied to the mass of water formed from the melted ice, its temperature rises to that of point **d**, its boiling point. The line **de** of Fig. 8-16 represents the heat required to change the liquid to a vapor (steam) without producing a change in temperature. Note that points **d** and **e** on Figs. 8-15 and 8-16 represent the same values. After the water is all converted to steam, the addition of heat energy causes the temperature of the steam to rise as indicated by **ef** in both figures.

In order to keep the pressure constant, for example at one atmosphere, while heat is applied to change ice from $-2\overline{0}$°C to steam at $12\overline{0}$°C, the volume of the container must be greatly increased. In our previous discussions, we noted that ice expands slightly as its temperature is raised to 0°C, that it contracts as it is melted to water at 0°C, that the water formed contracts to its minimum volume at 4°C, and then expands as its temperature is raised to $10\overline{0}$°C. As the water at $10\overline{0}$°C is changed to steam at $10\overline{0}$°C by the addition of heat, at constant pressure, the expansion is about 1700 times. As the vapor (steam) is heated further, it continues to expand at a rate which would be somewhat like, but not the same as, a Charles' law expansion. The vapor is too near its condensation temperature to obey Charles' law closely.

The vaporization curve **TA** in Fig. 8-15 is not unlimited in extent. The lower limit is the temperature and pressure of the triple point. The upper limit is the *critical point*. The temperature and pressure of the critical point are called the *critical temperature* and the *critical pressure*. A substance cannot exist as a liquid at a temperature above its critical temperature; no matter how great the pressure, it cannot be condensed to the liquid state. At the critical point the densities of the liquid and the vapor are equal, and the heat of vaporization is zero. At temperatures above the critical temperature a substance is usually called a gas, while at temperatures below the critical temperature it is called a vapor. The critical temperature of water is 374°C and the critical pressure is 218 atmospheres. This simply means that the temperature of liquid water cannot be raised to 374°C unless it is under a pressure of 218 atmospheres, and that at any higher temperature water can exist only in its gaseous phase, no matter how high the pressure.

Substances which are known to us as gases, such as oxygen and nitrogen, have very low critical temperatures. The critical temperature for oxygen is −119°C and for nitrogen, −147°C. These gases must first be cooled to these low temperatures before they can be liquefied. Helium has the lowest critical temperature which is 5°K.

8.23 The critical point

We have described several effects of addition or loss of heat on water. These are summarized in a somewhat different manner in Fig. 8-21 than has been shown previously. The figure shows what happens from the time heat is added to ice at $-2\overline{0}$°C until it is steam at $12\overline{0}$°C. Since the specific heat of ice is 0.53 cal/g C°, 1.0 g of ice absorbs 11 cal in being warmed to 0°C. As this ice melts there is *no temperature change* while $8\overline{0}$ cal of heat is being absorbed. As heating continues, the next $10\overline{0}$ cal increases the temperature to $10\overline{0}$°C. As the water boils, 539 cal of heat converts the water into steam at $10\overline{0}$°C; during this change of phase there is *no temperature change*. If the steam is under one atmosphere pressure, its specific heat is

8.24 Summary of effects of heat on water

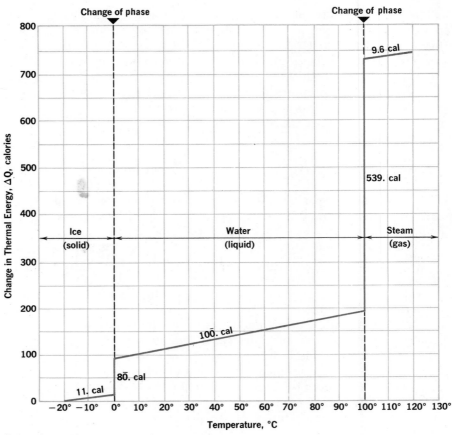

8-21 Graph showing the heat absorbed as 1.0 g of ice at $-2\overline{0}°$C is converted into steam at $12\overline{0}°$C.

0.48 cal/g C°, and 9.6 cal is needed to heat it to 120°C. Thus 740 cal are required to change 1.0 g of ice at $-2\overline{0}°$C into 1.0 g of steam at $12\overline{0}°$C. Conversely, 740 cal are evolved if 1.0 g of steam at $12\overline{0}°$C is changed into 1.0 g of ice at $-2\overline{0}°$C.

In Fig. 8-20 we saw that 539 calories of heat are absorbed when 1.0 gram of water changes to steam at 100°C. The same amount of heat is released when 1.0 gram of steam changes back to water at 100°C. Similar exchanges of heat can take place at other temperatures and with other liquids. Whenever a liquid evaporates, heat is absorbed from the environment. This cooling effect of evaporation can be very useful.

8.25 Evaporation is a cooling process

The human body uses evaporation to help control its temperature. When it becomes too warm, sweat glands produce water which evaporates. Since much of the required heat of vaporization comes from the skin, the body is cooled. If you sit in a breeze where perspiration can evaporate more rapidly, you cool off faster. When the air is humid, you may have difficulty keeping cool because perspiration does not evaporate readily under such conditions.

The cooling effect of an alcohol rub or ether poured on your hand is the result of rapid evaporation of these liquids. Since the heat of vaporization is obtained from your body, the liquids feel cold on your skin.

Liquefied gases behave in a similar fashion. Gases which can be liquefied easily by pressure alone at room temperature are important refrigerants. These gases are compressed and then cooled to room temperature; in this process they give off heat and condense to liquids. Then they are allowed to expand and evaporate; for this process they must gain heat from their surroundings. By recycling the gas through this process, the gas transports heat from one location to another. In practice, the heat required for evaporation and expansion is absorbed from the freezing compartment of the refrigerator. This heat is given up to the air of the room as it cools the gas in the condenser coils.

Electric refrigerators are *heat pumps*. They use energy in order to transfer heat from one place to another. This kind of heat transfer will be discussed in greater detail in the next chapter.

QUESTIONS

Group A

1. Draw the temperature-pressure equilibrium curves for a water-like substance.
2. (a) What is heat of fusion? (b) What is the value for the heat of fusion of ice?
3. What is supercooling?
4. For what purposes are (a) pressure cookers, (b) vacuum pans used?
5. Explain the processes of (a) distillation, (b) fractional distillation.
6. (a) What is heat of vaporization? (b) What is the magnitude of heat of vaporization of water?
7. Why does steam at 100°C produce a more severe burn to the skin than water at 100°C?
8. Why does an easily vaporized liquid, such as acetone or ether, feel cool to the skin?
9. The air above the ice of a pond is −10°C. What is the probable temperature of (a) the upper suface of the ice; (b) the lower surface; (c) the water just beneath the surface; (d) the water at the bottom of the pond?

Group B 10. How do the curves drawn in Question 1 differ from those that would be drawn for a substance that contracts as it changes from a liquid to a solid?

11. Assume you have a sample of pure water at the triple point. What happens if you (a) increase the pressure while the temperature is held constant? (b) increase the temperature while the pressure is held constant? (c) reduce the temperature while the pressure is held constant? (d) reduce the pressure while the temperature is held constant?

12. Refer to Fig. 8-14. What is the location of the set of points which indicates the temperature-pressure values for situations where the solid and vapor of this water-like substance are in equilibrium?

13. Isolate one point of the set referred to in Question 12. Assume that the pressure is held constant while the temperature of the substance is increased. What happens?

14. (a) Why does the boiling temperature of a liquid depend on the pressure exerted on its surface? (b) How does the boiling temperature of a liquid vary with the pressure exerted on its surface?

15. How is fractional distillation used in separating the different materials found in petroleum?

16. What data are required in order to determine the heat of vaporization of water by the method of mixtures?

17. Why does the heat of vaporization vary with the boiling temperature?

18. What are the limits of the vaporization curve **TA** in Fig. 8-15?

19. What is the physical meaning of the critical point?

PROBLEMS

Group A 1. How many calories will be absorbed by 1.50 kg of ice at 0.0°C as it melts?

2. To what temperature must a 2270 g iron ball be heated so that it can completely melt 1150 g of ice at 0.0°C?

3. A 50$\bar{0}$-g aluminum block is heated to 350°C. How many grams of ice at 0.0°C will the aluminum block melt on cooling?

4. A copper calorimeter has a mass of 220.0 g. It contains 450.0 g of water at 21.0°C. How many grams of ice at 0.00°C must be added to reduce the temperature of the mixture to 5.00°C?

5. To what temperature must a 500.0-g brass weight be heated to convert 60.0 g of ice at −20.0°C to water at 20.0°C?

6. How many calories are given off by 50.0 g of steam at 10$\bar{0}$°C when it condenses?

7. How many calories are required to vaporize 20.0 kg of water at 10$\bar{0}$°C?

8. Calculate the number of calories evolved when 4.00 kg of steam at 10$\bar{0}$°C is condensed, cooled, and changed to ice at 0°C.

162 g 9. How many grams of mercury can be vaporized at its boiling point, 356.58°C, by the addition of 1.00×10^3 calories?

10. What is the final temperature attained by the addition of 11.4 g of steam at 100.0°C to 681.0 g of water at 25.0°C in an aluminum calorimeter having a mass of 182.0 g? *34.6°C*

11. A calorimeter contains 400.0 g of water at 20.0°C. How many grams of steam at 100.0°C are needed to raise the temperature of the water and calorimeter to 80.0°C? The calorimeter has a mass of 100.0 g; its specific heat is 0.100 cal/g C°. *44 g*

12. What is the final temperature of a mixture of 50.0 g of ice at 0.00°C and 50.0 g of water at 80.0°C? *0°C* **Group B**

13. What is the final temperature when 300.0 g of ice at 0.00°C, 500.0 g of ice water at 0.00°C, and 120$\bar{0}$ g of water at 100.0°C are mixed? *48°C*

14. A calorimeter, specific heat 0.100 cal/g C°, mass 200.0 g, contains 300.0 g of water at 40.0°C. If 50.0 g of ice at 0.0°C is dropped into the water and stirred, the temperature of the mixture when all the ice has melted is 23.8°C. Calculate the heat of fusion of ice. *79.9 cal/g*

15. A block of silver, mass 500.0 g, temperature 100.0°C, is put in a calorimeter with 300.0 g of water, temperature 30.0°C. The mass of the calorimeter is 50.0 g, and its specific heat is 0.100 cal/g C°. A 50.0-g mass of ice at −10.0°C, is also put in the calorimeter. Calculate the final temperature. *20.2°C*

16. What is the final temperature attained when 90$\bar{0}$ g of ice at 0.0°C is dropped into 340$\bar{0}$ g of water at 93.3°C in a calorimeter having a mass of 135$\bar{0}$ g, with specific heat 0.090 cal/g C°? *58.1°C*

17. In an experiment to determine the heat of vaporization of water, 15.0 g of steam at 100.0°C is added to 150.0 g of water at 20.0°C in a calorimeter. The mass of the calorimeter is 75.0 g; its specific heat is 0.100 cal/g C°. The equilibrium temperature of the mixture is 73.9°C. What is the heat of vaporization of water? *539 cal/g*

18. A mixture of ice and water, mass 200.0 g, is in a 100.0-g calorimeter, specific heat 0.200 cal/g C°. When 40.0 g of steam is added to the mixture, the temperature is raised to 60.0°C. How many grams of ice were originally in the calorimeter? *124 g*

19. An aluminum cylinder, mass 50.0 g, is placed in a 100.0-g brass calorimeter with 250.0 g of water at 20.0°C. What equilibrium temperature is reached after the addition of 25.0 g of steam at 120.0°C? *73.2°C*

20. A copper ball with a mass of 4.54 kg is removed from a furnace and dropped into 1.36 kg of water, temperature 22.0°C. After the water stops boiling, the combined mass of the ball and water is 5.45 kg. What was the furnace temperature? *931°C*

360 g

An artist's conception of a space shuttle liftoff (top). The shuttle is the first reusable space transportation system, which greatly reduces the cost of each mission. The winged component of the system, called the orbiter, returns to Earth for a landing similar to that of a jet airplane (center). The utilization of metals with very high melting points and specific heats enables both the booster and orbiter to withstand extreme reentry temperatures for as many as two hundred consecutive flights. After landing, the orbiter can be returned to the launch site atop a large jet transport (bottom). Space shuttles can be used to deploy earth satellites and planetary probes, retrieve or repair malfunctioning equipment, and service space stations. More than a dozen countries are participating in the program.

Chapter 9

Heat and Work

The temperature of two blocks can be raised by briskly rubbing them together. The temperature of a nail can be raised by pounding it with a hammer. This is evidence that work and heat are related.

It was not until 1800 that Count Rumford discovered that work done against friction produces internal energy (see Chapter 1). From 1842 to 1870 James Prescott Joule carefully conducted a series of work and heat experiments. He wished to determine the amount of mechanical work which must be done on a body to produce the same temperature change as that produced by the addition of a given quantity of heat to the body. These experiments were called *mechanical equivalent of heat* experiments. Joule found that the internal energy produced by a definite quantity of mechanical energy was always the same. These discoveries showed that heat was another form of energy, and could therefore be related to work.

The study of the quantitative relationships between heat and other forms of energy is called **thermodynamics**. In this chapter we shall be concerned with the relation of heat energy to mechanical energy.

Joule used an apparatus similar to that shown in Fig. 9-1 to determine the relation between mechanical energy and heat energy. The system on which work was done was a mass of water, m_w, in an insulated vessel designed to reduce the transfer of heat to a minimum. A set of movable paddles was attached to a shaft turned by a falling mass attached to the shaft by a cord. The paddles turned past stationary vanes, churned the water, and increased its temperature from T_i to some final value

9.1 Relation between heat and work

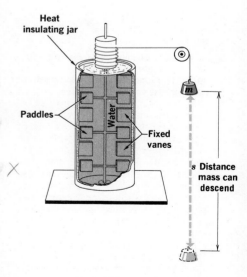

9-1 A simplified diagram of Joule's apparatus for observing the conversion of mechanical energy into internal energy.

209

The Granger Collection

An artist's conception of the English physicist, James Prescott Joule, measuring the heating of a metal wire by the passage of an electric current.

T_f. The work done on the water equals the loss of potential energy of mass m as it descends through a distance s, less the kinetic energy it possesses as it reaches the bottom of its path. The loss in potential energy is mgs. The final kinetic energy of the mass is $\frac{1}{2}mv^2$. (In these experiments, v was small.) Hence, the amount of work W, done on the system by the falling mass is

$$W = mgs - \tfrac{1}{2}mv^2$$

The amount of heat which would be needed to produce the observed temperature change in the water is

$$Q = m_w c_w (T_f - T_i)$$

W, the work done on the system, is expressed in units of mechanical energy (work). Q is the equivalent energy expressed in heat units. The results of many careful experiments have shown that

1 calorie = 4.19 joules

This equality is known as the *mechanical equivalent of heat*. (See Fig. 9.2)

If we wish to set up an equation involving W and Q we must introduce a conversion factor. J, the symbol for the *mechanical equivalent of heat* is used. Thus

$$W = JQ \qquad \text{where} \qquad J = 4.19 \text{ joules/calorie}$$

Dimensionally, $W = $ joules/calorie $\times$ calories and W is expressed in joules.

Just as in the case of the hot brass chips in Count Rumford's cannon-boring experiments it is possible to produce internal energy indefinitely in the Joule apparatus provided we continue to supply mechanical energy to it. Thus we must conclude that *heat* is a form of energy and not a substance.

A different kind of energy transfer takes place in the gasoline engine. As the piston moves down, air and gasoline vapor are brought into the cylinder through special valves. As the piston moves up again, the valves close and the air-vapor mixture is compressed to a fraction of its original volume. This compression causes the temperature of the mixture to rise. A spark then starts a chemical reaction between the gasoline vapor and the oxygen in the air. Heat produced by the chemical reaction increases the pressure of the gas in the cylinder. The heated gas does work by pushing the piston. Changing some of the internal energy into mechanical energy causes the temperature of the gases to decrease, but not to the temperature of the outside air. The heat that was added from the chemical reaction

| 4.19 joules of work | Converting **work into heat** → ← Converting **heat into work** | 1 calorie of heat |

9-2 The mechanical equivalent of heat in the metric system.

was partly converted to work and was partly used to increase the internal energy of the gases that escape through the exhaust.

We can now broaden the statement of the conservation of energy (Section 1.11) to include heat energy and internal energy as well as mechanical energy. This follows from the work of Count Rumford, Joule, and others, and is known as the ***first law of thermodynamics***: *the quantity of energy supplied to any system in the form of heat is equal to the work done by the system plus the change in internal energy of the system.* Thus, the energy input to a system equals the energy gained by the system plus the energy output in the form of work. We may also state the first law of thermodynamics as follows: *when heat is converted to another form of energy, or when other forms of energy are converted to heat, there is no loss of energy.*

As an application of the first law of thermodynamics, let us assume that an amount of heat, Q, is added to a substance whose total internal energy is E_i. Generally we would find that the addition of this energy increases the internal energy of the substance to E_f, and also causes the substance to do a quantity of work W on its surroundings. This can be stated algebraically as

$$Q = (E_f - E_i) + W$$

Q is positive when heat is added to the substance, and W is positive when the body does work on surrounding objects. All quantities must be expressed in the same units. If E_f and E_i are expressed in calories, the expression becomes

$$Q = (E_f - E_i) + \frac{W}{J}$$

When E_f and E_i are expressed in joules the equation becomes

$$JQ = (E_f - E_i) + W$$

In situations where no work is done by or on the substance, the change in internal energy equals the quantity of heat added to or removed from the substance. Adding heat to water which undergoes no change of state, will cause each gram of water to increase in temperature by one Celsius degree for each calorie of heat added. Here, we neglect the very small amount of work involved in changing the volume of the water. We know that the internal energy of the water is changed because we observe that the temperature of the water is changed.

A process in which no heat is added to or removed from a substance is called an ***adiabatic process***. In such a case, $Q = 0 = (E_f - E_i) + W$. An example is the Joule experiment for determining the mechanical equivalent of heat. When the vessel containing the

9.2 First law of thermodynamics

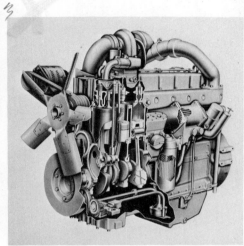

Caterpillar Tractor Co.

Cutaway view of an industrial Diesel engine. In this type of engine, the fuel and air mixture is ignited directly by the high temperatures resulting from compression.

water permits no heat to enter or leave during the churning process, the work done on the water equals the change in its internal energy.

In another example let us assume that we have a quantity of air trapped in an *insulated* cylinder with a tight-fitting but freely moving piston. When the air is compressed by pushing the piston into the cylinder, the change in the internal energy of the air must equal the work done on it. This relationship is shown by the change in volume, pressure, and temperature of the air. This situation is similar to that in a Diesel engine cylinder where the compression of the air occurs so rapidly that practically no heat escapes. Under these conditions the temperature of the air becomes high enough to ignite the gas-air mixture produced when the fuel is injected.

9.3 Conversion of heat into work

The conversion of work to heat is reversible — heat can be changed to work. One calorie of heat can be converted to 4.19 joules of work. See Fig. 9-2. This equivalence of work and heat has already been expressed as

$$W = JQ$$

There are several methods by which heat can be converted to useful work. Two examples are the following:

1. By means of steam. Heat from burning wood, coal, or oil is used to generate steam. Since this is usually done by burning the fuel outside the engine, most steam engines and steam turbines are *external combustion engines*. When water is changed to steam under normal atmospheric pressure it expands about 1700 times. In a boiler, however, the steam is confined and exerts pressure in all directions. Steam under pressure can do work by

This steam turbine-generator is capable of producing more than 550,000 kilowatts of electric power, enough to supply the power demands of a city of over a half million people.

The General Electric Co.

moving the piston of a steam engine or the blades of a steam turbine. In either case, a portion of the heat of the burning fuel is transformed to work through the use of steam. Nuclear power plants use heat from a nuclear reactor to produce steam.

2. By means of burning gases. When heat is obtained through the combustion of gases we may eliminate the need for a boiler. The pressure built up by burning compressed gases may convert heat to work by exerting a force to move a piston or turn the blades of a turbine. Since the burning of the fuel occurs within the cylinder or turbine chambers, such engines are called *internal combustion engines.*

In nearly all situations involving gases, they are confined by barriers on which they exert a force, and which, in turn, exert an equal and opposite force on them. A gas may be under pressure in a storage tank or in a cylinder above a movable piston of an internal combustion engine. A quantity of air (an air mass) in the atmosphere is under pressure exerted by the air around it. In any of these cases, expansion of the gas requires it to do work against an external force. Thus work is done on the external medium. On the other hand, the quantity of gas may be compressed by the action of an outside force; that is, work may be done on the gas.

To calculate the work done by a gas in expanding, let us enclose it in a cylinder with a tight-fitting piston as illustrated in Fig. 9-3. The piston rod is connected to a device on which it may exert a force. The force F acting on the piston due to the pressure p exerted by the gas on area A of the piston head is

$$F = pA$$

Suppose the piston is moved a given distance s by the expanding gas in the cylinder. Suppose further that heat is applied to the gas with the pressure remaining constant during the expansion. The work done by the expanding gas in moving the piston will be

$$W = Fs = pAs$$

where the quantity As is the change in volume of the expanding gas. Thus the work done by the gas expanding at constant pressure is

$$W = p(V_f - V_i)$$

where V_f and V_i are the final and initial volumes respectively of the confined gas. We may conveniently show the work done by the gas expanding at constant pressure by using a graph. On this graph volumes are plotted as abscissas and pressures as ordinates. See Fig. 9-4. The expansion at constant pressure is

9.4 Work done by a gas

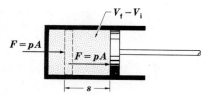

9-3 Expansion of a burning gas at constant pressure.

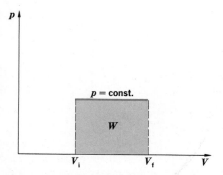

9-4 Graphic representation of work done by a gas expanding at constant pressure.

represented by a horizontal line extending from V_i to V_f. The work W, done by the gas in expanding, is given by the area between this line and the X axis and between V_i and V_f (the light portion shown in Fig. 9-4). This graph is for the *expansion* of a gas at constant pressure. If the gas is *compressed* at constant pressure, the work done is represented in the same manner. It is considered negative, however, since the volume is decreasing because work is done on the gas.

If, during the expansion, the pressure of the gas changes, the calculation becomes somewhat more complicated. Let us consider a situation where sufficient heat is supplied to keep the temperature constant during an expansion. Then, for a dry gas, the relationship between pressure and volume is given by Boyle's law

$$pV = \textbf{constant}$$

This relationship can be shown graphically as in Fig. 9-5. The area under the pV curve between V_f and V_i represents the work involved. This can be computed by dividing the total volume change into a number of very small volume changes. Each of these volume changes must be so small that the pressure remains practically constant for the change considered. The work associated with each minute change in volume is determined by multiplying the change in volume by the pressure at that volume. The sum of all these quantities of work equals the total work involved. *A process that takes place at constant temperature is known as an* **isothermal process**.

The common methods of converting heat to work make use of the expansion of hot compressed gases. To understand this better we must further describe the isothermal and adiabatic processes.

As stated earlier, isothermal expansion and compression of ideal gases occur in accordance with Boyle's law. If the volume of an ideal gas increases at constant temperature, its pressure decreases. Similarly, if the volume of an ideal gas decreases at constant temperature, its pressure increases. Since the internal energy of an ideal gas is determined by its temperature, there can be no change in the internal energy of an ideal gas during isothermal processes. However, work is done by a gas during expansion. Some work is done on the gas molecules, against external pressure, since the volume occupied by the gas becomes greater. (In a real gas, some work is also done on the gas molecules, increasing their potential energy by moving them farther apart.) The heat equivalent of the work done isothermally *by* an ideal gas during expansion *must be absorbed from its surroundings*. In a similar manner, work must be done *on* an ideal gas during isothermal compression and the equivalent amount of heat *must be evolved to its surroundings*.

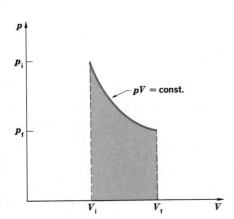

9-5 Graphic representation of work done during the expansion of a gas kept at constant temperature.

A sealed plastic bag will increase in volume as the atmospheric pressure drops during an approaching storm, even if the room temperature remains constant. The plastic bag pushes out against the atmosphere and does work, yet there are no temperature changes.

During an adiabatic expansion of an ideal gas, work is done just as it is during an isothermal expansion. Now, however, the equivalent amount of heat is not withdrawn from the surroundings, but is obtained at the expense of the thermal energy of the gas. Thus during adiabatic expansion not only the pressure, but also the temperature of the ideal gas is lowered. Similarly, when work is done on a gas as it is adiabatically compressed, the heat equivalent of the work is not lost to the surroundings, but increases the internal energy of the gas. Hence, during adiabatic compression both the pressure of the gas and its temperature increase.

Practical examples of adiabatic changes are not common because there is no perfect heat insulator. They do occur in fast processes when there is not enough time for much heat to be lost. As one example, adiabatic expansion occurs in any large atmospheric up-current. An imaginary cubic meter of air in the center of such an up-current is surrounded by a huge volume of air undergoing the same temperature change. Thus there is no transfer of heat to or from this central cubic meter. Its changes in pressure and volume are strictly adiabatic, though they may be slow.

While the specific heat of a solid or liquid is a fixed value to several significant figures for the substance at a given temperature, this is not true for gases. When heat is added to a mass of gas, its pressure, or volume, or both, may change; and its temperature may rise. Let us select the conditions for addition of heat to a unit mass of gas and describe special, but significant cases.

9.5 Specific heats of gases

First, we shall hold the volume of a unit mass of gas constant as heat is added. The quantity of heat required to change the temperature of this unit mass of gas by 1 C° is called its *specific heat at constant volume* c_v.

Second, we will hold the pressure of the same unit mass of gas constant as heat is applied to raise its temperature 1 C°. The quantity of heat required in this case is called its *specific heat at constant pressure* c_p.

The numerical value of c_v differs from that of c_p even though the same mass of the same gas is taken through the same temperature interval. This difference can be easily explained. The internal energy of the unit mass of gas must be changed by the same amount in each instance. Where the pressure is held

Table 9-1 SPECIFIC HEATS OF GASES

Gas	c_p $\left(\dfrac{cal}{g\,C°}\right)$	c_v $\left(\dfrac{cal}{g\,C°}\right)$
air	0.242	0.173
ammonia	0.523	0.399
carbon dioxide	0.200	0.154
hydrogen	3.40	2.40
nitrogen	0.248	0.176
oxygen	0.218	0.156

constant, added energy must be provided to do the work required to produce the volume increase. That is, work must be done on the movable part of the gas container or the surrounding atmosphere. This added work equals the pressure times the change in volume. As a result c_p is greater than c_v. In addition to increasing the internal energy as evidenced by the increased temperature of the gas, some of the added heat energy is transformed into mechanical energy as a result of the necessary expansion.

The same situation exists for liquids and solids. However the amount of expansion is so small that the two specific heats are numerically the same to the number of significant figures with which we work, even in most research situations.

The values of c_p and c_v at room temperature and atmospheric pressure are given in Table 9-1 for some of the common gases.

9.6 Efficiency of ideal heat engines

The processes occurring in the operation of an engine which converts heat energy into mechanical work are complex. However, we can simplify things by replacing the actual heat-engine cycle with an ideal cycle which can produce the same transformations of heat and work. The fact that there are many different types of heat engines, utilizing a variety of working substances such as steam, a mixture of fuel and air, or a mixture of fuel and oxygen, need not specifically concern us here.

In an engine the working substance is taken through a series of operations known as a *cycle*. The result of this is that some of the heat supplied to the substance from a high temperature source is converted into work which is delivered to an external object. For example, high temperature steam drives a turbine which in turn does work on an electric generator. Experimental and theoretical evidence indicate that not all the heat supplied to the engine can be converted into work. The heat which is not converted into work is delivered by the engine to some external reservoir at lower temperature. Such a reservoir is often called a *heat sink*. It is a system which absorbs the exhausted heat, preferably without a significant increase in its own temperature.

In an ideal heat engine, the working substance is a gas that is returned at the end of the cycle to its original pressure, volume, and temperature conditions. Thus, there is no permanent loss or gain of internal energy; the internal energy of the working substance remains unchanged.

The operation of an ideal heat engine is schematically shown in Fig. 9-6. A quantity of heat Q_1 is delivered to the engine during the beginning of a cycle. This comes from a high temperature heat source. The engine performs an amount of work W

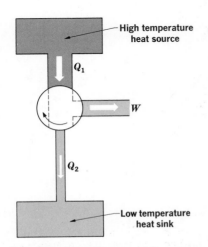

9-6 Schematic diagram of the operation of a heat engine.

on some outside object, and exhausts an amount of heat Q_2 to a low temperature heat sink. Low temperature in this case means any temperature below that of the heat source, and ideally much lower. Applying the first law of thermodynamics to this cycle, we get

$$W = J(Q_1 - Q_2)$$

The thermal efficiency e of the heat engine is defined as

$$e = \frac{\textbf{work done during one cycle}}{\textbf{heat added during one cycle}}$$

or

$$e = \frac{W}{JQ_1}$$

Since

$$W = J(Q_1 - Q_2)$$

then

$$e = \frac{J(Q_1 - Q_2)}{JQ_1} = 1 - \frac{Q_2}{Q_1}$$

From this equation we see that the thermal efficiency of an operating heat engine must always be less than 100%.

It can be shown that the ratio Q_2/Q_1 is always equal to the ratio of the absolute temperatures T_2/T_1, provided only that the engine is considered frictionless. Therefore we can write

$$e = \frac{T_1 - T_2}{T_1} = 1 - \frac{T_2}{T_1}$$

(Incidentally, the Kelvin temperature scale is defined by this equation.)

We can see by examining the above equation that the efficiency of a heat engine may be increased by making the tempera-

A wood engraving of the Corliss engine, an early form of a steam engine, as exhibited at the Philadelphia Centennial Exhibition of 1876.

The Granger Collection

ture of the heat source as high as possible and the temperature of the heat sink as low as possible.

From experience we know that gasoline and steam engines expel some heat during the exhaust part of the cycle. The efficiency of any real heat engine will be less than the efficiency of an ideal heat engine because of heat loss from engine parts and friction.

It is interesting to note that the efficiency of steam engines has increased from 0.17% for the first reciprocating engines of the 17th century to 40% for the 1,000,000 kilowatt turbines used in modern power plants.

9.7 The second law of thermodynamics

We have already seen that not all the heat supplied to a heat engine can be converted into mechanical work. This fact is true for all types of heat engines and it is the basis for a far-reaching generalization known as the *second law of thermodynamics: it is not possible to construct an engine whose sole effect is the extraction of heat from a heat source at a single temperature and the conversion of this heat completely into mechanical work.* Thus, if a heat engine takes a quantity of heat Q_1 from a source at a high temperature T_1 it must transfer some of this heat to a heat sink at a lower temperature.

One interpretation of the second law of thermodynamics is that it is impossible to attain the absolute zero of temperature. Values only a few thousandths of a degree above absolute zero have been attained. The experimental difficulties increase enormously as still lower temperatures are sought. The unattainability of absolute zero is sometimes called the third law of thermodynamics.

Some have considered extracting heat from the internal energy of the ocean and using this to operate the engines of a ship. If the water surrounding the ship is considered a heat source at a single temperature, the second law of thermodynamics indicates that it would be impossible to operate the engines of the ship from the internal energy of the sea water.

It also follows from the second law of thermodynamics that transfer of internal energy from a low temperature heat source to a high temperature heat sink requires work. This type of internal energy transfer takes place in refrigerators and air conditioners.

In order to express the second law of thermodynamics in quantitative form we must be able to measure the amount of the mechanical work a system can do. For example, consider placing a hot and a cold body in thermal contact. They will, after a time, reach thermal equilibrium; that is, the two bodies will come to the same temperature. There was no loss of energy in the process, but the system as a whole has lost its capacity for doing work. (The temperature of the environment is disregarded in this discussion.) Before being placed in contact, a heat engine connected between the two bodies could have done useful work. After contact, when a temperature difference no longer exists between the bodies, work cannot be done by an engine connected between the two.

The amount of energy that cannot be converted into mechanical work is called **entropy**. Entropy is a measurable property as important in the study of thermodynamics as is energy. As with potential energy, or internal energy, it is the difference in entropy that is significant rather than the actual value of entropy. If an amount of heat ΔQ is added to a system that is at an absolute temperature T, the change in entropy is

$$\Delta S = \frac{\Delta Q}{T}$$

If heat is removed from the system, the quantity ΔQ is negative, and the change in entropy is therefore also negative. Note that this equation defines the change in entropy and not entropy itself. Common units for denoting the change in entropy are calories per degree or joules per degree.

Let us refer again to the heat transfer taking place between the two bodies of different temperature which were brought into thermal contact. Assume that these bodies are insulated from their surroundings, and that the initial temperature T_1 of the first body is greater than the temperature T_2 of the second body. Then, the moment they touch, a small quantity of heat ΔQ will be transferred from body **1** to body **2**. The entropy change is $+\dfrac{\Delta Q}{T_2}$ for body **2** and $-\dfrac{\Delta Q}{T_1}$ for body **1**. The net change in entropy for the system is $\dfrac{\Delta Q}{T_2} - \dfrac{\Delta Q}{T_1}$. Since $T_1 > T_2$, the change in entropy is positive; the entropy of the system increased. This is an example of an irreversible process in which a loss of capacity for work results in an increase in entropy for the system. It can be shown that for any transformation occurring in an isolated system, the entropy of the final state can never be less than that of the initial state. Only in cases where the transformation is reversible will the system undergo no change in entropy.

The *second law of thermodynamics* can now be restated as **the law of entropy**: *a natural process usually takes place in such a direction as to cause an increase in the entropy of the system. In the case of an isolated system it is the entropy of the system that tends to increase.*

All natural processes are irreversible and therefore involve increases in entropy. Thus, the second law of thermodynamics is equivalent to the statement that the entropy of the universe is increasing, and, the first law of thermodynamics is equivalent to the statement that the total energy of the universe is constant.

Heat may be considered to be disordered energy. An example of ordered energy is a flying rifle bullet, having the kind of energy we call kinetic. When the bullet is stopped suddenly by impact, the energy of its motion is transformed to random motion of atoms. This disordered energy is evidenced by the heating of the bullet and the area of impact.

Work involves orderly motion. But when work is done against friction and dissipated into internal energy, the disorderly motion of molecules is increased. Thus, there is an accompanying increase in disorder.

There are many examples in nature where energy processes are observed to go toward a state of greater disorder. The melting of an isolated crystalline solid is an example. When heat is added, the system goes from a well-ordered array of molecules in a crystal to a less well-ordered array of molecules in the liquid without a change in the temperature of the sample. Entropy may thus be thought of as a measure of the order-disorder in the system.

Most natural processes proceed toward a state of greater entropy as well as toward increased disorder. Thus, it is not surprising to note that physicists have found a connection between the thermodynamic concept of entropy and the statistical concept of disorder.

Two quantities can be used to describe heat—one to measure the energy (the calorie or the joule), and the other to measure the quantity of disorder (entropy, a mathematical concept).

QUESTIONS

Group A
1. What is thermodynamics?
2. State (a) the first law of thermodynamics, (b) the second law of thermodynamics.
3. What is the meaning of the term *mechanical equivalent of heat*?
4. What is the metric value for the mechanical equivalent of heat?
5. What is (a) an isothermal process, (b) an adiabatic process?
6. What is the purpose of (a) a heat source, (b) a heat sink?
7. On what does the efficiency of an ideal engine depend?
8. How can we cause heat to flow from a body at a lower temperature to one at a higher temperature?

handwritten top margin: $Kg\ m/s^2 = N\cdot m$ $\frac{Kg\,m^2}{s^2} = a\ joule$

9. How does the first law of thermodynamics differ from the mechanical conservation of energy principle?
10. Describe Joule's method for determining the mechanical equivalent of heat.
11. What physical law governs the isothermal expansion and compression of an ideal gas?
12. What physical laws govern the adiabatic expansion and compression of an ideal gas?
13. (a) What is the source of the heat equivalent of the work done by an ideal gas during isothermal expansion? (b) What happens to the heat equivalent of the work done on an ideal gas during isothermal compression?
14. (a) What is the source of the heat equivalent of the work done by an ideal gas during adiabatic expansion? (b) What happens to the heat equivalent of the work done on an ideal gas during adiabatic compression?
15. When an ideal gas expands isothermally, it does work on its surroundings. (a) Does the energy of the gas change during this process? (b) What is the source of the energy for this work?
16. (a) Does a gas do work on its surroundings when it expands adiabatically? (b) What is the source of energy by which the gas can do this work?

Group B

handwritten: internal energy measured in cal.

handwritten: $\Delta w = \Delta q$

PROBLEMS

handwritten: 900 joule

Group A

1. How many joules can ideally be obtained from 1.00×10^4 cal? *(handwritten: 41,)*
2. Gasoline, mass density 0.700 g/cm³ liberates 1.15×10^4 cal/g when it is burned. How many joules of work can be obtained by burning 1.00 liter of gasoline? *(handwritten: 3.37 × 10⁷ joules)*
3. The water going over Niagara Falls drops 50.6 m. How much warmer is the water at the bottom of the falls than it is at the top? Disregard any possible effects of evaporation of water during the fall. *(handwritten: .118 °C)*

Group B

4. The natural gas burned in a gas turbine has a heating value of 1.00×10^5 cal/g. If 2.00 g of gas is burned in the turbine each second, and the efficiency of the turbine is 25.0%, what is the output in kilowatts? *(handwritten: 209 kw)*
5. How much heat will be produced if a 1.25-kg mass, moving at 26.6 m/sec, strikes a wall and all the energy is converted to heat? *(handwritten: 106 cal.)*
6. The powder used in firing a 5.00-g bullet from a rifle produces 750 calories of heat when burned. In the process of firing the rifle, 30.0% of the energy is converted into the kinetic energy of the bullet. Determine the muzzle speed of the bullet. *(handwritten: 614 m/s)*
7. A lead block falls from a height of 125 m and strikes a cement block. Assume that half the energy of the lead block is converted into in- *(handwritten: 4.79 C°)*

handwritten bottom: $m\,g\,h =$ $(9.8)\,125\,m$

ternal energy in the lead. Determine the rise in temperature of the lead block.

8. What must be the speed in meters per second of a snowball at 0°C, if the snowball is completely melted by its impact against a wall assuming that all the energy is absorbed by the snowball?

817 m/s

9. The following data were obtained by the use of an apparatus like that shown in Fig. 9-1: descending mass, 2.50 kg; distance moved, 1.50 m; number of descends, 25; temperature rise of water and calorimeter, 0.31 C°; mass of water, 0.700 kg; mass of copper calorimeter, 0.150 kg. Calculate the mechanical equivalent of heat. (Assume that the mass has no kinetic energy when it stops descending.)

4.16 j/cal

10. What is the theoretically highest efficiency of a steam engine which has a steam input temperature of 200.0°C and a steam exhaust temperature of 100.0°C?

21.1 %

11. Referring to Problem 10, assume the temperature of the heat sink to remain at 100.0°C. What input temperature would be required to increase the efficiency of this engine to 30.0%?

260°C

Chapter 10

Waves

THE NATURE OF WAVES

10.1 Energy transfer

We know that some mechanism must be provided to transport energy from one point to another. The place where energy is available is often different from the place where it is needed. One way of transporting energy is by the movement of materials or objects from one place to another. Winds and projectiles in flight are well-known examples. When a baseball strikes a window, the glass is shattered by energy transferred from the ball during impact. Thermal convection is a familiar process for transferring heat energy from one point to another by the gross movement of quantities of heated gas or liquid between the points.

A more interesting, but more complicated way of transporting energy involves waves. We shall recognize several natural phenomena that are examples of waves. We study these phenomena all together because of a very important simplifying fact: the ideas and language used to describe waves are the same, regardless of the kind of wave involved. The basic concept in our use of the term *wave* is that the wave involves some quantity or disturbance which *changes in magnitude with respect to time at a given location* and *changes in magnitude from place to place at a given time.* The common characteristic of all types of waves is that energy is transferred by the wave without the transport of matter.

A stone dropped into a quiet pond produces a familiar wave pattern on the surface of the water. A sound is heard because a wave travels from the source through the intervening atmosphere. The energy released by a great explosion can shatter

South African Tourist Corp.

The periodic nature of water waves is evident as they break over this beach.

14 *Wave*

15

223

windows far from its source because a wave of compression moves out from the source in all directions. The "shock wave" of a sonic boom can have similar destructive effects. *These waves are disturbances that move through a material medium.*

We are able to explain some properties of light by means of waves. Physicists have demonstrated that light waves, radio waves, infrared and ultraviolet waves, X rays, and gamma rays are fundamentally similar. These are *electromagnetic waves.* Their transmission through space does not require a material medium.

The nature of electromagnetic waves will be discussed in later chapters. For the present we shall be concerned with waves traveling in a material substance, a medium composed of matter. We call these waves *mechanical waves.* Such wave motion is related to harmonic motion. However, when we described harmonic motion earlier in Section 5.10, we were concerned with a single particle vibrating about its equilibrium position. Now we must consider many particles vibrating about their respective equilibrium positions as the wave travels through the medium. It is important to understand the behavior of waves because the language and ideas of wave motion are needed to correctly describe the motions of very small particles of matter.

As particles at some distance away from a source of vibrational energy are made to vibrate, their vibration shows that they possess energy. The energy has been transmitted to particles far from the source. This behavior reveals a very important characteristic of waves. They provide a mechanism by which energy is transmitted from one place to another *without the physical transfer of matter between these places.*

10.2 Mechanical waves

*A **mechanical wave** is a disturbance in the equilibrium positions of particles in matter.* To produce mechanical waves, we need a *source of energy* which produces a disturbance, and an *elastic medium* to transmit the disturbance. An elastic medium behaves as if it were an array of particles connected by springs, with each particle having an equilibrium position. A simple model of such a medium is shown in Fig. 10-1.

If particle **1** is displaced from its equilibrium position by being pulled away from particle **2**, it is immediately subjected to a force from particle **2** which attempts to restore particle **1** to its original position. At the same time, particle **1** exerts an equal but opposite force on particle **2** which attempts to displace it from its equilibrium position. Similar events occur, but in opposite directions, if particle **1** is displaced from its equilibrium position by being pushed toward particle **2**.

Suppose particle **1** is displaced by an energy source. It exerts a force which displaces particle **2**. Particle **2**, in turn, being dis-

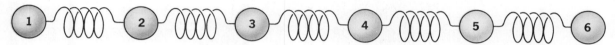

10-1 An elastic medium behaves as if it were an array of particles connected by springs, with each particle occupying an equilibrium position.

placed from its equilibrium position, exerts a force on particle **3**, which is in turn displaced. In this way, the displacement travels along from particle to particle. Because the particles have inertia, the displacements do not all occur at the same time, but successively as the disturbance affects particles farther and farther from the source. The energy initially imparted to particle **1** by the energy source is transmitted from particle to particle in the medium.

Now let us use as an elastic medium a long spiral spring stretched between two rigid supports, as shown in Fig. 10-2(A). Suppose a portion of the spring is displaced at point **2** to form a *crest* or upward displacement. See Fig. 10-2(B). To force the spring into this shape, we had to pull up on point **2** while points **1** and **3** were held in place. When we suddenly release the spring at points **2** and **3**, point **2** accelerates downward and point **3** accelerates upward. The crest moves toward the right as in Fig. 10-2(C). Similarly, as the spring in the region of point **3** moves downward, the spring in the region of point **4** is displaced upward. In this manner the crest travels along the spring—Figs. 10-2(D) and (E). A *trough* or downward displacement formed at **2** travels along the spring in similar fashion.

A single nonrepeated disturbance such as a single crest is called a single-wave pulse, or simply a *pulse*. The displacements of the particles of the medium (the coiled spring) caused by the pulse are *perpendicular* to the direction in which the pulse travels. Such a pulse is said to be *transverse*.

If a regular succession of pulses is applied to the coiled spring, a series of crests and troughs travels through the medium. This wave disturbance is called a *continuous wave* or a *wave train*. Again, the displacements of the particles of the medium are perpendicular to the direction in which the wave train travels. The wave motion is transverse. ***Transverse waves*** *are those in which the displacements of particles of the medium are perpendicular to the direction of propagation of the wave.*

Now, let us use a similar spiral spring, but instead of pulling the spring out of line, we pinch several coils closer together at one end, as in Fig. 10-3(A). Such a distortion is called a *compression*. When these compressed coils are released, they attempt

10.3 Transverse wave

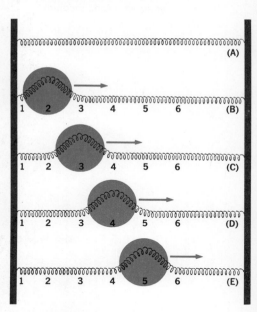

10-2 A transverse pulse traveling along an elastic medium.

16

10.4 Longitudinal wave

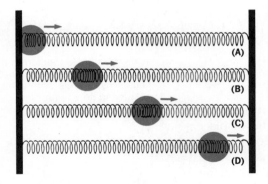 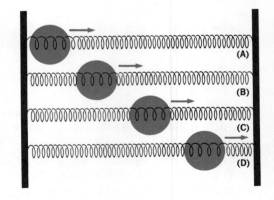

10-3 (Left) A compression pulse traveling along an elastic medium.

10-4 (Right) A rarefaction pulse traveling along an elastic medium.

to spread out to their equilibrium positions. In doing so, they compress the coils immediately to the right. In this way the compression moves toward the right. See Figs. 10-3(B), (C), and (D).

If the coils at the left end of the spring are stretched apart, instead of compressed, a *rarefaction* is formed. When released, the rarefaction travels along the spring just as the compression did. This effect is shown in Fig. 10-4.

These pulses propagate along the spring by displacing the particles of the spring in directions *parallel* to the direction the pulses are traveling. They are examples of *longitudinal pulses.* Similarly, a continuous wave disturbance of this type gives rise to *longitudinal wave motion.* Energy is transferred from particle to particle along the medium without motion of the medium as a whole. **Longitudinal waves** *are those in which the displacements of particles of the medium are parallel to the direction of propagation of the wave.*

10.5 Periodic waves

We have examined the effect of a single, nonrecurring wave disturbance on one end of a long, rigidly mounted spring. Now let us consider what happens if similar disturbances are repeated periodically.

Suppose we attach the left end of a long spring to a weight suspended by a second spring as in Fig. 10-5. Assume that the weight can move up and down without friction between its vertical guides. If the weight is pulled down slightly and then released, it will vibrate within the guides with simple harmonic motion. Such a motion is *periodic.* That is, the weight repeats its motion once every certain time interval T, called the *period* of vibration. Since the vibrating weight is attached to the end of the long spring, it acts as a source of periodic disturbances generating a *transverse wave train* which moves to the right along the spring. The transverse wave is shown in Fig. 10-5 at the

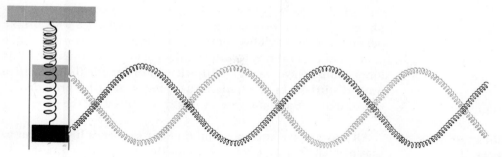

instant the vibrating weight is at the upper limit of its excursion and again at the instant it is at the lower limit of its excursion.

This periodic transverse wave carries energy away from the vibrating weight. Unless energy is supplied to it, the weight loses amplitude and comes to rest. In order for a source to generate a continuous wave of uniform amplitude, energy must be supplied to the source at the same rate as the source transmits it to the medium. Then the successive wave disturbances will be identical. When the periodic wave is a simple harmonic wave, it gives each particle of the medium a simple harmonic motion.

A periodic longitudinal wave can be generated by the apparatus shown in Fig. 10-6(A). The long spring is attached to a metal ball fastened to one end of a hacksaw blade. The other

10-5 The oscillating weight generates a periodic transverse wave. The waves in color and the black waves represent a time difference of 1/2T.

10-6 (A) An apparatus for generating longitudinal waves. (B) A periodic longitudinal wave in a section of the spring.

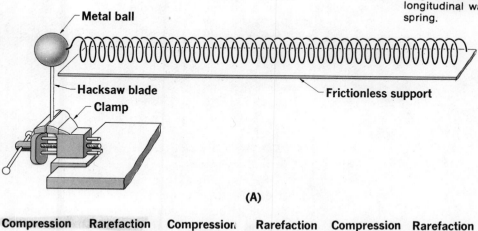

Metal ball

Hacksaw blade
Clamp

Frictionless support

(A)

Compression   Rarefaction   Compression   Rarefaction   Compression   Rarefaction

(B)

end of the blade is rigidly clamped. If the metal ball is displaced slightly to one side and released, it vibrates with simple harmonic motion. This motion produces a series of periodic compressions and rarefactions in the spring, and thus a periodic longitudinal wave. See Fig. 10-6(B). In order for the successive wave disturbances to be identical, energy must be provided to the source at the same rate as it is transmitted by the wave.

10.6 Characteristics of waves

All waves have several common characteristics in addition to that of transferring energy without the transport of matter. As a periodic wave travels through a medium, the particles of the medium vibrate about their equilibrium positions in identical fashion. However, the particles are in corresponding positions of their vibratory motion at different times. The position and motion of a particle indicate the *phase* of the wave. Particles which have the same displacement and are moving in the same direction are said to be *in phase*. Particles **a** and **b** in both waves of Fig. 10-7 are in phase. Those with opposite displacement and moving in the opposite direction (particles **b** and **c**) are in *opposite phase,* or 180° out of phase.

10-7 Characteristics of transverse and longitudinal waves. The black open circles show the equilibrium positions of the particles of the medium. The white dots show their displaced positions. The black arrows indicate the displacements of the particles from their equilibrium positions. The white arrows are the velocity vectors for the particles above them.

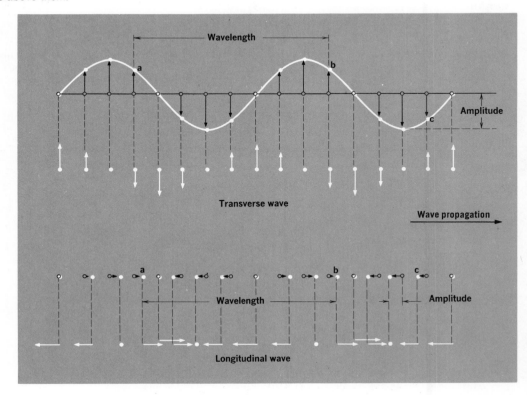

2 0

The *frequency, f,* of a periodic wave is the number of crests (or troughs) passing a given point in unit time. It is the same as the frequency of the simple harmonic motion of the source and is conventionally expressed in terms of the vibrating frequency of the source. Thus, the frequency of a motion is the number of vibrations, oscillations, or cycles per unit of time. The **MKS** unit of frequency is the *hertz* (hz), 1 hz being equivalent to the expression "one cycle per second." Observe that "cycle" is not a unit of measure and, therefore, is not a part of the dimensional structure of the hertz. The dimension of the hertz is simply sec^{-1}. For example, a wave generated at 60 cycles per second has a frequency of 60 hz, which is expressed dimensionally as 60/sec.

$$f = \textbf{60 cycles per second} = \textbf{60 hz} = \textbf{60/sec}$$

The *period, T,* of a wave is the time between the passage of two successive crests past a given point. It is the same as the period of the simple harmonic motion of the source. Period is, therefore, the reciprocal of frequency.

$$f = \frac{1}{T} \quad \text{and} \quad T = \frac{1}{f}$$

The *wavelength,* represented by the Greek letter λ (lambda), is the distance between any particle in a wave and the nearest particle that is in phase with it. The distance between particles **a** and **b** in either of the waves shown in Fig. 10-7 is one wavelength. It is the distance advanced by the wave motion in one period, T.

An advancing wave has a finite *speed, v,* for a given transmitting medium. Wave speed may be quite slow, as that of water waves. It may be moderately fast, as that of sound waves which travel with speeds of the order of 10^2–10^3 m/sec. It may be the speed of light or radio waves, 3×10^8 m/sec. The speed of a wave depends primarily on the nature of the wave disturbance and on the medium through which it passes. Wave speed may also depend on wavelength in certain media.

An interesting aspect of a surface wave on a liquid is that its speed of propagation depends on its wavelength. Ripples produced by a very gentle wind or vibrations of high frequency have very short wavelengths. The wave speed is governed by the surface tension of the liquid, a measure of the tendency of the surface to resist stretching. In this case, the *shorter* the wavelength, the higher is the wave speed.

A strong steady wind may produce surface waves of very long wavelength. Here, the wave speed is governed by gravity which provides a restoring force. Such waves are called *gravity waves.* In this case, the *longer* the wavelength, the higher is the wave speed.

When the speed of a wave depends on its wavelength (or frequency), we say the transmitting medium is *dispersive.* A glass prism separates (disperses) a beam of white light into a color spectrum, with light of different wavelengths emerging in different directions. Glass is a dispersive medium for light waves. We can observe rainbows because water droplets in the atmosphere disperse sunlight in the same way. In fact, all electromagnetic waves propagating through matter (but not in vacuum) show dispersion.

Since a wave travels the distance λ in the time T for a complete vibration of the source, its speed v is given by the expression

$$v = \frac{\lambda}{T}$$

and because

$$f = \frac{1}{T}$$

then

$$v = f\lambda$$

This important equation is true for all periodic waves, whether transverse or longitudinal, no matter what the medium is.

The maximum displacement of the vibrating particles of the medium from their equilibrium positions is called the *amplitude* of the wave. It is related to the energy flow in the system.

10.7 Amplitude and energy

In all forms of traveling waves, energy is transmitted from one point to another. By expending energy a vibrating source can cause a harmonic disturbance in a medium. The energy expended per unit of time depends on the amplitude, the frequency, and the mass of the particles of the medium at the source. Simple harmonic motion (vibrational motion) of a particle of the medium represents an amount of energy, part kinetic and part potential, that it has at any instant. The disturbance is transferred through the medium because of the influence that a particle has on other particles adjacent to it. Thus the wave carries energy away from the source.

Assuming no losses in the system, the energy transported by the advancing wave during a given time is the same as the energy expended by the source during that time. The energy transported (and the energy expended) per unit of time is the *power* transmitted by the wave.

If the wave amplitude is doubled, the vibrational energy is increased fourfold. Doubling the vibrating frequency has the same effect. *The rate of transfer of energy, or the power transmitted by a wave system is proportional to the square of the wave amplitude and the square of the wave frequency.*

Surface waves on water emanating from a point source undergo a decrease in amplitude as they move away from their source. Each advancing wave crest is an expanding circle. The energy contained in each crest is a fixed amount and the crest is expanding. The energy per unit length of crest must decrease. Thus, the amplitude of the wave must diminish. This effect is greater for sound waves as the advancing crests are expanding spheres.

We know from experience that the amplitude of a vibrating pendulum or spring gradually decreases with time and the vibrations eventually stop. Frictional and resistance effects which oppose the motion slowly remove energy from the vibrating system. Similarly, in a wave system energy is dissipated and the wave amplitude gradually diminishes. *The reduction in amplitude of a wave due to the dissipation of wave energy as it travels away from the source is called **damping**.* Damping effects may be quite small over relatively short distances.

South African Tourist Corp.

A surfer makes use of the energy in wave motion.

2 6

QUESTIONS

Group A

1. In what ways may energy be transferred?
2. Distinguish between mechanical waves and electromagnetic waves.
3. What are three requirements for the production of mechanical waves?
4. (a) What is a disturbance? (b) What constitutes the disturbance when a wave moves across the surface of a pond? (c) What constitutes the disturbance when a longitudinal wave travels through the air?
5. How does an elastic material behave as a wave medium?
6. (a) Distinguish between transverse and longitudinal waves. (b) Give an example of each.
7. Define (a) pulse; (b) crest; (c) trough; (d) compression; (e) rarefaction.
8. For wave motion, define (a) speed; (b) phase; (c) frequency; (d) period; (e) wavelength; (f) amplitude.
9. What does a wave source supply to the medium through which the wave passes?
10. A pebble is dropped into a quiet pond of water. Neglecting damping losses, how does the amplitude of the resulting wave disturbance vary with the distance from the source?
11. Neglecting damping losses, would you expect the amplitude of an advancing surface wave on a pond to diminish with distance from its point source at the same rate as an advancing sound wave diminishes with distance from its point source in air? Justify your conclusion qualitatively.

27 Torsional wave

PROBLEMS

Group A

1.5m/s

1. What is the speed of a periodic wave disturbance, frequency 2.5 hz and wavelength 0.60 m?

8 m

2. Calculate the wavelength of water waves which have frequency 0.50 hz and speed 4.0 m/sec.

3 m

3. The speed of transverse waves in a string is 15 m/sec. If a source produces a disturbance, frequency 5.0 hz, what is the wavelength of the wave produced?

3 m , 30 m/s

4. A periodic transverse wave, frequency 10.0 hz, travels along a string. The distance between a crest and either adjacent trough is 1.50 m. What is (a) the wavelength, (b) the speed of the wave?

8 m/s

5. A periodic longitudinal wave, frequency $\overline{2}0$ hz, travels along a coil spring. If the distance between successive compressions is 0.40 m, calculate the speed of the wave.

2.5 m

6. What is the wavelength of a periodic longitudinal wave in a coil spring, frequency 8.0 hz, and speed $\overline{2}0$ m/sec?

per 2.5s freq 4Hz

7. A wave generator produces 16 pulses in 4.0 seconds. (a) What is its period? (b) What is its frequency?

3.3cm/s

8. One pulse is generated every 0.10 sec in a tank of water and the wavelength of the surface wave measures 3.3 cm. What is the propagation speed?

$f \frac{v}{\lambda} \lambda$

$T = \frac{1}{f}$ *$v = f\lambda$*   *$.10 \times 3.3$*

WAVE INTERACTIONS

10.8 Properties of waves

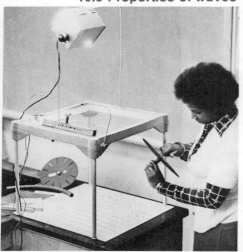

Alex Mulligan

10-8 The ripple tank provides a means of observing the properties of waves in the laboratory.

In any study of wave behavior, the various properties common to all kinds of waves should be recognized. These common properties are: *rectilinear* (straight line) *propagation, reflection, refraction, diffraction,* and *interference.* Being familiar with the properties of waves helps to determine whether an observed phenomenon involves a wave or not.

Surface waves on water are particularly useful in studying wave properties. A surface wave is easily generated, its speed is quite slow, and the transparency of the water to light allows the wave pattern to be projected on a screen. A continuous wave can be established on the water surface by allowing a probe to dip into the surface periodically. An apparatus for observing wave motion on the surface of water is shown in Fig. 10-8. It is called a ripple tank.

The diagram in Fig. 10-9 shows how images of surface wave crests can be projected on a screen. The ripple tank has a glass bottom which allows light to be projected down through the water and the glass onto a screen below the tank. The crests appear on the screen as bright regions and troughs as dark regions.

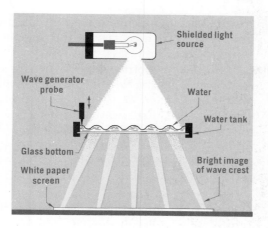

10-9 A functional diagram of a ripple tank.

We can generate a train of straight waves in a ripple tank by placing a long straight edge (like that of a ruler) along the surface of the water and causing it to vibrate up and down. A photograph of the image of such a continuous wave is shown in Fig. 10-10. The wave crests are the parallel white lines. The wave troughs are the dark spaces separating the crests. The surfaces whose particles are all in the same phase of motion are called *wavefronts.* The paths of the two points, **a** and **b**, show that *the direction of propagation of the advancing straight wave is perpendicular to the wavefront.*

By changing from a straight to a pointed probe such as the tip of a pencil, we can generate a train of circular waves. See Fig. 10-11. Here the advancing wave crests are expanding circles; the wavefronts are moving out in all directions from the center of disturbance. The letters **a** and **b** locate two points on an expanding crest. Their paths show that *the directions of propagation of these two segments of the advancing circular wave lie along radial lines away from the center of disturbance.* The same is

10.9 Rectilinear propagation

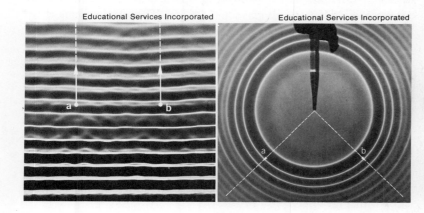

Educational Services Incorporated   Educational Services Incorporated

10-10 (Left) Periodic straight wave moving across a ripple tank. The wavelength is the distance between adjacent troughs.

10-11 (Right) Periodic circular wave generated by a point source in a ripple tank. The wave moves outward from the point of generation in everwidening circles.

true of all other points on any circular wave crest. The radial lines are perpendicular to the segments of the wavefront through which they pass.

From these experiments with the ripple tank we observe that *continuous waves traveling in a uniform medium propagate in straight lines perpendicular to the advancing wavefronts.* The uniform spacing between the wave crests suggests that the wave speed in the medium is constant. Considering the speed and direction of propagation of traveling waves, we can state that *the wave velocity at every point along the advancing wavefront is perpendicular to the wavefront.*

10.10 Reflection

Ken Chen

The waves generated at one end of this wave machine are propagated through a twisting wire.

Familiar examples of reflection are the sound echoes that return from a distant canyon wall, the reflection of light from a mirror, and the reflection of waves from the edge of a pool. Our image as seen in a mirror appears to be reversed, right for left. The crest of a water wave is reflected from the pool side as a crest traveling in a different direction. The echo of a sound retains the character of the original sound.

About the only inference we can draw from these casual observations is that *a wave is turned back, or **reflected**, when it encounters a barrier that is the boundary of the medium in which the wave is traveling.* A close examination of the boundary conditions might reveal much more about the nature of reflection.

Suppose we generate a single straight pulse in the ripple tank with a straight barrier placed across the tray parallel to the advancing wavefront. When the pulse reaches the barrier, it is reflected back in the direction from which it came. No disturbance appears in the water behind the barrier. The paths of the incident pulse (approaching the barrier) and the reflected pulse lie perpendicular to the surface of the barrier.

The angle formed by the path of incidence and the perpendicular (normal) to the reflecting surface at the point of incidence is called the *angle of incidence, i.* The angle formed by the path of reflection and the normal is the *angle of reflection, r.* In this instance both the incident and reflected angles are 0° and i is equal to r.

Certainly i and r equal 0° only when the incident wave approaches the barrier along a line perpendicular to it. We may then ask whether the equality between i and r is coincidental in this situation, or is characteristic of reflection in general. To investigate the relationship of i and r further, we need to change the position of the barrier so it is no longer parallel to the wavefronts and then send more pulses against it. A diagram of the reflection of a single pulse from a diagonal barrier is shown in Fig. 10-12.

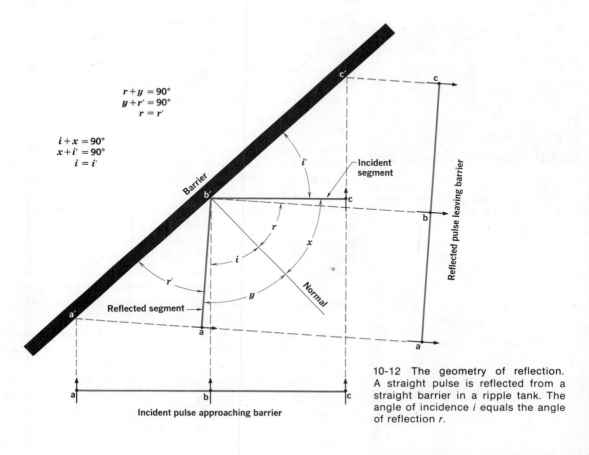

$$r + y = 90°$$
$$y + r' = 90°$$
$$r = r'$$

$$i + x = 90°$$
$$x + i' = 90°$$
$$i = i'$$

Barrier

Incident segment

Reflected pulse leaving barrier

i'

r

x

i

r'

y

Normal

Reflected segment

Incident pulse approaching barrier

10-12 The geometry of reflection. A straight pulse is reflected from a straight barrier in a ripple tank. The angle of incidence *i* equals the angle of reflection *r*.

Reasonably good measurements can be made of the angles that the incident and reflected pulse make with the barrier by placing suitable markers on the screen parallel to the projected images of the pulse. We shall call these angles i' and r' respectively. Measurements of i' and r' for several positions indicate consistently that these angles are equal. Figure 10-12 shows that i' and i are equal angles and r' and r are equal angles, thus i and r are equal.

$$i = r$$

We can state this relationship as a ***law of reflection***. *When a wave disturbance is reflected at the boundary of a transmitting medium, the angle of incidence i is equal to the angle of reflection r.* A photograph of a periodic straight wave reflected from a diagonally placed barrier is shown in Fig. 10-13.

The reflection of a circular wave from a straight barrier is shown in Fig. 10-14. Each segment of the expanding wavefront

Education Services Incorporated

10-13 Reflection of a periodic straight wave from a diagonal barrier. The left portion of each wave crest has already been reflected toward the right.

10-14 A circular wave generated at the center of the photograph is reflected from a straight barrier.

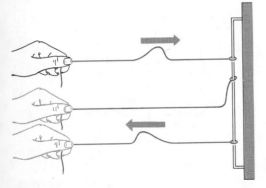

10-15 Reflection of a pulse at the "free" end of a taut string. The string is shown terminated in a frictionless ring which allows the end segment unrestrained displacement in the plane of the pulse.

reflected from the barrier surface rebounds according to the principle just stated. Observe that the reflected portions of the wave crests are arcs of circles. The apparent center of these reflected wave crests is as far behind the reflecting surface as the real center of disturbance is in front of it.

Reflection may be partial or complete, depending on the severity of the change at the reflecting boundary. If there is no boundary mechanism for extracting energy from the wave, all of the energy incident with the wave is reflected back with it.

When a surface wave in the ripple tank encounters the straight barrier, a rigid vertical bulkhead, the vertical transverse component of the wave is unrestrained. The wave crest is reflected *as a crest*, the trough *as a trough*. The surface wave is reflected without a change in phase. *A boundary that allows unrestrained displacement of the particles of a medium reflects waves with no change in phase.* The bulkhead acts as a *free-end* or *open-end* termination to the wave medium.

Suppose we send a transverse pulse traveling along a stretched string, the far end of which is free. Having such a string presents no problem in a "thought" experiment. In practice, the free-ended termination might be approximated as shown in Fig. 10-15. To the extent that the termination is frictionless, the end of the string is free to move in the plane of the pulse.

After arriving at the free end of the string, the pulse is reflected as shown in Fig. 10-15. Observe that it has not been inverted. Displacement of the particles of the string is in the same direction as that for the incident pulse. During the time interval that the pulse is arriving at the free end of the string and the reflected pulse is leaving it, the combined effect of the two pulses causes the free end to experience twice the displacement as from either pulse alone. *Reflection at the free-end termination of a medium occurs without a change in phase.*

Now, suppose we clamp the far end of the string in a fixed position and send a transverse pulse toward this termination. See Fig. 10-16. When the pulse arrives at the fixed end, it applies an upward force to the clamp. An equal but opposite reaction force is applied to the string generating a reflected pulse which is inverted with respect to the incident pulse. *Reflection at the fixed termination of a medium occurs with a phase shift of 180°.* In general, we may conclude that *a boundary which restrains the displacement of the particles of a medium reflects waves inverted in phase.*

Some examples of reflecting terminations for different kinds of wave disturbances are given in Table 10-1. The first three systems listed summarize the phase relations discussed in this section.

Table 10-1   REFLECTION BEHAVIOR

Type of wave	Example	Termination	
		For in-phase reflection	For out-of-phase reflection
transverse (mechanical)	stretched string	free-ended	fixed ended
longitudinal (sound)	air motion in organ pipe	open pipe	closed pipe
liquid surface (vertical component)	water	solid bulkhead	(no simple analog)
optical (electromagnetic)	light	(no simple analog)	mirror
electric	transmission line	short circuit	open circuit

Generally, something less than total reflection occurs at the termination of a transmitting medium. The "free" end of a vibrating string as well as the fixed end must be supported in some manner and some of the wave energy is transferred to the medium providing this support.

The speed of the wave disturbance depends on the properties of the transmitting medium. Thus, waves in the string and in the terminating medium travel at different speeds. If this difference in speed is very great, the portion of wave energy reflected at the boundary will be very large. If the two wave speeds are very similar, little reflection will occur at the boundary. An intermediate effect is seen in Fig. 10-18, where partial reflection at the boundary is evident. Light is partially transmitted and partially reflected when it passes from air into glass because of the difference in the transmission speeds in the two media.

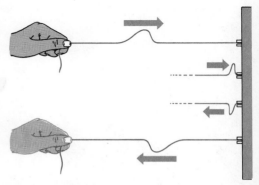

10-16 Reflection of a pulse at the clamped end of a taut string. The string is terminated in a fixed position and displacement of the end segment is restrained.

10.11 Impedance

If we were to apply the same wave-producing force to a light string and to a heavy rope, two entirely different *displacement velocities* would result. The string would experience a very large displacement velocity compared to that of the rope. We could say that the ratio of the *wave producing force* to the *displacement velocity* is quite small for the string and quite large for the rope. In the study of waves, this *ratio of the applied wave-producing force to the resulting displacement velocity is called the* **impedance** *of the medium.*

$$\text{Impedance} = \frac{\text{wave-producing force}}{\text{resulting velocity of the medium}}$$

By this definition, the string is said to have a relatively low impedance and the rope a relatively high impedance. Thus, the impedance of a wave medium denotes the ease (or difficulty) with which a wave disturbance of a given amplitude can be launched in it.

The concept of impedance is quite general and can be applied to wave media of all kinds. For a stretched string, the wave-producing force is the transverse oscillatory force applied to the end of the string. The displacement velocity is the oscillating transverse velocity imparted to the particles of the first portion of the string. In an organ pipe, the ratio of the alternating compressional force applied to the molecules of the air to the longitudinal oscillating velocity acquired by these molecules defines the acoustic impedance of the air column.

In cases of *total* in-phase reflection discussed in Section 10.10, the impedance of the terminating media may be considered to be zero. For *total* out-of-phase reflection, the impedance of the terminating medium is infinite. In systems having infinite or zero impedance terminations, reflection is complete and no wave energy is transferred to the termination.

If the terminating impedance exactly matches that of the transmitting medium, the wave energy is completely transferred to the termination and there is no reflection. What about systems that fall in between the extreme mismatch (zero or infinite impedance terminations) and the perfect impedance match? In these cases some energy is transferred to the termination and some is reflected back through the medium of the incident wave.

In practical energy transfer systems, an abrupt impedance discontinuity between two wave propagation media causes unwanted wave reflection which wastes energy. Numerous devices and techniques are used to smooth over an impedance mismatch and reduce or prevent reflections. They are called *impedance transformers.*

A cheerleader's megaphone is a simple approximation of an acoustic impedance transformer. It effectively matches the impedance of the air column of the throat and mouth to the free air. The coating on an optical lens acts as an impedance transformer. It reduces reflection at the air-glass boundary and causes a greater portion of the total incident light energy to be transmitted through the lens. There are many applications of impedance transformers in electric and electronic systems. In general, whenever a device intended to receive wave energy efficiently cannot be designed to have the same impedance as the transmitting medium, it must be coupled to the medium by means of an impedance transformer.

10.12 Refraction   The properties of the medium through which a certain wave disturbance moves determine the propagation speed of that disturbance. It is not surprising, therefore, to find that traveling waves passing from one medium into another experience a change in speed *at the boundary* of the two media.

From the wave equation, $v = f\lambda$, we see that the wavelength λ for a wave disturbance of a given frequency f is a function of its speed v in the medium through which it is propagating. If the speed decreases when the wave enters a second medium, the wavelength is shortened proportionately. If the speed increases, the wavelength is lengthened proportionately.

A useful aspect of water waves is the relation of the speed of surface waves to the depth of the water. Such wave disturbances travel faster in deep water than in shallow water. For a given wave frequency, the wavelength in deep water is longer than it is in shallow water. Therefore water of two different depths acts just like two different transmitting media for wave propagation.

This difference is easily observed in the ripple tank by arranging the tray to have two different depths of water. Then surface waves are generated that travel across the boundary of the two regions. In Fig. 10-17 the deep water representing the medium of higher propagating speed is in the lower portion of the photograph. The wave moves toward the shallow water in the upper portion. The boundary between the deep and shallow water is parallel to the advancing wavefront. Thus each incident wave crest approaches the shallow region along the normal to the boundary.

Observe that the change in wavelength is abrupt. It occurs simultaneously over the entire wavefront at the boundary of the deep and shallow water. All segments of the advancing wavefront change speed at the same time and the wave continues to propagate in its original direction.

Suppose we adjust the deep and shallow regions of the tray so that the boundary is no longer parallel to the advancing straight wave but cuts diagonally across its path. This arrangement is shown in Fig. 10-18. Each advancing wave crest now approaches the boundary obliquely. Adjacent segments of the wavefront pass from deep to shallow water successively rather than simultaneously. At the boundary, the direction of the wavefront changes; the advancing wave has undergone *refraction*. **Refraction** *is the bending of the path of a wave disturbance as it passes obliquely from one medium into another of different propagation speed.*

The refraction of surface waves on water is shown by diagram in Fig. 10-19. As the wave passes into the shallow water where its speed is less and its wavelength is shorter, it is refracted *toward* the normal drawn to the deep-shallow boundary. The angle of refraction r is smaller than the angle of incidence i. (The angle r is the angle between the path of the refracted wave and the normal.)

Had we generated the wave in the shallow region and directed it obliquely toward the boundary, it would have been refracted

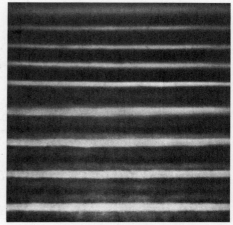

Educational Services Incorporated

10-17   The passage of a surface wave from deep to shallow water. The shallow water is at the top of the picture.

Educational Services Incorporated

10-18   Refraction of a surface wave at the boundary of deep and shallow water in a ripple tank.

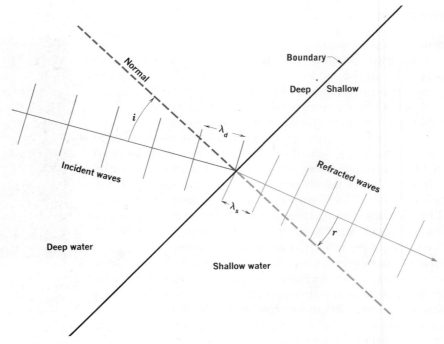

Normal

Boundary

Deep / Shallow

i

λ_d

Incident waves

Refracted waves

λ_s

r

Deep water

Shallow water

10-19 The geometry of refraction. Water of two depths in the ripple tank represents two media of different speeds.

away from the normal on entering the deep water. Angle r would have been larger than i. The change in direction and the change in speed occur simultaneously. How are these two changes related? We shall investigate this question quantitatively later when we study optical refraction. There the measurements we need can be made with reasonable precision.

10.13 Diffraction

Sounds can be heard even though they may originate around the corner of a building. The source of the sound disturbance cannot be seen around the corner, however. Rectilinear propagation appears to hold in this situation for light but not for sound. The building is an obstruction which prevents the straight-line transmission of light from the source of the sound disturbance to the observer.

Perhaps, where sound waves are concerned, the corner of the building creates a discontinuity in the transmitting medium which causes the waves to *spread.* Even if we find support for this idea, the question of the different behavior of light remains to be answered.

We will again use the ripple tank to observe wave behavior, this time with obstructions inserted into the transmitting medium. This may be done by placing two straight barriers across the tray on a line parallel to the straight wave generator. An opening (called an *aperture*) is left between them approximately equal to the wavelength of the wave to be used. When a periodic straight wave is sent out, the wave pattern beyond the barrier opening appears as shown in Fig. 10-20. As a segment of each wave crest passes through the aperture, it clearly spreads into the region beyond the barriers. *This spreading of a wave disturbance beyond the edge of a barrier is called* **diffraction**.

Sound waves spread around the edges of doorways in the same way water waves spread around the edges of obstructions. Audible sounds have wavelengths in air ranging from a few centimeters to several meters. The doorway of a room or building has dimensions within this range. This suggests, but does not prove, that a discontinuity such as an aperture in the path of an advancing wave will diffract the wave if its dimensions are comparable to the wavelength of the oncoming wave.

We produced the diffraction pattern in the ripple tank with a barrier aperture approximately the same width as the wavelength of the surface wave used. Suppose we shorten the wavelength by increasing the frequency of the wave generator stepwise and observe a series of patterns with waves of decreasing wavelengths.

The spreading of the wave at the edges of the aperture diminishes as the wavelength of the wave sent against them is shortened. When the wavelength is a small fraction of the width of the opening between the barriers, the wave segments passing through show little tendency to spread into the shadow regions beyond the barriers. These observations suggest that if the wavelength is very much smaller than the width of the aperture there will be no diffraction. The part of the straight wave that passes through the opening will continue in straight-line propagation.

How are these observations related to the fact that light is not diffracted at the edges of a doorway as is sound? The speed of light in air is high, being of the order of 3×10^8 m/sec. We have not yet dealt with light frequencies, but if they were extremely high, light wavelengths (v/f) would be very short. Then it would not be surprising to find that light is diffracted only by apertures having very small dimensions.

Indeed, the wavelength of visible light ranges from approximately 7.5×10^{-7} m down to about 4×10^{-7} m. This range of wavelengths suggests that the diffraction of light occurs in the realm of extremely small dimensions. Diffraction phenomena associated with light waves will be presented in Chapter 15.

PSSC Physics, D. C. Heath and Company, Boston

10-20 The diffraction of a periodic straight wave as it passes through a small aperture.

10.14 The superposition principle

We have described the passage of a single pulse and a continuous wave through a medium. It is possible for two or more wave disturbances to move through a medium at the same time. Sound waves from all the musical instruments of an orchestra move simultaneously through the air to our ears. Electromagnetic waves from many different radio and television stations travel simultaneously through regions of space to our receiving antennas. Nevertheless, we can listen to the sound of a particular musical instrument, or select a particular radio or television station. These facts suggest that each wave system proceeds independently along its pathway as if the other wave systems were not present.

Let us consider the effects of two periodic transverse waves traveling along a taut string in the same direction. The displacements they produce *at a particular instant* are shown in Fig. 10-21. These two waves have different amplitudes and frequencies. The displacements y_1 produced by one wave are represented by the black solid curve. The displacements y_2 produced by the other wave are represented by the black dashed curve. The resultant displacements Y all along the string at this instant are represented by the colored curve. These resultant displacements are determined by adding (algebraically) the displacements y_1 and y_2 for every point along the string.

In effect, the displacement of any particle of the medium by one wave at any instant is superimposed on the displacement of that particle by the other wave at that instant. The action of each wave on a particle is independent of the action of the other, and the particle displacement is the resultant of both wave actions. This phenomenon is known as *superposition*. The two waves are said to *superpose*.

The superposition principle: When two or more waves travel simultaneously through the same medium, (1) each wave proceeds independently as if no other waves were present, and (2) the resultant displacement of any particle at a given time is the vector sum of the displacements that the individual waves acting alone would give it.

This principle holds for light and all other electromagnetic waves as well as for sound waves and waves on a string or on a liquid surface, providing the displacements are small. For example, it does not hold for shock waves produced by violent explosions.

The component waves, y_1 and y_2 in Fig. 10-21, are simple sine waves. Either wave alone would cause each particle of the string to undergo simple harmonic motion about its equilibrium point as the wave traveled along the string. The resultant wave is periodic. However, it has a complicated (or complex) wave form. The superposition principle makes it possible to analyze a complex wave in terms of a combination of simple waves.

Actual wave disturbances generally have complex wave forms. For example, the sound waves produced by musical instruments

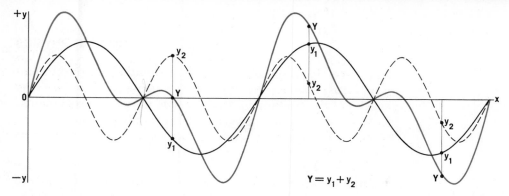

$$Y = y_1 + y_2$$

may be very complicated compared to simple sine wave variations. Wave forms of musical tones from a French horn and a trumpet are shown in Fig. 11-14 in Chapter 11. Each of these complex waves can be represented by a certain combination of simple waves which, by superposition, yield the complex wave form.

The general term *interference* is used to describe the *effects* produced by two or more waves which superpose while passing through a given region. Special consideration is given to *waves of the same frequency*, particularly in the case of sound and light. Interference phenomena are exclusively associated with waves. In fact, the existence of interference in experiments with light first established the wave character of light.

Let us consider two waves of the same frequency traversing the same medium simultaneously. *Each particle* of the medium is affected by *both* waves. Suppose the displacement of a particular particle caused by one wave at any instant is in the same direction as that caused by the other wave. Then the total displacement of *that particle at that instant* is the *sum* of the separate displacements (superposition principle). The resultant displacement is *greater* than either wave would have caused separately. This effect is called *constructive interference*.

On the other hand, if the displacement effects of the two waves on the particle are in opposite directions, they tend to cancel one another. The resultant displacement of *that particle at that instant* is the *difference* of the two separate displacements and is in the direction of the larger (superposition principle). The resultant displacement of the particle is *less* than one of the waves would have caused separately. This effect is called *destructive interference*.

If two such opposite displacement effects are equal in magnitude, the resultant displacement is zero. The destructive interference is complete. The particle is not displaced at all, but is in its equilibrium position *at that instant*.

Notice that we have been considering the effect of two waves on the position of just *one particle* of the medium at *one particular*

10-21 An instantaneous view of the superposition of two periodic transverse waves of different amplitude and frequency. The component waves y_1 and y_2 are shown in black; the resultant wave Y is in color.

10.15 Interference

instant. We shall continue to fix our attention on one instant in time, as we consider the displacements of many *different* particles of the medium in which the two waves are propagating. We find that the interference effects on different particles are different. There is constructive interference at some locations and destructive interference at others.

In Fig. 10-22(A) two periodic waves with the same frequency and in phase are traveling in the same direction. They interfere constructively. The resultant periodic wave (shown in color) has the same frequency as the component waves but has an amplitude equal to the sum of the component amplitudes.

In Fig. 10-22(B) the two periodic waves have the same frequency but are opposite in phase (180° out of phase). The displacements of the two waves are opposite in sign and they interfere destructively. The amplitudes of the two waves are equal in Fig. 10-22(C) and the destructive interference is complete.

The arrangement of interference effects (called an *interference pattern*) depends on the relative characteristics of the interfering waves. Figure 10-23 is a photograph of an interference pattern produced in a ripple tank by two identical circular waves emanating from two points. The two waves are in phase at their sources. That is, the two probes which generate the waves by their vibrations are moving up and down together.

A diagram of this interference pattern is shown in Fig. 10-24. Points **A** and **B** are the sources of two periodic circular waves of the same frequency and amplitude. The sources are acting in phase. Solid circular lines represent wave crests and dashed circular lines represent wave troughs.

At each point similar to those marked **C** the crest of a wave from one source is superposed with the crest of a wave from the other source. At points similar to **C′** the troughs are superposed. A half period later the crests are at **C′** and the troughs are at **C**. Constructive interference occurs along the lines **CC′** giving the resultant wave an amplitude twice the amplitudes of the individual waves.

At each point similar to those marked **D** the crest of a wave from one source is superposed with the trough of a wave from the other source. Destructive interference occurs along the lines **DD′**, displacements being reduced to zero.

Points of zero displacement in the interference pattern are called *nodes*. The lines **DD′** along which they occur are *nodal lines*. Similarly, points of maximum displacement are called *antinodes* (or loops) and the lines **CC′** along which they occur are *antinodal lines*. Observe these nodal and antinodal regions in the photograph of the interference pattern shown in Fig. 10-23.

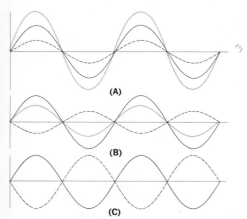

10-22 Interference of two periodic waves of the same frequency and traveling in the same direction. The component waves are in black, the resultant wave is in color. (A) Constructive interference. (B) Destructive interference. (C) Complete destructive interference.

10-23 A photograph of the interference pattern of water waves from two point sources. Locate the nodal and antinodal lines.

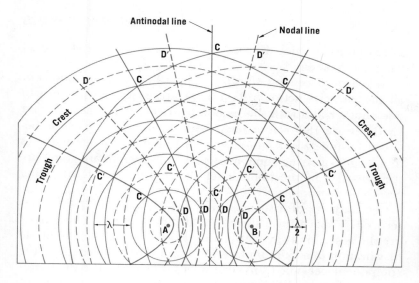

10-24 A diagram of the interference pattern of two periodic circular waves of the same frequency emanating in phase from points A and B.

At any nodal point where the destructive interference is complete, there is no motion of the medium and no energy. This does not mean that the energy of the two interfering waves has been destroyed or otherwise lost. Instead, it appears at points of constructive interference such as points **C** in Fig. 10-24. Recall from Section 10.7 that where the amplitude of the resultant wave crest is double that of a single interfering wave, the energy is four times greater. The total energy of the two wave systems remains unchanged, but the *energy distribution* resulting from the interference is different.

We found in Section 10.10 that a transverse pulse traveling on a taut string is inverted when reflected at the clamped end. So it is with a train of transverse waves. If no energy is lost in reflection at the fixed end, a continuous wave will be reflected back upon itself giving two wave trains of the same wavelength, frequency, and amplitude, but traveling in opposite directions.

Portions of two such wave trains are shown at a certain instant in time in (A) and (B) of Fig. 10-25. If their displacements are added at this instant, as in (C), the resultant displacement is zero. When the wave patterns have moved $\frac{1}{4}$ wavelength, each in its own direction of travel, superposition gives the resultant shown in (D). Another $\frac{1}{4}$ wavelength of movement gives the resultant in (E), and an additional movement of $\frac{1}{4}$ wavelength gives the resultant displacement in (F). Such a wave pattern is a *standing wave*. The particles in a standing wave vibrate in simple harmonic motion with the same frequency as each of the component waves. The amplitude of their motion is not the same for all points along the string. It varies from a minimum of zero amplitude at scale positions $\frac{1}{4}\lambda$, $\frac{3}{4}\lambda$, $\frac{5}{4}\lambda$, $\frac{7}{4}\lambda$, etc., to

10.16 Standing waves

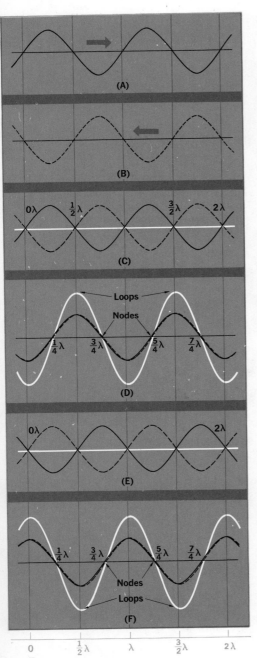

10-25 Standing wave (shown in color) produced by the interference of two periodic waves of the same frequency and amplitude traveling in opposite directions.

a maximum of twice the amplitude of one component wave at 0λ, $\frac{1}{2}\lambda$, 1λ, $\frac{3}{2}\lambda$, etc.

In the displacement shown in Fig. 10-25(F), the motions of all the particles between 0λ and $\frac{1}{4}\lambda$ are exactly in phase with one another and with the motion of particles between $\frac{3}{4}\lambda$ and $\frac{5}{4}\lambda$. They are 180° out of phase with the motion of particles between $\frac{1}{4}\lambda$ and $\frac{3}{4}\lambda$ and those between $\frac{5}{4}\lambda$ and $\frac{7}{4}\lambda$. When particles in a length of string equal to one-half wavelength are going up, the particles in the immediately adjacent parts of the string are going down.

Certain parts of a string vibrating with a standing wave pattern never move from their equilibrium positions. These parts are the *nodes*. Halfway between the nodes, where the amplitude of vibration is maximum, are the *loops*. The wavelength of the component periodic transverse waves which produce the standing wave is *twice* the distance between adjacent nodes or loops in a standing wave.

A standing wave is produced by the interference of two periodic waves of the same amplitude and wavelength, traveling in opposite directions. No standing wave can be produced if the two waves have different wavelengths.

When a stretched string is clamped at both ends, a standing wave pattern can be formed only for certain definite wavelengths. In such a vibrating string both ends must be nodes. Four possible standing wave patterns in a stretched string are shown in Fig. 10-26. Loops are indicated by the letter **L** and nodes by the letter **N**. The wavelength, λ, for each standing wave is expressed in terms of the length of the string, l. Part (A) is a time-exposure view showing the envelopes of the standing waves. Part (B) is a strobe-flash view showing positions of the strings at different instants of time.

In a standing wave, particles of the string at the nodes are continuously at rest. Energy is not transported along the string, but remains "standing" in the string. The energy of each particle remains constant as that particle executes its simple harmonic motion. When the string is straight (undistorted), particles have their maximum velocities and the energy is all kinetic. The energy is all potential when the string has its maximum displacement and all particles are momentarily at rest.

Standing waves are established in water, in air, or in other elastic bodies just as they are in taut strings. Standing waves can also be produced with electromagnetic waves. A standing wave pattern can occur in a circular ripple tank in which a periodic circular wave is generated at the center of the tank. Nodal rings appear where the surface of the water is at rest. The surface oscillates up and down between the nodal rings.

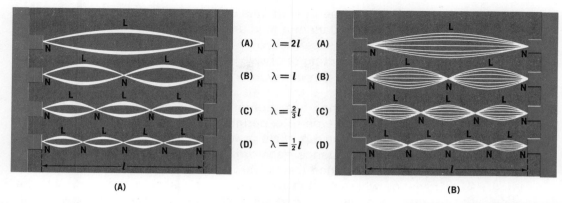

(A) $\lambda = 2l$ (A)

(B) $\lambda = l$ (B)

(C) $\lambda = \frac{2}{3}l$ (C)

(D) $\lambda = \frac{1}{2}l$ (D)

(A)

(B)

Many vibrating objects vibrate normally in a way that establishes standing waves in the object. The strings or the air columns of musical instruments establish various modes of standing waves.

10-26 Standing wave patterns in a stretched string. (A) A time-exposure view. (B) A strobe-flash view. Wavelength λ is expressed in terms of the length *l* of the string.

QUESTIONS

1. How does a pulse on a taut string differ from the incident pulse after being reflected at a fixed termination?
2. List the common properties of waves and give an illustration of each.
3. Make a drawing showing two transverse waves of the same wavelength but of different amplitudes, which are in phase. Graphically find the wave pattern which results if these two waves are superposed.
4. Repeat Question 3 with waves of the same amplitude, but with one having twice the wavelength of the other. At $t = 0$, the displacement of both waves is zero. At $t = T/4$ later for each, the displacement is maximum positive.
5. Repeat Question 4, but take the displacement as zero for the wave of longer wavelength, and as positive maximum for the wave of shorter wavelength at $t = 0$ while the reverse applies at $t = T/4$.
6. In your drawings of Questions 4 and 5 mark the points of maximum displacement and zero displacement. Do they occur at the same points at $t = 0$ as at $t = T/4$? Would you consider the resulting pattern as a standing wave or a progressing wave?
7. What are the requirements for production of a standing wave pattern?
8. What are *loops* and *nodes* in a standing wave pattern?
9. When two waves interfere, what influence does each exert on the progress of the other? Explain.
10. When two waves interfere, is there a loss of energy in the system? Explain.

Group B

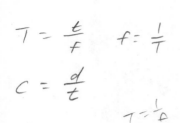

$$T = \frac{t}{f} \qquad f = \frac{1}{T}$$

$$C = \frac{d}{t}$$

$$T = \frac{1}{f}$$

11. Distingush between the effects of a "fixed" and a "free" termination at the boundary of a medium.

12. Two rooms are separated by a special sound-proof partition except for a connecting doorway. How can you explain the fact that a sound produced anywhere in one room can be heard anywhere in the other?

13. A new phenomenon has been observed in which there is a transfer of energy. What type of experiments would you propose to determine whether it is a particle or wave phenomenon?

14. What is an impedance transformer?

15. A wave disturbance travels through a uniform medium to its termination where a small part of the wave energy is transferred to the terminating medium and the remainder is reflected. How would you describe the impedance of the terminating medium relative to that of the transmitting medium?

16. Suggest two possible ways of modifying the wave-transfer system described in Question 15 to eliminate the reflection of wave energy.

$$V = f \lambda \qquad \lambda = \frac{V}{f} \qquad f = \frac{V}{\lambda}$$

PROBLEMS

Group B

3.9×10^{14} Hz
to
7.5×10^{14} Hz

1. Electromagnetic waves travel through space at a speed of 3.0×10^8 m/sec. The visible region of the spectrum has wavelengths ranging from about 4.0×10^{-7} m in the violet region to about 7.6×10^{-7} m in the red region. What is the frequency range of visible light?

28 m/s

$$T = \frac{t}{f} = \frac{1\,s}{7}$$

2. A string stretched between two clamps is 2.0 m long. When plucked at the center, a standing wave is produced which has nodes at the clamped ends and a single loop at the center. By means of a stroboscope, the string is observed to complete 7.0 vibrations per second. (a) What is the wavelength of the component traveling waves? (b) What is the speed of the transverse waves in the string?

615 cm/s

3. Periodic longitudinal waves are generated in a coil spring from a vibrating source at one end of the spring as shown in Fig. 10-6. The frequency of the vibrating source is 15.0 hz. The distance between successive compressions is 41.0 cm. What is the speed of each compression moving along the spring?

$$C = \frac{d}{t} = \frac{}{30}$$

5.5 m/s

4. An observer determined that 2.5 m separated a trough and an adjacent crest of surface waves on a lake and counted 33 crests passing in $3\bar{0}$ sec. What was the speed of these surface waves?

$$T = \frac{t}{f}$$

6.4 m

$$T = \frac{1}{f}$$

5. Two physics students were fishing from a boat anchored in a lake 24 m from shore. One student observed that the boat rocked through 11 complete oscillations in 19 sec and that one wave crest passed the boat with each oscillation. The other student noted that each crest required 6.5 sec to reach the shore. (a) What was the period of the surface wave? (b) What was the wavelength?

$$V = 3.7 \, m/s$$

Chapter 11

Sound Waves

THE NATURE OF SOUND

The energy-transfer mechanism of compression waves is a major interest of physicists. Waves propagate in elastic media as longitudinal disturbances consisting of compressions and rarefactions which give rise to elastic forces in the medium. Through these elastic forces the energy of the wave is transferred along to the particles next in line. The energy exchange is continuous as particles receive energy and pass it on.

The frequency range over which these compressional disturbances occur is very large. It is called the *sonic spectrum*.

11.1 The sonic spectrum

Australian Information Service photo by J. Tanner

A well-designed auditorium, like the main hall of the Opera House in Sydney, Australia, permits the audience to enjoy the full range of sound produced on the stage.

249

There is no clearly defined lower limit of frequency that falls within this vibrational framework. However, the frequency of an earthquake wave may be a fraction of a cycle per minute and its wavelength may be measured in kilometers.

The upper limit of the sonic spectrum is well defined. For a constant-velocity condition, periodic waves of increasing frequency have proportionally decreasing wavelength. A wave is not transported in the usual sense by a medium in which the wavelength is small compared to the inter-particle spacing of the medium. For a gas the mean free path of the molecules is the limiting dimension. Thus, at ordinary temperatures and pressures the upper range of sonic frequencies is of the order of 10^9 hertz in a gaseous medium. In liquids and solids the upper frequency limit is higher because of the smaller inter-particle spacing.

Within the sonic spectrum lies the region of **sound**, *a range of compression-wave frequencies to which the human ear is sensitive.* This audible range of frequencies, called the *audio range* and the *audio spectrum*, extends from approximately 20 to 20,000 hertz. Compression waves at frequencies above the audio range are referred to as *ultrasonic*, those below the audio range as *infrasonic*.

11.2 The production of sound

We produce a sound by initiating a series of compression waves in a medium capable of transmitting the vibrational disturbance. The particles of the medium acquire energy from the vibrating source and enter the vibrational mode themselves. As they do, they pass on the energy to adjacent particles. If the energy source continues to vibrate, a train of periodic waves travels through the medium and a transfer of energy takes place.

Suppose we clamp one end of a very thin strip of wood or steel in a vise to serve as a vibrating reed. When struck sharply, the free end vibrates to and fro, as shown in Fig. 11-1. If the reed vibrates rapidly, it produces a humming sound. This and other experiments which produce vibrations of a guitar string, a tuning fork, or an air column, show that *sounds are produced by vibrating matter.*

When the reed in Fig. 11-1 vibrates, its motion approximates simple harmonic motion. A graph of its displacement with time produces the sine wave shown in Fig. 11-2(B). As the vibrating reed moves from **a** to **b**, it does work on the gas molecules to the right by compression; the reed thus transfers energy to the molecules in the direction in which the compression occurs. At the same time, the gas molecules to the left expand into the space behind the reed as it moves, and become rarefied. This motion also represents energy which is transferred to

11-1 Sounds are produced by vibrating matter.

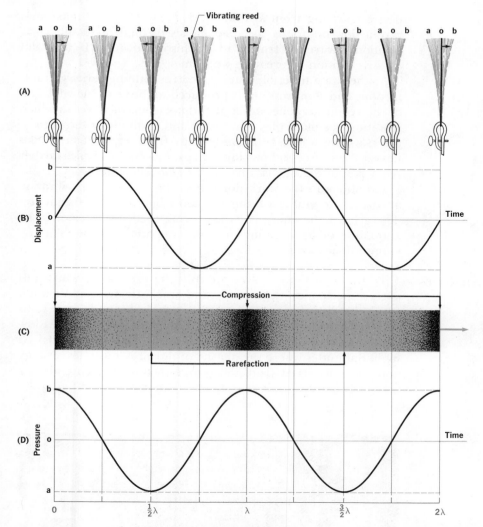

other molecules in the medium to the left of the reed. The combined effect of the simultaneous *compression* and *rarefaction* transfers energy to the molecules in both directions of the motion of the reed.

As the reed moves in the reverse direction from **b** to **a**, it compresses the gas molecules to the left of it, while the gas molecules to the right become rarefied. The combined effect of this simultaneous compression and rarefaction transfers energy to the molecules in both directions as before. However, this energy is not confined entirely to the line of motion.

If we consider just the series of compressions and rarefactions produced to the right, it is apparent that the maximum compression occurs as the reed moves through its equilibrium posi-

11-2 Variations of the vibrating reed in (A) produce the displacement variations with time in (B). The regions of compression and rarefaction of the longitudinal sound wave produced to the right of the reed are shown in (C). The pressure, or density variations of the sound wave with time are plotted in (D). Observe that the displacement and pressure curves are 90° out of phase.

tion **o** traveling from **a** to **b**. See Fig. 11-2(C). The maximum rarefaction occurs as the reed moves through its equilibrium position **o** traveling from **b** to **a**. This is shown in (D) as a plot of the variation of pressure with time.

At the same time, of course, a corresponding series of rarefactions and compressions is produced to the left. The vibration of the reed thus generates longitudinal trains of waves in which vibrating gas molecules move back and forth along the path of the traveling waves, receiving energy from adjacent molecules nearer the source and passing it on to adjacent molecules farther from the source. *Sound waves are longitudinal waves.*

Variations in the work done in setting the reed in vibration alter the amplitude of the vibration but not the frequency. The greater the energy of the moving reed, the greater is the amplitude of its vibrations and the amplitude of the resulting longitudinal waves.

11.3 Sound transmission. To produce sound waves, we must have a source which initiates a mechanical disturbance and an elastic medium through which the disturbance can be *transmitted.* Most sounds come to us through the air which acts as the transmitting medium. At low altitudes, we usually have little difficulty hearing sounds. At higher altitudes where the density of the air is lower, less energy may be transferred from the source to the air. Dense air is a more efficient transmitter of sound than rarefied air.

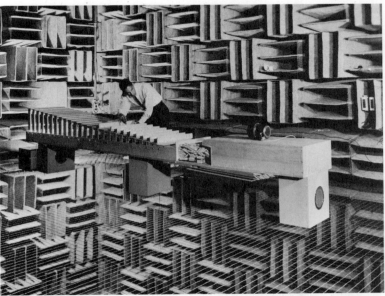

In this specially designed room, 99.9% of reflected sound is eliminated. The acoustical conditions here are similar to those in the atmosphere one mile above the earth's surface.

Bell Telephone Laboratories

The following experiment provides evidence that a material is required for the transmission of sound. An electric bell under a bell jar, Fig. 11-3, is connected to a source of energy so that it rings. While it is ringing, air is removed from the bell jar. As the remaining air becomes less and less dense, the sound becomes fainter and fainter. When air is allowed to reenter, the sound becomes louder. These effects show that it is increasingly difficult to get sound energy transferred to the air as its density decreases. This demonstration suggests that if all the air could be removed from the bell jar, no sound would be heard. *Sound does not travel through a vacuum; it is transmitted only through a material medium.*

The sound of two rocks being struck together under water can be heard quite plainly by a swimmer submerged in the water. If the swimmer is near the source of the disturbance, the effect can be painful. Liquids are efficient transmitters of sound.

Sometimes a loose faucet washer vibrates when water is drawn from a water pipe. The sound of this vibration is carried to all parts of the house by water pipes and wood framework. A train can be heard from a great distance by the sound transmitted through the rails. Many solids are efficient sound transmitters. In long rods or pipes, the sound propagation may be restricted to one dimension instead of spreading in space.

During a thunderstorm a distant lightning flash can be seen several seconds before the accompanying thunder is heard. The timer at the finish line during a track meet may see the smoke from the starter's gun before he hears the report. Over short distances, light travels practically instantaneously. Therefore, the time which elapses between a lightning flash and hearing the thunder, or between a gun firing and hearing the report, must be the time required for the sound to travel from its source to the observer. The speed of sound in air is 331.5 m/sec at 0°C. This speed increases with temperature about (0.6 m/sec)/C°.

The speed of sound in water is about four times that in air; in water at 25°C sound travels about 1500 m/sec. In some solids, the speed of sound is even greater. In a steel rod, for example, sound travels approximately 5000 m/sec—about 15 times the speed in air. In general, the speed of sound varies with the temperature of the transmitting medium. For gases the change in speed is rather large. For liquids and solids, however, this change in speed is small and usually is neglected. Representative values for the speed of sound waves in various media are given in Table 11-1. A more extensive list will be found in Table 17, Appendix B.

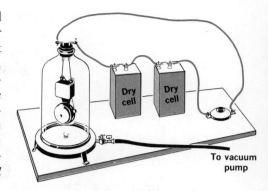

11-3 As air is pumped from the bell jar, the sound of the bell becomes fainter. Such a demonstration is evidence that a material medium is needed for the transmission of sound.

11.4 The speed of sound

Table 11-1 SPEED OF SOUND (25°C)

Medium	Speed (m/sec)
air	346
hydrogen	1339
alcohol	1207
water	1498
glass	4540
aluminum	5000
iron (steel)	5200

11.5 The properties of sounds

A nearby clap of thunder is loud; a whisper is soft. A cricket has a shrill, high chirp; a bulldog has a deep growl. A violin string bowed by a virtuoso produces a note of fine quality and is far more pleasing to hear than that produced by the novice. Each of these sounds has characteristics clearly associated with it. Sounds differ from each other in several fundamental ways. We shall consider three physical properties of sound waves, *intensity, frequency,* and *harmonic content.* The effects of these properties on the ear are called *loudness, pitch,* and *quality* respectively.

11.6 Intensity and loudness

*The **intensity** of a sound is the time rate at which the sound energy flows through a unit area normal to the direction of propagation.* Intensity thus has the dimension of power/area.

$$I = \frac{P}{A}$$

Where P is sound power in watts and A is area in square centimeters, the sound intensity I is expressed in watts per square centimeter. The intensity of a sound wave of given frequency is dependent on its amplitude.

Sound waves emanating from a vibrator which approximates a point source and traveling in a uniform medium spread out in a spherical pattern. Thus the area of the expanding wave front is directly proportional to the square of its distance from the source. Since the total power of the wave is constant, the intensity of the wave diminishes as it moves away from the source. The sound produced by a whistle is only one-fourth as intense at a distance of one kilometer as it is at a distance of half a kilometer from the source. The intensity of sound in a uniform medium is inversely proportional to the square of its distance from the point source.

*The **loudness** of a sound depends on an auditory sensation in the consciousness of a human listener.* In general, sound waves of higher intensity are louder, but the ear is not equally sensitive to sounds of all frequencies. Consequently, a high frequency sound may not seem as loud as one of lower frequency having the same intensity.

An increase in the intensity of a sound of fixed frequency causes it to seem louder to the listener. Suppose we generate a 1000-hz tone but of such low intensity that it is barely audible. The intensity can be increased approximately 10^{12} times before the tone becomes so loud that it is painful to the listener. The degree of loudness of a sound is not directly measurable with instruments since it depends on the ear and subjective judgment of the listener.

Intensity is measured with acoustical apparatus and does not depend on the hearing of an observer. The intensity of the average faintest audible sound, called the *threshold of hearing*, is 10^{-16} watt/cm^2 at 1000 hz. In measuring the *intensity level* of a sound, its intensity is compared with the intensity of this threshold of hearing. Because of the great range of intensities over which the ear is sensitive, a *logarithmic* rather than an arithmetic intensity scale is used. The intensity level of a sound is given by the equation

$$\beta = 10 \log \frac{I}{I_0}$$

where β (Greek letter beta) is the intensity level in *decibels* (db) of a sound of intensity I. I_0 is the intensity of the threshold of hearing. I and I_0 are measured in the same units, usually w/cm^2. Therefore the decibel is a dimensionless quantity. The following example illustrates the use of this equation. Intensity levels of several familiar sounds are listed in Table 11-2.

11.7 Intensity level measurements

Table 11-2 INTENSITY LEVELS OF SOUNDS (at 1000 hz)

Type of sound	Intensity (db)
threshold of hearing	0
whisper	10–20
very soft music	30
average residence	40–50
conversation	60–70
heavy street traffic	70–80
thunder	110
threshold of pain	120
jet engine	170

Example

Sound energy is radiated uniformly in all directions from a small source at a rate of 1.2 watts. (a) What is the intensity of the sound at a point 25 m from the source? (b) What is the intensity level at this reception point?

Solution

Assuming no absorption of sound energy by the transmitting medium, the 1.2 watts of sound power flows through a spherical area having a radius of 25 m.

(a) $I = \dfrac{P}{A} = \dfrac{1.2 \text{ w}}{4\pi(2500 \text{ cm})^2} = 1.5 \times 10^{-8} \text{ w/cm}^2$

(b) $\beta = 10 \log \dfrac{I}{I_0} = 10 \log \dfrac{1.5 \times 10^{-8} \text{ w/cm}^2}{10^{-16} \text{ w/cm}^2} = 10 \log (1.5 \times 10^8) = 82 \text{ db}$

The decibel is the practical unit for sound intensity levels. The word decibel means one-tenth of a *bel*, a unit named in honor of Alexander Graham Bell (1847-1922).

$$\text{Intensity level in bels} = \log \frac{I}{I_0}$$

Originally the bel was defined as the unit to describe intensity level differences, but it was too big. Today the decibel is used almost exclusively.

Ken Chen

A drummer carefully controls the sound levels produced by his instruments.

Table 11-3 RELATIVE INTENSITIES

I/I_0	bel	db
10	1	10
4		6
2		3
1	0	0
0.5		−3
0.25		−6
0.1	−1	−10

In the human sensory response, a change in the sound power level of 1 db is just barely perceptible. This change of 1 db represents a change in sound intensity of 26 per cent. Table 11-3 shows several power ratios and their decibel equivalents.

We stated in Section 1 that the audio spectrum extends from approximately 20 to 20,000 hz. This lower frequency is called the *lower limit of audibility* and the higher frequency the *upper limit of audibility*. However, there is considerable variation in the ability of individuals to hear sounds of high or low frequencies.

The graph in Fig. 11-4 shows the characteristics of audible sound waves. Since the graph is a composite of results obtained by testing many persons, it refers to the performance of the "average" ear.

The lower curve, the *threshold of hearing*, shows the minimum intensity level at which sound waves of various frequencies can be heard. Observe that the lowest intensity which will produce audible sound is for frequencies between 2000 and 4000 hz. The ear is most sensitive in this frequency range. At the lower and higher limits of audibility the intensities of sound waves must be higher to be heard.

The upper curve, the *threshold of pain*, indicates the upper intensity level for audible sounds. Sounds of greater intensity produce pain rather than hearing.

The graph shows the general frequency limits for the audio range to be between 20 and 20,000 hz. The intensity limits in

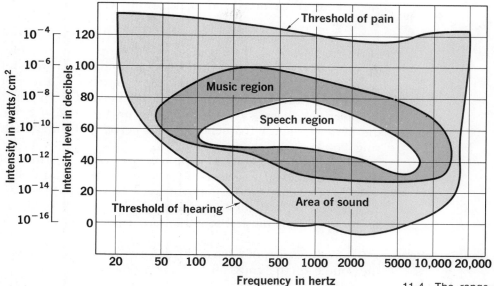

11-4 The range of audibility of the human ear.

the region of maximum sensitivity are between 0 and 120 decibels, corresponding to intensities of from 10^{-16} watt/cm² to 10^{-4} watt/cm².

11.8 Frequency and pitch

A perforated disc, like that in Fig. 11-5, can be used to show that the frequency of a sound determines its pitch. The disc has five concentric rings of holes. The holes of the inner-most ring are irregularly spaced and the holes in the other four rings are regularly spaced. There are 24, 30, 36, and 48 holes in these rings, respectively.

A stream of air, directed against a ring of holes, is interrupted by the metal between the holes as the disc rotates rapidly. These interruptions give rise to a series of air blasts which pro-duces a sound characteristic of the frequency of the blasts. A sound of steady *pitch* is heard if the holes are evenly spaced and the disc rotates with a constant speed; the pitch rises as the disc rotation is accelerated, it falls if the disc rotation is decelerated. If the air stream is directed at the 24-, the 30-, the 36-, and the 48-hole rings successively while the disc rotates steadily, tones of successively higher pitch are produced. ***Pitch*** *is the identifica-tion of a certain sound with a definite tone and depends on the fre-quency which the ear receives.*

We usually distinguish between a musical tone and a noise by the fact that the former is a pleasing sound and the latter is a disagreeable one. If the stream of air is directed at the inner-most ring of holes with the disc at constant speed, an unpleasant noise will be heard. The noise is characterized by a random

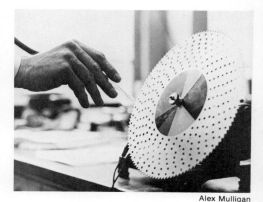

Alex Mulligan

11-5 The pitch of a sound depends on the frequency of the sound waves received by the ear.

mixture of frequencies and is not easily identified in terms of pitch.

The pitch of a tone produced by directing the air against one of the regularly spaced rings of holes is appropriately described in terms of the frequency of the sound produced. If the disc is rotating at the rate of 20 rps, the frequency of the tone produced by the ring with 24 holes is 480 hertz. The ring with 30 holes produces a tone having a frequency of 600 hertz; the 36-hole ring, a frequency of 720 hertz; and the 48-hole ring, 960 hertz.

The two tones produced by the outermost and innermost of these four regularly spaced rings are an *octave* apart, their frequencies being in the ratio of 2:1. The four tones have frequencies in the ratios 4:5:6:8 and, when produced simultaneously, comprise a musical sound known as a *major chord*.

11.9 The Doppler effect

Skip

In our discussion of pitch and frequency in Section 11.8, both the source of the emission and the listener were assumed to be stationary. Here the pitch of the sound heard is characteristic of the frequency of the emission. If the source emits 1000 vibrations per second, the listener hears a 1000-hz tone.

When there is relative motion between the source of sound and the listener, the pitch of the sound heard is not the same as that when both listener and source are stationary. Two situations are common: the source may be moving and the listener is stationary, and the listener may be moving and the source is at rest.

The first situation prevails when the listener stands at a railroad crossing while a train passes. He observes that the pitch of the warning horn of the locomotive drops abruptly as it passes his position. The second situation prevails when the listener rides in the train as it passes through a highway intersection. He observes that the pitch of the warning bell at the crossing drops abruptly as he passes through the intersection.

In both of these illustrations the steady pitch of the sound heard by the observer is higher than the frequency of the source would indicate as the distance between the observer and the source decreases at a constant rate. Also, in both cases described, the steady pitch of the sound heard is lower than the frequency of the source would indicate as the distance between the observer and the source increases at a constant rate. *The change in pitch produced by the relative motion of the source and the observer is known as the **Doppler effect**.* Of course, the frequency of the sound emitted by the source remains unchanged as does the velocity of the sound in the transmitting medium.

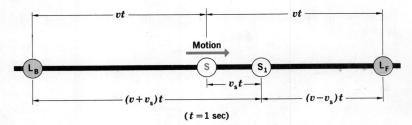

11-6 Sound waves emitted in unit time by the source **S** during its movement from **S** to **S₁** with speed v_S are contained within the distance **S₁L_F** in the direction of listener **L_F** in front of the source, and within the distance **S₁L_B** in the direction of the listener **L_B** behind the source.

Let us suppose that a source of sound is stationed at **S** in Fig. 11-6, and that one listener is at **L_F** and another is at **L_B**. If the source emits a sound of frequency f_S and the velocity of sound in the medium is v, the wavelength λ is

$$\lambda = \frac{v}{f_S} \qquad \text{(Equation 1)}$$

The time t in this diagram is unit time of 1 second. Thus, the distance $\mathbf{SL_F} = \mathbf{SL_B} = vt$, the distance the sound travels in 1 second. Then there will be f_S waves in both distances $\mathbf{SL_F}$ and $\mathbf{SL_B}$, each of wavelength λ.

Now suppose that the source is moving toward **L_F** and away from **L_B** with speed v_S and in 1 second travels from **S** to $\mathbf{S_1}$, a distance v_St. During this time, f_S vibrations were emitted by the source. The first one was emitted at **S** and at the end of the 1-second interval is at **L_F** in front of the source, and also at **L_B** behind the source (the advancing wave fronts are spherical). The last vibration just emitted at the end of the 1-second interval is at $\mathbf{S_1}$. Therefore, the same number of vibrations, f_S, are in the front region $\mathbf{S_1L_F}$ and the back region $\mathbf{S_1L_B}$ in the 1-second interval. These two distances are respectively

$$\mathbf{S_1L_F} = (v - v_S)t \qquad \text{(Equation 2a)}$$

and

$$\mathbf{S_1L_B} = (v + v_S)t \qquad \text{(Equation 2b)}$$

The wavelength λ' of the sound reaching the stationary listener in front of the moving source is shorter than λ of Equation 1 and is given by

$$\lambda' = \frac{v - v_S}{f_S} \qquad \text{(Equation 3)}$$

The velocity of the sound in the medium, v, is independent of the motion of the source. Thus the frequency of the sound reaching the stationary listener in front of the moving source, f_{LF}, is

$$f_{LF} = \frac{v}{\lambda'} \qquad \text{(Equation 4)}$$

Substituting the expression for λ' given in Equation 3 in Equation 4 yields

$$f_{LF} = \frac{v}{\dfrac{v - v_S}{f_S}}$$

or,

$$f_{LF} = f_S \frac{v}{v - v_S} \qquad \text{(Equation 5)}$$

Equation 5 shows us that *the frequency of the sound reaching the stationary listener in front of the moving source is higher than the frequency of the source.* Therefore he hears a sound of higher pitch than that emitted by the source.

We shall now turn to the other listener, L_B of Fig. 11-6, and show how the pitch of the sound heard by him is related to the frequency of the source. *The wavelength λ' of the sound reaching the stationary listener behind the moving source is longer than λ of Equation 1* and can be expressed as

$$\lambda' = \frac{v + v_S}{f_S} \qquad \text{(Equation 6)}$$

As in Equation 4, the frequency of the sound reaching the listener behind the moving source, f_{LB}, is

$$f_{LB} = \frac{v}{\lambda'} \qquad \text{(Equation 7)}$$

Substituting the expression for λ' given in Equation 6 in Equation 7, we get

$$f_{LB} = f_S \frac{v}{v + v_S} \qquad \text{(Equation 8)}$$

Equation 8 indicates that *the frequency of the sound reaching the stationary listener behind the moving source is lower than the frequency of the source.* Thus, he hears a sound of lower pitch than that emitted by the source.

If the listener is moving toward a stationary source, the pitch of the sound he hears will be higher than f_S but it will not be exactly that indicated by Equation 5. If the listener has a closing velocity v_{LC}, he will receive v_{LC}/λ waves per second in addition to the f_S emitted by the source. From Equation 1,

$$f_S = \frac{v}{\lambda}$$

so,

$$f_{LC} = \frac{v}{\lambda} + \frac{v_{LC}}{\lambda}$$

or

$$f_{LC} = \frac{v + v_{LC}}{\lambda} \qquad \text{(Equation 9)}$$

Substituting the expression for λ given in Equation 1 in Equation 9, we have

$$f_{LC} = f_s \frac{v + v_{LC}}{v} \qquad \text{(Equation 10)}$$

Equation 10 shows the frequency of the sound reaching the listener moving toward the stationary source. Thus he hears a sound of higher pitch than that emitted by the source, but not the same pitch as given in Equation 5.

The listener moving away from the stationary source with an opening velocity v_{LO} will receive v_{LO}/λ waves per second fewer than f_s emitted by the source.

$$f_{LO} = \frac{v - v_{LO}}{\lambda} \qquad \text{(Equation 11)}$$

Substituting for λ as before,

$$f_{LO} = f_s \frac{v - v_{LO}}{v} \qquad \text{(Equation 12)}$$

From Equation 12 we can determine the frequency of the sound reaching a listener moving away from the stationary source. Observe that the pitch is lower than that emitted by this source, but is not the same pitch as given in Equation 8.

We have considered the special cases in which the velocities of the source and the listener lie along the line common to both. If the medium has a velocity along this line joining the source and the listener, it must be considered also.

The Doppler effect is most easily observed in connection with sound waves. Astronomers have observed slight changes in the wavelength of light received from distant stars, and interpret this as being a Doppler effect caused by the relative motions of the stars toward or away from the earth. Light from many distant stars is shifted to longer wavelengths, toward the red region of the light spectrum. This effect, called the *red shift*, suggests that the universe is expanding. Doppler radar techniques can be used to detect moving objects, and some satellite tracking systems also use the Doppler principle.

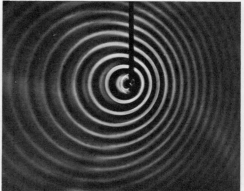

Educational Services Incorporated

11-7 Doppler effect in a ripple tank produced by the source moving from left to right.

QUESTIONS

Group A

1. How are sounds produced?
2. Why is sound not transmitted through a vacuum?
3. (a) What is the speed of sound in air at 0°C in the MKS system of measurement? (b) What is the rate of increase of speed with rise in temperature?
4. Distinguish between intensity and loudness.

5. Distinguish between frequency and pitch.
6. The engineer of a Diesel locomotive sounds the horn as the train approaches you. How does the pitch you hear compare with the pitch he hears?
7. How do the vibrations of the source of a musical tone differ from the vibrations of the source of a noise?
8. (a) What is the range of audio frequencies? What name is applied to sound vibrations (b) below the audio range; (c) above the audio range?
9. (a) What is the threshold of hearing? (b) What is the threshold of pain? (c) From Fig. 11-4, what is the threshold of hearing at 1000 hz? (d) What is the threshold of pain at 1000 hz?

Group B 10. Describe how a vibrating reed sets up longitudinal waves in the air surrounding it, and thereby transfers its energy to the surrounding air.
11. (a) How does variation in the work done in setting a reed in vibration affect the sound produced? (b) How does variation in the length of the vibrating portion of the reed affect the sound?
12. Explain why the audibility of a sound disturbance in an enclosed gaseous medium diminishes as the density of the gas is lowered.
13. Why is the intensity level of sound measured on a logarithmic scale?
14. What condition determines the upper limit of the sonic spectrum in a given transmitting medium?
15. Explain the meaning of the statement, "the sound level in the room is 40 db."

PROBLEMS

Group A 1. What time is required for sound to travel 5.00 km if the temperature of the air is 10.0°C?
2. What is the wavelength, in meters, of the sound produced by a tuning fork which has a frequency of $32\overline{0}$ hz? The temperature of the air is 15°C.
3. The echo of a ship's fog horn, reflected from an iceberg, is heard 5.0 sec after the horn was sounded. The temperature is −10.0°C. How many meters away is the iceberg?
4. A rifle is fired in a valley with parallel vertical walls. The echo from one wall is heard in 2.0 sec; the echo from the other wall 2.0 sec later. The temperature is $2\overline{0}$°C. What is the width of the valley?
5. What is the intensity level in decibels of a sound which has an intensity of 10^{-11} watt/cm²?

6. A man drops a stone into a mine shaft $25\bar{0}$ m deep. The temperature is 5.0°C. How many seconds pass before he hears the stone strike the bottom? (Neglect the effect of air resistance on the stone.)

7. A woman throws a stone over a cliff and hears it strike at the bottom after 8.00 sec. The temperature is 25°C. What is the height of the cliff in meters? (See note in Problem 6.)

8. A locomotive approaches a crossing at 95.0 km/hr. Its horn has a frequency of 288 hz and the temperature is 15°C. What is the frequency of the sound heard by the watchman at the crossing?

9. What is the drop in frequency of the sound a listener hears as a train, with its horn sounding, passes at 145 km/hr? The frequency of the horn is $32\bar{0}$ hz; the temperature is 25.0°C.

10. What is the intensity in watt/cm² of a sound which has an intensity level of $3\bar{0}$ decibels?

11. The intensity of a sound is determined to be 10^{-14} watt/cm². What is its intensity level?

CHARACTERISTICS OF SOUND WAVES

Suppose we stretch a piano wire about a meter in length between two clamps, drawing it tight enough to vibrate when plucked. If plucked in the middle, the wire vibrates *as a whole*, as shown in Fig. 11-10(A). *A taut wire or string which vibrates as a single unit produces its lowest frequency, called its* **fundamental**.

To study sounds produced by vibrating strings, physicists use an instrument called a *sonometer*, Fig. 11-10. This consists of two or more wires or strings stretched over a sounding board, which intensifies the sounds produced by the wires. Since the strings may vary in diameter, tension, length, or material, a

Group B

9

$$V = \frac{d}{t} =$$

.6

11.10 Fundamental tones

4 4

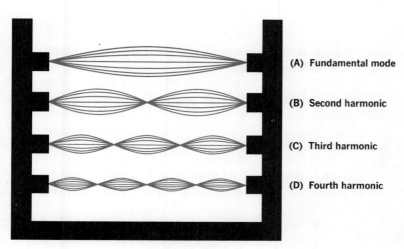

(A) Fundamental mode

(B) Second harmonic

(C) Third harmonic

(D) Fourth harmonic

11-10 Vibration modes of a single string.

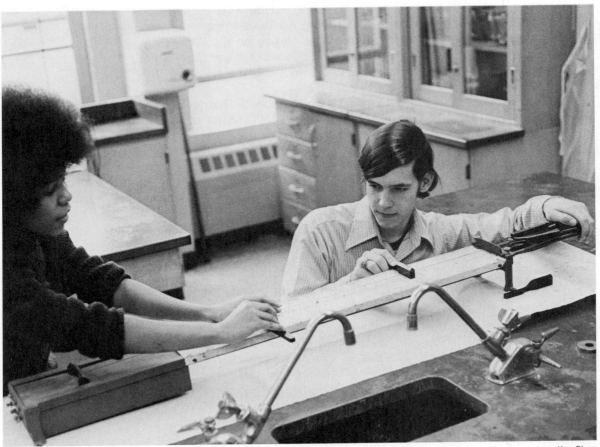

Ken Chen

11-11 The sonometer is used to study the laws of strings.

sonometer is useful for testing the frequency of strings and for showing how they vibrate.

By plucking a string, energy is transferred to the string and causes it to vibrate in transverse wave motion. Just as a vibrating reed transfers energy to molecules of air gases and causes them to exhibit longitudinal wave motion, so a vibrating string transfers energy to these gas molecules and causes them to vibrate and transmit a longitudinal wave. The frequency of the longitudinal vibration of the molecules (the frequency of the sound wave) is the same as the frequency of the transverse vibration of the string. Since the production of sound by a vibrating string dissipates energy, energy must be continuously supplied to the string by plucking or bowing to maintain the sound.

A string may vibrate as an entire unit, but may also vibrate in two, three, four or more segments depending on the standing wave pattern which is set up in the string. See Fig. 11-10(B-D). When a string is plucked or bowed near one end, it may vibrate in several segments.

We have already described how a string vibrates in two segments. Our study of standing waves indicates that its frequency of vibration must be twice that required to cause it to vibrate

11.11 Harmonics

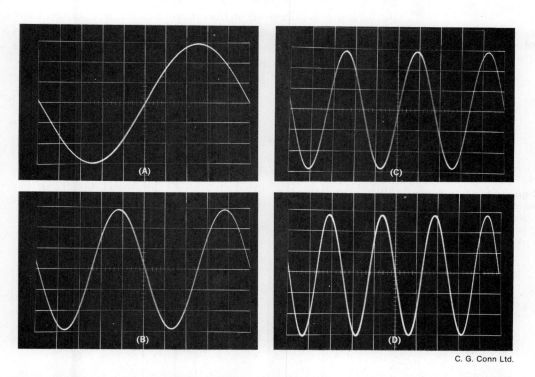

C. G. Conn Ltd.

as a single segment. Doubling the frequency of a sound wave raises the pitch one octave. If the string vibrates in four segments, the frequency of vibration of the string and the sound waves is four times as great, and the pitch of the sound produced is two octaves above the fundamental. *The fundamental and the tones having frequencies which are whole number multiples of the fundamental are called* **harmonics**. The fundamental is also the *first harmonic* since it is one times the fundamental. The tone having a frequency twice that of the fundamental is the *second harmonic*, the tone of frequency three times that of the fundamental is the *third harmonic*, and so on. Oscillograms of a fundamental tone and several orders of harmonics are shown in Fig. 11-12.

11-12 Oscillograms of (A) a fundamental, (B) the second harmonic, (C) the third harmonic, and (D) the fourth harmonic.

45

11.12 The quality of sound

It is not difficult to pick out the sounds produced by different instruments in an orchestra, even though they may be producing the same tone with equal intensity. The difference is a property of sound called *quality*, or *timbre*.

If the string of a sonometer is touched very lightly in the middle while being bowed, it can be made to vibrate in two segments and as a whole at the same time. See Fig. 11-13. The fundamental is audible, but added to it is the sound of the second harmonic. The combination is richer and fuller; the quality of the sound is improved by the addition of the second harmonic to the fundamental. See Fig. 11-14(A). *The **quality** of a sound depends on the number of harmonics produced and their relative intensities.* When stringed instruments are played, they are bowed, plucked, or struck near one end, instead of in the middle, to produce other harmonics which blend with the fundamental and give a richer sound. See Fig. 11-14(B).

The quality of the tones produced by orchestral instruments varies greatly. For example, the tone produced by a French horn consists almost entirely of the fundamental and the second harmonic. You can readily see this by comparing Figs. 11-14(A) and 11-14(C). The tonal quality of an instrument like the trumpet, however, is due to the great intensity of its high-frequency harmonics. See Fig. 11-14(D).

11-13 A single string vibrating with its fundamental and second harmonic modes simultaneously.

11-14 Oscillograms of (A) a fundamental and second harmonic, (B) a fundamental and fourth harmonic, (C) the sound of a French horn, and (D) the sound of a trumpet.

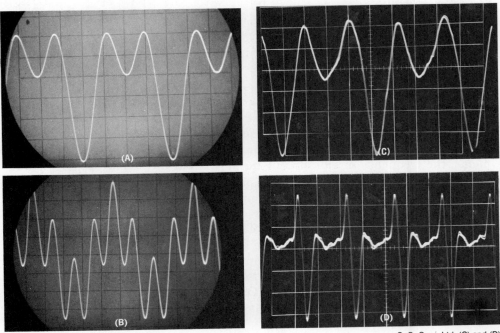

C. G. Conn Ltd. (C) and (D)

SOUND OUT

Thomas Edison, in 1877, built a phonograph. (The name was coined from the Greek words for "sound" and "writing.") It recorded and played back the phrase "Mary had a little lamb." Shouting into the mouthpiece caused a needle attached to a diaphragm to make "hills" and "valleys" in a sheet of tin foil wrapped around a grooved cylinder. To play back the recording, the needle was run through the same grooves so the "hills" and "valleys" made the diaphragm vibrate in a crude approximation of the original sound. Even though this machine showed that sound could be recorded, it was an impractical toy. The records were neither permanent nor did they faithfully reproduce the original sound. Edison and others eventually developed commercially successful mechanical phonographs.

With electronic amplification, phonograph sound has improved. Instead of using the record groove to generate sound mechanically, electric signals from a phonograph pickup are used to control an outside source of power. Mechanical distortion is reduced and loudness is increased.

The same principle, controlling a power source with the electric output from a microphone or an instrument pickup, have made large-audience rock concerts possible. Now, amplifiers drive loudspeakers that can fill a large stadium with powerful sound.

Thomas Edison demonstrating his first phonograph. By turning the crank, the cylinder rotated under the needle. The heavy wheel at the left increased rotational inertia and reduced variations in rotational velocity caused by uneven cranking.

Photoworld, Inc.

Culver Pictures

(Left) A mechanical phonograph popular for home entertainment in the early 1900's. (Below) An early mechanical recording studio. Before the invention of electronic amplifiers, recordings were made mechanically. In this method, the sound itself powered the movements of the recording needle. The long cone-shaped object at the left was designed to increase the effect of the orchestra's sound on the movements of the recording needle (out of view to the left). Notice that some of the violins have horns to concentrate and direct the instrument's sound toward the recorder. The small tube leading to the violinist's ear permitted him to hear his own inment.

Culver Pictures

Acoustic Control Corporation

Art and technology combine in a modern rock concert. To achieve the desired musical effect, the instruments' sounds are sometimes intentionally distorted by operating the amplifiers above their recommended power output. Electronic devices such as Moog organs, echo chambers, and "fuzz boxes" produce sounds that differ in quality from the sound of an instrument such as a guitar. Some rock performers suffer permanent hearing loss from performing near their high-powered loudspeakers.

Zenith Radio Corporation

Stereophonic 2-channel and 4-channel sound reproduction systems simulate a three dimensional sound effect around the listeners. This example of a 4-channel system requires four amplifiers (contained in the center case) and four loudspeakers arranged as shown.

Culver Pictures

An electric jukebox, popular for entertainment in the late 1930's.

The frequency of a string varies with its *length, diameter, tension,* and *density.* The strings of a piano produce tones with a wide range of frequencies. If we examine them we find that the strings which produce low-frequency tones are long, thick, and loose, while the strings that produce high-frequency tones are short, thin, and taut. One string produces a loud enough tone for the low notes, but three strings are needed to produce high notes of comparable loudness.

The conditions affecting the frequency of vibrating strings are summarized in four *laws of strings.*

1. Law of lengths. When a musician wishes to raise the pitch produced by a stringed instrument, she may shorten the vibrating length of the string. A violinist shortens the length of the A string about 2.5 cm to produce the note B. *The frequency of a string is inversely proportional to its length, if all other factors are constant.*

$$\frac{f}{f'} = \frac{l'}{l}$$

Here f and f' are the frequencies corresponding to the lengths l and l'.

2. Law of diameters. In a piano, and other stringed instruments like the cello and the guitar, the strings which produce higher frequencies have smaller diameters. A string with a diameter of 0.1 cm has twice the frequency of a similar string 0.2 cm in diameter. *The frequency of a string is inversely proportional to its diameter, if all other factors are constant.*

$$\frac{f}{f'} = \frac{d'}{d}$$

Here f and f' are frequencies corresponding to the diameters d and d'.

3. Law of tensions. When stringed instruments are tuned, the strings are tightened to increase their frequency, or loosened to decrease it. *The frequency of a string is directly proportional to the square root of the tension on the string, if all the other factors are constant.*

$$\frac{f}{f'} = \frac{\sqrt{F}}{\sqrt{F'}}$$

Here f and f' are the frequencies corresponding to the tensions F and F'. See the example at the top of page 270.

4. Law of densities. The more dense a string is, the lower its frequency. Usually three of the strings on a violin are of plain gut; the fourth is wound with fine wire to increase its density so that it can produce the low frequency tones. *The frequency of*

11.13 The laws of strings

Ken Chen

A guitarist uses the law of strings to vary the pitch of the sound from his instrument.

a string is inversely proportional to the square root of its density, if other factors are constant.

$$\frac{f}{f'} = \frac{\sqrt{D'}}{\sqrt{D}}$$

Here f and f' are the frequencies corresponding to the densities D and D'.

Example

A string stretched with a force of 50.0 n produces the note C, 261.6 hz. What force must be applied to this string to make it produce the note C', one octave higher in frequency?

Solution

The frequency of C is 261.6 hz; that of C' is 523.2 hz.

Basic equation:
$$\frac{f}{f'} = \frac{\sqrt{F}}{\sqrt{F'}}$$

Working equation:
$$F' = \frac{f'^2 F}{f^2} = \frac{(523.2 \text{ hz})^2 \times 50.0 \text{ n}}{(261.6 \text{ hz})^2} = 20\overline{0} \text{ n}$$

11.14 Forced vibrations

When we strike a tuning fork with a rubber hammer, it vibrates. This vibration is at a natural frequency which depends upon the fork's length, its thickness, and the material of which it is made. When we strike a key on a piano, the piano string vibrates at its fundamental frequency and at harmonics of this frequency. The only external forces which affect these natural rates of vibration are friction and gravitation.

Suppose we strike a tuning fork and then press its stem against a table top. The tone becomes louder when the fork is in contact with the table because the fork *forces* the table top to vibrate with the same frequency. Since the table top has a much larger vibrating area than the tuning fork, these *forced vibrations* produce a more intense sound.

A vibrating violin string stretched tightly between two clamps does not produce a very intense sound. When the string is stretched across the bridge of a violin, however, the wood of the violin is forced to vibrate in response to the vibrations of the string; the intensity of the sound is increased by these forced vibrations. The sounding board of a piano acts in the same way to intensify the sounds produced by the vibrations of its strings.

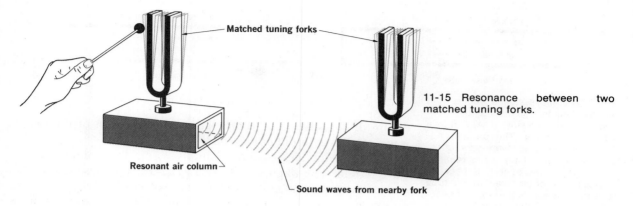

11-15 Resonance between two matched tuning forks.

11.15 Resonance

The two tuning forks in Fig. 11-15 have the same frequency. They are mounted on sounding boxes, each with one end open, which increase the intensity of the sound through forced vibrations. Suppose we place these forks a short distance apart, with the open ends of the boxes toward each other. Now let us strike one fork, and after it has vibrated several seconds, touch its prongs to stop them. We find that the other fork is vibrating weakly. The compressions and rarefactions produced in the air by the first tuning fork act on the second fork in a regular fashion, causing it to vibrate. Such action is called *resonance*, or *sympathetic vibrations*. A person who sings near a piano may cause the piano strings which produce similar frequencies to vibrate. Resonance occurs when the natural vibration rates of two objects are the same, or when the vibration rate of one of them is equal to one of the harmonics of the other. Changing the frequency of one of the tuning forks by adding mass to one of its prongs alters the conditions of the experiment and no resonance is evident; both forks should have the same natural frequency to produce this resonant effect.

In Fig. 11-16 we have illustrated a method of producing resonance between a tuning fork and a column of air. The vibrating fork is held above the hollow cylinder immersed in water. The length of the air column is gradually increased by raising the cylinder. At the position shown in Fig. 11-16(A) there is a marked increase in the loudness of the sound. Here the column of air in the tube vibrates vigorously at the frequency of the tuning fork and the two are in resonance.

This behavior is similar to the production of a standing wave on a stretched string. During resonance, a compression of the reflected wave unites with a compression of the direct wave and a rarefaction of the reflected wave unites with a rarefaction

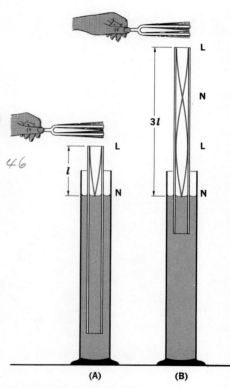

11-16 Resonance between a tuning fork and a vibrating air column. (A) gives greater sound reinforcement than (B). The curves represent maximum displacements of air particles. Nodes are at **N** and loops are at **L**.

Particle displacement:

before reflection ⟶
after reflection ⟵

(A) Closed tube

Particle displacement:

before reflection ⟶
after reflection ⟶

(B) Open tube

11-17 A compression traveling from left to right is reflected at the right end as a compression in (A) and as a rarefaction in (B). The particle displacement vector is inverted by reflection in the closed tube, but remains unchanged in the open tube because displacement of air layers in this tube is in the same direction for a rarefaction traveling to the left as for a condensation traveling to the right.

of the direct wave. The constructive superposition of the two waves in phase amplifies the sound.

The resonant air column is simply a standing longitudinal wave system. The water surface in Fig. 11-16(A) closes the lower end of the tube and prevents longitudinal displacement of the molecules of the air immediately adjacent to it. This termination effectively clamps the air column at the closed end and gives rise to a displacement node. The upper end of the tube, being open, provides a free-ended termination for the air column and is a displacement antinode or loop. These are shown in Fig. 11-16(A) as **N** and **L** respectively.

The air particles at the closed end of the tube, being unable to undergo longitudinal displacement, experience maximum changes in pressure. This position of a displacement node is also a pressure antinode, a point of maximum pressure change. (Refer to Fig. 11-2 for the phase relationship between displacement and pressure waves.) Compressions are reflected as compressions and rarefactions are reflected as rarefactions. This behavior amounts to a change in phase upon reflection from a rigid termination in the sense that the displacement vector of the air particles is inverted. See Fig. 11-17(A).

The open end of the tube is a displacement loop and, consequently, a pressure node. Here the pressure remains at the constant value of the outside atmosphere and air rushes into and out of the tube as the air column vibrates. It is this large movement of air at the open end of the tube that transfers energy to the atmosphere and provides the reinforcement of the sound produced by the tuning fork.

The fundamental frequency of the resonant column corresponds approximately to a displacement node at the closed end and an adjacent displacement loop at the open end as shown in Fig. 11-16(A). Since the distance separating a node and an adjacent loop of a standing wave is one-fourth wavelength, *the length of the closed tube is approximately one-fourth the wavelength of its fundamental resonant frequency.*

$$\lambda \simeq 4l$$

By applying a small empirical correction proportional to the diameter of the tube (because the motion of molecules of the air at the open end of the tube is not strictly in one dimension), we can state the relationship more precisely as follows:

$$\lambda = 4(l + 0.4d)$$

in which λ is the wavelength of the fundamental resonant frequency, l is the length of the closed tube, and d is its diameter.

If the cylinder of Fig. 11-16(A) is lifted higher out of the water, resonance will occur again when the length is three-quarters of a wavelength. This length of air column also corresponds to a displacement node at the closed end and a loop at the open end and allows a standing wave to develop. See Fig. 11-16(B). For a tube that is long enough, successively weaker resonance points could be found at $5/4\ \lambda$, $7/4\ \lambda$, etc. Thus, *a closed tube is resonant at odd quarter-wavelength intervals.*

The quarter-wave resonant column for the fundamental frequency of the tuning fork of Fig. 11-16(A) is three-quarters of a wavelength long for the third harmonic of this frequency. It is $5/4\ \lambda$ for the fifth harmonic, and is $7/4\ \lambda$ for the seventh

Gress-Miles Organ Co.

Rows of open and closed tubes are used in a pipe organ. The air in each pipe resonates to a sound with a specific frequency.

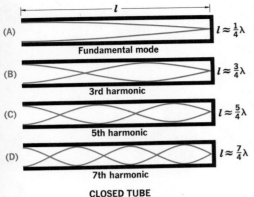

11-18 The normal modes of oscillation of a closed tube. The fundamental frequency is half that of an open tube of the same length, and only odd harmonics are produced.

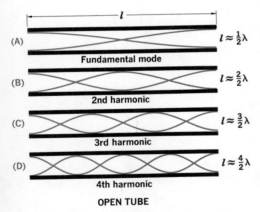

11-19 The normal modes of oscillation of an open tube. The fundamental frequency is twice that of a closed tube of the same length, and all harmonics are produced.

harmonic. Therefore, *the resonant frequencies of a closed tube are harmonics, but only odd harmonics of the fundamental mode are present*. This relationship is illustrated in Fig. 11-18.

Many musical instruments employ vibrating air columns open at one end and closed at the other *(closed tube)*, or open at both ends *(open tube)*. From the above discussion we have shown that the normal modes of oscillation of air columns are characterized by

1. *a displacement node (or pressure loop) at a closed end*, and
2. *a displacement loop (or pressure node) at an open end*.

Compressions traveling in an open tube are reflected at the open ends as rarefactions and rarefactions are reflected as compressions. In such reflections, the longitudinal displacement vector of the air particles is *not* inverted and in this sense there is no change in phase at the open termination of the air column. This condition is illustrated in Fig. 11-17(B).

The fundamental frequency of a resonant air column in an open tube corresponds approximately to displacement loops at opposite ends and a displacement node in the middle as shown in Fig. 11-19(A). Since adjacent loops of a standing wave are one-half wavelength apart, *the length of an open tube is approximately one-half the wavelength of its fundamental resonant frequency*.

$$\lambda \simeq 2l$$

Again, by applying a small empirical correction proportional to the diameter of the tube, we can state the relationship more precisely as follows:

$$\lambda = 2(l + 0.8d)$$

in which λ is the wavelength of the fundamental resonant frequency, l is the length of the open tube, and d is its diameter.

An open tube, which is a half-wave resonant column at its fundamental frequency, is a full wavelength long at the second harmonic of this frequency. It is $3/2 \lambda$ at the third harmonic. In each case displacement loops occur at both open ends and the column resonates in these modes. Therefore, *the resonant frequencies of an open tube are harmonics, and all harmonics of the fundamental mode are present*. See Fig. 11-19.

The quality of a musical tone generally is enhanced by its harmonic content. The open tube resonator has both odd and even harmonics of the fundamental mode present whereas the closed tube resonator has only odd harmonics. Thus, the quality of the sounds from open tubes and closed tubes is not the same.

We have already discussed interference of transverse waves in strings and of water waves in the ripple tank in Chapter 10. We have been concerned with standing waves in resonant air columns in the preceding section. There is abundant experimental evidence that two or more wave disturbances can travel through the same medium independently of one another. The superposition principle shows us that the displacement of a particle of a medium at any time is the vector sum of the displacements it would experience from the individual waves acting alone.

A standing wave is formed by two wave trains of the same frequency and amplitude traveling through a medium in opposite directions. We are generally concerned with the conditions or behavior of the space in which the standing wave exists. This generalization is true for resonant air columns used in musical instruments. The standing wave is characterized by an amplitude *which varies with distance, or position in space.*

Two wave trains of slightly different frequencies traveling in the same direction through a medium will interfere in a different way. At any fixed point in the medium through which the waves pass, their superposition gives a wave characterized by an amplitude *which varies with time.*

In Fig. 11-20 the resultant displacement of two wave trains of slightly different frequencies is plotted as a function of time. In curve (A) the frequency is 8 hz and in (B) it is 10 hz. Curve (C) shows the combined effect of these two waves at a fixed point in their pathway. This resultant wave varies periodically in amplitude with time. Such amplitude pulsations are called *beats.*

Observe that waves (A) and (B) come into phase two times each second and out of phase the same number of times each

11.16 Beats

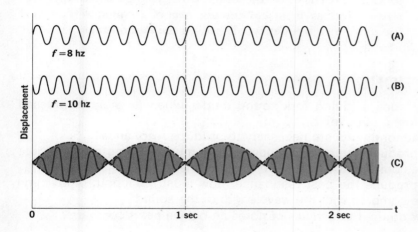

11-20 Beats. Waves (A) and (B) of slightly different frequencies combine to give a wave (C) which varies in amplitude with time.

second. The *beat frequency* can be described as *two beats per second. The number of beats per second equals the difference between the frequencies of the component waves.*

When the interfering frequencies are audible sounds, the amplitude variations, or beats, are recognized as variations in loudness. The average human ear can distinguish beats up to a frequency of approximately ten per second.

The beat phenomenon is frequently used to tune vibrating systems with great precision. Two vibrating strings can be tuned to the same frequency by adjusting the tension of one until the beats disappear. This procedure is called "zero beating." The piano-tuner adjusts frequencies precisely by systematically beating harmonics of notes against each other.

To illustrate, let us assume that two vibrating strings have fundamental frequencies of 165 hz and 325 hz respectively. One (who possesses a "trained" ear) may distinguish 5 beats per second as a consequence of the 325-hz tone beating against the second harmonic of the 165-hz tone.

A precision tuning fork vibrates only in its fundamental mode and produces a tone which is free of harmonics. Suppose a tuning fork of frequency 260 hz is sounded together with one of 264 hz. A listener will hear 4 beats each second of sound having an average frequency of 262 hz.

If the lower frequency is represented by f_l and the higher frequency by f_h, the average frequency f_{av} can be expressed as follows:

$$f_{av} = 1/2 (f_l + f_h)$$

The sound is a sine wave of average frequency f_{av} and varying amplitude which reaches a maximum $(f_h - f_l)$ times each second (the beat frequency). When the frequency separation of the two tones is too large for the beats to be distinguished by the listener, she may hear a difference *tone* of frequency $(f_h - f_l)$ if the difference frequency falls within the audio range.

QUESTIONS

Group A

1. Why does a tuning fork sound louder when its stem is pressed against a table top?
2. What conditions are necessary to produce resonance?
3. To produce the best resonance, how must the length of a closed tube compare with the wavelength of the sound?
4. To produce the best resonance, how must the length of an open tube compare with the wavelength of the sound?
5. How do the frequencies of notes an octave apart compare?

6. (a) What is a fundamental? (b) How does a string vibrate to produce the fundamental?

7. Which law of strings is used (a) in tuning a guitar; (b) in playing the instrument?

8. In sound waves, what is (a) constructive interference; (b) destructive interference? (c) What are beats?

Group B

9. Why is it easy to distinguish between the sound produced by a piano and a trombone even if both play the same note?

10. How do the strings on a piano illustrate the laws of strings?

11. Suggest a function of the bridge between the strings and the sounding board of a musical instrument such as a cello.

12. Suppose a piano-tuner has tuned the notes middle C and G to frequencies of 262 hz and 392 hz respectively. Then she beats G against low C which is one octave below middle C. What should she hear to indicate that she has adjusted low C to its proper frequency?

13. Given two tuning forks which vibrate at the same frequency, suggest a way to hear beats between them.

PROBLEMS

1. What is the frequency of a tuning fork which resonates with an open tube 25.0 cm long and 2.0 cm in diameter when the temperature is 20°C?

Group A

646 Hz

2. A tuning fork, frequency 384 hz, produces resonance with a closed tube 20.0 cm long and 4.0 cm in diameter. What is the speed of sound?

332 m/s

$$f = \frac{v}{\lambda}$$

3. A tuning fork has a frequency of 440 hz. If another fork of slightly lower pitch is sounded at the same time, the beats produced were 5/sec. What is the frequency of the second tuning fork?

4. How many beats will be heard each second when a string, frequency 288 hz, is plucked simultaneously with another string, frequency 296 hz?

5. If the string on a violin is 25.4 cm long and produces a fundamental tone of frequency $44\bar{0}$ hz, by how much must it be shortened to produce a tone of frequency 523.3 hz?

$$\frac{f}{f'} = \frac{l'}{l}$$

shorten by 4 cm

6. Compare the frequency of one string 25 cm long and 0.50 mm in diameter with that of another 100 cm long and 0.25 mm in diameter, assuming all other factors are constant.

7. Two tuning forks of $32\bar{0}$ hz and 324 are sounded simultaneously. What sound will the listener hear?

8. When a string 0.500 m long is stretched with a force of 2.50×10^2 n, its frequency is $44\bar{0}$ hz. If the string is shortened to 0.400 m and the stretching force is increased to 5.00×10^2 n, what is the new frequency?

Group B

9. Sound intensity at the hearing threshold is approximately 10^{-14} w/cm² for a sound frequency of 200 hz. The pain threshold is reached for sound at this frequency when the intensity is increased by 110 db. Calculate the intensity of this sound at the pain threshold.

10. Middle C on the piano keyboard is tuned to 261. 6 hz when the temperature is 20.0°C. Calculate (a) the frequency, and (b) the wavelength in air of the highest note on the keyboard which is exactly 4 octaves above middle C.

11. An organ pipe open at both ends is 1.23 m long and has a diameter of 10 cm. (a) What is its fundamental frequency when the air temperature is 15°C? (b) What are the frequencies of the two lowest harmonics produced along with the fundamental tone?

12. An organ pipe closed at one end is 0.76 m long and has a diameter of 5.0 cm. The air temperature is 12°C. (a) Determine its fundamental frequency. (b) What are the frequencies of the two lowest harmonics produced along with this fundamental tone?

Chapter 12

The Nature of Light

WAVES AND PARTICLES

The properties of waves in general were described in Chapter 10. They may be summarized as follows:

1. Propagation within a uniform medium is along straight lines.

2. Reflection occurs at the surface, or boundary, of a medium.

3. Refraction, or bending, may occur where a change of speed is experienced.

4. Interference is found where two waves are superposed.

5. Diffraction, or bending around corners, takes place when waves pass the edges of obstructions.

These properties are easily recognized in the behavior of sound and water waves. Such disturbances occur in matter, the particles of the medium being set in motion about their equilibrium positions by the passing waves.

Matter is not required for the propagation of light. While light does pass readily through certain kinds of matter, its transmission is unhindered in interstellar space, or through an evacuated vessel.

The regular reflection of light from smooth surfaces was known in the time of Plato, four hundred years before the Christian era. (Reflection is the subject of Chapter 13.)

Observations concerning the refraction of light at the interface of two transparent media of different optical densities were made by the Greeks as early as the second century A.D. The Arabian mathematician, Alhazen (965–1038) studied the refraction of light and disputed the ancient theory that visual rays emanated from the eye. He demonstrated the behavior of

12.1 Properties of light

Bausch & Lomb

12-1 Alhazen, an Arabian mathematician, studied the refraction of light nearly a thousand years ago.

light as it passes from a less dense to a more dense optical medium and recognized that the angles of incidence and refraction were related. He was unable to discover the law connecting them, however. This relationship, now known as Snell's law, was established six hundred years later. (Refraction and Snell's law are discussed in Chapter 14.)

The practical use of sight lines for placing objects in straight lines and the shape of shadows give evidence of the straight-line propagation of light. This, too, was known to the Greek philosophers. Sir Isaac Newton conducted experiments on the separation of light into colors by means of a prism and was aware of the colors produced by thin films.

We have listed the principal light phenomena familiar to observers in the seventeenth century when Newton was alive. It must have been evident to Newton and to other scientists in his day that only two general theories could explain the properties of light, since the transmission of energy from one place to another was involved.

A window pane may be shattered by a moving object, such as a baseball thrown from a distance, or by the concussion resulting from a distant explosion. In general, energy can be propagated either by particles of matter or by wave disturbances traveling from one place to another.

Arguments favoring both a particle (corpuscular) theory and a wave theory were plausible when applied to the properties of light observed in the seventeenth century. The principal advocate of the corpuscular theory was Newton, whose arguments were supported by the French mathematician, Laplace (1749–1827). The wave theory was upheld principally by Christian Huygens (*hi*-ganz) (1629–1695), a Dutch mathematician, physicist, and astronomer. He was supported by Robert Hooke of England. Because of the plausibility of both theories, a scientific debate concerning the nature of light developed between the followers of Newton and Huygens which continued unresolved for more than a century. Let us consider some of the arguments which support each of these classical theories of light.

12.2 The corpuscular theory

Sir Isaac Newton believed that light consists of streams of tiny particles (which he called corpuscles) emanating from a luminous source. Let us examine the arguments used by those who believed the particle theory best explained the various light phenomena known to them.

1. Rectilinear propagation. A ball thrown into space follows a curved path because of the influence of gravity. Yet if the ball is thrown with greater and greater speed, we know that its path curves less and less. We can easily imagine minute particles traveling at such enormous speed that their paths form essentially straight lines.

Newton experienced no difficulty in explaining the rectilinear propagation of light by means of his particle model. In fact, this property of light provided the supporters of the corpuscular theory with one of their strongest arguments against a wave theory. How, they asked, could waves travel in straight lines? A sound can easily be heard around the corner of an obstruction, but a light certainly cannot be seen from behind an obstruction. The former is unquestionably a wave phenomenon. How can the latter also be one?

The simple and direct explanation of rectilinear propagation provided by the particle model of light, together with the great prestige of Sir Isaac Newton, were largely responsible for the preference shown for the corpuscular theory during the seventeenth and eighteenth centuries.

2. Reflection. Where light is incident on a smooth surface such as a mirror, we know that it is regularly reflected. How do particles behave under similar circumstances? Steel ball bearings thrown against a smooth steel plate rebound in much the same way light is reflected. Perfectly elastic particles rebounding from a resilient surface, then, could provide a suitable model for the reflection of light. See Fig. 12-2.

3. Refraction. Newton was able to demonstrate the nature of refraction by means of his particle model. We can duplicate this experimentally by arranging two level surfaces, one higher than the other, with their adjacent edges joined by an incline as in Fig. 12-3. A ball may be rolled across the upper surface, down the incline, and across the lower surface. Of course, it will experience an acceleration due to the force of gravity while rolling down the incline and will move across the lower surface at a higher speed than it had initially.

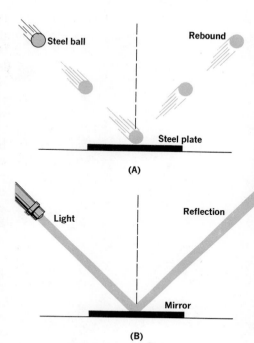

12-2 The rebound of a steel ball from a resilient surface resembles the reflection of light from a mirror surface. This example was used as an early argument to "prove" that light rays were streams of tiny particles.

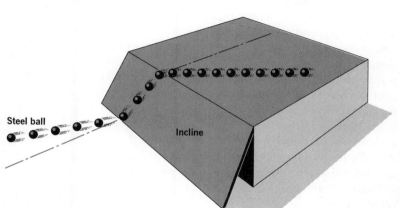

12-3 A ball bearing rolling from a higher to a lower surface illustrates one aspect of the refraction of light. In what way does this rolling-ball model of refraction fail?

Suppose the ball is set rolling on the higher surface toward the incline at a given angle with the normal to the edge. At the incline, the accelerating force exerts a pull on the ball causing it to roll across the lower surface at a smaller angle with the normal to its edge. Now if we think of the upper surface as representing air, the lower surface as an optically more dense medium like water, and the incline as the interface of the two transmitting media, the rolling ball behaves like particles of light being redirected, or refracted, as they pass from air into water.

By varying the grade of the incline while maintaining both constant rolling speed and constant angle with the normal on the upper surface, the refractive characteristics of different transmitting media can be illustrated by the rolling-ball model.

Newton believed that the water attracted the approaching particles of light in much the same way that gravity attracts the rolling ball on the incline. The rolling ball experiments imply, as they did to Newton, that light particles accelerate as they pass from air into an optically more dense medium such as water or glass. The corpuscular theory required that the speed of light in water be greater than in air. Newton recognized that if it should ever be determined that the speed of light is less in water than it is in air, his corpuscular theory would have to be abandoned. It was not until 1850, one hundred and twenty-three years after Newton's death, that the lesser speed in water was demonstrated experimentally by the French physicist Jean Foucault (foo-*koh*) (1819–1868).

12.3 The wave theory

Christian Huygens is generally considered to be the founder of the wave theory of light. Although somewhat different in its modern form, Huygens' basic concept is still very useful to us in predicting and interpreting the behavior of light. Let us recall a familiar characteristic of water waves as an introduction to this important principle.

If a stone is dropped into a pool of quiet water, it creates a disturbance in the water and a series of concentric waves travels out from the disturbance point. The stone quickly comes to rest on the bottom of the pool, so its action on the water is of short duration. However, wave disturbances persist for a considerable time thereafter and cannot reasonably be attributed to any activity on the part of the stone. It must be that the disturbances existing at all points along the wave fronts at one instant of time generate those in existence at the next instant.

Huygens recognized this logical deduction as a basic aspect of wave behavior and devised a geometric method of finding

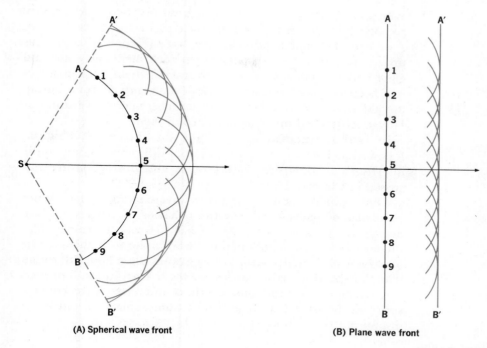

(A) Spherical wave front   (B) Plane wave front

12-4 By Huygens' principle, every point on an advancing wave front is regarded as a source of disturbance.

new wave fronts. His concept, published in 1690 and now recognized as **Huygens' principle**, may be stated as follows: *each point on a wave front may be regarded as a new source of disturbance.*

According to this principle, a wave front originating at a source **S** of Fig. 12-4(A) arrives at the position **AB**. Each point in this wave front may be considered as a secondary source sending out wavelets. Thus, from points **1, 2, 3**, etc., a series of wavelets develops simultaneously which, after a time, t, have a radius equal to vt, where v is the velocity of the wave.

The principle further states that the surface **A'B'**, tangent to all the wavelets, constitutes the new wave front. It is apparent from Fig. 12-4 that spherical wave fronts are propagated from spherical waves and plane wave fronts from plane waves.

The wave theory treats light as a train of waves having wave fronts perpendicular to the paths of the light rays. In contrast to the particle model discussed earlier, the light energy is considered to be distributed uniformly over the advancing wave front. Huygens thought of a ray merely as a line of direction of waves propagated from a light source.

The supporters of the wave theory were able to explain reflection and refraction of light satisfactorily, that of the latter requiring the speed of light in optically dense media such as water and glass to be *less* than in air. They had trouble, however, explaining rectilinear propagation. This was the primary reason why Newton rejected the wave theory.

Before the nineteenth century, interference of light was unknown, and the speed of light in such media as water and glass had not been measured. Diffraction fringes or shadows had been observed as early as the seventeenth century, but, in the absence of knowledge of interference, neither Newton nor Huygens attached much significance to them.

In 1801 the interference of light was discovered. This was followed in 1816 by the explanation of diffraction based on the interference principles. (Interference and diffraction are discussed in Chapter 15.)

These two phenomena imply a wave character and cannot be explained satisfactorily by the behavior of particles. Thus, despite the great prestige of Sir Isaac Newton, the corpuscular theory was largely abandoned in favor of the wave theory. The final blow to the corpuscular theory came when Foucault found that the speed of light was less in water than in air. Through the remainder of the nineteenth century the wave concept supplied the basic laws from which came remarkable advances in optical theory and technology.

12.4 The electromagnetic theory

Hot objects transfer heat energy by radiation. If the temperature is high enough, these objects radiate light as well as heat. If a light source is blocked off from an observer, its heating effect is cut off as well. For this reason, a cloud which obscures the sun cuts off some of the sun's heat at the same time.

Michael Faraday, the great English physicist, became concerned with the transfer of another kind of energy while investigating the attraction and repulsion of electrically charged bodies. These experiments led him in 1831 to the principle of the electric generator.

Faraday's practical mind required a model to interpret and explain physical phenomena. It was difficult for him to visualize electrically charged objects attracting or repelling each other at some distance with nothing taking place in the intervening space. Thus, he conceived a space under stress and visualized *tubes of force* between charged bodies.

Faraday was not an astute mathematician and so did not put his model for this "transmission of electric force" into abstract mathematical form.

James Clerk Maxwell, a Scot, and the first great mathematical physicist after Newton, set out to determine the properties of a medium which would transmit the energies of heat, light, and electricity. By the year 1865 he had developed a series of mathematical equations from which he predicted that all three are

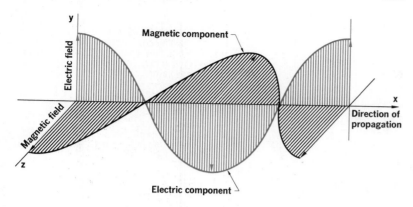

12-5 Electromagnetic wave. The electric and magnetic fields are each at right angles to the direction of propagation. This is a graph of the two fields at a given instant.

propagated in free space at the speed of light as *electromagnetic disturbances*. This unification, the *electromagnetic theory*, brought into common focus the various phenomena of radiation. Maxwell determined that the energy of an electromagnetic wave is equally divided between an electric field and a magnetic field, each perpendicular to the other, and both perpendicular to the direction of propagation of the wave. A model of an electromagnetic wave at a given instant is shown in Fig. 12-5.

By 1885 experimental confirmation of the electromagnetic theory was achieved by the German physicist, Heinrich Rudolph Hertz (1857–1894), who showed that light transmissions and electrically generated waves are of the same nature. Of course, many of their properties are quite different because of the very great differences in frequency.

Maxwell's theory of electromagnetic waves seemed to provide the final architecture for optical theory; all known optical effects could now be fully explained. Many physicists felt at this time that all the significant laws of physics had been discovered and that there was little left to do other than develop new and more sophisticated techniques for measuring everything more accurately. In this connection Hertz stated, "The wave theory of light is, from the point of view of human beings, a certainty." Ironically, it was Hertz who was soon to discover a most important phenomenon having to do with the absorption of light energy, one which would create a dilemma involving the wave theory and at the same time set the stage for the *new physics* that was to emerge in the early years of the twentieth century.

Electromagnetic energy can be detected and measured by physical means only when it is intercepted by matter and changed into another form of energy such as thermal, electric, kinetic, potential, or chemical energy. Today, the electromag-

The Bettmann Archive

Heinrich Hertz, one of the 19th century scientists who studied electromagnetic waves.

12.5 The electromagnetic spectrum

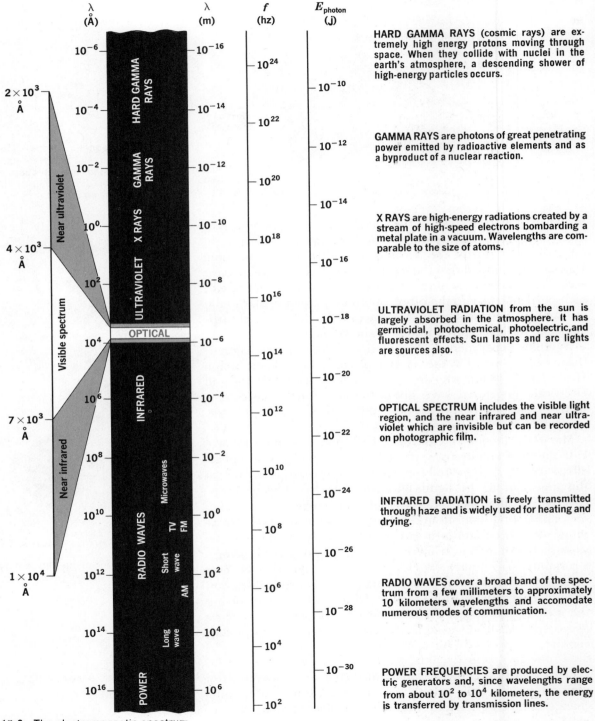

λ (Å)	λ (m)	f (hz)	E_{photon} (J)

HARD GAMMA RAYS (cosmic rays) are extremely high energy protons moving through space. When they collide with nuclei in the earth's atmosphere, a descending shower of high-energy particles occurs.

GAMMA RAYS are photons of great penetrating power emitted by radioactive elements and as a byproduct of a nuclear reaction.

X RAYS are high-energy radiations created by a stream of high-speed electrons bombarding a metal plate in a vacuum. Wavelengths are comparable to the size of atoms.

ULTRAVIOLET RADIATION from the sun is largely absorbed in the atmosphere. It has germicidal, photochemical, photoelectric, and fluorescent effects. Sun lamps and arc lights are sources also.

OPTICAL SPECTRUM includes the visible light region, and the near infrared and near ultraviolet which are invisible but can be recorded on photographic film.

INFRARED RADIATION is freely transmitted through haze and is widely used for heating and drying.

RADIO WAVES cover a broad band of the spectrum from a few millimeters to approximately 10 kilometers wavelengths and accomodate numerous modes of communication.

POWER FREQUENCIES are produced by electric generators and, since wavelengths range from about 10^2 to 10^4 kilometers, the energy is transferred by transmission lines.

12-6   The electromagnetic spectrum.

netic spectrum is known to consist of a tremendous range of radiation frequencies extending from about 10 hz to more than 10^{25} hz. Since all electromagnetic radiations travel in free space with a speed of 3×10^8 meters per second, the range of wavelengths is from about 3×10^7 meters in the low-frequency region to less than 3×10^{-17} meters in the high-frequency region. In angstroms (Å), the units commonly used to express the wavelengths of electromagnetic radiations, the range is from 3×10^{17} Å to 3×10^{-7} Å. One angstrom equals 10^{-10} m.

The electromagnetic spectrum may be divided into eight major regions depending on the general character of the radiations: (1) electric waves; (2) radio waves; (3) infrared; (4) optical; (5) ultraviolet; (6) X rays; (7) gamma rays; and (8) hard gamma rays. See Fig. 12-6.

The optical spectrum includes those radiations, commonly called light, that can be detected visually. They range from approximately 7600 Å to 4000 Å. Accordingly, *light may be defined as radiant energy which a human observer can see.* The optical spectrum extends into the near infrared and into the near ultraviolet. These radiations, although our eyes cannot see them, can be detected by means of photographic film.

As mentioned in Section 12.4, Hertz conducted experiments that led to confirmation of the electromagnetic theory. While studying the radiation characteristics of oscillatory discharges, he observed that a spark discharge occurred more readily between two charged spheres when they were illuminated by another spark discharge. At about the same time other investigators found that negatively charged zinc plates lost their charge when illuminated by the ultraviolet radiations from an arc lamp. Positively charged plates, on the other hand, were not discharged when similarly illuminated.

Observations of the peculiar effects of ultraviolet radiation on metal surfaces led to the discovery of the photoelectric effect, a phenomenon which defied explanation based on the electromagnetic wave theory of light.

Suppose two freshly polished zinc plates **A** and **B** are sealed in an evacuated tube with a quartz window and are connected externally to a battery and galvanometer (a sensitive current-indicating meter) as shown in Fig. 12-7. The quartz window transmits ultraviolet radiation which does not pass through glass. The galvanometer indicates a small current in the circuit when ultraviolet light falls on the negative plate **A**. If a sensitive electrometer circuit is substituted for the battery, it may be shown that the plate exposed to the ultraviolet light acquires a positive charge.

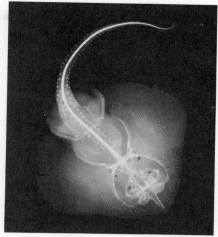

Eastman Kodak Co.

X-ray photo of a sting ray. The wavelengths of X rays are shorter than those of visible light and are more penetrating. Special film is required to take photos in this region of the electromagnetic spectrum.

12.6 The photoelectric effect

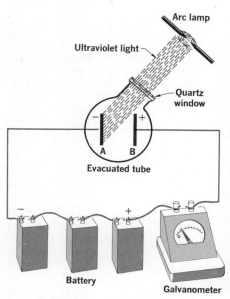

12-7 Apparatus for demonstrating the photoelectric effect.

The results of these experiments imply that the action of the light on the zinc plate causes it to lose electrons. The German physicist Philipp Lenard (1862–1947) published the results in the first quantitative studies of the photoelectric phenomenon in 1902. By measuring the charge-to-mass ratio of the negative electricity derived from an aluminum plate illuminated by ultraviolet light, he was able to prove that electrons were ejected from the metal surface. Such electrons are called *photoelectrons*. Subsequent investigations have shown that all substances exhibit photoemission of electrons. *The emission of electrons by a substance when illuminated by electromagnetic radiation is known as the photoelectric effect*.

12.7 Laws of photoelectric emission

Plate **B** of Fig. 12-7, having a positive potential V with respect to the emitter plate **A**, acts as a collector of photoelectrons ejected from the emitter. If the positive potential is increased enough, all photoelectrons are collected by plate **B** and the photoelectric current I reaches a certain limiting or *saturation* magnitude.

Curve **a** of Fig. 12-8 is a graph of photoelectric current as a function of collector plate potential for a given source of light. Curve **b** shows the result of doubling the intensity of the light. Observe that the magnitude of the saturation current is doubled. This means, of course, that the rate of emission of photoelectrons is doubled. Here we have evidence of the ***first law of photoelectric emission***: *the rate of emission of photoelectrons is directly proportional to the intensity of the incident light.*

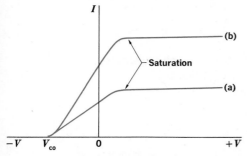

12-8   Photoelectric current as a function of collector plate potential. Curve (b) shows the effect of doubling the intensity of the same incident light.

For an electron to escape through the surface of a metal, work must be done against the forces that bind it within the surface. This work is known as the *work function* of the substance. Photoelectrons must acquire the energy needed to overcome this surface barrier from the incident light radiation. If electrons acquire less energy than the work function of the metal they cannot be ejected. On the other hand, if they acquire more energy than is required to pass through the surface, the excess appears as kinetic energy and, consequently, as velocity of the photoelectrons.

We may assume that light penetrates a few atom layers into the metal and that the photoelectric effect will occur at varying depths beneath the surface. Photoelectrons ejected from atom layers below the surface will lose energy through collisions in reaching the surface and must then give up energy equal to the work function of the metal in escaping through the surface. Photoelectrons ejected from the surface layer of atoms lose only the energy necessary to overcome the surface attractions. Thus, in any photoelectric phenomenon, we should expect photoelectrons to be emitted at various velocities ranging up to a maximum value possessed by electrons having their origin in the surface layer of atoms.

We can test the logic of these deductions by experimenting further with the photoelectric cell of Fig. 12-7. A positive potential of a few volts on the collector plate **B** produces a saturation current as shown in Fig. 12-8. If the collector plate potential is lowered towards zero, the photoelectric current decreases slightly, but at zero potential may still be close to the saturation magnitude.

As the collector plate potential is made slightly negative with respect to the emitter, the photoelectric current decreases also. By increasing this negative potential, a value is soon reached where the photoelectric current drops to zero. This is called the *stopping* or *cut-off* potential V_{co} of Fig. 12-8.

A negative potential on the collector plate repels the photoelectrons, tending to turn them back to the emitter plate. Only those electrons having enough kinetic energy (and velocity) to overcome this repulsion reach the collector. As the cut-off potential is approached, only those photoelectrons with the highest velocity reach the collector. These are the electrons with the maximum kinetic energy emitted from the surface layer of the metal. At the cut-off potential, these electrons are also repelled back to the emitter.

Thus the negative collector potentials, which repel rather than attract photoelectrons, reveal something about the kinetic energy distribution of the ejected electrons. As this potential is made more negative a nearly linear decrease in photoelectron current shows us that the photoelectrons do have a variety of velocities. The cut-off potential measures the kinetic energy of the *fastest* photoelectrons.

Observe, from curves **a** and **b** of Fig. 12-8, that the photoelectric currents produced by different intensities of incident light from a certain source reach zero at the same collector potential. Thus the cut-off potential for a given photoelectric system, and *the velocity of the electrons expelled*, are independent of the intensity of the light source. From these observations we may formulate a **second law of photoelectric emission:** *the kinetic energy of photoelectrons is independent of the intensity of the incident light.*

The American physicist, Robert A. Millikan (1868–1953), performed many experiments with various emitters and light sources. By illuminating emitters made of sodium metal with light radiations of different frequencies, Millikan found that the cut-off potential had different values for the various frequencies of incident light. By plotting the cut-off potentials V_{co} as a func-

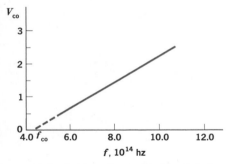

12-9 A plot of cut-off potentials for sodium as measured by Millikan at various frequencies of illumination. The cut-off frequency of sodium is 4.4×10^{14} hz.

tion of light frequencies f, he obtained the straight line shown in Fig. 12-9. He demonstrated that *the cut-off potential depends only on the frequency of the incident light.*

Recalling that the cut-off potential measures the kinetic energy of the fastest photoelectrons ejected in a particular photoelectric system, we must conclude that the *maximum kinetic energy of photoelectrons increases with the frequency of the light illuminating the emitter.*

Other physicists, notably Hughes at the Cavendish Laboratory in England and K. T. Compton at Princeton University, obtained similar results in numerous experiments. All these experiments showed further that *there is, for each kind of surface, a characteristic threshold or cut-off frequency f_{co} below which the photoelectric emission of electrons ceases* no matter how intense the illumination.

Only a few elements, in particular the alkali metals, exhibit photoelectric emission with ordinary visible light. The cut-off frequency of cesium is in the infrared region of the electromagnetic spectrum. Millikan determined f_{co} of sodium to be 4.4×10^{14} hz, red light with a wavelength of about 6800 Å. The cut-off frequency of potassium is in the visible green region. Those of copper and platinum are in the ultraviolet and deep ultraviolet.

Incident light radiations, to cause photoelectric emission, must contain frequencies higher than the cut-off frequency characteristic of each surface. The maximum kinetic energy of photoelectrons emitted from any surface can be increased only by raising the frequency of the light illuminating the surface. These facts provide us with a ***third law of photoelectric emission:*** *within the region of effective frequencies, the maximum kinetic energy of photoelectrons varies directly with the difference between the frequency of the incident light and the cut-off frequency.*

12.8 Failures of the wave theory

The experiments of Hertz, together with those which followed, confirmed that Maxwell's electromagnetic theory correctly describes the transmission of light and other kinds of radiation. This wave theory requires the radiated energy to be distributed uniformly and continuously over a wave front. The higher the intensity of the radiating source, the greater should be the energy distributed over the wavefront.

The first law of photoelectric emission does not imply any deviation from the electromagnetic theory, since the magnitude of the photoelectric current is proportional to the incident light intensity. The surprising thing is that the velocity of the photoelectrons is not raised with an increase in the intensity of the illumination on the surface of an emitter, as the wave theory suggests. Measurements of emission cut-off potentials over very large ranges of intensities show that the maximum kinetic energy of photoelectrons is independent of the light intensity.

According to the wave theory, light of any frequency should cause photoelectric emission provided it is intense enough. Experiments show, however, that all substances have characteristic cut-off frequencies below which emission does not occur, no matter how intense the illumination. On the other hand, a very feeble light containing frequencies above the threshold value causes the ejection of photoelectrons.

Again, from the wave theory we could argue that, given enough time, an electron in an area illuminated by a very feeble light would "soak up" enough energy to escape from the surface. No such time lag between the illumination of a surface and the ejection of a photoelectron has ever been measured. The emission of photoelectrons begins simultaneously with the illumination of a photosensitive surface.

The wave theory which serves so well in the explanation of radiation transmission phenomena is incapable of describing the processes of radiation absorption observed in the photoelectric effect. In this instance a particle model of light appears to be useful. Had Newton perhaps been on the right track after all? The classical particles of Newton's theory could explain the relation between photoelectron emission rate and intensity of illumination, but not that between photoelectron velocities and frequency of illumination.

The discovery of the photoelectric effect, coming as it did from the experiments that established the correctness of the electromagnetic wave theory, presented a paradox to twentieth-century physicists. Was there no theory to explain these widely divergent phenomena?

12.9 The quantum theory

Aside from the disturbing implications which the photoelectric effect introduced into twentieth-century physics, physicists were much concerned about discrepancies between their experimental studies of absorption and emission of radiant energy and the requirements derived from the electromagnetic radiation theory.

The first great step toward the resolution of these discrepancies was taken by Max Planck (1858–1947), a German theoretical physicist. In 1900 Planck was investigating the spectral distribution of electromagnetic radiation from a hot body. Classical electromagnetic theory predicted that the emission intensity would increase as the square of the radiation frequency. Accordingly, an infinite amount of energy should be radiated at the

Physics Today

Max Planck, a German physicist, developed the initial assumptions on which the quantum theory is based while studying radiation phenomena.

higher temperatures and higher radiating frequencies. The spectral distribution of radiated energy which had been experimentally measured was very different from that predicted by theory.

Planck found that he could bring radiation theory and experiment into agreement by assuming the energy emitted by the radiating sources to be an intergral multiple of a fundamental quantity hf, where h is a universal constant now known as *Planck's constant,* and f is the frequency of these radiating sources. To explain why this bold assumption worked, he postulated that light is radiated and absorbed in indivisible packets or quanta we now call *photons.*

The amount of energy comprising a photon is determined by the frequency of the radiation. It is directly proportional to this frequency since

$$E = hf$$

When f is given in hertz and h in joule seconds ($h = 6.63 \times 10^{-34}$ j sec), the energy E of a photon is expressed in joules.

Planck published his quantum hypothesis in 1901 and, although not immediately accepted, it was destined to influence profoundly the *new physics* emerging with the twentieth century. Certainly there is nothing in the classical physics of Newton to suggest that certain values of energy should be allowed and others should not.

Albert Einstein recognized the value of Planck's quantum hypothesis in connection with the photoelectric effect. He reasoned that, since emission and absorption of light radiation occur discontinuously, certainly the transmission field should be discontinuous. Proceeding on this hypothesis, Einstein published in 1905 a very simple and straightforward explanation of the photoelectric effect. A few years later, the very accurate experimental work of Millikan, Hughes, and Compton established the correctness of Einstein's explanation. The bold extension of Planck's quantum ideas by Einstein firmly established *the* **quantum theory** *which assumes that the transfer of energy between light radiations and matter occurs in discrete units called quanta, the magnitude of which depends on the frequency of the radiation.*

12.10 Einstein's photoelectric equation.

According to Einstein, light radiation illuminating an emitter surface consists of a stream of photons. When a photon is absorbed by the emitter its quantum of energy hf is transferred to a single electron within the surface. If the acquired energy is sufficient to overcome the surface barrier and the electron is moving in the right direction, it will escape from the surface. In penetrating the surface, the electron must give up a certain energy w, the work function of the substance. If the energy hf imparted by the photon is greater than w, the electron will have kinetic energy as indicated by its velocity after leaving the surface.

The maximum kinetic energy possessed by photoelectrons ejected from an emitter illuminated by light of frequency f was given by Einstein as

$$\tfrac{1}{2}mv^2_{max} = hf - w$$

where m and v are the mass and velocity respectively of the photoelectrons, h is Planck's constant, f is the frequency of the impinging light radiation (the product hf is the energy of the photon), and w is the work function of the emitting material.

Now, recalling the failures of the wave theory to explain photoelectric emission, we find no such difficulties in the application of Einstein's photon hypothesis. A lower light intensity means fewer photons impinging on the emitter surface in a given period of time, and fewer photoelectrons ejected. However, as long as the frequency of the incident light remains unchanged, each photon transfers the same energy hf to the electron when a collision occurs.

Einstein's photoelectric equation shows clearly why light of too low a frequency will not cause photoelectric emission from a given material no matter how intense the illumination. Photon energy is a linear function of the frequency of the light since it equals the product hf. Now if $\tfrac{1}{2}mv^2_{max} = 0$, it follows that

$$hf_{co} = w$$

Here the photon can impart to the electron just enough energy to penetrate the surface barrier. No energy is left over to appear as electron velocity. The frequency in this situation is the cut-off frequency f_{co}. Illumination of any lower frequency on this emitter will consist of photons with energy $hf < w$ and photoelectric emission cannot occur no matter how many photons there are.

If photons have enough energy to eject electrons, no "soaking up" time is required before a feeble light can start the photoelectric emission process because the ejection energy for each photoelectron is delivered in a single concentrated bundle.

The quantum theory, which provides a particle model of light, meets every objection raised when the electromagnetic wave theory is employed to interpret photoelectric emission phenomena. Yet many experiments have proved the correctness of the wave theory. When we consider the full range of radiation phenomena, light must have a dual character. In some circumstances it behaves like waves, and in others like particles.

The modern view of the nature of light recognizes this dual character: radiant energy is transported in photons which are guided along their path by a wave field.

12.11 The quantized atom

Striking evidence favoring the quantum theory was given by Niels Bohr, who in 1913 devised a model of the atom based on quantum ideas. Rutherford had conducted experiments (described in Section 23.7) that led him to postulate the nuclear atom with its planetary arrangement of electrons in 1911. This model of Rutherford's encountered difficulties immediately when subjected to the classical laws of physics, i.e., the known laws of mechanics and electromagnetism as formulated by Newton and Maxwell.

The electromagnetic theory predicts that charged particles undergoing acceleration must radiate energy. Indeed, this accounts for the radiation of energy from a radio transmitting antenna. A planetary electron moving about the nucleus of an atom experiences acceleration and, accordingly, should radiate energy. As energy is drained from the electron it should spiral in toward the nucleus causing the atom to collapse. Of course atoms do not collapse and so this classical model cannot be correct.

Bohr assumed that an electron in an atom can move about the nucleus in certain discrete orbits without radiating energy. Such orbits represent "allowable" energy levels in the Planck concept, the level closest to the nucleus being the lowest. This postulate could account for the stability of an atom. However, atoms do radiate energy. Bohr assumed further that an electron may "jump" from one discrete orbit to another of lower energy. In the process a photon is emitted. Its energy represents the energy difference between the initial and final states of the atom. The frequency of the emission depends on the magnitude of this energy change ΔE and can be expressed as $\Delta E/h$.

Danish Information Office

Niels Bohr, the Danish physicist, received the Nobel Prize in 1922 for his work in atomic physics.

12-10 Representative lines in the hydrogen spectrum. The small letter below each line indicates which of the energy-level transitions in Figure 12-11 produces it.

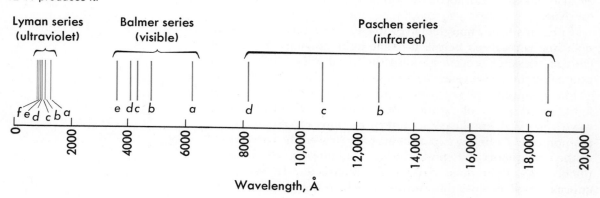

Lyman series
(ultraviolet)

Balmer series
(visible)

Paschen series
(infrared)

f e d c b a   e dc b   a   d   c   b   a

0   2000   4000   6000   8000   10,000   12,000   14,000   16,000   18,000   20,000

Wavelength, Å

The return of excited atoms to their stable state results in the emission of *bright line spectra*. (See Color Plate VII, Chapter 14.) Excited hydrogen atoms produce the simplest such atomic spectra. Hydrogen lines appear in several series in and beyond the visible region of the radiation spectrum. These include the *Balmer series* in the visible region, the *Lyman series* in the ultraviolet region, and the *Paschen series* in the near infrared region. See Figs. 12-10 and 12-11.

Numerous attempts had been made by physicists to account for the discrete frequencies of the bright lines observed in these spectra. However, it remained for Bohr to associate spectral lines with pairs of energy levels. This hypothesis marked the initial step in the development of the *quantum mechanics* of atomic structure.

Bohr's atom model provided no information about the mechanics of photon emission when an electron passes from a higher to a lower energy level; but his concept of energy levels provided a great stimulus for theoretical studies in this field. About 1924 the French physicist Louis de Broglie suggested that the dual particle-and-wave nature of light provided evidence of the wave nature of particles as well. Accepting Einstein's idea of the equivalence between mass and energy, he postulated that *in every mechanical system, waves are associated with matter particles.* The application of this concept of matter waves to the study of the structure of matter is known as *wave mechanics*. Just as the ordinary laws of mechanics are essential to any explanation of the behavior of objects of large dimensions, *wave mechanics* is necessary in dealing with objects which have atomic and subatomic dimensions.

A photon has energy which is the product of Planck's constant and its radiation frequency.

$$E = hf$$

In Einstein's equation $E = mc^2$ for mass-energy equivalency, m is the mass of the particle while in motion. When at rest its mass m_0, known as the rest mass is smaller than m.

If we consider the energy of the photon to be equivalent to that of a moving particle, then

$$hf = mc^2$$

and we could solve for m. However, this would imply also a certain rest mass for the photon. But a photon is never at rest; it always moves with the speed c. Photons do have momentum and can transfer it to any surface on which they impinge. Cal-

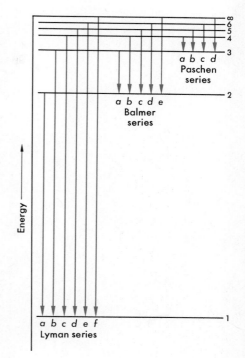

12-11 An electronic energy-level diagram for hydrogen showing some of the transitions which are possible in this atom.

culating this momentum mc we get

$$mc = \frac{hf}{c}$$

Since $$c = f\lambda$$

by substitution,

$$mc = \frac{h}{\lambda}$$

or $$\lambda = \frac{h}{mc}$$

The wavelength of the photon may be expressed in terms of its momentum mc. Similarly, the wavelength of any matter particle having a velocity v may be expressed in terms of its momentum mv.

$$\lambda = \frac{h}{mv}$$

There is abundant evidence today of the wave nature of subatomic particles. Accelerated electrons have been found to behave like X rays. The electron microscope is an application of electron waves. The development of the quantum theory and the system of wave mechanics have provided physicists with their most powerful means of studying the structure and properties of matter. Matter waves will be discussed more extensively in Chapter 25.

12.12 Production of X rays

In the photoelectric effect, photons of frequency f cause the ejection of electrons from atoms of a substance with a maximum velocity given by the equation

$$\tfrac{1}{2}mv^2_{max} = hf - w$$

It is not surprising that the converse of this phenomenon can be produced also. High-speed electrons projected against the surface of a target with velocity v cause the emission of photons of radiation having a maximum frequency given by the photoelectric equation

$$\tfrac{1}{2}mv^2 = hf_{max} - w$$

The work function w of target material is negligible compared to the photon energy at X-ray frequencies and is usually omitted from the above equation.

This phenomenon is sometimes referred to as the *inverse photoelectric effect*. A well-known example is the production of

X rays by bombardment of a metal target in an X-ray tube by accelerated electrons. Each electron that strikes the target loses its energy, and this energy reappears as photons of radiation. No more than the full kinetic energy of the electron can appear in the X-ray photons as the energy hf. Since h is constant, the maximum frequency f_{max} of the X-ray radiation is determined by the velocity v of the electron.

The penetrating properties of X rays and their many practical uses stemming from these properties are well known. X rays lie deep in the high frequency end of the electromagnetic spectrum beyond the ultraviolet region. The energy hf of X-ray photons is very high, being of the order of 10^4 times the energy of photons in the visible region. As a consequence of this high photon energy and the very short wave lengths, X rays are used extensively in numerous areas of research. Table 12-1 gives photon energies for important regions of the spectrum.

The electromagnetic theory of Maxwell predicted that incident light should exert a pressure applied in the direction of the radiation. According to Maxwell, the pressure on a totally reflecting surface should be twice that on a totally absorbing surface illuminated by the same radiation.

In 1901, Nichols and Hull in the United States and Lebedev in Russia succeeded in measuring the pressure of light experimentally. Their results were in such close agreement with theory as to provide proof of the existence of light pressure.

What does the particle model tell us about the pressure of light? Our common experiences with pressure are those involving collisions of particles in motion. Since particle collisions are momentum problems, conservation of momentum applies.

A perfectly elastic ball rebounding from an object transfers twice the momentum that a perfectly inelastic ball having the same mass and velocity would transfer. In Section 12.11 we expressed the momentum of a photon in terms of its frequency as

$$mc = \frac{hf}{c}$$

When a beam of photons is incident on a totally absorbing surface, the pressure exerted depends on the rate of change of photon momentum per unit area of illuminated surface. (Pressure, p, is defined as force per unit area).

$$p = \frac{F}{A} = \frac{\Delta(hf/c)}{\Delta t \times A} = \frac{\Delta hf}{c\Delta tA}$$

Table 12-1 PHOTON ENERGIES

Radiation	Typical value of f (hz)	hf (j)
radio waves	3.0×10^{15}	2.0×10^{-28}
heat waves	3.0×10^{13}	2.0×10^{-26}
visible light	6.0×10^{14}	4.0×10^{-19}
X rays	3.0×10^{18}	2.0×10^{-15}
gamma rays	3.0×10^{19}	2.0×10^{-14}

12.13 The pressure of light

In the MKS system, p has the dimensions

$$p = \frac{\mathbf{j} \text{ sec/sec}}{\mathbf{m/sec} \times \mathbf{sec} \times \mathbf{m}^2} = \frac{\mathbf{j}}{\mathbf{m}^3} = \frac{\mathbf{n}}{\mathbf{m}^2}$$

If the photon energy hf is totally reflected from the surface of a body, the momentum change is $2hf/c$ and the pressure of light is twice that for the totally absorbing surface illuminated by the same beam.

The pressure of light is exceedingly small in comparison to pressures we commonly experience. The pressure of sunlight on the earth is approximately 4×10^{-11} standard atmosphere. The tails of comets always point away from the sun, apparently due to the pressure of sunlight and solar particles on the extremely diffuse matter in comet tails. See Fig. 12-12.

Lowell Observatory

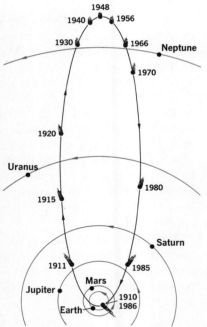

12-12 Halley's comet (left) as it looked during its last appearance in 1910. The comet's tail, millions of miles long, may be produced by pressure of radiation from the sun. In the diagram of the comet's orbit (above), notice that the tail always points away from the sun and gets longer as the distance between the two bodies decreases.

QUESTIONS

1. What is the modern view of the nature of light?
2. Arrange the following in order of increasing wavelength: visible light; infrared radiations; ultraviolet radiations; X rays; radio waves; gamma rays.
3. Compare visible light and sound as to: (a) origin; (b) transmitting media; (c) wavelength; (d) type of wave; (e) speed.
4. How does an atom of a substance radiate energy according to the quantum theory?
5. The flatiron is a source of radiations that cannot be detected by the eye. (a) Would you expect an ordinary photoelectric cell to detect these radiations? Explain. (b) Suggest a way to prove that such radiations are emitted.

6. A beam of light passes through a small aperture and illuminates the blackened bulb of a thermometer. A piece of ordinary glass is placed over the aperture and the thermometer reading drops two degrees. The glass is replaced by a quartz window and the thermometer reading returns approximately to the original value. What do the results suggest concerning the nature of the light source? Explain.
7. (a) State the three laws of photoelectric emission. (b) To what extent is a wave model of light successful in explaining these laws?
8. Given a monochromatic (single frequency) light source to illuminate a photocell, how can you explain the fact that photoelectrons are ejected at various velocities ranging up to a maximum value?
9. How does the pair of curves of Fig. 12-8 show that the velocity of photoelectrons is independent of the intensity of the light illuminating the photocell?
10. What special significance can you attach to the photoelectric situation in which the photon energy hf transferred to an electron is just equal to the work function w of the emitter?
11. How would you defend the assertion that the production of X rays illustrates the inverse photoelectric effect?

ILLUMINATION

Nearly all the natural light we receive comes from the sun. Distant stars account for an extremely small amount. Of course, moonlight is sunlight reflected from the surface of the moon.

We produce light from artificial sources in several ways. Materials may be heated until they glow, or become incandescent, as in an electric lamp. Molecules of a gas at reduced pressure may be bombarded with electrons to produce light, as in

12.14 Luminous and illuminated objects

a neon tube. Most of the visible light from fluorescent tubes results from the action of ultraviolet radiations on phosphors that coat the inside surface of the glass tubes. The firefly produces light by means of complex chemical reactions.

Most artificial sources of light are hot bodies which radiate energy in the infrared region of the spectrum as well as visible light. The energy of the *thermal radiation* emitted by hot bodies depends upon the temperature of the body and the nature of its surface. The radiation is distributed over a range of wavelengths.

At a temperature of 300° C the most intense radiation emitted by a hot body has a wavelength of about 5×10^{-4} cm, well down in the infrared region of the electromagnetic spectrum. As the temperature is raised to 800° C, enough radiation is emitted in the visible region to cause the body to appear "red hot" although the bulk of the energy radiated is still in the infrared region. If the temperature of the body is raised to 3000° C, the most intense emission remains in the near infrared region; however, there is enough blue visible radiation to cause the body to appear "white hot."

This last temperature is near that of the filament of an incandescent lamp. Hence such lamps have low efficiencies as producers of visible radiation. Generally the efficiency improves as the filament temperature is raised.

The white-hot filament of an incandescent lamp is said to be *luminous*. It is visible primarily because of the light it emits. *An object which gives off light because of the energy of its accelerated particles is said to be **luminous**.* The sun and the other stars are luminous objects.

Just as radiant heat may be reflected, light may be reflected from the surfaces of objects. Mirrors reflect a beam of light in a definite direction. Other surfaces scatter the light which is incident on them in all directions. *An object that is seen because of the light scattered from it is said to be **illuminated**.* The moon is illuminated, for it reflects radiant energy from the sun. Some of the light energy arriving at the surface of a substance is

12-13 The formation of beams and pencils of light.

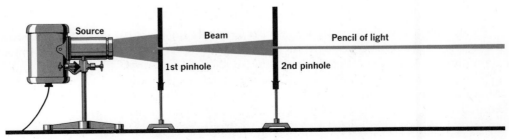

Source   Beam   Pencil of light

1st pinhole   2nd pinhole

reflected, some is transmitted, and some is absorbed by the substance.

Any dark-colored object absorbs light, but a black one absorbs nearly all the light it receives. When the rays of the sun strike a body of water vertically, most of them are either absorbed or transmitted. Most of the rays are reflected, however, when they strike the water at an oblique angle. For this reason the image of the sun can be seen in the water without discomfort when the sun is directly overhead, but not when the sun is near the horizon.

Air, glass, and water transmit light readily and are said to be *transparent*. Other substances transmit light but scatter or diffuse it so that objects seen through them cannot be identified; these are *translucent* substances, typical examples being frosted electric lamps and parchment lampshades. *Opaque* substances do not transmit light at all.

From a luminous point-source, light waves travel outward in all directions. If the medium through which they pass is of the same nature throughout, the light progresses along the normal to the wave front. A single line of light from a luminous point is called a *ray*; a group of closely spaced rays form a *beam* of light. Small beams are referred to as *pencils*. See Fig. 12-13. Light coming from the sun is in rays so nearly parallel that it may be considered as a parallel beam. When several rays of light come from a point, they are called a *diverging* pencil, while rays proceeding toward a point form a *converging* pencil. When the sun's rays pass through a magnifying glass, they converge at a point called a *focus*.

Since an opaque object absorbs light, it produces a shadow in the space behind it. When the source of light is a point, as in Fig. 12-14(A), an opaque ball, **B**, cuts off all the rays which strike it, and produces a shadow of uniform darkness on screen **S**. If the light comes from an extended source, the shadow varies in intensity as shown in Fig. 12-14(B). The part from which all the rays of light are excluded is called the *umbra*; the lighter part of the shadow is the *penumbra*. Within the region of the penumbra the luminous source is not entirely hidden from an observer.

The speed of light is one of the most important constants used in physics and the determination of the speed of light represents one of the most precise measurements achieved by man. Before 1675, light propagation was generally considered to be instantaneous, although Galileo had suggested that a finite time was required for it to travel through space. In that year a Danish astronomer, Olaus Roemer, determined the

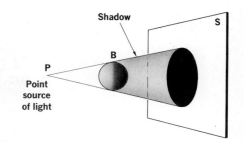

(A)

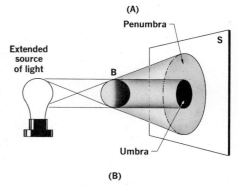

(B)

12-14 An obstruction in the path of light from a point source (A) casts a shadow of uniform density. If the light is from an extended source (B), the shadow is of varying density.

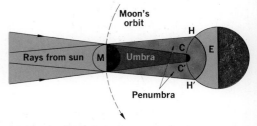

12-15 A diagram of a total solar eclipse showing the umbral and penumbral regions of the moon's shadow. CC' is the region of totality on the earth; CH and C'H' are the regions from which a partial eclipse is seen. (Sizes and distances are not to scale.)

12.15 The speed of light

first value for the speed of light to be 140,000 miles per second. This is approximately equivalent to 225,000 kilometers per second. He had been puzzled by a variation in his calculations of the time of eclipse of one of Jupiter's satellites as seen from different positions of the earth's orbit about the sun. Roemer concluded that the variation was due to differences in the distance which the light traveled to reach the earth.

Very precise modern measurements of the speed of light are made using laboratory methods. The most notable experiments were performed by Albert A. Michelson (1852–1931), a professor of physics at the University of Chicago, who measured the speed of light in air and in a vacuum with extraordinary precision.

1. The speed of light in air. Michelson measured the speed of light over the accurately determined distance between Mt. Wilson and Mt. San Antonio, California. His method is illustrated in principle, by Fig. 12-16. The light source, octagonal mirror, and telescope were located on Mt. Wilson and the concave mirror and plane mirror were located on Mt. San Antonio, approximately 22 miles away. The octagonal mirror, **M**, could be rotated rapidly under controlled conditions and was timed very accurately.

With mirror **M** stationary, a pencil of light from the slit opening was reflected by M_1 to the distant mirror **M′**, from which it was returned to M_3. The image of the slit in the mirror at the M_3 position could be observed accurately through the telescope. The octagonal mirror was then set in motion and the speed of rotation brought up to the value which moved M_2 into the position formerly occupied by M_3 during the time required for the light to travel from M_1 to Mt. San Antonio and

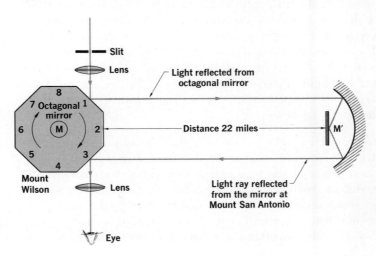

12-16 Michelson's octagonal-mirror method for measuring the speed of light.

return. The slit image was again seen in the telescope precisely as it was when the octagon was stationary. The light traveled twice the optical path of approximately 22 miles in one-eighth of the time of one revolution of the octagonal mirror. Thus,

$$c = \frac{2MM'}{t}$$

where MM' is the optical path, t is the time of one-eighth revolution of the octagon, and c is the speed of light in air.

Michelson's investigation of the speed of light in air required several years to complete and extremely high precision was attained in making the necessary observations. The optical path was measured by the U.S. Coast and Geodetic Survey and found to be 35,385.5 meters, accurate to about one part in seven million. The rate of the revolving mirror was measured by stroboscopic comparision with an electric signal of standard frequency. The average of a large number of determinations yielded a speed of light in air of 299,729 km/sec.

2. The speed of light in a vacuum. Michelson conducted similar experiments using an evacuated tube one mile long to eliminate the problems of haze and variations in air density. In these investigations he determined the speed of light to be 299,796 km/sec, which he believed to be accurate to within 1 km/sec.

12-17 A laser beam is directed down a 30-meter vacuum tube in an experiment to measure the speed of light. The apparatus is installed in an abandoned gold mine and is so sensitive that it records "tides" in the earth's crust caused by the sun and moon.

National Bureau of Standards

Modern laboratory methods of measuring the speed of light are considered to be more accurate than those used by Michelson and require very complex apparatus. In some experiments electromagnetic waves much longer than light waves have been used, good agreement being found between their speed and that of visible light. These findings provide experimental confirmation of Maxwell's electromagnetic theory which requires that all electromagnetic waves throughout the electromagnetic spectrum have the same speed c in free space. Thus, we must consider the speed of light within the larger framework of the speed of electromagnetic radiations in general.

As Michelson's figures show, the speed of light is slightly higher in a vacuum than in air; the speed in free space generally accepted as most accurate is

$$c = 2.99792458 \times 10^8 \text{ m/sec}$$

with an uncertainty of 1.2 m/sec. New laser experiments may soon provide the physicist with the techniques for measuring the speed of light with even greater accuracy.

12.16 Light measurements

*The quantitative study of light is called **photometry**.* Three quantities are generally measured in practical photometry; the *luminous intensity* of the source, the *luminous flux* or light flow from a source, and the *illumination* on a surface.

1. Luminous intensity. In order to derive a set of photometric units it is necessary to introduce an additional fundamental unit into our measurement system. The unit for luminous intensity I is the arbitrary choice. It is the *candle*(cd). The candle is known internationally as *candela*.

Originally the light from a certain type of candle was used as a standard, but this has been replaced by a more readily reproducible source of luminous intensity. *The **candle** is one-sixtieth of the luminous intensity of a square centimeter of a black-body radiator maintained at the temperature of freezing platinum (2046°K).* In practice it is convenient to use incandescent lamps which have been rated by comparison with the standard.

Incandescent lamps used for interior lighting generally have an intensity ranging from a few candles to several hundred candles. The common 40-watt lamp has an intensity of about 35 candles; a 100-watt lamp gives about 130 candles, while a 40-watt fluorescent lamp has an intensity of about 200 candles. The intensity of any lamp depends on the direction from which it is measured; the average candle power in all directions in space (spherical candle power) is often given.

2. Luminous flux. Not all of the energy radiated from a luminous source is capable of producing a visual sensation. Most of the radiation is in the infrared region and a small amount is in the ultraviolet region. For example, only about 2.3% of the energy supplied to a 100-watt incandescent lamp is radiated as visible light. The rate of flow of visible radiation is called *luminous flux*, the symbol for which is the Greek letter Φ (phi). **Luminous flux** *is that part of the total energy radiated per unit of time from a luminous source which is capable of producing the sensation of sight.* The unit of luminous flux is the *lumen* (lm).

Suppose a standard light source of 1 candle is placed at the center of a hollow sphere having a radius of 1 meter as illustrated in Fig. 12-18. The luminous source is presumed to radiate light equally in all directions and to have such small dimensions that it may be termed a "point source." The area of the surface of a sphere of radius r is equal to $4\pi r^2$. Since the radius of the unit sphere is 1 meter, its surface area is $4\pi \times (1\text{ m})^2$. One lumen of flux is radiated by the 1-candle source to each square meter of inside surface of the sphere. *The **lumen** is the luminous flux on a unit surface all points of which are at unit distance from a point source of one candle.* The lumen is not a measure of a total quantity of luminous energy but a *rate* at which luminous energy is being emitted, transmitted, or received.

The unit surface area of the unit sphere is intercepted by a solid angle (ω) of 1 *steradian* (sr). The unit surface area of a sphere of radius r is intercepted by a solid angle of $1/r^2$ steradians. *The ratio of the intercepted surface area of a sphere to the square of the radius is the measure of the solid angle in steradians.*

$$\omega = \frac{A}{r^2} \text{ (in sr)}$$

Observe that the steradian is dimensionless.

The luminous flux of the standard light source of 1 candle is 1 lumen per steradian.

Since the unit sphere has 4π unit areas of surface, there are 4π steradians per sphere. The total luminous flux emitted by a point source is, therefore, 4π lumens per candle of luminous intensity.

$$\Phi = \frac{4\pi \text{ lm}}{\text{cd}} \times I \text{ cd}$$

$$\Phi = 4\pi I \qquad\qquad \text{(in lumens)}$$

Thus a luminous source having an intensity of 1 candle emits light at the rate of 4π lm, or 12.57 lumens. In fact, light sources are usually rated in terms of the total flux emitted, with 12.57 lumens being radiated by 1 candle. A 40-watt incandescent lamp is rated at about 450 lumens and a 40-watt fluorescent lamp at about 2600 lumens.

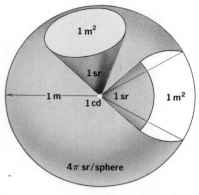

12-18 A 1-candle point source radiates luminous flux at the rate of 4π lumens.

3. Illumination. In Fig. 12-18 it is evident that as the intensity of the source is increased, the luminous flux transmitted to each unit area of surface and the flux on each unit area are similarly increased. The *illumination* on the surface is said to be increased. **Illumination** *is the density of the luminous flux on a surface.* When the surface is uniformly illuminated, the illumination E is the quotient of the flux on the surface divided by the area of the surface and is expressed as the luminous flux per unit area.

$$E = \frac{\Phi}{A}$$

Where Φ is the luminous flux in lumens and A is the area in square meters, the illumination E is in *lumens per square meter.*

Suppose the radius of the unit sphere shown in Fig. 12-18 is increased to 2 meters. The surface area is $4\pi(2m)^2$, or approximately 50 m², and is *four* times the area of the unit sphere. Similarly, a radius of 3 meters gives an area of $4\pi(3m)^2$ which is *nine* times the area of the unit sphere. It is apparent that, as the radial distance from the luminous source is increased, the area illuminated is increased in proportion to the *square* of the distance.

If a point source of constant intensity is located at the center of the sphere, *the illumination decreases as the square of the distance from the source.* See Fig. 12-19. If the intensity of the source is doubled, of course the luminous flux transmitted to the surface is doubled, and the illumination is doubled. Thus the illumination E on a surface perpendicular to the luminous flux falling on it is dependent on the intensity I of the source and its distance r from the source.

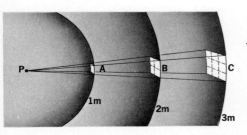

12-19 The illumination on a surface varies inversely as the square of the distance from the luminous point source.

The distance r from the point source is the radius of a spherical surface of area $4\pi r^2$ illuminated by the source I at its center. Thus the proper dimensions of E become apparent from the following:

$$E = \frac{\Phi}{A} = \frac{4\pi I}{4\pi r^2}$$

$$E = \frac{I}{r^2}$$

If r is expressed in meters and I in candles, then

$$E = \frac{4\pi \text{ lm/cd} \times I \text{ cd}}{4\pi \ r^2 \ \text{m}^2}$$

$$E = \frac{I}{r^2} \text{ (in lm/m}^2\text{)}$$

The *inverse square law* is used to calculate the illumination from an individual point source on planes perpendicular to the beam. In practice, if the dimensions of the source are

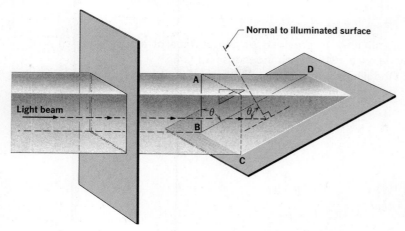

12-20   The illumination on a surface varies directly with the cosine of the angle between the luminous flux and the normal to the surface.

negligible compared with its distance from the illuminated surface, it is considered a point source. For long fluorescent tubes, the illumination varies inversely as the distance, over distances somewhat smaller than the length of the tube.

When a surface is not perpendicular to the beam of light illuminating it, the luminous flux spreads over a greater area and the level of illumination is reduced. In Fig. 12-20 the perpendicular surface **ABC** illuminated by the beam is square, having an area equal to **AB** × **BC**. As the surface is tilted away from the source the illuminated area becomes rectangular, the width remaining the same and the length increasing to **BD**. In the right triangle **ABD**

$$BD = \frac{AB}{\cos \theta}$$

where θ equals the tilt angle of the surface from its perpendicular position with respect to the beam. (It is evident that θ also represents the angle which the light beam makes with the perpendicular to the illuminated surface.)

As θ reaches 60°, cos θ equals 0.5 and the length **BD** becomes twice the width **AB**. Thus the area is doubled and, since the same flux is spread over twice the area, the illumination is reduced to half the original level. In the general case,

$$E = \frac{I \cos \theta}{r^2}$$

The illumination on a surface varies inversely with the square of the distance from the luminous source and directly with the cosine of the angle between the luminous flux and the normal to the surface. A surface that is perpendicular to the luminous flux is simply a special case of the general expression for illumination in which the angle θ becomes zero and cos $\theta = 1$. See the following example.

Example

(a) What illumination is provided on the surface of a table located 4.00 m directly below a 1610-lumen incandescent lamp?

(b) What is the illumination on the surface of the table at a spot 3.00 m to one side of its original position?

Solution

(a) $E = \dfrac{I}{r^2}$

$\Phi = 4\pi I, \; I = \dfrac{\Phi}{4\pi}$

$E = \dfrac{\Phi}{4\pi r^2} = \dfrac{1610 \text{ lm}}{4\pi \times (4.00 \text{ m})^2}$

$E = 8.00 \text{ lm/m}^2$

(b) $E = \dfrac{I \cos \theta}{r^2}$

$I = \dfrac{\Phi}{4\pi}$

$E = \dfrac{\Phi \cos \theta}{4\pi r^2}$

$E = \dfrac{1610 \text{ lm} \times 0.800}{4\pi \times (5.00 \text{ m})^2}$

$E = 4.08 \text{ lm/m}^2$

12.17 The intensity of a source

The candle power of a light source can be measured by comparing its intensity with that of a standard light source having the same color quality, by using an instrument called a *photometer*. See Fig. 12-21. Photometric measurements are made in a darkened room.

1. Bunsen photometer. The Bunsen photometer is sometimes called the grease-spot photometer. If a disc of white paper with a grease spot in the center is held toward a light, the grease spot will appear lighter than the rest of the paper because it transmits more light. On the other hand, because it is a poorer reflector of light than the paper, the grease spot will appear darker than the paper when held away from a light so that it is seen by reflected light. A laboratory model of the Bunsen photometer consists of such a paper screen supported on a meter stick between a standard lamp and a lamp of unknown candle power. The screen is moved back and forth along the meter stick until it is equally illuminated on both sides in which case the grease spot seems to disappear. When the screen is correctly positioned, illuminations E_1 and E_2 of the two sides of the screen are equal.

Since $E_1 = E_2$ then $\dfrac{I_1}{r_1{}^2} = \dfrac{I_2}{r_2{}^2}$

I_1 and I_2 are the intensities of the two sources producing illuminations E_1 and E_2, and r_1 and r_2 are their respective distances from the screen. Observe that each distance r is a radial distance from a source.

2. Joly photometer. The Joly photometer generally gives more satisfactory results than the grease-spot photometer. It consists of two blocks of paraffin separated by a thin sheet of metal. The light from either side is transmitted by the paraffin, but is stopped by the metal. By looking at the edges of the blocks of paraffin it is easy to adjust the photometer so that both sides are equally illuminated. Then distances from the sheet of metal to the lamps are measured and calculations made as with the Bunsen photometer.

3. Photoelectric photometer. The Bunsen or Joly photometer head can be replaced by a photoelectric cell connected to a meter suitable for measuring the photoelectric current of the cell. The photoelectric cell is placed a given distance from a standard lamp of known luminous intensity and the photocurrent is measured. An unknown lamp is then substituted for the standard lamp and the position of the photocell is adjusted to give the same photocurrent as for the standard lamp. The luminous intensity of the unknown lamp can then be calculated as with the Bunsen photometer.

4. Spherical photometer. The light source being tested is placed in the center of a large sphere, painted white on the inside. The luminous flux is received by a photocell located inside the sphere, but shielded from direct light from the source. The light on this cell is equal to that received by any other similar portion of the sphere interior, due to cross-reflections, and is therefore proportional to the total light emitted by the test

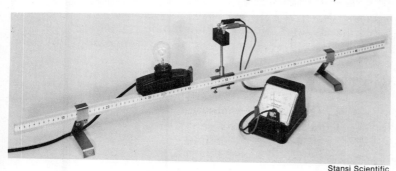

Stansi Scientific

12-21 A photoelectric photometer.

source. A meter outside the sphere is connected to the cell and is calibrated to read the mean spherical candle power or lumens directly. This accurate photometer is used commercially.

12.18 The amount of illumination

When planning lighting installations or taking photographs, it is helpful to know the amount of available illumination. Instruments used to measure this illumination are photoelectric cells called "light meters" or "exposure meters." The light-sensitive cell transforms light energy into electric energy, the amount of illumination and the electric current produced being proportional within the range of the instrument. Consequently, a light meter can be calibrated directly in lumens/meter², although most of them have an arbitrary scale. (Light meters calibrated in English units may give readings directly in lumens/foot², loosely called foot-candles.)

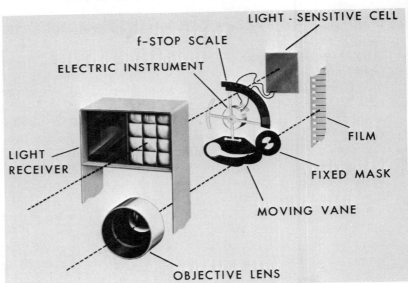

LIGHT - SENSITIVE CELL
f-STOP SCALE
ELECTRIC INSTRUMENT
FILM
LIGHT RECEIVER
FIXED MASK
MOVING VANE
OBJECTIVE LENS

Eastman Kodak

12-22 An exploded view of a photoelectric cell used to control film exposure in a movie camera.

QUESTIONS

Group A

1. Distinguish between luminous and illuminated objects.
2. Define and illustrate the following terms: (a) transparent; (b) translucent; (c) opaque.
3. What are the physical quantities generally measured in practical photometry?
4. Define luminous flux.
5. (a) Which of the quantities from Question 3 is measured in fundamental units? (b) Which are measured in derived units?
6. What is our chief method of providing artificial light?

7. By using Fig. 12-16, explain how Michelson determined the speed of light in air.

8. Devise an experiment which would enable you to verify the inverse-square law with a light meter. Describe it.

9. Suggest a procedure by which a light meter with an arbitrary scale could be used in the absence of a photometer to determine the intensity of an unknown light source.

10. A member of a television studio audience in New York is seated 30 m from the performer while a viewer observes the performance in her home in Chicago, 1200 km away. Which person hears the performer first?

PROBLEMS

Note: Assume filament lamps to be point sources.

1. The distance from the earth to the sun is approximately 1.5×10^8 km. What time, in minutes, is required for light from the sun to reach the earth?

2. What is the illumination on the page of a book 1.20 m directly below a source whose intensity is 125 cd?

3. It is recommended that the illumination be 540 lm/m² for newspaper reading. How far from the paper should a 265-cd source be placed to provide this illumination? (Assume the paper to be perpendicular to the luminous flux reaching it.)

4. What is the maximum illumination 1.50 m from a lamp whose intensity is 150 candles?

5. The amount of illumination thrown on a screen by two sources of light is the same when the distances from the lamps to the screen are 3.0 m and 2.0 m respectively. If the intensity of the first lamp is $2\bar{0}$ candles, what is the intensity of the second lamp?

6. A lamp, intensity 16.0 candles, is placed at the 0.0-cm mark on a meter stick. A lamp of unknown intensity is placed at the 100.0-cm mark. If a Bunsen photometer is equally illuminated at the 60.0-cm mark, what is the intensity of the unknown lamp?

7. A photometer is in balance on a meter stick when a 40.0 cd lamp and a second lamp are 100.0 cm apart and the grease spot is 30.0 cm from the second lamp. Find the intensity of this lamp.

8. The illumination on a screen located 3 m from a source of light is 4 times as much as that on a second screen which is illuminated by the same source. The intensity of the source is 25 candles. How far is the second screen from the source?

9. The intensity of a lamp is 60.0 cd. At what distance does it provide an illumination of 10.0 lm/m² on a table located directly beneath it?

10. How far away is the nearest star if it takes 4.3 years for the light from the star to reach the earth?

11. An incandescent lamp of 30.0 candles is placed at the 0-cm mark on a meter stick and a lamp of 20.0 candles is placed at the opposite end. Where must the screen of a photometer be placed so that both sides are equally illuminated?

12. A 100-watt lamp placed at one end of a meter stick and a 10-candle source placed at the other end equally illuminate a photometer which is 75 cm from the 100-watt lamp. How many candles per watt does the lamp supply?

13. How many revolutions per second did Michelson's octagonal mirror make if light traveled 70.8 km while the mirror made one-eighth of a revolution?

14. What is the range of frequencies of visible light?

15. A surface is 75 cm from a luminous source of 150 cd. At what angle can it be tilted and still have an illumination of 0.025 lm/cm^2?

Chapter 13

Reflection

A light beam passing through any material medium will become progressively weaker due to two effects. Part of its energy will be *absorbed* by molecules of the medium and part will be *scattered* in all directions by them. A light beam striking the boundary between two media can be partly *transmitted* and partly returned to the first medium. See Fig. 13-1. Light returned to the first medium is said to be *reflected* at the boundary. Reflection is described as a wave property in Section 10.10.

Part of the reflected light proceeds in one direction but part can be returned in all possible directions as scattered light. These effects are shown in Fig. 13-2. That portion which returns in one direction provides us with a method for controlling the direction of a light beam.

13.1 Reflectance

13-1 A diagram showing the effects on light rays of a material medium and a boundary between two media.

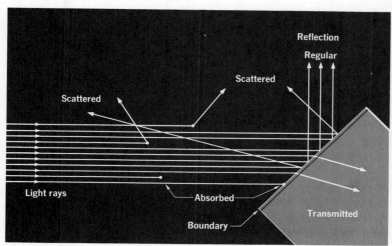

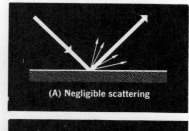

(A) Negligible scattering

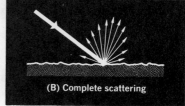

(B) Complete scattering

13-2 Reflecting surfaces vary in the extent to which reflected rays are scattered.

The amount of light reflected at the surface of an object, whether by scattering or by unidirectional reflection, depends on the kind of material underlying the surface, the smoothness of the surface, and the angle at which the light strikes it. *The ratio of the light reflected from a surface to the light falling on it is called* **reflectance**. This ratio is commonly expressed as a percentage. Materials differ widely in their reflectance. The material of highest reflectance is magnesium carbonate, a white chalky substance which reflects about 98% of incident light with practically complete scattering. The reflectance of a smooth surface of silver is about 95 percent, with negligible scattering. Some black surfaces have reflectances of 5 percent or less.

13.2 Regular and diffused reflection

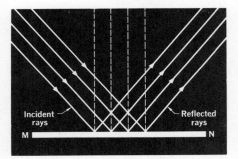

13-3 Regular reflection of light from a specular surface.

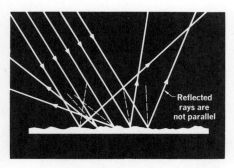

13-4 Irregular reflection promotes the diffusion of light.

13.3 Mirrors as reflectors

The reflection of sunlight by a mirror produces a blinding glare. The rays of the sun reaching the earth are practically parallel and thus have the same angle of incidence. They remain practically parallel after being reflected from a plane mirror. Such reflection, in which scattering of the reflected rays is negligible, is called *regular* reflection. Polished, or *specular*, surfaces cause regular reflection and the image of the luminous source is sharply defined. The nature of regular reflection is shown in Fig. 13-3.

Regular reflection from highly polished surfaces provides for relatively accurate control of light rays. Searchlights, beacons, and automobile spotlights use concentrated light sources of high intensity and highly polished regular reflectors to redirect light rays in the desired direction.

In Fig. 13-4 we observe what happens to a beam of light incident on an irregular surface. The laws of reflection hold true for each particular ray of light, but the normals to the surface are not parallel, and the light is reflected in many different directions. Such scattering, or *diffusion*, of light is extremely important.

If the sun's rays were not diffused by rough and irregular surfaces, the corners of a room and the spaces under shade trees would be in almost total darkness and the glare would be dazzling in sunlit areas. Astronauts have found that it is possible for them to see in the shadows on the lunar surface where there is no air, but they cannot see as easily as we can on the surface of the earth.

The reflection of light is similar to the reflection of sound or to the rebound of an elastic ball. The line **MN** in Fig. 13-5(A) represents a reflecting surface; **AD** is a ray of light incident upon the reflector at **D**; **DB** is the path of the reflected ray. The line **CD**, perpendicular to the reflecting surface at the point of incidence, is called a *normal*. In Fig. 13-5(B), the normal is perpendicular to the tangent to the curved reflecting surface at the point of incidence. Recall from Section 10.10 that the *angle of incidence* (*i*) is the angle between the incident ray and the normal at the point of incidence [angle **ADC** in Fig. 13-5(A)]. In Chapter 10 we examined the nature of reflection by sending water waves against a barrier in the ripple tank. At that time we recognized *the **first law of reflection**: the angle of incidence i is equal to the angle of reflection r*. The *angle of reflection r* is the angle between the reflected ray and the normal at the point of incidence [angle **BDC** in Fig. 13-5(A)].

The relationships between an incident ray of light and the reflected ray, and between the angles they form with the normal, are easily determined in the laboratory. Critical observation of the specular reflection of light reveals a **second law of reflection**: *the incident ray, the reflected ray, and the normal to the reflecting surface lie in the same plane*. As mentioned in Section 10.10 these laws are true for all forms of wave propagation.

Any highly polished surface which forms images by the regular reflection of light can act as a mirror. *Plane* mirrors of plate glass are silvered on one surface to reflect light efficiently and their reflectance is quite high. The plane parallel surfaces of the plate glass allow essentially distortion-free images to be observed.

Spherical mirrors, the surfaces of which are sections of spheres, are commonly used for special purposes. The laws of reflection hold for spherical mirrors; however, the size and position of the images formed are quite different from those of images formed by plane mirrors. When the mirror is a portion of the polished outer surface of a sphere, it is said to be *convex*. The reflecting surface is curved toward the observer. When the mirror is a portion of the polished inner surface of a sphere, it is said to be *concave*. Here the reflecting surface is curved away from the observer. These curved mirrors are shown diagrammatically in Fig. 13-6.

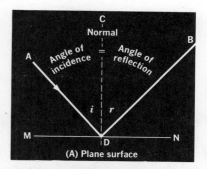

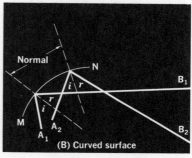

13-5 Reflection from plane and curved surfaces. Which law of reflection is not clearly illustrated here?

13-6 Circular sections of spheres form spherical mirrors.

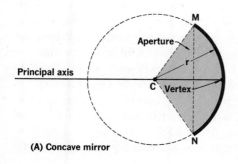

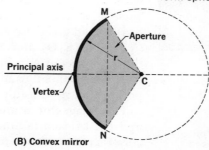

(A) Concave mirror

(B) Convex mirror

13.4 Images by reflection

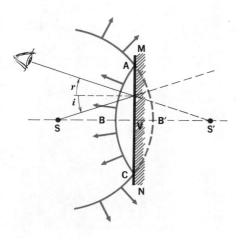

13-7 A wave-front diagram of reflection of light from a point source by a plane mirror.

Light rays reflected from a concave mirror may meet in front of the mirror and form an image of the object from which the light comes. Such an image can be projected on a screen placed at the image location. *An image formed by rays of light actually passing through the image point is called a **real image***. Real images are inverted relative to the object and can be larger or smaller than the object.

Your image observed in a plane mirror seems to be behind the mirror, although the rays forming it actually are reflected forward from the mirror surface. *This image is called a **virtual image**. Rays of light which appear to have diverged from the image point do not actually pass through that point.* Virtual images cannot be projected on a screen. They are erect with respect to the object; they also can be enlarged or reduced in size.

In Fig. 13-7, light traveling from a point source in spherical wave fronts is reflected from a plane mirror. At the instant that points **A** and **C** on the wave front reach the mirror, point **B** has been reflected back towards the source at **S**, having traveled the distance **VB**. The reflected wave front **ABC** has a center of curvature **S'** whose apparent distance behind the mirror **VS'** is equal to the distance of the source in front of the mirror **VS**. The reflected wave front approaches an observer, the eye, as though its source were **S'**, **S'** being the virtual image of the source **S**.

13.5 Images formed by plane mirrors

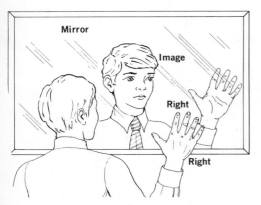

13-8 The image formed by a plane mirror is reversed right and left. Observe that the image of the right hand has the symmetry of a left hand.

The image formed by a plane mirror is neither enlarged nor reduced, but is always virtual, erect, and appears as far behind the mirror as the object is in front of it. The image differs from the object in that right and left are interchanged. In Fig. 13-8 it is apparent that the image of the right hand has the appearance of a left hand. If an object is spinning clockwise about its axis, its image appears to be spinning counterclockwise about its image axis.

Let us examine the ray diagram of Fig. 13-9 for a simple graphical method of locating the image formed by a plane mirror. The triangle **ABC**, drawn on paper, is used as the object in front of a mirror, **MN**. A pin is placed at each vertex of the triangle. Rays **AO₁** and **AO₂** from pin **A** strike the mirror so as to be reflected to the two eyes, **E₁** and **E₂**, of the observer. When the sight lines **E₁O₁** and **E₂O₂** are produced behind the mirror, they intersect at **A'** which is the location of the image of pin **A**. A comparison of triangles **AO₂O₁** and **A'O₂O₁** makes it apparent that **A'** is as far behind the mirror as **A** is in front of it.

The images of **B** and **C** are located in similar fashion at **B'** and **C'**. In each instance *the image appears to be as far behind the mirror as the object is in front of it*. When the image points **A'B'C'** are joined, it becomes evident that *the image is the same size as the object and reversed left and right.*

This method of constructing images is based on the laws of reflection. The light ray AO_1 is reflected at point O_1 and is sighted at E_1. By drawing a normal to the mirror at O_1, the angle AO_1E_1 is bisected and the angle of reflection E_1O_1R is equal to the angle of incidence AO_1R. The incident ray AO_1, the reflected ray O_1E_1, and the normal O_1R all lie in the same plane.

Sound waves bound and rebound between parallel cliffs or walls and produce multiple echoes. In a similar fashion, light reflects back and forth between parallel mirrors, or mirrors set at an acute angle, and forms multiple images. The image formed in one mirror appears to act as the object forming the image in the next mirror. Because some light energy is absorbed and some is scattered at each mirror, the succeeding images become fainter. A thick plate-glass mirror produces multiple reflection, as shown in Fig. 13-10, some light being reflected each time a boundary is encountered.

Multiple reflections can be avoided by aluminizing or silvering the front surface of a glass mirror. Mirrors for astronomical telescopes and other precision instruments are usually coated with aluminum in this manner. Such reflecting surfaces are exposed and can be easily damaged.

Before we discuss image formation by curved mirrors, several terms must be defined. As an aid to understanding these terms, refer to Fig. 13-11, in which **MN** represents a spherical mirror in two dimensions.

1. The center of curvature, **C**, is the center of the sphere of which the mirror forms a part.

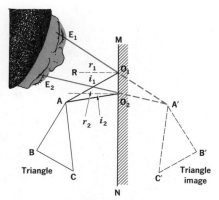

13-9 A ray diagram used to construct an image formed by a plane mirror.

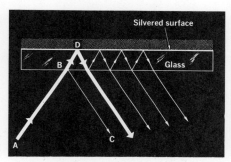

13-10 Multiple reflections result from the use of a back-silvered mirror.

13.6 Curved-mirror terminology

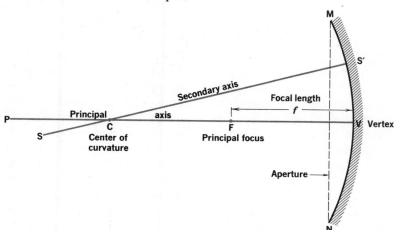

13-11 A plane diagram for defining terms used with curved mirrors.

2. The aperture is a measure of the portion of the sphere included by the mirror. Only a small section of the total surface of the sphere is used as the reflecting surface for clear image formation. The angle **MCN** is a measure of the aperture.

3. The vertex, **V**, is the center of the mirror itself.

4. The principal axis is the line **PV** drawn through the center of curvature and the vertex.

5. A secondary axis is any other line drawn through the center of curvature, **SS′** for example.

6. A normal to the surface of a concave mirror is a radius drawn from a point of incidence. (The radius is perpendicular to the tangent to the surface drawn through the point of incidence.) In a convex mirror, a normal is a radius produced or extended beyond the mirror.

13.7 Rays focused by spherical mirrors

In Fig. 13-12(A) the rays **AD** and **BE**, parallel to the principal axis, are shown incident on a concave spherical mirror at points **D** and **E** respectively. The normals **CD** and **CE** are drawn to the points of incidence and, by the second law of reflection, the reflected rays converge on the principal axis at **F**. *The point on*

13-12 Locating the principal focus of spherical mirrors.

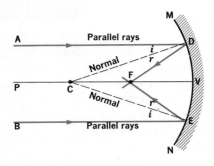

(A) Concave mirror

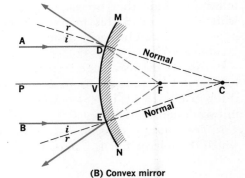

(B) Convex mirror

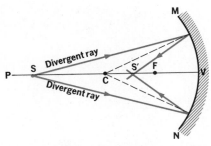

13-13 The reflection of diverging rays by a concave mirror.

the principal axis to which rays parallel to the principal axis converge (or from which they diverge) is known as the **principal focus**. Since the incident rays converge upon being reflected, concave mirrors are known as *converging* mirrors. The distance **FV** is the *focal length* of the mirror. For spherical mirrors of small aperture, the focal length is one-half the radius of curvature.

Parallel rays incident on the surface of a convex spherical mirror are shown in Fig. 13-12(B). The normals **CD** and **CE**, produced beyond the mirror surface, show the reflected rays to be divergent along the lines **FD** and **FE** produced, **F** being the principal focus of the mirror. Rays parallel to the principal axis appear to diverge from the principal focus of a convex mirror. Since incident rays diverge on being reflected, convex mirrors are known as *diverging* mirrors.

Diverging rays from a point **S** incident on a concave mirror, Fig. 13-13, converge to a focus at some point **S'** beyond the principal focus of the mirror. If **S** is located on the principal axis, the image **S'** will be on the principal axis also. Points **S** and **S'** are known as *conjugate foci.* Thus rays from **S'** will be focused at **S**.

Converging rays are also focused by concave mirrors. As shown by Fig. 13-14, the point of focus is between the vertex and the principal focus. In every instance, the direction of a reflected ray is determined by the law of reflection.

If the aperture of a spherical mirror is large, the parallel rays of light striking the mirror near its edge are not reflected through the principal focus, but are focused at a point nearer the mirror, as shown in Fig. 13-15. Only those parallel rays which are incident on the mirror near its vertex are reflected to the principal focus. This characteristic of spherical mirrors of large aperture, known as *spherical aberration,* results in the formation of fuzzy images.

In order to reduce spherical aberration the aperture of the mirror can be made very small. For apertures no larger than about 10°, the distortion of the image is negligible. This aberration can be avoided for parallel rays if the mirror surface is made parabolic instead of spherical. A parabolic mirror, as shown in Fig. 13-16, can bring all parallel rays to a focus at one point and reflect those originating at the focus as parallel rays. Automobile headlights generally have parabolic reflectors. Large reflecting telescopes also use parabolic mirrors to collect and focus light rays from distant objects.

In Fig. 13-17, the image of point **S** formed by a concave mirror is to be located. First the principal axis **PV** is drawn through **C**. Because light is given off in all directions from point **S**, *any two lines* can be drawn from **S** to represent rays of light

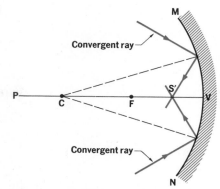

13-14 The reflection of converging rays by a concave mirror.

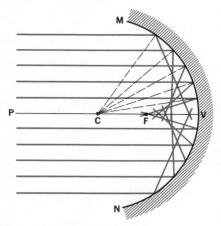

13-15 Spherical aberration.

13.8 Constructing the image of a point

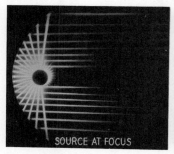

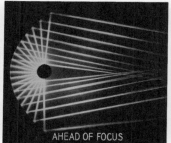

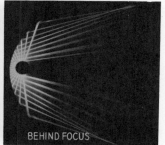

SOURCE AT FOCUS   AHEAD OF FOCUS   BEHIND FOCUS

13-16 Reflections from a parabolic mirror.

General Electric

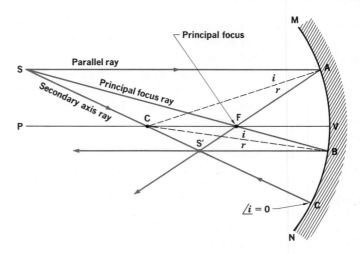

13-17 Locating an image formed by a
concave mirror.

incident on the mirror. The point of intersection of the *reflected* rays locates the image of **S** at **S'**.

The construction is greatly simplified if incident rays are selected for which the directions of the reflected rays are known from the geometry of the system. Three such special rays are shown in Fig. 13-17. Note that two are required to locate an image point. **SA**, *parallel to the principal axis*, is reflected through the principal focus. Ray **SB** *passes through the principal focus* and is reflected parallel to the principal axis. **SC** *lies along the secondary axis*. It is reflected back along itself because the angle of incidence is zero. The convergence of these reflected rays at a common point **S'** forms the image of **S**. Observe that if the object were located at **S'**, the image would be formed at **S**. The object and image are thus interchangeable, or *conjugate*. Points **S** and **S'** are *conjugate foci*.

13.9 Images formed by concave mirrors

We can construct the image formed by a concave mirror by locating the images of enough different points. If the object is an arrow, the entire image can be located by finding the positions of the images of the head and tail of the arrow. Concave mirror images may be grouped into six cases.

Case 1. Object at an infinite distance. Rays emanating from an object at an infinite distance from a mirror would be parallel as they arrive at the mirror, and if parallel to the principal axis, would be reflected through the principal focus, as shown in Fig. 13-18(A). We therefore, conclude that *the image formed by a concave mirror when an object is at an infinite distance is a point at the principal focus.* The sun's rays reaching the earth are very

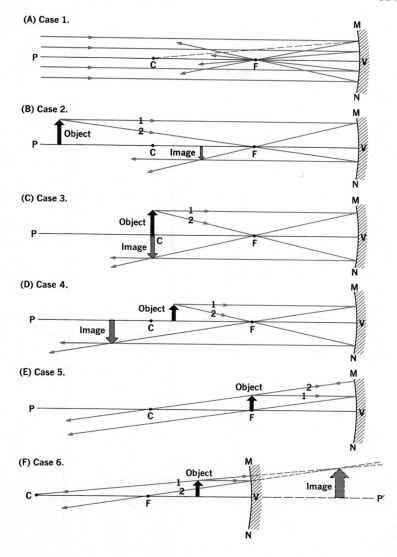

(A) Case 1.

(B) Case 2.

(C) Case 3.

(D) Case 4.

(E) Case 5.

(F) Case 6.

13-18 Ray diagrams of image formation by concave mirrors.

nearly parallel and provide a simple method of finding the approximate focal length of a concave mirror.

Case 2. Object at a finite distance beyond the center of curvature. In Fig. 13-18(B), the image of the object arrow can be located using the method illustrated in Section 13.8. Two known rays, **1** and **2**, emanating from the head of the arrow, intersect after reflection to locate the image of the arrow head. The image of the tail lies on the principal axis as shown earlier in Fig. 13-13. *The image in this case is real, inverted, reduced, and located between the center of curvature and the principal focus.* The nearer the object

Images are distorted where a mirror is not flat or does not have regular curvature. Which part of this mirror do you think is convex and which part is concave?

13.10 Images formed by convex mirrors

approaches the center of curvature, the larger the image becomes and the nearer the image approaches **C**.

Case 3. Object at the center of curvature. When the object arrow is at the center of curvature, as shown in Fig. 13-18(C), the image of the arrow head is found inverted at **C**. *When the object is at the center of curvature, the image is real, inverted, the same size as the object, and located at the center of curvature.*

Case 4. Object between the center of curvature and principal focus. This case is the converse of Case 2 and is shown in Fig. 13-18(D). *The image is real, inverted, enlarged, and located beyond the center of curvature.* The nearer the object approaches the principal focus of the mirror, the larger the image becomes and the farther it is beyond **C**.

Case 5. Object at principal focus. This case is the converse of Case 1; all rays originating from the same point on the object are reflected from the mirror as parallel rays. See Fig. 13-18(E). *When the object is at the principal focus, no image is formed.* If the object is a point source, all reflected rays are parallel to the principal axis.

Case 6. Object between principal focus and mirror. The reflected rays from any point on the object are divergent; they can never meet to form a real image. They appear to meet behind the mirror, however, to form a virtual image as shown in Fig. 13-18(F). In this case, *the image is virtual, erect, enlarged, and located behind the mirror.*

A convex mirror forms an erect image of reduced size. The diagram, Fig. 13-19, can be used to show how such an image is formed. The arrow **AB** represents the object. The secondary

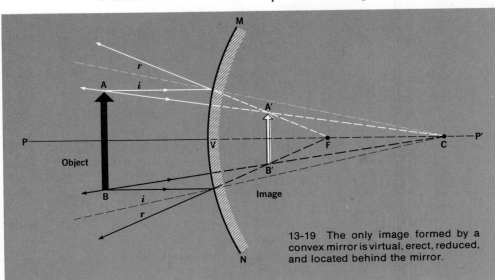

13-19 The only image formed by a convex mirror is virtual, erect, reduced, and located behind the mirror.

axes and the normals at the points of incidence of the parallel rays are *radii produced.* The parallel rays are reflected from the surface of the mirror and made divergent. When extended behind the mirror, they *appear* to meet at the principal focus, the image being formed where the reflected parallel rays and secondary-axis ray extended appear to intersect. In a convex mirror, *all images are virtual, erect, smaller than the object, and located behind the mirror between the vertex and the principal focus.* The size of the image increases as the object moves closer to the mirror, but it can never become as large as the object itself.

The largest optical telescopes in the world are reflecting telescopes using large concave mirrors to collect and focus light rays. A reflecting telescope can be made much larger than a refracting (lens) telescope because it is difficult to obtain a large piece of glass of sufficiently high optical quality for a lens, grind and polish two surfaces with precision, and support it appropriately.

When objects being viewed with a reflecting telescope are at a finite distance beyond the center of curvature of the mirror,

13.11 The reflecting telescope

Perkin-Elmer

13-20 An automatic optical missile tracking system employing a 600-mm aperture reflecting telescope with focal lengths from 250 cm to 1250 cm.

Case 2 applies. The image is real, inverted, and located near the principal focus of the mirror. This real image can be reflected out of the path of the rays of light incident on the mirror so that it can be viewed or photographed from a position outside the telescope. The inversion of the image is not objectionable when reflecting telescopes are used for viewing astronomical objects.

13.12 Object-image relationships

A simple relationship exists between the distance of an object s_o from a curved mirror, the distance of its image s_i, and the focal length f of the mirror. This relationship, known as the *mirror equation*, can be derived by considering the diagram of Fig. 13-21 in which a real image of the object **AB** is formed by a concave mirror. (In this derivation we will consider as insignificant the very slight error introduced by the curvature **MV**.)

In similar triangles **A′B′F** and **MVF**

$$\frac{\mathbf{A'B'}}{\mathbf{MV}} = \frac{\mathbf{B'F}}{\mathbf{VF}} \qquad \text{(Equation 1)}$$

Taking **MV** = **AB**, **VF** = f, and **B′F** = $s_i - f$, we have

$$\frac{\mathbf{A'B'}}{\mathbf{AB}} = \frac{s_i - f}{f} = \frac{s_i}{f} - 1 \qquad \text{(Equation 2)}$$

In similar triangles **ABV** and **A′B′V**,

$$\frac{\mathbf{A'B'}}{\mathbf{AB}} = \frac{\mathbf{B'V}}{\mathbf{BV}} \qquad \text{(Equation 3)}$$

Taking **BV** = s_o and **B′V** = s_i,

$$\frac{\mathbf{A'B'}}{\mathbf{AB}} = \frac{s_i}{s_o} \qquad \text{(Equation 4)}$$

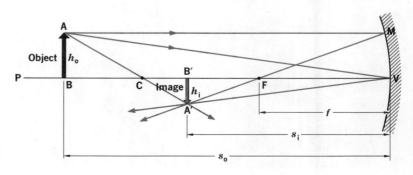

13-21 A diagram for the derivation of the mirror equation for curved mirrors.

Substituting in Equation 2

$$\frac{s_i}{s_o} = \frac{s_i}{f} - 1$$

Dividing by s_i,

$$\frac{1}{s_o} = \frac{1}{f} - \frac{1}{s_i} \qquad \text{(Equation 5)}$$

Or,

$$\frac{1}{f} = \frac{1}{s_o} + \frac{1}{s_i} \qquad \text{(Equation 6)}$$

where s_o is the distance of the object from the mirror, s_i the image distance, and f the focal length of the mirror.

The mirror equation is applicable to all concave and convex mirrors. When an object is located less than one focal length in front of a concave mirror, the image is virtual. It lies behind the mirror, and the image distance s_i is a *negative quantity*. In the case of convex mirrors, the radius of curvature is negative and the image is virtual. Therefore, both the focal length f and the image distance s_i are *negative quantities*. The use of these negative quantities is illustrated in the following example.

Wide World Photos

The 200-inch mirror of the observatory on Mt. Palomar, California. Visible in the huge reflector are various images, all silhouetted against a daytime sky.

Example

An object located $2\overline{0}$ cm in front of a convex mirror forms an image $1\overline{0}$ cm behind the mirror. What is the focal length of the mirror?

Solution

$$\frac{1}{s_o} + \frac{1}{s_i} = \frac{1}{f}$$

Solving for f:

$$f = \frac{s_o s_i}{s_o + s_i} = \frac{2\overline{0}\ \text{cm} \times (-1\overline{0}\ \text{cm})}{2\overline{0}\ \text{cm} + (-1\overline{0}\ \text{cm})} = -2\overline{0}\ \text{cm}$$

The relative heights of an object and the image formed by a curved mirror depend on their respective distances from the center of curvature of the mirror. This can be seen from similar triangles **ABC** and **A′B′C** of Fig. 13-21.

We can demonstrate that, for mirrors of small aperture, the relative heights of the object and image also depend on their respective distances from the vertex of the mirror. If the height of object **AB** in Fig. 13-21 is represented by h_o and the height of the image **A′B′** by h_i, Equation 4 of Section 13.12 becomes

$$\frac{h_i}{h_o} = \frac{s_i}{s_o}$$

As stated previously, the focal length f is considered to be positive for a concave mirror and negative for a convex mirror. For *real* objects and images, the object and image distances s_o and s_i are positive; for *virtual* objects and images, s_o and s_i are negative. Observe that mirror equations are always expressed symbolically with positive signs. Negative signs are introduced with the numerical values substituted for these symbols only when the sign convention requires them.

QUESTIONS

Group A

1. What three factors determine the amount of light an object will reflect?
2. What are the two laws of reflection?
3. When you look in a plane mirror, do you see yourself as others see you? Explain.
4. Illustrate the following by diagram as they are related to curved mirrors: center of curvature, vertex, principal axis.
5. What type of mirror produces real images?
6. In what ways can spherical aberration in mirrors be reduced?

Group B

7. Suppose we write the word "light" on a mirror with white paint. When the mirror is placed in a beam of sunlight, the reflection of the sunlight on a smooth wall consists of a bright area in which the letters of the word "light" appear dark. Explain.
8. What kind of trick mirror produces (a) a short, fattened image; (b) a tall, thin image?
9. What kinds of mirrors could be used and where should the object be placed to produce (a) an enlarged real image, (b) a reduced real image, (c) a real image the same size as the object, (d) an enlarged virtual image, (e) a reduced virtual image?
10. (a) Construct a ray diagram to show the formation of an image by a concave mirror when the object is at a finite distance beyond the center of curvature. (b) Describe fully the image that is formed.
11. (a) Construct a ray diagram to show the formation of an image by a concave mirror when the object is between the principal focus and the center of curvature. (b) Describe fully the image that is formed.
12. (a) Construct a ray diagram to show the formation of an image by a convex mirror. (b) Describe fully the image that is formed.

PROBLEMS

1. A concave mirror has a focal length of 10.0 cm. What is its radius of curvature?
2. If the radius of curvature of a curved mirror is 8 cm, what is its focal length?
3. While you are looking at the image of your feet in a plane vertical mirror, you see a scratch in the glass. Assuming your height to be 1.76 m, what is the approximate height of the scratch from the floor?
4. The light from a distant star is collected by a concave mirror. If the radius of curvature of the mirror is 150 cm, how far from the mirror is the image formed?
5. An object is placed 25.0 cm from a concave mirror whose focal length is 5.00 cm. Where is the image located?
6. An object 25.4 cm high is located 91.5 cm from a concave mirror, focal length 15.0 cm. (a) Where is the image located? (b) How high is it?
7. An object placed 50.0 cm from a spherical concave mirror gives a real image 33.3 cm from the mirror. (a) What is the radius of curvature of the mirror? (b) If the image is 30.5 cm high, what is the height of the object?
8. An object and its image in a concave mirror are the same height when the object is 36.4 cm from the mirror. What is the focal length of the mirror?

9. An object is placed 5.0 cm from a concave mirror whose focal length is 15 cm. (a) Where is the image located? (b) If the object is 2.0 cm high, what is the height of the image?
10. An object 5.00 cm tall stands at the 0.0-cm mark on a meter stick. (a) If a convex mirror having a focal length of 25.0 cm is placed at the 50.0-cm mark, where is the image formed? (b) How tall is the image?
11. The image of the moon is formed by a concave mirror whose radius of curvature is 4.00 meters at a time when the distance to the moon is 236,000 mi. What is the diameter of the image in centimeters if the diameter of the moon is 2160 mi?
12. The image of an incandescent lamp filament is to be formed on a screen 5.00 m from a concave mirror. The lamp filament is 5.00 mm long and the image is to be 50.0 cm long. (a) What should be the radius of curvature of the mirror? (b) How far in front of the vertex of the mirror should the filament be placed?
13. A spherical concave shaving mirror has a radius of curvature of 30.0 cm. When the face is 10.0 cm from the vertex of the mirror, what is the magnification of the image?

14. A physics student stands in front of a mirror admiring his image. He is 1.80 m tall and his eyes are 10 cm below the top of his head. (a) What is the smallest vertical mirror that will enable him to see his entire image? (b) Is the length of the mirror dependent upon the distance between the student and the mirror? (c) Construct a ray diagram which supports your answers to (a) and (b).

15. The mirror for Problem 14 is hung at an angle of 30.0° from the vertical toward the student. What is the minimum length mirror in which he will be able to see his full image, if his line of vision cannot be depressed below the horizontal? For this problem, assume that the student's eyes are at the top of his head.

Chapter 14

Refraction

OPTICAL REFRACTION

In Section 10.12, we discussed refraction as a property of waves. Now we shall examine the refractive behavior of light and relate this behavior to its wave-like nature.

When aiming a rifle at a target, one relies on the common observation that light travels in straight lines. It does so, however, only if the transmitting medium is of the same *optical density* throughout. **Optical density** *is a property of a transparent material which is an inverse measure of the speed of light through the material.*

Consider a beam of light transmitted through air and directed onto the surface of a body of water. Some of the light is reflected at the boundary between the air and water, and the remainder enters the water. Because water is transparent, the light entering the water is transmitted through it. Water has a higher optical density than air, consequently the speed of light is reduced as the light enters the water. This change in the speed of light at the air-water interface is shown diagrammatically in Fig. 14-1.

A ray of light that strikes the surface of the water at an *oblique* angle (less than 90° to the surface) changes direction abruptly as it enters the water because of the change in speed. The reason for this change in direction with a change in speed can be illustrated if we redraw the wave-front diagram of Fig. 14-1, making the angle of the incident ray oblique, as in Fig. 14-2. When interpreting this diagram, you should remember that a light ray indicates the direction the light travels and is perpendicular to the wave front. We have already defined refraction as a bending of a wave disturbance. (See Section 10.12.) This bending of a light ray is called **optical refraction**. *It is the*

14.1 The nature of optical refraction

Magnum Photos

In this photograph the sun appears to be flattened. After studying this chapter, see if you can devise a plausible explanation.

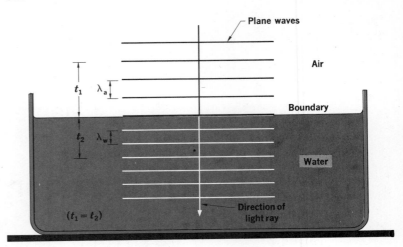

14-1 A wave-front diagram illustrating the difference in the speed of light in air and water.

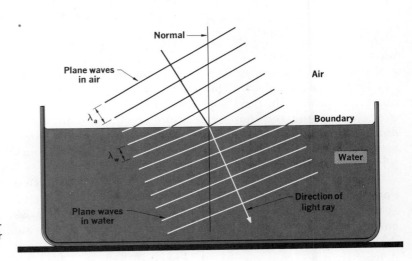

14-2 A wave-front diagram illustrating the refraction of light at the air and water boundary.

bending of light rays as they pass obliquely from one medium into another of different optical density.

Because of refraction, a fish observed from the bank appears nearer to the surface of the water than it actually is. A stick or teaspoon in a tumbler of water appears to be bent or broken at the surface of the water. A coin in the bottom of a teacup, out of the line of vision of an observer, may become visible when the cup is filled with water.

14.2 Refraction and the speed of light

Suppose **MN** of Fig. 14-3 represents the surface of a body of water. The line **AO** represents a ray of light through the air, striking the water at **O**. Some of the light is reflected along **OE**.

The light ray entering the water, instead of continuing in a straight line along **OF**, is bent as it passes from air into water, taking the path **OB**.

The incident ray **AO** makes the angle **AOC** with the normal, the *angle of incidence, i*. The refracted ray **OB** makes the angle **DOB** with the normal produced. *This angle between the refracted ray and the normal at the point of refraction is called the **angle of refraction**, r.*

In the examples given so far, the light rays have passed from one medium into another of *higher* optical density, with a resulting reduction in speed. When a ray enters the denser medium normal to the boundary, no refraction occurs; when a ray enters the denser medium at an oblique angle, refraction does occur and the ray is bent *toward* the normal.

What is the nature of the refraction if the light passes obliquely from one medium into another of *lower* optical density? Suppose the light source were at **B**, in Fig. 14-3, and the light ray, line **BO**, met the surface at point **O**, angle **BOD** being the angle of incidence. Of course, some light would be reflected at this boundary; however, the main portion of the light would be refracted along the line **OA** on entering the air. The angle of refraction in this case would be **COA**, showing that the light was bent *away* from the normal.

The speed of light in a vacuum is approximately 300,000 kilometers per second. The speed of light in water is approximately 225,000 kilometers per second, just about three-fourths of that in a vacuum. The speed of light in ordinary glass is approximately 200,000 kilometers per second, about two-thirds of that in a vacuum. *The ratio of the speed of light in a vacuum to its speed in a substance is called the **index of refraction** for that substance.* For example,

$$\text{Index of refraction (glass)} = \frac{\text{speed of light in vacuum}}{\text{speed of light in glass}}$$

Using the approximate values just given, the index of refraction for glass would be about 1.5 and for water about 1.3. The index of refraction of a few common substances is given in Table 18, Appendix B. The speed of light in air is only slightly different from the speed of light in a vacuum. Therefore, with negligible error, we can use the speed of light in a vacuum for cases where light travels from air into another medium.

The fundamental principle of refraction was discovered by Willebrord Snell (1591–1626), a Dutch mathematician and astronomer. He did not publish his discovery, but his work was taught at the University of Leyden where he was a professor

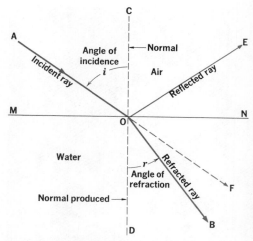

14-3 A ray diagram of refraction showing the angle of incidence and the angle of refraction.

14.3 The index of refraction

American Optical Co.

A beam of light from a laser is reflected by two plane mirrors and is then refracted as it enters and leaves a semi-circular piece of clear plastic.

Bausch & Lomb

Willebrord Snell discovered the law of refraction in 1621. This law makes possible precise computation of modern lenses and optical instruments.

of mathematics and physics. Rene Descartes (1596–1650), a French mathematician, published Snell's work in 1637.

Snell's discoveries about refraction were not stated in terms of the speed of light. The speed of light in empty space was determined in 1676, but the speed in water was not measured until 1850. From his observations, however, Snell defined the index of refraction as the ratio of the sine of the angle of incidence to the sine of the angle of refraction. This relationship is known as Snell's law. If n represents the index of refraction, i the angle of incidence, and r the angle of refraction,

$$n = \frac{\sin i}{\sin r}$$

The sines of angles from 0° to 90° are given in Table 6, Appendix B.

The relationship between Snell's law and the ratio of the speeds of light in air and a refracting medium can be recognized from Fig. 14-4. Rays of light travel through the first medium (air) with a speed v_1, and enter the refracting medium in which the speed is v_2.

A wave front **MP** approaches the refracting interface **MN** in the first medium at an incident angle i, the wavefront at **P** traveling to **N** in the time t with a speed v_1. Simultaneously the wavefront at **M** travels in the second medium to **Q** in the same time t but with a speed v_2. The new wavefront is **NQ** which travels forward in the second medium at a refractive angle r. The distances **PN** and **MQ** are respectively $v_1 t$ and $v_2 t$, so that

$$\frac{\mathbf{PN}}{\mathbf{MQ}} = \frac{v_1 t}{v_2 t} = \frac{v_1}{v_2}$$

In triangle **MNP**
$$\sin i = \frac{\mathbf{PN}}{\mathbf{MN}}$$

In triangle **MNQ**
$$\sin r = \frac{\mathbf{MQ}}{\mathbf{MN}}$$

The ratio
$$\frac{\sin i}{\sin r} = \frac{\mathbf{PN/MN}}{\mathbf{MQ/MN}} = \frac{\mathbf{PN}}{\mathbf{MQ}} = \frac{v_1}{v_2}$$

From Snell's law
$$n = \frac{\sin i}{\sin r}$$

Therefore
$$n = \frac{v_1}{v_2}$$

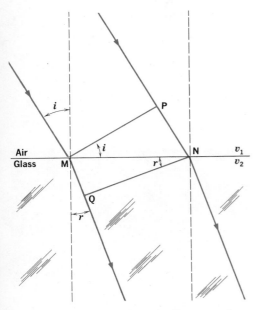

14-4 A wave-front diagram of refraction.

These relationships are illustrated in the following example.

Example

A ray of light travels from air into water at an angle with the surface of 60.0°. The index of refraction of the water is 1.33. Find (a) the angle of refraction and (b) the speed of light in the water.

Solution

(a) From Snell's law,

$$n = \frac{\sin i}{\sin r} \text{ and } \sin r = \frac{\sin i}{n}$$

$(i = 90.0° - 60.0° = 30.0° \text{ and } n = 1.33)$

$$\sin r = \frac{\sin 30.0°}{1.33} = \frac{0.500}{1.33} = 0.376$$

$$r = 22.0°$$

(b) From the definition of the index of refraction,

$$n = \frac{v_1}{v_2} \text{ and } v_2 = \frac{v_1}{n}$$

$(v_1 = 3.00 \times 10^8 \text{ m/sec and } n = 1.33)$

$$v_2 = \frac{3.00 \times 10^8 \text{ m/sec}}{1.33} = 2.26 \times 10^8 \text{ m/sec}$$

The index of refraction of a homogeneous substance is a constant quantity which is a definite physical property of the substance. Consequently, the identity of such a substance can be determined by measuring its index of refraction with an instrument known as a *refractometer*. For example, butterfat and margarine have different indexes of refraction: one of the first tests made in a food-testing laboratory to determine whether butter has been mixed with margarine is the measurement of the index of refraction. The exceedingly high index of refraction of a diamond furnishes one of the most conclusive tests for its identification.

Because light travels very slightly faster in outer space than it does through air, light from the sun or the stars is refracted when it enters the earth's atmosphere obliquely. Since the atmosphere is denser near the earth's surface, a ray of light from the sun or a star striking the atmosphere obliquely follows a path suggested by the curve in Fig. 14-5. There is no abrupt refraction such as that which occurs at the boundary between two media of different optical densities.

Atmospheric refraction prevents the sun and stars from being seen in their true positions except when they are directly over-

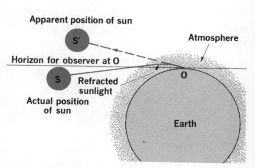

14-5 The sun is visible before actual sunrise and after actual sunset because of atmospheric refraction.

head. In the figure, the sun appears at **S'** instead of in its true position at **S**. Since the index of refraction from outer space to air is only 1.00029, the diagram is greatly exaggerated to show the bending. Refraction of light by the earth's atmosphere makes the sun at this time appear about one diameter ($\frac{1}{2}°$) higher than it really is.

14.4 The law of refraction

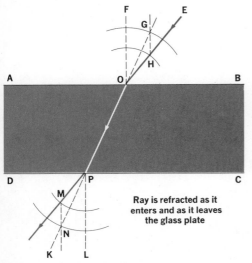

14-6   An illustration of a method of tracing a light ray through a glass plate.

If the index of refraction of a transparent substance is known, it is possible to trace the path that a ray of light will take in passing through the substance. In Fig. 14-6, **ABCD** represents a piece of plate glass with parallel surfaces, and **EO** represents a ray of light incident upon it at point **O**. From **O** as a center two arcs are drawn having the ratio 3 to 2, the index of refraction of glass being taken as 1.5. The normal **OF** is drawn; then the line **GH** is drawn parallel to **OF**, passing through the point **H** where the incident ray intersects the *smaller* arc. The line **OP**, determined by the points **G** and **O**, marks the path of the refracted ray through the glass.

If the ray were not refracted as it left the glass, it would proceed along the line **PK**. To indicate the refraction at **P**, **P** is used as a center and arcs are drawn having the same ratio, 3 to 2, as before. The normal **PL**, and a line **MN**, parallel to the normal, are drawn. The parallel line passes this time through the point **N** where the larger arc is intersected by the refracted ray produced. The points **P** and **M** determine the line which marks the path of the refracted ray as it leaves the glass.

If the ray of light **AD** is incident upon a triangular glass prism, Fig. 14-8, the ray is bent toward the normal along the

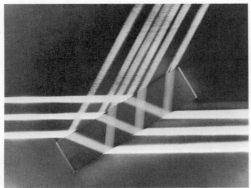

14-7   Parallel beams of light incident upon a rectangular glass plate. The beams are mainly refracted at both surfaces, however, some reflection occurs at each surface.

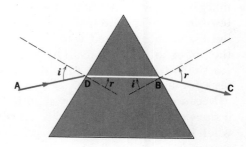

14-8   The path of a light ray through a prism. As the light ray AD passes from the optically less dense to the optically more dense medium at D, its path is diverted toward the normal. As the beam passes out of the glass at B, its path is diverted away from the normal.

line **DB**. Leaving the prism, it is refracted away from the normal along the line **BC**.

Refraction of light can be summarized in ***three laws of refraction:***

1. The incident ray, the refracted ray, and the normal to the surface at the point of incidence are all in the same plane.

2. The index of refraction for any medium is a constant that is independent of the angle of incidence.

3. When a ray of light passes obliquely from a medium of lesser to one of greater optical density, it is bent toward the normal. Conversely, a ray of light passing obliquely from an optically denser medium to an optically rarer medium is bent away from the normal to the surface.

Suppose an incident ray of light, **AO**, passes from water into air and is refracted along the line **OB**, as shown in Fig. 14-9. As the angle of incidence i is increased, the angle of refraction r also increases. When this angle approaches the limiting value, $r_l = 90°$, the refracted ray emerges from the water along a path that gets closer to the water surface. As the angle of incidence continues to increase, the angle of refraction finally equals 90° and the refracted ray takes the path **ON**, along the water surface. *The limiting angle of incidence in the denser medium, resulting in an angle of refraction of 90°, is known as the **critical angle**, i_c.* The critical angle for water is reached when the incident ray **DO** makes an angle of 48.5° with the normal; the critical angle for crown glass is 42°, while that of a diamond is only 24°.

In Section 14.3 we defined the index of refraction of a material as the ratio of the speed of light in a vacuum (air) to the speed of light in the material, or as the ratio sin i/sin r. In Fig. 14-9, the light passes from the denser material to the air. The angle of refraction r is thus related to the speed of light in air. The index of refraction of the water in this instance is

$$n = \frac{\sin r \text{ (air)}}{\sin i \text{ (water)}}$$

At the critical angle i_c, r is the limiting value r_l, which equals 90°, thus,

$$n = \frac{\sin r_l}{\sin i_c} = \frac{\sin 90°}{\sin i_c} = \frac{1}{\sin i_c}$$

Therefore, in general

$$\sin i_c = \frac{1}{n}$$

where n is the index of refraction of the optically denser medium relative to air and i_c is the critical angle of this medium.

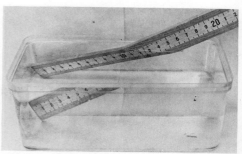

Refraction makes this meter stick seem to bend where it enters the water. Can you explain the image of the end of the stick at the lower left?

14.5 Total reflection

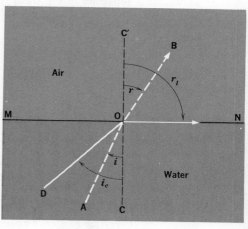

14-9 The critical angle i_c is the limiting angle of incidence in the optically denser medium which results in an angle of refraction of 90°.

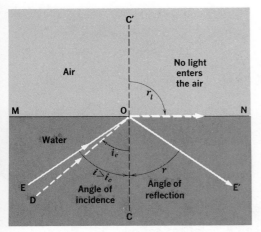

14-10 Total reflection at the water-air boundary occurs when the angle of incidence exceeds the critical angle.

If the angle of incidence of a ray of light passing from water into air is increased beyond the critical angle, no part of the incident ray enters the air; it is *totally reflected* from the water boundary. In Fig. 14-10, **EO** represents a ray of light whose angle of incidence exceeds the critical angle, the angle of incidence **EOC** being greater than the critical angle **DOC**. The ray of light is reflected back into the water along the line **OE'**, a case of simple reflection in which the angle of incidence **EOC** equals the angle of reflection **E'OC**. Total reflection always occurs when the angle of incidence exceeds the critical angle.

A diamond is a brilliant gem because its index of refraction is exceedingly high and its critical angle is therefore correspondingly small. Very little of the light that enters the upper surface of a cut diamond passes through the diamond; most of the light is reflected internally (total reflection), finally emerging from the top of the diamond.

QUESTIONS

Group A
1. Define (a) refraction, (b) angle of refraction, and (c) index of refraction.
2. What property of a transparent substance causes the refraction of light rays which strike it at an oblique angle?
3. What are the three laws of refraction?
4. What is meant by the terms (a) critical angle and (b) total reflection?
5. What practical use is made of the index of refraction of a substance?

Group B
6. You are looking diagonally down at a fish in a pond. To the fish, assuming that it can see you, does your head appear higher or lower than it actually is?
7. Explain why we see the sun before it actually rises above the horizon in the morning, and why we see it after it has dropped below the horizon in the evening.
8. Which is the better reflector of light, a right-angle prism or a plane silvered mirror? Explain.
9. Why are totally reflecting prisms usually designed so that light enters and leaves the prism at an angle of 90° with respect to the surface?
10. Why is a diamond more brilliant than a glass imitation cut the same way?

PROBLEMS

Group A
1. The speed of light in chloroform is 1.99×10^8 m/sec. What is its refractive index?

2. What is the speed of light in kilometers per second in a diamond whose refractive index is 2.42?

3. A penny at the bottom of a glass cylinder is 30.0 cm below the eye. If water is poured into the cylinder to a depth of 16.0 cm, how much closer does the coin appear?

4. A ray of light passes from a medium of refractive index 1.33 into a medium of refractive index 1.50. The angle of incidence is 45.0°. (a) By the construction method, determine the angle of refraction. (b) Compute the angle of refraction.

Group B

5. If the angles of incidence and refraction of a ray of light passing from air into water are 60.0° and 41.0°, what is the index of refraction of the water?

6. Find the critical angle for a carbon tetrachloride-to-air surface.

LENS OPTICS

A lens is any transparent object having two nonparallel, curved surfaces, or one plane surface and one curved surface. The curved surfaces can be spherical, parabolic, or cylindrical, although spherical surfaces are the most common. Lenses are usually made of glass and are of two kinds.

1. Converging lenses. Cross sections of converging lenses are shown in Fig. 14-11(A); all are thicker in the middle than at the edge. The concavo-convex lens is called a meniscus lens.

A converging lens bends the wave front of light passing through it, the thick portion retarding the light more than the thin portion. A plane wave incident on the surface of a converging lens parallel to the lens plane are refracted and converge at a point beyond the lens. See Fig. 14-12(A).

14.6 Types of lenses

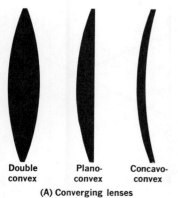

Double convex   Plano-convex   Concavo-convex

(A) Converging lenses

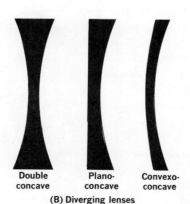

Double concave   Plano-concave   Convexo-concave

(B) Diverging lenses

14-11 Common lens cross sections.

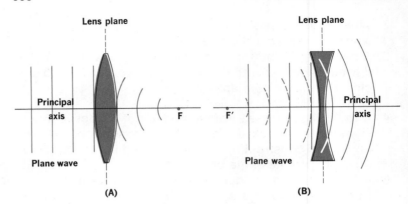

14-12 Refraction of plane wave (A) by a converging lens and (B) by a diverging lens.

2. *Diverging lenses.* Lenses that are thicker at the edge than in the middle are diverging lenses. Their cross sections are shown in Fig. 14-11(B). The convexo-concave lens is a meniscus lens.

A diverging lens bends the wave front of light passing through it, the thick portion retarding the light more than the thin portion. Plane waves incident on the surface of a diverging lens parallel to the lens plane are refracted and diverge from a point in front of the lens. See Fig. 14-12(B).

14.7 Ray diagrams

The nature and location of the image formed by a lens is more easily determined by a ray diagram than by a wave-front diagram. The plane waves of Fig. 14-12 can be represented by light rays drawn perpendicular to the wave fronts. Since these wave fronts approaching the lens are shown parallel to the lens plane, their ray lines are parallel to the *principal axis* of the lens.

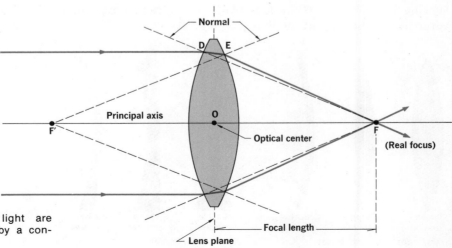

14-13 Parallel rays of light are brought to a real focus by a converging lens.

In Fig. 14-13 these parallel rays (which are also parallel to the principal axis) are shown incident on a converging lens. They are refracted as they pass through the lens and converge at a point on the principal axis called the *principal focus* of the lens. At point **D** the incident ray is bent toward the normal drawn to the front surface of the lens. At point **E** the incident ray is bent away from the normal drawn to the back surface of the lens. Because the rays of light actually pass through the principal focus, it is called a *real* focus **F**. *Real* images are formed on the same side of the lens as the real focus.

Rays parallel to the principal axis are shown incident on a diverging lens in Fig. 14-14. The rays of light are refracted as they pass through the lens and diverge as if they originated at the principal focus located in front of the lens. Because the rays do not actually pass through the principal focus, it is called a *virtual* focus **F'**. *Virtual* images are formed on the same side of the lens as the virtual focus.

Spherical lenses usually have two centers of curvature, the centers of the intersecting spheres which form the lens surfaces. The principal axis passes through the centers of curvature. In Fig. 14-15, the ray of light **AB**, parallel to the principal axis is refracted and passes through the real focus, **F**. The *secondary axes* pass through the *optical center* of a lens, which may coincide with its geometrical center. The ray **AOA'** travels along the secondary axis drawn from **A**. Rays of light passing through the optical center of a thin lens *are not appreciably refracted.*

Lenses refract rays which are parallel to the principal axis so they meet at the principal focus. However, this focus is not midway between the lens and the center of curvature as it is

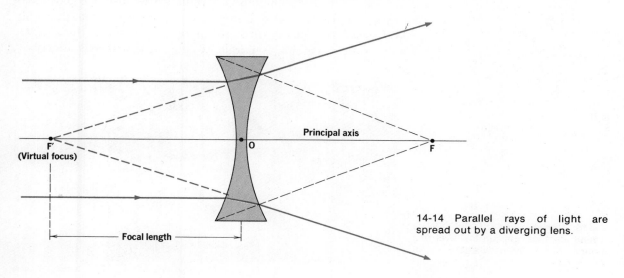

Principal axis

F'
(Virtual focus)

O

F

Focal length

14-14 Parallel rays of light are spread out by a diverging lens.

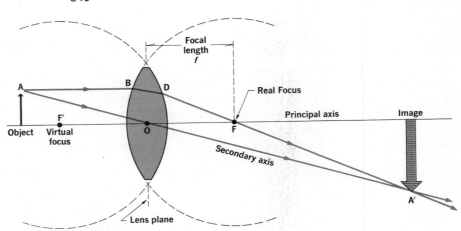

14-15 A ray parallel to the real axis of a converging lens is refracted so that it passes through the principal focus. A ray passing through the optical center is not appreciably refracted.

in spherical mirrors; *its position on the principal axis depends on the index of refraction of the lens.* With a common double convex lens of crown glass, the principal foci and the centers of curvature almost coincide, and the radius of curvature and the focal length are approximately equal. The *focal length, f,* of a lens is the distance between the optical center of the lens and the principal focus. Increasing the index of refraction shortens the focal length; also the more curved its surfaces are, the shorter its focal length is.

14.8 Images by refraction

To understand how images are formed by lenses, let us refer again to Fig. 14-15. As in the case with curved mirrors, any two rays coming from point **A** on the object are sufficient to locate its image point. For convenience we use two particular rays. One ray, **AO**, along the secondary axis, is not appreciably refracted as it passes through the optical center of the lens, **O**. The other ray, **AB**, is parallel to the principal axis and is re-

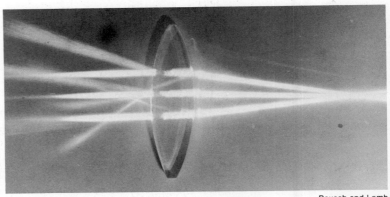

14-16 Convergence of light by a cylindrical lens. Explain the diverging pencils of low intensity at the left of the lens.

Bausch and Lomb

fracted as it enters the lens at **B** and as it leaves the lens at **D**. It passes through the real focus **F**, intersecting the secondary-axis ray at **A′**, thus locating the image of **A** at **A′**. Rays from other points on the object can be similarly treated, giving rise to the image shown.

Lenses and mirrors differ in several ways.

1. Secondary axes pass through the optical center of a lens and not through either of its centers of curvature.

2. The principal focus is usually near the center of curvature, depending on the refractive index of the glass from which the lens is made. Thus the focal length of a double convex lens is generally about equal to its radius of curvature.

3. Since the image produced by a lens is formed by rays of light which actually pass through the lens, a *real* image is formed on the side of the lens opposite the object. *Virtual* images formed by lenses appear to be on the same side of the lens as the object.

4. Convex lenses form images in almost the same manner as concave mirrors, while concave lenses are like convex mirrors in the manner in which they form images.

Spherical lenses, like spherical mirrors, have aberration defects. See Fig. 14-17. When such lenses are used with large apertures, images are generally sharp and well defined at the center but blurred near the edges because of *spherical aberration*.

Similarly, rays of light from horizontal and vertical lines in a plane in the object are not focused in the same plane on the edges of the image. This defect of lenses is known as *lens astigmatism*. By using a combination of lenses of suitable refractive indexes and focal lengths, lens makers produce *anastigmatic* lenses which give good definition over the entire image even when used with large apertures.

Lenses of short focal length that can be used with a large aperture are said to be *fast* and are used in high-speed photography. The effective aperture of a lens equals the diameter of the camera diaphragm when it is open as wide as possible. The *speed* of a lens depends upon the ratio of its focal length to the effective aperture and is called its *relative aperture*. In an f/4 lens, the focal length is 4 times the effective aperture. Such a lens is 4 times as fast as an f/8 lens, and 16 times as fast as an f/16 lens, the speed ratio being proportional to the squares of the relative apertures.

We shall consider six different cases of image formation.

Case 1. Object at infinite distance. The use of a small magnifying glass to focus the sun's rays upon a point approximates this first case. While the sun is not at an infinite distance, it is so far away that its rays reaching the earth are nearly parallel. When

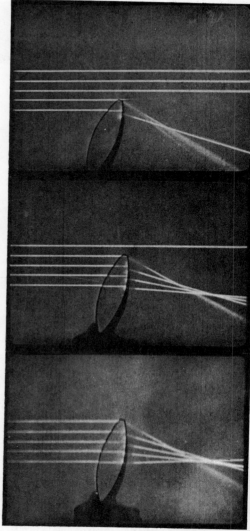

American Optical Company

14-17 Parallel rays of light incident on a converging lens near its edge are not refracted through the principal focus. How does this affect the use of the lens?

14.9 Images formed by converging lenses

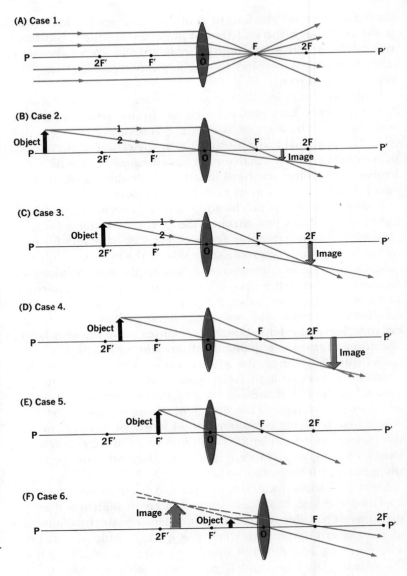

(A) Case 1.

(B) Case 2.

(C) Case 3.

(D) Case 4.

(E) Case 5.

(F) Case 6.

14-18   Ray diagrams of image formation by converging lenses.

an object is at an infinite distance, so that its rays are parallel, *the image formed is a point at the real focus.* See Fig. 14-18(A). This principle can be used to find the focal length of a lens by focusing the sun's rays on a white screen. The distance from the screen to the optical center of the lens is the focal length of the lens.

Case 2. Object at a finite distance beyond twice the focal length. Case 2 is illustrated in Fig. 14-18(B). Rays parallel to the principal axis and along the secondary axis and emanating from a point on the object are used to locate the corresponding image point. *The image is real, inverted, reduced, and located between F and 2F on the opposite side of the lens.* The lenses of the eye and the camera, and the objective lens of the refracting telescope are all applications of this case.

Case 3. Object at a distance equal to twice the focal length. The construction of the image is shown in Fig. 14-18(C). *The image is real, inverted, the same size as the object, and located at 2F on the opposite side of the lens.* An inverting lens of a field telescope, which inverts an image without changing its size, is an application of Case 3.

Case 4. Object at a distance between one and two focal lengths away. This is the converse of Case 2 and is shown in Fig. 14-18(D). *The image is real, inverted, enlarged, and located beyond 2F on the opposite side of the lens.* The compound microscope, slide projector, and motion picture projector are all applications of a lens used in this manner.

Case 5. Object at the principal focus. This case is the converse of Case 1. *No image is formed*, since the rays of light are parallel as they leave the lens. See Fig. 14-18(E). The lenses used in lighthouses and searchlights are applications of Case 5.

Case 6. Object at a distance less than one focal length away. The construction in Fig. 14-18(F) shows that the rays are divergent after passing through the lens and cannot form a real image on the opposite side of the lens. These rays appear to converge behind the object to produce *an image that is virtual, erect, enlarged, and located on the same side of the lens as the object.* The simple magnifier and the eyepiece lenses of microscopes, binoculars, and telescopes form images as shown in Case 6.

The only kind of image of a real object that can be formed by a diverging lens is one that is *virtual, erect, and reduced in size.*

14.10 Images formed by diverging lenses

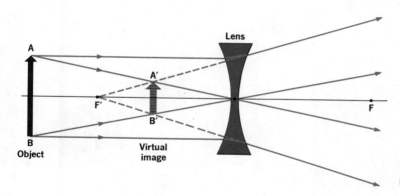

14-19   The image of an object formed by a diverging lens.

Such lenses are used to neutralize the effect of a converging lens, or to reduce, to some extent, its converging effect. The image formation is shown in Fig. 14-19.

14.11 Object-image relationships

For thin lenses, the ratio of object size to image size equals the ratio of the object distance to image distance. This rule is the same as that for curved mirrors. Thus,

$$\frac{h_i}{h_o} = \frac{s_i}{s_o}$$

where symbols h_o and h_i represent the heights of the object and the image respectively, and s_o and s_i represent the respective distances of the object and image from the optical center of the lens.

The equation for curved mirrors used to determine the distances of the object and image in relation to focal length applies also to lenses, and therefore can be restated here as

$$\frac{1}{f} = \frac{1}{s_o} + \frac{1}{s_i}$$

where s_o represents the distance of the object from the lens, s_i the distance of the image, and f the focal length. When the image is virtual, s_i has a *negative* value. For diverging lenses, both s_i and f have *negative* values. The derivations of these lens equations follow the same logic used in deriving the mirror equations in Section 13.12 and are left for the student to develop.

14.12 The simple magnifier

A converging lens of short focal length can be used as a simple magnifier. The lens is placed slightly nearer the object than one focal length and the eye is positioned close to the lens on the opposite side. This is a practical example of Case 6; the image is virtual, erect, and enlarged as shown in Fig. 14-21. A

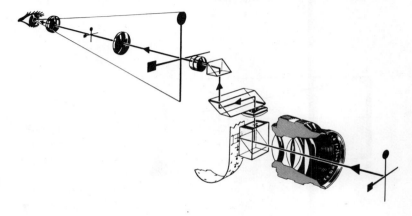

14-20   The optical system of a motion picture camera. Observe the real inverted image produced on the film and the virtual erect image for viewing produced by an auxillary optical system.

reading glass, a simple microscope, and an eyepiece lens of a compound microscope or telescope are applications of simple magnifiers.

Magnification M is simply the ratio of the image height to the object height.

$$M = \frac{h_i}{h_o}$$

But,

$$\frac{h_i}{h_o} = \frac{s_i}{s_o}$$

So,

$$M = \frac{s_i}{s_o}$$

Suppose an object is viewed by the unaided eye. As it is moved closer and closer to the eye, the image formed on the retina becomes larger and larger. Eventually a *nearest* point is reached for the object at which the eye can still form a clear image. This minimum distance for distinct vision is approximately 25 cm from the eye. Although the nearest point varies among individuals, 25 cm is taken as the standard *distance for most distinct vision;* it is called the *near point.*

When a converging lens is placed in front of the eye as a simple magnifier, the object can be brought much closer and the eye focuses on the virtual image. The lens is used to best advantage when the object is just inside the principal focus ($s_o \simeq f$). The image then is formed approximately at the near point. Magnification, shown above to be equal to the ratio s_i/s_o, can now be expressed for a simple magnifier as the ratio of the distance for most distinct vision to the focal length of the lens. When f is given in centimeters, the magnification becomes approximately

$$M = \frac{25 \text{ cm}}{f}$$

Magnifiers are sometimes labeled to show their magnifying power. Thus a magnifier with a focal length of 5 cm would be marked 5X. One with a focal length of 2.5 cm would be marked 10X, etc. Observe that the shorter the focal length of a converging lens, the higher is its magnification.

14.13 The microscope

The compound microscope, thought to be invented in Holland by Zacharias Janssen about 1590, uses a lens, the *objective*, to form an enlarged image as in Case 4. This image is then magnified, as in Case 6, by a second lens, called the *eyepiece*.

In Fig. 14-22 a converging lens is used as the objective, with the object **AB** just beyond its focal length. At **A'B'**, a distance

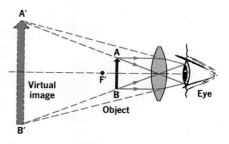

14-21   The simple magnifier.

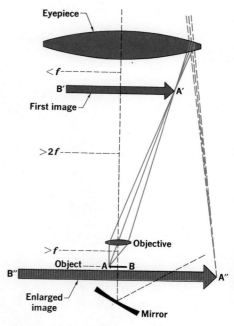

14-22   Image formation by a compound microscope.

greater than twice the focal length of the objective lens, an enlarged, real, and inverted image is formed. The eyepiece lens acts as a simple magnifier to enlarge this image.

The magnifying power of the objective is approximately equal to the length of the tube l, divided by the focal length, f_o, of the objective, or l/f_o. The magnifying power of the eyepiece, acting as a simple magnifier, is approximately $25 \text{ cm}/f_e$. The total magnification is the product of the two lens magnifications. (The equation is again an approximation.)

$$M = \frac{25 \text{ cm} \times l}{f_e \times f_o}$$

14.14 Refracting telescopes

A refracting astronomical telescope has two lens systems. The *objective lens* is of large diameter so that it will admit a large amount of light. The objects to be viewed in telescopes are always more distant than twice the focal length of the objective lens. As a consequence, the image formed is smaller than the object. The *eyepiece lens* magnifies the real image produced by the objective lens. The magnifying power is approximately equal to the focal length of the objective, f_o, divided by the focal length of the eyepiece, f_e, or f_o/f_e.

The lenses of a *terrestrial*, or field, telescope form images just as their counterparts do in the refracting astronomical telescope. Since it would be confusing to see objects inverted in a field telescope, another lens system is used to reinvert the real image formed by the objective. This additional inverting lens system makes the final image erect, as shown in Fig. 14-23.

A field telescope in use.

U.S. Navy

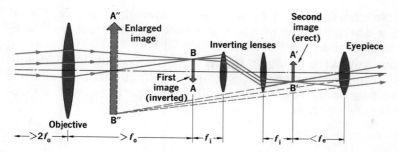

14-23 Image formation in a terrestrial telescope.

The inverting lens system does not magnify the image because the lens system is placed exactly its own focal length from the image formed by the objective.

The *prism binocular* is actually a double field telescope, using two sets of totally reflecting prisms instead of a third lens system to reinvert the final image. This method of reinverting the first image, which also has the effect of folding the optical path, makes possible a shorter distance between the objective and eyepiece. Thus binoculars are usually more compact and easier to use than field telescopes.

Bausch and Lomb

14-24 A pair of totally reflecting prisms reinvert the image in binoculars.

QUESTIONS

Group A

1. (a) What causes spherical aberration in lenses? (b) How can it be remedied?
2. Of which case of converging lenses is the simple magnifier an application?
3. Explain the lens system and image formation of a compound microscope in terms of the lens cases used.
4. Explain the lens system and image formation of a refracting astronomical telescope in terms of the lens cases used.
5. How does a terrestrial telescope compare with a refracting astronomical telescope?

Group B

6. What kinds of lenses could be used and where should the object be placed to produce (a) an enlarged real image, (b) a reduced real image, (c) a real image the same size as the object, (d) an enlarged virtual image, (e) a small virtual image?
7. When the distance between a projector and the screen is increased, what adjustment must be made in the distance between the film and the objective lens to bring the image back into focus?
8. Is the focal length of a crown-glass diverging lens changed when the lens is immersed in water? Justify your answer.

9. A double convex lens in air acts as a converging lens. (a) Can it act as a diverging lens in another medium? Construct a ray diagram to illustrate your response to (a).
10. Suppose you were going to use a clear plastic bag inflated with air as an underwater converging lens. (a) What shape should the inflated bag have? (b) Illustrate your response to (a) with an appropriate ray diagram.

PROBLEMS

Group A

1. A converging lens has a focal length of 20.0 cm. If it is placed 50.0 cm from an object, at what distance from the lens will the image be?
2. If an object is $1\bar{0}$ cm from a converging lens of 5 cm focal length, how far from the lens will the image be formed?
3. The focal length of the lens in a box camera is 10.0 cm. The fixed distance between the lens and the film is 11.0 cm. If an object is to be clearly focused on the film, how far must it be from the lens?
4. An object 3.0 cm tall is placed $2\bar{0}$ cm from a converging lens. A real image is formed $1\bar{0}$ cm from the lens. What is (a) the focal length of the lens, (b) the size of the image?
5. An object $3\bar{0}$ cm from a converging lens forms a real image $6\bar{0}$ cm from the lens. (a) Find the focal length of the lens. (b) What is the size of the image if the object is 5 cm high?
6. The focal length of a camera lens is 5.00 cm. How far must the lens be from the film to produce a clear image of an object 3.00 m away?
7. What is the focal length of the lens in your eye when you read a book 35.0 cm from your eye? Distance from lens to retina is 19.0 mm.
8. What is the focal length of the lens in your eye when you are looking at a person standing 15.0 m away? The distance from the lens to the retina is 19.0 mm.
9. What is the magnifying power of a simple magnifier whose focal length is $1\bar{0}$ cm?

Group B

10. An object 3 cm tall is placed 16 cm from a converging lens with a focal length of 24 cm. (a) Find the location of the image. (b) What is its size?
11. When an object 5.0 cm tall is placed 12 cm from a converging lens, an image is produced on the same side of the lens as the object, but 61 cm away from the lens. What is (a) the focal length of the lens, (b) the size of the image?
12. An optical bench pointer 1.0 cm tall is placed at the 55.0-cm mark on the meter stick. When a diverging lens is placed at the 0.0-cm mark, an image is formed at the 5.0-cm mark. What is (a) the focal length of the lens, (b) the size of the image?
13. The objective lens of a compound microscope has a focal length

of 0.500 cm. The eyepiece has a focal length of 2.00 cm. If the lenses are 15.0 cm apart, what is the magnifying power of the microscope?

14. The dimensions of the picture on a slide are 6.4 cm by 7.6 cm. This slide is to be projected to form an image 1.5 m by 1.8 m at a distance of 9.0 m from the objective lens of the projector. (a) What is the distance from the slide to the objective lens? (b) What focal length objective lens must be used?

15. The tube of a microscope is 160 mm long. If the focal length of the eyepiece is 30.0 mm and the focal length of the objective is 5.00 mm, find the magnifying power.

16. What is the distance between the objective lens and the eyepiece lens of a terrestrial telescope when an object 1.5 kilometers away is being observed? The focal length of the objective lens is 15 cm and the focal length of the eyepiece lens is 5 cm. Each lens of the two-lens inverting system has a focal length of 3 cm and these two lenses are 6 cm apart.

DISPERSION

Suppose a narrow beam of sunlight is directed onto a glass prism in a darkened room. If the light which leaves the prism falls on a white screen, a band of colors is observed, one shade blending gradually into another. *This band of colors produced when sunlight is dispersed by a prism is called a* **solar spectrum**. The dispersion of sunlight was described by Newton, who observed that the spectrum was "violet at one end, red at the other, and showed a continuous gradation of colors in between."

We can recognize six distinct colors in the visible spectrum. These are *red, orange, yellow, green, blue,* and *violet*. Each color gradually blends into the adjacent colors giving a *continuous* spectrum over the range of visible light. A continuous spectrum is shown in **Plate VII** of the color insert between pages 356 and 357. *Light consisting of several colors is called* **polychromatic** *light; light consisting of only one color is called* **monochromatic** *light.*

The dispersion of light by a prism is shown in **Plate I** of the color insert. It is evident that the refraction of red light by the prism is not as great as that of violet light, and that the refractions of other colors lie between these two. Thus the index of refraction of glass is not the same for light of different colors. If we wish to be very precise in measuring the index of refraction of a substance, monochromatic light must be used and the monochrome color must be stated. Some variations in the index of refraction of glass are given in Table 14-1.

A hot solid radiates an appreciable amount of energy which increases as the temperature is raised. At relatively low tempera-

14.15 Dispersion by a prism

Table 14-1   VARIATION OF THE INDEX OF REFRACTION

Color	Crown glass	Flint glass
red	1.515	1.622
yellow	1.517	1.627
blue	1.523	1.639
violet	1.533	1.663

14.16 The color of light

tures, the energy is radiated only in the infrared region. As the temperature of the solid is raised, some of the energy is radiated at higher frequencies, ranging into the red portion of the visible spectrum as the body becomes "red hot." At still higher temperatures the solid may be "white hot" as the major portion of the radiated energy shifts toward the higher frequencies.

Suppose we have a clear-glass tungsten-filament lamp connected so the current in the filament, and thus the temperature of the filament, can be controlled. A small electric current in the filament does not change its appearance, but as we gradually increase the current, the filament begins to glow with a dark red color. To produce this color, the electrically charged particles in the atoms of tungsten must vibrate fast enough to radiate energy with wavelengths of about 7600 Å. Even before the lamp filament glows visibly, experiments show that it radiates infrared rays which we detect as heat. As the current is increased further, the lamp filament gives off orange light in addition to red; then the filament adds yellow, and finally at higher temperatures it adds enough other colors to produce white light.

A photographer's tungsten-filament flood lamp operates at a very high temperature. If the white light of such a lamp is passed through a prism, a band of colors similar to the solar spectrum is obtained. Figure 14-25 shows the distribution of radiant energy from an "ideal" radiator for several different temperatures.

Considering the wavelengths of various colors shown in **Plate I**, it is evident that our eyes are sensitive to a range of frequencies equivalent to about one octave. The wavelength of the light at the upper limit of visibility (7600 Å) is about twice

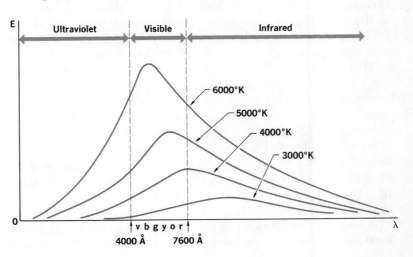

14-25 Distribution of radiant energy from an ideal radiator.

visibility (4000 Å). We use the word *color* to describe a sensation received through our eyes. The color perceived for monochromatic light depends on the frequency of the light.

Color is a property of the light that reaches our eyes. Objects may absorb certain wavelengths from the light falling upon them and reflect other wavelengths. For example, a cloth which appears blue in sunlight appears black when held in the red portion of a solar spectrum in a darkened room. A red cloth held in the blue portion of the solar spectrum also appears black. *The color of an opaque object depends upon the frequencies of light it reflects.* If all colors are reflected, we say it is white. It is *black* if it absorbs all of the light that falls upon it. It is called *red* if it absorbs all other colors and reflects only red light.

A piece of blue cloth appears black in the red portion of the spectrum because there is no blue light there for it to reflect, and it absorbs all other colors. For the same reason, a red cloth appears black in the blue portion of the spectrum. *The color of an opaque object depends on the color of the light incident upon it.*

Ordinary window glass, which transmits all colors, is said to be colorless. Red glass absorbs all colors but red, which it transmits. The stars of the United States flag would appear red on a black field if viewed through red glass. *The color of transparent objects depends upon the color of the light which they transmit.*

14.17 The color of objects

Since polychromatic light can be dispersed into its simple colors, it is reasonable to suppose that we can combine simple colors to form polychromatic light. There are three ways in which this can be done.

1. A prism placed in the path of the solar spectrum formed by another prism will recombine the different colors to produce white light. Other colors can be compounded in the same manner.

2. A disk which has the spectral colors painted on it can be rotated rapidly to produce the effect of combining the colors. The light from one color forms an image which persists on the retina of the eye until each of the other colors in turn has been reflected to the eye. If pure spectral colors are used in the proper proportion, they will blend to produce the same color sensation as white light.

3. Wavelengths from the mid-region of the visible spectrum combined with wavelengths from the two end regions produce white light. This method is described in Section 14.19.

14.18 Complementary colors

Using two prisms as described above, instead of permitting all the colors produced by dispersion from the first prism to enter the second prism, we can block off the red light from the first prism. The remaining spectral colors combine as they pass through the second prism to produce a blue-green color called *cyan*. Red light and cyan should therefore combine to produce white light, and a rotating color wheel shows this to be true. *Any two colors which combine to form white light are said to be* **complementary**.

In similar fashion, it can be shown that blue and yellow are complementary colors. White fabrics acquire a yellowish color after continued laundering. Bluing, or a bluish dye added to laundry detergents, neutralizes the yellow color and the fabrics appear white. Iron compounds in the sand used for making glass impart a green color to the glass. Manganese gives glass a *magenta*, or purplish-red color. However, if both these elements are present in the right proportion, the resulting glass will be colorless. The complements of the six simple spectral colors are shown in **Plate II**.

14.19 The primary colors. The six regions of color in the solar spectrum are easily observed by the dispersion of sunlight. Further dispersion within a color region fails to reveal any other colors of light. We generally identify the range of wavelengths comprising a color region by the color of light associated with that region. These are the six *elementary* colors of the visible spectrum; they combine to produce white light. However, the complement of an elementary color is not monochromatic, but is a mixture of all of the elementary colors remaining after the one elementary color has been removed.

Experiments with beams of different colored lights have shown that most colors and hues can be described in terms of three different colors. Light from one end of the visible spectrum combined with light from the middle region in various proportions will yield all of the color hues in the half of the spectrum that lies in between. Light from the opposite end, when combined with light from the middle region, will also yield all hues in the half of the spectrum that lies in between. Colored light from the two end regions and the middle region can be combined to match most of the hues, when mixed in the proper proportions. The three colors which can be used most successfully in color matching experiments of this sort are *red, green,* and *blue*. Consequently, these have been called the **primary colors**.

Suppose we project the three primary colors onto a white screen as shown in **Plate III(A)**. The three beams can be adjusted to overlap, producing additive mixtures of these primary colors. Observe that green and blue lights combine to produce cyan, the complement of red; green and red lights combine to produce yellow, the complement of blue; and red and blue lights combine to produce magenta, the complement of green. Thus two primary colors combine to produce the complement of the third primary color, and where the three overlap, white light is produced.

14.20 Mixing pigments

When the complements, blue light and yellow light, are mixed, white light results by an additive process. If we mix a blue pigment with a yellow pigment, a green mixture results. This is a subtractive process, since each pigment subtracts or absorbs certain colors. For example, the yellow pigment subtracts blue and violet lights and reflects red, yellow, and green. The blue pigment subtracts red light and yellow light and reflects green, blue, and violet. Green light is the only color reflected by both pigments; thus the mixture of pigments appears green under white light.

The subtractive process can be demonstrated by the use of various color filters which absorb certain wavelengths and transmit others from a single white-light source.

When pigments are mixed, each one subtracts certain colors from white light, and the resulting color depends on the light waves that are not absorbed. *The **primary pigments** are the complements of the three primary colors.* They are cyan (the complement of red), magenta (the complement of green), and yellow (the complement of blue). When the three primary pigments are mixed in the proper proportions, all the colors are subtracted from white light and the mixture is black. See **Plate IV**.

14.21 Color vision

Scientists do not fully understand the complex processes of visual perception and the relationship between light wavelengths and color sensations. A generally useful theory of color vision was proposed many years ago by Thomas Young, an English physician and scientist. It was later elaborated on by Hermann Helmholtz (1821–1894), a noted German physicist.

According to the *Young-Helmholtz color vision theory*, the retina of the eye has three types of nerve receptors with unequal sensitivity over the range of the visible spectrum. Maximum sensitivity for each type of receptor lies in a different region of the spectrum, so that there is one type for each of the primary colors.

If all three types of receptors are equally stimulated, we receive the sensation which the brain interprets as white. Lack of stimulation gives the sensation of darkness or blackness.

When light from a red source enters the eye, it stimulates chiefly the receptors that produce the sensation of red, and we see that color. If only those receptors sensitive to green are stimulated, the sensation of green is produced in the brain. When yellow light enters the eye, however, the receptors for both red and green are stimulated and we see yellow. We see purple if the receptors sensitive to red and blue are stimulated. Thus, according to the Young-Helmholtz theory, all colors, shades, and hues are seen through varying stimulation of one, two, or three types of color receptors.

A diagram for mixing colored lights, called a *chromaticity diagram*, is shown in **Plate V**. The wavelengths of the spectral colors are listed around the perimeter in angstroms. Any point not on the solid-line curve, but within the diagram, represents some additive mixture of colors and not a simple spectral color. White light, being such a mixture, is within the bound area at **C**. The primary colors are located at the three extremities of the curve.

A straight line joining any two points within the curve will indicate all of the color variations that can be obtained by combining these two colored lights in varying intensities, an additive process. The line **RG** is an example. Observe that straight lines passing through point **C** join colors which are complementary. Colors, shades, and hues that can be seen on a color television screen are inside the smaller triangle **BGR**.

Recent experiments in color vision have shown the eye to be a far more versatile instrument than is indicated by the three-color theory. These experiments suggest that the rays of light themselves may not be colormaking, but that they may be carriers of information which enable the eye to assign appropriate colors to the various parts of an image.

In one of these experiments, two photographs of a multicolored object are taken simultaneously on black-and-white film with a special dual camera, through two different color filters. Black-and-white positive transparencies are then made from the two negatives. These transparencies have no color and, although they are photographs of the same scene, are not identical. The degree of transparency of corresponding areas of the two films is different since different wavelengths of light were used to form the two images originally. When the images of the two transparencies are projected and superimposed on a screen, the long-wavelength transparency being projected through a red filter and the short-wavelength transparency being projected with white light without a filter, the composite image reproduces the full range of color of the object originally photographed.

Certainly, red light and white light mixed on a screen produces pink. How then can the full range of color of this photographic image be explained? Perhaps the color of the image results not from the choice of light wavelengths but from the relative balance of the longer and shorter wavelengths over the entire scene. This suggests that the eye needs information about the long and short wavelengths to see color, without regard to any particular wavelengths. The eye-brain mechanism may separate the incoming rays into long- and short-wavelength images, average together all those on the long side and all those on the short side, and then compare the two averaged images to develop the color sensation.

14.22 Chromatic aberration

Since a lens has some similarity to a prism, some dispersion occurs when light passes through a lens. Violet light is refracted more than the other colors, and is brought to a focus by a converging lens at a point nearer the lens than other colors. Because red is refracted the least, the focus for the red rays is farthest from the lens. See Fig. 14-26. Thus, images formed by ordinary spherical lenses are always fringed with spectral colors. *The non-focusing of light of different colors is called **chromatic aberration***. Sir Isaac Newton developed the reflecting telescope to avoid the objectionable effects of chromatic aberration when observations are made through a refracting telescope.

John Dollond (1706–1761), an English optician, discovered that the fringe of colors could be eliminated by means of a combination of lenses. A double convex lens of crown glass used with a suitable plano-concave lens of flint glass corrects for chromatic aberration without preventing refraction and image formation. A lens combination of this type is called an *achromatic* (without color) lens.

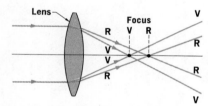

14-26 Chromatic aberration is caused by unequal refraction of the different colors.

QUESTIONS

Group A

1. Why does a prism disperse sunlight into a band of colors?
2. What property of light determines its color?
3. What name is given to electromagnetic radiations having wavelengths slightly (a) longer, (b) shorter, than visible light?
4. If a black object absorbs all light rays incident upon it, how can it be seen?
5. What is the appearance of a red dress in a closed room illuminated only by green light? Explain.
6. (a) What are the primary colors? (b) Define a complementary color. (c) Name the complement of each primary color.

Group B   7. Why is it not possible to make white paint from orange paint by adding a pigment of another color?

8. How could you demonstrate that a piece of white-hot iron gives off red light?

9. The focal length of a converging lens is determined experimentally using red light. (a) How will this focal length compare with that for green light? (b) Construct a ray diagram to support your conclusion in (a).

10. Suppose a diverging lens is substituted for the converging lens in Question 9. (a) How will the focal length of the lens for red light compare with that for green light? (b) Construct an appropriate diagram to support your conclusion.

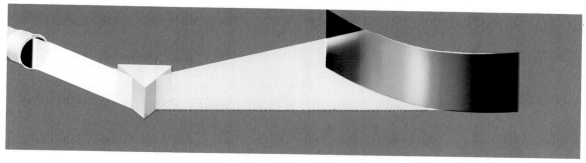

A. The prism spreads a narrow beam of white light out into the visible spectrum, the shorter wavelengths being bent more than the longer wavelengths.

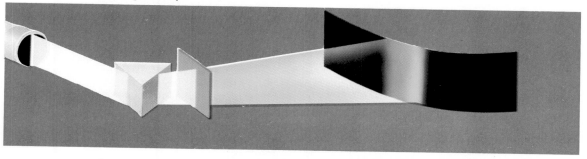

B. A red filter between the prism and the screen allows only light of the longer wavelengths to pass.

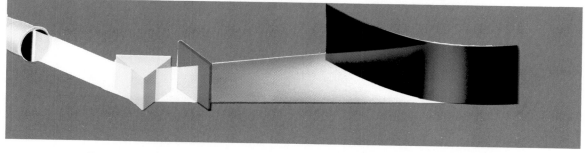

C. A green filter allows only light from the middle region of the spectrum to pass.

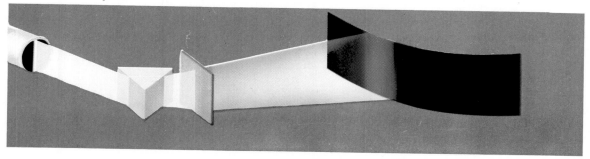

D. A blue filter passes only light of the shorter wavelengths.

(Adapted from COLOR AS SEEN AND PHOTOGRAPHED, Eastman Kodak)

Plate I

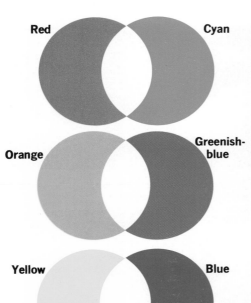

Red   Cyan

Orange   Greenish-blue

Yellow   Blue

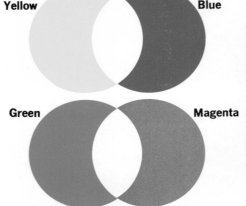

Green   Magenta

Blue   Yellow

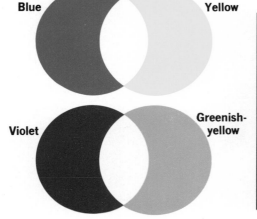

Violet   Greenish-yellow

A.   Complementary colors.

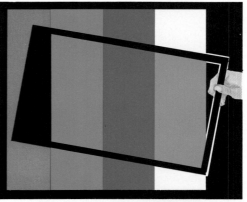

B.   A cyan filter absorbs its complement, red light, and transmits blue and green light.

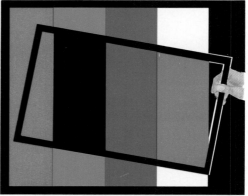

C.   A magenta filter absorbs its complement, green light, and transmits red and blue light.

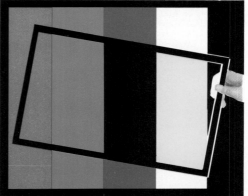

D.   A yellow filter absorbs its complement, blue light, and transmits red and green light.

(Adapted from COLOR AS SEEN AND PHOTOGRAPHED, Eastman Kodak)

Plate II

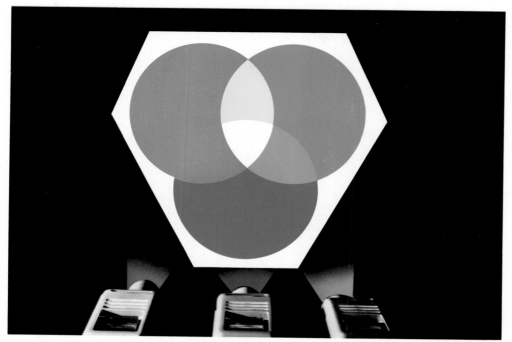

A. Primary colors. The additive mixture of red, green, and blue lights produces white light. Combined in pairs, two primaries give the complement of the third: cyan, magenta, and yellow. (Adapted from COLOR AS SEEN AND PHOTO-GRAPHED, Eastman Kodak)

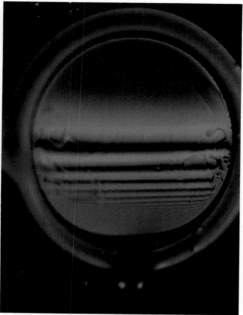

B. Interference produced by reflecting white light from a soap film. The picture on the right shows the fringes produced by red light.

Plate III

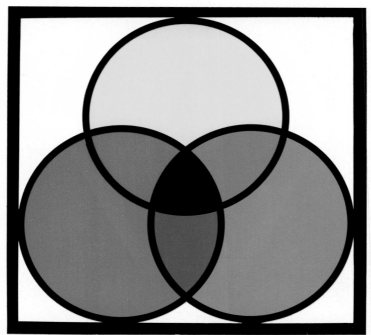

A. Primary pigments. The subtractive combination of cyan, magenta, and yellow filters transmits no light. Combined in pairs, two primary pigments give the complement of the third by subtraction: red, green, and blue.

B. Subtractive process. The range of colors produced by mixing the three primary pigments is shown on the left. The quantities are decreased toward the center allowing the white background to show through. At the right, magenta, yellow, and cyan water colors are mixed in varying amounts to give black shading through gray to white. (Adapted from COLOR AS SEEN AND PHOTOGRAPHED, Eastman Kodak)

Plate IV

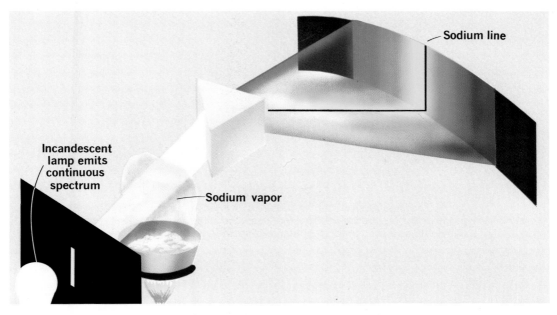

Sodium line

Incandescent
lamp emits
continuous
spectrum

Sodium vapor

A. Nonluminous sodium vapor absorbs yellow light of the same wavelength as that emitted by luminous sodium vapor.

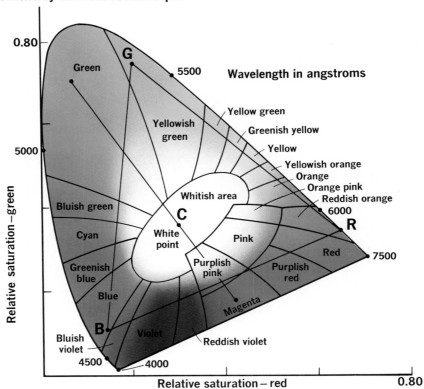

B. Chromaticity diagram. In the chromaticity diagram colors are specified in terms of theoretical colored lights and all possible colors can be described mathematically.

Plate V

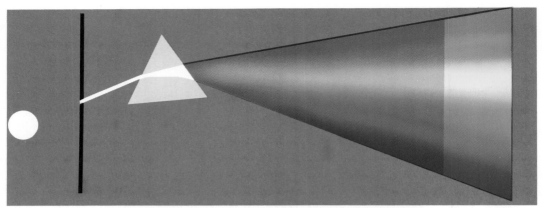

A. A continuous spectrum is produced by incandescent solids, liquids, and gases under high pressure. The very dense incandescent gases in the main body of the sun and stars produce continuous spectra.

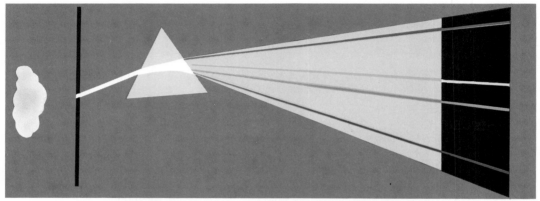

B. A bright-line spectrum is produced by incandescent gases of low density. Each chemical substance yields a characteristic pattern of lines that differ from all others.

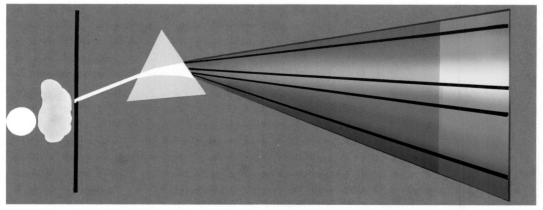

C. A dark-line spectrum is produced by a nonluminous (cooler) gas in front of an incandescent source of a continuous spectrum. The cooler gas absorbs light energy from the parts of the spectrum where it would emit bright lines if heated to incandescence. (Adapted from THE UNIVERSE, Time, Inc.)

Plate VI

EMISSION SPECTRA

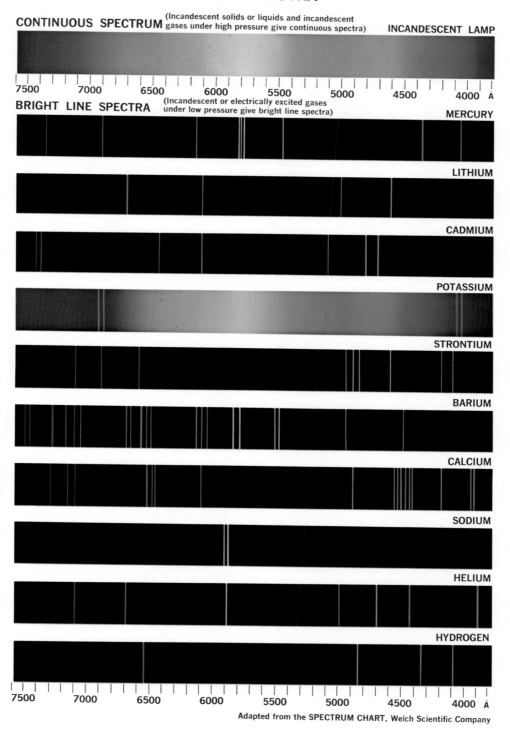

CONTINUOUS SPECTRUM (Incandescent solids or liquids and incandescent gases under high pressure give continuous spectra) **INCANDESCENT LAMP**

7500   7000   6500   6000   5500   5000   4500   4000 Å

BRIGHT LINE SPECTRA (Incandescent or electrically excited gases under low pressure give bright line spectra)

MERCURY

LITHIUM

CADMIUM

POTASSIUM

STRONTIUM

BARIUM

CALCIUM

SODIUM

HELIUM

HYDROGEN

7500   7000   6500   6000   5500   5000   4500   4000 Å

Adapted from the SPECTRUM CHART, Welch Scientific Company

Plate VII

A. Interference pattern produced by light of a single
spectral color passing through two narrow slits.

B. Passing white light through a single slit
produces this diffraction pattern.

Red light passed through the same slit
produces this pattern.

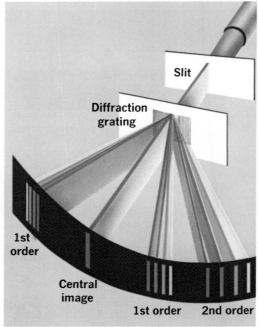

C. Mercury light through a diffraction grating.
First and second order spectra appear to the
right of the central image.

Plate VIII

Chapter 15

Diffraction and Polarization

INTERFERENCE AND DIFFRACTION

The superposition of two identical wave trains traveling in the same or opposite direction illustrates the phenomenon of *interference*. Sound waves of the same amplitude and wavelength projected in the same direction by two loudspeakers provide an interference pattern in which alternate regions of reinforcement and cancellation can be found. Two identical waves traveling in opposite directions on a stretched string interfere to produce a standing wave pattern.

The interference of two water waves of identical wavelength is easily observed in the laboratory using the common ripple tank. More precise studies of such wave behavior are made by photographing light reflections from the surface of a mercury ripple tank. Interference and superposition topics can be reviewed by referring to Sections 10.15 and 10.16.

The superposition principle holds for these wave disturbances which occur in material media, and for light waves and electromagnetic waves in general in free space. Thus light shows *interference: the mutual effect of two beams of light resulting in a loss of intensity in certain regions (destructive interference) and reinforcement of intensity in others (constructive interference).*

In 1801, Thomas Young first demonstrated interference of light and showed how this phenomenon supports the wave theory of Huygens. Suppose the two narrow slits of Fig. 15-1, about 1 mm apart in a piece of black paper, are used to observe a narrow source of light **S** placed 2 or 3 meters away. A series

15.1 Double-slit interference

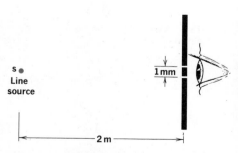

15-1   A method of observing double-slit interference.

of alternately dark and light narrow bands is seen in the center of a fairly wide band of light similar to that of Fig. 15-2. If a red filter is placed between the source and the slits to provide a single spectral color as a light source, a series of red and black bands is seen. A double-slit interference pattern from a monochromatic light is shown in **Plate VIII(A)**.

A wave-front diagram of double-slit interference with a monochromatic light source is shown in Fig. 15-3. Slits **S₁** and **S₂** are equidistant from the source **S**. As light from **S** reaches **S₁** and **S₂**, each slit can be considered as a new light source producing new wave fronts in phase with each other. These waves travel out from **S₁** and **S₂**, producing bright bands of reinforced light where constructive interference occurs, and dark bands due to cancellation where destructive interference occurs.

From *Foundations of Physics*, by Lehrman and Swartz—Holt, Rinehart and Winston

15-2 A double-slit interference pattern.

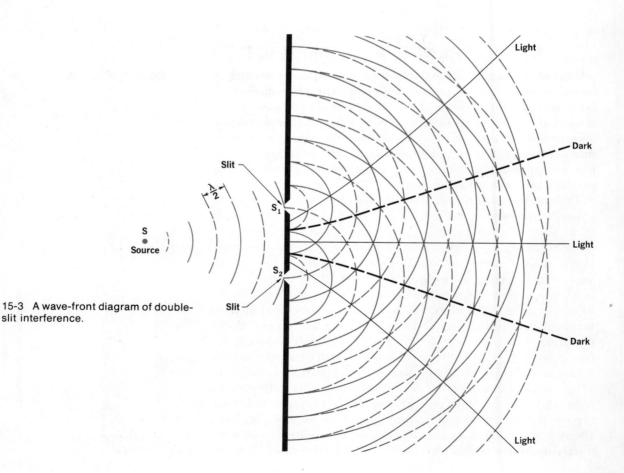

15-3 A wave-front diagram of double-slit interference.

Sir Isaac Newton knew of the color fringes produced by thin films and he devised experiments to determine the film thickness corresponding to a specific color. Interference of light was unknown in his time, however, and his corpuscular explanation of the partial reflection and partial refraction of light at the interface of two different transmitting media is inadequate in view of modern theories of light.

Thin transparent soap films, oil slicks, and wedge-shaped films of air show a varying pattern of colors when viewed by reflected white light. When illuminated by monochromatic light, alternate light and dark regions are observed, the positions of the bands shifting as the color of the monochromatic light is changed.

Thomas Young explained this thin-film phenomenon by the interference of light waves. Suppose a ray of monochromatic light is incident on a thin transparent film at a small angle i as shown in Fig. 15-4. Some light is reflected at **B** and some is refracted toward **C**. The refracted light is then partially reflected at **C** emerging from the film along **DE′** parallel to **BE**. If the wave fronts traveling along **BE** and **DE′** reach the eye, interference occurs since the paths **ABE** and **ACE′** differ in length and the partial path **BCD** of the latter is in a medium of different optical density. The nature of the interference will depend on the phase relation between the waves arriving at the eye.

Assume that the incidence angle i is very small and the film at **B** has an optical thickness of a quarter wavelength for the monochromatic light used. Light emerging from the film at **D** will then be a half wavelength behind that reflected at **B** and would be expected to interfere destructively causing the film to appear dark.

15.2 Interference in thin films

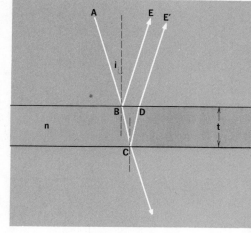

15-4 Partial reflection and refraction of light in a thin film results in interference.

15-5 Interference patterns. (Left) Straight interference fringes obtained from tests made against an optical flat. (Right) An interference pattern obtained from a spherical mirror being tested in an interferometer. The white spots are reflections from the interferometer light source.

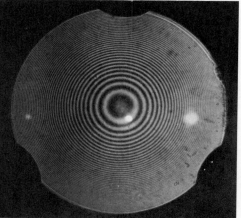

American Optical Company

Now if we assume the film has an optical thickness of a half wavelength, light reflected at **D** from the lower surface of the film will emerge a whole wavelength behind that reflected from the upper surface. The waves would be expected to interfere constructively causing the film to appear bright at this point. *Observation of reflected light from thin films shows that a reverse effect actually occurs.* The quarter-wave point appears *bright* and the half-wave point appears *dark*.

This abnormal situation prevails whenever air is on both sides of the film. It is easily observed in soap films. If a soap film is supported vertically, its upper region will become quite thin as it drains becoming a very small fraction of a wavelength in thickness just before it breaks. If observed by reflected monochromatic light at this moment, this upper region appears dark. See **Plate III(B)**.

Applying the same line of argument used before to this film of almost negligible thickness, we would expect the light reflected from the front surface and that reflected from the back surface to reach the eye so nearly in phase that this upper region of the film would appear bright by reflected light. Here is a clear-cut discrepancy between observation and theory. How can it be reconciled?

Thomas Young resolved the difficulty by suggesting that *one of the interfering waves undergoes a phase inversion during reflection* giving a phase difference of a half wavelength between the two reflected waves in addition to the phase difference resulting from the unequal lengths of their optical paths. This phase inversion occurs because the two reflections are opposite in kind. One reflection takes place at an interface where the medium beyond has a higher index of refraction; here the reflected wave is inverted in phase. The other reflection occurs at an interface where the medium beyond has a lower index of refraction; here the reflected wave experiences no change in phase. Refer to Section 10.10 to review the phase relations of incident and reflected waves at a reflecting interface.

Because of this phase-inverting effect of one of the two reflecting interfaces, the rules for constructive and destructive interference for thin films are just the opposite from those we might expect. *Maximum constructive interference occurs with thin films if the optical path difference is an odd number of half wavelengths.* This is the case where the film thickness is an *odd* number of quarter wavelengths. *Maximum destructive interference occurs if the optical path difference is a whole number of wavelengths.* Here the film thickness is an *even* number of quarter wavelengths.

An air film between two optically flat glass plates produces a regular pattern of interference fringes. Irregular surfaces produce irregular patterns of interference fringes. Inspection techniques using interference patterns have been developed which make extremely high precision measurements possible. Test plates can be polished optically flat with a tolerance of approximately 5×10^{-7} cm. Interference techniques are used to establish standards of measurement in many mechanical processes. The *interferometer* is an instrument that uses interference in the measurement of distance in terms of known wavelengths of light or in the measurement of wavelengths in terms of a standard of length.

15.3 Diffraction of light

According to the wave theory of light, light waves should bend around corners, although our common experience with light shows that it travels in straight lines. However, under some conditions, light waves do bend out of their straight course. When light waves encounter an obstruction with dimensions comparable to their wavelengths, the light spreads out and produces spectral colors due to interference. *The spreading of light into a region behind an obstruction is called* **diffraction**. A slit opening, a fine wire, a sharp edged object, or a pinhole can serve as a suitable obstruction in the path of a beam of light from a point source. It is possible to see diffraction fringes if one peers between two fingers at a distant light source. With the fingers held close to the eye and brought together to form a slit opening, dark fringes will be seen just before the light is shut out.

Diffraction effects, such as indistinct edges of shadows and shadow fringes, are known to have been observed as early as the seventeenth century. However, before the discovery of interference in 1801, neither the wave theory nor the corpuscular theory could offer a suitable explanation. In 1816 the French physicist A. J. Fresnel (fray-*nel*) demonstrated that the various diffraction phenomena are fully explained by the interference of light waves.

Very useful diffraction patterns can be produced by illuminating an optical surface, either plane or spherical concave, which has many thousands of straight, equally spaced, parallel grooves ruled on it. These ruled surfaces are known as *diffraction gratings*. Light is diffracted on being transmitted through, or reflected from the narrow spaces between the ruled lines.

Standard gratings can have as many as 12,000 ruled lines per centimeter of grating surface. X rays are investigated with ordinary diffraction gratings set with their surface at a low angle to the rays giving them the equivalent of many lines per centimeter. Gratings are generally superior to optical prisms for displaying the length or spread of spectra. However, grating spectra tend to be less intense than those formed by prisms.

Bausch and Lomb

15-6 A master diffraction grating being ruled by a diamond-pointed scribe.

15.4 Wavelength by diffraction

A transmission grating placed in the path of plane waves disturbs the wave front, since the ruled lines are opaque to light and the narrow spacings between the lines are transparent. These spaces provide a large number of fine, closely spaced transmission slits. New wavelets, generated at these slits, interfere in such a way that several new wave fronts are established, one traveling in the original direction and the others traveling at various angles from this direction depending on their wavelength.

Suppose a single narrow slit is illuminated by white light and viewed through a transmission grating. A white image of the illuminated slit is seen directly in line with the slit opening. In addition, pairs of continuous spectra are observed, each pair equally spaced on opposite sides of the principal image.

If we illuminate the slit with monochromatic light, successive pairs of slit images of decreasing intensity will appear on opposite sides of the principal image. The two images forming the first pair are known as *first order* images, those forming the second pair as *second order* images, etc.

Referring to Fig. 15-7, **A** and **B** are parallel spaces between the ruled lines on a diffraction grating. They act as adjacent transmission slits, being uniformly separated by the distance *d*, called the *grating constant*. Monochromatic light from a distant illuminated slit traveling normal to the grating surface produces secondary wavelets simultaneously at **A** and **B**. A new wave front of these wavelets proceeds along **MN** and produces the principal image of the distant slit at **N**.

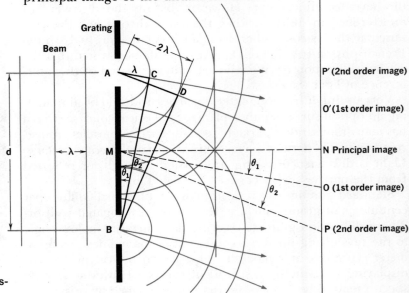

15-7   The optical geometry of a transmission grating.

A given wavelet from **B** and the first preceding wavelet from **A** produce a wave front **CB** that travels along **MO** and gives a *first order* image of the slit at **O**. Similarly, a given wavelet from **B** and the second preceding wavelet from **A** give a wave front **DB** that yields a *second order* image at **P**, etc. Of course, corresponding images appear at **O'**, **P'**, etc., on the other side of **N**.

In the right triangle **ABC**, side **AC** equals the wavelength λ of the incident light and angle θ_1 is the angle of the first order diffracted wave front from the grating plane, the *diffraction angle*.

It is evident that

$$\lambda = d \sin \theta_1$$

Side **AD** of triangle **ABD** is equal to 2λ and θ_2 is the second order diffraction angle. Thus, for second order images,

$$\lambda = \frac{d \sin \theta_2}{2}$$

In the general case, for n orders the grating equation becomes

$$\lambda = \frac{d \sin \theta_n}{n}$$

The diffraction angle θ can be determined experimentally. Knowing the order of image n observed, the diffraction angle θ, and the grating constant d, the wavelength of the light can be calculated from this equation. Of course, if the grating constant of a particular diffraction grating is not known, it can be calculated from an experimental determination of θ_n in which a monochromatic light of known wavelength is used. In the example, the grating equation is used to determine the wavelength of a monochromatic light from experimental data.

Example

An optical grating with 6.00×10^3 lines/cm gives a second order image at a diffraction angle of 44.8°. Calculate the wavelength of the light used.

Solution

$$\lambda = \frac{d \sin \theta_n}{n}$$

where $n = 2$ and $d = \dfrac{1}{6.00 \times 10^3/cm} = 1.67 \times 10^{-4}$ cm

$$\lambda = \frac{1.67 \times 10^{-4} \text{ cm} \times \sin 44.8°}{2}$$

$$\lambda = \frac{1.67 \times 10^{-4} \text{ cm} \times 0.705}{2} \times \frac{\text{Å}}{10^{-8} \text{ cm}}$$

$$\lambda = 5890 \text{ Å}$$

15.5 Single-slit diffraction

According to Huygens' principle, every point on an advancing wave front can be regarded as a new source of disturbance from which secondary waves spread out as spherical wavelets.

If a barrier with a narrow slit opening is placed in the path of advancing plane waves, the disturbance will be transmitted to the region beyond the barrier by the slit. When the width of the slit opening is reduced to only a few wavelengths of the light [see Fig. 15-8(A)] a broad region **MN** is illuminated by the slit. Experiments show that the central portion of this region is always brighter than the remote portions which reveal diffraction fringes of diminishing intensity. Examples of single-slit diffraction patterns are shown in **Plate VIII(B)**.

In Fig. 15-8(B) the point b_0 lies on the perpendicular bisector of the slit and is equidistant from points **B** and **C**. Because the distance from the slit to the screen is very large compared to the width of the slit, point b_0 is essentially equidistant from all points along the line **BAC**. Thus the wavelets originating simultaneously from all points along **BA** and from all points along **AC** will reach b_0 in phase and the screen in this region will be bright.

At points d_1 above and below b_0, where the distance from **B** and **C** is different by a whole wavelength, the distance from **A** and **C** is different by a half wavelength. For every point along **CA** there is a corresponding point along **BA** that is a half wavelength different in distance from d_1. Therefore wavelets arriving at d_1 from one half of the slit will be annulled by the wavelets arriving from the other half and the region of d_1 will be dark.

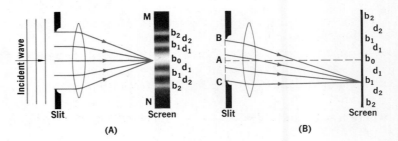

15-8   Single-slit diffraction. Slit size is exaggerated relative to the lines and screen.

Beyond points d_1 there are points b_1 where the distance from **B** and **C** is different by 1.5 wavelengths. Now we can think of the slit opening as being divided into three equal parts. Wavelets from one part arrive at b_1 a half wavelength behind wavelets from the second part. Thus wavelets from these parts of the slit opening interfere destructively, while wavelets arriving from the third part produce brightness at b_1. However, the illumination at b_1 will be lower than that at b_0 since only one-third of the slit opening contributes to the brightness of these regions.

By the same reasoning the regions of d_2, where the difference in distance from **B** and **C** is 2 wavelengths, will be dark. Similarly, the regions of b_2 will be bright. Thus, a series of alternate bright and dark regions appear on either side of b_0, the intensity decreasing as the distance from b_0 increases.

QUESTIONS

Group A

1. How do the colors of a soap bubble originate?
2. Why are the various colors of white light separated by a diffraction grating?
3. Will the angular separation between red and blue rays be greater in the first-order or second-order spectrum of white light produced by a diffraction grating?
4. Given two diffraction gratings, one with 400 lines per centimeter and the other with 4000 lines per centimeter. Which grating yields more orders of images of an illuminated slit?
5. What advantage is realized by increasing the number of ruled lines per centimeter of grating surface?

Group B

6. Explain why the following appear red: (a) glowing charcoal, (b) a ripe cherry, (c) a neon sign, (d) the sunrise, (e) objects viewed through red sunglasses.
7. How can you explain that, in observations of thin films by reflected light, the interference effects are the reverse of those we would normally expect?
8. Given two optical gratings, one with fewer lines per centimeter than the other, and a single monochromatic light source. For which grating will the angular separation of orders be greater? Justify your conclusion.
9. What part of Young's double-slit experiment depended on diffraction and what part depended on interference?
10. Monochromatic light of known wavelength was transmitted by a grating and the diffraction angle of a first order image was determined. Set up an equation by means of which the grating constant of the transmission grating can be found.

PROBLEMS

Group B

1. A transmission grating with 5800 lines/cm is illuminated by monochromatic light with a wavelength of 4920 Å. What is the diffraction angle for the first order image?

2. In Problem 1, the perpendicular distance from the grating to the image screen was 34.5 cm. How far from the principal image was the first order image found?

3. Monochromatic light illuminates a grating having 5900 lines/cm. The diffraction angle for a second order image is found to be 38.0°. (a) Determine the wavelength of the light in angstroms. (b) What is its color?

4. White light falls on a grating which has 3500 lines/cm. The perpendicular distance from the grating to the image screen is 50.0 cm. (a) Find the distance of the near edge of a first order image from the principal image on the screen. (b) Find the distance of the far edge of the same image.

5. In the experiment of Problem 4, a marker was placed in the first order image on the screen 9.25 cm from the principal image. (a) Determine the wavelength (in angstroms) at the marker position. (b) What color corresponds to this wavelength?

POLARIZATION

15.6 Polarization of transverse waves

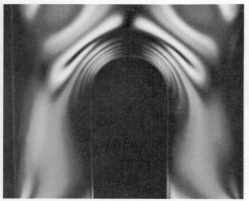

Polaroid Corp.

Polarized light reveals the strain patterns in a transparent plastic model under stress. This technique is used extensively in the field of mechanical stress analysis.

The general wave properties of rectilinear propagation (in a homogeneous medium), reflection, refraction, interference, and diffraction are clearly recognized in the behavior of light as well as in sound and water disturbances.

In Chapter 12 we considered a particle model of light that was once as successful as the wave model in explaining rectilinear propagation, reflection, and refraction. Only interference and diffraction failed to accommodate the particle model, but required a wave model. Thus, interference and diffraction give the best evidence that light has wave-like characteristics.

Sound is a longitudinal wave disturbance and water waves have both transverse and longitudinal motions. We can infer nothing from interference or diffraction experiments concerning the transverse nature of light waves since both sound and water waves show these properties.

Before the introduction of the electromagnetic theory, light was generally assumed to be a longitudinal wave disturbance. Fresnel observed that a beam of light falling on a calcite crystal was separated into two beams which were incapable of producing interference fringes. Thomas Young suggested that this could be accounted for if one could assume the light to consist of transverse waves which were separated into component waves having oscillating planes at right angles to each other, *a plane-polarization effect.*

Many experiments with calcite and other similar materials have demonstrated the correctness of Young's polarization hypothesis. Transverse waves can be polarized but longitudinal waves cannot. ***Plane-polarized light*** *is light in which the oscillations are confined to a single plane which is perpendicular to the line of propagation.*

Light radiated by ordinary sources is unpolarized since the primary radiators, the atoms and molecules of the light source, oscillate independently. Beams of unpolarized light are made up of independent wavetrains with oscillation planes oriented in a random manner about the line of propagation. Diagrammatically, we can represent unpolarized light being propagated in space by a system of *light vectors* as shown in Fig. 15-9. It is customary to resolve these vectors into vertical and horizontal components, a convenient but entirely arbitrary orientation.

Ordinary light can become plane-polarized through interactions with matter. The scattering effect of small particles (see Section 15.11) is accompanied by a polarization effect. Polarization can result from the reflection of light from various surfaces, from refraction of light through some crystals, and from selective absorption of light in some crystals.

A simple mechanical model can be used to illustrate the polarization concept. Suppose we set up transverse waves in a rope passed through a slot as shown in Fig. 15-10. We can readily see that vibrations are transmitted beyond the slot only when the vibrating plane of the rope and the plane of the slot are aligned. We shall call this frame of slots the *polarizer.* A second slot, parallel to the first, will transmit the waves. If the second slot is perpendicular to the first slot, it obstructs them. We shall call this second frame of slots the *analyzer.*

If the rope is replaced by a long coiled spring, longitudinal waves set up in the spring will pass through both slots regardless of their orientation. *Polarization is a property of transverse waves.*

It has long been known that certain crystalline substances transmit light in one plane of polarization and absorb light in other polarization planes. Tourmaline is such a material. Unpolarized light incident on a tourmaline crystal emerges as green, plane-polarized light of low intensity. This property of crystals in which one polarized component of incident light is absorbed and the other is transmitted is called *dichroism.* See Fig. 15-11.

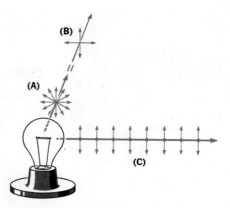

15-9 The vectors representing random oscillation planes of unpolarized light (A) may be arbitrarily resolved into vertical and horizontal component vectors as in (B) for an end-on view, and as in (C) for a side view.

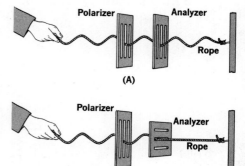

15-10 A mechanical analogy of polarization.

15.7 Selective absorption

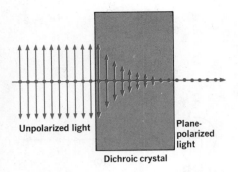

Unpolarized light

Plane-polarized light

Dichroic crystal

15-11 Polarization by selective absorption.

Dichroic crystals of quinine iodosulfate transmit plane-polarized light very efficiently but the crystals are too small for practical use. In 1935 Edwin H. Land developed a method of imbedding these crystals in cellulose film so that the dichroic properties of the crystals were retained. This highly efficient polarizing film is known commercially as Polaroid. Improved Polaroid sheets have now been developed in which polarizing molecules, rather than crystals, are imbedded in appropriate films.

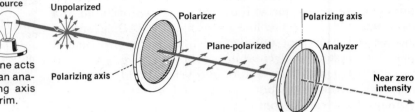

Source

Unpolarized

Polarizer

Polarizing axis

Plane-polarized

Analyzer

Polarizing axis

Near zero intensity

15-12 Polaroid discs in use. One acts as a polarizer and the other as an analyzer. Notice that the polarizing axis of each disc is marked on the rim.

15.8 Polarization by reflection

Sunlight reflected from the surface of calm water or from a level highway can be quite objectionable to the observer. Sunglasses made of polarizing films reduce the intensity of these reflections. By rotating the lenses slightly from side to side the reflections are seen to pass through a minimum, indicating that these rays are partially polarized.

Ordinary light incident obliquely on the surface of a glass plate is partly reflected and partly refracted. Both the transmitted and the reflected beams are partly polarized. This can be verified by observing the light through a polarizing disc used as an analyzer. By rotating the disc in a plane perpendicular to the light axis, one can determine the direction of the dominant light vectors in each beam.

The component of the incident light lying in the plane parallel to the surface of the glass is largely reflected while the component lying in the plane perpendicular to the surface is largely refracted. A particular angle of incidence known as the *polarizing angle* can be found experimentally at which polarization of the reflected light is complete. Polarization by reflection is illustrated in Fig. 15-13.

At the polarizing angle the reflected beam is of low intensity, the reflectance being about 15%. The refracted beam, which is not completely polarized, is bright. By stacking several plates, the combined reflections increase the intensity of the plane-polarized reflected beam. The combined refracted beam becomes less intense but more completely plane-polarized.

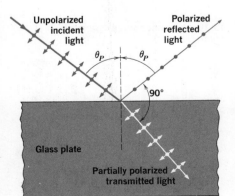

Unpolarized incident light

Polarized reflected light

θ_P θ_P

90°

Glass plate

Partially polarized transmitted light

15-13 At the polarizing angle, the reflected light is completely polarized but of low intensity.

If a thick glass plate is placed on the printed page of this book, the print viewed through the glass may appear displaced due to refraction. A natural crystal of calcite placed on the page would show *two* refracted images of the print. See Fig. 15-14. Calcite, along with many other crystalline materials, exhibits this property of *double refraction*.

A beam of unpolarized light can divide into two beams at the crystal surface on entering a doubly refracting crystal such as calcite. This separation is shown diagrammatically in Fig. 15-15. Analyzing these separate beams with polarizing discs reveals that they are plane-polarized with their planes of polarization perpendicular to each other.

One of the polarized beams can be shown experimentally to follow Snell's law; the other beam does not. Using monochromatic sodium light of 5893 Å and measuring the angles of incidence and refraction, one beam yields a constant index of refraction of 1.66. However, the other beam shows an index of refraction that varies from 1.49 to 1.66 depending on the angle of incidence. This difference suggests that the light energy is propagated through the crystal at different speeds determined by the orientation of the light planes with the crystal lattice.

Calcite crystals are sometimes polished, cut through, and cemented back together in such a way that one of the polarized beams is totally reflected at the cemented face. Such a crystal, known as a *Nicol prism*, can be used to produce a beam of completely polarized light.

The two plane-polarized beams of light that emerge from a doubly refracting crystal cannot be made to interfere with each other even though they are transmitted through the crystal at different speeds. This is because their planes of polarization are perpendicular to each other. It follows that *if two light waves interfere their oscillations must lie in the same plane.*

If *polarized light* is incident on a doubly refracting crystal at the proper angle, the emerging beams *are* found to interfere as they pass through an analyzer disc. The analyzer passes only the components of these rays that lie in its transmission plane. Those waves from the two beams having a phase difference of an odd number of half wavelengths interfere destructively, the corresponding color is removed, and its complement is observed.

Materials such as glass and lucite, which become doubly refracting when strained, are said to be *photoelastic*. When one of these materials is placed between polarizing and analyzing discs, the strain patterns are revealed by interference fringes.

15.9 Polarization by refraction

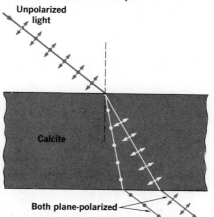

Alex Mulligan

15-14 Double refraction in calcite.

15.10 Interference patterns

15-15 Double refraction. Light in one polarization plane conforms to Snell's law; light in the other plane does not.

15.11 Scattering

A beam of light traveling in dust-free air cannot be seen even in a darkened room. If, however, there is dust or smoke in the path of the beam, it becomes visible by reflection of light from the surface of the particles.

Suppose a beam of white light travels in a medium. The medium contains particles in suspension having diameters smaller than the mean wavelength of visible light. When observed at right angles to its path, the beam then has a distinctly bluish cast. With certain concentrations of suspended particles the bluish light sent off sideways becomes quite intense and the transmitted light acquires a red-orange shade. In other words, an excess of shorter wavelengths is emitted at right angles to the path of the beam and an excess of longer wavelengths is transmitted along the path of the beam. This phenomenon, known as *scattering*, occurs when a beam of light encounters particles whose dimensions are small compared to the wavelengths in the beam.

If we look at blue skylight through a polarizing disc, we observe that it is plane polarized. By selecting a point in the blue sky near the horizon, with the sun overhead, we find the scattered light to be horizontally polarized. Airplane navigators have devices to locate the direction of the sun in Arctic regions that depend upon the polarization of skylight. Horseshoe crabs and bees are said to navigate by the sun; they have analyzer capabilities with respect to polarized light.

In the late afternoon, near the time of sunset, sunlight must travel a maximum distance through the atmosphere to reach an observer. The setting sun has a yellow to red hue and the sunlight reflected to an observer from clouds near the sight line of the observer has the yellow or red hue characteristic of the sunset. Much of the energy in the blue region of the sunlight

Scattering of light by particles in the air brightens the daytime sky on earth (left). An observer on the lunar surface, however, sees a dark daytime sky (right) because the moon has almost no atmospheric particles.

Bruce Roberts of Rapho-Guillumette   NASA

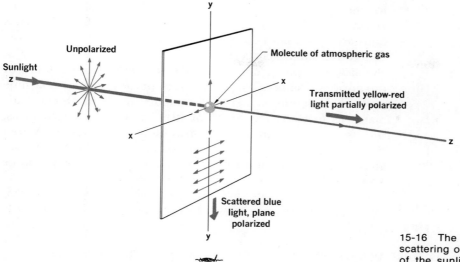

y

Unpolarized

Sunlight

z

Molecule of atmospheric gas

x

Transmitted yellow-red
light partially polarized

z

x

Scattered blue
light, plane
polarized

y

15-16 The sky is blue due to the
scattering of the shorter wavelengths
of the sunlight passing overhead in
the atmosphere.

has been removed by the scattering effect of the atmospheric gas
molecules. The transmitted light under these conditions is
largely yellow-red. This accounts for the blue appearance of
the sky and the reddish appearance of the setting sun. See
Fig. 15-16.

If the earth had no envelope of atmospheric gases, the sky
would appear black to an observer on the surface since there
would be no scattering of sunlight passing overhead. Astronauts
have observed the blackness of outer space while in flight
beyond the earth's atmosphere.

Scattering is responsible for certain other natural color
phenomena known as *structural colors*, in contrast to the pigment
colors which we have already considered. The colors of many
minerals are structural. The blue color of a bluejay's feathers
results from scattering of light by tiny bubbles of air dispersed
through the feather structure. The blue color in the eyes of a
human being is also a structural color, since there is no blue
pigment in the irises of blue eyes.

15.12 Optical rotation

A number of substances, among them quartz, sugar, tartaric
acid, and turpentine, are said to be *optically active* because they
rotate the plane of polarized light. A water solution of cane
sugar (sucrose) rotates the plane of polarization to the right.
For a given path length through the solution, the angle of rotation is proportional to the concentration of the solution.

Chemists find numerous applications of this property of
optically active substances in analytical procedures. Instruments

Carl Zeiss Inc.

A modern polarimeter in use.

for measuring the angle of rotation under standard conditions are known as *polarimeters*; those used specifically for sugar solutions are called *saccharimeters*.

Because substances vary in their ability to polarize light, chemists can use polarized light to examine small crystals of unknown substances. Manufacturers of automobiles, machine parts, and building materials use models made of photo-elastic materials to study the effects of stresses on various structures, because the strains in the structures show clearly when analyzed by polarized light. Polarizing sunglasses eliminate the annoying glare of bright sunlight reflected from the surface of a road or a smooth body of water.

QUESTIONS

Group A

1. What phenomenon provides evidence of the transverse wave character of light?
2. How do Polaroid sunglasses reduce the glare of bright sunlight?
3. Distinguish between a structural color and a pigment color.
4. Define the polarizing angle.
5. How could you determine whether a beam of light is plane polarized or unpolarized?
6. Suggest a way to identify the polarizing axis of a sheet of Polaroid film.

Group B

7. Explain why a Polaroid disc used as an analyzer blocks the beam of light transmitted by the polarizer disc when it is properly oriented?
8. The two beams of light that emerge from a doubly refracting crystal travel through the crystal at different speeds. Can they be made to produce an interference pattern? Explain.
9. A physics student observes that the setting sun near the horizon is red while the sky overhead is blue. Explain.
10. For a given optically active substance, upon what does the magnitude of the rotation angle for the plane of polarized light passing through the substance depend?
11. If scattering of sunlight is more pronounced in the shorter wavelength regions, violet light must be scattered more than blue. Why does the sky appear to be light blue rather than violet?
12. A tube filled with a sucrose solution is placed between two crossed polarizing discs. (a) Explain why some light is transmitted through the analyzer. (b) In what direction must the analyzer be rotated to reduce the light intensity to a minimum? (c) The tube is now filled with a more dilute solution of the same substance. How must the analyzer be adjusted to reestablish the light minimum?

A "SNAPSHOT" OF CAMERAS

(Top) This 35 mm camera uses film that is 35 mm wide. To produce high-quality pictures on small film, all parts of the camera must be precisely made. The first ring around the lens next to the camera body is used to adjust the aperture. The second ring is used to focus the lens. To adjust shutter speed, the photographer turns the dial under her thumb. (Center) While in the air, a skydiver may have attached to his helmet a specially designed camera that takes pictures on 70 mm film. To aim the electrically operated camera, the skydiver turns his head and sights through the viewfinder in front of his eye. (Bottom) Many commercial photographers use studio view cameras that take pictures on large film. The photographer composes the picture on a screen at the back of the camera before inserting a sheet of film. The knobs on the front permit tilting, raising, or lowering the lens with respect to the film.

Ken Chen

Swedish
Information
Service

The essential parts of a camera are a lens, a shutter, and a material that is sensitive to light (usually called film). These parts are usually supported by a body that also prevents light from reaching the film until the shutter is opened. The lens focuses an image of the subject onto the film. The aperture of the lens (the diameter of the opening that admits light) and the length of time the shutter is open, control the amount of light reaching the film.

In a simple camera, such as the original Kodak invented by George Eastman (right), the aperture, shutter speed, and distance from the lens to the film are all fixed. With a camera designed so the distance between the lens and the film can be varied, clear pictures are possible under a greater variety of photographic conditions. The image of a distant object is focused closer to the lens than a nearby object. (See Section 14.8.) A moveable lens permits focusing clearly on near or distant objects. If the aperture of the lens and the shutter speed can be varied, pictures can be taken under different lighting conditions using different kinds of film.

Cameras made about the year 1900, such as the Kodaks, press cameras, and Lawrence's 1,400 pound monster, were designed to use large-sized film. The picture quality of early enlargements was poor. Using a process called *contact printing,* high-quality pictures could be made, but only the same size as the film. Therefore, to make large pictures, large film and large cameras were needed.

Now, with improvements in enlarging techniques, most amateur and many professional photographers use small, light cameras that use small-sized film. However, many professional photographers still use studio view cameras designed for large film sizes. (See page 373.)

International Museum
of Photography
at George Eastman House

George Eastman, a manufacturer of photographic materials, perfected photographic roll film. His simple "box" camera, designed to use this invention, opened photography to millions of amateur photographers. This snapshot shows Eastman aboard a ship taking a picture with his Kodak while a friend took his picture with another Kodak. Photographs made with this camera were circular because the lens could not form a clear image out to the edges of a rectangular piece of film.

Culver Pictures

Three examples of early types of cameras. The box camera on the left is a variation of Eastman's original Kodak.

George R. Lawrence in 1900 built this camera weighing
1,400 pounds. Fifteen men were required to operate it.
Lawrence's assignment was to make "a perfect contact
picture not less than eight feet long," of the Chicago
and Alton Railroad's new train.

In contrast with the older cameras on this page, the
astronauts used special cameras on the moon. Notice
that the image of the astronaut who took this picture
is reflected from the curved faceplate of his subject.
About 1905, press photographers used cameras designed
for large-sized film. Without enlargement, large pictures
for newspapers and magazines were produced from this
film.

(Above) If the photographer uses a slow shutter speed, the image of the car moves so much that a blurred picture results. (Below) If the shutter speed is fast enough, the image of the car does not move enough during the exposure to blur the picture.

Amateur and professional photographers alike seek technical and artistic solutions to photographic problems. One of these problems is to stop the motion of moving objects. Another is to focus clearly on objects at different distances.

The viewing screen and film holder on many studio view cameras can be rotated and tilted with respect to the lens. (See page 373.) This flexibility permits the photographer to solve many focusing problems. Since most small cameras are made to be hand carried, this flexibility is often sacrificed for lightness. Small camera users solve these problems by using a small aperture. Up to a certain limit, the smaller the aperture, the greater is the distance range of objects that are acceptably clear. See examples at the right.

(Above) If the photographer uses a large aperture and focuses on the subject in the middle, the images of the nearest and most distant subjects are blurred. With this aperture, these subjects are not included in the distance range of objects that form acceptably clear images. (Below) A small aperture increases the distance range of objects that form acceptably clear images. Focusing again on the middle subject, this range now includes the nearest and most distant subjects.

Chapter 16

Electrostatics

ELECTRIC CHARGE

Rubbing pieces of dry matter sometimes produces a number of physical effects which we can observe about us every day. An annoying shock is sometimes felt when the door handle of an automobile is touched after sliding over the plastic-covered seat. We may feel a shock after walking on a woolen carpet and then touching a doorknob or other metal object. The slight crackling sound heard when dry hair is brushed and the tendency of thin sheets of paper to resist separation are other common observations of these physical effects.

When an object shows effects of the type we have described, we say that it has an *electric charge. The process which produces electric charges on an object is called **electrification**.* An object that is electrically charged can attract small bits of cork, paper, or other lightweight particles. Electrification is most apparent when the air is dry. Because the electric charge is confined to the object and is not moving, it is called an *electrostatic charge.* Thus **static electricity** *is stationary electricity in the form of an electric charge.* Static electricity is commonly produced by friction between two surfaces in close contact.

We can detect the presence of an electrostatic charge by means of an instrument called an *electroscope.* The simplest kind of electroscope is a small ball of wood pith or Styrofoam suspended by a silk thread. This electroscope is more sensitive if the pith ball is coated with aluminum or graphite. Such an instrument is shown in Fig. 16-1.

Suppose a hard rubber or Bakelite rod is charged by stroking it with flannel or fur. If the end of the charged rod is then held

16.1 Electrification

Black Star Photos

Can you explain why electrification from the generator in the foreground makes this person's hair stand out?

16.2 Two kinds of electric charges

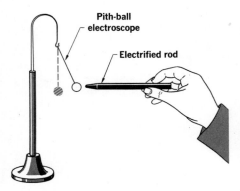

Pith-ball electroscope

Electrified rod

16-1 The pith-ball electroscope may be used to detect an electrostatic charge.

near a simple electroscope, the pith ball is attracted to the rod.

If the pith ball is allowed to come in contact with the charged rod, it immediately rebounds and is then repelled by the rod. We can reasonably assume that some of the *charge* has been transferred to the pith ball so that both the rod and the ball are now similarly charged.

Now suppose a glass rod is charged by stroking it with silk. If the glass rod is held near the charged electroscope, the pith ball is attracted rather than repelled as it was with the charged rubber rod. These effects of attraction and repulsion can be explained if we assume that there are two kinds of electric charge.

The electric charge produced on the rubber rod when the rod is stroked with flannel or fur is called a *negative* charge, and the rod is said to be charged negatively. The electric charge produced on the glass rod when the rod is stroked with silk is called a *positive* charge, and the rod is said to be charged positively.

From a study of atomic structure it is known that all matter contains both positive and negative charges, but for simplification, the drawings which follow will show only the excess charges. If a body is neutral, it will have no sign; if it is negative, this charge will be indicated by negative signs; if it is positive, this charge will be indicated by plus signs.

Two pith balls, negatively charged by contact with a charged rubber rod, repel each other. Similarly, two pith balls, positively charged by contact with a charged glass rod, also repel each other. However, if a negatively charged pith ball is brought near a positively charged pith ball, they attract each other. See Fig. 16-2. These observations are summarized in *a **basic law of electrostatics**: objects that are similarly charged repel each other; those with unlike charges attract each other.*

16.3 Electricity and matter

To understand the nature of static electricity, it may be helpful to review briefly some basic concepts of the structure of matter. (These concepts will be discussed more fully in Chapter

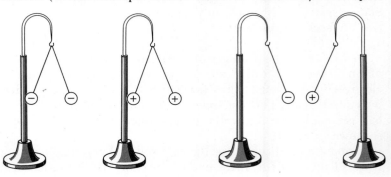

16-2 Like charges repel each other and unlike charges attract each other.

23.) All matter is composed of atoms, of which there are many different kinds. Each atom consists of a positively charged nucleus surrounded by negatively charged electrons.

Protons and neutrons are tightly packed into the very dense nucleus, which is positively charged because each proton possesses a single unit of positive electric charge. Neutrons, as their name suggests, are neutral particles. The positive charge on the nucleus is determined by the number of protons it contains.

All electrons surrounding the nucleus are exactly alike. They all carry the same amount of negative electric charge, one unit of negative charge per electron. Because an atom is electrically neutral, we know that the nucleus has a positive charge equal in size to the total negative electronic charge. Thus the number of electrons around the nucleus of a neutral atom equals the number of protons in the nucleus.

The rest mass of an electron is 9.1095×10^{-31} kg. The mass of a proton is 1.6726×10^{-27} kg and that of a neutron is 1.6750×10^{-27} kg. Both the proton and the neutron have masses that are nearly 2000 times greater than the mass of an electron. The mass of an atom is almost entirely concentrated in the nucleus.

Protons and neutrons are bound together within the nucleus by strong forces acting through very short distances. The repulsions between protons due to their similarity of charge are weak forces by comparison.

The electrons are retained in the atom structure by the electric attraction exerted by the positive nuclear charge. In general, the outermost electrons are held less firmly in the atom structure than inner electrons of lower energies. The outer electrons of the atoms of metallic elements in particular are loosely held and are easily influenced by outside forces.

When two appropriate materials are brought into close contact, some of the loosely held electrons can be transferred from one material to the other. Thus, if a hard rubber rod is stroked with fur, some electrons can be transferred from the fur to the rod. The rubber rod thus becomes negatively charged because of an *excess of electrons,* and the fur becomes positively charged because of a *deficiency of electrons.*

Similarly, when a glass rod is stroked with silk, some electrons are transferred from the glass to the silk. The glass is consequently positively charged because of a *net deficiency of electrons* and the silk is negatively charged because of an *excess of electrons.* All of these charged states result from *the transfer of electrons.*

Electric charge is a scalar quantity. The net charge on an object is the sum of its positive charges minus the sum of its negative charges.

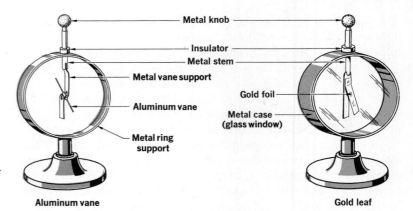

16-3 Two types of sensitive electroscopes.

Aluminum vane   Gold leaf

16.4 The electroscope

Two common types of electroscopes more sensitive than the
simple pith-ball device are shown in Fig. 16-3. The *leaf electroscope* consists of very fragile strips of gold leaf suspended from
a metal stem which is capped with a metal knob. The leaves are
enclosed in a metal case with glass windows for their protection,
and the metal stem is well insulated from the case. When electrified, the leaves diverge because of the force of repulsion of
their similar charge. Good sensitivity is derived from the very
low mass of the gold leaf.

The *vane electroscope* consists of a light aluminum rod mounted
by means of a central bearing on an insulated metal support.
When charged, the vane is deflected by electrostatic repulsion
at an angle depending on the magnitude of the charge.

A *proof plane* is frequently used with an electroscope to test
or transfer charges. The proof plane is made of a small metal
disc and an insulating handle. A proof plane can be made
easily by cementing a small coin to a glass rod. To transfer a
charge with such a proof plane, the coin is brought in contact
with the charged object and then with the electroscope.

16.5 Conductors and insulators

Let us suspend an aluminum-coated pith ball by a silk thread
and then join the ball to the knob of a leaf electroscope by means
of a copper wire as shown in Fig. 16-4. If we now place a charge
on the ball, the leaves of the electroscope diverge. Apparently
the charge on the ball is transferred to the electroscope by the
copper wire.

Suppose we substitute a silk thread for the copper wire. Now
when we charge the ball, the leaves of the electroscope do not
diverge because the charge has not been conducted to the
electroscope by the silk.

*A **conductor** is a material through which an electric charge is readily
transferred.* Most metals are good conductors. At normal tem-

peratures, silver is the best solid conductor; copper and aluminum follow in that order.

*An **insulator** is a material through which an electric charge is not readily transferred.* Good insulators are such poor conductors that for practical purposes they are considered to be nonconductors. Glass, mica, paraffin, hard rubber, sulfur, silk, shellac, dry air, and many plastics are good insulators.

Liquid solutions and confined gases conduct electricity in a different way than solids. At this time we are primarily interested in the conductivity of solids. We can use our knowledge of the structure of matter to describe why some materials are conductors and why some are insulators.

A few grams of matter contain a very large number of atoms and, except for hydrogen, an even larger number of electrons. For example, 27 g of aluminum consists of 6.02×10^{23} aluminum atoms containing 7.83×10^{24} electrons.

On an atomic scale, there is one electron in about each 2.2 atomic mass units of matter. (One atomic mass unit $= 1.66 \times 10^{-24}$ g of matter.)

Metals have close-packed crystal structures in which the crystal lattice consists of positively charged particles permeated by a cloud of *free electrons* commonly referred to as the *electron gas.* The binding force in such structures is the attraction between the positively charged metal ions and the electron gas. The loosely-held outermost electrons of the metal atoms can be considered to have been donated to the electron gas and to belong to the crystal as a whole. These electrons are free to migrate throughout the crystal lattice and give rise to the high electric conductivity commonly associated with metals.

A good conductor contains a large number of free electrons whose motions are relatively unimpeded within the material. Since like charges repel, the free electrons spread throughout the material so as to relieve any local concentration of charge. If such a material is brought into contact with a charged body, the free electrons surge in a common direction. If the charged object is deficient in electrons (positively charged), this surge is in the direction of the object. If the charged object has an excess of electrons (negatively charged), the surge is away from the object. See Fig. 16-5. In either case, a transfer of electric charge continues until the repulsive forces between the free electrons are in equilibrium throughout the entire system.

An insulator has no free electrons because even the outermost electrons are rather firmly held within the atom structure. Thus, the transfer of charge through an insulator is usually negligible. If an excess of electrons is transferred to one particular region of such a material, the extra electrons remain in that region for some time before they gradually leak away.

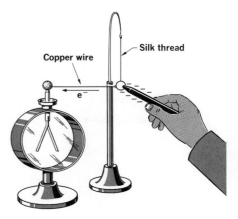

16-4 A charge is conducted to the electroscope by the copper wire.

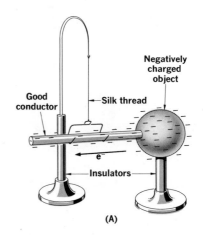

(A)

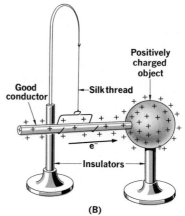

(B)

16-5 Free electrons of a conductor surge in the direction which reduces the net charge.

16.6 Transferring electrostatic charges

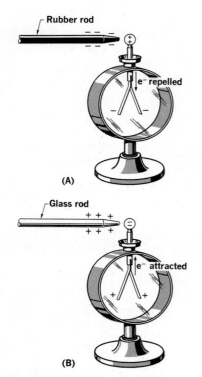

16-6 An electroscope may be charged temporarily by induction due to a redistribution of the free electrons of the metallic conductor.

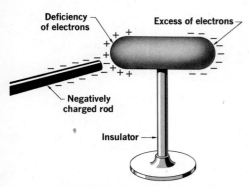

16-7 A charged rod brought near an isolated conductor induces electricity of the same sign in the far end of the conductor.

Suppose we charge a rubber rod negatively by stroking it with fur. If the rod is brought near the knob of an electroscope, the leaves diverge. If the rod is removed, the leaves collapse; no charge remains on the electroscope. The charge that makes the leaves diverge is called an *induced* charge. The electroscope is said to be charged temporarily by *induction*.

We can reason that the negative charge on the rod, when brought near the metal knob of the electroscope, repels free electrons in the knob and metal stem down to the leaves. See Fig. 16-6(A). The force of repulsion of the extra electrons on the leaves causes them to diverge. The knob is then deficient in electrons and is consequently positively charged. As soon as the force of repulsion exerted by the charged rod is withdrawn, the excess free electrons on the leaves scatter throughout the stem and knob, restoring the normal uncharged state throughout the electroscope.

Similarly, a glass rod that has been stroked with silk temporarily induces a positive charge on the leaves of an electroscope by attracting electrons through the stem to the knob. See Fig. 16-6(B). (This experiment does not work well unless the air is quite dry, for a sufficient charge cannot be maintained on the glass rod.)

Any conducting object, when properly isolated in space, can be temporarily charged by induction. The region of the object nearest the charged body will acquire a charge of the *opposite* sign; the region farthest from the charged body will acquire a charge of the same sign. See Fig. 16-7. This statement is seen to be reasonable by recalling the basic law of electrostatics stated in Section 16.2.

A charge can be transferred by conduction. If we touch a negatively charged rubber rod to the knob of an electroscope, the leaves diverge. When the rod is removed, the leaves remain apart, indicating that the electroscope retains the charge. How can we determine the nature of this residual charge on the electroscope?

We can reason that some of the excess electrons on the rod have been repelled onto the knob of the electroscope. This would be true only for the region of the rod immediately in contact with the electroscope, since rubber is a very poor conductor and excess electrons do not migrate freely through it. Any free electrons thus transferred to the electroscope, together with other free electrons of the electroscope itself, would be repelled to the leaves by the excess electrons remaining on the parts of the rod not in contact with the electroscope.

When the rod is removed, and with it the force of repulsion, the electroscope is left with a residual negative charge of a

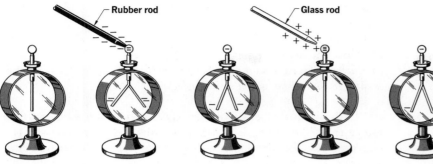

somewhat lower density. This deduction can be verified by bringing a positively charged glass rod near the electroscope to induce a positive charge on the leaves. The leaves collapse and diverge again when the glass rod is removed. See Fig. 16-8.

Any conducting object, properly isolated in space, when charged by conduction, always acquires a residual charge of the same sign as that of the body touching it. Thus, an electroscope with a known residual charge can be used to identify the nature of the charge on another object. This second object need merely be brought near the knob of the charged electroscope.

16-8 The residual charge on an electroscope, when charged by conduction, is of the same sign as the charge on the object which touches it.

When a charged rubber rod is held near the knob of an electroscope, there is no transfer of electrons between the rod and the electroscope. If a path is provided (to ground) over which electrons can pass from the electroscope while the repelling force is present, free electrons will escape. Then, if the escape path is removed before removing the repelling force, the electroscope will be left with a deficiency in electrons, giving it a residual positive charge. We can verify this conclusion by bringing a positively charged glass rod near the knob of an electroscope which has been charged in this manner. The steps in

16.7 Residual charge by induction

16-9 Steps in placing a residual charge on an electroscope by induction.

| Uncharged electroscope | Leaves charged negatively by induction | Electrons repelled to earth | Electroscope deficient in electrons | Positively charged electroscope |

placing a residual charge on an electroscope by induction are shown in Fig. 16-9.

Similarly, we can induce a residual negative charge on an electroscope using a positively charged glass rod. *When an isolated conductor is given a residual charge by induction, the charge is opposite in sign to that of the object inducing it.*

16.8 The force between charges

The basic law of electrostatics has been stated earlier to the effect that like charges repel and unlike charges attract. If a charge is uniformly dispersed over the surface of an isolated sphere, the influence on another charged object some distance away is the same as if the charge were concentrated at the center of the sphere. Thus, the charge on such an object can be considered to be located at a particular point and is called a *point charge.*

The quantity of charge on a body, designated by the letter Q, is determined by the number of electrons in excess of (or less than) the number of protons. In the MKS system of units, the practical system for the study of electricity, the quantity of charge is expressed in *coulombs* (c) named for the French physicist, Charles Augustin de Coulomb (1736–1806).

$$\textbf{1 coulomb} = \textbf{6.25} \times \textbf{10}^{18} \textbf{ electrons}$$

Thus, the charge on one electron, expressed in coulombs, is the reciprocal of this number and the sign of Q is −.

$$\textbf{e}^- = \textbf{1.60} \times \textbf{10}^{-19} \textbf{ c}$$

Similarly, the charge on the proton is 1.60×10^{-19} coulomb and the sign of Q is +.

The coulomb is a very large unit of charge for the study of electrostatics. Frequently, it is convenient to work with a fraction of this unit called the microcoulomb (μc)

$$\textbf{1 } \boldsymbol{\mu}\textbf{c} = \textbf{10}^{-6} \textbf{ c}$$

Coulomb's many experiments with charged bodies led him to conclude that the forces of electrostatic attraction and repulsion obey a law similar to Newton's law of universal gravitation. We now recognize his conclusions as ***Coulomb's law of electrostatics****: the force between two point charges is directly proportional to the product of their magnitudes and inversely proportional to the square of the distance between them.* Charged bodies approximate point charges if they are small compared to the distances separating them. See Fig. 16-10.

Coulomb's law can be expressed as follows:

$$F \propto \frac{Q_1 Q_2}{s^2}$$

If we use a proportionality constant which takes into account the properties of the medium separating the charged bodies, and which has the proper dimensions, Coulomb's law becomes

$$F = k \frac{Q_1 Q_2}{s^2}$$

In the MKS system, k has the numerical value 8.987×10^9 for vacuum and 8.93×10^9 for air. The dimensions of k are n m²/c². The point charges Q_1 and Q_2 are in coulombs and are of proper sign to indicate the nature of each charge. As s is distance in meters, F is expressed in newtons of force.

In Fig. 16-10(A) the charges Q_1 and Q_2 have opposite signs and the force F acts on each charge to move it toward the other. In (B), charges Q_1 and Q_2 have the same sign and the force F acts on each charge to move it away from the other. The force between the two charges is a vector quantity which acts on each charge.

Suppose the objects in Fig. 16-10(B) are charged to 0.01 coulomb each and placed 10 meters apart. Since the charges are of like sign, the force between them is one of repulsion. Using k for air (to one significant figure it is 9×10^9 n m²/c²), the Coulomb's law expression for this force becomes

$$F = 9 \times 10^9 \frac{\text{n m}^2}{\text{c}^2} \times \frac{(10^{-2}\text{ c})(10^{-2}\text{ c})}{(10 \text{ m})^2}$$

$$F = 9 \times 10^9 \frac{\text{n m}^2}{\text{c}^2} \times \frac{10^{-4}\text{ c}^2}{10^2 \text{ m}^2}$$

$$F = 9 \times 10^3 \text{ n of repulsive force}$$

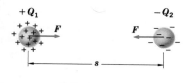

(A) Unlike charges

(B) Like charges

16-10 When Q_1 and Q_2 are of opposite sign, F is negative and is interpreted as a force of attraction. When Q_1 and Q_2 are of the same sign, F is positive and is interpreted as a force of repulsion.

Example

Find the force between charges of $+100.0$ μc and -50.0 μc located 50.0 cm apart in air.

Solution

The charges must be expressed in coulombs and the distance in meters.

$$F = 8.93 \times 10^9 \frac{\text{n m}^2}{\text{c}^2} \times \frac{(100.0 \text{ μc} \times \text{c}/10^6 \text{ μc})(-50.0 \text{ μc} \times \text{c}/10^6 \text{ μc})}{(50.0 \text{ cm} \times \text{m}/10^2 \text{ cm})^2}$$

$$F = 8.93 \times 10^9 \frac{\text{n m}^2}{\text{c}^2} \times \frac{(1.000 \times 10^{-4}\text{ c})(-5.00 \times 10^{-5}\text{ c})}{(5.00 \times 10^{-1}\text{ m})^2}$$

$$F = 8.93 \times 10^9 \frac{\text{n m}^2}{\text{c}^2} \times \frac{-5.00 \times 10^{-9}\text{ c}^2}{2.50 \times 10^{-1}\text{ m}^2}$$

$$F = -1.78 \times 10^2 \text{ n (the negative sign indicating } \textit{attraction} \text{ between the two charges.)}$$

16.9 Electric fields of force

The concept of a field of force can be helpful as we consider the region surrounding an electrically charged body. A second charge brought into this region experiences a force according to Coulomb's law. Such a region is an *electric field*. *An* **electric field** *is said to exist in a region of space if an electric charge placed in that region is subject to an electric force.*

Let us consider a positively charged sphere isolated in space, $+Q$ of Fig. 16-11(A). A small positive charge $+q$, which we shall call a *test charge*, is brought near the surface of the sphere. Since the test charge is in the electric field of the sphere and the charges are similar, it experiences a repulsive force directed radially away from $+Q$. Were the charges on the sphere negative, as in Fig. 16-11(B), the force acting on the test charge would be directed radially toward $-Q$.

An **electric line of force** *is a line so drawn that a tangent to it at any point indicates the orientation of the electric field at that point.* We can imagine a line of force as the path of a test charge moving slowly in a very viscous medium in response to the force of the field. By convention, electric lines of force *originate* at the surface of a positively charged body and *terminate* at the surface of a negatively charged body, each line of force showing the direction that a positive test charge would be accelerated in that part of the field. A line of force must therefore be *normal* to the surface of the charged body where it joins that surface.

The *intensity*, or strength, of an electrostatic field, as well as its direction, can be represented graphically by lines of force. *The electric field intensity is proportional to the number of lines of force per unit area normal to the field.* Where the intensity is high, the lines of force will be close together. Where the intensity is low, the lines of force will be more widely separated in the graphical representation of the field.

In Fig. 16-12(A), electric lines of force are used to show the electric field near two equally but oppositely charged objects.

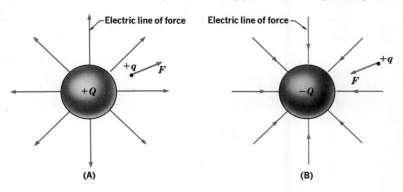

16-11 The electric field surrounding a charged sphere isolated in space.

(A)   (B)

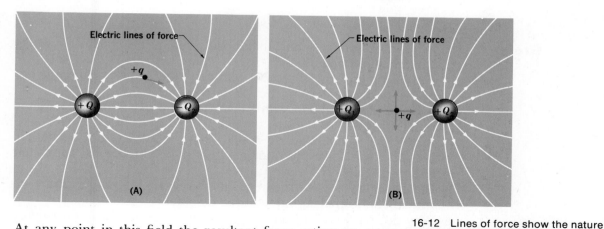

(A)   (B)

At any point in this field the resultant force acting on a test charge $+q$ can be represented by a vector drawn tangent to the line of force at that point.

The electric field near two objects of equal charge of the same sign is shown by the lines of force in Fig. 16-12(B). The resultant force acting on a test charge $+q$ placed at the midpoint between these two similar charges would be zero.

*The **electric field intensity**, $\mathscr{E}$, at any point in an electric field is the force per unit positive charge at that point.* In the MKS system the electric field intensity has the dimensions *newton per coulomb.* Thus,

$$\mathscr{E} = \frac{F}{q}$$

where $\mathscr{E}$ is the electric field intensity and F is the force in newtons acting on the test charge q in coulombs.

The following example illustrates the use of this equation.

16-12 Lines of force show the nature of the electric field near two equal charges of opposite sign (A), and near two equal charges of the same sign (B).

Example

A charge of 2 μc placed in an electric field experiences a force of 0.08 n. What is the magnitude of the electric field intensity?

Solution

The charge of 2 μc expressed in coulombs becomes 2 μc $\times$ c/10^6 μc or 2×10^{-6} c. The force of 0.08 n is most conveniently expressed as 8×10^{-2} n.

$$\mathscr{E} = \frac{F}{q} = \frac{8 \times 10^{-2} \text{ n}}{2 \times 10^{-6} \text{ c}}$$

$\mathscr{E} = 4 \times 10^4$ n/c, the electric field intensity.

QUESTIONS

Group A   1. List five examples (other than those given in this chapter) in which electrification occurs.
2. A hard rubber rod is rubbed with fur. What kind of charge is acquired (a) by the rubber rod, (b) by the fur?
3. A glass rod is rubbed with silk. What kind of charge is acquired (a) by the glass rod, (b) by the silk?
4. A pith ball suspended on a silk thread is attracted to a charged rubber rod. Does this indicate that the pith ball is oppositely charged? Explain.
5. State the law of electrostatics which reveals the nature of the attraction and repulsion of charged objects.
6. Why do the leaves of an uncharged electroscope diverge when a charged object is brought near?
7. Why is it necessary to ground an electroscope temporarily while inducing a residual charge on it with a negatively charged object?
8. What determines the property of a metal as a conductor of electricity?
9. Explain why sulfur is a very poor conductor.
10. What is the unit of electric charge in the MKS system?
11. State Coulomb's law of electrostatics.
12. Define an electric field.

Group B   13. How can you explain (a) the presence of a charge on a rubber rod after it has been rubbed with fur, (b) the charge remaining on the fur?
14. Which would you consider offers the more conclusive proof of the presence of a charge on a pith-ball electroscope, an observed force of repulsion or one of attraction? Explain.
15. Given a charged sphere, describe a simple experiment which would enable you to determine conclusively the nature of the charge on the sphere.
16. A negatively charged rod is brought near the knob of a charged electroscope. The leaves first collapse and then, as the rod is brought nearer, they again diverge. (a) What is the residual charge on the electroscope? (b) Explain the action of the leaves.
17. (a) In order for a coulomb force to be expressed in newtons, what must be the dimensions of the MKS proportionality constant in the Coulomb's law equation, $F = k\, Q_1 Q_2 / s^2$? (b) Verify your answer.
18. A very small sphere is given a positive charge and is then brought near a large negatively charged plate. Draw a diagram of the system showing the appearance of the electric lines of force.
19. An electron of mass m and charge e^- is projected into a uniform electric field with an initial velocity v_i at right angles to the field. Describe its motion in the electric field.

PROBLEMS

Group B

1. A small sphere is given a charge of $+2\bar{0}$ μc and a second sphere of equal diameter located $1\bar{0}$ cm away is given a charge of -5.0 μc. What is the force of attraction between the charges?

2. The two spheres of Problem 1 are allowed to touch and are again spaced $1\bar{0}$ cm apart. What force exists between them?

3. Two small spheres, each having a mass of 0.050 g, are suspended by silk threads from the same point. When given equal charges, they separate, the threads making an angle of $1\bar{0}°$ with each other. What is the force of repulsion acting on each sphere? (Suggestion: Construct the vector diagram and solve for the horizontal component of the force on one thread.)

4. Two small spheres, each having a mass of 0.10 g, are suspended from the same point on silk threads $2\bar{0}$ cm long. When given equal charges they are found to repel each other, coming to rest 24 cm apart. Find the charge on each sphere. (Suggestion: Construct a vector diagram and determine the force of repulsion by similar triangles.)

5. A charge of 0.52 μc is placed in an electric field where the field intensity is 4.5×10^5 n/c. What is the magnitude of the force acting on the charge?

POTENTIAL DIFFERENCE

16.10 Electric potential

Let us consider the work done by gravity on a wagon coasting down a hill. The wagon is within the gravitational field of the earth and experiences a gravitational force causing it to travel downhill. Work is done by the gravitational field, so the energy expended comes from within the gravitational system. The wagon has less potential energy at the bottom of the hill than it had at the top, and in order to return the wagon to the top, work must be done on it. However, in this instance, the energy must be supplied from an outside source to pull against the gravitational force. The energy expended is stored in the system, imparting to the wagon more potential energy at the top of the hill than it had at the bottom.

Similarly, a charge in an electric field experiences an electric force according to Coulomb's law. If the charge moves in response to this force, work is done by the electric field. Energy is removed from the system. If the charge is moved against the Coulomb force of the electric field, work is done on it using energy from some outside source, this energy being stored in the system.

If work is done as a charge moves from one point to another in an electric field, or if work is required to move a charge from one point to another, these two points are said to *differ in electric potential. The magnitude of the work is a measure of this difference of potential.* The concept of potential difference is very important in the understanding of electric phenomena. It is analogous to gravitational potential in mechanical energy transformations. *The **potential difference**, V, between two points in an electric field is the work done per unit charge as a charge is moved between these points.*

$$\text{potential difference } (V) = \frac{\text{work } (W)}{\text{charge } (q)}$$

The unit of potential difference in the MKS system is the *volt* (v). *One **volt** is the potential difference between two points in an electric field such that 1 joule of work is done in moving a charge of 1 coulomb between these points.*

$$1 \text{ volt} = \frac{1 \text{ joule}}{1 \text{ coulomb}}$$

Small differences of potential are commonly expressed in *millivolts* (mv) or *microvolts* (μv), large differences of potential in *kilovolts* (kv) and *megavolts* (Mv).

$$1 \ \mu v = 10^{-6} \ v$$
$$1 \ mv = 10^{-3} \ v$$
$$1 \ kv = 10^{3} \ v$$
$$1 \ Mv = 10^{6} \ v$$

Suppose the potential difference between two points in an electric field is 6.0 v. The work required to move a charge of 3.00×10^2 μc between these points can be determined as follows.

$$V = \frac{W}{q}$$

$$W = Vq = 6.0 \text{ v} \times 3.00 \times 10^2 \ \mu c \times c/10^6 \ \mu c$$
$$W = 6.0 \text{ v} \times 3.00 \times 10^{-4} \ c$$
$$W = 1.8 \times 10^{-3} \ j$$

Since a joule of work is a force of 1 newton applied through a distance of 1 meter, it follows that

and

$$v = \frac{j}{c} = \frac{n \ m}{c}$$

$$\frac{v}{m} = \frac{n}{c}$$

In Section 16.9 it was shown that $\mathscr{E}$, the electric field intensity, is expressed in newtons per coulomb. Thus,

$$\mathscr{E} = \frac{n}{c} = \frac{v}{m}$$

General Electric Co.

Simulated lightning in General Electric's high voltage lab in Pittsfield, Mass. demonstrates how proper lightning protection prevents failure in an electric distribution system.

The electric field intensity is commonly expressed in terms of *volts per meter* and can be referred to as the *potential gradient. The **potential gradient** of an electric field is the change in potential per unit of distance.*

We can consider the earth to be an inexhaustible *source* of electrons, or limitless *sink* into which electrons can be "poured" without changing its potential. For practical purposes, the potential of the earth is arbitrarily taken as *zero*. Any conducting object connected to the earth must be at the same potential as the earth; that is, the potential difference between them is zero. Such an object is said to be *grounded*.

The potential at any point in an electric field is the potential difference between the point and earth taken as zero. This potential can be either positive or negative depending on the nature of the charge producing the electric field.

Michael Faraday performed several experiments to demonstrate the distribution of charge on an isolated object. He charged a conical silk bag like that of Fig. 16-13, and found that the charge was on the outside of the bag. By pulling on the silk thread, he turned the bag inside out and found that the charge was again on the outside. The inside of the bag showed no electrification in either position.

Faraday connected the outer surface of an insulated metal pail to an electroscope by means of a conducting wire, as shown in Fig. 16-14(A). He then lowered a positively charged ball

16.11 Distribution of charges

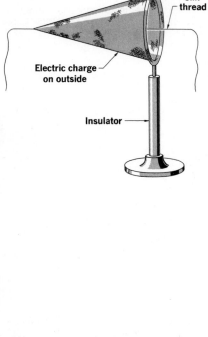

16-13 The type of conical silk bag used by Faraday to demonstrate that electric charges reside on the outside.

Silk thread

Electric charge on outside

Insulator

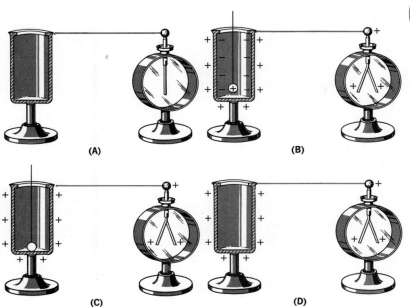

(A)

(B)

(C)

(D)

16-14 Faraday's ice-pail experiment.

into the pail, supporting it by a silk thread. The leaves of the electroscope diverged (B), indicating a charge by induction: the positively charged ball attracted the free electrons in the pail to the inner surface, leaving the outside of the pail and the electroscope positively charged. The leaves remained apart without change when the ball was allowed to contact the inside of the pail (C). The positive charge on the ball was exactly neutralized by the equal and opposite charge induced on the inside of the pail; the charge on the ball was therefore lost. After the ball was removed, it was evident that the outside of the pail (and the electroscope) had acquired all the charge originally placed on the ball (D).

From these and other experiments with isolated conductors, we can conclude that

1. All the static charge on a conductor lies on its surface. Electrostatic charges are at rest. If the charge were beneath the surface, so that an electric field existed within a conductor, free electrons would be acted upon by the Coulomb force of this field. Work would be done, the electrons would move because of a difference of potential, and energy would be given up by the field. Since movement is not consistent with a static charge, the charge must be on the surface and the electric field must exist only externally to the surface of a conductor. See Fig. 16-15.

2. There can be no potential difference between two points on the surface of a charged conductor. A difference of potential is a measure of the work done in moving a charge from one point to another. As no electric field exists within the conductor, no work is done in moving a charge between two points on the same conductor. No difference of potential can exist between such points.

3. The surface of a conductor is an equipotential surface. All points on a conductor are at the same potential and no work is done by the electric field in moving a charge residing on a conductor. If points of equal potential in an electric field near a charged object are joined, an *equipotential line* or *surface* within the field is indicated. No work is done when a test charge is moved in an electric field along an equipotential surface.

4. Electric lines of force are normal to equipotential surfaces. A line of force shows the direction of the force acting on a test charge in an electric field. It can be shown that there is no force acting normal to this direction. Thus no work is done when a test charge is moved in an electric field normal to the lines of force. See Fig. 16-16.

5. Lines of force originate or terminate normal to the surface of a charged object. Since the surface of a conductor is an equipotential surface, lines of force must start out perpendicularly from the

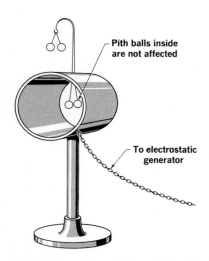

Pith balls inside are not affected

To electrostatic generator

16-15 When the metal cylinder is charged by the electrostatic generator, the pith balls outside diverge, while those inside are not affected. What does this tell us about the location of the charge?

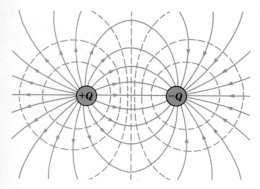

16-16 Lines of force (solid lines) and equipotential lines (dashed lines) define the electric field near two equal but opposite charges.

surface. For the same reason, a line of force cannot originate and terminate on the same conductor.

A charged spherical conductor, perfectly isolated in space, has a uniform charge density, or charge per unit area, over the outer surface. Lines of force extend radially from the surface in all directions and the equipotential surfaces of the electric field are spherical and concentric. Such symmetry is not found in all cases of charged conductors.

A charge acquired by a nonconductor such as glass is confined to its original region until it gradually leaks away. The charge placed on an isolated metal sphere quickly spreads uniformly over the entire surface. If the conductor is not spherical, the charge distributes itself according to the surface curvature, concentrating mainly around points. The pear-shaped conductor of Fig. 16-17 shows the charge more concentrated on the curved regions and less on the straight regions. If the small end is made more pointed, the charge density will increase at that end.

In Fig. 16-17, the lines of force and equipotential lines are shown more concentrated at the small end of the charged conductor. This geometry indicates that the intensity of the electric field, or potential gradient, in this region is greater than elsewhere around the conductor. If this surface is reshaped to a sharply pointed end, the field intensity can become great enough to cause the gas molecules in the air to *ionize*. Ionized air consists of electrically charged particles responsive to the electric force. When the air is ionized, the point of the conductor is rapidly discharged.

When a molecule of a gas loses electrons because of some stress condition, it becomes a positively charged *ion*. There are always a few of these positive ions and free electrons present in the air. The intense electric field near a sharp point of a charged conductor will set these charged particles in motion, the electrons being driven in one direction and the positive ions in the opposite direction. Violent collisions with other gas molecules will knock out some electrons and produce more charged particles. In this way air can be ionized quickly when it is subjected to a sufficiently large electric stress.

In dry air at atmospheric pressure, a potential gradient of 30 kv/cm is required between two charged surfaces to ionize the intervening column of air. When such an air gap is ionized, a *spark discharge* occurs. There is a rush of free electrons and ionized molecules across the ionized gap, discharging the surfaces and producing heat, light, and sound. Usually the quantity of static electricity involved is quite small and the time duration

16.12 Effect of the shape of conductors

16.13 Discharging effect of points

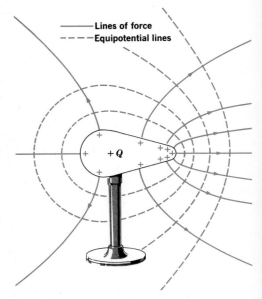

16-17 The charge density is greatest at the point of greatest curvature.

of the spark discharge is very short. Atmospheric lightning, however, is a spark discharge in which the quantity of charge is great.

The intensity of an electric field near a charged object can be sufficient to produce ionization only at sharp projections or sharp corners of the object. A slow leakage of charge will occur at these locations, producing a *brush* or *corona discharge*. A faint violet glow is sometimes emitted by the ionized gases of the air. A glow discharge, called St. Elmo's fire, can be observed at night at the tips of the masts of ships and at the trailing edges of wing and tail surfaces of aircraft. "Pigtails" are usually attached to the trailing edges of aircraft wings to aid in removing the charges acquired by the plane in flight.

The escape of charges from sharply pointed conductors is of great importance in the operation of electrostatic generators and in the design of lightning rods.

Lightning is a gigantic electric discharge in which electric charges rush to meet their opposites. The interchange can occur between clouds or between a cloud and the earth. According to the Lightning Protection Institute, one hundred bolts of lightning strike the earth every second, each bolt initiated by a potential difference of millions of volts.

There are no known ways of preventing lightning. However, there are effective means of protection from its destructiveness. Lightning rods, an invention of Benjamin Franklin, are often used to protect buildings made of nonconductors, such as wood or masonry, from lightning damage. Sharply pointed rods are strategically located above the highest projections of the building, and by their discharging effect, normally prevent the

Streaks of lightning brighten the night-time sky. Each flash requires a potential difference of millions of volts.

accumulation of a dangerous electrostatic charge. Lightning rods are thoroughly grounded. If lightning strikes, they provide a good conducting path into the ground. The steel frames of large buildings, being well grounded, offer excellent protection from lightning damage.

Television receiving antennas, even though equipped with lightning arresters, do not protect a building from lightning. Without lightning arresters they are a distinct hazard since they are not grounded.

Any isolated conductor is able to retain an electrostatic charge to some extent. If we place a positive charge on such a conductor by removing electrons, the potential is raised to some positive value with respect to ground. Conversely, a negative charge placed on the conductor results in a negative potential with respect to ground. By increasing the charge, we increase the potential of the conductor, since the potential of an isolated conductor is a measure of the work done in placing a charge on the conductor. It is evident that we can continue to increase the charge until the potential, with respect to ground or other conducting surface, becomes so high that corona or spark discharges occur. However, if the conductor were in an evacuated space, it could have been raised to a much higher potential by continuing the addition of charge.

Suppose a charged conductor is connected to an electroscope as shown in Fig. 16-18(A). The leaves of the electroscope will diverge indicating the potential of the charged conductor, because there can be no difference of potential between different regions of a single charged conducting surface.

16.14 Capacitors

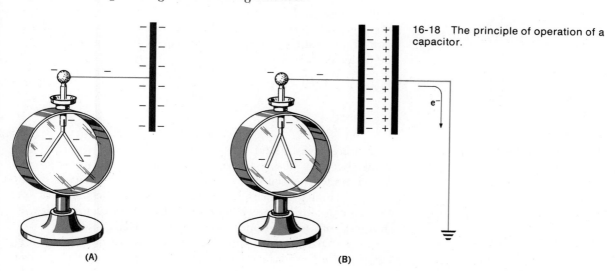

16-18   The principle of operation of a capacitor.

(A)   (B)

Materials used in making a low-loss miniature capacitor. The first vial contains chloroform which is mixed with the contents of the second vial, a polycarbonate resin. Aluminum (second from right top row) is coated with the polycarbonate resin on a polyester support (top center). About fifteen feet of this aluminized polycarbonate lacquer film from each roll (bottom row) is required for the manufacture of a one-microfarad capacitor (bottom center).

Now suppose a grounded conductor is brought near the charged conductor, as shown in Fig. 16-18(B). A positive charge is induced on this second conductor as free electrons are repelled to ground by the negative field of the first conductor. The leaves of the electroscope partially collapse. The closer we move the grounded plate the more pronounced is this effect. Because of the attractive force of the induced charge on the grounded plate, less work is required to place the same negative charge on the first conductor. Its potential is consequently reduced accordingly. A greater charge can now be placed on this conductor to raise the potential back to the initial value.

A combination of conducting plates separated by an insulator, used to store an electric charge, is known as a **capacitor**. The area of the plates, their distance of separation, and the character of the insulating material separating them determine the charge that can be placed on a capacitor. The larger the charge, the greater is the potential difference between the plates of a capacitor. The ratio of charge Q to the potential difference V is a *constant* for a given capacitor and is known as its *capacitance, C*. **Capacitance** *is the ratio of the charge on either plate of a capacitor to the potential difference between the plates.* Thus,

$$C = \frac{Q}{V}$$

where C is the capacitance of a capacitor, Q is the quantity of charge on either plate, and V is the potential difference between the conducting plates.

In the MKS system, the unit of capacitance is the *farad*, f, named in honor of Michael Faraday. *The capacitance is 1* **farad** *when a charge of 1 coulomb on a capacitor results in a potential difference of 1 volt between the plates.* The farad is an extremely large unit of capacitance. Practical capacitors have capacitances of the order of *microfarads*, μf or *picofarads*, pf.

$$1 \ \mu\mathbf{f} = 10^{-6} \ \mathbf{f}$$
$$1 \ \mathbf{pf} = 10^{-12} \ \mathbf{f}$$

16.15 Dielectric materials

Faraday investigated the effects of different insulating materials between the plates of capacitors. He constructed two capacitors with equal plate areas and equal plate spacing. Using air at normal pressure in the space between the plates of one and an insulating material between the plates of the other, he charged both to the same potential difference.

These capacitors are shown as C_1 and C_2 respectively in Fig. 16-19. Faraday measured the quantity of charge on each capaci-

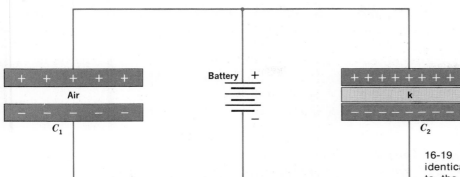

16-19 Capacitors C_1 and C_2 have identical dimensions and are charged to the same potential difference by the battery. C_2 accumulates the larger quantity of charge.

tor and found that C_2 had a greater charge than C_1 by a factor k.

$$Q_2 = kQ_1$$

Since the two capacitors are identical except for the material separating the plates, and have the same potential difference across their plates, the factor k must be due to a property of the insulating material of C_2. The ratio Q_2/V is larger than Q_1/V by this factor k.

$$\frac{Q_2}{V} = k \frac{Q_1}{V}$$

Thus, the capacitance of C_2 is larger than the capacitance of C_1 by the factor k.

$$C_2 = kC_1$$

Many materials such as mica, paraffin, oil, waxed paper, glass, plastics, and ceramics can be used instead of air in the space between the plates of a capacitor. For each material, the resulting capacitance Q/V will have a different value.

Materials used to separate the plates of capacitors are known as *dielectrics*. *The ratio of the capacitance with a particular material separating the plates of a capacitor to the capacitance with a vacuum between the plates is called the* **dielectric constant**, *k, of the material.* Dry air at atmospheric pressure has a dielectric constant of 1.0006. In practice this is taken as *unity* (the same as vacuum) for dielectric constant determinations. Dielectric constants are dimensionless numbers ranging from 1 to 10 for materials commonly used in capacitors. The dielectric constant k of the dielectric material used in Fig. 16-19 is

$$k = \frac{C_2}{C_1}$$

Typical dielectric constants are given in Table 16-1 for some common dielectric materials.

Table 16-1 DIELECTRIC CONSTANTS

Dielectric	Dielectric constant (typical value)	Proportionality constant (n m²/c²)
air	1.0	8.9×10^9
paper (oiled)	2.0	4.5×10^9
paraffin	2.2	4.1×10^9
polyethylene	2.3	3.9×10^9
polystyrene	2.5	3.6×10^9
hard rubber	2.8	3.2×10^9
mica	6.0	1.5×10^9
glass	8.0	1.1×10^9

Instead of charging the identical capacitors of Fig. 16-19 to the same potential difference, suppose we place the same charge Q on them. The experiment now shows that the potential difference across C_2 is smaller than that across C_1 by the factor $1/k$.

$$V_2 = \frac{V_1}{k}$$

This leads us to our previous conclusion about the influence of the dielectric material separating the plates of a capacitor. Since $C = Q/V$ and Q_1 and Q_2 are equal,

$$\frac{Q_2}{V_2} = \frac{Q_1}{V_1/k} \qquad \text{and} \qquad C_2 = kC_1$$

16.16 The effect of dielectrics

The molecules of some dielectrics have a permanent separation of their positive and negative centers of charge. This property is described as a permanent *electric dipole moment*. These molecules are called *polar* molecules or simply *dipoles*. When placed in an electric field, polar molecules tend to become aligned with the external field to a degree characteristic of the molecules.

Other dielectrics are composed of molecules that are essentially *nonpolar* and which show no permanent electric dipole moments. When placed in an electric field, these molecules can acquire a temporary polar character by *induction*. While in the electric field, they have induced electric dipole moments.

The space between the plates of a charged capacitor is permeated by a uniform electric field. If a dielectric slab is inserted into such an electric field denoted by the potential gradient $\mathscr{E}_0$, the slab as a whole becomes polarized by induction. The surface near the positive plate of the capacitor acquires a negative charge and the surface near the negative plate acquires a positive charge. See Fig. 16-20. These surface charges result from the dipole moments of the dielectric molecules and not from the transfer of electrons as in the case of metallic conductors.

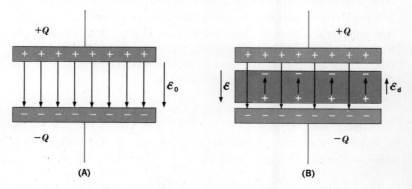

16-20 A dielectric slab placed in an electric field tends to weaken the field within the dielectric. What should be the effect on the potential differences across the plates?

The electric field established in the dielectric slab by the surface charge *opposes* the external field $\mathscr{E}_0$ of the capacitor. This opposing field is shown in Fig. 16-20(B) as $\mathscr{E}_d$. Its effect is to weaken the original field within the dielectric. The net electric field $\mathscr{E}$ is the vector sum of the two fields $\mathscr{E}_0$ and $\mathscr{E}_d$ and is always a weaker field in the direction of $\mathscr{E}_0$.

$$\vec{\mathscr{E}} = \vec{\mathscr{E}}_0 + \vec{\mathscr{E}}_d$$

The net effect of a dielectric between the plates of a charged capacitor is to lower the potential gradient of the electric field. If a parallel-plate capacitor with an air dielectric is charged and then isolated, a potential difference of Q/C volts remains across the plates. The introduction of a dielectric slab between the plates causes a decrease in this potential difference and reveals its weakening effect on the electric field of the capacitor.

If the charged spheres of Fig. 16-10 are immersed in some dielectric medium, the medium would also become polarized by induction. Clustered around each of the charged spheres would be opposite charges from the medium. The result would be an effective reduction in the values of Q_1 and Q_2. An exact analysis shows that the force between the two spheres is reduced in value by the factor k which is the dielectric constant of the medium. Thus, in the equation for Coulomb's law

$$F = k\,\frac{Q_1 Q_2}{s^2},$$

the value of k is 8.987×10^9 n m^2/c^2 for vacuum, but is less for material media. Its value for various materials is given in the last column of Table 16-1.

Capacitors find wide application in all kinds of electronic circuits, ignition systems, and telephone and telegraph equipment. Large capacitances are achieved by using large plate areas, insulators with high dielectric constants, and small separation of the plates. Physical size limits the plate area while cost limits the choice of dielectric. *Dielectric strength* of the insulator limits the reduction in spacing between the plates.

Dielectric strength should not be confused with the dielectric constant of a material. The dielectric strength defines the quality of the material as an insulator; that is, the potential gradient it will withstand without being punctured by a spark discharge. Some typical values are given in Table 16-2.

Suppose we connect three capacitors in *parallel*: that is, with one plate of each capacitor connected to one conductor while the other plate is connected to a second conductor. See Fig. 16.21(A).

Table 16-2   DIELECTRIC STRENGTHS

Dielectric material	Dielectric strength (kv/cm to puncture)
air	30
oil	75
paraffin	350
paper (oiled)	400
mica	500
glass	1000

16.17 Combinations of capacitors

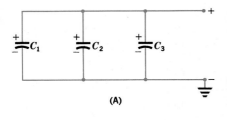

(A)

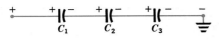

(B)

16-21   Capacitors connected in parallel (A) and in series (B).

The plates connected to the $+$ conductor are parts of one conducting surface. Those connected to the $-$ conductor form the other conducting surface. If the three capacitors are charged, it is apparent that they must have the same difference of potential, V, across them. The quantity of charge on each must be respectively

$$Q_1 = C_1V, \; Q_2 = C_2V, \text{ and } Q_3 = C_3V$$

The total charge, Q_T, must be the sum of the separate charges on the three capacitors,

$$Q_T = Q_1 + Q_2 + Q_3$$

then

$$Q_T = C_1V + C_2V + C_3V$$

Since the total charge is equal to the product of the total capacitance, C_T, and the potential difference, V, it is evident that

$$Q_T = C_T V$$

Substituting,

$$C_T V = C_1 V + C_2 V + C_3 V$$

and

$$C_T = C_1 + C_2 + C_3$$

For capacitors connected in parallel, the total capacitance is the sum of all the separate capacitances.

Now suppose we connect the three capacitors in *series* as shown in Fig. 16-21(B). A positive charge placed on C_1 from the $+$ source induces a negative charge on the second plate, the electrons being attracted away from the plate C_2 connected to C_1. A positive charge of the same magnitude is left on the $+$ plate of C_2. Similarly, the plates of C_3 acquire the same magnitude of charge. Thus,

$$Q = Q_1 = Q_2 = Q_3$$

The negative plate of C_1 must be at the same potential with respect to ground as the positive plate of C_2, since they are connected and are parts of the same conducting surface. Similarly, the negative plate of C_2 must be at the same potential as the positive plate of C_3. Thus the total difference of potential, V_T, across the three series capacitors must be equal to the sum of the separate potential differences across each capacitor: V_1, V_2, and V_3.

$$V_T = V_1 + V_2 + V_3$$

Since the charge received from the source is Q, then by definition

$$V_T = \frac{Q}{C_T}$$

and

$$V_1 = \frac{Q}{C_1}, V_2 = \frac{Q}{C_2}, V_3 = \frac{Q}{C_3}$$

Substituting,

$$\frac{Q}{C_T} = \frac{Q}{C_1} + \frac{Q}{C_2} + \frac{Q}{C_3}$$

or

$$\frac{1}{C_T} = \frac{1}{C_1} + \frac{1}{C_2} + \frac{1}{C_3}$$

For capacitors connected in series, the reciprocal of the total capacitance is equal to the sum of the reciprocals of all the separate capacitances. See the following example.

Example

Three capacitors have capacitances of 0.200 μf, 0.300 μf, and 0.500 μf. (a) If they are connected in parallel and charged to a potential difference of $10\bar{0}$ v, what is the charge on each capacitor? (b) What is the total charge acquired? (c) If these three capacitors are discharged, then connected in series, and a charge of +30.0 μc is transferred to the ungrounded terminal, what potential difference appears across each? (d) What total potential difference exists across the three capacitors?

Solution

(a) The diagram of Fig. 16-21(A) applies to this part of the problem. In parallel,

$$V = V_1 = V_2 = V_3 = 10\bar{0} \text{ v}$$

Then

$$Q_1 = C_1 V = 0.200 \ \mu\text{f} \times 10\bar{0} \text{ v} = 20.0 \ \mu\text{c}$$
$$Q_2 = C_2 V = 0.300 \ \mu\text{f} \times 10\bar{0} \text{ v} = 30.0 \ \mu\text{c}$$
$$Q_3 = C_3 V = 0.500 \ \mu\text{f} \times 10\bar{0} \text{ v} = 50.0 \ \mu\text{c}$$

(b) In parallel,

$$Q_T = Q_1 + Q_2 + Q_3 = (20.0 + 30.0 + 50.0) \ \mu\text{c}$$
$$Q_T = 100.0 \ \mu\text{c}$$

(c) The diagram of Fig. 16-21(B) applies to this part of the problem. In series,

$$Q = Q_1 = Q_2 = Q_3 = 30.0 \ \mu c$$

Thus each capacitor is charged to 30.0 μc, the ungrounded terminal being positive. Then,

$$V_1 = \frac{Q}{C_1} = \frac{30.0 \ \mu c}{0.200 \ \mu f} = 15\overline{0} \ v$$

$$V_2 = \frac{Q}{C_2} = \frac{30.0 \ \mu c}{0.300 \ \mu f} = 10\overline{0} \ v$$

$$V_3 = \frac{Q}{C_3} = \frac{30.0 \ \mu c}{0.500 \ \mu f} = 60.0 \ v$$

(d) In series,

$$V_T = V_1 + V_2 + V_3 = 15\overline{0} \ v + 10\overline{0} \ v + 60.0 \ v$$
$$V_T = 31\overline{0} \ v \text{ (positive with respect to ground)}$$

QUESTIONS

Group A

1. In what region of an insulated ellipsoidal conductor is the greatest charge density found to be concentrated?
2. What determines whether a difference of potential exists between two points?
3. Define (a) potential difference, (b) the MKS unit of potential difference.
4. A conducting object connected to the earth is at zero potential. Explain.
5. Is work required to move a charge along the surface of a charged conductor isolated in space? Explain?
6. How does a spark discharge occur between two charged surfaces?
7. (a) Define capacitance. (b) What is the MKS unit of capacitance?
8. What is the effect of connecting capacitors (a) in parallel, (b) in series?

Group B

9. (a) Express the dimensions of the volt in fundamental MKS units. (b) Demonstrate that the electric field intensity can have the dimensions of volt per meter.
10. (a) Why is it not possible to maintain a charge on an electroscope indefinitely? (b) What shape should the knob have for a minimum rate of loss of charge?
11. Why are the tips of lightning rods shaped into sharp points?
12. Why are the occupants of a modern steel-frame building not harmed when the building is struck by lightning?

13. Would you expect to be very successful in conducting experiments with static electricity on a humid day? Explain.
14. The electrostatic force between two charges immersed in oil is found to be one-half of the electrostatic force when the same two charges are in air. Explain.
15. A solid metal sphere and a hollow metal sphere have the same dimensions, both perfectly insulated. Which will hold the larger maximum charge in air without breaking down?

PROBLEMS

Group B

1. A force of 0.032 n is required to move a charge of 42 μc in an electric field between two points 25 cm apart. What potential difference exists between the two points?
2. An electron is accelerated in a machine in which it is subjected to a potential difference of 5.0 megavolts. What energy has the electron acquired?
3. (a) What is the potential gradient between two parallel plates 0.50 cm apart when charged to a potential difference of 1.2 kv? (b) Convert your result to an expression of electric field intensity in terms of n/c.
4. A capacitor consisting of two parallel plates separated by a layer of air 0.3 cm thick and having a capacitance of 15.0 pf is connected across a 15$\overline{0}$-volt source. (a) What is the charge on the capacitor? The air dielectric is replaced by a sheet of mica 0.3 cm thick. (b) What is the capacitance with the mica dielectric? (c) What additional charge does the capacitor take up?
5. Three paper capacitors having capacitances of 0.15 μf, 0.22 μf, and 0.47 μf are connected in parallel and charged to a potential difference of 240 volts. (a) Determine the charge on each capacitor. (b) What is the total capacitance of the combination? (c) What is the total charge acquired?

Chapter 17

Direct-Current Circuits

SOURCES OF DIRECT CURRENT

17.1 Electric charges in motion

The quantity of charge on a capacitor is indicated by the potential difference between the plates.

$$Q = CV$$

If the capacitance C for given capacitor is a constant, then the charge Q is proportional to the potential difference V across it.

$$Q \propto V \quad (C \text{ constant})$$

A potential difference across a charged capacitor, and therefore a charge on the capacitor, can be indicated by an electroscope connected across the capacitor plates. See Fig. 17-1. Suppose the two plates of the capacitor are now connected by a heavy copper wire as in Fig. 17-2(A). The leaves of the electroscope immediately collapse, indicating that the capacitor has been discharged rapidly. Free electrons flow from the negative plate of the capacitor, and from the electroscope, through the copper wire to the positive plate. This action quickly establishes the normal distribution of electrons characteristic of an uncharged capacitor.

Considering the charged capacitor of Fig. 17-1 again, suppose the plates are connected by means of a long, fine wire made of nichrome, which has few free electrons compared to copper. The leaves of the electroscope collapse more gradually than before. See Fig. 17-2(B). This delay means that a longer time is required to completely discharge the capacitor. When any

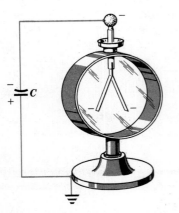

17-1 The charge on a capacitor may be indicated by an electroscope.

conductor connects the plates of the capacitor, electrons move from the negative plate through the conductor to the positive plate. This transfer decreases the charge on each plate and the difference of potential between the plates.

The charge Q on either plate of a capacitor is proportional to the potential difference V between the plates. The *rate* at which the charge decreases, in c/sec, is proportional to the rate at which the potential difference decreases, in v/sec. Now the rate of decrease of charge on the capacitor must represent the rate of flow of the charge, in c/sec, through the conductor. Thus the rate at which the leaves of the electroscope collapse indicates the rate of flow of the charge through the conductor. During the time the capacitor is discharging, a *current* is said to exist in the conducting wire. *An **electric current** (I) in a conductor is the rate of flow of charge through a cross section of the conductor.*

$$\text{current } (I) = \frac{\text{charge } (Q)}{\text{time } (t)}$$

The unit of current in the MKS system is the *ampere*, a. *One ampere is a current of 1 coulomb per second.*

$$1 \text{ a} = \frac{1 \text{ c}}{\text{sec}}$$

Recall that 1 coulomb of charge consists of 6.25×10^{18} electrons, or a like number of protons. Small currents can be expressed in *milliamperes* ma or *microamperes* μa:

$$1 \text{ ma} = 10^{-3} \text{ a}$$
$$1 \text{ } \mu\text{a} = 10^{-6} \text{ a}$$

A moving charge is basic for an electric current. The character of a conducting substance determines the nature of the charge set in motion in an electric field. In solids the charge carriers are electrons; in gases or electrolytic solutions they can be positive or negative ions or both. *An **electrolyte** is a substance whose solution conducts an electric current.*

A negative charge moving in one direction in an electric circuit is equivalent to a positive charge moving in the opposite direction insofar as external effects are concerned. Negative charges departing from a negatively charged surface and arriving at a positively charged surface leave the former surface less negative and the latter surface less positive. Positive charges departing from the positively charged surface and arriving at the negatively charged surface would have a similar effect, leaving the positively charged surface less positive and the negatively charged surface less negative.

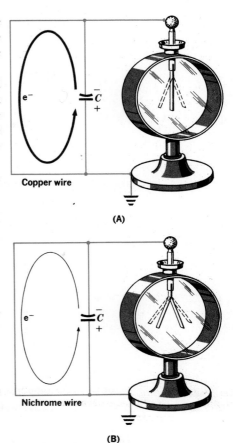

Copper wire

(A)

Nichrome wire

(B)

17-2 The rate of discharge of a capacitor depends on the conducting path provided.

If both positive and negative charges are set in motion in a conducting medium, the current in the medium is the sum of the currents due to the motion of the positive charges in one direction and the negative charges in the opposite direction.

The directional sense of electron flow through an electric field in a metallic conductor is from negative to positive. The directional sense of a positive ion flow in an ionized gas is from positive to negative. In our study of electric circuits we will be concerned generally with current in metallic conductors and thus will deal mainly with electron flow in which the directional sense is from negative to positive. In any case, confusion about current direction can be avoided by indicating the directional sense of the charge carriers that are in motion.

The above reference to an electric field in a conductor does not contradict the assertions of Section 16.11, which require the electric field in a conductor to equal zero. In this earlier discussion we were concerned with static electric charges on an isolated conductor. The charges reside on the surface of such a conductor and there is no net charge motion on this equipotential surface. We are presently dealing with moving charges and with conductors across the ends of which potential differences are deliberately maintained. Thus this earlier restriction does not apply.

Free electrons in empty space are accelerated by an electric field. The effect of an electric field on the free electrons of a metallic conductor is quite different. A net acceleration of these electrons is not realized because of their frequent collisions with the fixed particles of the conductor, the metallic ions. With each collision the electron loses whatever velocity it had acquired in the direction of the accelerating force, transfers energy to the fixed particle, and makes a fresh start.

The kinetic energy transferred in these collisions increases the vibrational energy of the conductor particles and heat is given up to the surroundings. The free electrons move in the direction of the accelerating force with an average velocity called the *drift velocity*. This drift velocity has a constant average value for a given conductor carrying a certain magnitude of current. It is much smaller than the speed with which changes in the electric field propagate through the conductor, which is approximately 3×10^8 m/sec.

It has been estimated that the free electrons of a copper conductor of 1 mm² cross section have an average drift velocity of about 1 mm/sec when a current of 20 a   is in the conductor. The situation is somewhat analogous to that of a ball rolling down a flight of stairs. With the proper conditions, the successive collisions of the ball with the steps effectively cancel the acceleration it acquires between steps and it rolls down with a constant average speed.

As we have seen, collision between the free electrons and the fixed particles of a conductor is an energy dissipating process which opposes the flow of charge through the conductor. *This opposition to the electric current is called **resistance**, R.* The practical MKS unit of resistance is the *ohm*, represented by the Greek letter omega, Ω. The laws of electric resistance will be discussed in Section 17.11.

17.2 Continuous current

The current from a discharging capacitor persists for a very short interval of time; it is known as a *transient* current. The effects of such a current are also transient, but those effects are very important in certain types of electronic circuits. In the general applications of electricity, more continuous currents are required.

The effects of current electricity are quite different from those of static electricity. The electric current is one of our most convenient means of transmitting energy. A *closed-loop* conducting path is needed if energy is to be utilized outside the source; this conducting loop is known as an *electric circuit,* and the device or circuit component utilizing the electric energy is called the *load.* The basic components of an electric circuit are illustrated in simple form in Fig. 17-3. Some conventional symbols used in schematic diagrams of electric circuits are shown in Fig. 17-4.

A capacitor would be useful as a source of continuous current over a prolonged period of time only if some means were available for keeping it continuously charged. We would need to supply electrons to the negative plate of the capacitor as rapidly as they were removed by the current in the conducting loop. Similarly, we would need to remove electrons from the positive plate of the capacitor as rapidly as they were deposited by the current. This is to say, we must maintain the potential differ-

17-3 An electric circuit is a conducting loop in which a current can transfer electric energy from a suitable source to a useful load.

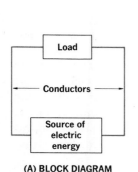

(A) BLOCK DIAGRAM

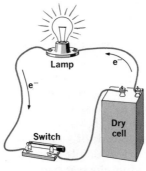

(B) PICTORIAL DIAGRAM

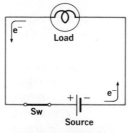

(C) CIRCUIT DIAGRAM

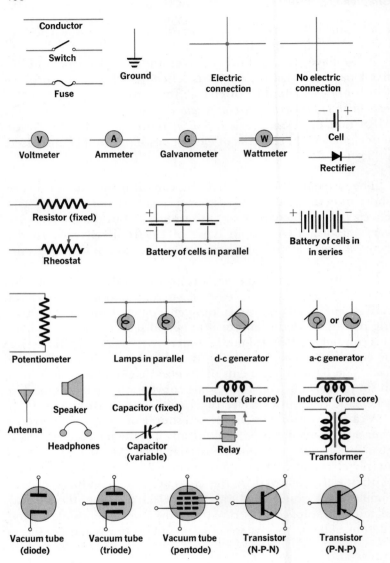

17-4 Conventional symbols used in schematic diagrams of electric circuits.

ence across the source during the time a continuous current is in the circuit.

This is an energy-consuming process in which work is done on the electrons in opposition to the force of the electric field between the charged plates. Some of this energy becomes available to do useful work in the external circuit. What is needed is some kind of "electron pump." Several practical energy sources are available to maintain a difference of potential across an operating electric circuit.

The transformation of available energy into electricity is accomplished by one of two basic methods called *dynamic conversion* and *direct conversion*. Dynamic converters are rotating machines, and these machines supply most of our requirements for electric energy today. Direct conversion methods produce energy transformations without moving parts. We shall consider the following sources of continuous current:

1. Electromagnetic. The major source of electric current in practical circuits today depends on the principle of *electromagnetic induction*. If a conducting loop is rotated in a magnetic field, the free electrons of the conductor are forced to move around the loop and constitute a current. This is the basic principle of operation of electric generators. It is an example of the transformation of mechanical energy into electric energy, a dynamic conversion process. Electromagnetic induction and the electric generator will be studied in Chapter 20.

2. Photoelectric. The photoelectric effect was first observed by the German physicist Hertz. He noticed that a spark discharge occurred more readily when charged metal spheres were illuminated by another spark discharge. See Section 12.6.

Electrons are emitted from the surface of a metal illuminated by light of sufficiently short wavelength. For most metals, the light must contain energy radiated in the ultraviolet region. The alkali metals are particularly sensitive to this action; potassium and cesium will respond to rays of ordinary visible light. When a photon of the incident light is absorbed by the metal, its energy is imparted to an electron, which can then possess sufficient energy to break away from the forces which bind it within the surface of the metal. (Refer to the discussion of the photoelectric effect, Sections 12.6 and 12.7.)

The metal surface, if properly isolated, acquires a positive charge as photo-electrons are emitted. As the charge increases, other electrons are prevented from escaping from the metal and the action stops. If, however, the metal is placed in an evacuated tube and made part of a circuit, as in Fig. 17-5, it can act as a source of current whenever light is incident upon its surface. Such a tube is called a *photoelectric cell.*

The photoelectric cell shown in Fig. 17-5 has a coating of potassium metal deposited on the inner surface of a glass tube, leaving an aperture through which light can enter. A metallic ring near the focus of the emitter surface acts as a collector of photoelectrons. The emitter is connected externally to the negative terminal of a battery and the collector is connected to the positive terminal. The collector is thus maintained at a positive potential with respect to the emitter. The force of the resulting electric field acts on the emitted electrons, driving those elec-

17.3 Sources of continuous current

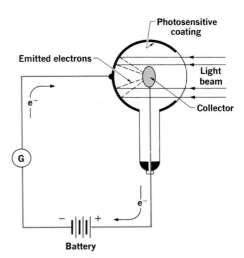

17-5 The circuit of a photoelectric cell.

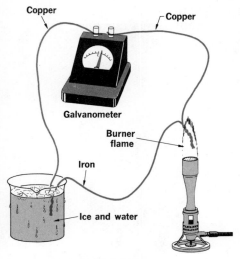

Copper

Copper

Galvanometer

Burner flame

Iron

Ice and water

17-6   A thermocouple.

trons to the collector and producing a small current in the external circuit. A *galvanometer*, an electric meter sensitive to very feeble currents, can be placed in the circuit to indicate the relative magnitude and direction of the current.

A bright light causes the ejection of many electrons from the surface of the photosensitive metal, while light of the same frequency but lower intensity produces fewer photoelectrons. Thus the current produced by the photoelectric cell is determined by the intensity of the incident light; this is a case in which radiant energy' is transformed into electric energy. Some form of photosensitive cell is used in devices that are controlled or operated by light.

3. Thermoelectric. Suppose we form a conducting loop circuit consisting of a length of iron wire and a length of copper wire and a sensitive galvanometer, as shown in Fig. 17-6. One copper-iron junction is put in a beaker of ice and water to maintain a low temperature; the other junction is heated by a gas flame. As the second junction is heated, the galvanometer indicates a current in the loop. An electric circuit incorporating such junctions is known as a *thermocouple*.

The magnitude of the current is related to the nature of the two metals forming the junctions and the temperature difference between the junctions. A thermocouple can be used as a sensitive thermometer designed to measure radiant energy. The iron-copper junction is useful for temperatures up to about 275°C. Junctions of copper and constantan (a copper-nickel alloy) are widely used in lower temperature ranges. Junctions of platinum and rhodium are used to indicate temperatures ranging up to 1600°C.

The thermocouple is a thermoelectric source of current, since heat energy is transformed directly into electric energy. If a sensitive galvanometer is properly calibrated, temperatures can be read directly. Thus the hot junction can be placed in a remote location where it would not be possible to read an ordinary mercury thermometer.

Recall that the first law of thermodynamics tells us that heat can be converted into other forms of energy, but in a closed thermodynamic system, energy can be neither created nor destroyed. Thermoelectric converters are fundamentally heat engines and, as in all other heat engines, are limited to the efficiency of the conversion process. The actual efficiency with which heat is converted to electricity is a function of the temperature difference within the operating system.

The heating effect of an electric current in the resistance of a conductor is an irreversible phenomenon. On the other hand, there are *three* basic thermoelectric effects, each of which is

A thermoelectric generator on the surface of the moon. Heat is supplied by nuclear energy. The shadow of an astronaut is seen at the right.

reversible. The best known of these effects was described in the first paragraph of this section; when the junctions of two dissimilar metals are subjected to a difference in temperature, a current is set up in the loop. This is known as the *Seebeck effect*, being named after its discoverer who first observed the phenomenon in 1821. See Fig. 17-7(A).

The second thermoelectric effect, known as the *Peltier effect*, is produced when a direct current is passed through a junction formed by two dissimilar metals. The junction becomes warmer or cooler depending on the direction of the current. This effect is shown in Fig. 17-7(B).

The third thermoelectric effect, called the *Thomson effect*, is observed in certain homogeneous materials. If a single solid is subjected to a temperature gradient between opposite faces, a difference of potential is established across it. This potential difference can be used to supply an electric current in an external circuit connected to the solid.

Certain semiconductor materials show thermoelectric properties and perform the heat-to-electricity conversion more efficiently than metals. In addition to the application of semiconductor converters as electric generators, the Peltier effect makes possible their use as cooling devices such as refrigerators.

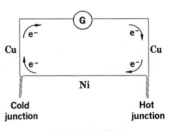

(A) Seebeck effect

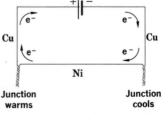

(B) Peltier effect

17-7   The Seebeck and Peltier effects for copper and nickel. One is the inverse of the other.

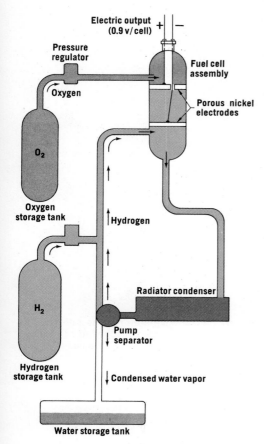

17-8 Functional diagram of a hydrogen-oxygen fuel cell.

Thermoelectric modules composed of stacked wafers of these semimetals may ultimately replace metal thermocouples and provide a practical means of converting heat energy directly into electric energy on a large scale. Thermoelectric generators made with ceramic wafers may eventually provide a means of converting the wasted heat in a rocket-engine exhaust to electricity.

Thermocouples using heat from radioactive isotopes to generate electricity are presently being used in some unmanned satellites. Nuclear heat sources which produce electric current by thermoelectric conversion are used by astronauts on the surface of the moon to provide power for their lunar experiments. These energy converters use plutonium-238 as the heat source.

4. Piezoelectric. When certain crystals, such as Rochelle salt and quartz, are subjected to a mechanical stress, the opposite surfaces become electrically charged. The difference of potential between the stressed surfaces is proportional to the amount of stress applied to the crystal. Reversing the stress reverses the charges also.

If the crystal is suitably supported, and a conducting circuit is connected between surfaces having a difference of potential, electricity will flow through the circuit. Thus, mechanical energy is transformed into electric energy. This transformation is known as the *piezoelectric effect*, and the crystal with its supporting mechanism is called a *piezoelectric cell.*

Crystal microphones use the piezoelectric effect to transform the alternating pressure of sound waves into an electric current that varies as the pressure of the sound waves varies. A crystal phonograph pickup responds in a similar manner to the varying stress caused by the needle riding in the groove of the record.

The piezoelectric effect is reversible; that is, the crystal experiences a mechanical strain when subjected to an electric stress. An alternating difference of potential properly placed across the crystal will cause mechanical vibrations proportional to the variations of the voltage. Crystal headphones use this reciprocal effect.

5. Chemical. Certain chemical reactions involve a transfer of electrons from one reactant to the other. These reactions that occur *spontaneously* (that is, of and by themselves) can be used as sources of continuous current. During the chemical reaction, electrons are removed from one reactant. A like number of electrons is added to the other reactant. By separating the reactants in a conducting environment, the transfer of electrons can take place through an external circuit connected between them for as long as reactants are available. Such an arrangement is known as an *electrochemical cell.* Chemical energy is transformed into electric energy during the chemical reaction.

Electrochemical cells include primary, storage, and fuel cells. A primary cell, a flashlight cell for example, is ordinarily replaced when its reactants are used up. Storage cells, as in an automobile battery, are reversible. Electric energy is initially stored as chemical energy and the cell can be repeatedly "recharged" with energy. If the reactants in a primary cell are supplied continuously, the arrangement is called a fuel cell. A functional diagram of the hydrogen-oxygen fuel cell used as the source of electric current in the Apollo spacecraft is shown in Fig. 17-8.

17.4 The dry cell

The essential components of a primary cell are an *electrolyte* and two *electrodes* of unlike materials, one of which reacts chemically with the electrolyte. Let us examine the carbon-zinc dry cell as a common example of the primary cell. A cut-away diagram of this cell is shown in Fig. 17-9. The electrolyte is a moist paste of ammonium chloride. One electrode is a carbon rod. The other electrode, a zinc cup, is consumed as the cell is used.

When an external circuit is connected across the cell, zinc atoms react with the electrolyte and give up electrons. This reaction leaves the zinc electrode *negatively charged*. We shall refer to the negative electrode as the **cathode**. *It is the electron-rich electrode.*

Simultaneously, the electrolyte removes a like number of electrons from the carbon electrode. This reaction leaves the carbon electrode positively charged. We shall call the positive electrode the **anode**. *It is the electron-poor electrode.*

Electrons move through the external circuit from cathode to anode because of the difference in potential between the electrodes. Thus, the cell acts as a kind of electron pump. See Fig. 17-10. It removes electrons with low potential energy from the anode and supplies electrons with high potential energy to the cathode while current is in the external circuit. Electrons flow through the external circuit from cathode to anode. This unidirectional current is an example of *direct current* (dc).

If we open the circuit and stop the current, the *maximum* potential difference is quickly established across the cell. The magnitude of this *open circuit* potential difference is dependent solely on the materials that make up the electrodes. For the carbon-zinc cell it is approximately 1.5 volts.

The open circuit potential difference can be referred to as the *emf,* or electromotive force of the cell. The MKS symbol for emf is E and the unit is the *volt*. The cell itself must supply a definite amount of energy for each unit of charge that is stored

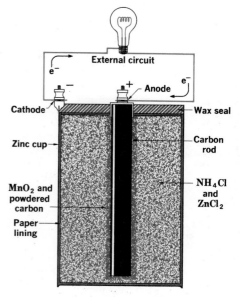

17-9   The dry cell is a practical source of direct current in the physics laboratory.

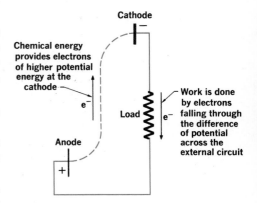

17-10   A voltaic cell provides electrons of higher potential energy because of chemical action in the cell.

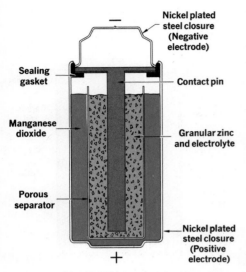

Nickel plated steel closure (Negative electrode)

Sealing gasket

Contact pin

Manganese dioxide

Granular zinc and electrolyte

Porous separator

Nickel plated steel closure (Positive electrode)

17-11 Cross-section of an alkaline-manganese cell. An outer jacket (not shown) and appropriate terminal connections provide the conventional appearance of the carbon-zinc cell.

on either electrode; *the **emf** of a source is the energy per unit charge supplied by the source.* Thus the potential difference across the cell on an *open circuit* is equal to the emf of the cell.

$$V_{oc} = E$$

We will see in Section 17.6 that the potential difference V across a source of emf on a *closed circuit* is less than the emf E.

The carbon-zinc cell has an emf of 1.5 volts, regardless of the size of the cell. However, the larger the electrode surfaces, the higher the current the cell can deliver. The standard No. 6 dry cell is capable of supplying a *momentary* current up to 35 amperes. It should not be required to furnish more than 0.25 ampere of continuous current, however. The internal resistance can vary from less than 0.1 ohm in the No. 6 cell to over 1 ohm in small special-purpose cells.

Alkaline-manganese cells can be substituted directly for carbon-zinc cells in many applications. While more expensive to produce, alkaline cells have lower internal resistance, higher efficiency, and the ability to deliver from 50 to 100% more current than their carbon-zinc counterparts.

A sectional view of an alkaline-manganese cell is shown in Fig. 17-11. The positive electrode consists of manganese dioxide in conjunction with a steel can that serves as the electrode terminal. The negative electrode is granulated zinc which is mixed with a highly conductive potassium hydroxide electrolyte. The nominal potential difference across the cell is 1.5 volts.

17.5 Combination of cells

Energy-consuming devices that form the loads of electric circuits are designed to draw the proper current for their operation when a specific potential difference exists across their terminals. For example, a lamp designed for use in a 6-volt electric system of an automobile would draw an excessive current and burn out if placed in a 12-volt system. A lamp that is intended for use in a 12-volt system, on the other hand, would not draw sufficient current at 6 volts to function as intended.

Electrochemical cells are sources of emf. Each cell furnishes a certain amount of energy to the circuit for each coulomb of charge that is moved. It is often necessary to combine cells in order to provide either the proper emf or an adequate source of current. Groups of cells can be connected in *series*, in *parallel*, or in *series-parallel* combinations. *Two or more cells connected together form a **battery**.* The emf of a battery depends on the emf of the individual cells and the way they are connected.

A *series* combination of cells is shown in Fig. 17-12. Observe that the positive terminal of one cell is connected to the external

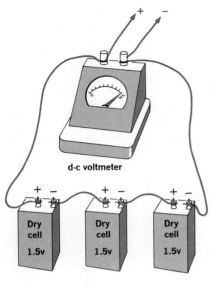

(A) Pictorial diagram

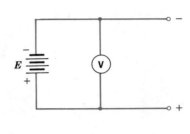

(B) Circuit diagram

17-12 Dry cells connected in series to form a battery. The same quantity of electricity flows through each cell.

circuit and the negative terminal is connected to the positive terminal of a second cell. The negative terminal of this cell is connected to the positive terminal of a third cell, and so on. The negative terminal of the last cell in the series is connected to the load to complete the circuit. Thus the cells are joined end to end and *the same quantity of electricity must flow through each cell.*

Suppose we think of the battery as a group of electron pumps connected in *series* (adding). Each electron pump (cell) removes electrons of low potential energy from its anode and supplies electrons of high potential energy to its cathode. The first pump lifts electrons to a certain level of potential energy, the second pump takes them from this level to the next higher level, the third lifts them to a still higher potential energy, and so on. We can readily see that the emfs of the cells are added to give the emf of the battery.

A battery made up of cells connected in *series* has the following characteristics:

1. The emf of the battery is equal to the sum of the emfs of the individual cells.

2. The current in each cell and in the external circuit has the same magnitude throughout.

3. The internal resistance of the battery is equal to the sum of the internal resistances of the individual cells.

In a *parallel* combination of cells, all negative terminals are connected together. One side of the external circuit is then connected to any one of these common terminals. The positive

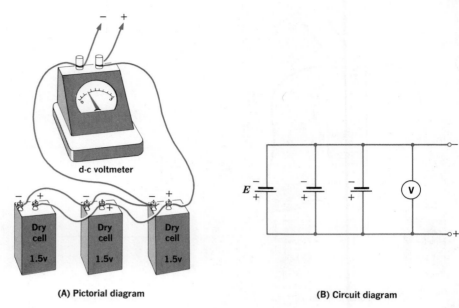

(A) Pictorial diagram

(B) Circuit diagram

17-13 Dry cells connected in parallel
to form a battery.

terminals are connected together and the other side of the
external circuit can be connected to any one of these common
terminals to complete the circuit. This arrangement, in effect,
simply increases the total cathode and anode surface areas.
The battery is then roughly the equivalent of a single cell having
greatly enlarged electrodes in contact with the electrolyte and,
a lower internal resistance. Each cell of a group in parallel
merely furnishes its proportionate share of the total circuit
current. Of course, cells should not be connected in parallel
unless they have equal emfs. See Fig. 17-13.

A battery of *identical* cells connected in *parallel* has the following characteristics:

1. The emf is equal to the emf of each separate cell.

2. The total current in the circuit is divided equally among the cells.

*3. The reciprocal of the internal resistance of the battery is equal to
the sum of the reciprocals of the internal resistances of the cells.*

The lead-acid storage battery for automobiles with 6-volt
electric systems consists of three cells connected in series. The
emf is approximately 6.6 volts. Six cells are connected in series
to make up the battery for 12-volt systems.

As mentioned previously, a No. 6 dry cell, if properly used,
should not be required to deliver more than 0.25 ampere of
continuous current. Suppose we have an electric device designed to perform in a 3-volt circuit which requires a continuous
current of 0.75 ampere. How should the 1.5-volt dry cells be
grouped to make up the battery to operate the device?

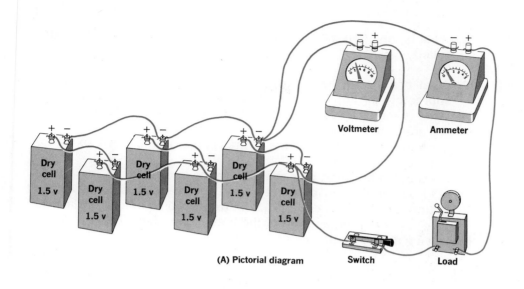

(A) Pictorial diagram

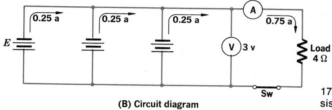

(B) Circuit diagram

17-14 A circuit using a battery consisting of a series-parallel arrangement of cells.

Certainly, two dry cells in series would provide an emf of 3 volts for the circuit. Three cells in parallel would require no more than 0.25 ampere from each cell. Thus, a series-parallel arrangement of dry cells, as shown in Fig. 17-14, is appropriate.

QUESTIONS

Group A

1. What is an electric current?
2. What is the MKS unit of current?
3. Define the unit of current in terms of fundamental MKS units.
4. What is electric resistance?
5. Name five basic sources of continuous current.
6. Name a current-producing device for each of these sources.
7. What are the essential parts of a primary cell?
8. Define an electrolyte.
9. What term is used to identify (a) the negative electrode of an electric cell, (b) the positive electrode?
10. What is the distinguishing characteristic of direct current electricity?
11. Distinguish between the terms "open circuit" and "closed circuit."

12. What is the open-circuit potential difference of a source of current called?

Group B 13. What change in the energy of an electron is produced (a) by a source of emf, (b) by a load connected across a source of emf?

14. What is the distinguishing difference between a primary cell and a storage cell?

15. Explain the meaning of the expression "spontaneous oxidation-reduction reaction."

16. Distinguish between potential difference and emf.

17. (a) How would you connect 1.5-volt dry cells to provide a 6-volt battery to supply a continuous current of 0.25 ampere to a load? (b) Draw a circuit diagram of the battery you describe.

18. Does a storage battery store electricity? Justify your answer.

SERIES AND PARALLEL CIRCUITS

17.6 Ohm's law for d-c circuits

George Ohm, the German physicist for whom the unit of resistance is named.

Resistance R is defined as the opposition to the flow of electric charge. Metallic substances in general are classed as good conductors of electricity. Silver and copper, because of their abundance of free electrons, are excellent conductors, but even these metals offer some opposition to the current in them. There is some inherent resistance in every conductor through its normal range of operating temperatures, and therefore every device or component in an electric circuit offers some resistance to the current in the circuit.

Copper wire is used in electric circuits to connect various circuit components because ordinarily its resistance is low enough to be neglected. Certain metallic alloys offer unusually high resistance to the flow of electricity; *nichrome* and *chromel* are notable examples. Spools wound with wire made from these alloys can be used in an electric circuit to provide either *fixed* amounts of resistance, or *variable* resistance in definite amounts.

Carbon granules can be mixed with varying amounts of clay and molded into cylinders having a definite resistance. These devices, called *carbon resistors*, are commonly used in electronic circuits.

Georg Simon Ohm (1787–1854), a German physicist, discovered that *the ratio of the emf of the source in a closed circuit to the current in the circuit is a constant*. This constant is the *resistance* of the circuit. The above statement, known as **Ohm's law of resistance**, is a relationship of the utmost importance in the study of current electricity. It can be stated mathematically as follows:

$$\frac{E}{I} = R \quad \text{or} \quad E = IR$$

The MKS units are the volt, ampere, and ohm respectively. The *ohm* (Ω) has the following dimensions:

$$\Omega = \frac{v}{a} = \frac{j/c}{c/sec}$$

$$\Omega = \frac{j \ sec}{c^2} = \frac{n \ m \ sec}{c^2}$$

$$\Omega = \frac{kg \ m^2 \ sec}{sec^2 \ c^2} = \frac{kg \ m^2}{c^2 \ sec}$$

Suppose an emf of 12 v exists in an electric circuit which has 33 Ω resistance. The current in the circuit is:

$$E = IR \quad so \quad I = E/R$$

$$I = \frac{12 \ v}{33 \ \Omega} = 0.36 \ a$$

Now suppose the circuit resistance is doubled. In this situation the opposition to the current is doubled but the emf remains the same, so we should expect the current in the circuit to be reduced to one-half the former value.

$$I = \frac{12 \ v}{66 \ \Omega} = 0.18 \ a$$

The emf, E, applied to a circuit equals the drop in potential across the *total* resistance of the circuit, but Ohm's law applies equally well to *any part* of a circuit that does not include a source of emf. Suppose we consider the circuit shown in Fig. 17-15. Points **A** and **B** are the terminals of the battery, which supply an emf of 12.0 volts to the circuit. The total resistance of the circuit is 12.0 ohms. Of this total, 0.20 ohm is *internal resistance*, r, of the battery and is conventionally represented as a resistor in series with the battery inside the battery terminals. The remaining 11.8 ohms of resistance consists of a *load resistor*, R_L, in the external circuit.

For the entire circuit, the total resistance, R_T, is equal to the sum of internal and external resistances.

$$R_T = R_L + r$$

The current in the entire circuit is

$$I = \frac{E}{R_T} = \frac{E}{R_L + r}$$

$$I = \frac{12.0 \ v}{11.8 \ \Omega + 0.20 \ \Omega} = 1.00 \ a$$

When we apply Ohm's law to a part of a circuit that does not include a source of emf, we are concerned with the potential

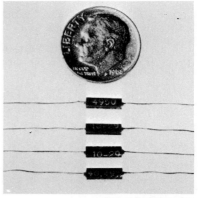

General Resistance, Inc.

Small resistors such as those used in a transistor radio. A dime indicates their actual size.

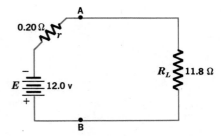

17-15 Ohm's law applies equally well to all or any part of an electric circuit.

difference V, the current I, and the resistance R that apply only to that part of the circuit. Thus, Ohm's law for a part of the circuit becomes

$$V = IR$$

The drop in potential across the external circuit of Fig. 17-15 must be

$$V_L = IR_L$$
$$V_L = 1.00 \text{ a} \times 11.8 \ \Omega = 11.8 \text{ v}$$

The drop in potential across the internal resistance of the battery due to current in the battery can be found by a similar application of Ohm's law.

$$V_r = Ir$$
$$V_r = 1.00 \text{ a} \times 0.20 \ \Omega = 0.20 \text{ v}$$

This is a fall of potential across the battery resistance, which removes energy from the electrons. It is, therefore, opposite in sign to the emf of the battery and subtracts from the emf to give the potential difference across the battery terminals on closed circuit with a current I.

$$V = E - Ir$$

The closed-circuit potential difference across the terminals of a source of emf which is applied to the external circuit will always be less than the emf by the amount Ir volts. This is not an important difference for a source of emf of low internal resistance unless an excessive current is in the circuit. (In much of the discussion of Sections 17.8-17.10 the internal resistance of a source of emf will be neglected and the emf will be assumed to be applied to the external circuit.)

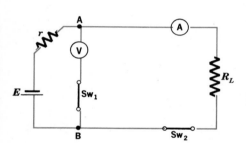

17-16 A circuit for measuring the internal resistance of a cell.

17.7 Determining internal resistance

A good quality voltmeter is an instrument of very high resistance. When a voltmeter is connected across the terminals of a source of emf, even one with low internal resistance, negligible current is drawn from the source. For all practical purposes the meter reading is an "open-circuit" reading and indicates the emf of the source. This provides a convenient method of measuring the internal resistance of a cell or battery. The following example, based on Fig. 17-16, illustrates this method.

Example

A dry cell gives an open-circuit voltmeter reading of 1.5 v. The voltmeter is then removed and an external load of 2.8 ohms is connected across the cell. An ammeter in the external circuit reads 0.50 ampere. (a) Find the internal resistance of the cell. (b) What would the voltmeter have read if it had been left connected while the current was in the load?

Solution

(a) We are given the following information: the emf of the cell, $E = 1.5$ v; $I = 0.50$ a; and $R_L = 2.8$ Ω. We are asked to find r. We know that E is the work done per coulomb of charge moved through the total resistance of the circuit. Thus,

$E = IR_T$.   But $R_T = R_L + r$

Substituting for R_T: $E = I(R_L + r)$

Solving for r: $r = \dfrac{E - IR_L}{I}$

$r = \dfrac{1.5 \text{ v} - (0.50 \text{ a} \times 2.8 \text{ } \Omega)}{0.50 \text{ a}} = 0.20 \text{ } \Omega$, the internal resistance

(b) $V = E - Ir = 1.5$ v $- (0.50$ a $\times 0.20$ $\Omega)$

$V = 1.4$ v, the potential difference across the circuit

17.8 Resistances in series

If several electric devices are connected end to end in a circuit, electricity must flow through each in succession. There is a single path for the moving charge, and so the same current must be in each device. Otherwise there would be an accumulation of charge at different points around the conducting circuit. We know that a charge can be accumulated on a conductor only if it is isolated. *An electric circuit with components arranged to provide a single conducting path for current is known as a **series circuit**.*

Series-circuit operation has several inherent characteristics. If one element of a series connection fails to provide a conducting path, the circuit is opened. Also, each component of the circuit offers resistance to the flow of electricity, and resistance in a circuit limits the current in the circuit according to Ohm's law. When connected in series, resistance is cumulative; the more resistive components, the higher the total resistance, and the smaller the current in the circuit for a given applied emf. Obviously, since the current must be the same at all points in the circuit, *all devices connected in series must be designed to function at the same current magnitude.*

From Ohm's law, the drop in potential across each component of a series circuit is the product of the current in the circuit and the resistance of the component. Electrons lose energy as they fall through a difference of potential; in a series circuit these losses occur in succession and are therefore cumulative. *The drops in potential across successive components in a series circuit are*

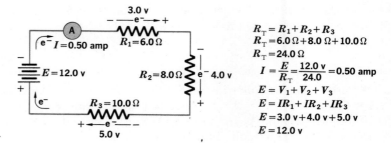

17-17   A series circuit.

additive, and their sum is equal to the potential difference across the whole circuit.

We can summarize these observations by stating three cardinal rules for resistances in series:

1. The current in all parts of a series circuit has the same magnitude.

$$I_T = I_1 = I_2 = I_3 = \text{etc.}$$

2. The sum of all the separate drops in potential around a series circuit is equal to the applied emf.

$$E = V_1 + V_2 + V_3 + \text{etc.}$$

3. The total resistance in a series circuit is equal to the sum of all the separate resistances.

$$R_T = R_1 + R_2 + R_3 + \text{etc.}$$

Suppose these rules are applied to a circuit consisting of several resistors connected in series as shown in Fig. 17-17. The computations are shown at the right of the circuit diagram. Observe that the "positive" side of R_1 is 3.0 volts positive with respect to the cathode of the battery and is 9.0 volts negative with respect to the anode of the battery. The three voltage drops in the external circuit are in series and their sum equals the applied emf in magnitude, but their signs are opposite.

Stated in another way, *the algebraic sum of all the changes in potential occurring around the complete circuit is equal to zero.* This is a statement of **Kirchhoff's second law** credited to Gustav Robert Kirchhoff (1824–1887), an eminent German physicist. Since potential difference is an expression of work (or energy) per unit charge involved in transporting a charge around a closed circuit, Kirchhoff's second law can be recognized as an application of the law of *conservation of energy* to electric circuits.

17.9 Resistances in parallel

Some of the characteristics of series operation of electric devices were mentioned in the preceding section. It would be quite disconcerting to have all the lights go out in your home each time one lamp were turned off. For this reason each lamp is on a separate circuit, so that each is operated independently. Such lamps are said to be connected in parallel. *A **parallel circuit** is one in which two or more components are connected across two common points in the circuit to provide separate conducting paths for current.*

Since there can be only one difference of potential between any two points in an electric circuit, *electric devices or appliances connected in parallel should usually be designed to operate at the same voltage.* The currents in the separate branches must vary inversely with their separate resistances since the same potential difference exists across each branch of the parallel circuit.

By Ohm's law, which can be applied to any part of a circuit, the current in each branch is

$$I = \frac{V}{R}$$

But V is constant for all branches in parallel. Then

$$I_{\text{(for each branch)}} \propto \frac{1}{R_{\text{(of that branch)}}}$$

In Fig. 17-18 it is apparent that there is more opportunity for the flow of electricity between points **A** and **B** with two parallel branches in the circuit than with one branch removed. The current I entering junction **A** must be the same as the current $(I_1 + I_2)$ leaving junction **A**. Similarly, the current $(I_1 + I_2)$ entering junction **B** must be the same as the current I leaving junction **B**. Then I must be equal to $I_1 + I_2$.

Let us consider the currents entering and leaving junctions **A** and **B** in another way. Electric current is the rate of transfer of charge, $I = Q/t$. In the steady-state operation of the circuit, the charge of **A** can neither increase nor decrease. Current I carries charge toward this junction and I_1 and I_2 carry charge away from it. Thus,

$$I - I_1 - I_2 = 0$$

Similarly, currents I_1 and I_2 carry charge toward junction **B** and I carries charge away from it. Using the same sign convention for current direction as before,

$$I_1 + I_2 - I = 0$$

These expressions tell us that *the algebraic sum of the currents at any circuit junction is equal to zero.* This is known as **Kirchhoff's first law**. It states, in effect, a law of *conservation of charge* in electric circuits. Kirchhoff's two laws define the basic principles we must employ in our interpretation of electric circuits: *that energy and charge are conserved.*

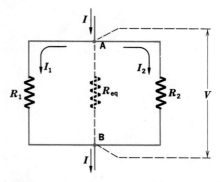

17-18 Two resistances in parallel.

Assume that $R_1 = 1\overline{0} \ \Omega$, $R_2 = 15 \ \Omega$, and $V = 3\overline{0}$ v. From Ohm's law, the current in R_1 is

$$I_1 = \frac{V}{R_1} = \frac{3\overline{0} \text{ v}}{1\overline{0} \ \Omega} = 3.0 \text{ a}$$

The current in R_2 is

$$I_2 = \frac{V}{R_2} = \frac{3\overline{0} \text{ v}}{15 \ \Omega} = 2.0 \text{ a}$$

and

$$I = I_1 + I_2 = 5.0 \text{ a}$$

According to Ohm's law, the current from **A** to **B**, which is I, is the quotient of the potential difference across **A-B** divided by the effective resistance between **A** and **B**. It is convenient to think of the effective resistance due to resistances in parallel as a single *equivalent resistance* (R_{eq}) which, if substituted for the parallel resistances, would provide the same current in the circuit.

$$I = \frac{V}{R_{eq}}$$

Then

$$R_{eq} = \frac{V}{I} = \frac{3\overline{0} \text{ v}}{5.0 \text{ a}} = 6.0 \ \Omega$$

The equivalent resistance for the parallel combination of R_1 and R_2 is *less than* either resistance present. As the current approaching junction **A** *must be larger* than either branch current, clearly the equivalent resistance of the parallel circuit *must be smaller* than the resistance of any branch.

Since

$$I = \frac{V}{R_{eq}}, \ I_1 = \frac{V}{R_1}, \ I_2 = \frac{V}{R_2}$$

and

$$I = I_1 + I_2$$

then,

$$\frac{V}{R_{eq}} = \frac{V}{R_1} + \frac{V}{R_2}$$

Dividing by V, we get

$$\frac{1}{R_{eq}} = \frac{1}{R_1} + \frac{1}{R_2} \qquad \text{(Equation 1)}$$

Equation 1 shows that the sum of the reciprocals of the resistances in parallel is equal to the reciprocal of their equivalent resistance. Then solving Equation 1 for R_{eq},

$$R_1 R_2 = R_{eq}(R_1 + R_2)$$

and

$$R_{eq} = \frac{R_1 R_2}{R_1 + R_2}$$

$$R_{eq} = \frac{1\overline{0}\ \Omega \times 15\ \Omega}{1\overline{0}\ \Omega + 15\ \Omega} = \frac{150\ \Omega^2}{25\ \Omega}$$

$$R_{eq} = 6.0\ \Omega$$

Let us summarize these observations by stating three cardinal rules for resistances in parallel.

1. The total current in a parallel circuit is equal to the sum of the currents in the separate branches.

$$I_T = I_1 + I_2 + I_3 + \text{etc.}$$

2. The potential difference across all branches of a parallel circuit must have the same magnitude.

$$V = V_1 = V_2 = V_3 = \text{etc.}$$

3. The reciprocal of the equivalent resistance is equal to the sum of the reciprocals of the separate resistances in parallel.

$$\frac{1}{R_{eq}} = \frac{1}{R_1} + \frac{1}{R_2} + \frac{1}{R_3} + \text{etc.}$$

Practical circuits can be quite complex compared to the series and parallel circuits we have considered. There can be resistances in series, other resistances in parallel, and different sources of emf. Such complex circuits are commonly called *networks*.

A simple network is shown in Fig. 17-19(A). There is a single source of emf and one resistor in series with the combination of two resistors in parallel. We will use this circuit to demonstrate the steps that can be taken to simplify a network and reduce circuit problems to simple relationships.

We are given the emf and internal resistance of the battery and the resistance of each component resistor in the circuit. The first step is to find the total current in the circuit. To do this we must know the total resistance. To find the total re-

17.10 Resistances in simple networks

17-19 A simple network and its equivalent circuit.

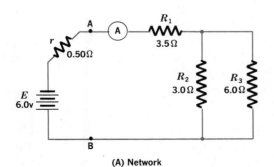

(A) Network

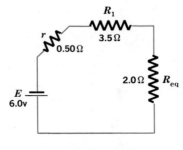

(B) Equivalent circuit

sistance we must reduce the parallel resistances to an *equivalent* value.

$$\frac{1}{R_{eq}} = \frac{1}{R_2} + \frac{1}{R_3} \quad \text{and} \quad R_{eq} = \frac{R_2 R_3}{R_2 + R_3}$$

$$R_{eq} = \frac{3.0 \ \Omega \times 6.0 \ \Omega}{3.0 \ \Omega + 6.0 \ \Omega}$$

$$R_{eq} = 2.0 \ \Omega, \text{ the equivalent resistance}$$

We can now draw a simpler *equivalent* circuit showing this equivalent resistance in series with R_1 and r. See Fig. 17-19(B). The total resistance is now readily seen to be 6.0 ohms.

$$R_T = R_1 + R_{eq} + r = 6.0 \ \Omega$$

And

$$I_T = \frac{E}{R_T} = \frac{6.0 \ v}{6.0 \ \Omega} = 1.0 \ a$$

The drop in potential across R_1 is

$$V_1 = I_T R_1 = 1.0 \ a \times 3.5 \ \Omega$$
$$V_1 = 3.5 \ v$$

Since R_2 and R_3 are in parallel, the same potential drop must appear across each. This is found by considering the total current in the equivalent resistance of the parallel segment.

$$V_{eq} = I_T R_{eq} = 1.0 \ a \times 2.0 \ \Omega$$
$$V_{eq} = 2.0 \ v$$

The potential difference across the terminals of the battery is the difference between the emf and the $I_T r$ drop.

$$V = E - I_T r = 6.0 \ v - (1.0 \ a \times 0.50 \ \Omega)$$
$$V = 5.5 \ v$$

This is verified by the fact that V must equal $V_1 + V_{eq}$.

The current in R_2 may be found since the potential difference, V_{eq}, is known.

$$I_2 = \frac{V_{eq}}{R_2} = \frac{2.0 \ v}{3.0 \ \Omega}$$
$$I_2 = 0.67 \ a$$

The current in R_3 is

$$I_3 = \frac{V_{eq}}{R_3} = \frac{2.0 \ v}{6.0 \ \Omega}$$
$$I_3 = 0.33 \ a$$

This is verified by the fact that I_3 must equal $I_T - I_2$.

A more complex network is shown in Fig. 17-20(A). The battery is a series-parallel arrangement of similar cells, so the magnitude of the emf will depend on the number of cells in

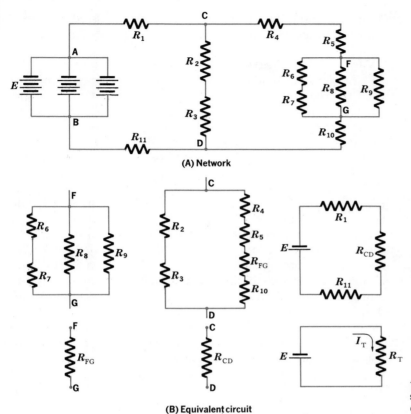

(A) Network

(B) Equivalent circuit

17-20 A network may be reduced to a simple circuit by the use of equivalent circuit analysis techniques.

series. The total current must be known. The approach is the same as that in our earlier example. First, reduce the segment **F-G** to its equivalent value. We will label this R_{FG}. Now R_{FG} is in series with R_4, R_5, and R_{10} to form one branch of the segment **C-D**. When the two branches of **C-D** are reduced to their equivalent, R_{CD}, we can consider R_1, R_{CD}, and R_{11} to be in series. This reduction provides R_T, and I_T may be calculated. See the diagrams in Fig. 17-20(B).

Suppose we need to know the magnitude of current in R_7 and the drop in potential across this resistor. Now the current in R_{CD} must be I_T and the drop in potential across **C-D** must be $I_T R_{CD}$, or V_{CD}. The current in the branch of **C-D** containing R_{FG} is the quotient of V_{CD} divided by the sum of $(R_4 + R_5 + R_{FG} + R_{10})$. This current (we will label it I_{FG}) is in R_{FG} and the potential drop, V_{FG}, across R_{FG} is the product $I_{FG} R_{FG}$.

Since R_6 and R_7 are in series, the resistance of this branch of **F-G** is equal to their sum. The current in R_7 is V_{FG} divided by $(R_6 + R_7)$. With I_7 known, the drop in potential across R_7 is the product $I_7 R_7$. You will observe that we have depended on

Ohm's law and the six extensions of Ohm's law listed as cardinal rules for series and parallel circuits in Sections 17.8 and 17.9.

17.11 The laws of resistance

Various factors affect the resistance of a conductor.

1. Temperature. The resistance of all substances changes to some degree with changes in temperature. *In the case of pure metals and most metallic alloys, the resistance increases with a rise in temperature.* Carbon, semiconductors, and many electrolytic solutions, on the other hand, show a decrease in resistance as their temperature is raised. A few special alloys, such as constantan and manganin, show very slight changes in resistance over a considerable range of temperatures. For practical purposes, the resistance of these alloys can be considered independent of temperature.

Thermal agitation of the particles composing a metallic conductor rises as the metal is heated. As the temperature is lowered, thermal agitation diminishes. The electric resistance of metals is related to this thermal agitation; their resistance approaches zero as the temperature approaches absolute zero (0°K). The graph of resistance against temperature of a metallic conductor is essentially linear over the normal temperature range of the solid state of a metal. Thus, when the electric resistance of a conductor is stated, the temperature of the material at which this resistance applies should be indicated. See Fig. 17-21.

17-21 The resistivity of copper as a function of temperature.

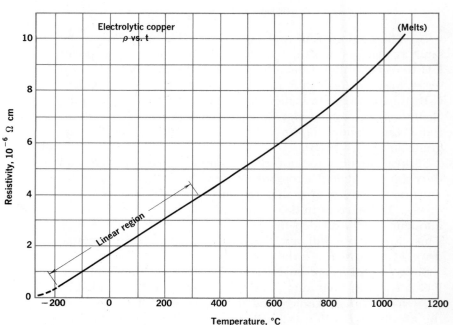

2. Length. Resistances in series are added to give the total resistance of the series circuit. From this fact we can conclude that 10 meters of a certain conductor should have a resistance 10 times that of 1 meter of the same conductor. Experiments prove this relationship to be true; *the resistance of a uniform conductor is directly proportional to the length of the conductor*

$$R \propto l$$

where l is the length of the conductor.

3. Cross-sectional area. If three *equal* resistances are connected in parallel in an electric circuit, the equivalent resistance is one-third the resistance of any one branch. The equal currents in the three branches add to give the total current in the circuit.

Assuming the three resistances to be three similar wires 1 meter in length, each having a cross-sectional area of 0.1 cm², we can think of the equivalent resistance as a similar wire of the same length but having a cross-sectional area of 0.3 cm². This deduction is reasonable, since a wire carrying a direct current of constant magnitude has a constant current density throughout its cross-sectional area. If the parallel resistances are designated R_1, R_2, and R_3, then

$$\frac{1}{R_{eq}} = \frac{1}{R_1} + \frac{1}{R_2} + \frac{1}{R_3}$$

But

$$R_1 = R_2 = R_3$$

So

$$\frac{1}{R_{eq}} = \frac{3}{R_1}$$

And

$$R_1 = 3R_{eq}$$

We can conclude that the resistance of the large wire, R_{eq}, is one-third the resistance of the small wire, R_1, and experiments prove this conclusion to be true. *The resistance of a uniform conductor is inversely proportional to its cross-sectional area*

$$R \propto \frac{1}{A}$$

where A is the cross-sectional area of the conductor.

4. Nature of the materials. A copper wire having the same length and cross-sectional area as an iron wire offers about one-sixth the resistance to the flow of electricity. A similar silver wire presents even less resistance. *The resistance of a given conductor depends on the material of which it is made.*

Taking these four factors into account, several useful conclusions become apparent. For a uniform conductor of a given material and temperature, the resistance is directly proportional to the length and inversely proportional to the cross-sectional area.

$$R \propto \frac{l}{A}$$

Suppose we introduce a proportionality constant, called *resistivity*, represented by the Greek letter ρ (rho). The laws of *resistance* for wire conductors can then be summarized by the following expression:

$$R = \rho \frac{l}{A}$$

Resistivity is dependent only on the material composing the wire and its temperature. See Fig. 17-21. If R is in ohms, l is in centimeters, and A is in centimeters², then ρ has the dimensions *ohm centimeter*.

$$\rho = \frac{RA}{l}$$

$$\rho = \frac{\Omega \text{ cm}^2}{\text{cm}} = \Omega \text{ cm}$$

Resistivity, ρ, is equal to the resistance of a wire 1 cm long and having a uniform cross-sectional area of 1 cm². (The resistivities of various materials are listed in Appendix B, Table 20. The wire gauge scale and the dimensions of wire by gauge number are given in Table 21.) If the resistivity of a material is known, the resistance of any other wire composed of the same material can be calculated. See the following example.

Example

What is the resistance of a copper wire $2\bar{0}$ m long and 0.81 mm in diameter at 20°C? The resistivity of annealed copper at 20°C is 1.72×10^{-6} Ω cm.

Solution

We are given the resistivity of copper at 20°C, $\rho = 1.72 \times 10^{-6}$ Ω cm. The length of wire can be converted to centimeters and is most conveniently expressed as $l = 2.0 \times 10^3$ cm. The diameter of the wire in millimeters can be converted to 0.081 cm. The area, A, of a circle with diameter, d, $= \frac{\pi d^2}{4}$.

$$R = \rho \frac{l}{A}$$

$$R = 1.72 \times 10^{-6} \text{ } \Omega \text{ cm} \times \frac{2.0 \times 10^3 \text{ cm}}{\frac{\pi (0.081 \text{ cm})^2}{4}}$$

$$R = \frac{1.72 \times 10^{-6}\ \Omega\ \text{cm} \times 4 \times 2.0 \times 10^{3}\ \text{cm}}{\pi \times 6.56 \times 10^{-3}\ \text{cm}^{2}}$$

$R = 0.67\ \Omega$, the resistance of the wire

The enormous range of resistivities of common materials is shown in Fig. 17-22. The resistance of the best insulator can be greater than that of the best conductor by a factor of approximately 10^{25}. Insulators and semiconductors can decrease in resistivity with increasing temperature and with increasing potential gradient. We can interpret this latter behavior to mean that Ohm's law is not obeyed by these materials.

17.12 Range of resistivities

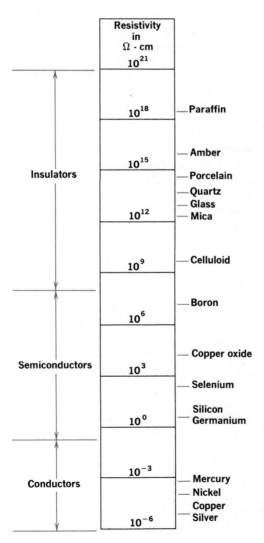

17-22 A resistivity spectrum. Observe the enormous range of resistivities exhibited by substances.

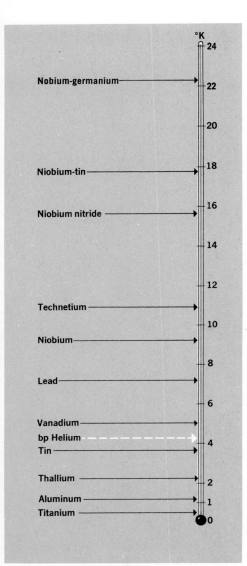

°K

Nobium-germanium —————————→ 22

Niobium-tin ——————————→ 18

Niobium nitride ——————————→ 16

Technetium ——————————→

Niobium ——————————→

Lead ——————————→

Vanadium ——————————→
bp Helium - - - - - - - - - - - →
Tin ——————————————→

Thallium ——————————→ 2

Aluminum ——————————→ 1
Titanium ——————————→ 0

17-23 **Temperature on the Kelvin scale at which various materials become superconductive.**

A small group of *semiconductors* has assumed considerable importance because of unusual variations in resistance with changes in temperature and potential gradient. Copper oxide rectifiers will pass a current when a potential difference is applied in one direction but not in the opposite direction. Silicon and germanium *transistors* are substituted for vacuum tubes in many electronic circuit applications.

At extremely low temperatures, some metals exhibit the unusual property of zero resistance. The production of very low temperatures and the study of the properties of materials at low temperatures is called *cryogenics*. Cryogenic temperatures are generally considered to be those below the boiling point of liquid oxygen (below $80°K$). Ultra-low temperature research began with the liquefaction of helium in 1908 by the Dutch physicist, Heike Kamerlingh Onnes (1853–1926). The boiling point of liquid helium is about $4°K$ $(-269°C)$.

We have learned that the resistivity of a conductor is a function of its temperature. We would therefore expect that the resistivity will become less and less as the temperature of a conductor drops, until the conductor offers no resistance to the passage of electrons at all. In 1911 Kamerlingh Onnes found that resistivity did indeed continue to drop with falling temperature. However, instead of gradually approaching zero resistivity, some materials had a specific temperature at which the resistivity dropped suddenly to zero. This temperature is called the *transition temperature. The condition of zero resistivity below the transition temperature of a material is called* **superconductivity.** Temperatures at which some materials become superconductive are shown in Fig. 17-23.

The region of very low temperatures at which superconductivity prevails poses a severe limitation for the utilization of superconductors. Obviously, superconductors offer great promise for such applications as power transmission, electric energy storage, and superelectromagnets that operate without power loss. However, the problem of keeping a power line below the transition temperature is a formidable one.

17.13 Measuring resistance

There are several methods of measuring the resistance of a circuit component. Two methods utilizing apparatus normally available in the physics laboratory will be discussed here. These are the *voltmeter-ammeter* method and the *Wheatstone bridge* method.

1. The voltmeter-ammeter method. Ohm's law applies equally well to any part of an electric circuit which does not contain a source of emf and to an entire circuit to which an emf is applied.

For a part of a circuit:

$$V = IR \quad \text{and} \quad R = \frac{V}{I}$$

If the potential difference V across a resistance component is measured with a voltmeter and the current I in the resistance is measured with an ammeter, the resistance R can be computed.

Suppose we wish to measure the resistance of R_1 in the circuit shown in Fig. 17-24. We connect the ammeter in series with the resistance R_1 to determine the current in R_1. We connect the voltmeter in *parallel* with R_1 to determine the potential difference across R_1.

If the resistance of R_1 is very low, it can have an excessive loading effect on the source of emf, causing an excessive current in the circuit. We can avoid this difficulty by placing a variable resistance, or rheostat, in series with R_1. The rheostat provides additional series resistance and limits the current in the circuit. By adjusting the rheostat we can provide an appropriate magnitude of current in the circuit. See Fig. 17-25. Observe that the voltmeter is connected across that part of the circuit for which resistance is to be determined.

The voltmeter-ammeter method of measuring resistance is convenient but not particularly precise. A voltmeter is a high resistance instrument. However, as it is connected in parallel with the resistance to be measured, there is a small current in it. The ammeter reading is actually the sum of the currents in these two parallel branches. Precision is limited by the extent to which the resistance of R_1 exceeds the equivalent resistance of R_1 and the meter in parallel.

2. The Wheatstone bridge method. A precise means of determining resistance utilizes a simple *bridge* circuit known as the *Wheatstone bridge*. It consists of a source of emf, a galvanometer, and a network of four resistors. If three are of known resistance, the resistance of the fourth can be calculated.

The circuit diagram of a Wheatstone bridge is shown in Fig. 17-26, in which an unknown resistance, R_x, may be balanced against known resistances R_1, R_2, and R_3. A galvanometer is *bridged* across the parallel branches **ADB** and **ACB**. By adjusting R_1, R_2, and R_3, the bridge circuit can be balanced, and the galvanometer shows zero current.

When the bridge is balanced in this manner, there can be no potential difference between **C** and **D**, since the galvanometer indicates zero current. Thus

$$V_{AD} = V_{AC}$$

and

$$V_{DB} = V_{CB}$$

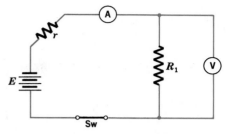

17-24 Determining resistance by the voltmeter-ammeter method.

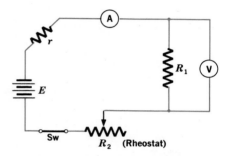

17-25 A rheostat provides a means of limiting the current in a circuit.

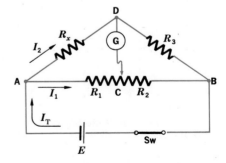

17-26 The electric circuit of the Wheatstone bridge.

The current in the branch **ACB** is I_1, and the current in **ADB** is I_2. Then

$$I_2 R_x = I_1 R_1$$

and

$$I_2 R_3 = I_1 R_2$$

Dividing one expression by the other, we have

$$\frac{R_x}{R_3} = \frac{R_1}{R_2}$$

or

$$R_x = R_3 \frac{R_1}{R_2}$$

In the laboratory form of the Wheatstone bridge, resistances R_1 and R_2 usually consist of a uniform resistance wire, such as constantan, mounted on a meter stick. See Fig. 17-27. The length of wire comprising R_1, and the length comprising R_2, are determined by the position of the contact **C**. If we let l_1 be the length of wire forming R_1 and l_2 the length of wire forming R_2, it is apparent that

$$\frac{l_1}{l_2} = \frac{R_1}{R_2}$$

We do not need to know the resistances of R_1 and R_2, for the lengths of wire, l_1 and l_2, can be taken directly from the meter stick. Our Wheatstone bridge expression then becomes

$$R_x = R_3 \frac{l_1}{l_2}$$

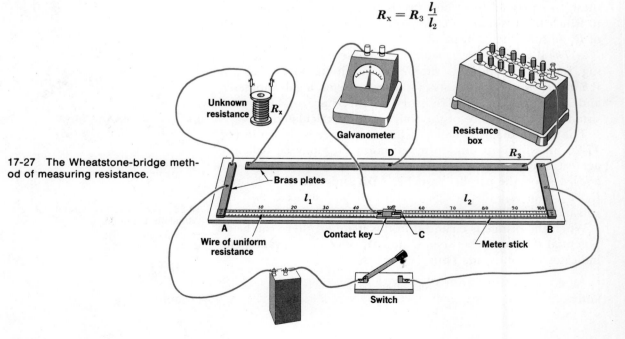

17-27　The Wheatstone-bridge method of measuring resistance.

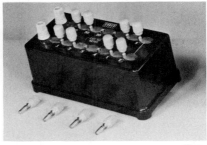

Cenco

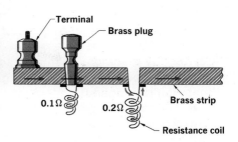

Terminal
Brass plug
0.1Ω
0.2Ω
Brass strip
Resistance coil

17-28 A plug-type resistance box providing resistance between the terminals from 0.1 ohm to 111 ohms in 0.1-ohm steps. The total resistance across the terminals depends on which plugs are removed.

A precision resistance box of the type shown in Fig. 17-28 is often used to provide a suitable known resistance R_3, in the bridge circuit. The internal arrangement is shown in the diagram. Resistance coils are wound with manganin or constantan wire to minimize changes in resistance with temperature. The free ends of each resistance coil are soldered to heavy brass blocks which can be electrically connected by inserting brass plugs between them. Each plug in place provides a low-resistance path across a resistance coil and thus effectively removes the coil from a circuit. Each plug removed places a coil in the circuit. The resistance between the terminals of the box is the sum of the resistances of all coils whose plugs are removed.

QUESTIONS

Group A

1. State Ohm's law (a) verbally, (b) mathematically.
2. What is the mathematical expression for Ohm's law as it applies to a part of a circuit which does not contain a source of emf?
3. What is the identifying characteristic of a series circuit?
4. State the three cardinal rules for circuits in which resistances are in series.
5. Define a parallel circuit.
6. What change occurs in the total resistance of a circuit as additional resistances are added (a) in series, (b) in parallel?
7. State the three cardinal rules for circuits in which resistances are connected in parallel.
8. (a) What is the usual relationship between resistance and temperature of metallic conductors? (b) Is this true of all conducting materials in general?
9. How does the resistance of a conductor vary with its length?
10. What is the relationship between the resistance of a conductor and its cross-sectional area?
11. Define the resistivity constant, rho, which appears in the mathematical expression for the Laws of Resistance.
12. Demonstrate that resistivity, rho, has the dimensions "ohm-centimeter."

Group B   13. Explain why the fall of potential, which appears across the internal resistance of a source of emf when a current is in the circuit, is always opposite in sign to the emf of the source.

14. What condition must be assumed in order to determine the emf of a battery by placing a voltmeter across it?

15. Why are lamps in a house-lighting circuit not connected in series?

16. What would happen if a 6-volt lamp and a 120-volt lamp were connected in parallel across a 120-volt circuit?

17. Draw a diagram of an electric circuit which would be classed as a simple network. Include the internal resistance of the source of emf. Assign values to all resistances and to the source of emf, and be prepared to analyze your network for the class.

18. Explain how the voltmeter-ammeter method is used for measuring resistance.

19. Why is the voltmeter-ammeter method not a particularly precise way to measure resistance?

20. In the laboratory form of the Wheatstone bridge, in Fig. 17-17, resistors R_1 and R_2 are lengths of wire. Why can we use the lengths of wire rather than their actual resistances in determining the unknown resistance once the bridge is balanced?

21. Lamps **A**, **B**, and **C** have equal resistances and are connected in series-parallel across an appropriate source of emf, **A** being in series with the parallel combination of **B** and **C**. (a) Draw the circuit diagram. (b) Discuss the relative brightness of the three lamps. (c) If **C** burns out, what change in relative brightness occurs in the remaining lamps. Explain.

PROBLEMS   (Refer to Appendix Tables 20 and 21)

Group A   1. A resistance of 18 ohms is connected across a 4.5-volt battery. What is the current in the circuit?

2. The load across a 12-volt battery consists of a series combination of three resistance R_1, R_2, and R_3, which are 15 ohms, 21 ohms, and 24 ohms respectively. (a) Draw the circuit diagram. (b) What is the total resistance of the load? (c) What is the magnitude of the circuit current?

3. What is the potential difference across each of the three resistances of Problem 2?

4. A small lamp is designed to draw $30\bar{0}$ ma in a 6.0-v circuit. What is the resistance of the lamp filament?

5. Resistances R_1 of 2 ohms and R_2 of 4 ohms are connected in series across a combination of 1.5-volt dry cells. An ammeter in the circuit reads 0.5 a. (a) What potential difference is applied across the circuit by the battery? (b) If the continuous current of each cell is limited to 0.25 a, how many cells are used and how are they arranged? (c) Draw the circuit diagram.

6. The resistance of an electric lamp filament is $23\overline{0}$ ohms. The lamp is switched on when the line voltage is 115 volts. What current is in the lamp circuit?

7. If the line voltage of Problem 6 rises to $12\overline{0}$ volts, what current is in the lamp circuit?

8. What would be the filament resistance of a lamp designed to draw the same current as the lamp in Problem 6 but in a 230-volt circuit?

9. Prove algebraically that the equivalent resistance of two resistances, R_1 and R_2, connected in parallel is:

$$R_{eq} = \frac{R_1 R_2}{R_1 + R_2}$$

10. Two resistances, one 12 ohms and the other 18 ohms, are connected in parallel. What is the equivalent resistance of the parallel combination?

11. Solve the following expression algebraically for R_{eq}:

$$\frac{1}{R_{eq}} = \frac{1}{R_1} + \frac{1}{R_2} + \frac{1}{R_3}$$

12. Three resistances of 12 ohms each are connected in parallel. What is the equivalent resistance?

13. (a) What potential difference must be applied across the parallel combination of resistances in Problem 12 to produce a total current of 1.5 amperes? (b) What is the current in each branch?

14. A 3.0-ohm, a 5.0-ohm, and an 8.0-ohm resistance are connected in parallel. What is the equivalent resistance?

15. A 4.0-ohm resistance, R_1, and a 6.0-ohm resistance, R_2, are connected in parallel across a 6.0-volt battery. (a) Draw the circuit diagram. (b) What is the total current in the circuit? (c) What is the current in R_1? (d) in R_2?

16. A 24-volt lamp has a resistance of 8.0 ohms. What resistance must be placed in series with it, if it is to be used on a 117-volt line?

17. At 20°C, $10\overline{0}$ m of No. 18 gauge copper wire has a resistance of 2.059 ohms. What is the resistance of $50\overline{0}$ m of this wire?

18. The diameter of the copper wire in Problem 17 is 1.024 mm. What is the resistance of $10\overline{0}$ m of No. 30 gauge copper wire which has a diameter of 0.2546 mm?

19. What is the resistance of 125 m of No. 20 gauge aluminum wire at 20°C?

20. No. 24 gauge German silver wire has a diameter of 0.511 mm at 20°C. How many centimeters are needed to make a resistance spool of $10\overline{0}$ ohms?

21. Three cells of a storage battery, each with a resistance of 0.0100 ohm and an emf of 2.20 volts, are connected in series with a load resistance of 3.27 ohms. (a) Draw the circuit diagram. (b) Determine

Group B

the current in the circuit. (c) What is the potential difference across the load?

22. Two identical dry cells connected in series provide an emf of 3.1 volts. When a load of 5.8 ohms is connected across the battery an ammeter in the external circuit reads 0.50 ampere. Find the internal resistance of each cell.

23. A load connected across a 12.0-volt battery consists of the resistance R_1, 40.0 ohms, in series with the parallel combination of R_2 and R_3, 30.0 ohms and 60.0 ohms respectively. (a) Draw the circuit diagram. (b) What is the total current in the circuit? (c) What is the potential difference across R_1? (d) What is the current in the R_2 branch?

24. A 6.0-ohm, a 9.0-ohm, and an 18.0-ohm resistance are connected in parallel and the combination is connected across a battery having an internal resistance of 0.10 ohm and an emf of 6.2 volts. (a) Draw the circuit diagram and the equivalent circuit. (b) Determine the total current in the circuit. (c) What is the potential difference across the load? (d) What is the current in each of the three load resistances?

25. Resistors R_1, R_2, and R_3 have resistances of 15.0 ohms, 9.0 ohms, and 8.0 ohms respectively. R_1 and R_2 are in series and the combination is in parallel with R_3 to form the load across two 6-volt batteries connected in parallel. (a) Draw the circuit diagram. (b) Determine the total current in the circuit. (c) What is the current in the R_3 branch? (d) What is the potential drop across R_2?

26. A battery with an internal resistance of 1.5 ohms is connected across a load consisting of two resistances, 3.0 ohms and 3.5 ohms in series. The potential difference across the 3.0 ohm resistance is 9.0 volts. What is the emf of the battery?

27. Two resistances, R_1 and R_2, of 12.0 ohms and 6.00 ohms are connected in parallel and this combination is connected in series with a 6.25-ohm resistance R_3, and a battery which has an internal resistance of 0.250 ohm. The current in R_2, the 6.00-ohm resistance, is $80\overline{0}$ milliamperes. (a) Draw the circuit diagram. (b) Determine the emf of the battery.

28. The resistance of a uniform copper wire 50.0 meters long and 1.15 mm in diameter is 0.830 ohm at 20°C. What is the resistivity of the copper at this temperature?

29. In determining the resistance of a component of an electric circuit by the voltmeter-ammeter method, the voltmeter reads 1.4 volts and the ammeter reads 0.28 ampere. What is the resistance of the component?

30. (a) Reduce the accompanying circuit to its series equivalent circuit. (b) Determine the potential difference across the 1-Ω resistance.

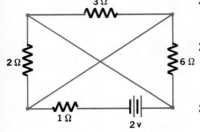

Chapter 18

Heating And Chemical Effects

HEATING EFFECTS

Basic concerns of physics are with the relationships between objects, time, and space. Work, power, and energy are important physical concepts involved in these relationships. We have described energy as the ability to do work and have measured it in units of work and heat. To maintain an electric current, energy must be supplied by the source of emf. Chemical energy, which can be thought of as the potential energy of chemical bonds, is transformed into electric energy in an electrochemical cell. Thus a moving charge acquires energy within the cell, or other source of emf, and expends this energy in the electric circuit.

In Chapter 16 we learned that one joule of work is done when one coulomb of charge is moved through a potential difference of one volt. One coulomb of charge transferred in one second constitutes one ampere of current. Thus,

$$W = VIt \qquad \text{(Equation 1)}$$

Within a source of emf, the charge is moved in opposition to the potential difference, and work W is done *by the source* upon the electrons. As the charge moves through the circuit in response to the potential difference across the circuit, work W is done *by the electrons* upon the components of the circuit. It is this electric energy, expended in the external circuit, that is available to perform useful work.

We can observe the work done by an electric current in a variety of ways. If a lamp is in the circuit, part of the work appears as light; if an electric motor is in the circuit, part of the

18.1 Energy of an electric current

General Electric—Nela Park

Light and heat appear as part of the work done by the electrons passing through the filament of this incandescent bulb.

439

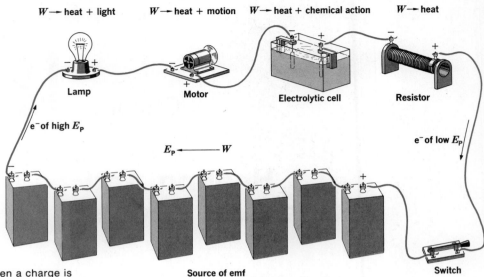

$W \rightarrow$ heat + light $W \rightarrow$ heat + motion $W \rightarrow$ heat + chemical action $W \rightarrow$ heat

Lamp   Motor   Electrolytic cell   Resistor

e^- of high E_P

$E_P \longleftarrow W$

e^- of low E_P

Source of emf

Switch

18-1   Work is done when a charge is moved through a potential difference.

work appears as rotary motion; if an electroplating cell is in the circuit, part of the work promotes chemical action in the cell. In all cases, *part* of the work W appears as *heat* due to the inherent resistance of the circuit components. If an ordinary resistor comprises the circuit, *all* of the work goes to the production of heat, since no mechanical work or chemical work is done. See Fig. 18-1.

18.2 Energy conversion in resistance

Suppose short lengths of No. 30 gauge copper wire and German silver wire are connected in series and placed in the circuit shown in Fig. 18-2. When the switch is closed the German silver wire may become red hot and melt. The copper wire will become warm, but is less likely to melt. The melting point of German silver is about 30C° higher than that of copper, but its resistivity is nearly 20 times higher than that of copper. Since the two wires were in series, the same magnitude of current was in each. We may infer that *a greater quantity of electric energy was converted to heat in the wire having the higher resistance.*

Now let us connect a single piece of No. 30 copper wire in the circuit in place of the copper-German silver link. When the switch is closed, the copper wire may warm to a red heat and even melt. Since the resistance of this copper wire is less than that of the copper-German silver link, the current in the circuit is higher. We may infer that *the quantity of electric energy converted to heat in the wire is greater when the current is increased.* We may reason also that *the longer the switch is closed* (assuming the wire does not melt), *the greater will be the quantity of electric energy converted to heat.*

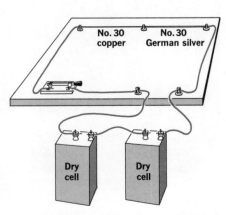

No. 30 copper   No. 30 German silver

Dry cell   Dry cell

18-2   A circuit for studying the heating effect of an electric current.

Bethlehem Steel Corp.

A 150 ton capacity high power electric furnace capable of producing steel in three hours. Since temperature and atmosphere can be closely controlled in an electric furnace, it is ideal for producing steel to exacting specifications.

From Ohm's law, the potential difference across the resistance of an external circuit is the product of the current in the circuit and the resistance of the circuit.

$$V = IR$$

Substituting this product for V in Equation 1, we have an expression for the energy transferred to the resistance of a circuit.

$$W = I^2 Rt \qquad \text{(Equation 2)}$$

18.3 Joule's law

James Prescott Joule, the English physicist who first studied the relationship between heat and work, also pioneered the quantitative study of the heating effect of an electric current. From the results of his experiments he formulated the generalization known as *Joule's law*: *The heat developed in a conductor is directly proportional to the resistance of the conductor, the square of the current, and the time the current is maintained.*

Since all of the work done by a current in a resistance appears as heat, the electric energy expended in the resistance is directly proportional to the heat energy that appears.

$$W = JQ \qquad \text{(Equation 3)}$$

where W is the electric energy in joules, J is the proportionality constant we have known previously as the mechanical equivalent of heat (4.19 joules/calorie), and Q is the quantity of heat given up in calories.

Solving Equation 3 for Q we have an expression for Joule's law.

$$Q = \frac{W}{J} \qquad \text{(Equation 4)}$$

By substituting the expression for W in Equation 2 into Equation 4, a useful form of Joule's law evolves from which the quantity of heat developed in the resistance of an electric circuit can be calculated directly.

$$Q = \frac{I^2 Rt}{J} \qquad \text{(Equation 5)}$$

Observe that the quantity of heat Q is expressed in kilocalories by introducing the conversion factor $kcal/10^3$ cal.

$$\frac{I^2 Rt}{J} = \frac{(a \times \Omega)(a \times sec)}{j/cal} \times \frac{kcal}{cal}$$
$$= \frac{v \times c \times kcal}{j} = \frac{j \times kcal}{j}$$
$$= kcal$$

The following example illustrates an application of Joule's law.

Example

The heating element in a percolator has a resistance of 22.0 ohms and is designed for use across a 117-volt circuit. How long will it take to heat 1.00 kg of water at 20.0°C to the boiling point, 100.0°C, assuming no loss of heat to surroundings?

Solution

The problem is concerned basically with the heating effect of an electric current, Joule's law. However, the specific heat capacity of water is a factor in determining the time of the circuit operation. The basic equation is

$$Q = \frac{I^2 Rt}{J}$$

The quantity of heat Q required to warm a given mass of water through a change of temperature ΔT is

$$Q = mc\Delta T$$

From Ohm's law: $I = \dfrac{V}{R}$

Substituting for Q and I in the basic equation,

$$mc\Delta T = \frac{V^2 Rt}{R^2 J} = \frac{V^2 t}{RJ}$$

We now have an expression which makes use of the quantities given in the problem. Since time is required, we will solve this expression for t yielding our working equation.

$$t = \frac{mc \Delta TRJ}{V^2}$$

Substituting and solving:

$$t = \frac{1.00 \text{ kg} \times 1 \text{ kcal/kg C}° \times 80.0 \text{ C}° \times 22.0 \text{ }\Omega \times 4.19 \text{ j/cal} \times 10^3 \text{ cal/kcal}}{(117 \text{ v})^2}$$

$$t = 538 \frac{\Omega \text{ j}}{\text{v}^2} = 538 \text{ sec}$$

Dimensional analysis: $\dfrac{\Omega \text{ j}}{\text{v}^2} = \dfrac{\text{v}}{\text{a}} \times \dfrac{\text{v c}}{\text{v}^2} = \dfrac{\text{c}}{\text{a}} = \dfrac{\text{a sec}}{\text{a}} = \text{sec}$

18.4 Power in electric circuits

Power is defined as the rate of doing work. The symbol for power is P, and in the MKS system the unit of power is the watt (w), a rate of one joule of work per second. In electric circuits, it is convenient to think of power *as the rate at which electric energy is delivered to the circuit.*

$$P = \frac{W}{t} \qquad \text{(Equation 6)}$$

Recalling Equation 1 of Section 18.1, $W = VIt$, let us solve this expression for W/t.

$$\frac{W}{t} = VI \qquad \text{(Equation 7)}$$

Combining Equations 6 and 7 yields a basic power equation for electric circuits.

$$P = VI \qquad \text{(Equation 8)}$$

If I is in amperes and V is in volts, then P is in watts.

$$P = VI = \frac{\text{joule}}{\text{coulomb}} \times \frac{\text{coulomb}}{\text{second}}$$

$$P = \frac{\text{joule}}{\text{second}} = \text{watt}$$

By Ohm's law, the potential difference across a load resistance in a circuit is equal to the product IR_L. Substituting for V in Equation 8,

$$P_L = I \times IR_L$$

or

$$P_L = I^2 R_L \qquad \text{(Equation 9)}$$

This shows us that *the power expended by a current in a resistance is proportional to the square of the current in the resistance.*

Similarly, the power dissipated in the internal resistance of a source of emf is

$$P_r = I^2 r \qquad \text{(Equation 10)}$$

The total power consumed in a circuit must be the sum of the power dissipated within the source of emf and the power expended in the load of the external circuit.

$$P_T = I_T{}^2 R_T = I_T{}^2 (R_L + r)$$

Recall that

$$E = I_T (R_L + r)$$

Therefore

$$P_T = I_T E \qquad \text{(Equation 11)}$$

There are instances in which the current in a circuit is unknown or of no interest. Power can then be expressed in terms of voltage and resistance since, by Ohm's law,

$$I_T = \frac{E}{R_T}$$

Substituting for I_T in Equation 11, we get

$$P_T = \frac{E^2}{R_T} \qquad \text{(Equation 12)}$$

and for the external circuit,

$$P_L = \frac{V^2}{R_L} \qquad \text{(Equation 13)}$$

18.5 Maximum transfer of power

There are some electric-circuit applications in which the transfer of maximum power to the load is of great importance. An example is the circuit of the starter motor of an automobile engine. To operate the starter, a large amount of electric energy must be supplied by a battery during a short interval of time. Other less familiar examples are the transfer of audio-frequency power from the output stage of a radio to the speaker, and the transfer of radio-frequency power from the transmission line to the antenna.

Consider the circuits of Fig. 18-3 to determine the circum-

18-3 In which circuit is the most power expended in the load?

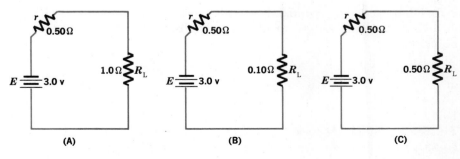

(A) (B) (C)

stances under which maximum power from a given source of emf is expended in the load. Observe that in all three circuits the same source of emf is used, and that loads greater than, less than, and equal to the internal resistance of the source are supplied. In each circuit I_T, P_L, P_r and P_T can be determined by inspection, using equations derived in Section 18.4. These values are listed below for comparison.

Circuit **A**	Circuit **B**	Circuit **C**
$I_T = 2.0$ a	5.0 a	3.0 a
$P_L = 4.0$ w	2.5 w	4.5 w
$P_r = 2.0$ w	12.5 w	4.5 w
$P_T = 6.0$ w	15.0 w	9.0 w

From such calculations it can be shown that the power expended in the load of circuit **C**, 4.5 w, is the maximum that can be transferred from this source of emf. *Maximum power is transferred to the load when the load resistance is equal to the internal resistance of the source of emf.* The source and the load are said to be *matched*. In circuit **B**, where the load resistance is less than the internal resistance of the source, most of the power generated is dissipated as heat in the source itself. This power is wasted. In circuit **A**, where the load resistance is greater than the internal resistance of the source, little power is lost in the internal resistance of the source. However, the power expended in the load is not as high as in circuit **C**.

An operating circuit which requires 100 watts of power converts 100 joules of energy per second. Obviously, the longer this circuit continues to operate, the larger will be the total quantity of energy transformed. Since

18.6 Purchasing electric energy

$$\textbf{power} = \frac{\textbf{energy}}{\textbf{time}}$$

then

$$\textbf{energy} = \textbf{power} \times \textbf{time}$$

In the MKS system, current, potential difference, and resistance are measured in amperes, volts, and ohms respectively; power is expressed in watts, and time in seconds. The energy can be expressed in *watt seconds* (w sec). The MKS unit, the watt second, is inconveniently small for electric energy sold on a commercial scale. For example, a 100-watt lamp operated for 1 hour transforms 3.6×10^5 watt seconds of energy. By dividing by 3.6×10^3 sec/hr we can convert this quantity to 1×10^2 w hr. By dividing again by 1×10^3 w/kw we have 1×10^{-1} kw hr (0.1 kilowatt hour), a more practical unit of electric energy.

Observe the magnitude of this combined conversion constant:

$$\mathbf{kw\ hr} \times \frac{10^3\ \mathbf{w}}{\mathbf{kw}} \times \frac{3.6 \times 10^3\ \mathbf{sec}}{\mathbf{hr}} = 3.6 \times 10^6\ \mathbf{w\ sec}$$

A kilowatt hour of electric energy usually costs between 1 and 6 cents. The cost of electric energy is calculated in the example which follows:

Example

A small electric furnace connected across a 117-v line expends 2.0 kw of power. (a) What current is in the circuit? (b) What is the resistance of the furnace? (c) What is the cost of operation for 24 hr at $0.050 per kw hr? (d) What quantity of heat, in kcal, is developed in 1.0 hr?

Solution

(a) The potential difference across the furnace and the power expended in the furnace are given. We can find the current since

$$P = IV \text{ and, therefore, } I = \frac{P}{V}$$

$$I = \frac{2.0\ \text{kw}}{117\ \text{v}} \times \frac{10^3\ \text{w}}{\text{kw}}$$

$I = 17$ a, the current in the circuit

(b) Knowing both the current in the furnace and the potential drop across it, we can apply Ohm's law to find the resistance.

$$R = \frac{V}{I} = \frac{117\ \text{v}}{17\ \text{a}}$$

$R = 6.9\ \Omega$, the resistance of the furnace

(c) We are given the power requirement of the furnace, the time of operation, and the cost per kw hr.

$$\text{cost} = \text{kw hr} \times \frac{\text{cost}}{\text{kw hr}} = \frac{2.0\ \text{kw} \times 24\ \text{hr} \times \$0.050}{\text{kw hr}}$$

$\text{cost} = \$2.40$, the cost for 24 hr operation

(d) We are given the time of operation and we have found the current and the resistance.

$$Q = \frac{I^2 R t}{J}$$

$$Q = \frac{(17\ \text{a})^2 \times 6.9\ \Omega \times 1.0\ \text{hr}}{4.19\ \text{j/cal}} \times \frac{3.6 \times 10^3\ \text{sec}}{\text{hr}} \times \frac{\text{kcal}}{10^3\ \text{cal}}$$

$Q = 1.7 \times 10^3$ kcal, the heat in 1 hr

(Proof of answer unit is left to the student.)

QUESTIONS

1. State four ways in which the work done by an electric current in a load may be observed, and name the kind of load responsible in each instance.
2. Equal lengths of silver wire and iron wire having the same diameters are connected in series to form the external circuit across a dry cell. Which wire becomes hotter? Explain.
3. One length of platinum wire is connected across the terminals of a single dry cell. A second platinum wire, identical with the first, is connected across a battery of two dry cells in series. Which wire becomes hotter? Explain.
4. State Joule's law.
5. How may electric power be defined?
6. (a) What change occurs in the heating effect of an electric circuit if the source of emf remains the same but the total resistance is cut in half? (b) Devise a simple circuit problem to prove your answer.
7. If a battery is short-circuited by means of a heavy copper wire, its temperature rises. Explain.
8. Under what circumstance is the power expended in a load the maximum the source is capable of delivering?
9. Suppose you have just paid the electric utility bill for your home. (a) What did you purchase? (b) In what units was it measured?
10. What change occurs in the resistance in the external circuit connected to a source of emf when the load across the source is increased?

11. Demonstrate that Q in Joule's law can be expressed in kilocalories.
12. Suggest a reason why it is not safe to place a coin behind a fuse in a house-lighting circuit to avoid "blowing" the fuse.
13. Two resistors of equal resistance were originally connected in parallel. By what factor does their combined resistance change when they are connected in series instead?
14. Why is it important that an automobile battery have a very low internal resistance?
15. What special characteristics should a toaster wire have?
16. Express the rate of energy dissipation in a resistance in terms of (a) current and potential difference, (b) current and resistance, (c) potential difference and resistance.

PROBLEMS

1. The current in an electric heater is 7.5 amperes. What quantity of electric charge flows through the heater in 15 minutes?
2. Determine the current in a lamp circuit if 4800 coulombs of electric charge flow through the lamp in 25 minutes.

3. An electric lamp connected across a 117-volt line has a current of 0.52 ampere in it. How much work is done in 12 minutes?

4. What is the approximate wattage rating of the lamp in Problem 3?

5. How many kilocalories of heat are produced by a resistance of 55 ohms connected across a 110-volt line for $1\bar{0}$ minutes?

6. A heating coil across a 117-volt line draws 9.00 amperes. How many kilocalories are liberated if the heater operates for 30.0 minutes?

7. The heating element of an electric iron has a resistance of 24 ohms and draws a current of 5.0 amperes. How many kilocalories are developed if the iron is used for 45 minutes?

8. A battery has an emf of 26.4 volts and an internal resistance of 0.300 ohm. A load of 3.00 ohms is connected across the battery. How much power is (a) delivered to the load, (b) dissipated in the battery?

9. (a) To what value would the load resistance of Problem 8 have to be changed in order that maximum power is delivered to the load using the same source of emf? (b) What is the magnitude of the maximum power delivered to this load? (c) What power is now dissipated in the battery?

10. A wire for use in an electric heater has a resistance of 5.25 Ω/m. What length of this wire is needed to make a heating element for a toaster which will draw 8.70 a across a $12\bar{0}$-v line?

Group B 11. If electric energy costs 5.0¢ per kw hr, what is the cost of heating 4.6 kg of water from 25°C to the boiling point, assuming no energy is wasted?

12. A percolator with a heating coil of 20.0 ohms resistance is connected across a $12\bar{0}$-volt line. (a) What quantity of heat is liberated per second? (b) If it contains $50\bar{0}$ g of water at 22.5°C, how much time is required to heat the water to boiling, assuming no loss of heat?

13. An electric iron has a mass of 1.50 kg. The heating element is a 2.00-m length of No. 24 gauge nichrome wire. What time is required for the iron to be heated from 20.0°C to $15\bar{0}$°C when connected across a 115-volt line, assuming no loss of heat?

14. An electric hotplate draws 10.0 amperes on a $12\bar{0}$-volt circuit. In 7.00 minutes the hotplate can heat $60\bar{0}$ g of water at 20.0°C to boiling, and boil away 60.0 g of water. What is the efficiency of the hotplate?

15. Each coil of a plug-type resistance box is capable of dissipating heat at the rate of 4.0 watts. What is the maximum voltage that should be applied across (a) the 2.0-ohm coil, (b) the 20.0-ohm coil?

16. A dial-type rheostat of 10.0 ohms resistance is capable of dissipating heat at the rate of 4.0 watts. (a) What is the maximum current the rheostat can carry? (b) What is the maximum voltage that can be applied across it?

17. How many meters of No. 30 gauge nichrome wire are needed to form the heating element of a 100̄0-watt electric iron, used on a 117-volt line?
18. A lamp operates continuously across a 117-v line dissipating 10̄0 w. How many electrons flow through the lamp per day?

ELECTROLYSIS

The close relationship between chemical energy and electric energy has already been discussed. Spontaneous reactions which involve the transfer of electrons from one reactant to the other were described in Chapter 17. Such reactions can be sources of emf. In the electrochemical cell, chemical energy is converted to electric energy while the spontaneous electron-transfer reaction proceeds. The products of the reaction have less energy than did the reactants.

Similar reactions *that are not spontaneous* can be forced to occur if electric energy is supplied from an external source, as in charging a storage battery. In such forced reactions, the products have more chemical energy than did the reactants. This means that electric energy from the external source of emf is transformed into chemical energy while the reaction proceeds. An arrangement in which a forced electron-transfer reaction occurs is known as an *electrolytic cell.*

The basic requirements for an electrolytic cell are shown in Fig. 18-4. The conducting solution contains an electrolyte, furnishing positively and negatively charged ions. Two electrodes are immersed in the electrolytic solution. The negative terminal of a battery or other source of direct current is connected to one electrode, forming the *cathode* of the cell; the positive terminal of the source is connected to the other electrode to form the *anode* of the cell.

When the circuit is closed, the cathode becomes negatively charged and the anode positively charged. Positive ions migrate to the cathode, where they acquire electrons of high potential energy from the cathode and are discharged. Negatively charged ions migrate to the anode and are discharged by giving up electrons of low potential energy to the anode. Note that the electrode reactions in electrochemical cells, presented in Chapter 17, are just the reverse of those occurring in an electrolytic cell.

The loss of electrons by the cathode and the acquisition of a like number of electrons by the anode is, in effect, the conduction of an electric charge through the cell. *The conduction of an electric charge through a soultion of an electrolyte or through a fused ionic compound, together with the resulting chemical changes, is called* **electrolysis**.

18.7 Electrolytic cells

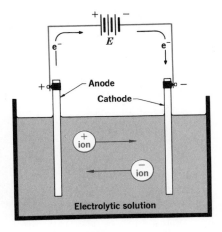

18-4 The essential components of an electrolytic cell.

Ken Chen

The principles of electrolysis are illustrated in this laboratory model of an electrochemical cell.

The end result of electrolysis depends on the nature of the electrolyte, the kinds of electrodes, and to some extent, the emf of the source. Electrolytic cells are useful in decomposing compounds, plating metals, and refining metals.

18.8 Electroplating metals

Suppose positively charged metallic ions, such as copper(II) ions, Cu^{++}, or silver ions, Ag^+, are in solution in an electrolytic cell whose anode consists of that same metal. The metallic ions acquire electrons from the cathode and from metallic atoms (at the cathode) when a small potential difference is placed across the cell.

$$Cu^{++} + 2e^- \rightarrow Cu^0 \quad \text{(Cathode reaction)}$$

or

$$Ag^+ + e^- \rightarrow Ag^0 \quad \text{(Cathode reaction)}$$

The copper or silver atoms plate out on the cathode surface.

This is the basic action which makes an electrolytic cell useful for the *electrolytic deposition* or *electroplating* of one metal on the surface of another. The metallic object to be plated is used as the cathode of the cell. The conducting solution contains a salt of the metal to be plated out; for example, copper(II) sulfate or silver nitrate. The anode consists of the plating metal, copper or silver for the examples given.

The metallic atoms of the anode give up electrons (to the anode) and form metallic ions which replace those being plated out. Metallic ions pass into solution from the anode at the same rate as similar metallic ions leave the solution to form the plate. Thus the anode is used up in the plating process to maintain the concentration of metallic ions in the electrolytic solution.

$$Cu^0 - 2e^- \rightarrow Cu^{++} \quad \text{(Anode reaction)}$$

or

$$Ag^0 - e^- \rightarrow Ag^+ \quad \text{(Anode reaction)}$$

A simplified diagram of an electrolytic cell illustrating its use for copper plating is shown in Fig. 18-5.

Metallic copper of the highest purity is required for electric conductors. Even very small amounts of impurities in copper cause a marked increase in its electric resistance. These impurities can be removed almost completely from the copper by electrolysis. For this purpose, an electroplating cell is used in which the anode is composed of impure copper. During electrolysis, refined copper is plated onto the cathode made of pure copper. This electrolytically refined copper metal deposited on the cathode is more than 99.9% pure.

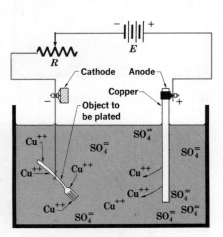

18-5 An electrolytic cell used for copper plating.

Michael Faraday investigated the distribution of charge on isolated bodies and the nature of electric fields. He also performed experiments on the conduction of electric charge by solutions. Faraday found that a current which deposited a half-penny-weight of silver in ten minutes would deposit one penny-weight of silver in twenty minutes. This discovery suggests an important relationship between the quantity of electricity which passes through an electrolytic cell and the quantity of a substance liberated by the chemical action.

Suppose we consider the quantitative significance of Faraday's discovery by imagining several cells connected in series and supplied by a source of emf. Each cell has a pair of inert platinum electrodes immersed in a water solution of an electrolyte. See Fig. 18-6. Each cell has a different electrolyte: cell No. **1** has sulfuric acid (hydrogen sulfate), cell No. **2** has silver nitrate, No. **3** has copper(II) sulfate, and No. **4** has aluminum sulfate. Since this is a *thought experiment* we need not be concerned with the possibility of running out of ions in the cells. The cells are in series, so a certain constant current in the circuit for a given time interval signifies that *the same quantity of charge has passed through each cell.*

Hydrogen, silver, copper, and aluminum are liberated at the respective cathodes. The quantity of each liberated substance must be proportional to the quantity of charge that passed through each cell; that is, to the product of the current and the time.

Faraday's first law: *The mass of an element deposited or liberated during electrolysis is proportional to the quantity of charge that passes.*

$$m \propto Q$$

where

$$Q = It$$

By varying either current or time interval, we merely vary the

18.9 Faraday's laws of electrolysis

The Royal Institution

Michael Faraday, the English scientist who formulated the laws of electrolysis and for whom the unit of electric capacitance is named.

18-6 Electrolytic cells in series must have the same magnitude of current for the same length of time.

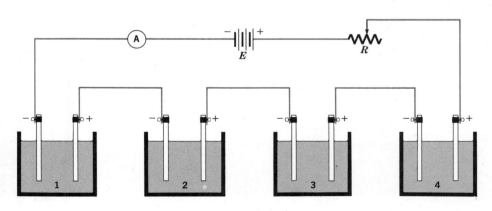

Table 18-1   ELECTROCHEMICAL EQUIVALENTS

Element	g-at wt (g)	Ionic Charge (oxidation state)	z (g/c)
aluminum	27.0	3	0.0000932
copper	63.5	2	0.0003294
hydrogen	1.01	1	0.0000104
silver	108	1	0.0011179

Russell Dian

A workman holds the silver-coated master disc of a phonograph record. This disc will be immersed in the electroplating tanks at the right where a coating of nickel will be applied. A series of such processes is required to produce a finished master disc.

quantity of charge passing through each cell. By Faraday's first law, the masses of the elements deposited or liberated vary accordingly. It follows that whatever the charge through the cells, the relationship between the quantities of the elements deposited remains *constant*. Such quantities of the elements may be said to be *electrochemically equivalent*. The **electrochemical equivalent**, *z, of an element is the mass of the element, in grams, deposited or liberated by 1 coulomb of electricity*. See Table 18-1. A more extensive table of electrochemical equivalents of common elements is given in Appendix B, Table 19.

Suppose we allow the charge to flow through our cells until 1 g of hydrogen has been liberated in cell No. **1**. We would find 108 g of silver deposited in No. **2**, 31.8 g of copper in No. **3**, and 9 g of aluminum in No. **4**.

Using the information, we can make two very interesting and important observations. *First*, the hydrogen ion, H^+, and silver ion, Ag^+, are deficient by 1 electron and carry 1 unit of positive charge. The elements hydrogen and silver are said to have an ionic charge of 1, which means they lose 1 electron per atom in a chemical action. Similarly the charge of the copper(II) ion, Cu^{++}, is 2 and that of the aluminum ion, Al^{+++}, is 3. *For a given quantity of charge, the quantity of each element deposited or liberated, in grams, is proportional to the ratio of its gram-atomic weight (g-at wt) to its ionic charge*. This ratio is known as the **chemical equivalent** of an element.

$$\text{chemical equivalent} = \frac{\text{g-at wt}}{\text{ionic charge}}$$

Thus, the chemical equivalents of hydrogen, silver, copper, and aluminum are respectively 1, 108, 31.8, and 9 grams.

Second, the product of the current in amperes, and the time in seconds during which the cells operated to deposit the chemical equivalents of these elements, is found to be approximately 96,500 coulombs. This product is a constant and is called a *faraday*:

1 faraday = 96,500 coulombs

*One **faraday**, 96,500 coulombs, is the quantity of electricity required* *to deposit one chemical equivalent of an element.* This unit has many significant applications in electrolysis and electrochemistry.

Faraday's second law: *The mass of an element deposited or liberated during electrolysis is proportional to the chemical equivalent of the element.*

$$m \propto \textbf{chemical equivalent}$$

From our definition of the electrochemical equivalent of an element, we can see that

$$z = \frac{\textbf{chemical equivalent}}{\textbf{faraday}}$$

and has the dimensions g/c. The electrochemical equivalent z is a constant for a given element, but of course is different for different elements.

We can combine Faraday's Laws of Electrolysis into the following equation:

$$m = zIt$$

where m is the mass in grams of an element deposited or liberated, z is the electrochemical equivalent in g/c of the element, I is the current in amperes, and t is the time in seconds.

Faraday's laws give us a precise method of measuring the quantity of electricity flowing through a circuit. If we know the length of time the electricity flows, we can determine the average current magnitude as shown in Fig. 18-7. A platinum dish is connected with the negative terminal of a source of about 2 volts emf and then the dish is partly filled with a solution of silver nitrate. A platinum spiral rod is connected to the positive terminal of the source of current and dipped into the silver solution.

One coulomb of electricity (one ampere second) flowing through such a silver solution will deposit on the walls of the dish 0.001118 g of silver. If the average current in the circuit is one ampere for one hour, 3600 coulombs will deposit 4.025 g of silver. From the mass of the silver deposited the number of coulombs of electricity can be determined with good accuracy.

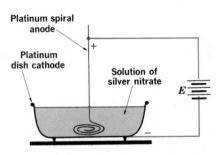

18-7 A silver coulombmeter.

QUESTIONS

Group A

1. How can electron-transfer reactions that are not spontaneous be forced to occur?
2. What is an electrolytic cell?
3. What may be the effect of the conduction of electric charge through a fused ionic compound?
4. What are the basic requirements for a silver-plating cell?
5. Why is electrolytically refined copper used to make electric

        conductors?

6. State Faraday's Laws of Electrolysis.
7. What part of a silver coulombmeter is used as the cathode?

Group B 8. Distinguish between an electrochemical cell and an electrolytic cell.
9. Compare the cathode and anode reactions in an electrolytic cell to the corresponding electrode reactions in an electrochemical cell.
10. The atomic weight of aluminum is 27 and of gold is 197; both ions have a charge of 3. Which has the higher electrochemical equivalent?
11. Demonstrate that the mass of an element deposited according to Faraday's law can be expressed in grams.
12. How could you define the ampere in relation to Faraday's laws and the silver coulombmeter?

PROBLEMS

Group A 1. How much silver can be deposited by a steady current of 0.500 ampere in 8.00 minutes?
2. An electroplating cell connected across a source of direct current for 15.0 minutes deposits 0.750 g of copper. What is the average current in the cell?
3. How many hours are required for an electrolytic cell to liberate 0.160 g of oxygen using a steady current of 0.300 ampere?
4. A water-decomposition cell is maintained in continuous operation with a constant current of 25.0 a. How much hydrogen is recovered per day?
5. How many hours would it take to plate 25.0 g of nickel onto an automobile bumper if the current in the plating bath is 3.40 a?

Group B 6. An electroysis-of-water cell is operated until 1 faraday of electricity has been passed. How many atoms of hydrogen are liberated?
7. (a) What magnitude of electric charge must pass through an electrolysis-of-water cell to liberate one g-at wt of hydrogen? (b) How much oxygen will be liberated during the same time?
8. How long will it take a current of 4.50 a to produce 1.00 liter of hydrogen by the electrolysis of water? Assume STP conditions.
9. Two coulombmeters are connected in series, one of silver and the other of an unknown metal which is known to form ions having a +3 charge. A constant current of 2.00 a is maintained in the coulombmeter circuit for 2.00 hr and 2.73 g of the unknown metal are deposited. How much silver is deposited?
10. What is the g-at wt of the unknown metal deposited in Problem 9?

FAR OUT

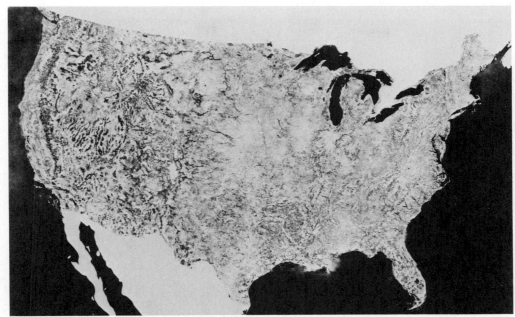

NASA

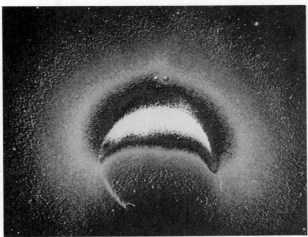

NASA

During the flight of Apollo 16 to the moon, astronaut John W. Young took a picture of the crescent earth with film that was sensitive to ultraviolet light (1216 Angstroms, or about one-third the wavelength of visible blue light). The halo of light around the Earth is due to the presence of hydrogen gas, which accompanies our planet in its journey around the sun. The significance of this ''geocorona'' is not yet fully understood. (The spike of light at the lower left of the picture is an auroral display over the south magnetic pole.)

This map of the United States was made by assembling 595 cloud-free black-and-white satellite photos, all of which were taken from the first American Resources Technology Satellite (ERTS-1) at an altitude of 912 kilometers. The images were assembled into a 10 x 16 foot montage by the Soil Conservation Service of the USDA.

Through space technology, a vast amount of new information is being gathered about the planet Earth. This information plays a key role in the wise management of the world's natural resources. Photos like the one at the top are providing vital data for the fields of geology, forestry, agriculture, water and land use.

Some space flights have revealed information not previously known about the planet Earth. An example is the ''geocorona'', a halo of hydrogen gas around the earth, revealed in the photograph to the left.

After a two-year journey from Earth, cameras aboard Pioneer 10 took this spectacular photo of Jupiter. The mysterious Red Spot (perhaps a violent storm in the giant planet's atmosphere) is partially visible at the left. Io, one of Jupiter's thirteen known moons, is at the right. Its shadow is clearly projected against the planet. This photo was transmitted over a distance of more than 500 million miles with power provided by on-board nuclear batteries. In 1986, Pioneer 10 will cross the orbit of Pluto and become the first object made by human beings to travel beyond the solar system.

NASA

Eight other planets and countless smaller or more diffuse objects move in orbits around the sun. Unmanned space vehicles are transmitting data about these objects that may yield clues to the history of the solar system—and perhaps to its future as well.

A hydrogen halo, similar to the one around the Earth, has also been found around comets. The composition of these wispy bodies has long been debated, but the mystery is slowly being solved through photos like the one at the bottom of this page.

NASA

The Comet Kohoutek on December 25, 1973, three days before its closest approach to the sun (about 19 million miles). The elongated halo is about 1.6 million miles in diameter. This photo was made with ultraviolet film during a space walk from Skylab, the huge American space laboratory.

The 1000-foot radar-radio telescope of the Arecibo Observatory in Puerto Rico. Besides mapping radio signals from spacecraft and natural celestial objects, the giant dish is also being used to search for clues of extraterrestrial beings and to transmit messages to possible listeners among the stars.

Meanwhile, back on Earth, scientists and technologists are developing ever larger and more sophisticated instruments, such as those shown at the left, in their reach for the stars. With techniques and tools like these, astrophysicists hope to come closer to answering the ultimate question of the origin and destiny of the universe itself. Did matter begin with a Big Bang and will it end in a gradual diffusion through endless reaches of space over eons of time? Or, will it, as some theorists suppose, collapse into a series of cataclysmic black holes (below)? Do such black holes already exist? Evidence is beginning to accumulate that they do.

Kitt Peak National Observatory

Helmut K. Wimmer

(Above) The four-meter reflecting telescope atop Kitt Peak Arizona was the first to photograph details in the atmosphere of the giant star Betelgeuse (right). Previously, no telescope was able to show even the largest and closest stars (other than the sun) as more than mere pinpoints of light.

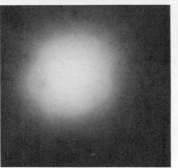

Kitt Peak National Observatory

(Above) A black hole in space as envisioned by artist H. K. Wimmer. Stars that have spent their fuel and ejected their orbital electrons may shrink into superdense masses that suck everything, even light, into irreversible oblivion.

A familiar probe in an unfamiliar setting. Scientist-astronaut Joseph P. Kerwin is giving an oral physical examination to astronaut Charles Conrad, Jr., aboard Skylab. Conrad is floating upside down in the zero-g environment of the space ship. (Or is it Kerwin who is upside down?) Note the floating piece of paper at the right.

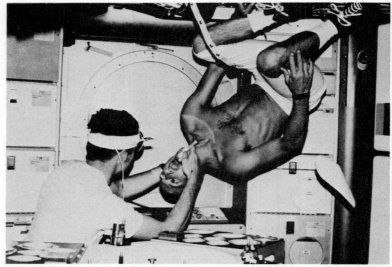

NASA

In the final analysis, the most important spinoff of the Space Age may turn out to be our better understanding of ourselves. The process of searching invariably reveals new information about the searcher. By probing for intelligent life forms in other parts of the universe, we may be better able to identify and apply the intelligence of earthbound life.

(Center) Two Applied Technology Satellites (ATS) in position for TV coverage of Alaska. Entertainment, health services, and education can be provided for any part of the world by these sophisticated space vehicles. (Bottom) The first hookup of two space ships with international crews took place on July 17, 1975. This successful American-Russian enterprise not only paved the way for future rescue operations in space but, perhaps more importantly, symbolized the increasing scientific cooperation between the two nations. As one of the participants in the linkup put it: "Like you, I want my children to be able to sleep peacefully."

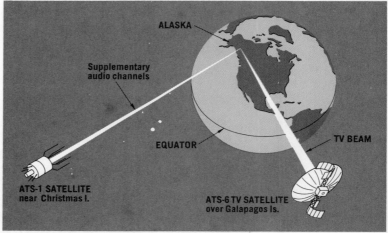

ALASKA

Supplementary audio channels

EQUATOR

TV BEAM

ATS-1 SATELLITE near Christmas I.

ATS-6 TV SATELLITE over Galapagos Is.

UNITED STATES

NASA

Chapter 19

Magnetic Effects

MAGNETISM

Today, physicists believe that all magnetic phenomena result from forces between electric charges in motion. Vast quantities of electric energy are now generated as a consequence of relative motion between electric conductors and magnetic fields. Electric energy is transformed into mechanical energy by relative motion between electric currents and magnetic fields. The function of many electric measuring instruments depends on the relationship between electricity and magnetism.

The basic theory of electric generators and motors is presented in Chapter 20. Electric measuring instruments are discussed later in this chapter. Before undertaking the study of magnetic effects of electric currents, we shall examine the magnetic properties of substances and learn something of the nature of magnetism and magnetic fields.

Deposits of a magnetic iron ore were discovered by the Greeks in a section of Turkey many centuries ago. The region was then known as Magnesia and the ore was called *magnetite*. Other deposits of magnetite are found in the Adirondack Mountains of New York and in other regions of the world. Pieces of magnetite are known as *natural magnets*. A suspended piece of magnetite aligns itself with the magnetic field of the earth. About the twelfth century men began to use these natural magnets, which they called lodestones (leading stones), as the first magnetic compasses.

A few materials, notably iron and steel, are strongly attracted by magnets; cobalt and nickel are attracted to a lesser degree. These substances are said to have *ferromagnetic* properties.

19.1 Magnetism and electricity

Ken Chen

The flying ring was repelled by the coil of wire when the circuit was completed. Try to explain this after studying the next two chapters.

19.2 Magnetic substances

W. Dawn

Metal filings attracted to a lodestone show the field of force surrounding the magnetic rock.

Special alloys, such as *permalloy* and *alnico*, have extraordinary ferromagnetic properties. Physicists have shown much interest in the structure of materials possessing the property of *ferromagnetism*.

Today very strong and versatile artificial magnets are made from ferromagnetic substances. Alnico magnets may support a weight over 1000 times that of the magnets themselves. Ferromagnetic substances are commonly referred to simply as "magnetic substances."

19.3 Nonmagnetic substances

Materials are commonly classified as magnetic or nonmagnetic. Those which do not demonstrate the strong ferromagnetism of the Iron Family of metals are said to be "nonmagnetic." However, if these materials are placed in the field of a very strong magnet, some are observed to be slightly repelled by the magnet, while others are very slightly attracted.

Zinc, bismuth, sodium chloride, gold, and mercury are a few of the substances that are feebly repelled, and are said to be *diamagnetic*. The property of *diamagnetism* is an important concept in the modern theory of magnetism, as we shall see in Section 19.4.

Wood, aluminum, platinum, oxygen, and copper(II) sulfate are examples of substances which are very slightly attracted by a strong magnet. Such materials are said to be *paramagnetic*, and this type of magnetic behavior is called *paramagnetism*.

19.4 The domain theory of magnetism

William Gilbert's report on his experiments with natural magnets, published in 1600, probably represents the first scientific study of magnetism. In the years that followed, discoveries by Coulomb, Oersted, and Ampère added to our knowledge of the behavior of magnets and the nature of magnetic forces. However, physicists believe that it is only within this century that they have begun to understand the true nature of magnetism. The present view is that the magnetic properties of matter are electric in origin, probably resulting from the movements of electrons within the atoms of substances. Since the electron is an electrically charged particle, this theory suggests that *magnetism is a property of a charge in motion.* If so, we can account for the energy associated with magnetic forces by using known laws of physics.

Two kinds of electron motions are important in this modern concept of magnetism. **First**, *an electron revolving about the nucleus of an atom imparts a magnetic property to the atom structure.* See Fig. 19-1. When the atoms of a substance are subjected to the magnetic force of a strong magnet, the force affects this magnetic property, opposing the motion of the electrons. The atoms are

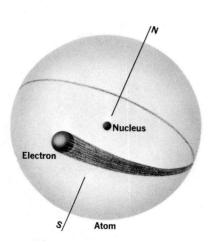

19-1 Revolving electrons impart a magnetic property to the atom.

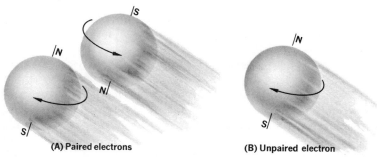

(A) Paired electrons   **(B) Unpaired electron**

19-2 Magnetism in matter stems basically from the spin of electrons.

thus repelled by the magnet; this is diamagnetism. If the movement of the electron about the nucleus were its only motion, all substances would be diamagnetic. Diamagnetic repulsion is quite feeble in its action on the total mass of a substance.

*The **second** kind of electron motion is the spinning of the electron on its own axis.* The magnetic property of matter stems basically from the spin of electrons as well as their orbital motions; *each spinning electron acts as a tiny permanent magnet.* Opposite spins are designated as + and − spins; electrons spinning in opposite directions tend to form *pairs* and so neutralize their magnetic character. See Fig. 19-2. The magnetic character of an atom as a whole may be weak because of the mutual interaction among the electron spins.

Magnetic properties are associated with both kinds of electron motion. The atoms of some substances may possess permanent magnet characteristics because of an imbalance between orbits and spins. These atoms act like tiny magnets, called *dipoles*, and are attracted by strong magnets. Substances in which this effect exceeds the diamagnetism common to all atoms show the property of paramagnetism.

In the atoms of ferromagnetic substances, there are unpaired electrons whose spins are oriented in the same way. The common metals iron, cobalt, and nickel; the rare earth elements gadolinium and dysprosium; some alloys of these and other elements; and certain metallic oxides called ferrites show strong ferromagnetic properties.

The inner electron quantum levels, or shells, of the atom structures of most elements contain only paired electrons. The highest quantum level, or outer shell, of each of the noble gases (except helium) consists of a stable octet of electrons made up of four electron pairs. The atoms of other elements achieve this stable configuration by forming chemical bonds. Only in certain transition elements, which have incomplete inner shells, do unpaired electrons result in ferromagnetic properties. The electron configuration of the iron atom, Fig. 19-3, shows four unpaired electrons in the third principal quantum level.

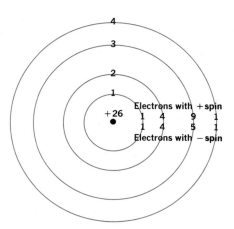

19-3 The iron atom has strong ferromagnetic properties.

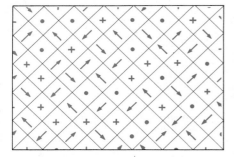

19-4 The domains of an unmagnetized ferromagnetic substance are polarized along the crystal axes. Dots and plus signs represent arrows going out of and into the page respectively.

Table 19-1	CURIE POINTS OF FERRO-MAGNETIC ELEMENTS
Element	**Curie Point**
iron	770°C
cobalt	1131°C
nickel	358°C
gadolinium	16°C

The similarly oriented spins of these electrons, enhanced by the influence of nearby atoms in the crystal, account for its strong ferromagnetism.

From the foregoing it would seem that every piece of iron should behave as a magnet. However, the atoms are grouped in microscopic magnetic regions called *domains*. The atoms in each domain are magnetically polarized parallel to a crystal axis. Ordinarily, these domains are oriented in every possible direction parallel to the crystal axes, so that they tend to cancel one another and the net magnetism is essentially zero. In Fig. 19-4 the polarity of each domain in an unmagnetized material is represented by an arrow.

When a ferromagnetic material is placed in an external magnetic field and becomes magnetized, two effects occur. The domains favorably oriented in the magnetic field may increase in size at the expense of adjacent domains. Other domains may become more favorably oriented with respect to the external field. If domain boundaries remain extended to some degree after the external magnetizing force is removed, the material is said to be "permanently" magnetized. When the direction of magnetization of a magnetic domain is altered by an external magnetic field, it must be understood that the *material* of the domain does not change its position in the specimen. It is only its direction of magnetization that changes.

When the temperature of a ferromagnetic material is raised above a certain critical value, the domain regions disappear and the material becomes merely paramagnetic. This temperature is known as the *Curie point*. It is usually lower than the melting point of the substance. The Curie points for some ferromagnetic substances are given in Table 19-1.

Physicists have developed a technique which enables them to see and photograph the microscopic domains in a ferromagnetic material, the domains being outlined with colloidal particles of iron oxide. Typical photomicrographs of magnetic domains are shown in Fig. 19-5. This technique can be used to

19-5 Photomicrographs of magnetic domains.

indicate what goes on inside a magnet when it is subjected to various experimental manipulations.

A recent magnet technology based on a group of ferromagnetic substances known as *ferrites* yields strong hard magnets with unique properties. Ferrites are iron oxides combined with oxides of other metals such as manganese, cobalt, nickel, copper, and magnesium. The combined oxides are powdered, formed into the desired shape under pressure, and fired. As oxides, the ferrites have very high electric resistance, a property that is extremely important in some applications of ferromagnetic materials. The original lodestone is a material of this type, commonly called magnetic iron oxide. Chemically, it is a combination of iron(II) oxide, FeO, and iron(III) oxide, Fe_2O_3. Its formula is considered to be $Fe(FeO_2)_2$.

The fact that iron filings cling mainly to the ends of a bar magnet indicates that the magnetic force acts on the filings primarily in these regions or *poles*; it does not mean that the middle region of the magnet is unmagnetized. The pole which points toward the north, when the magnet is free to swing about a vertical axis, is commonly called the *north-seeking pole* or simply the **N** pole. The opposite pole, which points toward the south, is called the *south-seeking pole* or **S** pole.

Suppose a bar magnet is suspended as shown in Fig. 19-6. When the **N** pole of a second magnet is brought near the **N** pole of the suspended magnet, the two repel each other. A similar action is observed with the two **S** poles. If the **S** pole of one magnet is placed near the **N** pole of the other magnet, they attract each other. Such experiments show that *like poles repel; unlike poles attract.*

Magnets usually have two well-defined poles, one **N** and one **S**. Long bar magnets sometimes acquire more than two poles, and an iron ring may have no poles at all when magnetized. A single isolated pole has never been found and physicists believe that only dipoles occur in nature. A magnet has an **S** pole for every **N** pole. An isolated **N** pole of unit strength is *assumed* when we use "thought" experiments. *A **unit pole** may be thought of as one which repels an exactly similar pole placed a centimeter away with a force of 1 dyne.* (a dyne = 10^{-5} newton.)

The first quantitative study of the force between two magnets is generally credited to Coulomb, who found this magnetic force to be governed by the same inverse-square relationship that applies to gravitational force and electrostatic force. ***Coulomb's law for magnetism*** *states that the force between two magnetic poles is directly proportional to the product of the strengths of the poles and inversely proportional to the square of the distance between*

19.5 Force between magnet poles

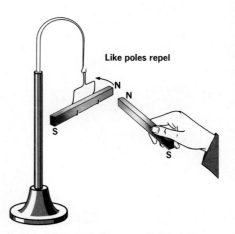

Like poles repel

19-6 Like poles repel. Unlike poles attract.

them. The force is one of repulsion or attraction, depending on whether the magnetic poles are alike or different.

19.6 Magnetic field of force

In Chapter 16, we described the electric field of force near an electrically charged object. Electric forces are not the only forces which act on charged particles. Sometimes we observe the effect of a force perpendicular to the velocity of a *moving* charge, and proportional to this velocity. This force defines a *magnetic field.* A dipole magnet in such a region of space experiences a torque. We speak of a magnetic field in the space around a bar magnet in the same way we speak of an electric field around a charged rod. Furthermore, *we can represent a magnetic field by lines of flux,* just as we represented an electric field by lines of force.

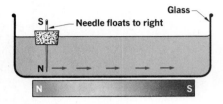

The behavior of our imaginary independent **N** pole in a magnetic field can be approximated by using a magnetized darning needle as illustrated in Fig. 19-7. The needle is supported by cork so it floats with the **N** pole extended below the surface of the water. The **S** pole is far enough away to have negligible influence on the movement of the needle. A bar magnet placed under the glass dish with its **N** pole near the needle causes the floating magnet to move approximately along the path that would be followed by an isolated **N** pole.

19-7 The path followed by the floating magnet in this experiment is approximately that of an independent N pole.

The path of an independent **N** pole in a magnetic field suggests a *line of flux. A **line of flux** is a line so drawn that a tangent to it at any point indicates the direction of the magnetic field.* Flux lines are assumed to emerge from a magnet at the **N** pole and to enter the magnet at the **S** pole, every line being a closed path running from **S** pole to **N** pole within the magnet. See Fig. 19-8.

The lines of flux perpendicular to a specified area in the magnetic field are collectively called the magnetic flux, for which the symbol Φ, the Greek letter Phi, is used. The unit of magnetic flux in the MKS system is the *weber* (wb).

*The **magnetic flux density**, B, is the number of flux lines per unit area that permeates the magnetic field.* The flux density B is a vector quantity, the direction of B at any point in the magnetic field being the direction of the field at that point.

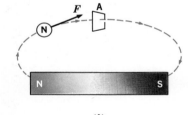

(A)

$$B = \Phi/A$$

Flux density in the MKS system is expressed in webers per square meter (wb/m²). It determines the *magnetic field intensity, H,* or *magnetizing force,* at any point in the magnetic field. The magnetic field intensity is given in newtons per weber (n/wb). Later we shall consider how these quantities are measured.

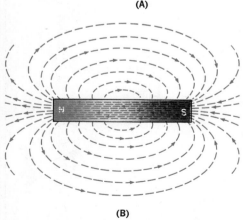

(B)

19-8 (A) The path taken by an independent N pole in a magnetic field suggests a line of flux. (B) Magnetic flux about a bar magnet.

Flux lines drawn to indicate how tiny magnets would behave when placed at various points in a magnetic field provide a means of *mapping* the field. A line drawn tangent to a flux line at any point would show the direction a very small magnet would take if placed there. An arrowhead can be added to the tangent line to indicate the direction in which the **N** pole of the tiny magnet would point, thus giving the direction of the magnetic field (and the *B* vector) at that point.

Using a suitable scale of flux lines per unit area perpendicular to the field, field density, *B*, and field intensity, *H*, at any point can be illustrated. Selection of a number of lines to represent a unit of magnetic flux is arbitrary. Usually, one flux line per square meter represents a flux density of 1 wb/m². In this sense, one line of flux is a weber.

The field of a single magnet, or a group of magnets, is suggested by the pattern formed by iron filings sprinkled on a glass plate laid over the magnet. Photographs of such patterns are shown in Figs. 19-9 through 19-12.

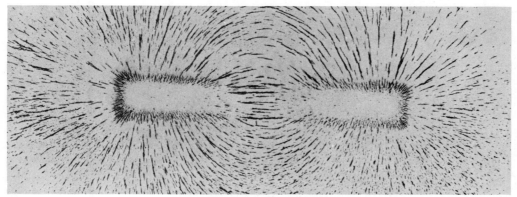

Alex Mulligan

19-9   Iron filings near a single bar magnet.

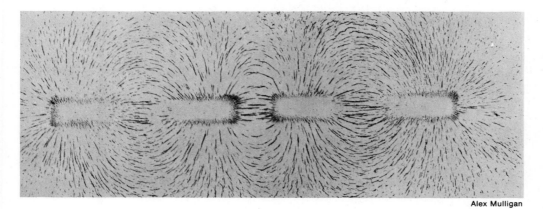

Alex Mulligan

19-10   Iron filings around two bar magnets with unlike poles facing each other.

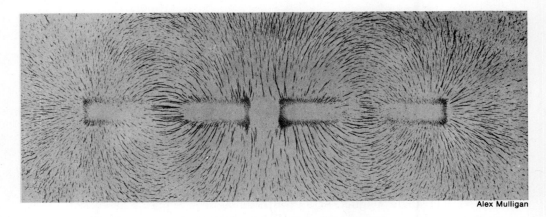

Alex Mulligan

19-11   Iron filings around two bar magnets with like poles facing each other.

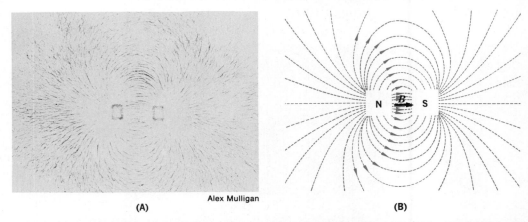

Alex Mulligan

(A)   (B)

19-12   (A) Iron filings near the poles of a horseshoe magnet, end view. (B) An idealized drawing of (A) showing lines of flux.

19.7 Magnetic permeability

In Section 19.6 we described the effect of a magnetic field of force on iron filings and on a magnetized needle through glass and water. Nonmagnetic materials, in general, are transparent to magnetic flux; that is, their effect on the lines of flux is not appreciably different from that of air. *The property of a material by which it changes the flux density in a magnetic field from the value in air is called its* **permeability** *(μ)*. The permeability of empty space is taken as unity and that of air is very nearly the same. The permeabilities of diamagnetic substances are slightly less than unity, while permeabilities of paramagnetic substances are slightly greater than unity. Permeability is a ratio of flux densities and therefore is without dimension.

If a sheet of iron covers a magnet, there is little magnetic field above the sheet. The flux enters the iron and follows a path

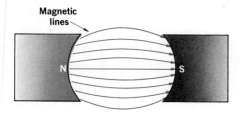

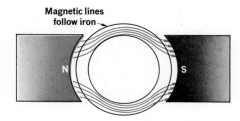

within the iron itself. Figure 19-13 illustrates this principle. The flux density in iron is greater than it is in air; therefore, iron is said to have a high permeability. The permeabilities of other ferromagnetic substances are also very high.

19-13 At left, magnetic flux crosses the air gap between the poles of a magnet. At right, magnetic flux follows the soft iron ring, which is more permeable than air.

Suppose a bar of soft iron lies in a magnetic field, as in Fig. 19-14. Because of the high permeability of the iron, the field is distorted, the magnetic flux passing through the iron in preference to the air. The soft iron bar becomes a magnet under these circumstances, with end **A** as the **S** pole and end **B** as the **N** pole. Such a bar is said to be magnetized by *induction*. *Magnetism produced in a ferromagnetic substance by the influence of a magnetic field is called* **induced magnetism**.

19-14 Magnetizing an iron bar by induction.

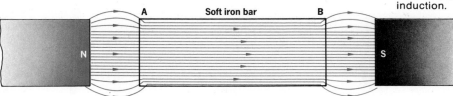

If the magnetic field is removed by withdrawing the two bar magnets, most of the induced magnetism is lost. Magnets produced by induction are known as temporary magnets. A piece of hardened steel is not so strongly magnetized by induction, but retains a greater *residual* magnetism when removed from the induction field.

There is no significant difference in the process if the iron bar in Fig. 19-14 is brought into contact with one of the magnet poles. The magnetization process is somewhat more efficient due to the reduction of the air gap. This effect is sometimes referred to as *magnetization by contact*. See Fig. 19-15.

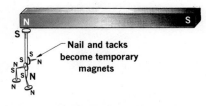

Nail and tacks become temporary magnets

19-15 The nail becomes a magnet by induction. Are the tacks also magnets?

The magnetic field intensity, H, acts as the *magnetizing force* in magnetic induction. As a ferromagnetic material is subjected to an increasing magnetizing force, the flux density, B, increases until the material is *saturated*. See curve **ab** of Fig. 19-16. If the magnetizing force is then reduced to zero, the magnetization

19.8 Magnetic hysteresis

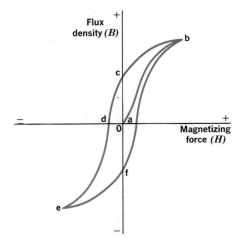

19-16   A typical hysteresis loop.

does not return to zero but lags behind the magnetizing force, segment **bc**. *The lagging of the magnetization behind the magnetizing force is known as* **hysteresis**. The greater the lag, the greater is the residual magnetism retained by the material, ordinate **0c**.

The flux density, and thus the magnetization, can be reduced to zero only by reversing the magnetic field and building up the magnetizing force in the opposite direction, segment **cd**. The reverse magnetizing force, if increased enough, causes the material to reach saturation again, but with its poles reversed, segment **de**. Reducing the magnetizing force to zero and then increasing it in the original direction again merely completes the segment **efb**. This process may be repeated and the magnetization of the material follows the closed loop **bcefb**, a curve called a *hysteresis loop*.

Hardened steel has a thick-loop hysteresis characteristic since the residual magnetism is high. Soft iron has a thin-loop characteristic. The area enclosed by a hysteresis loop gives an indication of the quantity of energy that is dissipated in taking a ferromagnetic substance through a complete cycle of magnetization. In the operation of many electric devices such as transformers and electric motors, this energy is wasted and appears as heat; the hysteresis characteristic of a ferromagnetic material is therefore an important design consideration in such electric devices.

19.9 Terrestrial magnetism

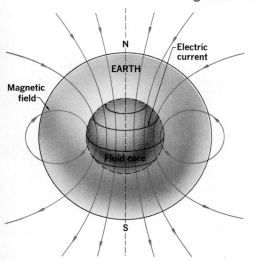

19-17   The magnetic field of the earth may be due to electric currents in the earth's core.

The earth behaves as a large magnet. Its magnetic poles do not coincide with the geographic poles, since the North Magnetic Pole is about 1200 miles south of the North Geographic Pole at latitude 73° N, longitude 100° W. Thus the N pole of the compass needle does not point due north from most locations on the earth. *The angle of compass variation from true north is called the* **angle of declination**. A succession of points of equal declination form an *isogonic* line, and a line of zero declination is called an *agonic* line.

A compass needle mounted on a horizontal axis, provided with a means of measuring the angle of the needle with the horizontal, is called a *dipping* needle. At certain places on the earth's surface, approximately midway between the magnetic poles, the angle of dip is zero and the needle is horizontal. A line drawn through a succession of such points identifies the *magnetic equator*; it is the *aclinic* line. Lines drawn through places of equal dip are called *isoclinic* lines. *The dip, or deviation between the equilibrium position of a dipping needle and the horizontal*, is known as **magnetic inclination**.

In 1600 William Gilbert published his scientific treatise,

De Magnete, dealing with the magnetism of the earth. This was one of the earliest publications on experimental science. Gilbert inferred that the earth behaved as a large magnet because the interior consisted of permanently magnetic material. Scientists believe the core of the earth is too hot to be a permanent magnet. They have not yet learned the source of the earth's magnetism.

Karl Friedrich Gauss (1777–1855), a German physicist, showed that the magnetic field of the earth must originate inside the earth. Walter M. Elsasser, professor of theoretical physics at the University of California, suggested in 1939 that the earth's magnetic field results from currents generated by the flow of matter in the earth's fluid core. See Fig. 19-17.

Space vehicles that travel to the outer limits of the earth's atmosphere and beyond have stimulated a growing interest in a region of the upper atmosphere called the *magnetosphere*. This is the region beyond approximately 200 km in which the motion of charged particles is governed primarily by the magnetic field of the earth. At lower altitudes where the density of the atmosphere is much greater, the motion of such particles is controlled largely by collisions.

The magnetosphere on the side facing the sun extends beyond the earth's surface approximately 57,000 km, or about 10 earth radii. On the side away from the sun, the magnetosphere probably extends outward for hundreds of earth radii. See Fig. 19-18. The elongated shape results from the influence of the onrushing *solar wind*, or *solar plasma*. The solar wind,

19.10 The magnetosphere

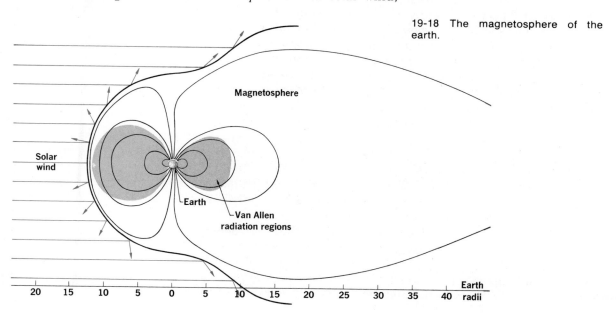

19-18 The magnetosphere of the earth.

consisting mainly of protons and electrons emitted by the sun, greatly compresses the magnetosphere on the side nearest the sun.

In 1958 huge regions of radiation were discovered within the magnetosphere. These regions, now known as the Van Allen radiation belts, contain energetic protons and electrons trapped by the earth's magnetic field. When these intense radiation belts were first discovered, scientists were apprehensive about the serious threat to space travel which the radiation belts appeared to present. Today it is believed that astronauts journeying into outer space are able to pass through these regions quickly with adequate protection from the Van Allen radiation.

QUESTIONS

Group A

1. (a) What is a lodestone? (b) Why are lodestones sometimes called natural magnets?
2. What is the distinguishing property of ferromagnetic materials?
3. Distinguish between diamagnetic and paramagnetic materials.
4. What two kinds of electron motion are important in determining the magnetic property of a material?
5. What are electron pairs and what is the significance in regard to their magnetic character?
6. (a) What three metals are the most important ferromagnetic materials? (b) What special alloy is often used to make very strong magnets?
7. How can you account for the ferromagnetic properties of the metals of the Iron Family?
8. What are magnetic domains?
9. Describe the condition of a ferromagnetic material in a state of magnetic saturation.
10. State Coulomb's law for magnetism.
11. Under what circumstances will a magnetic force be (a) one of repulsion, (b) one of attraction?
12. Describe a simple way to examine the fields of small magnets.
13. What is the advantage of making a magnet in the shape of a horseshoe?
14. Describe an experiment which illustrates induced magnetism.
15. Distinguish between a north-seeking pole and the North Magnetic Pole.
16. Why is a declination angle involved in the use of a compass over most of the earth's surface?

Group B

17. Explain, on the basis of atomic structure, the property of diamagnetism.

18. Explain paramagnetism on the basis of imbalance between orbits and spins.
19. Assume the dish in Fig. 19-7 to be located in the northern hemisphere. Will the magnetized needle be attracted to the north edge of the dish? Explain.
20. How would you prove that a steel bar is magnetized?
21. What is the significance of the area enclosed by the hysteresis loop of a ferromagnetic material?
22. If a watch mechanism is to be magnetically "insulated," should the case be made of diamagnetic, paramagnetic, or ferromagnetic material? Explain.

ELECTROMAGNETISM

It can be easily demonstrated that electrostatic charges and stationary magnets have no effect on one another. However, in 1820 Hans Christian Oersted (er-stet) (1777–1851), a Danish physicist and professor of physics at the University of Copenhagen, observed that a small compass needle is deflected when brought near a conductor carrying an electric current. This was the first evidence of a long suspected link between electricity and magnetism. Oersted discovered that forces exist between a magnet and electric charges in motion. His famous experiment is so significant that a brief description of it is in order.

A dry cell, compass, switch, and conducting wire are arranged as shown in Fig. 19-19(A). With the switch open, a straight section of the conductor is supported *above* the compass in the vertical plane of the compass needle. In (B) the dry-cell connection is such that the electron flow will be from north to south. When the switch is closed, the **N** pole of the compass is deflected toward the west. When the dry-cell connections are reversed so electron flow is from south to north, the **N** pole of the com-

19.11 The link between an electric current and magnetism

The New York Public Library

Hans Christian Oersted studied medicine before becoming professor of physics at the University of Copenhagen in 1806. Several years before he performed his famous experiment, he predicted that a link between electricity and magnetism would be found.

19-19 The Oersted experiment as viewed from above. In each diagram the compass needle is located below the conductor.

(A) (B) (C)

pass is deflected to the east. It is evident that *a magnetic field exists in the region near the conductor when the circuit is closed.* Furthermore, *the direction of the field is dependent on the direction of the current in the conductor.*

If the experiment is repeated with the conductor placed *below* the compass needle, the compass deflection is opposite to that in the first experiment. This suggests, but does not prove, that the magnetic field encircles the conductor.

19.12 The magnetic field surrounding an electric charge in motion

The Granger Collection

André Ampère, the French physicist for whom the unit of electric current is named, did fundamental work in electromagnetism.

Shortly after Oersted's discovery, the French physicist André Marie Ampère (1775–1836) determined the shape of the magnetic field about a conductor carrying a current. He had discovered that forces exist between two parallel conductors in an electric circuit, the force being one of attraction if the two currents are in the same direction, and one of repulsion if the currents are in opposite directions. See Fig. 19-20.

In a quantitative sense, two long straight parallel conductors of length l separated by a distance s and carrying currents I_1 and I_2, respectively, will each experience a force F of magnitude

$$F = \frac{2k\, l\, I_1 I_2}{s}$$

The constant k is exactly 10^{-7} n/a^2 in the MKS system. If I_1 and I_2 are expressed in amperes and l and s in meters, the force F is given in newtons.

These attractive and repulsive forces between current-carrying conductors are directly proportional to the currents in the conductors, thus providing a precise method of defining the practical unit of current, the ampere. In this sense, the

19-20 Forces between parallel currents (A) in the same direction, and (B) in opposite directions.

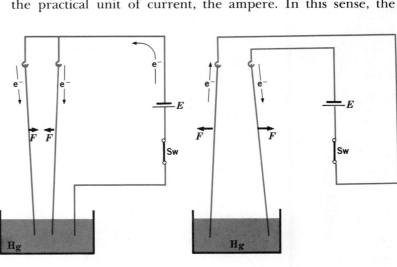

ampere may be defined as *the current in each of two long parallel conductors spaced one meter apart, which causes a magnetic force of 2×10^{-7} newton per meter length of conductor.*

Following this scheme, the ***coulomb*** as a quantity of charge (an ampere-second), may be defined as *the quantity of electricity which passes a given point on a conductor in one second when the conductor carries a constant current of one ampere.*

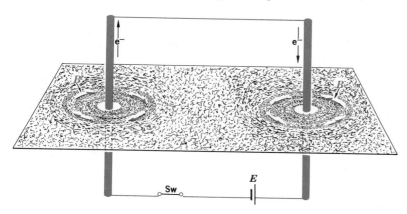

19-21 The magnetic field encircling a current in a straight conductor.

Ampère investigated the magnetic fields about conductors to find an explanation of the magnetic forces. Suppose a heavy copper wire passes vertically through the center of a horizontal sheet of stiff cardboard. When the ends of the vertical conductor are connected to a dry cell, iron filings sprinkled over the surface of the cardboard form a pattern of concentric circles around the conductor. See Fig. 19-21. If a small compass is placed at various points on a circle of filings, the needle always comes to rest tangent to the circle.

If the direction of current in the vertical conductor is reversed, the compass needle again becomes aligned tangent to the circle of filings, but with the **N** pole in the *opposite* direction. From these observations, we conclude that *a magnetic field encircles an electric charge in motion.* The lines of flux are closed concentric circles in a plane perpendicular to the conductor with the axis of the conductor as their center. The direction of the magnetic field is everywhere tangent to the flux and is dependent on the direction of the current.

Ampère devised a rule, known today as *Ampère's rule,* for determining the direction of the magnetic field around a current in a straight conductor when the direction of the electron flow is known.

Ampère's rule for a straight conductor: Grasp the conductor in the left hand with the thumb extended in the direction of the elec-

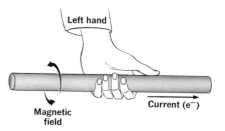

19-22 Ampère's rule for a straight conductor.

Ken Chen

A metal sphere is suspended in midair beneath a current-carrying coil of wire. The current is regulated by the amount of light striking the solar cell on the vertical support. When the sphere begins to fall, more light from a source at the left strikes the solar cell, and the current in the coil is increased, thus increasing the field strength of the coil and drawing the sphere up again.

tron current. The fingers then will circle the conductor in the direction of the magnetic flux.

The flux density B (also called the *magnetic induction*) at any point in the magnetic field of a long straight conductor carrying a current I is directly proportional to the current in the conductor and inversely proportional to the radial distance r of the point from the conductor.

$$B = 2k \frac{I}{r}$$

The constant k again is 10^{-7} n/a^2. When I is given in amperes and r is in meters, B is expressed in newtons per ampere meter which is equivalent to webers per square meter.

In Section 19.6 flux density was defined in terms of the lines of flux per unit area that permeate the magnetic field, $B = \Phi/A$. Thus,

$$\Phi = BA$$

When B is expressed in newtons per ampere meter, the MKS unit for Φ, the weber, can be shown to be 1 newton meter per ampere. Dimensionally,

$$\mathbf{wb} = \frac{\mathbf{n}}{\mathbf{a\ m}} \times \mathbf{m}^2 = \frac{\mathbf{n\ m}}{\mathbf{a}}$$

Whether Φ is expressed in webers or newton meters per ampere, and B in webers per square meter or newtons per ampere meter, is a matter of convenience in each situation.

Observe that the definition of B given in Section 19.6 was based on the force exerted on an isolated unit pole. An isolated pole exists only in the fiction of a thought experiment, consequently measurements based on this definition lack precision. The more modern definition given above involves quantities that can be measured precisely and should therefore be preferred.

19.13 Magnetic field about a current loop

Keeping Ampère's rule in mind, let us consider a loop in a conductor carrying a current. The magnetic flux from all segments of the loop must pass through the inside of the loop in the same direction, that is, *the face of the loop must show polarity.* See Fig. 19-23.

The pole strength of this loop magnet will be stronger if the flux density is increased. Because the magnetic field around a conductor varies with the current, the pole strength can be increased by increasing the magnitude of the current in the conducting loop, and by forming additional loops in the conductor, similar to the original loop and close to it.

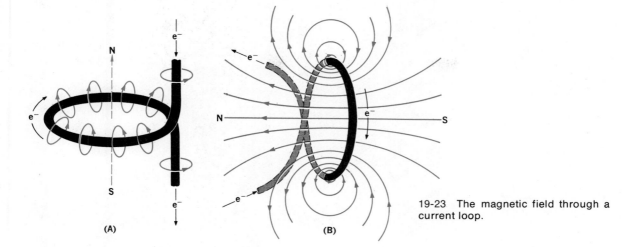

19-23 The magnetic field through a current loop.

A linear coil of such conducting loops takes the form of a helix, and is called a *solenoid*. The cylindrical column of air inside the loops, extending the length of the coil, is called the *core*. When a current is in a solenoid, the core of each loop, or *turn*, becomes a magnet; and the core of the solenoid is a magnetic tube through which practically all the magnetic flux passes. See Fig. 19-24.

Since a solenoid carrying a current acts like a bar magnet, we may determine its polarity by means of a compass. However, the magnetic flux in the core of the solenoid is derived from the magnetic field of each turn of the conductor. Thus we may modify Ampère's rule to fit this special case.

Ampère's rule for a solenoid: Grasp the coil in the left hand with the fingers circling the coil in the direction of the electron current. The extended thumb will point in the direction of the N pole of the core.

A solenoid having a core of air, wood, or some other non-magnetic material does not produce a very strong electromagnet, for the permeability of all nonmagnetic substances is essentially equal to that of air, unity. Substitution of such materials for air does not appreciably change the flux density.

Soft iron, on the other hand, has a high permeability. If an iron rod is substituted for air as the core material, the flux density is greatly increased. Strong electromagnets therefore have ferromagnetic cores with high permeability. For a given core material, the strength of the electromagnet depends on the magnitude of the current and on the number of turns. Thus, its strength is determined by *the number of ampere-turns.*

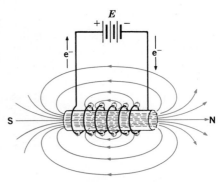

19-24 Magnetic field about a solenoid.

19.14 The electromagnet

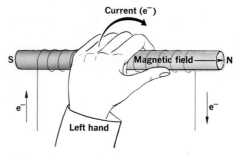

19-25 Ampère's rule for a solenoid.

A super-conducting electromagnet. In operation, the eight foot cylinder is immersed in liquid helium (−232°C). At this temperature, the niobium-titanium strips imbedded in the copper coils lose all resistance to electric current and the magnet produces a force field up to 5000 times greater than that of the earth.

d-c METERS

19.15 The galvanometer

Suppose we form a wire loop in a vertical plane, place a compass needle (free to rotate in a horizontal plane) in the center of it, and introduce a current into the loop. The needle is deflected. If we increase the number of turns sufficiently, even a feeble current produces a deflection of the needle. Such a device, called a *galvanoscope,* may be used to detect the presence of an electric current or to determine its direction. A simple galvanoscope is shown in Fig. 19-26.

A more versatile instrument for detecting feeble currents is the *galvanometer,* the essential parts of which are shown in Fig.

19-27. A coil of wire is pivoted on jeweled bearings between the poles of a permanent horseshoe magnet. The coil becomes a magnet when current passes through it. Thus our instrument has two magnets: a permanent horseshoe magnet, in a fixed position; and an electromagnet, free to turn on its axis. Electric connections to the coil are made through two control springs, which hold it so that the pointer attached to the electromagnet shows a zero reading when no current is present. In a galvanometer, the zero position is often located at the midpoint of the scale.

When there is a current in the movable coil, its core is magnetized. The poles of the core are then attracted and repelled by the poles of the permanent magnet. A torque acts upon the coil, which rotates in an attempt to align its plane perpendicular to the line joining the poles of the permanent magnet. As the coil rotates, however, it does work against the two control springs. Its final position is reached when the torque acting on it is just neutralized by the reaction of the springs. Since the permanent field flux is constant, the torque on the coil is proportional to the current in it. We may assume, for small movements of the coil, that the reaction of the springs is proportional to the deflection angle. When the coil reaches its equilibrium position, these two opposing torques are equal, and the deflection angle of the coil is therefore proportional to the current in it.

The scale of the galvanometer is marked at intervals on either side of the zero center. Readings are made on this scale by means of a small, lightweight pointer attached to the coil. For a coil current in one direction, the needle deflection is to the left. If the current direction is reversed, the needle is deflected to the right.

The galvanometer is a sensitive instrument for detecting feeble currents of the order of microamperes, the scale graduations giving relative magnitudes of current. For translation of a reading into absolute current values, the *current sensitivity* of the specific instrument must be known. Current sensitivity is usually expressed in *microamperes per scale division.*

The pointer deflection, s, of a galvanometer is proportional to the current, I_M, in the coil

$$I_M \propto s$$

or

$$I_M = ks$$

and

$$k = \frac{I_M}{s}$$

Welch Scientific Co.

19-26   A simple galvanoscope.

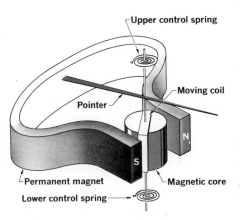

19-27   Magnet and moving coil of a galvanometer.

Upper control spring

Moving coil

Pointer

N

S

Permanent magnet

Lower control spring

Magnetic core

where k is the current sensitivity in microamperes per scale division.

The moving coil of the galvanometer has resistance. By Ohm's law, a potential difference appears across the resistance of the meter when a current is in the coil. We can express the *voltage sensitivity* of the instrument since it must be equal to the product of the meter resistance and the current per scale division.

$$\textbf{Voltage sensitivity} = kR_M = \frac{I_M}{\textbf{div}} \times R_M$$

where R_M is the resistance of the meter movement. Voltage sensitivity is given in microvolts per scale division.

If provision is made to prevent excessive currents from entering the coil, the galvanometer can be adapted for service as either a d-c ammeter or d-c voltmeter.

The following examples illustrate calculations involving the galvanometer.

Example

What current is required for full-scale deflection of a galvanometer having a current sensitivity of 50.0 μa per scale division? The meter has exactly 50 divisions on either side of the mid-scale index.

Solution

We are given the current sensitivity, $k = 50.0$ μa/div, and the number of divisions on either side of mid-scale (zero) position, $s = 50$ div.

$$I_M = ks = \frac{50.0 \ \mu\text{a}}{\text{div}} \times 50 \text{ div}$$

$I_M = 25\overline{0}0$ μa, or 2.50×10^{-3} a, the required current

Example

What potential difference appears across the galvanometer described in the previous example when the pointer is fully deflected? The meter resistance is 10.0 Ω.

Solution

We are given the current sensitivity, $k = 50.0$ μa/div, the resistance of the meter, $R_M = 10.0$ Ω, and the number of divisions of deflection, $s = 50$ div.

$$V_M = I_M R_M$$

But

$$I_M = ks$$

Then

$$V_M = ks R_M = \frac{50.0\ \mu a}{\text{div}} \times 50\ \text{div} \times 10.0\ \Omega$$

$V_M = 2.50 \times 10^4\ \mu v$ or 2.50×10^{-2} v, the potential difference across the meter.

The potential difference across a galvanometer is quite small even when the needle is fully deflected. If a galvanometer is to be used to measure voltages of ordinary magnitudes, we must convert it to a high-resistance instrument. The essential parts of a d-c voltmeter are shown in Fig. 19-28.

If a high resistance is added in series with the moving coil, most of the potential drop appears across this series resistor or *multiplier*. Since *a voltmeter is connected in parallel* with the part of a circuit across which the potential difference is to be measured, a high resistance prevents an appreciable loading effect. By the proper choice of resistance, we can calibrate the meter to read any desired voltage.

19.16 The d-c voltmeter

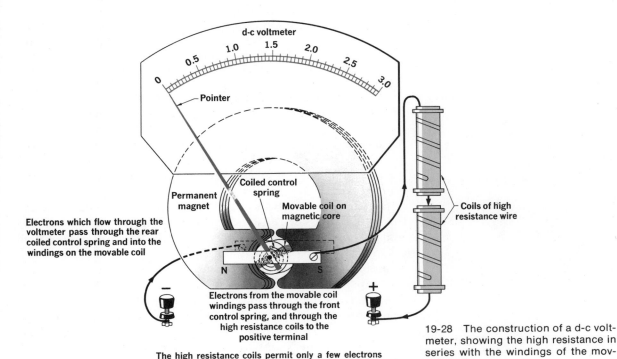

d-c voltmeter

Pointer

Coiled control spring

Permanent magnet

Movable coil on magnetic core

Coils of high resistance wire

Electrons which flow through the voltmeter pass through the rear coiled control spring and into the windings on the movable coil

Electrons from the movable coil windings pass through the front control spring, and through the high resistance coils to the positive terminal

The high resistance coils permit only a few electrons to flow through the movable coil of a voltmeter

19-28 The construction of a d-c voltmeter, showing the high resistance in series with the windings of the movable coil.

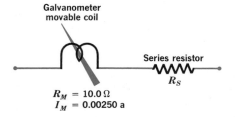

Galvanometer
movable coil

Series resistor

R_S

$R_M = 10.0\ \Omega$
$I_M = 0.00250\ a$

19-29   Converting a galvanometer to a voltmeter.

Suppose we convert the galvanometer used in the examples of Section 19.15 to a voltmeter reading 15.0 volts on full-scale deflection. The current required for full deflection has been found to be 2.50×10^{-3} ampere, and the resistance of the meter coil is 10.0 ohms. We must determine the value of the resistor R_S to be placed in series with the moving coil. Figure 19-29 illustrates this problem.

Since R_M and R_S (of Fig. 19-29) are in series,

$$V = I_M R_M + I_M R_S$$

Then

$$R_S = \frac{V}{I_M} - R_M$$

$$R_S = \frac{15.0\ v}{2.50 \times 10^{-3}\ a} - 10.0\ \Omega$$

$$R_S = 5990\ \Omega,\ \text{value of the series resistor}$$

Observe that the total resistance between the terminals of the meter is $60\overline{0}0$ ohms.

The voltmeter sensitivity is frequently expressed in terms of *ohms per volt*. When the ohms-per-volt sensitivity of a voltmeter is known, we can quickly estimate the loading effect it will have when placed across a known resistance component of a circuit. For example, at 400 ohms per volt, our meter which reads from 0 to 15 volts has $60\overline{0}0$ ohms between the terminals. If it were placed across resistances greater than about 600 ohms, the loading effect would result in serious errors.

19.17 The d-c ammeter

Leeds and Northrup Co.

Sensitive galvanometers use a mirror to indicate the position of a suspended coil by producing an image of a scale viewed through a telescope or by reflecting a beam of light onto a scale.

We could use the basic galvanometer of Section 19.15 as a microammeter merely by calibrating the graduated scale to read directly in microamperes. However, the meter would not be useful in circuits in which the current exceeded 2500 microamperes. Current in the resistance of a galvanometer coil produces I^2R heating, and an excessive current would burn out the meter.

To convert the galvanometer to read larger currents, an alternate (parallel) low-resistance path for current, called a *shunt*, must be provided across the terminals. By the proper choice of shunt resistance, we can calibrate the meter to read over the required range of current magnitudes. See Fig. 19-30.

Suppose we wish to convert the same galvanometer to an ammeter reading 10.0 amperes full scale. As before, the current required for the full deflection of the moving coil is 2.50×10^{-3} ampere and the resistance is $10.0\ \Omega$. We must determine the resistance of the shunt to be used across the coil. Fig. 19-31 applies.

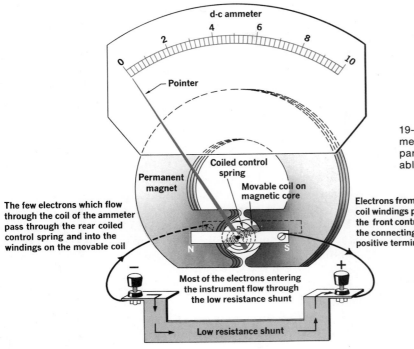

19-30 The construction of a d-c ammeter, showing the low resistance in parallel with the windings of the movable coil.

d-c ammeter

Pointer

Coiled control spring

Permanent magnet

Movable coil on magnetic core

The few electrons which flow through the coil of the ammeter pass through the rear coiled control spring and into the windings on the movable coil

Electrons from the movable coil windings pass through the front control spring and the connecting wire to the positive terminal

Most of the electrons entering the instrument flow through the low resistance shunt

Low resistance shunt

Since R_M and R_S are in parallel,

$$I_M R_M = I_S R_S$$

But

$$I_S = I_T - I_M$$

Then

$$R_S = \frac{I_M R_M}{I_T - I_M}$$

$$R_S = \frac{2.50 \times 10^{-3}\ \text{a} \times 10.0\ \Omega}{10.0\ \text{a} - 0.00250\ \text{a}}$$

$$R_S = 0.00250\ \Omega,\ \text{the value for the shunt resistor}$$

The total resistance of the ammeter is the equivalent value for 10.0 ohms and 0.00250 ohm in parallel; it will be less than 0.00250 ohm. This exercise demonstrates clearly why *an ammeter must be connected in series* in a circuit, and why it does not materially alter the magnitude of current in the circuit.

An ohmmeter provides a convenient means of measuring the resistance of a circuit component. A basic ohmmeter circuit is shown in Fig. 19-32. Its accuracy limitation is approximately the same as that of the voltmeter-ammeter method of measuring

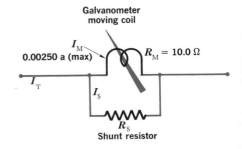

Galvanometer moving coil

I_M
0.00250 a (max)

$R_M = 10.0\ \Omega$

I_T

I_S

R_S
Shunt resistor

19-31 Converting a galvanometer to an ammeter.

19.18 The ohmmeter

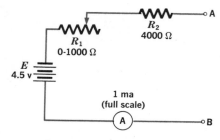

R_2
$4000 \,\Omega$

R_1
$0\text{-}1000 \,\Omega$

E
$4.5 \,v$

1 ma
(full scale)

A

19-32 A simple ohmmeter circuit.

Ken Chen

An ohmmeter being used to measure the resistance of a non-operating circuit.

resistance; actually, it is a modified version of this method. The ohmmeter must be used only on a completely de-energized circuit.

The ohmmeter circuit of Fig. 19-32 shows a milliammeter requiring 1 ma for full-scale deflection. With an emf of 4.5 volts, by Ohm's law, 4500 ohms of resistance will provide 1 ma of current when terminals **A-B** are short-circuited. A fixed resistor, R_2 of 4000 ohms and a rheostat, R_1, of 0-1000 ohms are provided.

To use this ohmmeter, **A** and **B** are short-circuited, R_1 is adjusted to give full deflection. If the emf is 4.5 v, R_1 will be set at 500 ohms. The pointer position at full-scale deflection is now marked as zero ohm (0 Ω). The rest position of the pointer is the open-circuit position with infinite resistance between **A** and **B**. This position is marked as $\infty \,\Omega$. Other resistance calibrations may be made from Ohm's law applications. For example, 4500 ohms between **A** and **B** will mean a total of 9000 ohms in the circuit and 0.5 ma of current. This mid-scale position of the pointer can be marked 4500 Ω. The meter, when recalibrated, will read the resistance between terminals **A-B**.

Each time the ohmmeter is used, it is first shorted across **A-B** and R_1 is adjusted to "zero" the meter. This operation calibrates the meter and accommodates any decrease in the terminal voltage of the battery with age. The resistance R_1 allows the ohmmeter to be used until E drops below 4.0 volts.

QUESTIONS

Group A

1. What important discovery was made by Oersted?
2. A conductor carrying a current is arranged so that electrons flow in one segment from north to south. If a compass is held over this segment of the wire, in what direction is it deflected?
3. Describe a simple experiment to show the nature of the magnetic field about a straight conductor carrying a current.
4. Suppose an electron flow in a conductor passing perpendicularly through this page is represented by a dot inside a small circle when the direction of flow is up out of the page. What is the direction of the magnetic flux about this current?
5. Upon what factors does the strength of an electromagnet depend?
6. What prevents the movable coil of a galvanometer from aligning its magnetic field parallel to that of the permanent magnet each time a current is in the coil?
7. (a) Why is it necessary that an ammeter be a low-resistance instrument? (b) Why must a voltmeter be a high-resistance instrument?

8. A solenoid with ends marked **A** and **B** is suspended by a thread so that the core can rotate in the horizontal plane. A current is maintained in the coil such that the electron flow is clockwise when viewed from end **A** toward end **B**. How will the coil align itself in the earth's magnetic field?

9. A stream of electrons is projected horizontally to the right. A straight conductor carrying a current is supported parallel to the electron stream and above it. (a) What is the effect on the electron stream if the direction of the current in the conductor is from left to right, (b) if the current is reversed?

10. Suppose the conductor in Question 9 is replaced by a magnet which produces a magnetic field directed downward. What is the effect on the electron stream? Explain.

11. Why might the potential difference indicated by a voltmeter placed across a circuit load be different from the potential difference with the meter removed?

12. Suppose the resistance of a high-resistance load is to be determined using the voltmeter method. Considering the design characteristics of ammeters and voltmeters, how would you arrange the meters in the circuit to reduce the error to a minimum? Draw your circuit diagram and justify your arrangement.

13. Suppose the resistance of a low-resistance load is to be determined using the voltmeter-ammeter method. How would you arrange the meters in this circuit to reduce the error to a minimum? Draw your circuit diagram and justify your arrangement.

Group B

PROBLEMS

1. Two parallel conductors 2.0 m long and 1.0 m apart and carrying equal currents experience a total force of 1.6×10^{-6} n. What magnitude of current is in each conductor?

2. An ammeter which has a resistance of 0.01 ohm is connected in a circuit and indicates a current of 10 amperes. A shunt having a resistance of 0.001 ohm is then connected across the meter terminals. What is the new reading on the meter? Assume the introduction of the shunt does not affect the total circuit current.

3. A galvanometer has a zero-center scale with 20.0 divisions on each side of zero. The pointer deflects 15.0 scale divisions when a current of 375 μa is in the movable coil. (a) What is the current sensitivity of the meter? (b) What current will produce a full-scale deflection?

4. A galvanometer has a resistance of 50.0 ohms and requires 75.0 milliamperes to produce a full-scale deflection. What resistance must be connected in series with the galvanometer in order to use it as a voltmeter for measuring a maximum of 300.0 volts?

Group B

5. A galvanometer movement has a resistance of 2.5 ohms and when fully deflected has a potential difference of $5\bar{0}$ millivolts across it. What shunting resistance is required to enable the instrument to be used as an ammeter reading 7.5 amperes full scale?

6. A repulsive force of 9.6×10^{-4} n is experienced by each of two parallel conductors 5.0 m long when a current of 3.2 a is in each conductor. By what distance are they separated?

Chapter 20

Electromagnetic Induction

INDUCED CURRENTS

In Chapter 19 we discussed Oersted's discovery of the link between magnetism and electricity. Soon after Oersted's work, other scientists attempted to find out whether an electric current could be produced by the action of a magnetic field. In 1831, Michael Faraday discovered that *an emf is set up in a closed electric circuit located in a magnetic field, whenever the total magnetic flux linking the circuit is changing.* Joseph Henry (1797–1878) made a similar discovery in America at about the same time. This phenomenon is called *electromagnetic induction.* The emf is called an *induced emf* and the resulting current in the closed conducting loop is called an *induced current.*

Modern technology is largely dependent on the production and distribution of inexpensive electric power. These accomplishments were made feasible by the discoveries of Faraday and Henry which led to the invention of electric generators and transformers.

We shall examine some of Faraday's experiments to understand their significance. Suppose we connect a sensitive galvanometer in a closed conducting loop as shown in Fig. 20-1. A segment of the conductor is poised in the field flux of a strong magnet. In Fig. 20-1(A), as the conductor is moved down between the poles of the magnet, there is a momentary deflection of the galvanometer needle, indicating an induced current. The needle shows no deflection when the conductor is stationary in the magnetic flux. This leads to the observation that *the induced current is related to the motion of the conductor in the magnetic flux.*

20.1 Discovery of induced current

Alex Mulligan
An induced electric current makes the light bulb glow.

20.2 Faraday's induction experiments

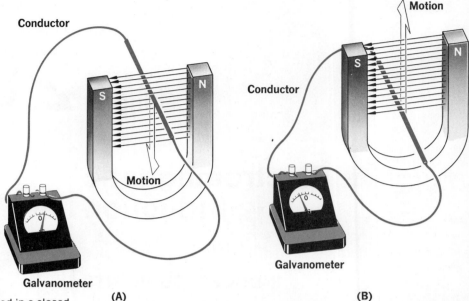

20-1   A current is induced in a closed conducting loop when the magnetic flux linked through the circuit is changing.

(A)   (B)

Raising the conductor between the poles of the magnet, as in Fig. 20-1(B), results in another momentary deflection of the galvanometer, this time in the opposite direction. This leads to the observation that *the direction of the induced current in the conductor is related to the direction of motion of the conductor in the field.* The emf induced in the conductor is of opposite polarity to that in the first experiment.

Faraday found that he could induce an emf in a conductor either by moving the conductor through a stationary field or by moving the magnetic field near a stationary conductor. He observed that the direction of the induced current in the conducting loop is reversed with a change in either the direction of motion or the direction of the magnetic field.

Supporting the conducting loop of Fig. 20-1 in a fixed position and lifting the magnet results in a deflection similar to that of Fig. 20-1(A). When the magnet is lowered, the galvanometer needle is momentarily deflected as in Fig. 20-1(B). The relative motion between the conductor and the magnetic flux is the same whether the conductor is raised through the stationary field or the field is lowered past the stationary conductor.

So far we have considered the relative motion of the conductor to be essentially *perpendicular* to the magnetic flux. If the conductor is moved in the magnetic field *parallel* with the flux lines, no emf is induced and no deflection is observed on the galvanometer. *When a conductor cuts across lines of flux, the magnetic flux linking the conducting loop changes;* a conductor moving

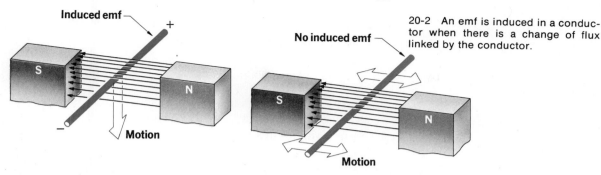

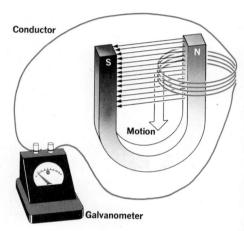

Induced emf

No induced emf

20-2   An emf is induced in a conductor when there is a change of flux linked by the conductor.

Motion

Motion

(A) Change in flux linkage   **(B) No change in flux linkage**

parallel with the flux experiences no change in flux linkage. See Fig. 20-2. This leads to the observation that *relative motion between a conductor and a magnetic field, which produces a change of magnetic flux linked by the conductor, results in an induced emf in the conductor.*

Suppose the conductor is looped so that several turns are poised in the magnetic field, as in Fig. 20-3. When the coil is moved down between the poles of the magnet as before, there is a greater deflection on the galvanometer. By increasing the rate of motion of the coil across the magnetic flux, or by substituting a stronger magnetic field, greater deflections are produced. In each of these cases the effect is to increase the number of flux lines cut by turns of the conductor in a given length of time. We can then state that *the magnitude of the induced emf, or of the induced current in a closed loop, is related to the rate at which the flux linked by the conductor changes.*

Faraday found that an emf is induced in a conductor whenever any change occurs in the magnetic flux (lines of induction) linking the conductor. Very careful experiments have shown that *the emf induced in each turn of a coiled conductor is proportional to the time rate of change of magnetic flux linking each turn of the coil.*

The total magnetic flux linking the coil is designated by the Greek letter Φ. If we let $\Delta\Phi$ represent the *change* in magnetic flux linking the coil during the time interval Δt, the emf E induced in a single turn of the coil can be expressed as

$$E \propto -\frac{\Delta\Phi}{\Delta t}$$

By introducing a proportionality constant k, the value of which depends on the system of units used, the expression can be written as

$$E = -k\,\frac{\Delta\Phi}{\Delta t}$$

Conductor

Motion

Galvanometer

20-3   A greater change in flux linkage occurs when several turns of a conductor cut through the magnetic flux.

**20.3 Factors affecting
          induced emf**

In the MKS system where E is measured in volts and Φ in webers, the numerical value of k is unity and the equation becomes

$$E = -\frac{\Delta \Phi}{\Delta t}$$

This is to say that a change in the magnetic flux linking a coil occurring at the rate of 1 weber/second will induce an emf of 1 volt in a single turn of the coil.

A coil consists of turns of wire that are, in effect, connected in series. Thus the emf induced in the coil is simply the sum of the emfs induced in the individual turns. A coil of **N** turns has **N** times the emf of the separate turns. This can be written as

$$E = -\text{N} \frac{\Delta \Phi}{\Delta t}$$

The negative sign merely indicates the relative polarity of the induced voltage. It expresses the fact that the induced emf is of such polarity as to oppose the change which induced it, a basic energy conservation principle discussed in detail in Section 20.6.

To illustrate this development, let us suppose that a coil of 150 turns linking the flux of a magnetic field uniformly is moved perpendicular to the flux and a change in flux linkage of 3.0×10^{-5} weber occurs in 0.010 second. The induced emf is then

$$E = -\text{N} \frac{\Delta \Phi}{\Delta t}$$

$$E = -150 \times \frac{3.0 \times 10^{-5} \text{ wb}}{1.0 \times 10^{-2} \text{ sec}}$$

$$E = -0.45 \text{ v}$$

$$\left(\frac{\text{wb}}{\text{sec}} = \frac{\text{n m/a}}{\text{sec}} = \frac{\text{j}}{\text{c}} = \text{v} \right)$$

20.4 The cause of an induced emf

A length of conductor moving in a magnetic field has an emf induced across it proportional to the rate of change of flux linkage, but an induced current exists *only* if the conductor is a part of a closed circuit. In order to understand the cause of an induced emf we shall make use of several facts that have already been established.

A length of copper wire poised in a magnetic field, as shown in Fig. 20-4, contains many free electrons, and moving charges constitute an electric current. In Section 19.15 we recognized that a force acts on the movable coil of a galvanometer in a magnetic field when a current is in the coil. This force, in effect, acts on the moving charges themselves.

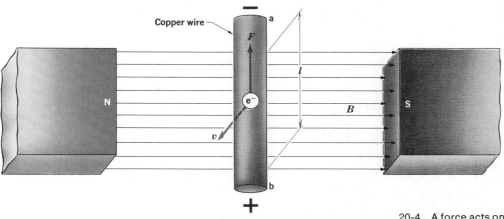

20-4 A force acts on a moving charge in a magnetic field.

Suppose the copper wire of Fig. 20-4, at right angles to the uniform magnetic field, is pushed downward (into the page) through the magnetic field of flux density B with a velocity v. The free electrons of the copper conductor may be considered to move perpendicular to the flux with the speed v as a consequence of the motion of the wire, and a force F acts on them in a direction perpendicular to both B and v. These electrons move in response to the force toward end **a** and away from end **b**, end **b** of the wire being left with a positive charge and end **a** acquiring a negative charge. Thus a difference of potential is established across the conductor with **a** the negative end and **b** the positive end. If either the motion of the wire or the magnetic field is reversed, the direction of F will be reversed and an emf will be induced so that end **a** is positive and end **b** is negative.

An electric field opposing the movement of electrons through the wire is consequently established between the ends of the conductor. Since the ends of the wire are not connected in a circuit, the force of the electric field soon balances the force due to the motion of the conductor, and the flow of electrons ceases. *The equilibrium potential difference across the open conductor is the induced emf*, and depends on the length l of wire linking the magnetic flux, the flux density B of the field, and the speed v imparted to the wire.

$$E = Blv$$

When B is in webers/meter^2 (or newtons/ampere meter), l in meters, and v in meters/second, E is given in volts.

Assume that the length of conductor linking the magnetic field in Fig. 20-4 is 0.075 m and the flux density is 0.040 wb/m^2.

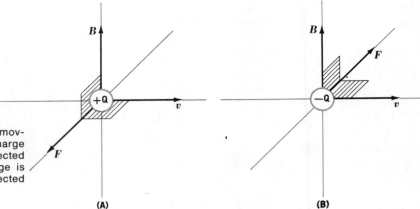

20-5 Force acting on a charge moving in a magnetic field. (A) The charge is positive and the force is directed out of the page. (B) The charge is negative and the force is directed into the page.

(A)   **(B)**

If the conductor is moved down through the flux with a velocity of 1.5 m/sec, the induced emf is

$$E = Blv$$
$$E = 0.040 \text{ wb/m}^2 \times 0.075 \text{ m} \times 1.5 \text{ m/sec}$$
$$E = 0.0045 \text{ v or } 4.5 \text{ mv}$$

In Fig. 20-4 a force equal but opposite to F will act on the positively charged protons in the copper nuclei. Since these are in the bound parts of the copper atoms, they will not move in response to this force. However, positively charged ions in a liquid or gas would move.

The vectors B, v, and F are all mutually perpendicular as shown in Fig. 20-5. If a charge Q moves with a velocity v through a magnetic field of flux density B, the force F acting on the charge becomes

$$F = QvB$$

In the MKS system F is in newtons, Q is in coulombs, v is in meters/second, and B is in newtons/ampere meter (or webers/meter^2).

20.5 The direction of induced current

If the wire of Fig. 20-4 is part of a conducting circuit, there will be an induced current in the circuit when the wire is moved. We will call the length of wire linked with the magnetic flux the *internal circuit* and the rest of the conducting path the *external circuit*.

When the movement of the straight conductor is downward, as shown in Fig. 20-4, electrons move from the negative end **a** through the external circuit to the positive end **b** and through the internal circuit from end **b** to end **a**. Work done by the current in the external circuit expends energy acquired by the electrons as potential energy in the internal circuit, and thus work must be done on the free electrons of the wire to move them in the magnetic field. *This movement must be opposed by a force if the free electrons are to acquire potential energy.*

By Ampère's rule (Section 19.12), the direction of the magnetic field encircling a current is known. This rule can be applied to the induced current considered in Section 20.5.

In Fig. 20-6 is shown a cross-sectional view of a wire poised in a magnetic field. The wire is a part of a closed circuit which cannot be shown in this cross-sectional diagram, but which corresponds to the end **b** of the wire in Fig. 20-4. As this conductor is moved downward through the magnetic field, Fig. 20-6(A), the induced electron current is directed into the page, indicated by the × symbol (tail of the arrow) in the wire cross section. By Ampère's rule, the magnetic field of this induced current is in a counter-clockwise direction.

It is apparent in Fig. 20-6(A) that the permanent magnetic field and the induced field are opposed in the region above the wire, reducing the total flux. Below the wire, the two fields are in the same direction and the flux density is increased. The magnetic field is stronger in the region into which the conductor is moving. The magnetic field of the induced current acts to weaken the field behind it and strengthen the field ahead of it. Thus we have the *additional* magnetic force which opposes the motion of the conductor. Figure 20-6(B) shows that a similar force opposes the reverse motion of the conductor.

This significant relationship between an induced current and the action inducing it was first recognized in 1834 by the German physicist, H. F. E. Lenz (1804–1864). **Lenz's law,** true of all induced currents, can be stated: *An induced current is in such direction as to produce a magnetic force that opposes the force causing the motion by which the current is induced.*

The fact that an induced current always opposes the motion that induces it illustrates the conservation-of-energy principle. Work must be done to induce a current in a closed circuit. The

20.6 Lenz's law

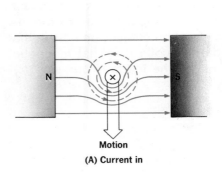

Motion

(A) Current in

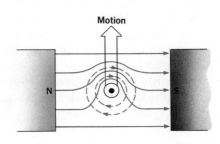

Motion

(B) Current out

20-6 An induced current always produces a magnetic force which opposes the force causing the motion.

energy expended comes from outside the system, and potential energy is stored within the system. The induced current can produce heat or do mechanical or chemical work in the external circuit as electrons of high potential energy fall through a difference of potential in the external circuit.

QUESTIONS

Group A

1. What is the essential condition under which an emf is induced in a conductor?
2. What determines the magnitude of the emf induced in a length of conductor moving in a magnetic field?
3. In what two ways may the rate of change of magnetic flux linking a conductor be increased?
4. Distinguish between an induced emf and an induced current.
5. What is the source of the energy expended as work is done in a load by an induced current resulting from the movement of the conductor in a magnetic field?
6. State Lenz's law.
7. What is the meaning of the negative sign in the expression $E = -N\Delta\phi/\Delta t$?

Group B

8. If a bar magnet is held in a vertical position with the **N** pole down and is dropped through a closed-loop coil whose plane is horizontal, what is the direction of the induced current as the **N** pole approaches the loop?
9. What is the direction of the force acting on the loop in Question 8 as the **N** pole approaches?
10. What physical quantities are measured in (a) webers, (b) webers per meter^2, (c) webers per second, (d) joules per coulomb?
11. Explain how Lenz's law illustrates conservation of energy.
12. Demonstrate that the product Blv is properly expressed in volts.
13. Demonstrate that the product QvB is properly expressed in newtons.
14. The S pole of a bar magnet is entering a solenoid. What is the direction of the flux lines of the induced current inside the solenoid?
15. A permanent magnet is moved away from a stationary coil as shown in the accompanying diagram. (a) What is the direction of the induced current in the coil? (Indicate direction of electron flow in the straight section of conductor below the coil.) (b) What magnetic polarity is produced across the coil by the induced current? (c) Justify your answers to (a) and (b).

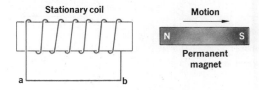

PROBLEMS

Group A

1. A coil of 325 turns moving perpendicular to the flux in a uniform magnetic field experiences a change in flux linkage of 1.15×10^{-5} weber in 0.00100 sec. What is the induced emf?
2. How many turns are required to produce an induced emf of 0.25 volt for a coil which experiences a change in flux linkage at the rate of 5.0×10^{-3} weber per sec?
3. A straight conductor $1\bar{0}$ cm long is moved through a magnetic field perpendicular to the flux at a velocity of 75 cm/sec. If the flux density is 0.025 weber/m², what emf is induced in the conductor?
4. A coil of 75 turns and an area of 4.0 cm² is removed from the gap between the poles of a magnet having a uniform flux density of 1.5 wb/m² in 0.025 sec. What voltage is induced across the coil?
5. A rod 15 cm long is perpendicular to a magnetic field of 4.5×10^{-1} n/a m and is moved at right angles to the flux at the rate of $3\bar{0}$ cm/sec. Find the emf induced in the rod.

GENERATORS AND MOTORS

An emf is induced in a conductor whenever it experiences a change in flux linkage. When the conductor is part of a closed circuit, an induced current can be detected in the circuit. Since, according to Lenz's law, work must be done to induce a current in a conducting circuit, this is a practical source of electric energy.

Moving a conductor up and down in a magnetic field is not a convenient method to induce a current. A more practical way is to shape the conductor into a loop which can be rotated in the magnetic field, with the ends of the loop connected to the external circuit by means of *slip rings*. See Fig. 20-7.

Such an arrangement is a simple *generator*. The loop across which an emf is induced is called the *armature*. The ends of the loop are connected to slip rings which rotate as the armature is turned. A graphite *brush* rides on each slip ring, connecting the armature to the external circuit. *An **electric generator** converts mechanical energy into electric energy.* The essential components of a generator are a *field magnet, an armature*, and *slip rings and brushes*.

The induced emf across the armature, and the induced current in the closed circuit, result from relative motion between the armature and the magnetic flux which effects a change in the flux linkage. Thus either the armature or the magnetic field may be rotated. In some commercial generators the field magnet is rotated and the armature is the stationary element.

20.7 The generator principle

Alex Mulligan

A magneto is a special kind of generator that produces electric current by mechanically changing the amount of magnetic flux associated with a coil. Since magnetos are compact, lightweight and reliable, they are often used for ignition in power mowers (shown above), motorcycles and piston-type airplane engines.

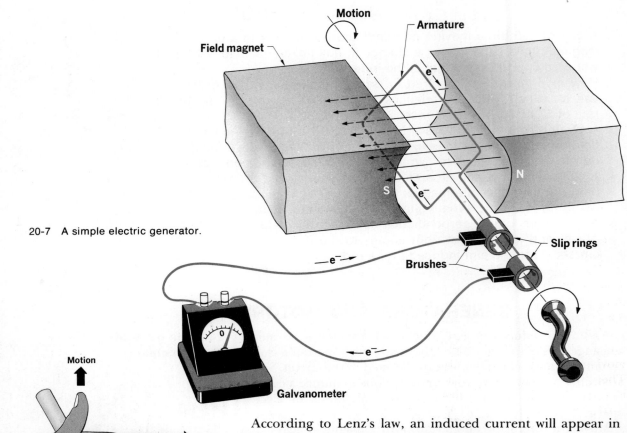

20-7   A simple electric generator.

20-8   The left-hand generator rule.

According to Lenz's law, an induced current will appear in such a direction that it opposes the motion producing it. The direction of induced current in the armature loop of a generator can be easily determined by use of a *left-hand rule* known as the *generator rule,* which takes into account Lenz's law and the fact that an electric current in a metal conductor consists of a flow of electrons. See the diagram, Fig. 20-8.

The generator rule: Extend the thumb, forefinger, and the middle finger of the left hand at right angles to each other. Let the forefinger point in the direction of the magnetic flux and the thumb in the direction the conductor is moving; then the middle finger points in the direction of the induced electron current.

20.8 The simple a-c generator

The two sides of the conducting loop in Fig. 20-7 move through the magnetic flux in opposite directions when the armature is rotated. By the generator rule, as applied to each side of the loop, the direction of the induced current is shown to be toward one slip ring and away from the other. Thus a single-

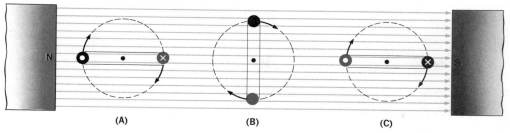

(A)   (B)   (C)

direction current loop is established in the closed circuit. As the direction of each side of the loop changes with respect to the flux, the direction of the induced current is reversed. As the armature rotates through a complete cycle, there are two such reversals in direction of the induced current.

In Fig. 20-9, one side of a conducting loop rotating in a magnetic field is shown cross-sectionally in color while the other side is shown in black. In (A), the colored side of the loop is shown moving down and cutting through the flux. By the generator rule, the induced current is directed into the page. The motion of the black side of the loop induces a current directed out of the page. (The white dot represents the tip of the arrow.)

An emf is induced in a conductor as a result of a change in the flux linking the conductor. In (B), both sides of the loop are moving parallel to the flux and there is no change in linkage. Therefore, no emf is induced across the loop and no current is in the closed circuit.

In (C), the black side of the loop is moving down and cutting through the flux; the induced current is directed into the page. The colored side is moving up through the flux, thus the induced current is directed out of the page. The direction of the current in the circuit is the reverse of that in (A). A quarter cycle later, the emf again drops to zero and there is no current in the circuit. The emf induced across the conducting loop reaches a maximum value when the sides of the loop are moving perpendicular to the magnetic flux. See Section 20.2.

It is not difficult to see from Fig. 20-9 that the magnitude of the induced emf across the conducting loop must vary between zero and a maximum during a half cycle of rotation. The emf must then vary in magnitude between zero and this maximum during the second half cycle but with the opposite polarity across the loop. The emf across the loop thus *alternates* in polarity.

Similarly, the current in a circuit connected to the rotating armature by way of the slip rings alternates in direction, electrons flowing in one direction during one half cycle and in the opposite direction during the other half cycle. *A current which has one direction during part of a generating cycle and the opposite*

20-9 An emf is induced only when there is a change in the flux linking a conductor.

Westinghouse

A large electric generator being tested before shipment.

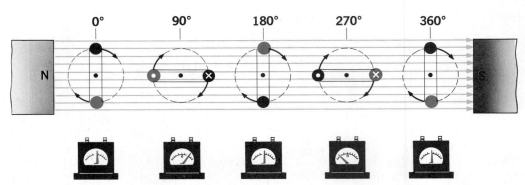

0°   90°   180°   270°   360°

20-10 One cycle of operation of an a-c generator.

direction during the remainder of the cycle is called an **alternating current**, *a-c.* A generator which produces an alternating current must, of course, produce an alternating emf. See Fig. 20-10.

Commercial electric power is usually supplied by the generation of alternating currents and voltages. Such power is referred to as *a-c power.* The expressions *a-c* and *d-c* are commonly used as prefixes to distinguish between alternating-current and direct-current properties. Examples are a-c voltage, d-c current.

20.9 Instantaneous current and voltage

The open-circuit voltage across a battery has a constant magnitude characteristic of the chemical makeup of the battery. The voltage across an armature rotating in a magnetic field, however, has no constant magnitude. It varies from zero through a maximum in one direction and back to zero during one half cycle. It then rises to a maximum in the opposite direction and falls back to zero during the other half cycle of armature rotation. At successive instants of time, different magnitudes of induced voltage exist across the rotating armature. *The magnitude of a varying voltage at any instant of time is called the* **instantaneous voltage** (symbol *e*).

20-11 The instantaneous value of an induced voltage varies with the sine of the displacement angle of the loop in the magnetic field.

The maximum voltage, E_{max}, is obtained when the conductor is moving perpendicular to the magnetic flux, since during this time the rate of change of flux linking the conductor is maximum. *If the armature is rotating at a constant rate in a magnetic field of uniform flux density, the magnitude of the induced voltage varies sinusoidally (as a sine wave) with respect to time.*

In Fig. 20-11 a single loop is rotating in a uniform magnetic field. When the plane of the loop is perpendicular to the flux (**MN** of Fig. 20-11) the conductors are moving parallel to the flux lines; the displacement angle of the loop is said to be zero. We shall refer to this angle between the plane of the loop and the perpendicular to the magnetic flux as θ (theta). When $\theta = 0°$ and $180°$, $e = 0$ v. When $\theta = 90°$, $e = E_{max}$ and when $\theta = 270°$, $e = -E_{max}$. These relationships are apparent from Fig. 20-10. In general the instantaneous voltage *e* varies with

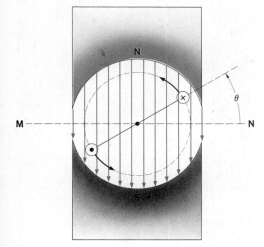

the sine of the displacement angle of the loop.

$$e = E_{max} \sin \theta$$

The current in the external circuit of a simple generator consisting of pure resistance will vary in a similar way, the *maximum current*, I_{max}, occurring when the induced voltage is maximum. From Ohm's law

$$I_{max} = \frac{E_{max}}{R}$$

The *instantaneous current*, i, is accordingly

$$i = \frac{e}{R}$$

but

$$e = E_{max} \sin \theta$$

so

$$i = \frac{E_{max}}{R} \sin \theta$$

and

$$i = I_{max} \sin \theta$$

The simple generator consists of a coil rotating in the magnetic field of a permanent magnet. Any small generator employing a permanent magnet is commonly called a *magneto*. Small magnetos are often used in the ignition systems of gasoline engines for lawn mowers, motor-bikes, and boats.

The generator output is increased in a practical generator by increasing the number of turns on the armature or increasing the field strength. The field magnets of large generators are strong electromagnets; in a-c generators they are supplied with direct current from an auxiliary d-c generator called an *exciter*. See Fig. 20-12.

The performance of large a-c generators is generally more satisfactory if the armature is stationary and the field rotates inside the armature. Such stationary armatures are referred to as *stators* and the rotating field magnets as *rotors*. Circuit current is taken from the stator at the high generated voltage without the use of slip rings and brushes, while the exciter voltage, which is much lower than the armature voltage, is applied to the rotor through slip rings and brushes.

In a simple two-pole generator one cycle of operation produces one cycle or two alternations of induced emf as shown in Fig. 20-13. If the armature (or the field) rotates at the rate of 60 cycles per second, the frequency, f, of the generated voltage sine wave is 60 hertz, the period T being $\frac{1}{60}$ second.

20.10 Practical a-c generators

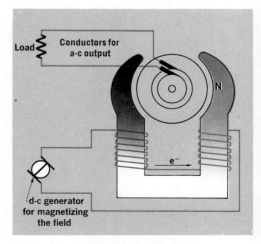

20-12 The field of an alternating-current generator is produced by an electromagnet.

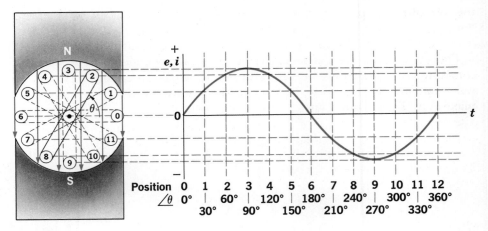

20-13 A sine curve representing current or voltage generated by a single-loop armature rotating at a constant rate in a uniform magnetic field. Positions 0 through 12 on the graph correspond to positions of the rotating armature in the magnetic field as shown to the left.

*The **frequency** of an alternating current or voltage is the number of cycles of current or voltage per second.* If the generator has a 4-pole field magnet, 2 cycles of emf are generated during 1 revolution of the armature or field. Such a generator turning at 30 rps would generate a 60 hz voltage. In general

f = No. of pairs of poles × revolution rate

Practically all commercial power is generated by *three-phase* generators having three armature coils spaced symmetrically, producing emfs spaced 120 degrees apart. The coils are usually connected so that the currents are carried by three conductors.

20-14 The principle of the three-phase alternator. Armature coils schematically diagrammed in (A) are spaced 120° apart generating peak voltage output in three phases as shown in (B). Part (C) shows this output as a vector diagram.

It is evident from Fig. 20-14(B) that three-phase power is smoother than the single-phase power of Fig. 20-13. Electric power is transmitted by a three-phase circuit but is commonly supplied to the consumer by a single-phase circuit.

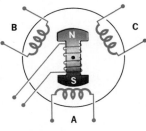

(A) Three-phase generator

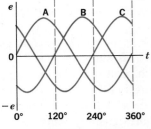

(B) Voltage output

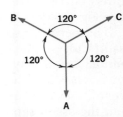

(C) Voltage vector diagram

20.11 The d-c generator

The output of an a-c generator is not suitable for circuits which require a direct current. However, it can be made to supply a *unidirectional* current to the external circuit by connecting the armature loops to a *commutator* instead of slip rings.

*A **commutator** is a split ring, each segment of which is connected to an end of a corresponding armature loop.*

The current and voltage generated in the armature are alternating, as we would expect. However, by means of the commutator, the connections to the external circuit are reversed at the same instant that the direction of the induced emf reverses in the loop. See Fig. 20-15. The alternating current in the armature appears as a *pulsating* direct current in the external circuit, and a pulsating d-c voltage appears across the load. A graph of the instantaneous values of the pulsating current from a generator with a two-segment commutator, plotted as a function of time, is shown in Fig. 20-16. A graph of the voltage across a resistance load would have a similar form. Compare this pulsating d-c output to the a-c output of the generator shown in Fig. 20-13.

The electrons in the external circuit of a d-c generator flow through the circuit in one direction, but this current is quite different from the steady direct current supplied by a battery. The split-ring commutator *rectifies* the alternating current induced in the armature, which is, at any displacement angle θ, $I_{max} \sin \theta$.

To secure a more constant voltage from a d-c generator, and one having a value at any instant which approaches the average value of the emf induced in the entire armature, many coils are wound on the armature. Each coil is connected to a different pair of commutator segments, and the two brushes are placed so as to be in contact with successive pairs of commutator segments while the induced emf is in the E_{max} region in their respective coils. See Fig. 20-17.

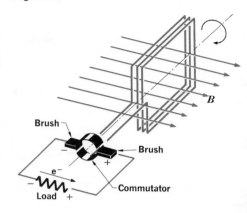

20-15 A split-ring commutator of two segments.

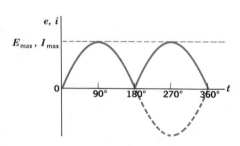

20-16 The variation of current or voltage with time in the external circuit of a simple generator with a two-segment commutator.

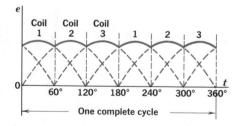

20-17 The output of a d-c generator having three armature coils and a six-segment commutator is fairly constant.

Most d-c generators employ part of the induced power to energize their field magnets, and are said to be *self-exciting*.

The field magnets may be connected in series with the armature loops, so that all of the generator current passes through the coil windings. In the *series-wound* generator an increase in the load increases the magnetic field and consequently the induced emf. See Fig. 20-18.

20.12 Field excitation

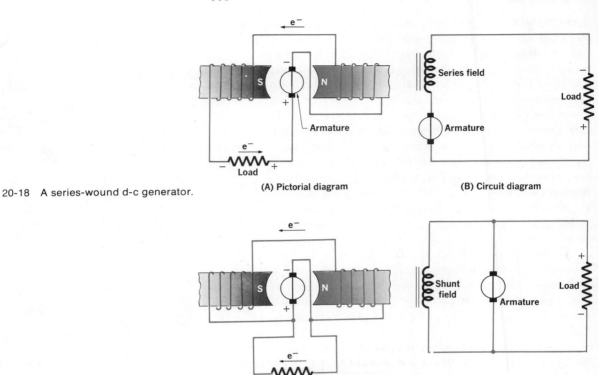

20-18 A series-wound d-c generator.

(A) Pictorial diagram

(B) Circuit diagram

20-19 A shunt-wound d-c generator.

(A) Pictorial diagram

(B) Circuit diagram

The field magnets may also be connected in parallel with the armature so that only a portion of the generated current is used to excite the field. In this *shunt-wound* generator, Fig. 20-19, an increase in load results in a decrease in the field and hence a decrease in the induced emf.

By using a combination of both series and shunt windings to excite the field magnets, the potential difference across the

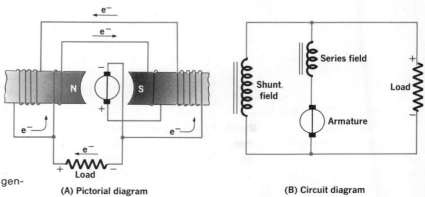

20-20 A compound-wound d-c generator.

(A) Pictorial diagram

(B) Circuit diagram

external circuit of a d-c generator may be maintained fairly constant, an increase in load causing an increase in current in the series windings and a decrease in current in the parallel windings. With the proper number of turns of each type of winding, a constant flux density can be maintained under varying loads. A compound-wound generator is shown in Fig. 20-20.

We can think of the armature turns as the source of emf in the d-c generator circuit. If the field magnet were separately excited, this emf would appear across the armature terminals on open-circuit operation since there would be no induced armature current.

However in a self-excited generator the armature circuit is completed through the field windings. The resistance of the armature turns, r_a, is in this current loop, producing a situation analogous to that of a battery with internal resistance furnishing current to an external circuit. A potential drop $I_a r_a$, of opposite polarity to the induced emf, must appear across the armature, the armature potential difference, V, being

$$V = E - I_a r_a$$

The resistance circuit of the series-wound generator is shown in Fig. 20-21. The resistance of the field windings, R_f, is in series with the internal resistance of the armature and the load resistance, so that the armature current is in all three resistances.

In Fig. 20-19, the resistance of the shunt windings is in parallel with the load. The resistance circuit of a shunt-wound generator is diagrammed in Fig. 20-22, the resistance of the shunt windings being shown as R_f. The total current of the circuit, I_a, must be in r_a producing an $I_a r_a$ drop across the armature. The potential difference V, which has been shown to be $E - I_a r_a$, then appears across the network consisting of R_f and R_L in parallel. The following Ohm s law relationships hold:

$$I_f = \frac{V}{R_f}$$

$$I_L = \frac{V}{R_L}$$

and

$$I_a = I_f + I_L$$

The total electric power in the generator circuit, P_T, derived from the mechanical energy source which turns the armature, is the product of the armature current, I_a, and the induced emf, E.

$$P_T = EI_a$$

20.13 Ohm's law and generator circuits

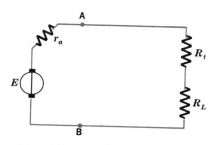

20-21 The resistance circuit of a series-wound d-c generator.

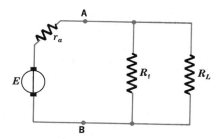

20-22 The resistance circuit of a shunt-wound d-c generator.

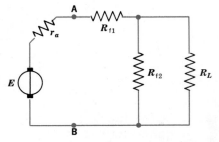

20-23 The resistance circuit of a compound-wound d-c generator.

Some of this power is dissipated as heat in the armature resistance, and some is dissipated in the field windings; the remaining power is delivered to the load.

$$P_T = P_a + P_f + P_L$$

or

$$EI_a = I_a^2 r_a + I_f^2 R_f + I_L^2 R_L$$

The application of these relationships to the d-c shunt-wound generator is illustrated in the example below.

Figure 20-23 shows the resistance circuit of a compound-wound generator. Observe the similarity between this circuit and the resistance network shown in Fig. 17-18 in Chapter 17. How would you proceed to analyze this resistance circuit of the compound-wound d-c generator?

Example

The armature resistance of a shunt-wound generator is 0.50 ohm, the resistance of the shunt winding is 60.0 ohms, and 0.960 kilowatt is delivered to a 15.0-ohm load. (a) What is the potential difference across the load? (b) What is the magnitude of the armature current? (c) What is the emf of the generator?

Solution

The circuit of Fig. 20-22 applies.

(a) $P_L = I_L^2 R_L = \dfrac{V_L^2}{R_L}$

$\quad V_L = \sqrt{P_L R_L} = \sqrt{960 \text{ w} \times 15.0\ \Omega}$

$\quad V_L = 12\overline{0}$ v

(b) $I_a = I_f + I_L$

$\quad I_f = \dfrac{V_f}{R_f}$ and $I_L = \dfrac{V_L}{R_L}$

But $V_L = V_f = V$

$\quad I_a = \dfrac{V}{R_f} + \dfrac{V}{R_L} = \dfrac{12\overline{0} \text{ v}}{60.0\ \Omega} + \dfrac{12\overline{0} \text{ v}}{15.0\ \Omega}$

$\quad I_a = 2.00 \text{ a} + 8.00 \text{ a} = 10.00 \text{ a}$

(c) $V = E - I_a r_a$

$\quad E = V + I_a r_a = 12\overline{0} \text{ v} + (10.00 \text{ a} \times 0.50\ \Omega)$

$\quad E = 125$ v

20.14 The motor effect   We have learned that a current is induced in a conducting loop when it is moving in a magnetic field so that the magnetic flux linking the loop is changing. This is the generator principle.

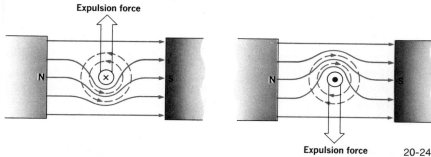

Expulsion force

(A) Electron current in   **(B) Electron current out**

Expulsion force

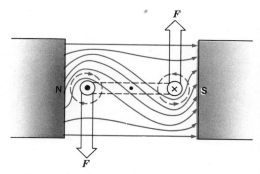

20-24 The motor effect: a current in a magnetic field distorts the field and experiences an expulsion force resulting from this distortion.

By Lenz's law, we have seen that work must be done against a magnetic force as an induced current is generated in the conducting loop. Recall that an induced current always produces a magnetic force that opposes the force causing the motion by which the current is induced.

Instead of employing a mechanical effort to move a conductor poised in the magnetic field, suppose a current is *supplied* to the conductor from an external source. The magnetic field is distorted, as discussed in Section 20.6, and the resulting magnetic force tends to expel the conductor from the magnetic field. This action is known as the *motor effect*, and is illustrated in Fig. 20-24.

If a current is supplied to an armature loop poised in a uniform magnetic field, as in Fig. 20-25, the field around each conductor is distorted. A force acts on each side of the loop proportional to the flux density and the current in the armature loop. These two forces, equal in magnitude but opposite in direction, constitute a *couple*, and produce a torque, T, which causes the armature loop to rotate about its axis. The magnitude of this torque is equal to the product of the force and the *perpendicular* distance between the two forces.

It is evident from Fig. 20-25 that the perpendicular distance between the torque-producing forces is maximum when the conductors are moving perpendicular to the magnetic flux. This distance is equal to the width of the armature loop. When the loop is in any other position with respect to the flux lines, the perpendicular distance between the forces is less than the width of the loop, and consequently the resulting torque must be less than the maximum value. See Fig. 20-26.

We shall refer to the angle between the plane of the loop and the magnetic flux as angle α (alpha). When the angle is zero, the plane of the loop is parallel to the flux lines and the torque is maximum.

$$T_{\max} = Fw$$

20-25 The forces acting on a current loop in a magnetic field.

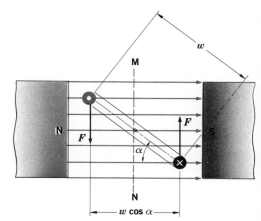

20-26 The torque on a current loop in a magnetic field is proportional to the perpendicular distance between the forces acting on the conductors.

where F is the magnetic force acting on either conductor and w is the width of the conducting loop.

As the armature turns, the angle α approaches 90° and the torque diminishes, since the perpendicular distance between the couple approaches zero. In general, the perpendicular distance between the forces acting on the two conductors is equal to $w \cos \alpha$, as shown in Fig. 20-26. Hence

$$T = Fw \cos \alpha$$

When the plane of the loop is perpendicular to the magnetic flux, angle α is 90°, and since the cosine of 90° = 0, the torque is zero. As the inertia of the conductor carries it beyond this point, a torque develops which reverses the motion of the conductor and returns it to the zero-torque position. In order to prevent this action, the direction of the current in the armature loop must be reversed at the proper instant. The conducting loop terminates in a commutator to reverse the current when the neutral position is reached.

An electric motor performs the reverse function of a generator. *Electric energy is converted to mechanical energy* using the same electromagnetic principles employed in the generator. We can easily determine the direction of motion of the conductor on a motor armature by use of a *right-hand rule* known as the *motor rule*, illustrated in Fig. 20-27.

The motor rule: Extend the thumb, forefinger, and middle finger of the right hand at right angles to each other. Let the fore-finger point in the direction of the magnetic flux and the middle finger in the direction of the electron current; then the thumb points in the direction of the motion of the conductor.

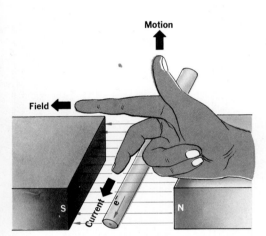

20-27   The right-hand motor rule.

20.15 Back emf in a motor

The simple d-c motor does not differ essentially from a generator; it has a field magnet, an armature, and a commutator ring. In fact, *the operating motor also acts as a generator.* As the conducting loop of the armature rotates in a magnetic field, an emf is induced across the armature turn. The magnitude of this emf depends on the speed of rotation of the armature.

Suppose an incandescent lamp and an ammeter are connected in series with the armature of a small battery-driven motor, as shown in Fig. 20-28. If the motor armature is held so that it cannot rotate as the circuit is closed, the lamp glows and the circuit current is indicated on the meter. Releasing the armature allows the motor to gain speed, and the lamp dims; the ammeter indicates a smaller current.

According to Lenz's law, the induced emf must be opposed to the motion inducing it. The emf induced by the generator

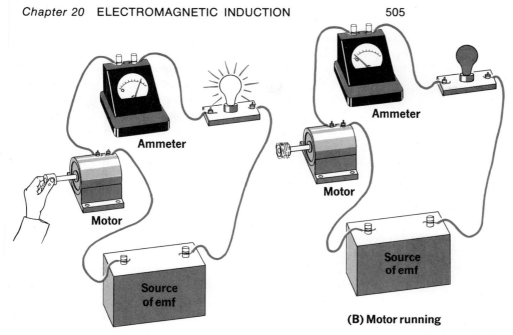

Ammeter

Motor

(A) Motor stalled

Ammeter

Motor

Source of emf

(B) Motor running

20-28 Demonstrating the back emf of a motor.

action of a motor consequently opposes the voltage applied to the armature. *Such an induced emf is called the **back emf** of the motor.* The difference between the applied voltage and the back emf determines the current in the motor circuit.

A motor running at full speed under no load generates a back emf nearly equal to the applied voltage; thus a small current is required in the circuit. The more slowly the armature turns, the smaller is the back emf and consequently the larger is the voltage difference and the circuit current. A motor starting under a full load has a large initial current which decreases due to the generation of a back emf as the motor gains speed.

The induced emf in a generator is equal to the terminal voltage *plus* the voltage drop across the armature resistance.

$$E = V + I_a r_a$$

In the motor, the induced emf is equal to the terminal voltage *minus* the voltage drop across the armature resistance.

$$E = V - I_a r_a$$

Hence, the back emf in a motor must always be less than the voltage impressed across the armature terminals.

A simple motor with a single armature coil would be impractical for many purposes because it has neutral positions and a pulsating torque. In practical motors a large number of coils

20.16 Practical d-c motors

is used in the armature; in fact there is little difference in the construction of motor and generator armatures. Multiple-pole field coils can be used to aid in the production of a uniform torque. The amount of torque produced in any given motor is proportional to the armature current and to the flux density.

Practical d-c motors are of three general types, depending on the method of exciting the field magnets. These are *series*, *shunt*, and *compound* motors. The excitation methods are similar to those of the d-c generators discussed in Section 20.12.

20.17 Practical a-c motors

Nearly all commercial distributors of electric power now supply alternating-current power. Thus a-c motors are far more common today than d-c motors, except for certain specialized applications. Unfortunately much of the theory and technology of a-c motors is quite complex. We will outline very briefly some important generalizations by considering three common types of a-c motors: *the universal motor, the induction motor*, and *the synchronous motor*.

1. The universal motor. Any small d-c series motor can be operated from an a-c supply. When this is done, the currents in the field windings and armature reverse direction simultaneously, maintaining torque in the same direction throughout the operating cycle. However, heat losses in the field windings are extensive unless certain design changes are incorporated in the motor. With laminated pole pieces and special field windings, small series motors operate satisfactorily on either a-c or d-c power. They are known as *universal* motors.

2. The induction motor. Induction motors are the most widely used a-c motors, for they are rugged, simple to build, and well adapted to constant speed requirements. They have two essential parts, a stator of field coils and a rotor. The rotor is usually built of copper bars laid in slotted, laminated iron cores. The ends of the copper bars are shorted by a copper ring to form a cylindrical cage; this common type is known as a *squirrel-cage* rotor.

By using three pairs of poles and a three-phase current the magnetic field of the stator is caused to rotate electrically, and currents are induced in the rotor, which by Lenz's law will then rotate so as to follow the rotating field. Since induction requires relative motion between the conductor and the field, the rotor must *slip* or lag behind the field in order for a torque to be developed. An increase in the load causes a greater slip, a greater induced current, consequently a greater torque.

An induction motor depends on a rotating magnetic field for its operation. Thus a single-phase induction motor is not self-starting without auxiliary means because the magnetic

Ken Chen

A 25-watt a-c motor. The field magnet is energized by the coil at the top.

field of its stator merely reverses periodically and does not rotate electrically. Single-phase induction motors may be started by hand, by an auxiliary motor, or by a *split-phase winding*, a *capacitor*, a *shading coil*, or a *repulsion winding*. The name of the motor usually indicates the auxiliary means for starting it.

3. *The synchronous motor.* We can illustrate the principle of synchronism by placing a thoroughly magnetized compass needle in a rotating magnetic field. The magnetized needle aligns itself with the magnetic field and rotates in synchronization with the rotating field.

The synchronous motor is a constant speed motor, running in synchronism with the a-c generator which supplies the stator current. However, it is not self-starting; the rotor must be brought up to synchronous speed by auxiliary means.

Electric clocks are operated by small single-phase synchronous motors which start automatically as a form of induction motor. Once synchronism is attained, they run as synchronous motors. Electric power companies exercise very accurate control of the 60-hz frequency of commercial power now that electric clocks are in general use.

In large industrial synchronous motors, the permanent-magnet rotor is replaced by an electromagnetic rotor supplied with d-c power, and the stator is commonly supplied with three-phase alternating current.

QUESTIONS

Group A

1. What are the essential components of an electric generator?
2. State the rule which helps us determine the direction of the induced current in the armature loops of a generator.
3. Distinguish between a direct current and an alternating current.
4. Under what circumstances does a simple generator produce a sine-wave variation of induced voltage?
5. What does the term θ (theta) represent in the expression $e = E_{max} \sin \theta$?
6. (a) What is a magneto? (b) For what is it used?
7. What is the function of an *exciter* in the generation of a-c power?
8. (a) What is meant by the frequency of an alternating current? (b) Under what circumstances will the frequency of a generated current be the same as the rps of the armature?
9. How can a generator be made to supply a direct current to its external circuit?
10. In what way is the output of a d-c generator different from the d-c output of a battery?
11. (a) What methods are used to energize the field magnets of d-c generators? (b) Draw a circuit diagram of each method.

12. What are the three power-consuming parts of a d-c generator circuit?
13. What is meant by the term α (alpha) in the torque expression $T = Fw \cos \alpha$?
14. State the rule which helps us determine the direction of motion of the armature loops of a motor.
15. (a) What is meant by back emf? (b) How is it induced in an electric motor?
16. What two quantities influence the amount of torque produced in a motor?
17. What are the three common types of a-c motors?

Group B
18. What is the advantage of having a 4- or 6-pole field magnet in a generator producing a 60-hz output?
19. How does an increase in the load on a series-wound d-c generator affect the induced emf? Explain.
20. How does an increase in the load on a shunt-wound d-c generator affect the induced emf? Explain.
21. How is torque produced on the armature loops of a motor?
22. Why is it true that an operating motor is also a generator?
23. The torque in a series motor increases as the load increases. Explain.
24. Explain why a single-phase induction motor is not self-starting.
25. Why are synchronous motors used in electric clocks?
26. Two conducting loops, identical except that one is silver and the other aluminum, are rotated in a magnetic field. In which case is the larger torque required to turn the loop?

PROBLEMS

Group A
1. A series-wound d-c generator turning at its rated speed develops an emf of 28 volts. The current in the external circuit is 16 amperes and the armature resistance is 0.25 ohm. What is the potential drop across the external circuit?
2. A d-c generator delivers $15\bar{0}$ amperes at $22\bar{0}$ volts when operating at normal speed connected to a resistance load. The total losses are $32\bar{0}0$ watts. Determine the efficiency of the generator.
3. A shunt-wound generator has an armature resistance of 0.15 ohm and a shunt winding of 75.0-ohms resistance. It delivers 18.0 kw at $24\bar{0}$ v to a load. (a) Draw the circuit diagram. (b) What is the generator emf? (c) What is the total power developed by the armature?
4. A magnetic force of 3.5 n acts on one conductor of a conducting loop in a magnetic field. A second force of equal magnitude but opposite direction acts on the opposite conductor of the loop. The conducting loop is 15 cm wide. Find the torque (a) acting on the

conducting loop when the plane of the loop is parallel to the magnetic flux, (b) after the loop has rotated through 30°.
5. The maximum torque which acts on the armature loop of a motor is 10 m n. At what positions of the loop with respect to the magnetic flux will the torque be 5 m n?
6. A shunt-wound motor connected across a 117-v line generates a back emf of 112 v when the armature current is 1$\overline{0}$ a. What is the armature resistance?

INDUCTANCE

An emf is induced across a conductor in a magnetic field when there is a change in the flux linking the conductor. In our study of the generator we observed that an induced emf appears across the armature loop whether the conductors move across a stationary field, or the magnetic flux moves across stationary conductors. *In either action there is relative motion between conductors and magnetic flux.*

This relative motion can be produced in another way. By connecting a battery to a solenoid through a contact key, an electromagnet is produced which has a magnetic field similar to that of a bar magnet. When the key is open, there is no magnetic field. As the key is closed, the magnetic field builds up from zero to some steady value determined by the number of ampere-turns. The magnetic flux spreads out and permeates the region about the coil. *An expanding magnetic field is a field in motion.* When the key in the solenoid circuit is opened, the magnetic flux collapses to zero. *A collapsing magnetic field is also a field in motion.* However, the motion is in the opposite sense to that of the expanding field.

Suppose the solenoid is inserted into a second coil whose terminals are connected to a galvanometer as in Fig. 20-29. The coil connected to a current source is called the *primary*; the coil connected to the load is called the *secondary*. At the instant the contact key is closed, a deflection shows on the galvanometer. There is no deflection, however, while the key remains closed. When the key is opened, a galvanometer deflection again occurs, but in the opposite direction. An emf is induced across the secondary turns whenever the flux linking the secondary is increasing or decreasing.

The relative motion between conductors and flux is in one direction when the field expands, and in the opposite direction when the field collapses. Thus the emf induced across the secondary as the key is closed is of opposite polarity to that induced as the key is opened. The more rapid this relative motion, the greater the magnitude of the induced emf; the

20.18 Mutual inductance

The New York Public Library

Joseph Henry, the American physicist for whom the unit of inductance is named.

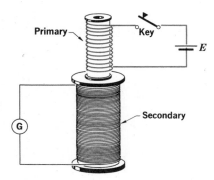

20-29 Varying the current in the primary induces an emf in the secondary.

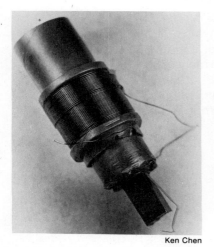

Ken Chen

The 12-volt induction coil of an automobile shown out of its housing. The primary, secondary and soft iron core are visible.

greater the number of turns in the secondary, the greater the magnitude of the induced emf. A soft iron core placed in the primary greatly increases the flux density and the induced emf.

Two circuits so arranged that a change in magnitude of current in one causes an emf to be induced in the other show *mutual inductance*. The **mutual inductance**, *M*, *of two circuits is the ratio of the induced emf in one circuit to the rate of change of current in the other circuit.*

The unit of mutual inductance in the MKS system is called the *henry*, h, after the American physicist Joseph Henry. The mutual inductance of two circuits is *one henry* if *one volt of emf* is induced in the secondary when the current in the primary changes at a rate of *one ampere per second.*

$$M = \frac{-E_S}{\Delta I_P / \Delta t}$$

Here *M* is the mutual inductance of the two circuits in henrys, E_S is the average induced emf across the secondary in volts, and $\Delta I_P / \Delta t$ is the time rate of change of current in the primary in amperes per second. The minus sign indicates that the induced voltage opposes the change in current according to Lenz's law. From this equation the emf induced in the secondary becomes

$$E_S = -M \frac{\Delta I_P}{\Delta t}$$

See the following example.

Example

Two coils have a mutual inductance of 1.25 henrys. Find the average emf induced in the secondary if the current in the primary builds up to 10.0 amperes in 0.0250 second after the switch is closed.

Solution

The primary current must build up from zero to 10.0 amperes during 0.0250 sec, so

$$\frac{\Delta I_P}{\Delta t} = \frac{10.0 \text{ a}}{0.0250 \text{ sec}}$$

The mutual inductance is given as 1.25 h

$$E_S = -M \frac{\Delta I_P}{\Delta t} = -1.25 \text{ h} \times \frac{10.0 \text{ a}}{0.0250 \text{ sec}}$$

$E_S = -50\overline{0}$ v, the emf induced in the secondary

Observe that since $h = \frac{v}{a/\text{sec}}$, the units $h \times \frac{a}{\text{sec}} = \frac{v \times \text{sec} \times a}{a \times \text{sec}} = v$

Suppose a coil is formed by winding many turns of insulated copper wire on an iron core and connecting it in a circuit to a 6-volt battery, a neon lamp, and a switch. See Fig. 20-30. Since the neon lamp requires about 85v-dc to conduct, it acts initially as an open switch in a 6-volt circuit.

When the switch is closed, a conducting path is completed through the coil; the fact that the lamp does not light is evidence that it is not in the conducting circuit. If now the switch is quickly opened, the neon lamp conducts for an instant, producing a flash of light. This means that the lamp is subjected to a potential difference considerably higher than that of the battery. What is the source of this higher voltage?

Any change in the magnitude of current in a conductor causes a change in the magnetic flux about the conductor. If the conductor is formed into a coil, a changing magnetic flux about one turn cuts across adjacent turns and induces a voltage across them. According to Lenz's law, the polarity of this induced voltage acts to oppose the motion of the flux inducing it. The sum of the induced voltages of all the turns constitutes a *counter emf* across the coil.

If a rise of current with its expanding magnetic flux is responsible for the counter emf, this rise of current will be opposed. Therefore, the counter emf is opposite in polarity to the applied voltage. When the switch in Fig. 20-30 was closed the rise of current from zero to the steady-state magnitude was opposed by the counter emf induced across the coil. Once the current reached a steady value, the magnetic field ceased to expand and the opposing voltage fell to zero.

If a fall in current with its collapsing flux is responsible for the induced voltage across the coil, the fall of current is opposed. In this case the induced emf has the same polarity as the applied voltage and tends to sustain the current in the circuit. A very rapid collapse of the magnetic field may induce a very high voltage. *It is the change in current, not the current itself, which is opposed by the induced emf.* It follows, then, that the greater the rate of change of current in a circuit containing a coil, the greater is the magnitude of the induced emf across the coil which opposes this change of current.

The property of a coil which causes a counter emf to be induced across it by the change in current in it is known as *self-inductance*, or simply *inductance*. *The **self-inductance**, L, of a coil is the ratio of the induced emf across the coil to the rate of change of current in the coil.*

The unit of self-inductance in the MKS system is the *henry*, the same unit used for mutual inductance. Self-inductance is *one henry* if *one volt of emf* is induced across the coil when the cur-

20.19 Self-inductance

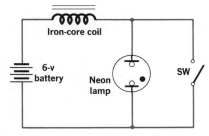

Iron-core coil

6-v battery   **Neon lamp**   **SW**

20-30 A circuit to demonstrate self-inductance.

rent in the circuit changes at the rate of *one ampere per second*.

$$L = \frac{-E}{\Delta I / \Delta t}$$

Here L is the inductance in henrys, E is the emf induced in volts, and $\Delta I / \Delta t$ is the rate of change of current in amperes per second. The minus sign merely shows that the induced voltage is in opposition to the change of current. From this expression the induced emf is given by the following:

$$E = -L \frac{\Delta I}{\Delta t}$$

The equation for inductance L is analogous to the defining equation for capacitance C as expressed in Section 16.14:

$$C = \frac{Q}{V}$$

The presence of a magnetic field in a coil conducting an electric current corresponds to the presence of an electric field in a charged capacitor.

Once a coil has been wound, its inductance is a constant property which depends on *the number of turns, the diameter of the coil, the length of coil,* and *the nature of the core*. Because of its property of inductance, a coil is commonly called an *inductor*.

Inductance in electricity is analogous to inertia in mechanics, which is the property of matter that opposes a *change* of velocity. If a mass is at rest, its inertia opposes a change which imparts a velocity; if the mass has a velocity, its inertia opposes a change which brings it to rest. The flywheel in mechanics illustrates the property of inertia. We know that energy is stored in a flywheel as its angular velocity is increased, and is removed as its angular velocity is decreased.

In an electric circuit inductance has no effect as long as the current is steady. An inductance does, however, oppose any change in the circuit current. An increase in current is opposed by the inductance and energy is stored in its magnetic field since work is done by the source against the counter emf induced. A decrease in current is opposed by the inductance, and energy is removed from its field, tending to sustain the current. *We can think of inductance as imparting a flywheel effect in a circuit having a varying current.* This concept is very important in alternating-current circuit considerations.

20.20 Inductors in series and parallel

The total inductance of a circuit consisting of inductors in series or parallel can be calculated in the same manner as total resistance. When inductors are connected in series the total inductance, L_T, is equal to the sum of the individual inductances, providing there is no mutual inductance between them.

$$L_T = L_1 + L_2 + L_3 + \text{etc.}$$

However, when two inductors are in series and so arranged that the magnetic flux of each links the turns of the other, the total inductance is

$$L_T = L_1 + L_2 \pm 2M$$

The $\pm$ sign is necessary in the general expression because the counter emf induced in one coil by the flux of the other may either aid or oppose the counter emf of self-induction. The two coils can be connected either in series "aiding" or series "opposing" depending on the manner in which their turns are wound.

Inductors connected in parallel so that each is unaffected by the magnetic field of another provide a total inductance according to the following general expression:

$$\frac{1}{L_T} = \frac{1}{L_1} + \frac{1}{L_2} + \frac{1}{L_3} + \text{etc.}$$

See Fig. 20-31 for schematic representation of these series and parallel connections for inductors.

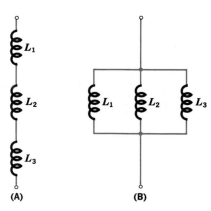

20-31 Inductors in series (A) and in parallel (B).

In principle, the transformer consists of two coils, a primary and a secondary, electrically insulated from each other and wound on the same ferromagnetic core. Electric energy is transferred from the primary to the secondary by means of the magnetic flux in the core. A transformer is shown in its simplest form in Fig. 20-32.

20.21 The transformer

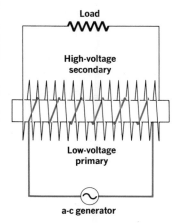

(A) Step-up transformer

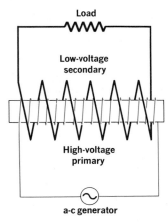

(B) Step-down transformer

20-32 The transformer in its simplest forms.

Refer back to the current sine wave produced by the a-c generator, in Fig. 20-13. The current is changing at its maximum rate as it passes through zero. Consequently, the emf induced across the secondary winding of a transformer is maximum as the primary current passes through zero. The polarity of the secondary emf reverses each time the primary current passes through a positive or negative maximum, since at these instants the current is changing at its minimum rate.

In a power transformer, a *closed* core is used to provide a continuous path for the magnetic flux, insuring that practically all of the primary flux links turns of the secondary. Since the same flux links both primary and secondary turns, the same emf per turn is induced in each, the ratio of secondary to primary emf being equal to the ratio of secondary to primary turns. Neglecting losses, we may assume the terminal voltages to be equal to the corresponding emfs. Thus

$$\frac{V_S}{V_P} = \frac{N_S}{N_P}$$

where V_S and V_P are the secondary and primary terminal voltages, and N_S and N_P are the number of turns in the secondary and primary windings respectively.

If there are 20 turns in the secondary winding for every turn of the primary, the transformer is said to have a *turns ratio* of 20.

$$\textbf{Turns ratio} = \frac{N_S}{N_P} = \frac{20}{1} = 20$$

If the primary voltage is 110 volts, the secondary terminal voltage is 2200 volts, and the transformer is called a *step-up transformer*. If the connections are reversed and the coil with the larger number of turns is made the primary, the transformer becomes a *step-down transformer*. The same primary voltage now produces a voltage across the secondary of 5.5 volts.

It can be shown that when power is delivered to a load in the secondary circuit, the product of the secondary current and secondary turns is essentially equal to the product of the primary current and primary turns.

$$I_S N_S = I_P N_P$$

or

$$\frac{I_S}{I_P} = \frac{N_P}{N_S}$$

Thus when the voltage is stepped up, the current is stepped down; there is no power gain as a result of transformer action. Ideally, primary and secondary power are equal, but actually there are power losses as in any machine.

General Electric

External view, low voltage side of a power transformer.

The efficiency of practical transformers is high and constant over a wide power range. Transformer efficiencies above 95% are common. Efficiency can be expressed as the ratio of the power dissipated in the secondary circuit to the power used in the primary.

$$\textbf{Efficiency} = \frac{P_S}{P_P} \times \textbf{100\%}$$

Power losses in the transformer are of three types: *copper losses, hysteresis losses*, and *eddy-current losses*. All represent wasted energy and appear as heat.

20.22 Transformer losses

1. Copper losses. These result from the resistance of the copper wires in the primary and secondary turns. Copper losses are I^2R heat losses and cannot be avoided.

2. Hysteresis losses. Energy is transformed into heat in reversing the magnetic polarity of the transformer core. The loss is minimized by using a core material with a narrow hysteresis loop.

3. Eddy-current losses. When a mass of conducting metal is moved in a magnetic field or is subjected to a changing magnetic flux, induced currents circulate in the mass. These are closed loops of induced current circulating in planes perpendicular to the magnetic flux, known as *eddy currents*.

Eddy currents in motor and generator armatures and transformer cores produce heat due to the I^2R losses in the resistance of the iron. They are induced currents which do no useful work, and they waste energy by opposing the change which induces them according to Lenz's law. Eddy-current losses are reduced by *laminating* the armature frames and cores. Thin sheets of metal with insulated surfaces are used to build up the armatures and cores, with the laminations set in planes parallel to the magnetic flux, so that eddy-current loops are confined to the width of the individual laminations.

QUESTIONS

1. Define (a) mutual inductance, (b) self-inductance.   **Group A**
2. What types of losses occur in a transformer?
3. What is the effect on the inductance of a coil when an iron core is inserted?
4. Why is a closed core used in a power transformer?
5. If an ideal transformer triples the voltage, how does the secondary current compare with the primary current?

6. Why is an inductor in an electric circuit said to impart a flywheel   **Group B** effect?
7. Why is a transformer considered to be an a-c circuit device?

8. The primary of a step-up transformer with negligible losses is connected to a source of emf and the secondary is connected to a resistance load. What is the relationship between primary and secondary (a) current, (b) power, and (c) number of turns?

9. Explain why the galvanometer of Fig. 20-29 indicates a current in the secondary at the time the key in the primary circuit is closed or opened, but not while it remains closed.

10. The voltage induced across the secondary of an ideal transformer is ten times the voltage applied across the primary. Explain why there is no power gain in the secondary circuit.

PROBLEMS

Group B

1. A step-up transformer is used on a 120-volt line to provide a potential difference of 2400 volts. If the primary has 75 turns, how many turns must the secondary have (neglecting losses)?

2. An initial rise of current in a coil occurs at the rate of 7.5 a/sec at the instant a potential difference of 16.5 v is applied across it. (a) What is the self-inductance of the coil? (b) At the same instant a potential difference of $5\bar{0}$ v is induced across an adjacent coil. Find the mutual inductance of the two coils.

3. A coil with an inductance of 1.2 h and a resistance of 65 ohms is connected across an $8\bar{0}$ v-dc line. What is the rate of current rise at the instant it is connected to the line? (Suggestion: Consider the inductance and resistance of the coil to be in series.)

4. A coil with an inductance of 0.42 h and a resistance of 25 ohms is connected across a 110 v-dc line. What is the rate of current rise (a) at the instant the circuit is closed, (b) at the instant it reaches 85% of its steady-state value?

5. A 5:1 step-down transformer with negligible losses is connected to a $12\bar{0}$ v-ac source. The secondary circuit has a resistance of 15.0 ohms. (a) What is the potential difference across the secondary? (b) What is the secondary current? (c) How much power is dissipated in the secondary resistance? (d) What is the primary current?

6. Assume that the transformer of Problem 5 is replaced by one having an efficiency of 92.5%. What is the primary current?

7. A transformer with a primary of $40\bar{0}$ turns is connected across a $12\bar{0}$ v-ac line. The secondary circuit has a potential difference of $30\bar{0}0$ v. The secondary current is 60.0 ma and the primary current is 1.85 a. (a) How many turns are in the secondary winding? (b) What is the transformer efficiency?

8. A $27\bar{0}$-ohm resistor, a 2.50-h coil, and a switch are connected in series across a 12.0-v battery. At a certain instant after the switch is closed the current is 20.0 ma. (a) What is the potential difference across the resistor? (b) Across the inductor? (c) What is the rate of change of current at this instant?

Chapter 21

Alternating-Current Circuits

a-c MEASUREMENTS

A single conducting loop rotating at a constant speed in a uniform magnetic field generates an alternating emf. Its magnitude varies with the sine of the angle which the plane of the loop makes with the perpendicular to the magnetic flux. The instantaneous value of the emf is

$$e = E_{max} \sin \theta$$

The instantaneous current in a pure resistance load comprising the external circuit of the generator is similarly expressed as

$$i = I_{max} \sin \theta$$

This current is a consequence of the alternating voltages impressed across the load, and its maxima and minima occur

21.1 Power in an a-c circuit

Thomas A. Edison, left, and Charles P. Steinmetz in Steinmetz's laboratory at Schenectady, N.Y., in 1922.

517

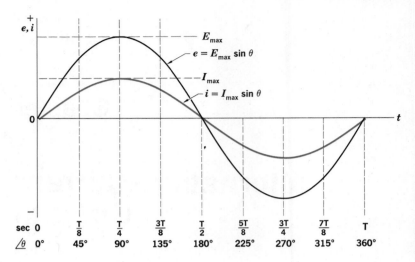

21-1 One cycle of alternating current and voltage in phase.

at the same instants as the voltage maxima and minima. The alternating current and voltage are said to be *in phase*, a relationship characteristic of a resistance load to which an alternating voltage is applied. Sine curves of in-phase alternating current and voltage are shown in Fig. 21-1.

Electric power in a d-c circuit is the product of E and I. In an a-c circuit the instantaneous power, p, is the product of e and i. These relationships are shown in Fig. 21-2.

The voltage and current in Fig. 21-2(B) are shown in phase as in a resistance load. The instantaneous power curve varies between some positive maximum and zero and has an average value, P. The instantaneous power gives a curve with a frequency twice that of e and i, whose ordinates are always positive since e and i are in phase. During the first half cycle e and i are both positive, so their products are positive. During the second half cycle both e and i are negative, but again their products are positive.

21-2 A comparison of d-c and a-c power.

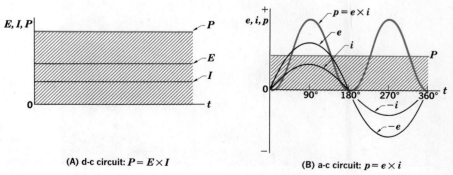

(A) d-c circuit: $P = E \times I$

(B) a-c circuit: $p = e \times i$

If a zero-centered d-c ammeter were placed in an a-c circuit, the pointer would tend to swing alternately in the positive and negative directions. At all but the very lowest frequencies, the inertia of the meter movement would cause the pointer to remain at zero, in effect, averaging out the sine-wave variations. The same would be true of an a-c voltage measurement. *The average value of a sine curve of alternating current or voltage is zero.* This is true regardless of the magnitude of the maximum values attained.

The most useful value of an alternating current is based on its heating effect in an electric circuit and is commonly referred to as the *effective value*. The **effective value** of an alternating current *is the number of amperes which, in a given resistance, produces heat at the same average rate as that number of amperes of steady direct current.*

Let us assume that a resistance element is immersed in water in a calorimeter and that a steady direct current of 1 ampere in the circuit raises the temperature of the water 25 C° in 10 minutes. An alternating current in the same resistance which would raise the temperature the same amount in the same time is said to have an effective value of 1 ampere. The symbol for the effective value of an alternating current is I, the same as that for steady direct current. When the magnitudes of alternating currents are given in amperes, effective values should be understood, unless other values are clearly stated.

From Joule's law, $Q = I^2Rt/J$, we know that the heating effect of an electric current is proportional to I^2. The average rate of heat production by an alternating current is proportional to the mean (average) of the instantaneous values of current squared. From Fig. 21-3 it is evident that the mean value of I^2 is $\frac{1}{2}I_{max}^2$, because the square of the instantaneous values of the alternating current of frequency f gives a curve of frequency $2f$ which varies between I_{max}^2 and zero. Thus

$$I^2 = \frac{I_{max}^2}{2}$$

and

$$I = \sqrt{\frac{I_{max}^2}{2}} = \frac{I_{max}}{\sqrt{2}}$$

$$I = 0.707\, I_{max}$$

Then

$$I_{max} = 1.414\, I$$

A sine curve of alternating current having a maximum value of 10.0 amperes is plotted in Fig. 21-3. *The effective value is the square root of the mean of the instantaneous values squared* and is

21.2 Effective values of current and voltage

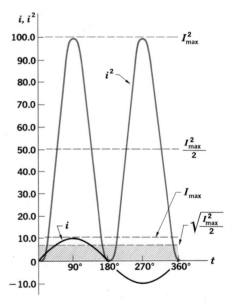

21-3 Current and current squared curves showing the effective value of an alternating current.

frequently called the *root-mean-square* (rms) value. In the example shown, the rms or effective value of current is

$$I = \sqrt{\frac{I_{max}^2}{2}} = \sqrt{\frac{10\overline{0} \text{ a}^2}{2}} = \sqrt{50.0 \text{ a}^2} = 7.07 \text{ a}$$

The rms or effective value of an a-c emf is expressed similarly.

$$E = 0.707 \ E_{max}$$

Then

$$E_{max} = 1.414 \ E$$

For a potential difference which does not include a source of emf, these expressions become

$$V = 0.707 \ V_{max}$$

and

$$V_{max} = 1.414 \ V$$

Thus a house-lighting circuit rated at 120 vac varies between +170 volts and −170 volts during each cycle. An appliance which draws 10.00 amperes when connected across this circuit has a current that varies between +14.14 amperes and −14.14 amperes.

If the load is a pure resistance, the current and voltage are in phase, and the average power consumed is

$$P = I^2R = VI$$
$$P = 120 \text{ v} \times 10.00 \text{ a}$$
$$P = 1200 \text{ w}$$
$$(\text{v} \times \text{a} = \text{j/c} \times \text{c/sec} = \text{j/sec} = \text{w})$$

If, however, the current and voltage are not in phase, *the average power of the circuit is not a simple product of the effective values of voltage and current.* The products I^2R and VI are no longer the same, the former giving the *actual* power dissipation and the latter the *apparent* power. This is a basic difference between d-c and a-c circuits and it stems from the fact that phase differences between current and voltage may be produced by capacitance and inductance in an a-c circuit. These effects add a new dimension to alternating-current circuits known as *impedance* which will be considered in Section 21.6.

21.3 a-c meters   A galvanometer, which provides the basic movement for d-c instruments, cannot be used directly in a-c circuits. At ordinary power frequencies inertia prevents the movement from following the alternations. The pointer simply vibrates about the zero-center position on the meter scale.

In some specialized applications, peak reading a-c meters can be used. The cathode-ray oscilloscope can be, in fact, a peak-to-peak voltmeter. In general, however, alternating-current instruments are designed to indicate *effective values* of current or voltage. The a-c instruments are of five common types: *moving iron-vane meters, hot-wire meters, electrodynamometers, rectifier-type meters,* and *induction watt-hour meters.*

1. Moving iron-vane meters. If two similar iron bars are subjected to a common magnetic field, a repelling force develops between them. This principle is used in iron-vane meters. One iron vane is fixed and the other is pivoted so that it can rotate when a magnetizing current is in the actuating coil, as shown in Fig. 21-4.

The repulsion that actuates the moving vane does not distinguish polarity of the magnetic field, and can be applied in either d-c or a-c meters. Inexpensive a-c instruments are commonly of the moving-vane type, the same basic mechanism being used for both voltmeters and ammeters. When a current is in the actuating coil, the moving vane exerts a force against a restoring spring, and the final pointer position is a measure of the coil current.

2. Hot-wire meters. Electric meters generally depend on some form of electrodynamic action of an electric current for their operation. The hot-wire meter is unique in that it depends on the heating action of a current. Consequently, it can be used to measure the magnitude of a steady direct current, the average value of a pulsating direct current, or the effective value of an alternating current. A diagram of a hot-wire mechanism is shown in Fig. 21-5.

A fine wire of a platinum alloy is used as the resistance **AB**. When a current passes through the meter circuit, the I^2R loss in wire **AB** raises its temperature. Expansion results, reducing the tension on wire **CD**. This allows the spring to pull thread **EF**, which is looped around the pulley, to the left. The pulley rotates, moving the pointer over the meter scale.

Hot-wire meters are sluggish and the pointer moves slowly to the final deflection. In some applications, however, this characteristic is advantageous. These meters are, of course, sensitive to temperature changes. When used as ammeters, they require a shunt for all except very small currents. A high resistance is connected in series with wire **AB** when the mechanism is used as a voltmeter.

3. Electrodynamometers. Better quality instruments for certain a-c measurements at common power frequencies are of the electrodynamometer type. The dynamometer mechanism is probably the most versatile device in general use for electric

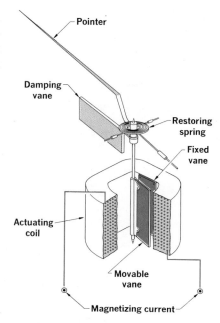

21-4 The basic mechanism of a moving iron-vane meter.

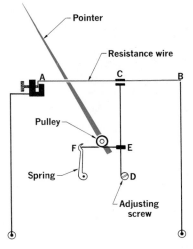

21-5 The hot-wire meter mechanism.

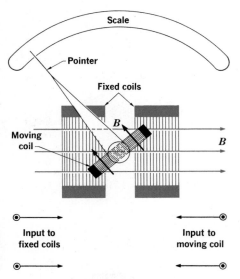

21-6   The electrodynamometer mechanism.

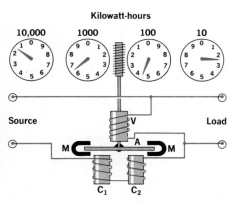

21-7   The induction-type watt-hour meter.

measurements. In principle, the electrodynamometer is similar to the galvanometer movement of d-c meters, but it does not include a permanent magnet. A moving coil rotates in a magnetic field created by a pair of fixed coils carrying a magnetizing current. These coils can be considered to be two parts of a single coil separated in the middle to allow the spindle of the moving coil to pass through. The basic components of a dynamometer mechanism are shown in Fig. 21-6.

A current in the fixed coils produces a magnetic flux, which at some instant is to the right as shown in Fig. 21-6. At the same instant the current in the moving coil produces a flux along its axis. The moving coil tends to turn so as to align the two magnetic fields; the resulting torque produces a pointer deflection indicative of the product of the two coil currents. The dynamometer mechanism can be used to produce ammeters, voltmeters, and wattmeters.

4. Rectifier-type meters. A d-c meter of the galvanometer type can be used for a-c measurements when a rectifier is provided to convert the alternating current to a pulsating direct current. The instrument responds to the average value of the pulsating direct current but is generally calibrated to read effective values. These meters are usually preferred for current measurements in the audio-frequency range.

5. Induction watt-hour meters. Electric power companies sell *electric energy* at a cost of a few cents for each kilowatt-hour. An induction type watt-hour meter is commonly used in a-c circuits to measure and record the quantity of electric energy supplied to a customer.

The watt-hour meter is essentially a small single-phase induction motor that turns at a rate proportional to the power used. The shaft of the motor armature is geared to a system of dials which indicate, in kilowatt-hours, the energy used in the load connected in the circuit.

In Fig. 21-7 a simplified diagram of the induction watt-hour meter is shown. A coil V is connected in parallel with the load and acts as a voltage winding. The coils C_1 and C_2 are connected in series with the load and act as current windings. An aluminum disk **A** turns as an induction-motor armature to follow the sweeping flux set up by the combination of coils. Permanent magnets **M** induce eddy currents in the rotating disk which oppose the motion of the disk and produce the slippage required for the induction-motor operation.

21.4 Inductance in an a-c circuit

In Chapter 20 inductance was described as an inertia-like property opposing any *change* in current in a coil and causing a counter emf proportional to the rate of change of current to be induced across the coil. Figure 21-8 shows the wave forms characteristic of a circuit consisting of pure inductance to which an alternating voltage is applied. The instant the current is passing through zero in a positive direction, it is changing at its maximum rate. Thus the counter emf induced across the coil at this instant must be at its negative maximum value. When the current reaches the positive maximum, the rate of change of current is zero, and the induced emf is zero. Again 90° later, the current is changing in a negative direction at its maximum rate and the counter emf is at its positive maximum.

The counter emf follows behind the current inducing it by 90°, and is opposite in polarity to the applied voltage as shown in Fig. 21-8. The current in the circuit must then *lag behind* the applied voltage by 90°. It is just as appropriate to consider that the voltage leads the current by 90°; the *difference in time phase* is 90°. We can think of alternating currents and voltages as vectors rotating counterclockwise in a polar coordinate system as shown in Fig. 21-9. The phase angle between the voltage and current vectors is commonly referred to as the

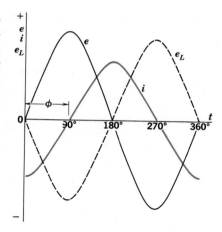

21-8 Current and voltages in an a-c circuit containing pure inductance.

21-9 Phase relation of an a-c current and voltage in pure resistance and pure inductance circuits.

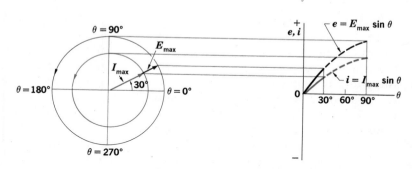

(A) *e* and *i* in pure resistance

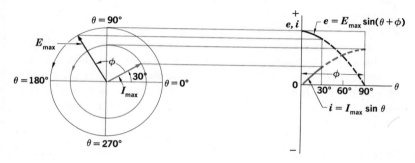

(B) *e* and *i* in pure inductance

angle ϕ (the lower case Greek letter phi). This relation in an a-c circuit can be expressed as follows:

$$i = I_{max}\ sin\ \theta$$
$$e = E_{max}\ sin\ (\theta + \phi)$$

The phase angle, ϕ, of a leading voltage is *positive*, and it indicates that the voltage is ahead of the current in phase. Suppose the effective value of voltage represented in Fig. 21-9(B) is 10.0 volts. When the displacement angle θ is 30°, the instantaneous value e will be

$$e = E_{max} \sin (\theta + \phi)$$
$$e = E_{max} \sin (30° + 90°)$$
$$e = E_{max} \sin 120°$$

But

$$E_{max} = 1.414\ E = 1.414 \times 10.0\ v$$
$$E_{max} = 14.1\ v$$

Then

$$e = 14.1\ v \times \sin 120°$$
$$\sin 120° = \sin 60° = 0.866$$
$$e = 14.1\ v \times 0.866$$
$$e = 12.2\ v$$

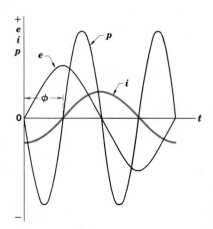

21-10 Power curve in a pure inductance.

Plotted as a function of time, the products of the instantaneous values of voltage and current in a pure inductance yield an instantaneous power curve as shown in Fig. 21-10. Observe that the average power is zero. While the current is changing from zero to a maximum, energy is taken from the source and stored in the magnetic field of the inductor. These portions of the power curve are positive. When the current is changing from a maximum to zero, all of the energy stored in the magnetic field is returned to the source. These portions of the power curve are negative. Therefore, the net energy removed from the source during a cycle by a pure inductance is zero, and the product of the rms voltage and current can indicate only an *apparent power*.

21.5 Inductance and resistance

An inductor cannot be entirely without resistance, since it is not possible to have pure inductance in a circuit. The ordinary resistance of the conductor is an inherent property of any coil. We can treat the resistance of an inductive circuit as a lumped value in series with a pure inductance. This arrangement is shown in Fig. 21-11(A).

The same current must be present in all parts of a series circuit, so the circuit current is used as a reference vector to show the phase relation between current and voltages in the

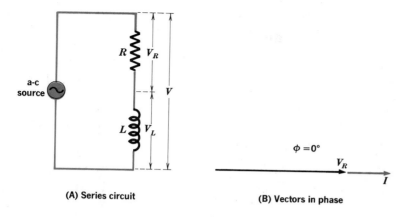

(A) Series circuit   **(B) Vectors in phase**

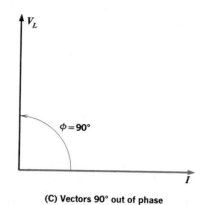

(C) Vectors 90° out of phase

21-11 An **L-R** circuit showing the phase relations between voltage and current in the resistance and in the inductance.

resistance and inductance. The voltage across the resistance is in phase with the circuit current; this in-phase relation is shown in Fig. 24-11(B). The voltage across the inductance leads the circuit current by 90°, as shown in (C) of the same figure. The voltage across the series combination of R and L then leads the circuit current by some angle between 90° and zero.

With the circuit current of Fig. 21-11 as a reference, we observe that V_R and V_L have a phase difference of 90°. Thus the two voltages in series cannot be added algebraically, but must be added *vectorially* to give the circuit voltage, V. The *vector sum* of V_R and V_L is shown in the *phase diagram*, Fig. 21-12. The phase angle, ϕ, has a positive value less than 90°.

No power is dissipated in the inductance. The average power dissipated in the resistance is equal to the product of the effective values of the circuit current and the voltage across the resistance.

$$P_R = V_R I$$

From the voltage diagram (see Fig. 21-12) it is apparent that

$$V_R = V \cos \phi$$

Thus the actual power consumed in the external circuit is

$$P = VI \cos \phi$$

The total power consumed in the internal and external circuits is, of course,

$$P_T = EI \cos \phi$$

When the phase angle ϕ is *zero* (a pure resistive load), $\cos \phi = 1$, and the product $VI \cos \phi = VI$. When the phase angle ϕ is +90° (a pure inductive load), $\cos \phi = 0$, and the

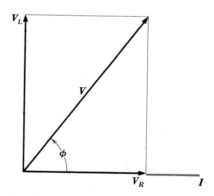

21-12 A phase diagram showing the vector addition of voltages in a series circuit containing inductance and resistance.

product $VI \cos \phi = 0$ (Fig. 21-10). The cosine of ϕ is known as the *power factor* (pf) of an a-c circuit. See Fig. 21-13.

$$\mathbf{pf} = \cos \phi = \frac{V_R}{V}$$

Electric power companies strive to maintain a power factor near unity in their distribution lines. Why?

21.6 Impedance in an a-c circuit

The potential drop across the resistance in the circuit of Fig. 21-11 is represented by the vector V_R in Fig. 21-12. This potential difference is, of course, equal to the product IR, R being the common resistance to current in the external circuit. The inductance, too, has a potential difference across it as a consequence of its opposition to the current in the circuit. This opposition is *nonresistive* as no power is dissipated in the inductance, and is called *reactance, X*. It is expressed in *ohms*. When reactance is due to inductance it is referred to as *inductive reactance, X_L*. **Inductive reactance**, X_L, *is the ratio of the effective value of inductive potential, V_L, to the effective value of current, I.*

$$\boldsymbol{X_L = \frac{V_L}{I}}$$

Thus the voltage V_L of Fig. 21-12 is equal to the product IX_L.

The inductive reactance of a coil is directly proportional to the inductance, and to the frequency of the current in the circuit since the rate of change of a given current increases with frequency. The larger the inductance, the greater is the opposition to the change in current at a given frequency.

$$X_L = 2\pi f L$$

When f is in hertz and L is in henrys, X_L is expressed in ohms of inductive reactance, 2π being a proportionality constant.

The vector sum of IX_L and IR is equal to the voltage applied to the external circuit, V of Fig. 21-12. This potential difference is the product of the circuit current I and the combined effect of the inductive reactance X_L and the resistance R in the load. The joint effect of reactance and resistance in an a-c circuit is called *impedance, Z*. It is expressed in ohms. Thus V is equal to the product IZ. See Fig. 21-14(A). Dividing each voltage IX_L, IR, and IZ by the current I yields respectively inductive reactance X_L, resistance R, and impedance Z as in the *impedance diagram* shown in Fig. 21-14(B).

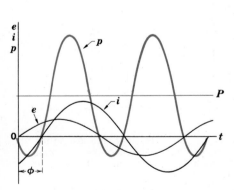

21-13   Power in an a-c circuit containing resistance and inductance.

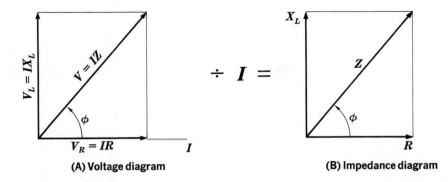

(A) Voltage diagram   **(B) Impedance diagram**

21-14 The derivation of an impedance diagram of an **L-R** series circuit.

From trigonometry, the tangent of the phase angle ϕ is defined by the ratio of the side opposite ϕ to the side adjacent. These sides of the right triangle in the impedance diagram are respectively X and R. Therefore

$$\frac{X}{R} = \tan \phi$$

This equation gives X/R as a *function* of ϕ. It also enables us to determine ϕ as a function of X/R, which is to say that ϕ *is an angle* whose tangent is X/R. This expression gives the *inverse function* of the above equation and is commonly written as

$$\phi = \arctan \frac{X}{R}$$

The impedance Z has a magnitude equal to $\sqrt{R^2 + X^2}$ and a direction angle ϕ (with respect to R) whose tangent is X/R. It can be written as a polar vector of the form $Z\lfloor\phi$ as

$$Z = \sqrt{R^2 + X^2} \; \lfloor \arctan X/R$$

When the reactance is inductive, $X = X_L$ and ϕ is a positive angle whose tangent is X_L/R.

We can now rewrite the Ohm's-law expression for d-c circuits in a form which applies to a-c circuits. For the entire circuit:

$$E = IZ$$

For the external circuit:

$$V = IZ$$

See the following example.

Example

A coil with a resistance of $3\bar{0}$ ohms and an inductance of 0.12 henry is connected across a 120-volt $6\bar{0}$-hertz source. (a) What is the magnitude of the circuit current? (b) What is the phase angle? (c) What power is expended in the external circuit?

Solution

The circuit of Fig. 21-11 and the vector diagram of Fig. 21-12 apply to this problem.

(a) The magnitude of Z will be determined since only the magnitude of the circuit current is required in part (a).

By Ohm's law, $I = \dfrac{V}{Z}$

where the magnitude of $Z = \sqrt{R^2 + X_L^2}$ and $\quad X_L = 2\pi fL$

So, $\quad Z = \sqrt{R^2 + (2\pi fL)^2}$

Thus, $\quad I = \dfrac{V}{\sqrt{R^2 + (2\pi fL)^2}} = \dfrac{120 \text{ v}}{\sqrt{(3\bar{0}\ \Omega)^2 + (2\pi \times 6\bar{0}/\text{sec} \times 0.12 \text{ h})^2}}$

$I = \dfrac{120 \text{ v}}{54\ \Omega} = 2.2$ a, the circuit current

(b) $\phi = \arctan \dfrac{X_L}{R} = \arctan \dfrac{45\ \Omega}{3\bar{0}\ \Omega} = \arctan 1.\dot{5}$

From Table 6 of the Appendix, $\phi = 56°$, indicating a leading voltage

(c) $P = VI \times \text{pf} = VI \cos \phi = 120 \text{ v} \times 2.2 \text{ a} \times \cos 56° = 120 \text{ v} \times 2.2 \text{ a} \times 0.56$

$P = 150$ watts

21.7 Capacitance in an a-c circuit

A capacitor in a d-c circuit charges to the applied voltage and effectively opens the circuit. The potential difference across a capacitor can change only as the charge on the capacitor changes. Since $Q = CV$, for a given capacitor the charge Q, in coulombs, is directly proportional to the potential difference V, in volts. Thus we can refer to the charge in terms of the voltage across the capacitor.

An uncharged capacitor offers no opposition to a charging current from a source of emf. However, as a charge builds up on the capacitor plates, a voltage develops across the capacitor which opposes the charging current. When the charge is such that the voltage across the capacitor is equal to the applied voltage, the charging current must be zero. Why? These two conditions are illustrated in Fig. 21-15. We can conclude that

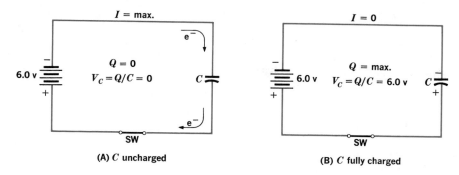

(A) C uncharged   (B) C fully charged

21-15 As a capacitor is charged, a voltage develops across it which opposes the charging current.

the current in a capacitor circuit is maximum when the voltage across the capacitor is zero, and is zero when the capacitor voltage is maximum.

Let us examine the effect of pure capacitance in an a-c circuit. When the initial charging current is a positive maximum, the voltage across the capacitor plates is zero. As the capacitor charges, the potential difference builds up and the current decays, the charging current reaching zero when the capacitor voltage is maximum.

As the charging current reverses direction and increases toward a negative maximum, electrons flow from the negative plate of the capacitor through the circuit to the positive plate, removing the charge. The capacitor then charges in the opposite sense and the potential difference reaches a maximum with opposite polarity as the current returns to zero. Thus, *the voltage across the capacitor lags the circuit current by 90°.* See Fig. 21-16.

The phase angle ϕ in an a-c circuit with a pure capacitance load is $-90°$, and the circuit has a *lagging* voltage. The phase relationship is expressed as

$$i = I_{max} \sin \theta \quad \text{and} \quad e = E_{max} \sin (\theta + \phi)$$

21-16 Pure capacitance in an a-c circuit.

(A) Circuit

(B) e_C and i vs. time

These expressions are similar to those given for i and e in Section 21.4. However, the phase angle of a lagging voltage is *negative*. Hence the sign of the phase angle ϕ must always be introduced properly.

Suppose the effective value of voltage across a capacitor is 10.0 volts. When the displacement angle θ is 30°, the instantaneous value of e is

$$e = E_{\max} \sin (\theta + \phi)$$
$$e = E_{\max} \sin [30° + (-90°)]$$
$$e = E_{\max} \sin (-60°)$$

Now

$$E_{\max} = 1.414 \ E = 1.414 \times 10.0 \text{ v}$$
$$e = 14.1 \text{ v} \times \sin (-60°)$$

and

$$\sin (-60°) = -0.866$$

Therefore

$$e = 14.1 \text{ v} \times (-0.866)$$
$$e = -12.2 \text{ v}$$

Compare this result with the similar computation in Section 21.4.

Plotted as a function of time, the product of the instantaneous values of current and voltage in a circuit of pure capacitance results in the instantaneous power curve shown in Fig. 21-17. As in a circuit with pure inductance, the average power is zero. Energy is taken from the source of emf and stored in the electric field between the capacitor plates, as the current changes from each maximum to zero. All this energy is returned to the source as the current rises from zero to either maximum. Thus the product of the effective values of current and voltage indicates an *apparent power*. The phase angle of −90° yields a power factor equal to zero [cos (−90°) = 0] and so the *actual power* dissipated must be zero.

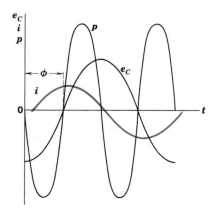

21-17 Power curve in a circuit of pure capacitance.

21.8 Capacitance and resistance

The opposition to the current in an a-c circuit due to capacitance is *nonresistive* since no power is dissipated in the capacitor; it is called *capacitive reactance*. The symbol used for capacitive reactance is X_C and the unit is the *ohm*.

The inherent resistance in any practical circuit containing capacitance can be represented in series with X_C. An *R-C* series circuit is shown in Fig. 21-18. The potential difference across the external circuit V is the vector sum of V_C and V_R, the series current being used as the reference vector. Of course there is no electron flow through the capacitor; it is alternately charged, first in one sense and then in the other, as the charg-

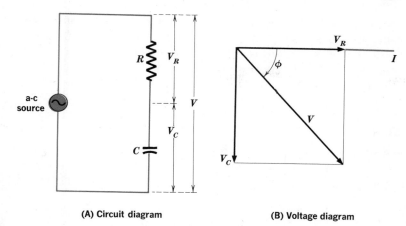

(A) Circuit diagram   **(B) Voltage diagram**

21-18 An *R-C* series circuit showing the phase relations of the different voltages to the circuit current.

ing current alternates. The phase angle ϕ is negative, characteristic of a lagging voltage.

We can produce the corresponding impedance diagram by dividing each voltage vector by the circuit current. See Fig. 21-19. Just as V_C is negative with respect to V_L of Fig. 21-14(B), so is X_C plotted in the opposite direction to X_L.

Since $V_C = Q/C$, the larger the capacitance, the lower the potential difference developed across it for a given charge. *Thus the reactance to a circuit current is inversely proportional to the capacitance in the circuit.* As the frequency of a charging current is increased, a shorter time is available during each current cycle for the capacitor to charge and discharge. Smaller changes in voltage occur across the capacitor. *Hence the capacitive reactance to the circuit current is inversely proportional to the current frequency.*

$$X_C = \frac{1}{2\pi fC}$$

When f is in hertz and C is in farads, X_C, the capacitive reactance, is expressed in ohms.

21-19 The derivation of an impedance diagram of an *R-C* series circuit.

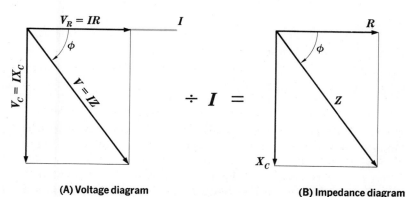

(A) Voltage diagram   **(B) Impedance diagram**

The impedance of a circuit containing capacitance and resistance in series has a magnitude equal to $\sqrt{R^2 + X^2}$ and a phase angle ϕ whose tangent is $-X_C/R$. The impedance in its general polar form $Z \underline{|\phi}$, is expressed as $\sqrt{R^2 + X^2}\ \underline{|\arctan X/R}$, where $X = X_C$. See the following example.

Example

A capacitance of 20.0 μf and a resistance of $10\overline{0}$ Ω are connected in series across a $12\overline{0}$-v 60.0-hertz source. (a) Find the impedance of the circuit. (b) What is the circuit current? (c) What is the potential difference across the capacitor?

Solution

(a) The circuit and diagrams of Fig. 21-18 and Fig. 21-19 apply.

$$Z = \sqrt{R^2 + X^2}\ \underline{|\arctan X/R}$$

But

$$X = X_C = \frac{1}{2\pi f C} = \left(\frac{1}{2\pi \times 60.0 \times 20.0 \times 10^{-6}}\right) \text{ohms}$$

$$X_C = 133\ \Omega$$

Magnitude of

$$Z = \sqrt{(10\overline{0}\ \Omega)^2 + (133\ \Omega)^2}$$

$$Z = 166\ \Omega$$

$$\phi = \arctan \frac{-X_C}{R} = \arctan \frac{-133\ \Omega}{10\overline{0}\ \Omega}$$

$$\phi = \arctan -1.33$$

$$\phi = -53°, \text{ the phase angle of a lagging voltage}$$

Therefore, the impedance can be expressed as

$$Z = 166\ \Omega\ \underline{|-53°}$$

(b) $I = \dfrac{V}{Z} = \dfrac{12\overline{0}\ \text{v}}{166\ \Omega}$

$$I = 0.723\ \text{a, the circuit current}$$

(c) $V_C = IX_C = 0.723$ a $\times$ 133 Ω

$$V_C = 96.2\ \text{v, the potential difference across } C.$$

21.9 L, R, and C in series   Inductance produces a leading voltage and a positive phase angle in an a-c circuit, and capacitance produces a lagging voltage and a negative phase angle. Of course, the voltage across a resistance must be in phase with the current in the resistance. Suppose values of L, R, and C are connected in series

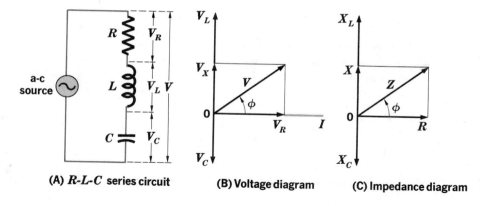

(A) *R-L-C* **series circuit**   **(B) Voltage diagram**   **(C) Impedance diagram**

across an a-c source of emf as in Fig. 21-20(A). The *total reactance* of the circuit is

$$X = X_L - X_C$$

21-20 An **R-L-C** series circuit with phase diagrams.

since X_L and X_C are 180° apart. The circuit is inductive if X_L exceeds X_C, having a positive phase angle and a leading voltage. If X_C exceeds X_L, the circuit is capacitive, having a negative phase angle and a lagging voltage.

The impedance has the general form, $Z \lfloor \phi$, as before.

$$Z = \sqrt{R^2 + X^2} \, \lfloor \mathbf{arctan\ X/R}$$

However, X can be either positive or negative (X^2 is always positive) since

$$X = X_L - X_C = 2\pi fL - \frac{1}{2\pi fC}$$

Therefore the magnitude of the impedance can be expressed as

$$Z = \sqrt{R^2 + (X_L - X_C)^2}$$

$$Z = \sqrt{R^2 + \left(2\pi fL - \frac{1}{2\pi fC}\right)^2}$$

When both X_L and X_C are involved in a circuit computation, it is quite important that the sign of the resulting value of X be introduced properly.

Suppose, for a given frequency, X_L is found to equal 24.0 ohms, X_C to equal 12.0 ohms, and the series resistance to be 16.0 ohms. From these values of R, X_L, and X_C, we may determine the impedance of the circuit as a vector quantity.

$$Z = \sqrt{R^2 + X^2} \, \lfloor \mathbf{arctan\ X/R}$$

But

$$X = X_L - X_C = 24.0\ \Omega - 12.0\ \Omega = 12.0\ \Omega$$

$$Z = \sqrt{(16.0\ \Omega)^2 + (12.0\ \Omega)^2} \, \lfloor \mathbf{arctan\ 12.0\ \Omega/16.0\ \Omega}$$

$$Z = 20.0\ \Omega \, \lfloor \mathbf{37.0°}$$

The direction angle of Z is positive and indicates a leading voltage.

The value found for Z tells us that the magnitude of the impedance is 20.0 ohms and the voltage across the external circuit must lead the series current by an angle of 37.0°. Assuming a line voltage across the external circuit of Fig. 21-20 of $10\bar{0}$ volts, the magnitude of the circuit current is

$$I = \frac{V}{Z} = \frac{10\bar{0} \text{ v}}{20.0 \text{ } \Omega} = 5.00 \text{ a}$$

We can now determine by inspection the magnitude of the three component voltages across L, R, and C, *which must have a vector sum equal to V*.

$$V_R = IR = 80.0 \text{ v}$$
$$V_C = IX_C = 60.0 \text{ v}$$
$$V_L = IX_L = 12\bar{0} \text{ v}$$

According to the voltage diagram, Fig. 21-20(B), the magnitude of the voltage, V, across the external circuit is

$$V = \sqrt{V_R{}^2 + V_X{}^2}$$

where

$$V_X = V_L - V_C$$

Then

$$V = \sqrt{(80.0 \text{ v})^2 + (60.0 \text{ v})^2}$$
$$V = 10\bar{0} \text{ v}$$

Of course, the direction angle of V must be 37.0° since this is the phase angle ϕ with I as the reference. It is important to recognize that the magnitude of the voltage across a reactance in an a-c circuit may exceed that of the applied voltage across the entire external circuit.

21.10 L, R, and C in parallel

In practical circuits the components are commonly connected in parallel rather than in series. Computations of parallel impedance networks become involved and cumbersome unless the student is familiar with *rectangular* and *polar* forms of complex notations and with the use of *vector algebra*.

Let us consider the simplest kind of parallel circuit: one consisting of pure inductance, pure capacitance, and pure resistance in parallel. We will use the same values as in the last example and we will assume the resistance of the L and C branches to be negligible. This simple network is shown in Fig. 21-21(A).

The same value of voltage must exist across each branch of a parallel network. The total current in the network, however,

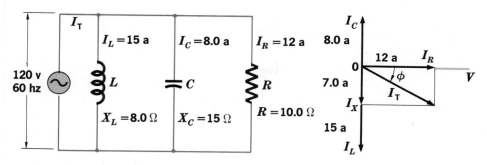

(A) L-C-R parallel circuit

(B) Current diagram

21-21   An **L-C-R** parallel circuit and phase diagram.

is the sum of the currents in the separate branches. This is a *vector sum* when there are differences in phase between the currents in the branches and the voltage across the network.

In the inductance branch, assumed to have no resistance, the current I_L lags the network voltage V by 90°. With this voltage as the reference vector, I_L is plotted as a lagging current of 15 amperes 90° behind V. See Fig. 21-21(B). The current I_C of 8.0 amperes leads the voltage by 90° and is plotted 90° ahead of V. The current in the resistance branch, I_R being in phase with V, is plotted along the line of the voltage reference. The total current I_T is the vector sum of the branch currents, and the phase relation is expressed with reference to the network voltage.

$$I_T = \sqrt{I_R^2 + I_X^2} \; \lfloor \mathbf{arctan}\ I_X/I_R$$

$$I_T = \sqrt{(12\ a)^2 + (-7.0\ a)^2} \; \lfloor \mathbf{arctan}\ -7.0\ a/12\ a$$

$$I_T = 14\ a \; \lfloor -30°$$

We have determined the circuit current I_T from the current diagram in the same way we determined Z in earlier examples. This current vector has a magnitude of 14 amperes and a phase angle of −30°, and is expressed in polar form.

Similarly the circuit voltage, plotted as the reference vector, has a magnitude of 120 volts and a direction angle of 0°. In polar notation, this vector quantity has the form

$$V = 120\ v\ \lfloor 0°$$

Multiplication and division operations with vector quantities can be handled very simply when these quantities are written in polar form. *The product of two polar vectors is found by taking the product of their magnitudes and the sum of their angles.* Thus

$$\mathbf{A} \lfloor \mathbf{a} \times \mathbf{B} \lfloor \mathbf{b} = \mathbf{AB} \lfloor \mathbf{a+b}$$

$$\mathbf{A} \lfloor \mathbf{a} \times \mathbf{C} \lfloor -\mathbf{c} = \mathbf{AC} \lfloor \mathbf{a + (-c)}$$

The quotient of two polar vectors is found by taking the quotient of their magnitudes and the difference of their angles. Thus

$$\frac{A\,\lfloor a}{B\,\lfloor b} = \frac{A}{B}\,\lfloor a - b$$

$$\frac{A\,\lfloor a}{C\,\lfloor -c} = \frac{A}{C}\,\lfloor a - (-c)$$

Unfortunately, polar vectors cannot be added or subtracted so easily. They are first converted to a rectangular form of complex notation.

The total impedance of the parallel branches can be determined by Ohm's law, now that the total current is known.

$$Z = \frac{V}{I_T} = \frac{120\text{ v}\,\lfloor 0°}{14\text{ a}\,\lfloor -30°}$$

$$Z = \frac{120\text{ v}}{14\text{ a}}\,\lfloor 0° - (-30°)$$

$$Z = 8.6\ \Omega\ \lfloor 30°$$

In practical parallel circuits having both resistance and reactance in each branch, we must deal with parallel impedances. In general,

$$\frac{1}{Z_T} = \frac{1}{Z_1} + \frac{1}{Z_2} + \frac{1}{Z_3} + \text{etc.}$$

However, each impedance is a vector quantity, and the computations involving such circuits are somewhat more sophisticated than the example demonstrated.

21.11 Impedance matching

We have recognized that maximum power can be transferred to the load in a d-c circuit if the load resistance is equal to the internal resistance of the source of emf. This is equally true of a-c circuits in which the loads may be complex impedances.

A device or circuit used as an a-c source may require a particular load impedance in order to perform satisfactorily. However, it may not be possible to supply a load that even approximates this value. A typical audio-frequency amplifier used to drive a loudspeaker may require a load impedance of 8000 ohms and the loudspeaker may have a nominal impedance of 8 ohms. In order for this combination to function properly, the load must appear as 8000 ohms to the amplifier and the source must appear as 8 ohms to the speaker. The loudspeaker, therefore, must be coupled to the amplifier by means of an *impedance matching* device.

A transformer is commonly used to match the impedance of a load to that of a source in order to obtain the greatest transfer of energy from one circuit to the other. The load impedance connected to the secondary is transformed to the value required by the source.

In a well-designed iron-core transformer practically all of the magnetic flux links both primary and secondary turns. In Section 20.21, we expressed the secondary voltage V_S in terms of the turns ratio and the primary voltage V_P.

$$V_S = V_P \frac{N_S}{N_P}$$

Similarly the secondary current is

$$I_S = I_P \frac{N_P}{N_S}$$

The secondary impedance, Z_S, and the primary impedance, Z_P, are respectively

$$Z_S = \frac{V_S}{I_S} \quad \text{and} \quad Z_P = \frac{V_P}{I_P}$$

But

$$\frac{V_S}{I_S} = \frac{\dfrac{V_P N_S}{N_P}}{\dfrac{I_P N_P}{N_S}} = \frac{V_P}{I_P}\left(\frac{N_S}{N_P}\right)^2$$

Then

$$\frac{Z_S}{Z_P} = \frac{N_S{}^2}{N_P{}^2}$$

or

$$\frac{N_S}{N_P} = \sqrt{\frac{Z_S}{Z_P}}$$

Let us use the expression we have just derived to determine the transformer turns ratio, primary to secondary, required to couple the amplifier and loudspeaker mentioned earlier.

$$\frac{N_P}{N_S} = \sqrt{\frac{Z_P}{Z_S}} = \sqrt{\frac{8000\ \Omega}{8\ \Omega}}$$

$$\frac{N_P}{N_S} = \sqrt{1000} = 31.6$$

Thus the primary must have 30 times the number of turns as the secondary. There are many instances in a-c circuits in which the impedance of the source and the load are fixed by the design requirements of the components, and are unequal in magnitude. By the insertion of a transformer with the proper turns ratio between the source and the load, the impedance of the load may be stepped up or stepped down to match that of the source.

QUESTIONS

Group A

1. What is the significant relationship between an alternating current and alternating voltage which are said to be in phase?
2. In a-c circuits what type of load has a current in phase with the voltage across it?
3. What is meant by instantaneous power?
4. (a) Why is it not possible to use a galvanometer-type meter in an a-c circuit? (b) What would happen to the meter if placed in an a-c circuit?
5. Upon what property of an alternating current is its effective value based?
6. Define the effective value of an alternating current.
7. Explain briefly the principle on which the moving iron-vane mechanism functions.
8. In what respect is the method of the hot-wire meter different from other meter mechanisms?
9. What is the phase relation between (a) the current in a pure inductance and the applied voltage, (b) the current and the induced voltage, (c) the applied voltage and the induced voltage?
10. What is the significance of the power factor pertaining to an a-c circuit?
11. Why is reactance described as being nonresistive?
12. (a) Define impedance. (b) What is an impedance diagram?
13. Describe the difference in the performance of a capacitor in a d-c circuit and in an a-c circuit.
14. What is the power factor of an a-c circuit containing (a) pure inductance, (b) pure resistance, (c) pure capacitance?
15. Express Ohm's law for an a-c circuit (a) including a source of emf, (b) which does not include a source of emf.

Group B

16. Explain why the instantaneous power curve for current in a resistive load varies between some positive maximum value and zero.
17. Demonstrate algebraically that the heating effect of an electric current is proportional to the effective value of current squared.
18. Plot the current and current squared curves for an alternating current having a maximum value of 5.7 amperes. Use cross-section paper and a suitable scale for the coordinate axes to produce a graph similar to Fig. 21-3. Show that the rms value of the current is 4.0 amperes.
19. If an a-c circuit has a pure inductance load, the average power delivered to the load is zero. Does this mean that there is no energy transfer between the source and the load? Explain.
20. (a) Considering the expression for X_L in terms of frequency and inductance, draw a rough graph of X_L as a function of frequency for a given inductance. (b) What is the nature of the curve? (c) What is

the significance of the fact that X_L is zero when f is zero regardless of the value of L?

21. Considering the expression for X_C in terms of frequency and capacitance, what is the significance of the fact that when the frequency is zero, X_C is infinitely high for any given capacitance?

22. (a) In a series circuit operating at a certain frequency and containing L, R, and C, what determines whether the load is inductive or capacitive? (b) Can you suggest a circumstance in which the load would be resistive?

23. What is the significance of the negative portions of the power curve shown in Fig. 21-17?

24. (a) Why is it sometimes desirable to match the impedance of a source to that of its load? (b) How may this be done in an a-c circuit?

25. Various meters are available, but they do not include a power-factor meter. Suggest a method by which you could determine the power factor of an a-c circuit.

26. How can a dynamometer be used to measure electric power?

PROBLEMS

Group A

Note: Compute angles to the nearest 0.5 degree.

1. A current in an a-c circuit measures 5.5 amperes. What is the maximum instantaneous magnitude of this current?

2. A capacitor has a voltage rating of $45\bar{0}$ v maximum. What is the highest rms voltage that can be impressed across it without danger of dielectric puncture?

3. The emf of an a-c source has an effective value of 122.0 volts. What is the instantaneous value when the displacement angle θ is $50.0°$?

4. An alternating current in a 25.0-ohm resistance produces heat at the rate of $25\bar{0}$ watts. What is the effective value (a) of current in the resistance, (b) of voltage across the resistance?

5. An inductor has an inductance of 2.20 henrys and a resistance of $22\bar{0}$ ohms. (a) What is the reactance if the a-c frequency is 25.0 hz? (b) Draw the impedance diagram and determine graphically the magnitude and phase angle of the impedance.

6. A 2.00 μf capacitor is connected across a 60.0-hertz line and a current of 167 milliamperes is indicated. (a) What is the reactance of the circuit? (b) What is the voltage across the line?

7. A capacitance of 2.65 μf is connected across a 120-volt line and is found to draw $12\bar{0}$ milliamperes. What is the frequency of the source?

8. When a resistance of 4.0 ohms and an inductor of negligible resistance are connected in series across a $10\bar{0}$-volt, $6\bar{0}$-hertz line, the current is $2\bar{0}$ amperes. What is the inductance of the coil?

9. A source of emf with an internal impedance of 2500 Ω is to be matched to a load impedance of 4.0 Ω using a matching transformer. What is the turns ratio of the transformer?

Group B 10. A 0.50-μf capacitor and a 3$\bar{0}$-ohm resistor are connected in series across a source of emf whose frequency is 8.0 × 10³ hz. (a) Draw the circuit diagram. (b) Find the capacitive reactance. (c) Draw the vector diagram and determine the magnitude and phase angle of the impedance.

11. The current in the circuit of Problem 10 is found to be 5$\bar{0}$ milli-amperes. (a) What is the magnitude of the voltage across the series circuit? (b) What is the phase relation of this voltage to the circuit current? (c) What is the voltage across the capacitor? (d) What is the voltage across the resistor?

12. A 60.0-hertz circuit has a load consisting of resistance and inductance in series. A voltmeter, ammeter, and wattmeter, properly connected in the circuit, read respectively 117 v, 4.75 a, and 40$\bar{0}$ w. (a) Determine the power factor. (b) What is the phase angle? (c) What is the resistance of the load? (d) What is the inductive reactance of the load? (e) Determine the voltage across the resistance. (f) Determine the voltage across the inductance. (g) Draw the voltage diagram with the circuit current as the reference vector. What is the applied voltage as found graphically? Express in polar form.

13. A coil has a resistance of 9$\bar{0}$ ohms and an inductance of 0.019 henry. (a) What is the impedance (complex) at a frequency of 1.0 × 10³ hz? (b) What is the magnitude of the current when a potential difference of 6.0 volts at this frequency is applied across it? (c) How much power is delivered to the coil?

14. A capacitance of 5$\bar{0}$ μf and a resistance of 6$\bar{0}$ ohms are connected in series across a 120-volt, 6$\bar{0}$-hertz line. (a) What is the magnitude of current in the circuit? (b) What power is dissipated? (c) What is the power factor? (d) Determine the voltage across the resistance. (e) Determine the voltage across the capacitance. (f) Draw the voltage diagram with the circuit current as the reference vector. What is the applied voltage found graphically? Express in polar form.

15. An inductance of 4.8 millihenrys, a capacitance of 8.0 μf, and a resistance of 1$\bar{0}$ ohms are connected in series and a 6.0-volt, 1.0 × 10³-hertz signal is applied across the combination. (a) What is the magnitude of the impedance of the series circuit? (b) What is the phase angle? (c) Determine the magnitude of the current in the circuit. (d) Find the potential drop across each component of the load and draw the voltage diagram.

16. An inductor, a resistance, and a capacitor are connected in series across an a-c circuit. A voltmeter reads 9$\bar{0}$ volts when connected

across the inductor, 16 volts across the resistor, and 120 volts across the capacitor. (a) What will the voltmeter read when placed across the series circuit? (b) Draw the voltage diagram and graphically verify your answer to (a). (c) Compute the power factor.

17. An inductance of 0.14 henry and a resistance of 56 ohms are connected in parallel across a 112-volt, 50-hertz line. (a) Determine the current in the resistance branch. (b) Determine the current in the inductance branch. (c) Draw the current diagram using the applied voltage as the reference vector. (d) Find the magnitude and phase angle of the total current in the circuit. (e) What is the impedance of the circuit?

RESONANCE

An inductor in a d-c circuit has no effect on the steady direct current except that due to the ordinary resistance of the wire forming the coil. A steady direct current can be thought of as an alternating current having a frequency of zero hz. Inductive reactance in the d-c circuit must then be zero, since $X_L = 2\pi fL$.

21.12 Inductive reactance vs. frequency

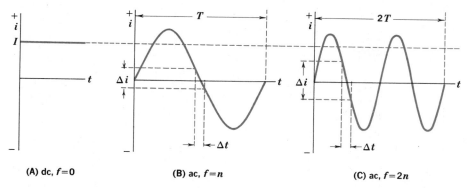

(A) dc, $f=0$ (B) ac, $f=n$ (C) ac, $f=2n$

An alternating current changes from its positive maximum to its negative maximum in a time equal to one-half the period, T; and if the frequency of this current is increased, the time rate of change of current is increased accordingly. See Fig. 21-22. The inductive reactance presented to the current in an a-c circuit by an inductor increases as the frequency of this current is increased.

Consider the reactance of a certain inductance over a range of frequencies. A plot of the values of inductive reactance as ordinates against frequencies as abscissas produces a linear curve, shown in Fig. 21-23. Any value of inductance yields a reactance curve which starts at the origin of the coordinate axes; the larger the value of inductance, the greater is the slope of the curve.

21-22 Current changes at a higher rate when the frequency is higher.

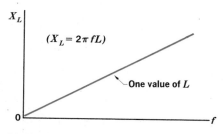

21-23 The reactance of a given inductance is plotted as a function of frequency.

21.13 Capacitive reactance vs. frequency

Capacitance in a d-c circuit, once the capacitor is charged to the applied voltage, acts as an open switch, and the current in the circuit is zero. Thus the capacitive reactance in the circuit is infinitely high regardless of the value of C.

In an a-c circuit containing a fixed value of capacitance, electrons flow in one direction during one half cycle to charge the capacitor in one sense; they flow in the opposite direction during the other half cycle, reversing the charge on the capacitor.

If the frequency is very low, the circuit current is small and the capacitive reactance is large since $X_C = 1/(2\pi fC)$. As the frequency increases, less change occurs in the charge on the capacitor during each half cycle, and there is less reactive opposition to the circuit current. At extremely high frequencies the change in the capacitor charge becomes negligible, and the capacitive reactance in the circuit ceases to be a significant factor in the control of the current. The larger the value of capacitance in the circuit, the more rapidly the capacitive reactance falls away with increasing frequency.

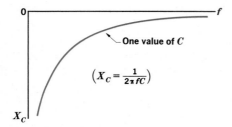

$$\left(X_C = \frac{1}{2\pi fC}\right)$$

21-24 The reactance of a given capacitance is plotted as a function of frequency.

Plotting the values of reactance for a certain capacitance over a range of frequencies produces a curve similar to that in Fig. 21-24. The curve is hyperbolic, typical of the inverse relation between capacitive reactance X_C and frequency. A larger capacitance would have a reactance-frequency curve with a greater slope.

21.14 Series resonance

In Section 21.9 it was stated that the voltages across an inductance and a capacitance in a series circuit are of opposite polarity. If X_L is larger than X_C, the circuit is inductive, and the voltage across the circuit leads the current. If X_C is the larger reactance, the circuit is capacitive and the circuit voltage lags behind the current. In either instance the impedance Z has a magnitude $\sqrt{R^2 + (X_L - X_C)^2}$ and a phase angle ϕ whose tangent is $(X_L - X_C)/R$.

The frequency of an a-c voltage applied to a series circuit with fixed values of L, R, and C determines the reactance of the circuit. Figures 21-23 and 21-24 show that the reactance of the circuit is inductive over a range of high frequencies, and is capacitive over a range of low frequencies. At some intermediate frequency the inductive and capacitive reactances are equal, and the reactance of the circuit $(X_L - X_C)$ equals zero. This is a special case known as *series resonance*; the frequency at which this occurs is called the *resonant frequency, f_r*. **Series resonance** *is a condition in which the impedance of an L-R-C series circuit is equal to the resistance, and the voltage across the circuit is in phase with the circuit current.*

Suppose an inductor of $1\overline{0}$ millihenrys inductance and 25

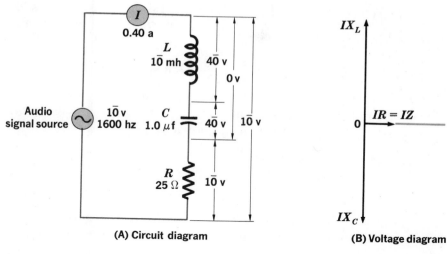

(A) Circuit diagram   **(B) Voltage diagram**

21-25 An *L-R-C* series circuit which has a resonant frequency of 1600 hz.

ohms resistance is placed in series with an ammeter and a capacitor of 1.0 microfarad capacitance, and a signal of $1\bar{0}$ volts rms from a variable frequency source such as an audio signal generator is applied. The circuit is shown in Fig. 21-25. When the frequency of the applied signal is varied through the audio range, a distinct rise in current occurs as the frequency approaches 1600 hz. The current magnitude quickly falls away as the frequency of the signal increases beyond this value. We can conclude that **the** series circuit is resonant at 1600 hz.

At resonance, $X_L = X_C$, and the value of each is found as follows:

$$X_L = 2\pi f_r L$$
$$X_L = (2\pi \times 1.6 \times 10^3 \times 1.0 \times 10^{-2})\ \Omega$$
$$X_L = 1.0 \times 10^2\ \Omega$$

$$X_C = \frac{1}{2\pi f_r C}$$

$$X_C = \left(\frac{1}{2\pi \times 1.6 \times 10^3 \times 1.0 \times 10^{-6}}\right)\Omega$$

$$X_C = 1.0 \times 10^2\ \Omega$$

The impedance at resonance is

$$Z = \sqrt{R^2 + X^2}\ \underline{|\mathbf{arctan\ }X/R}$$

But

$$X = X_L - X_C = 0\ \Omega$$

and the phase angle

$$\phi = \mathbf{arctan}\frac{X}{R} = 0°$$

Thus

$$Z = R = 25\ \Omega$$

Since the impedance of the series resonant circuit is the minimum value and equal to R, the current is the maximum value and equal to V/R.

$$I_r = \frac{V}{R} = \frac{1\bar{0}\ \text{v}}{25\ \Omega} = 0.40\ \text{a}$$

$$V_L = I_r X_L = 0.40\ \text{a} \times 1.0 \times 10^2\ \Omega$$

$$V_L = 4\bar{0}\ \text{v}$$

$$V_C = I_r X_C = 0.40\ \text{a} \times 1.0 \times 10^2\ \Omega$$

$$V_C = 4\bar{0}\ \text{v}$$

$$I_r X_L - I_r X_C = 4\bar{0}\ \text{v} - 4\bar{0}\ \text{v} = 0\ \text{v}$$

$$V_R = I_r \times R = 0.40\ \text{a} \times 25\ \Omega = 1\bar{0}\ \text{v}$$

Since the phase angle $\phi = 0°$, the power factor, $\cos \phi = 1$. Thus the power consumed in the series circuit is maximum at resonance.

$$P = VI_r \cos \phi = VI_r$$

The frequency at which a series circuit resonates is determined by the combination of L and C used. For a particular combination there is one resonant frequency, f_r. At series resonance

$$X_L = X_C$$

$$2\pi f_r L = \frac{1}{2\pi f_r C}$$

Solving for f_r

$$f_r^2 = \frac{1}{4\pi^2 LC}$$

$$f_r = \frac{1}{2\pi \sqrt{LC}}$$

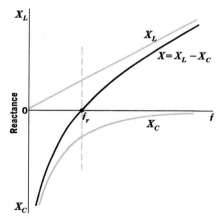

21-26 The reactance characteristic of an **L-R-C** series circuit on either side of the resonant frequency.

When L is in henrys and C is in farads, f_r is expressed in hertz.

At frequencies below the resonance point, the series circuit is capacitive, behaving as one with an X_C and R in series. At the resonant frequency, of course, the circuit behaves as one containing pure resistance. Above the resonant frequency it is inductive. These characteristics of the L-R-C series circuit are shown in Fig. 21-26 by the reactance curve X.

21.15 Selectivity in series resonance

A resonant circuit responds to impressed voltages of different frequencies in a very selective manner. The circuit presents a high impedance to a signal voltage far removed from the resonant frequency and the resulting current is correspondingly small. This same circuit presents a low impedance consisting of the circuit resistance to a signal voltage at the resonant frequency and the current is correspondingly large.

The property of a tuned circuit which discriminates between signal voltages of different frequencies is known as its **selectivity**. The lower the resistance of the series circuit, the higher is the resonant current and the more sharply selective is the circuit. The family of current-resonance curves shown in Fig. 21-27 illustrates the influence of circuit resistance on selectivity. Curves are shown for three different values of circuit resistance.

The usual series-resonant circuit consists of an inductor and a capacitor, the only resistance being that inherent in the circuit, which is almost entirely that of the coil. The characteristics of the series-resonant circuit depend primarily on the ratio of the inductive reactance to the circuit resistance, X_L/R. This ratio is called the Q (quality factor) of the circuit. It is essentially a design characteristic of the inductor; the higher the Q the more sharply selective the series-resonant circuit.

Resonant circuits can be tuned over a range of frequencies by making either the inductance or the capacitance variable. The position of a powdered-iron core in a coil can be varied to change its inductance, but it is more common to tune a circuit to resonance by varying capacitance; mechanical stability is more easily obtained in the case of a variable capacitor. Virtually all manual tuning of radio circuits is done with variable capacitors.

Circuit resonance is generally avoided in power circuits, since a high resonant current results in unusually high voltages across the reactance components. However, in electronic circuits resonance is a most important property.

Figure 21-28(A) represents an ideal case of parallel resonance, a pure inductance in parallel with a pure capacitance. Suppose a constant voltage from a variable frequency source is applied across the parallel circuit. The current in the inductance branch I_L, lags behind the circuit voltage by 90° since zero resistance is assumed. Similarly, the current in the capacitive branch, I_C, leads the applied voltage by 90°.

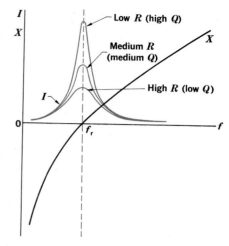

21-27 The magnitude of current in a series-resonant circuit is plotted as a function of frequency.

21.16 Parallel resonance

21-28 An ideal parallel-resonant circuit and its current diagram.

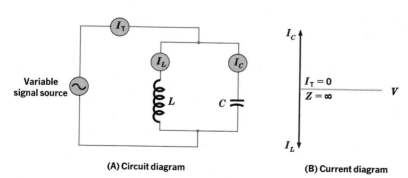

(A) Circuit diagram

(B) Current diagram

I_L varies inversely with f since

$$I_L = \frac{V}{X_L} = \frac{V}{2\pi f L}$$

where

$$\frac{V}{2\pi L} = \text{a constant}$$

I_C varies directly with f since

$$I_C = \frac{V}{X_C} = 2\pi f C V$$

where

$$2\pi C V = \text{a constant}$$

The total current, I_T, is the vector sum of the currents in the two branches, and in our ideal circuit which assumes no resistance in either branch I_L and I_C are fully 180° out of phase. Thus, signal voltages of low frequencies produce large currents in the inductive branch of the circuit and small currents in the capacitive branch. Signal voltages of high frequencies produce small values of I_L and large values of I_C.

There is some intermediate frequency at which the currents in these two ideal branches are equal. Since I_L and I_C are opposite in phase, their vector sum I_T is equal to zero. See Fig. 21-28(B). The equivalent impedance of the ideal network is infinitely high as $Z_r = V/I_T$. This is a condition of *parallel resonance*. Because $X_L = X_C$ at this resonant frequency, f_r can again be expressed as in the case of series resonance.

$$f_r = \frac{1}{2\pi \sqrt{LC}}$$

In this ideal case of parallel resonance we have the interesting situation in which a large current is in L and C and *no* current (I_T) is being supplied from the source. At resonance, the parallel network, called a *tank circuit*, is said to *oscillate*. The capacitor alternately charges and discharges through the inductance at the resonant frequency, energy being alternately stored in the electric field of the capacitor and in the magnetic field of the inductor. Since we have stipulated that both L and C are pure (having no resistance), no energy is dissipated. The situation is analogous to that of a frictionless pendulum after it has been given an initial push.

A practical parallel-resonant circuit is shown in Fig. 21-29. We shall assume that the two resistances R_1 and R_2 are equal. At the resonant frequency of the tank circuit, the rms currents in the two branches are equal in magnitude, one leading the applied voltage and the other lagging it by equal phase angles,

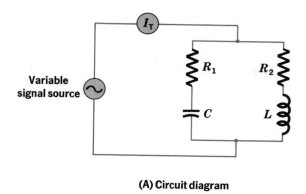

(A) Circuit diagram

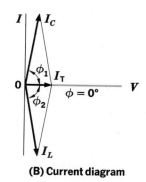

(B) Current diagram

21-29 A practical parallel-resonant circuit and its current diagram.

ϕ_1 and ϕ_2 respectively. If R_1 and R_2 are very small in comparison to X_C and X_L at resonance (a high Q circuit), these phase angles are very nearly 90°. Thus the resultant line current I_T in the external circuit is very small and is in phase with the applied voltage. The equivalent impedance of the tank circuit must be very large at resonance, since it is equal to V/I_T. It is interesting to observe that the smaller the resistance of the parallel-resonant circuit, the larger is its impedance.

In *L-R-C* parallel circuits the resonant rise of impedance can result in very high impedances if the circuit Q is high; this is one of the most important properties of parallel resonance. At resonance there is a very large current oscillating between the inductance and capacitance, and a line current outside the tank circuit which is just large enough to supply the resistance losses in the circuit.

At frequencies below f_r, a tank circuit acts inductively because of the large current in the inductance branch and the small current in the capacitance branch. At frequencies above f_r the tank circuit acts capacitively since a larger current is in the capacitance branch. Thus the reactance is inductive below f_r and capacitive above f_r. The reactance curve for the *L-R-C* parallel circuit has the form shown in Fig. 21-30. Observe the similarity between the impedance curve for parallel resonance and the current curve for series resonance in Fig. 21-27.

In Section 21.15 we expressed the Q of a resonant circuit as being essentially equal to X_L/R. When the Q of a parallel-resonant circuit is high, the impedance *at resonance* can be expressed very conveniently and with negligible error as

$$Z_r = 2\pi f_r L Q$$

See the following example.

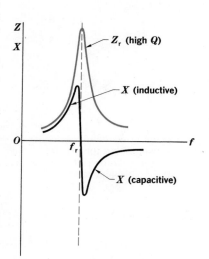

21-30 Impedance in a parallel-resonant circuit is plotted as a function of frequency.

Example

A tank circuit consisting of an inductance of 60.0 μh and 20.0 Ω resistance in parallel with a capacitor is resonant at a frequency of 1.00 megahertz. Find the magnitude of the circuit impedance at resonance.

Solution

$$Z_r = 2\pi f_r L Q$$

But, $\quad Q = \dfrac{X_L}{R} = \dfrac{2\pi f_r L}{R}$

Substituting,

$$Z_r = \frac{(2\pi f_r L)^2}{R}$$

$$Z_r = \frac{(2\pi \times 1.00 \times 10^6 \times 6.00 \times 10^{-5} \text{ h})^2}{\sec \times 20.0 \ \Omega}$$

$$Z_r = 71\overline{0}0 \ \Omega$$

Ken Chen

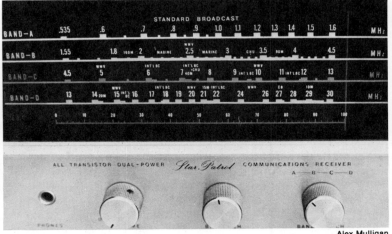

Alex Mulligan

A three-gang variable air capacitor (above) used in the tuning circuit of a radio receiver. At the right, the tuning dials of a multi-band radio.

QUESTIONS

Group A   1. Select three different values of inductance, determine the reactance of each at four different frequencies, and plot a curve of inductive reactance as a function of frequency for each using the same coordinate axes. (a) What is the shape of each curve? (b) Which has the greatest slope? (c) Why should each curve start at the origin of the coordinate axes?

2. How is an oscillating current produced in a resonant circuit?
3. Define series resonance.
4. What is the relation between the voltage across a series *L-R-C* circuit and the current in the circuit at a frequency below the resonant frequency? Explain.
5. What is the relation between the voltage across a series *L-R-C* circuit and the circuit current at a frequency above the resonant frequency? Explain.
6. What factor largely determines the sharpness of the rise of current near the resonance frequency in a series-resonant circuit?
7. What is the advantage of a resonant circuit having a high Q?
8. How is the Q of a resonant circuit affected by an increase in (a) resistance, (b) inductance, (c) frequency?

9. How can the resonant frequency of an *L-R-C* circuit be varied?
10. Suppose an inductor is connected in series with a lamp in an a-c **Group B** circuit. What is the effect? Explain.
11. A variable capacitor is connected in series in the circuit of Question 10 and, when adjusted, the lamp glows normally. Explain.
12. A series *L-R-C* circuit is connected across an a-c signal source of variable frequency. Draw a curve to show the way in which the circuit current varies with the frequency of the source.
13. Explain why the impedance of a parallel-resonant circuit reaches a maximum at the resonant frequency.
14. Sketch a curve of impedance of a parallel-resonant circuit as a function of frequency for a range of frequencies above and below f_r. Sketch a second curve on the same graph showing the circuit current as a function of frequency. Why cannot the circuit current fall to zero at f_r in a practical parallel-resonant circuit?
15. Compare the reactance characteristic of an *L-R-C* series circuit to that of an *L-R-C* parallel circuit at frequencies below the resonance frequency. (b) Compare the resistance characteristics of these circuits at frequencies above the resonance frequency.
16. How do the separate currents in the branches of a parallel-resonant circuit compare at frequencies (a) below the resonant frequency; (b) above the resonant frequency?

PROBLEMS

1. A resonant circuit has an inductance of 320 μh and a capacitance **Group B** of $8\bar{0}$ pf. What is the resonant frequency?
2. Assume that the frequency of the signal voltage applied to the resonant circuit of Problem 1 is varied from a value of 25 khz below

the resonant frequency to 25 khz above. (a) Obtain values of inductive reactance for every 5 khz over this range of frequencies and plot a curve showing inductive reactance as a function of frequency, using the frequency as the reference abscissa. (b) Obtain values of capacitive reactance for every 5 khz and plot a curve showing capacitive reactance as a function of frequency, using the same reference abscissa. (c) Determine the resonant frequency graphically from your curves by plotting the values for $(X_L - X_C)$.

3. The variable capacitor used to tune a broadcast receiver has a maximum capacitance of 350 pf. The lowest frequency to which we wish to tune the receiver is 550 khz. What value of inductance should be used in the resonant circuit?

4. The minimum capacitance of the variable capacitor of Problem 3 is 15 pf. What is the highest resonant frequency that may be obtained from the circuit?

5. A resonant circuit consists of an inductance of 25 mh and 180 ohms resistance in parallel with a capacitance of 15 pf. What is the magnitude of the impedance of the circuit at resonance?

6. Suppose the inductor in the circuit of Problem 5 fails and is replaced with one of equal inductance but of 360 ohms resistance. (a) What is the effect on the circuit Q? (b) What is the magnitude of the circuit impedance at resonance?

Chapter 22

Electronic Devices

VACUUM TUBES

The vacuum tube has been described as the most important single piece of equipment introduced into electrical engineering during the 20th century. Its development has produced the engineering art called *electronics*, which has given us radio, long-distance telephones, sound motion pictures, public-address systems, television, radar, electronic computers, and industrial automation. Many improvements have been made in vacuum tubes since the invention of the first crude models. Today vacuum tubes are used in electronic circuits to perform many different functions:

1. As *rectifiers*, they convert alternating current to direct current.

2. As *mixers*, they combine separate signals to produce a different signal.

3. As *detectors*, they separate the useful component from a complex signal.

4. As *amplifiers*, they increase the strength of a signal.

5. As *oscillators*, they convert a direct current to an alternating current of a desired frequency.

6. As *wave shapers*, they change a voltage wave form into a desired shape for a special use.

Vacuum-tube operation presents four inherent problems.

1. Vacuum tubes are power-dissipating devices. The power output of a vacuum-tube circuit is always considerably less than the total power input.

2. The size of vacuum tubes limits reduction in size of electronic circuits although tubes used today are smaller than early types.

22.1 Vacuum-tube applications

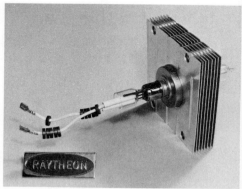

Amana

22-1 Modern vacuum tubes are designed to perform a variety of highly specialized functions. Shown here is a magnetron which serves as the radiation source in a microwave (radar) oven.

3. A vacuum tube requires a warm-up time, a delay between the time the device is activated and begins to perform.

4. The performance of a particular vacuum-tube circuit is limited to a relatively small range of frequencies. A circuit that is capable of amplifying one signal may produce a loss of signal strength at another frequency.

Transistors have provided a solution for the first three problems associated with vaccum-tube circuits. They require very little power for operation, they occupy a much smaller space than vacuum tubes, and they function immediately when activated. However, vacuum tubes continue to be used in many electronic circuits.

A vacuum tube usually contains a *cathode* as a source of electrons, an *anode* (commonly called a *plate*) which attracts electrons from the cathode, and one or more *grids* for controlling the flow of electrons between cathode and plate. These electrodes are enclosed in a highly evacuated, gas-tight envelope. Modified forms of the vacuum tube may contain only a cathode and a plate, or two independent sets of electrodes in a single envelope. In some, a small amount of a particular gas is introduced to obtain special operating characteristics.

Common tubes are classified as *diodes, triodes, tetrodes,* and *pentodes,* according to the number of electrodes. High-vacuum tubes are known as *hard* tubes and those containing a gas under very low pressure are known as *soft* tubes. Special tubes have special names. For example, the cathode-ray tube is a visual indicating tube used in cathode-ray oscilloscopes. It serves also as the picture tube in television sets, the indicator in radar equipment, and the visual-display tube in computers.

22.2 The Edison effect

While experimenting with the first electric lamp in 1883, Thomas Edison (1847–1931) was plagued by the frequent burning out of the carbon filament with an accompanying black deposit inside the bulb. While trying to correct this difficulty, he sealed a metal plate inside the lamp near the filament and connected it through a galvanometer to the filament battery. He observed a deflection on the galvanometer when the plate was connected to the positive terminal of the battery, but no deflection when the plate was connected to the negative terminal. Edison recorded these observations and continued his lamp experiments without attempting to explain the phenomenon.

Several years later, J. J. Thomson (1865–1940) discovered the electron and provided the explanation for the *Edison effect.* Electrons escaped from the heated carbon filament and moved unimpeded through the evacuated space to the plate when it was connected to the positive terminal of the filament battery.

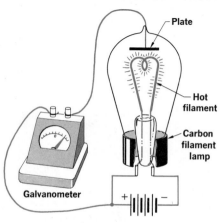

22-2   The Edison effect.

The negatively charged plate, on the other hand, repelled the escaping electrons and prevented an electron current in the galvanometer circuit.

Near the end of 1901, "wireless telegraphy," the forerunner of modern radio communications, was successfully used to transmit radio signals over long distances. In the early days of radio, crystals of semiconductors were used as receivers to *detect* (or recover) the message from the transmitted signals, but these crystals were unsatisfactory in many ways. A better method of detection was clearly needed.

In 1904 J. A. Fleming (1849–1945), an English physicist, patented the first diode, called the *Fleming valve*. He used the Edison effect to develop a crude detector for radio signals. Fleming's valve was so insensitive that it found little immediate application, yet it was an important link in the evolution of the vacuum tube.

Lee De Forest (1873–1961) was one of America's pioneers in wireless telegraphy, radio telephony, sound movies, and the development of the vacuum tube. In 1906, he succeeded in amplifying feeble radio signals which neither the Fleming valve nor the crystal detectors were sensitive enough to detect.

De Forest placed a third electrode, consisting of a *grid* of fine wire, between the filament and plate of the diode, as shown in Fig. 22-3. He found that a small variation in voltage applied to the grid produced a large variation of current in the plate circuit of the tube. Thus, the feeble radio signals from an antenna could be amplified by De Forest's *triode* and then suc-

22.3 The Fleming valve

22.4 The De Forest triode

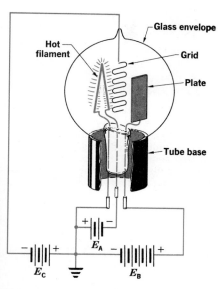

22-3 De Forest's three-element vacuum tube, the triode.

Lee De Forest earned his Ph.D. at Yale University in 1899. His triode is considered by many to be the single most important invention in radio.

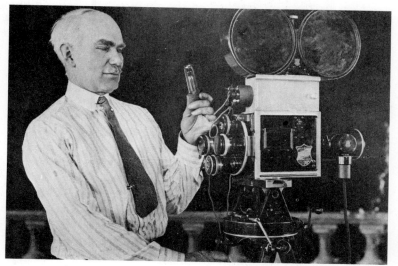

cessfully detected by the Fleming valve to provide the varying d-c signal necessary to operate headphones. The success of the De Forest triode led to the development of modern vacuum tubes.

22.5 Thermionic emission

Metallic substances conduct electricity because they have a great many free electrons. In all conduction of electricity there is a transfer of some kind of charged particle. In a highly evacuated tube the number of gas particles is so small that conduction by gas ionization is insignificant. Conduction in a high vacuum results from the introduction of charged particles into the electric field between the electrodes in the evacuated space. In high-vacuum (hard) tubes, the conducting particles are electrons, supplied through a process known as *thermionic emission.*

The free electrons of a metallic conductor are in continuous motion with speeds that increase with temperature. To escape from the surface of a conductor, an electron must do work to overcome the attractive forces at the surface of a material. At ordinary temperatures, the kinetic energies of electrons are not large enough to exceed the work function of the surface; thus, the electrons cannot escape.

At a *high* temperature the average kinetic energy of the free electrons is large, and a relatively large number will have enough energy to escape through the surface of the material. ***Thermionic emission*** *is the emission of electrons from a hot surface.* It is analogous to the evaporation of molecules from the surface of liquid water.

The rate at which electrons escape from an emitting surface increases as the temperature of the emitter is raised. In the photoelectric effect, photons of light supply the energy required to eject electrons through the surface barrier of the photosensitive material. In thermionic emission, thermal energy produces the same effect.

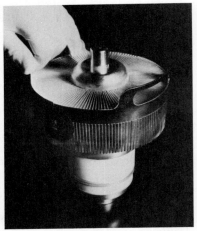

Westinghouse

Vacuum tubes vary widely in their appearance because different designs are manufactured for different circuit requirements. This vacuum tube, designed for high power applications, has radiation fins to dissipate heat.

22.6 Types of emitters

The high temperatures needed for satisfactory thermionic emission in vacuum tubes limit the number of suitable emitters to such substances as *tungsten, thoriated tungsten*, and certain *oxide-coated metals.* Tungsten and thoriated tungsten operate at very high temperatures and are connected directly to a source of filament current. These *directly-heated cathodes*, called *filament cathodes* or simply *filaments*, are used as the source of electrons in large transmitting tubes.

Oxide-coated emitters consist of a metal such as nickel, coated with a mixture of barium and strontium oxides over which is formed a surface layer of metallic barium and strontium. The electrons are emitted from this metallic surface layer. Such emitters can be heated to operating temperature either directly as a filament cathode or indirectly by radiation from an incandescent tungsten filament. *Indirectly heated cathodes* are commonly called *heater cathodes* or simply *cathodes*. See Fig. 22-4. Since practically all receiving tubes in use today have oxide-coated emitters, we shall concern ourselves principally with vacuum tubes of this type.

The simplest vacuum tubes are diodes containing two elements, a cathode and a plate. Diode circuit symbols are shown in Fig. 22-5. If the plate is made positive with respect to the cathode, the diode conducts because electrons flow from the cathode to the plate inside the tube, and from the plate through the plate circuit to the cathode outside the tube. If the plate is negative with respect to the cathode, the diode does not conduct and there is no plate current in the external circuit. Thus, a diode acts as a one-way valve for electrons; it allows electrons to flow one way through the circuit, but not the other.

As electrons are emitted from the hot cathode, the space about the cathode becomes negatively charged. This negative charge in the space between cathode and plate, called the *space charge*, opposes the escape of additional electrons from the cathode. The number of electrons emitted is dependent on the temperature of the cathode.

At low positive plate voltages only those electrons near the plate are attracted to it, producing a small plate current. As the plate voltage is increased, greater numbers of electrons are attracted, increasing the plate current and reducing the space charge. The emission of electrons from oxide-coated cathodes

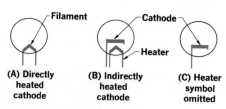

22-4 Circuit symbols for directly and indirectly heated cathodes.

22.7 Diode characteristics

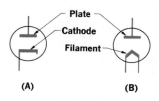

22-5 Circuit symbols for diodes with indirectly heated cathode (A) and directly heated cathode (B).

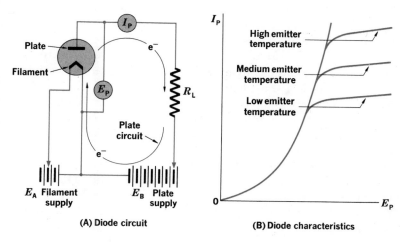

(A) Diode circuit

(B) Diode characteristics

22-6 A diode circuit and characteristic curves showing the plate current as a function of plate voltage at different filament temperatures.

is quite abundant and the diode might be damaged before the plate voltage could be raised enough to completely remove the space charge and produce current *saturation*. That is, the oxide coating might be pulled off the cathode.

In an ordinary resistor the proportionality of current to voltage is described by Ohm's law. The resistor is said to be a linear or *ohmic* element in the circuit. In the case of the diode, the plate current is not proportional to the plate voltage. The diode and other such devices are said to be nonlinear or nonohmic elements in the circuit.

A diode circuit from which we can determine the plate current I_P as a function of plate voltage E_P for different filament temperatures is shown in Fig. 22-6(A). The resulting family of I_P vs E_P curves is shown in Fig. 22-6(B).

Diode tubes can be classified as *power* diodes or *signal* diodes. The difference is primarily one of size and power-handling capabilities. Power diodes are used as rectifiers in power-supply circuits and must be large enough to dissipate the heat generated during their operation. Signal diodes handle signals of negligible power and are small, being used principally as detectors and wave-shapers. See Fig. 22-7. They are frequently enclosed in the same envelope with triodes and pentodes.

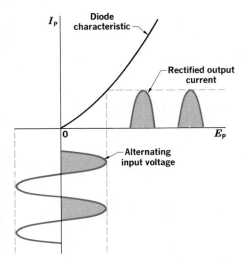

22-7 A diode characteristic used to show the rectifying action of a power diode.

22.8 Triodes can amplify

De Forest perfected the first *triode* amplifier by inserting a third electrode between the cathode and plate of a diode. This electrode consists of an open spiral of fine wire which presents a negligible physical barrier to electrons flowing from cathode to plate. However, a small potential difference between this electrode and the cathode has an important controlling effect on the flow of electrons from cathode to plate, and thus on the current in the plate circuit. For this reason the third electrode is called a *control grid*. We may think of a triode as an adjustable electron valve. The electrode configuration of a triode and the triode circuit symbol are shown in Fig. 22-8.

If the control grid is made sufficiently negative with respect to the cathode, all electrons are repelled toward the cathode. In this condition the plate current is zero, and the triode is said to be *cut off*. The grid-to-cathode voltage is called the *grid bias*. *The smallest negative grid voltage, for a given plate voltage, which causes the tube to cease to conduct is the **cut-off bias**.* This design characteristic of vacuum tubes containing control grids is important in the circuit applications of these tubes.

The effects of different grid-bias voltages on the plate current of a triode are shown in Fig. 22-9. If a negative grid bias less than the cut-off value is used, some electrons pass through the grid and reach the plate to provide some magnitude of plate

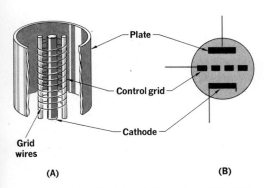

22-8 Sketch of the electrode configuration of a triode (A), and the triode circuit symbol (B).

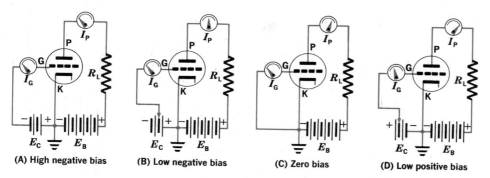

(A) High negative bias (B) Low negative bias (C) Zero bias (D) Low positive bias

current. As the negative grid bias is reduced toward zero, the plate current increases accordingly. At zero bias, the plate current is fairly large and depends primarily on the plate voltage. The performance of the triode is now essentially the same as that of a diode of similar construction.

If, on the other hand, the grid is made positive with respect to the cathode, it no longer repels the electrons of the space charge but accelerates them in the direction of the plate. The plate current is increased by this action; however, *some electrons are attracted to the grid and produce an appreciable current in the grid circuit.* Grid current causes power dissipation in the grid circuit which represents a waste of power. Thus the grid is normally maintained at some negative potential with respect to that of the cathode. .

The characteristics of triode vacuum tubes are based on the relationships between grid voltage, plate current, and plate voltage under normal operating conditions. These relationships provide three important tube constants: *amplification factor, dynamic plate resistance,* and *transconductance.* They depend on the structure of the electrodes, their spacing, and power-dissipation capabilities.

1. Amplification factor. The measure of the amplifying capability of a triode, that is, the relative effectiveness of grid and plate voltages in controlling plate current, is called the *amplification factor.* The symbol is the Greek letter *mu* (μ). The **amplification factor** of a tube is the ratio of a small change in plate voltage to a small change in grid voltage of the opposite sense, which maintains a constant plate current.

$$\mu = -\frac{\Delta e_P}{\Delta e_G} \ (i_P \text{ constant})$$

Where Δe_P is a small change in plate voltage and Δe_G is a small change in grid voltage, μ is the amplification factor (a dimensionless number). The negative sign indicates that the changes

22-9 The effects of control-grid bias on the plate current of a triode.

22.9 Triode characteristics

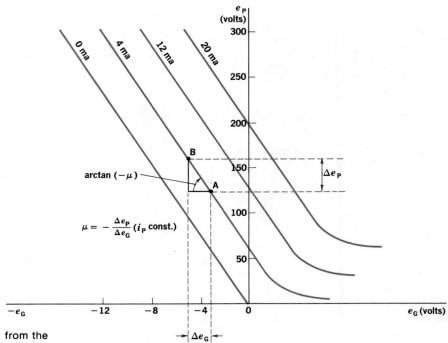

22-10 Determination of mu from the
e_P-e_G characteristic of a triode.

in plate voltage and grid voltage are not in the same sense (direction).

A family of e_P vs e_G characteristic curves for a typical triode is shown in Fig. 22-10. Let us select a value of plate voltage on the ordinate axis and adjust the grid voltage to operate the tube at point **A** on the 4-milliampere curve. If the plate voltage e_P is raised a certain amount, then the grid voltage e_G must be made more negative to hold the plate current i_P to 4 milliamperes. With these adjustments the tube operates at point **B**. The amplification factor is the ratio of this small change in plate voltage Δe_P to the small change in grid voltage Δe_G necessary to maintain i_P at the constant value of 4 milliamperes.

Triodes designed to have amplification factors of the order of 20 are called *medium-mu* triodes. *High-mu* triodes have amplification factors of from 70 to 100. A *mu* of 20 means that a change in grid voltage (an input signal) is twenty times more effective in changing the plate current than a change of plate voltage of the same magnitude.

2. Dynamic plate resistance. The dynamic plate resistance, r_p, of a vacuum tube is the internal resistance to electron flow from cathode to plate. It is analogous to the *internal* resistance of a generator. The type of emitter, the geometry of the tube, and the space charge largely determine the plate resistance.

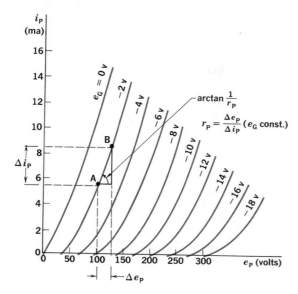

22-11 Determination of r_P from the i_P-e_P characteristic of a triode.

The **dynamic plate resistance** *is the ratio of a small change in plate voltage* Δe_P *to the small change in plate current* Δi_P *which it produces, when the grid voltage* e_G *is maintained at a constant level.*

$$r_P = \frac{\Delta e_P}{\Delta i_P} \; (e_G \text{ constant})$$

When Δe_P is expressed in volts and Δi_P in amperes, r_P is expressed in ohms.

An i_P vs e_P family of characteristic curves for a typical triode is shown in Fig. 22-11. Let us assume that a grid bias of -2 volts is maintained and the plate voltage e_P is raised from a value which locates the operation of the tube at point **A** to a value which changes the operating point to **B**. The ratio of the small change in plate voltage Δe_P to the small change in plate current Δi_P which it effects indicates the plate resistance of the tube.

Since the plate resistance is the reciprocal of the slope of the i_P vs e_P characteristic, it is *lowest* where the slope is *greatest*. The plate resistance of any particular tube depends on the grid and plate voltages *at the operating point* on the i_P vs e_P characteristic.

3. Transconductance. Perhaps the most important single constant of a vacuum tube is the *transconductance*, g_m. It indicates the effectiveness of the control grid in producing changes in plate current and, consequently, in signal output. **Transconductance** *is the ratio of the small change in plate current to the small change in grid voltage producing it, when the plate voltage is held constant.*

$$g_m = \frac{\Delta i_P}{\Delta e_G} \; (e_P \text{ constant})$$

From Ohm's law, resistance in ohms equals the quotient of potential difference in volts divided by the current in amperes. The unit of transconductance is the *reciprocal of the resistance unit*, the ohm, and is called the *mho* (ohm spelled backwards). In a general sense,

$$\text{conductance} = \frac{1}{\text{resistance}}$$

and

$$1 \text{ mho} = \frac{1}{1 \text{ ohm}}$$

Because the mho is too large a unit for practical use in expressing the transconductance of a vacuum tube, the *micromho* (μmho) is commonly used.

$$1 \text{ } \mu\text{mho} = 1 \times 10^{-6} \text{ mho}$$

Where Δi_P is in amperes and Δe_G is in volts, the g_m must be multiplied by 10^6 to be expressed in micromhos.

In Fig. 22-12 is shown an i_P vs e_G family of characteristic curves for a typical triode. Let us assume that the plate voltage e_P is held constant at 250 volts and the grid voltage is lowered from the value which locates the tube operation at point **A** to the value which locates the operating point at **B**. The ratio of the small change in plate current Δi_P to the small change in grid voltage Δe_G indicates the transconductance.

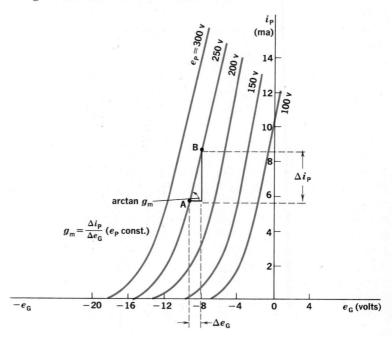

22-12 Determination of g_m from the i_P-e_G characteristic of a triode.

The relationship between the grid voltage e_G, the plate current i_P and the plate voltage e_P determines the three important tube constants (μ, r_p amd g_m). By combining equations for μ and r_P, we can find the relationship between the tube constants:

$$g_m = \frac{\mu}{r_P}$$

In the design of a vacuum tube, a low plate resistance and high amplification factor are desired. Thus the transconductance provides an indication of the design merit of a tube. In the common *tube tester*, the g_m of the tube under test is compared with the rated value of a new tube of the same type.

The simplified triode circuit of Fig. 22-13 may be used to illustrate the application of tube characteristics to vacuum-tube circuit problems. The plate-supply voltage E_B is a d-c source of $30\overline{0}$ volts and the plate-load resistance R_L is a resistance of 8.00×10^3 ohms. The control grid has a d-c biasing voltage E_C of -4 volts.

Let us assume first that the tube is cut off. In this condition the plate circuit is open, the plate current is zero, and there is no potential drop across the load resistance R_L. Thus the plate is at the full supply voltage of $30\overline{0}$ volts.

We assume next that the tube is a short circuit, that is, the plate resistance r_P is zero. The plate voltage must be zero and the full supply voltage appears across the load resistance. The plate current is the maximum value for this supply voltage and is determined as follows:

$$I_P = \frac{E_B}{R_L}$$

$$I_P = \frac{30\overline{0} \text{ v}}{8.00 \times 10^3 \ \Omega}$$

$$I_P = 37.5 \text{ ma}$$

22.10 A typical triode problem

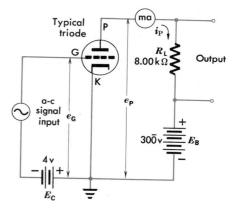

22-13   A basic triode circuit.

These two limiting conditions define the *load line* which we can construct on the i_P vs e_P characteristic as shown in Fig. 22-14. The steady state or *quiescent* operation of the tube is determined by the intersection of the load line with the -4-volt curve at point **Q**. By projection from point **Q** through the i_P axis, we can determine that the quiescent plate current I_P is 13.0 milliamperes when no a-c signal is impressed on the grid. By projection from point **Q** through the e_P axis, we can determine that the quiescent plate voltage E_P is about 195 volts. This leaves a potential drop of approximately 105 volts across R_L which is in good agreement with the Ohm's-law product $I_P R_L$.

$$(13.0 \times 10^{-3} \text{ a})(8.00 \times 10^3 \ \Omega) = 104 \text{ volts}$$

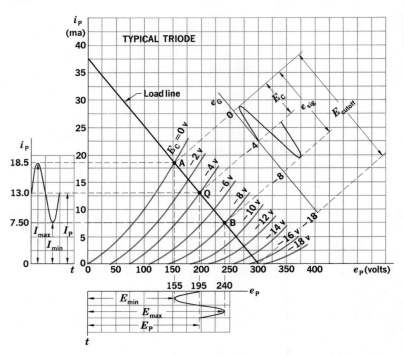

22-14 The application of a triode i_P-e_P characteristic to a typical tube problem.

Suppose an a-c signal of $E_{max} = 4$ volts is impressed on the control grid. From the quiescent grid bias of −4 volts, the signal swings the grid in a positive sense to 0 volts and in a negative sense to −8 volts. This establishes the *operating region* of the tube along the load line between points **A** and **B**. By projections from points **A** and **B** through the i_P axis, we can determine the plate-current variation produced by the a-c signal input. Similarly, by projections through the e_P axis, we can determine the plate-voltage variation.

By this graphic application of the i_P vs e_P characteristic of the triode, the operation of the circuit in Fig. 22-13 becomes apparent. A voltage variation of 8 volts (peak-to-peak) on the grid results in a variation of 85 volts on the plate.

22.11 Polarity inversion

The plate current inside the tube in Fig. 22-13 is from cathode to plate. Outside, it is from the plate, through the load, and back to the cathode. Thus the plate side of R_L *is negative with respect to the positive terminal of the plate-supply battery* when the tube conducts.

At the instant that a signal voltage applied to the grid is at its positive *maximum*, the plate current is maximum also. This maximum current in the load resistance produces a maximum potential drop across R_L and so the plate end of R_L is at its *minimum* instantaneous voltage. The plate, which is at the same

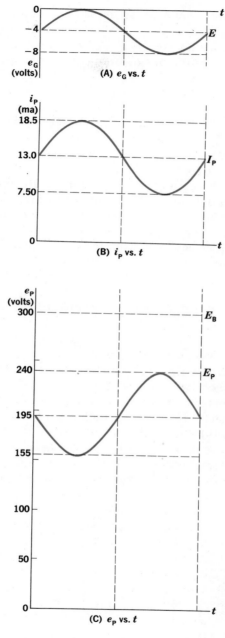

22-15 Grid voltage, plate current, and plate voltage variations of a vacuum tube circuit showing voltage inversion between grid and plate circuits.

potential as this end of R_L, must be at its minimum instantaneous value.

When the signal voltage on the grid is at its minimum instantaneous value, the plate current and the $i_P R_L$ drop across the plate-load resistance are minimum, and the voltage on the plate must be at its *maximum* instantaneous value. Thus the plate-voltage variations are opposite to those of the control grid. This reversal amounts to *polarity inversion* between the voltage variations of the plate and grid circuits. The grid voltage, plate current, and plate voltage relationships derived from the i_P vs e_P characteristic are shown in Fig. 22-15.

22.12 Interelectrode capacitance

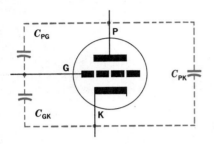

22-16 A schematic diagram of the interelectrode capacitances of a triode.

The electrodes of a triode form an electrostatic system in which capacitances exist between grid and plate, grid and cathode, and plate and cathode. Collectively these are known as *interelectrode capacitances*.

Interelectrode capacitances are quite small, having magnitudes of the order of 3 picofarads in triodes. However, the coupling effects they produce between the input and output circuits restrict the use of triodes as amplifiers at radio frequencies. As the operating frequency is increased, the capacitive reactances decrease and an a-c circuit exists for energy transfer from the plate back into the grid. The signal which is fed back to the grid tends to counteract the signal at the grid and limits the high-frequency response of the circuit.

22.13 Tetrodes

The interelectrode capacitance between grid and plate of a triode can be reduced by inserting a second grid, called the *screen grid*, between the control grid and plate. Such four-electrode tubes are known as *tetrodes*. See Fig. 22-17(A). Tetrodes extend the range of frequencies over which an ordinary vacuum tube can be used as an amplifier.

The screen grid is supplied with a positive potential somewhat less than that of the plate. Electrons in transit from the cathode are accelerated by the positive screen grid, increasing the plate current. Some electrons do strike the screen grid and produce

22-17 The circuit symbol and typical i_P-e_P characteristic curves of a tetrode.

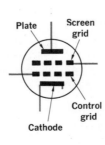

(A) Circuit symbol

(B) $i_P - e_P$ characteristic

a screen current which wastes power and serves no useful purpose.

A variation of plate voltage has little effect on the magnitude of plate current, because of the presence of the screen grid. The control grid, on the other hand, retains control over the plate current. Tetrodes have high plate resistance and amplification factors. A typical family of i_P vs e_P characteristic curves is shown in Fig. 22-17(B).

Observe that the $i_P - e_P$ curves have a negative slope at plate voltages below the fixed screen voltage. When accelerated by the screen grid, some electrons strike the plate with enough force to dislodge other electrons. *Emission as a result of bombardment of an electrode by high-velocity electrons is called* **secondary emission**. See Fig. 22-18. When the plate voltage is lower than the screen voltage, secondary-emission electrons are attracted to the screen grid. This effect lowers the plate current and necessitates operation of the plate at an abnormally high voltage in order to overcome the effects of secondary emission.

The introduction of a third grid, known as the *suppressor grid*, between the screen grid and plate eliminates the effects of secondary emission. This gives the five-electrode tube, or *pentode*, shown schematically in Fig. 22-19(A). The suppressor grid is usually connected to the cathode and serves to repel secondary electrons back to the plate.

Pentodes have replaced tetrodes in receiving-tube applications because of the advantage of the lower plate-voltage requirements. At radio frequencies the pentode makes possible a high voltage amplification at moderate values of plate voltage. A typical family of i_P vs e_P characteristic curves is shown in Fig. 22-19(B).

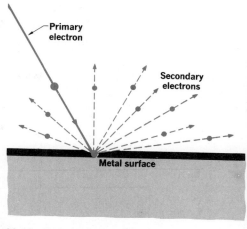

22-18 Secondary emission of electrons from the surface of a metal plate by the impact of a single high-speed electron.

22.14 Pentodes

22-19 The circuit symbol and typical i_P-e_P characteristic curves of a pentode.

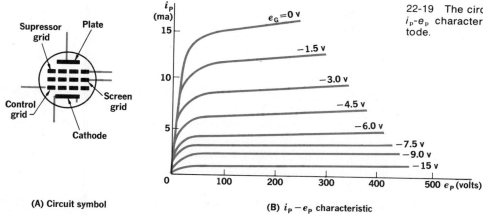

(A) Circuit symbol

(B) $i_P - e_P$ characteristic

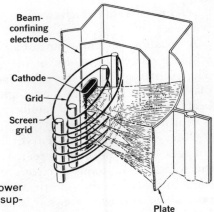

22-20 The structure of a beam-power tube employing space-charge suppression of secondary emission.

A *beam-power* tube is a special kind of tetrode with the performance characteristics of a pentode. It is highly efficient as a power amplifier. The electrodes are arranged so that secondary emission from the plate is suppressed by the negative space charge without the use of a suppressor grid. A beam-confining electrode, connected internally to the cathode, concentrates the transient electrons in the vicinity of the plate. The structure of a beam-power tube is shown in the diagram, Fig. 22-20.

22.15 The cathode-ray tube

The cathode-ray tube is a special kind of vacuum tube used in test equipment, radar, television receivers, and computers to present a visual display of information. Electrons are emitted from a cathode, accelerated to a high velocity, and brought to focus on a fluorescent screen. This screen is a translucent backing on the glass face of the tube, composed of certain chemicals which *fluoresce*, or emit visible light, at the point where the electron beam strikes.

Fluorescent substances emit light of characteristic colors when bombarded by electrons. All have some *phosphorescence* or after-glow, the persistence of which depends on the material and the energy of the bombarding electrons. Cathode-ray tubes used in test equipment such as the oscilloscope have short-persistence screens which emit predominantly green light. The picture tubes of television receivers have long-persistence screens.

The electron beam is moved about over the fluorescent screen in response to the information signals being presented. This means that the information, in the form of electric signals, must be used to deflect the beam from its quiescent path within the tube.

Since an electron has a mass of approximately 10^{-27} gram, it

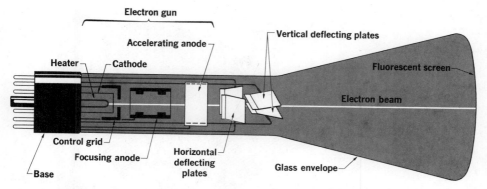

Electron gun

Accelerating anode

Vertical deflecting plates

Heater   Cathode

Fluorescent screen

Electron beam

Control grid

Focusing anode

Horizontal deflecting plates

Glass envelope

Base

22-21   The construction of a cathode-ray tube using electrostatic deflection.

has virtually no inertia. Thus a beam of electrons can be deflected back and forth across the screen of a cathode-ray tube at seemingly incredible speeds in response to very weak signals. In a television receiver, for example, the electron beam sweeps across the face of the picture tube 15,750 times per second at a speed of the order of 15,000 miles per hour.

There are two general methods of deflecting the electron beam in cathode-ray tubes: *electrostatic deflection* and *electromagnetic deflection.*

1. Electrostatic deflection systems. A cathode-ray tube employing electrostatic deflection is shown in Fig. 22-21. The arrangement of electrodes which produces a focused beam of electrons is called the *electron gun.* It consists essentially of an indirectly heated *cathode* capable of high emission, a *control grid* which regulates the intensity of the electron beam, a *focusing anode,* and an *accelerating anode.* The two anodes are maintained at high positive potentials with respect to the cathode, and produce a field which acts as an *electrostatic lens* to converge the electron paths at a point on the screen.

Deflection of the beam is accomplished by two sets of *deflecting plates* set at right angles to each other. Signal voltages applied to these pairs of plates establish electrostatic fields through which the electrons move. The electron beam is subjected to deflecting forces in both the horizontal and vertical planes. Since electrons have very little mass, they respond practically instantly to these forces, being deflected in the direction of the resultant force. Electrostatic deflection is generally used in the small cathode-ray tubes of test equipment.

2. Electromagnetic deflection. Large cathode-ray tubes use electromagnetic deflection because of the greater definition possible. The beam can be focused either electrostatically as in Fig. 22-21, or magnetically by an external focusing coil. Beam control is accomplished by coils formed into a deflection yoke placed on the neck of the tube.

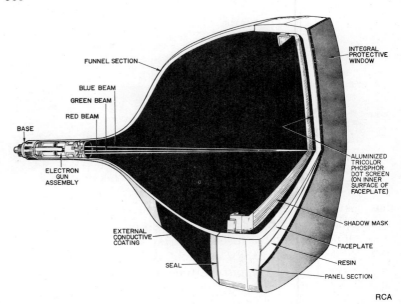

FUNNEL SECTION

BLUE BEAM

GREEN BEAM

RED BEAM

BASE

ELECTRON
GUN
ASSEMBLY

INTEGRAL
PROTECTIVE
WINDOW

ALUMINIZED
TRICOLOR
PHOSPHOR
DOT SCREEN
(ON INNER
SURFACE OF
FACEPLATE)

SHADOW MASK

FACEPLATE

RESIN

PANEL SECTION

EXTERNAL
CONDUCTIVE
COATING

SEAL

RCA

22-22   A cut-away view of a color-TV picture tube.

Color picture tubes use three electron guns, one for each primary color, which scan and stimulate color phosphors on a tri-color, phosphor-dot screen. The structure of a typical color television tube is shown in Fig. 22-22. Cathode-ray tubes with more than three electron guns have been developed for use in highly specialized electronic equipment.

22.16 Photomultiplier tube

Secondary emission, the liberation of electrons from a metal surface by the impact of a high-speed electron, can be utilized in conjunction with the photoelectric effect to detect light of very low intensity. This special form of photoelectric cell is known as a *photomultiplier tube*.

A diagram of a photomultiplier tube is shown in Fig. 22-23. The number of photoelectrons emitted by the light-sensitive cathode in a given time is proportional to the intensity of the incident light. These photoelectrons are attracted to the first secondary-emission electrode, which is 100 volts positive with respect to the emitter cathode. On impact, additional electrons are released by secondary emission.

Successive secondary-emission electrodes, each more positive (less negative) than the one preceding it, contribute additional electrons as the electron stream progresses toward the collector anode. Thus, a meager photoemission from a faint incident light can develop into an avalanche of electrons by the time they arrive at the collector plate. If each electron impact produces **n** secondary electrons, a photomultiplier tube with **x** secondary-

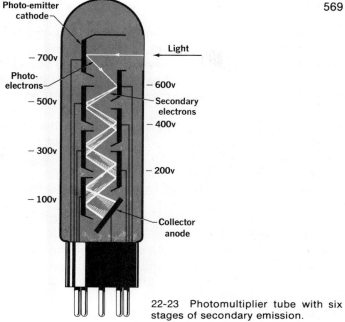

Photo-emitter cathode

Light

−700v

Photo-electrons

−600v

−500v

Secondary electrons

−400v

−300v

−200v

−100v

Collector anode

22-23 Photomultiplier tube with six stages of secondary emission.

emission electrodes will supply n^x electrons to the collector plate for each photoelectron emitted.

Suppose a faint light incident on the photoemission cathode of the tube shown in Fig. 22-23 produces *five* photoelectrons per millisecond. Also suppose that each electron impact produces *four* secondary electrons. Since the tube has *six* secondary-emission stages, the number of electrons arriving at the collector plate is of the order of 2×10^4 per millisecond.

$$5n^x = 5 \times 4^6 = 2 \times 10^4$$

This equation suggests the extraordinary gain with a photomultiplier tube compared to a regular photoelectric cell.

QUESTIONS

Group A

1. What device is primarily responsible for the development of electronics as a branch of engineering?
2. What discovery by J. J. Thomson provided the explanation for the Edison effect?
3. What significant advantage was realized by De Forest's triode which had not been possible with previously developed diodes?
4. (a) Define thermionic emission. (b) What type of emitter is commonly used in receiving tubes?
5. Why is the grid of a triode called a control grid?
6. What is meant when a vacuum tube is said to be cut off?

7. Why is the control grid of a vacuum tube normally maintained at some negative potential with respect to the cathode?
8. What determines the quiescent operation point of a vacuum tube?
9. What is meant by the interelectrode capacitances of a vacuum tube?
10. What is the function of the suppressor grid in a pentode?

Group B
11. Suggest two possible reasons why Edison did not offer an explanation for the phenomenon known as the Edison effect.
12. Explain voltage inversion between the control grid and plate in a vacuum-tube circuit.
13. What restricts the use of triodes as amplifiers at radio frequencies? Explain.
14. Why is the tetrode able to perform as an amplifier at higher frequencies than the triode?
15. Explain why the plate resistance of a vacuum tube is considered to be analogous to the internal resistance of a generator.
16. Why is the vacuum-tube transconductance considered the most important tube constant?
17. What is the load line used in conjunction with the i_P-e_P family of characteristic curves of a vacuum tube?
18. Explain, by the use of appropriate wave forms, what is meant by polarity inversion across a vacuum tube.
19. What is the electron gun of a cathode-ray tube?
20. What is the basic difference between the electrostatic and electromagnetic deflecting systems used in cathode-ray tubes?
21. (a) Explain why the first secondary-emission electrode of a photomultiplier tube is maintained at a positive (less negative) potential with respect to the photoemission electrode. (b) Why is each successive secondary-emission electrode at a positive potential with respect to the preceding electrode?

TRANSISTORS

22.17 Crystal diodes   One of the devices from the early days of radio that is found in modern electronic circuits is the *crystal diode*. The rectifying property of silicon or galena (lead sulfide) crystals was used in early receivers before the development of the diode tube. During World War II, improved crystal diodes were developed for use in radar receivers. They are now used extensively in many types of circuits to perform a variety of specialized functions. They have the advantage of small size and they require no heater or filament power.

A modern crystal diode can consist of a tiny wafer of silicon or germanium and a platinum *catwhisker*, contained in a sealed capsule. See Fig. 22-24. The crystal acts as the cathode of the diode and the catwhisker acts as the anode. The diode char-

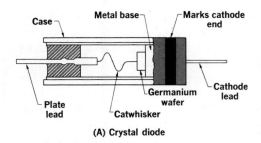

(A) Crystal diode

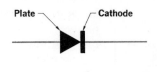

(B) Circuit symbol

22-24 A crystal diode and its circuit symbol.

acteristic depends on the unique property of a semiconductor which permits a relatively large flow of electrons in the *forward* direction with a small applied voltage, and only a very small flow of electrons in the *reverse* direction, even at a much larger applied voltage.

The *transistor* was developed by a team of physicists at the Bell Telephone Laboratories in 1948 after nearly ten years of basic research in the physics of semiconductors. Transistors are crystals of silicon or germanium containing traces of certain impurities. They have replaced vacuum tubes in many types of circuits. They are tiny, rugged structures which require very little power. The development of a family of transistor triodes, tetrodes, and pentodes has made possible the miniaturization of electronic circuits.

The first transistors were known as *point-contact* transistors. These devices have been superseded by *junction* transistors which can be further classified into several broad categories depending on the forming process and performance characteristics.

A relatively new addition to the semiconductor family is the *field-effect* transistor (FET). It has operating characteristics very similar to those of the pentode vacuum tube. New transistor configurations with improved frequency response and power-handling capabilities continue to appear as the physicist's knowledge of semiconductor materials expands.

Silicon and germanium are quite similar in their structure and chemical behavior. The atoms of both elements have *four* valence electrons bound in the same way in their respective crystals. In its transistor functions, germanium is the more versatile semiconductor. It has a diamond cubic crystal lattice in which each atom is bonded to four neighboring atoms through shared electrons, as illustrated in Fig. 22-25. This arrangement ties up the four valence electrons of each atom so that pure germanium would appear to be a nonconductor.

22.18 Transistor development

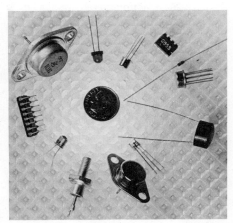

Ken Chen

Semiconductors and components manufactured for a variety of different circuit designs.

22.19 P- and N-type semiconductors

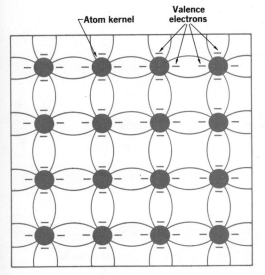

22-25 Electron-paired bonds in a pure germanium crystal.

Germanium acquires the diode property of rectification and the transistor property of amplification through the presence of certain impurities in the crystal structure. Two types of impurities are important; one is known as a *donor*, the other as an *acceptor*.

Arsenic and antimony are typical donor elements. The atoms of each have *five* valence electrons. When minute traces of antimony are added to germanium, each antimony atom joins the crystal lattice by *donating* one electron to the crystal structure. Four of the five valence electrons are paired, but the fifth electron is relatively free to wander through the lattice like the free electrons of a metallic conductor. The detached electron leaves behind an antimony atom with a unit positive charge bound into the crystal lattice. Germanium with this type of crystal structure is called *N-type*, or *electron-rich* germanium. *N-type germanium consists of germanium to which is added equal numbers of free electrons and bound positive charges, so that the net charge is zero.* An **N**-type semiconductor crystal is illustrated in Fig. 22-26.

Atoms with *three* valence electrons, such as those of aluminum and gallium, will act as acceptors. When minute traces of aluminum are added to germanium, each aluminum atom joins the crystal lattice by *accepting* a single electron from a neighboring germanium atom. This leaves a *hole* in the electron-pair bond from which the electron is acquired.

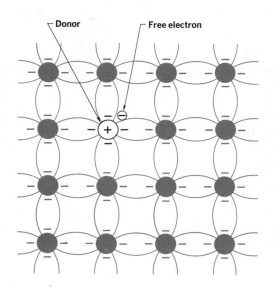

22-26 **N**-type germanium has donor atoms and free electrons in equal numbers.

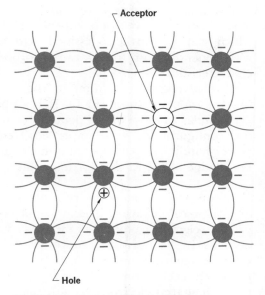

22-27 **P**-type germanium has acceptor atoms and free (positive) holes in equal numbers.

We can think of this hole as the equivalent of a *positive charge* since it acts as a trap into which an electron can fall. As an electron fills the hole, it leaves another hole behind, into which another electron can fall. In effect then, the hole (positive charge) detaches itself and becomes free to move, leaving behind the aluminum atom with a unit negative charge bound into the crystal lattice. Germanium with this crystal structure is called *P-type*, or *hole-rich* germanium. ***P-type*** *germanium consists of germanium to which is added equal numbers of free positive holes and bound negative charges, so that the net charge is zero.* A **P**-type semiconductor crystal is illustrated in Fig. 22-27.

Impurities can be added to germanium in such a way that, as a crystal is formed, a definite boundary is created between **P**-type and **N**-type regions. This boundary is a kind of electric barrier and is called the *P-N junction*. The crystal as a whole has properties of a diode and is called a *P-N junction diode*. The holes of the **P**-type crystal cannot pass through the electric barrier at the **P-N** junction to reach the **N**-crystal. The free electrons of the **N**-crystal cannot cross the **P-N** junction to reach the **P**-crystal.

A small potential difference impressed across the diode, as in Fig. 22-28(A), enables the free electrons to cross the junction and pass into the **P**-crystal. Similarly the holes cross into the **N**-crystal. Recall that the apparent movement of holes is in the opposite sense to the actual movement of electrons which fall in the holes of the **P**-type crystal. Thus an electron current is established across the **P-N** junction and in the external circuit.

If the battery connections are reversed, as shown in Fig. 22-28(B), the free electrons in the **N**-crystal and the free holes of the **P**-crystal are attracted away from the **P-N** junction. The junction region is left without current carriers; consequently, there is no conduction across the junction and no current in the circuit.

The junction has the diode characteristic of permitting unidirectional electron flow with ease when a small voltage is ap-

22.20 The P-N junction

22-28 The **P-N** junction is the rectifying element of semiconductor crystals.

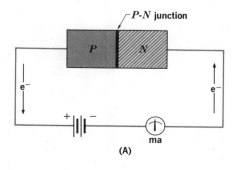

(A)

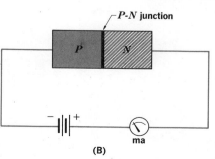

(B)

plied in the proper sense. Thus the **P-N** junction is the rectifying element of semiconductor crystals.

22.21 Two types of junction transistors

The amplifying property of a transistor is a result of current changes which occur in the different regions of the structure when proper voltages are applied. A transistor is a current amplifier much as a vacuum tube is a voltage amplifier.

Junction transistors consist of two **P-N** junctions back to back with a thin **P**-type or **N**-type region formed between them. The **P-N** junctions are formed as described in Section 22.20. If the center region is composed of **P**-type material, the transistor is designated **N-P-N**. The arrangement of an **N-P-N** transistor and its circuit symbol are shown in Fig. 22-29.

The **N**-type material at the left of the **P**-type center is the *emitter*. It is normally biased negatively with respect to the **P**-region, which is called the *base*. The **N**-type material on the right of the base is the *collector*. It is biased positively with respect to the base. The basic circuit of the **N-P-N** transistor is shown in Fig. 22-31(A).

Transistors in which the center region is composed of **N**-type semiconductor material are designated **P-N-P**. A diagram of a **P-N-P** transistor and its circuit symbol are shown in Fig. 22-30.

The basic circuit of **P-N-P** transistors is given in Fig. 22-31(B). Observe that it is the same as that for **N-P-N** transistors except that the battery connections are reversed.

Ken Chen

Transistors, resistors, capacitors and inductance coils in a small radio.

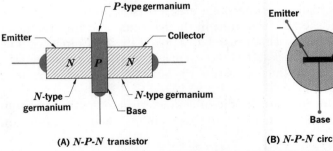

22-29 An **N-P-N** junction transistor and its circuit symbol.

(A) *N-P-N* transistor

(B) *N-P-N* circuit symbol

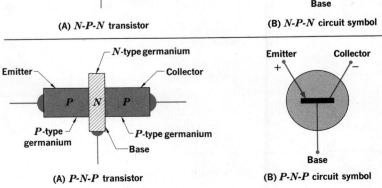

22-30 A **P-N-P** junction transistor and its circuit symbol.

(A) *P-N-P* transistor

(B) *P-N-P* circuit symbol

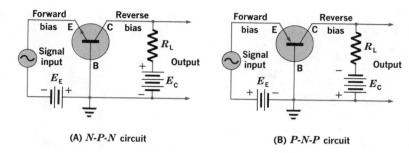

(A) *N-P-N* circuit   **(B)** *P-N-P* circuit

22-31 Basic junction transistor circuits. (A) **N-P-N** transistor and (B) **P-N-P** transistor.

In either **N-P-N** or **P-N-P** transistors, the emitter is biased to supply charges, electrons or holes, to be acquired by the collector through the two junctions of the base. An **N**-type emitter is biased negatively with respect to the base to supply electrons to its **N-P** junction and then to the **P**-type base. A **P**-type emitter is biased positively to withdraw electrons from its **P-N** junction and thus from the **N**-type base. This statement is equivalent to saying it supplies holes to its **P-N** junction and then to the **N**-type base. Both emitter types are said to have *forward* bias.

The arrow head at the emitter in the transistor circuit symbol indicates the direction of motion of the hole charge. Electron flow is in the opposite direction.

An **N**-type collector is biased positively with respect to the base to attract electrons from its **N-P** junction and from the **P**-type base. A **P**-type collector is biased negatively to transfer electrons to its **P-N** junction and into the **N**-type base. Again, this is equivalent to saying it attracts holes from its **P-N** junction and thus from the **N**-type base. Both collector types are said to have *reverse* bias.

The forward bias on emitters and the reverse bias on collectors have the effect of producing an electron current in the **N-P-N** transistor from emitter to base in the emitter circuit, and from base to collector in the collector circuit. Forward emitter bias and reverse collector bias in the **P-N-P** transistor produce an electron current from collector to base and from base to emitter.

The base section serves to isolate the emitter input circuit from the collector output circuit of a transistor. This isolation results from the barrier voltages established at the two junctions. The barrier polarities at these two junctions are reversed because the base has an **N-P** junction at one side and a **P-N** junction at the other.

Forward bias at the emitter junction overcomes the barrier voltage and enables the emitter to supply charge to the base.

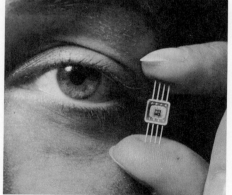

Texas Instruments

The integrated circuit mounted on the small black square performs the functions of 50 transistors, diodes, resistors, and capacitors.

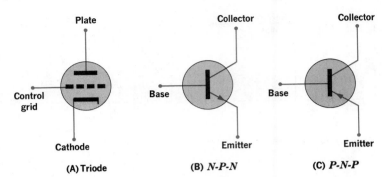

22-32 Transistor elements compared to those of a vacuum triode. (A) Triode, (B) **N-P-N** transistor, (C) **P-N-P** transistor.

(A) Triode   (B) *N-P-N*   (C) *P-N-P*

The reversed polarity of the barrier voltage at the collector junction, augmented by the reverse collector bias, aids the transfer of charge through the junction to the collector. Transistor performance is achieved when the collector current is controlled by the emitter current in the base.

When the operation of a transistor is compared to that of a vacuum triode, the emitter is equivalent to the cathode, the base to the control grid, and the collector to the plate. These relationships are illustrated in Fig. 22-32.

22.22 Transistor amplification

The transistor circuits shown in Fig. 22-31 are called *common-base* amplifiers. Small signals introduced into the emitter circuit are supplemented by energy from the collector battery and larger signals are transferred from the collector circuit. This effect is accomplished in spite of the fact that the collector current is slightly smaller than the emitter current.

Amplification in the common-base transistor amplifier is due to the ratio of output impedance to input impedance which may be of the order of 1000:1. Low emitter impedance is obtained by the *forward* biasing of the emitter junction, the junction between the emitter section and the base section. As stated in Section 22.21, the effect is to reduce the electric field across the emitter junction. High collector impedance is obtained by the *reverse* biasing of the junction between the collector

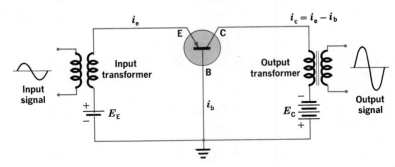

22-33 A **P-N-P** common-base amplifier.

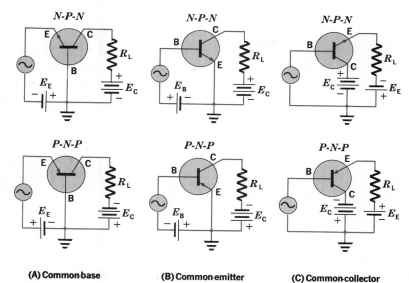

N-P-N N-P-N N-P-N

P-N-P P-N-P P-N-P

(A) Common-base   **(B) Common-emitter**   **(C) Common-collector**

22-34 Circuit configurations for N-P-N and P-N-P junction transistors.

section and the base section. This effect is to increase the electric field across the collector junction.

Only 1% to 5% of the emitter current passes through the base leg of the circuit. The remaining 95% to 99% passes through the collector circuit because of the thinness of the base section and the consequent ease with which positive holes from the emitter diffuse across it to be collected.

A typical **P-N-P** common-base amplifier circuit is shown in Fig. 22-33. A small signal current i_e in the emitter circuit will result in a low input power $i_e^2 Z_e$ since the input impedance is low. The slightly smaller collector current ($i_c = i_e - i_b$) will yield a higher output power $i_c^2 Z_c$ because of the high output impedance. The *power gain* of the circuit is the ratio of the output power to the input power.

The common-base transistor circuit which we have been considering is just one of three general circuit configurations for transistors. Others are the *common-emitter* and *common-collector* circuits. These transistor-circuit configurations are shown in Fig. 22-34. Observe that in all circuits the emitters have forward bias to provide low impedance and the collectors have reverse bias for high impedance.

22.23 Transistor characteristics

A transistor can amplify a small signal voltage applied to its input circuit because the magnitude of collector current in its output circuit can be controlled by the current in the input circuit. The performance of a transistor is indicated by its family

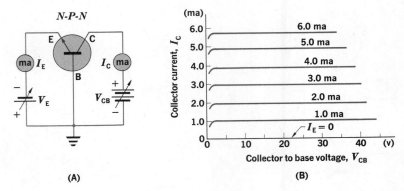

22-35 Typical common-base output characteristic curves for an **N-P-N** transistor. (A) Common-base test circuit, (B) $I_C - V_{CB}$ characteristics.

of characteristic curves. These curves describe the behavior of the transistor in a specific circuit configuration.

Typical output characteristics for an **N-P-N** transistor in a common-base configuration are shown in Fig. 22-35. Each curve shows how the collector current I_C varies with the output voltage V_{CB} measured between the collector and base terminals, for a given value of emitter current I_E. The family of curves is produced by using different values of emitter current.

These curves show that the collector current is independent of the collector voltage, but is dependent on the magnitude of emitter current. Variations in I_E produce variations in I_C. At a constant value of V_{CB}, the ratio of a change in I_C to a change in I_E expresses the *current gain* of the common-base circuit. It is expressed as a positive number without dimension and is denoted by the Greek letter *alpha* (α).

$$\alpha = \frac{\Delta I_C}{\Delta I_E} \ (V_{CB} \ \textbf{constant})$$

Referring to Fig. 22-35(B), suppose the emitter current I_E is varied from 2.0 ma to 4.0 ma (a change of 2.0 ma) while the voltage V_{CB} is held constant at 15 v. Reading from the collector current axis, I_C is found to vary from 1.9 ma to 3.8 ma (a change of 1.9 ma). The current gain can be determined from these data as follows:

$$\alpha = \frac{\Delta I_C}{\Delta I_E} = \frac{\textbf{1.9 ma}}{\textbf{2.0 ma}} = \textbf{0.95}$$

The forward current gain, or alpha characteristic, of a common-base circuit is always slightly less than unity. Typical values of α range from 0.95 to 0.99. The closer α is to unity, the better the quality of the transistor. As stated in Section 22.22, the signal gain across the common-base circuit depends on the high impedance of the collector circuit.

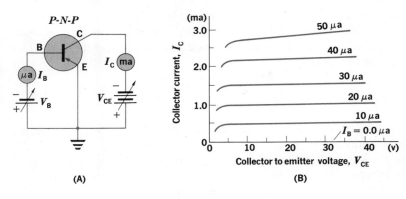

(A)   (B)

22-36 Typical common-emitter output characteristic curves for a **P-N-P** transistor. (A) Common-emitter test circuit, (B) $I_C - V_{CE}$ characteristics.

Fig. 22-36 shows a typical family of characteristic curves of transistor performance in a common-emitter configuration. Collector current I_C is plotted as a function of output voltage V_{CE} measured between collector and emitter, for each value of base current I_B.

Base currents are very small compared to emitter and collector currents. In the common-emitter circuit, small changes in I_B produce large variations in I_C. At a constant value of V_{CE}, the ratio of a change in I_C to a change in I_B expresses the *current gain* for the common-emitter circuit. This current-gain factor is denoted by the Greek letter *beta* (β).

$$\beta = \frac{\Delta I_C}{\Delta I_B} \; (V_{CE} \text{ constant})$$

Using the typical curves of Fig. 22-36(B), we will assume that the base current I_B is varied from $2\overline{0}$ μa to $4\overline{0}$ μa (a change of $2\overline{0}$ μa) while V_{CE} is held constant at $2\overline{0}$ v. Projecting to the collector current axis, we find that I_C varies from 1.0 ma to 2.3 ma (a change of 1.3 ma). The current gain, or β characteristic, of this common-emitter circuit is

$$\beta = \frac{\Delta I_C}{\Delta I_B} = \frac{1.3 \times 10^{-3}\text{a}}{2.0 \times 10^{-5}\text{a}} = 65$$

Typical values of β fall in the range from 20 to 200. Either the common-base or the common-emitter transistor circuit will provide amplification of an input signal. With a low impedance load, where high *current gain* is desired, the common-emitter circuit is preferred. With a high impedance load, where large *power gain* is desired, the common-base circuit will serve as well and is even preferable.

The common-collector circuit is essentially the reverse of the common-emitter circuit. This configuration can be recognized in Fig. 22-34. It has a high input impedance and a low output impedance and a voltage gain of less than unity. Thus, it has little value as an amplifier but can be used for impedance matching between a high impedance source and a low impedance load.

QUESTIONS

Group A

1. What is the property of a semiconductor crystal known as the diode characteristic?
2. Why is **N**-type germanium referred to as electron-rich germanium?
3. Why is **P**-type germanium referred to as hole-rich germanium?
4. What is the **P-N** junction of a semiconductor?
5. How are the two types of junction transistors designated?
6. Draw the circuit symbol for an **N-P-N** transistor, labeling the emitter, base, and collector.
7. Draw the circuit symbol for a **P-N-P** transistor. Label the emitter, base, and collector.
8. What is the significance of the arrow head at the emitter in a transistor circuit symbol?
9. Which sections of a junction transistor are equivalent to the cathode, control grid, and plate of a vacuum triode?
10. What are the different circuit configurations used for transistor service?

Group B

11. Distinguish between a germanium diode and a germanium transistor.
12. Distinguish between a **P-N-P** transistor and an **N-P-N** transistor.
13. The emitter of an **N-P-N** transistor is biased negatively and the emitter of a **P-N-P** transistor is biased positively with respect to the base. In both cases they are described as forward bias. Explain.
14. What is the alpha characteristic of a transistor and to what transistor configuration does it apply?
15. Why must the current gain in a common-base transistor circuit always be less than unity?
16. Which transistor circuit configuration most closely resembles the basic vacuum triode circuit? Explain why.
17. To what does the beta characteristic of a transistor refer?
18. How can you account for amplification in a common-base transistor circuit when the collector current in the output circuit can never be as large as the emitter current in the input circuit?

SMALLER AND BETTER

A crystal of the element silicon or the mineral galena (left) was used in early radio receivers. The radio operator had to "tickle" the crystal with the fine wire above the crystal (called a *catwhisker*) until a sensitive spot was found. Unfortunately, the slightest jiggle of the apparatus could disrupt reception by moving the catwhisker.

William Shockley (seated), John Bardeen (behind) and Walter H. Brattain (right) with the apparatus used in the investigations that led to their invention of the transistor.

General Electric

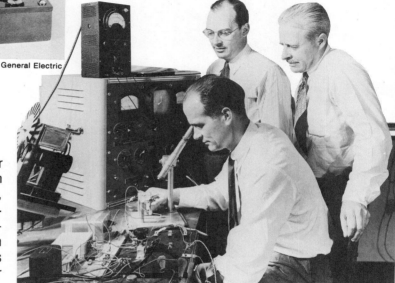

Bell Laboratories

TRANSISTORS DISCOVERED

As long ago as 1874, the peculiar flow of electric current in certain minerals was reported. Over the years, these materials were known as *semiconductors.* They conduct an electric current better than insulators such as glass, but they do not conduct as well as conductors such as silver or copper.

By 1945, much had been learned at Bell Laboratories about the behavior of many semiconductor materials. Satisfactory theories had been developed to explain their behavior. Then, on December 24, 1947, William Shockley, Walter H. Brattain, and John Bardeen demonstrated that a semiconductor crystal with two wires attached two-thousandth of an inch apart, was amplifying a voice about forty times. The phenomenon came to be known as the *transistor effect.* This discovery was so fundamental that these men were awarded the Nobel Prize in Physics in 1956.

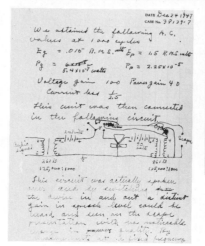

Bell Laboratories

The laboratory notebook on which Walter H. Brattain recorded the events of December 24, 1947, when the transistor effect was demonstrated.

HOW TRANSISTORS ARE MADE

A silicon crystal 28 inches long and 2 inches in diameter. It takes about twelve hours and very precise control of temperatures to grow a crystal this size.

Western Electric

There are two kinds of silicon, P for positive and N for negative depending upon the direction in which the flow of electric charge is favored. Small amounts of specific impurities are introduced to the purified crystal chips to make transistor material of the P or N type. For example, the steps in making an N-P-N transistor are:

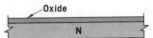

1. An oxide coating is produced on the surface of a chip of silicon.

2. The oxide coating is covered by a material that is sensitive to light. A mask is placed over this material in the desired pattern.

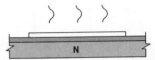

3. The chip is exposed to ultraviolet light. A protective layer remains over the parts of the oxide coating that are to be retained.

There is a big step between a fundamental discovery, such as the *transistor effect,* and production of reliable transistors for computers and radios. In their natural state, transistor materials consist of many crystals of varying purity. To manufacture reliable transistors, crystals of near-perfect purity and uniformity are needed. Metallurgists and chemists developed ways of growing single crystals of the necessary purity.

A crystal of the element silicon is so hard that a diamond saw is used to slice it. Each two-inch wafer forms the base material for up to 9,000 transistor chips.

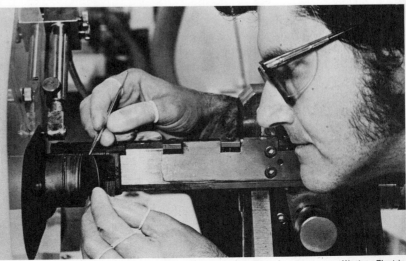

Western Electric

4. A chemical dissolves away the unprotected oxide. The protective coating is also removed.

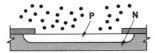

5. The surface is exposed to vapor impurities that produce a layer of P silicon.

6. The oxidation, masking, chemical treatment and impurities treatment are repeated to produce a layer of N silicon.

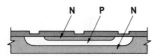

7. Again, with a different mask, the surface is reoxidized and chemically treated to produce openings into which metal is deposited to connect to the N and P layers.

Western Electric

Silicon wafers are highly polished before controlled amounts of impurities are added in specific areas.

Western Electric

Connections of gold wire, 0.025 mm in diameter, are attached to transistor chips. These assembly steps are controlled by operators peering through microscopes.

Chapter 23

Atomic Structure

THE ELECTRON

23.1 Subatomic particles

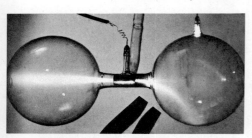

23-1 Evidence of subatomic particles. The dumbbell-shaped apparatus contains hydrogen gas. With a d-c voltage, hydrogen atoms separate into streams of oppositely charged particles. These photos show that hydrogen atoms are composed of at least two different parts.

Toward the end of the 19th century, evidence began to appear that atoms were not the ultimate particles of the universe. Some of this evidence will be discussed in greater detail in Chapter 24. A simple way of demonstrating the existence of subatomic particles is shown in Fig. 23-1. In each picture, the glass tube contains hydrogen gas under low pressure. The conductor leading to the center of the tube is connected to the negative terminal of a direct-current source of electricity. The conductor at the top of the right bulb in each picture is connected to the positive terminal. When a high voltage is impressed across the tubes, two beams shoot out in opposite directions from the hollow electrode in the center. Furthermore, the two beams have different colors.

Since the tubes contain only hydrogen atoms, the differently colored beams show that the hydrogen atom has at least two different parts. The fact that the beams are flowing in opposing directions also shows that the two parts of the hydrogen atom have opposite electric charges. One beam is negatively charged, since it passes into the part of the tube where the positive electrode is located. The other beam is positively charged, since it is attracted through the negative electrode at the center and into the left side of the tube.

The magnets in the pictures tell still more about the parts of the hydrogen atom. In the first picture, the magnet is held near the positive beam. The effect on the beam is not very pronounced. In the other picture, the magnet is held near the negative beam. This time, the bending effect is more noticeable. This suggests that the particles composing the two beams have differences in addition to that of opposite charge. Further studies show that the main reason for the way in which the beams react to magnetism is that the positive particles have much larger masses than do the negative particles.

Starting from evidence of this kind, scientists have developed a comprehensive theory of atomic structure. Various parts of this theory will be presented in the remainder of this chapter and in later chapters. It is important to remember, however, that all these discussions are based on the best current knowledge of atomic structure. Revisions will frequently become necessary as new investigations and new interpretations are made. What sort of picture of the atom will finally emerge from this research no one can fully predict. It is certain, however, that the atom is made up of a number of still smaller particles which are arranged in various complex ways and which interact with each other and compose different kinds of atoms in much the same way that atoms interact in forming different molecules.

American Institute of Physics, Niels Bohr Library

23-2 Nobel Prize winner Marie Sklodowski Curie in her laboratory.

The first subatomic particle to be identified and studied by scientists was the electron. Actually, the discovery of this particle was a by-product of other investigations. Toward the end of the 19th century physicists were using tubes similar to the one described in the preceding section to study the conduction of electricity through various gases. When such a tube was filled with air (at atmospheric pressure), electricity would not flow between the electrodes even under high voltages. When some of the air was removed, however, electricity began to flow from one electrode to the other through rarefied air. The air in the tube glowed with a purplish light. When still more air was pumped from the tube, the purplish light faded and the glass walls of the tube glowed with a greenish fluorescence.

Further work with evacuated tubes showed that the greenish glow on the glass walls was produced by particles emitted from the negative electrode, the cathode. Fig. 23-3(A) shows how this was deduced. With the electrodes placed as shown in the figure, the walls of the tube glowed everywhere except where the cross inside the tube cast a shadow on the face of the tube. The shadow is in a direct line with the cross and the cathode. This means that the green glow is produced by something coming from the cathode in straight lines. These so-called *cathode rays* are invisible to the eye unless they produce a visible effect in some other substance (such as a glow in the glass walls

23.2 Discovery of the electron

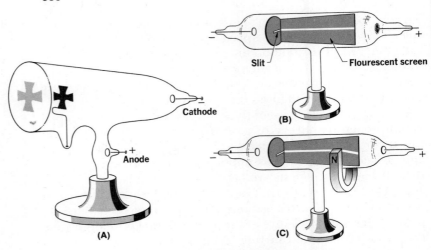

23-3 Properties of cathode rays. The shadow cast by the cross in (A) shows that cathode rays travel in straight lines. The coated screen in (B) shows the ability of cathode rays to produce fluorescence. In (C) the negative charge of cathode rays is determined by means of a magnet.

of the tube) and they can be stopped by substances like the cross inside the tube.

In 1895, the French scientist Jean Perrin (1870–1942) discovered another property of cathode rays. He arranged an evacuated tube as shown in Fig. 23-3(B). The slit in the tube forms a broad beam of cathode rays which strikes the fluorescent screen and causes it to glow. The screen is placed at an angle so that the beam is visible along the entire length of the screen. Ordinarily, the beam would trace a straight horizontal path on the screen. But when Perrin placed a magnet in the position shown in Fig. 23-3(C), the beam was deflected downward. When he reversed the poles of the magnet, the beam bent upward. Since light beams are not deflected by magnets, Perrin concluded that cathode rays were really streams of negative electricity coming from the cathode.

In Chapter 22, you learned that the modern television picture tube makes use of many of the principles discovered by scientists working with the cathode rays many years ago. The face of the picture tube glows when cathode rays strike it. In color television, different chemicals are used on the face of the tube so that multicolored glows are produced. The position of the picture on the tube is adjusted by magnets surrounding the neck of the tube inside the set.

Other scientists continued the investigations of cathode rays begun by Perrin. Among these were Sir William Crookes (1832–1919) and J. J. Thomson. Thomson was able to show that cathode-ray particles are much lighter than atoms and that they are present in all forms of matter. He arrived at this conclusion by observing that the nature of the particles did not change when he changed the composition of the cathode or of the gas in his tubes. Thus, Thomson is credited with the first discovery of a subatomic particle—the *electron*.

It is obviously impossible to use a laboratory balance to determine the mass of something as small as an electron. Even if you could pile as many as 10^{13} electrons on the balance, the total mass would still only amount to 10^{-17} kg. An indirect method must therefore be used. Thomson developed such a method in a famous series of experiments in 1897. The basic parts of this experiment are shown in Fig. 23-4. The cathode rays (electrons) emanating from the electrode at the left are accelerated and focused by the positively charged disc with a small hole in its center. The potential difference V between the cathode and the disc determines the kinetic energy of each electron, since $eV = \frac{1}{2}mv^2$ where e is the electric charge on a single electron. A second disc further narrows the electron beam.

The beam then passes between two oppositely charged plates on its way to a fluorescent screen. Surrounding the neck of the tube is a magnetic field that is set at right angles to the electric field produced by the two charged plates in the tube. In the arrangement of Fig. 23-4, the electron beam is under the influence of a downward force due to the electric field and an upward force due to the magnetic field. Both forces depend on the charge of the electrons but that force due to the magnetic field also depends on the speed of the electrons. By varying these forces until they exactly balance each other, the speed of the electrons, v, can be deduced and used in $eV = \frac{1}{2}mv^2$. Two unknowns, e and m, still remain. Though neither e nor m can be determined individually by this method, their ratio e/m can be determined from the measured values of the potential difference, the electric field, and the magnetic field. In other words, Thomson was able to calculate the quantity of electric charge per unit mass of electrons. This is expressed in coulombs per kilogram of electrons. The presently accepted value for this ratio is 1.758796×10^{11} c/kg.

This measurement is a step in the right direction, but it still

23.3 Measuring the mass of the electron

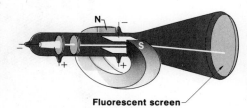

Fluorescent screen

23-4 The Thomson experiment. By means of an evacuated tube such as this, Thomson found that cathode radiation particles are subatomic in mass and are present in all forms of matter.

does not tell us the mass of an electron. If the charge on a single electron could be measured, of course, the charge-to-mass ratio could be used to calculate the mass. Similarly, if the mass could be determined, the ratio would tell us the charge. In 1912, the American physicist Robert A. Millikan succeeded in measuring the charge on the electron, and the problem was solved. His experiment will be described in the next section. But first we shall take a look at a completely different way of measuring the electron's mass.

It was seen in Chapter 1 that mass and energy are related, as shown by Einstein's equation, $E = mc^2$. Consequently, if an electron could be converted into energy, this equation could be used to calculate the original mass of the electron from the resulting energy. Or, conversely, if a form of energy, such as a beam of X rays, could be converted into an electron, the

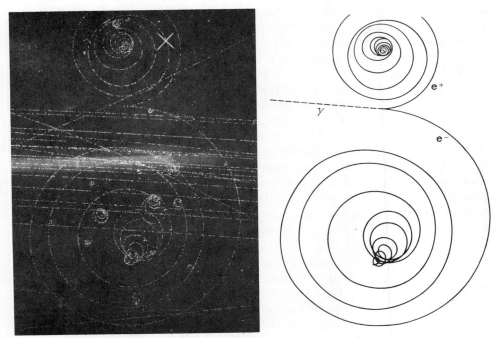

Brookhaven National Laboratory

23-5 Pair production, as photographed in a bubble chamber. X rays entering from the left were converted into a positron-electron pair.

mass could again be calculated from the known energy of the X rays. Figure 23-5 shows the results of such an experiment. As the diagram to the right of the photograph indicates, X rays entered from the left and then changed into a pair of electrons, one with a positive charge (called a positron) and one with a negative charge. The cloud chamber in which the photograph was taken was in a magnetic field which caused the two particles to spiral off in opposite directions after their formation.

Repeated experiments have shown that in order to produce an electron pair X rays must have an energy value of 1.64×10^{-13} joule. Since X rays with this energy produce two particles (a single electron is never produced), and assuming that the two particles have equal masses, the mass of each particle is equal to half of this energy, or 8.2×10^{-14} joule. Solving Einstein's equation for m and substituting:

$$m = \frac{E}{c^2} = \frac{8.2 \times 10^{-14}\,\text{j}}{(3.0 \times 10^8\,\text{m/sec})^2}$$

$$m = 9.1 \times 10^{-31}\,\text{kg}$$

The mass of the electron varies with its velocity (as explained in Chapter 1). In this case the two particles have low velocities so that they can be considered almost at rest and the mass computed above is called the *rest mass*. In terms of atomic mass units, this amounts to 0.0005486, or $\frac{1}{1837}$ of the mass of an atom of hydrogen. Obviously, electrons do not account for a very large share of the mass of substances. Other subatomic particles must be responsible for most of the mass. We shall see later in this chapter how these particles are identified.

The determination of the charge on the electron by Millikan is one of the classic experiments of physics. A diagram of the apparatus is shown in Fig. 23-6. Charged capacitor plates were placed inside a metal box in which temperature and pressure conditions could be held constant. The top plate had a small hole in the center. The plates were connected to a high potential source of power which could be varied at will. The plates were parallel and the distance between them was

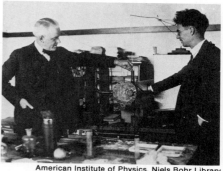

American Institute of Physics, Niels Bohr Library

Robert Millikan, the American physicist, with the apparatus he used to measure the charge on the electron.

23.4 The electronic charge

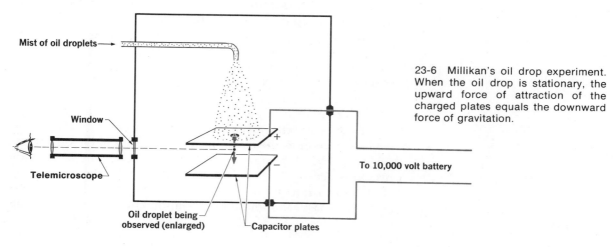

23-6 Millikan's oil drop experiment. When the oil drop is stationary, the upward force of attraction of the charged plates equals the downward force of gravitation.

Mist of oil droplets →

Window

Telemicroscope

Oil droplet being observed (enlarged)

Capacitor plates

To 10,000 volt battery

carefully measured. From the voltage and the plate spacing, the electric field could be computed. The space between the plates was illuminated by a spotlight and could be viewed through a telemicroscope, a combination of two instruments for viewing small objects at intermediate distances.

A mist of light oil was sprayed into the region above the plates. Eventually, a single oil drop fell through the opening in the top capacitor plate. The spray was then turned off so that this single drop could be studied as it fell between the plates. When the plates were uncharged, the drop fell through the field of view with a constant terminal velocity which depended on its weight. By means of crosshairs in the eyepiece of the telemicroscope, this velocity could be accurately measured. When the voltage was turned on, however, the behavior of the oil drop changed. Depending on the weight of the drop, the amount of charge it acquired in the oil spraying process, and the strength of the electric field between the capacitor plates, the drop slowed its descent, stopped in midair, or even began to rise.

Consider, for the moment, the case of a drop that was suspended motionless between the two plates. The force of gravity on the drop was then exactly balanced by the force of the electric field between the two plates. This could happen only if there were an electric charge on the oil drop upon which the electric field could exert a force. Hence, the field strength between the capacitor plates needed to suspend the drop was a measure of the electric charge on the drop. But it still did not tell how many charged particles were on the drop, and so the value of the unit charge was still unknown.

By studying the behavior of thousands of oil drops in the apparatus, however, Millikan was able to solve this problem. By shooting X rays at the drops, he was even able to change the charge on a drop in midair as a result of the photoelectric effect. Finally, he was able to arrive at these two important conclusions:

1. Even though the equipment was capable of detecting much smaller values, the charges on the oil drops never fell below a certain minimum value.

2. All charges were integral multiples of the minimum charge.

Millikan correctly concluded that the minimum charge he had measured was the electronic charge—the charge on a single electron. This important fundamental unit of physics has the presently accepted value of 1.60210×10^{-19} c. The mass of the electron can now be computed by dividing the charge by the charge-to-mass ratio found by Thomson (given in the preceding section):

$$m = \frac{e}{e/m} = \frac{1.60210 \times 10^{-19} \text{ c}}{1.75880 \times 10^{11} \text{ c/kg}}$$

$$m = 9.10905 \times 10^{-31} \text{ kg}$$

This result agrees with the mass of the electron as determined by the cloud chamber method described earlier, except that it is much more precise.

Measuring the size of the electron presents a problem that is not encountered in the determination of mass and charge. Mass and charge can be determined by the methods just described without "seeing" the electron in any way. It is far too small to be seen with visible light. Some indirect way to measure its size has to be devised.

Since the electron is a subatomic particle it must be smaller than the smallest atom, which is only about 1 Å across (see Section 7.3). Suppose we fire a narrow beam of electrons through a thin metal foil and then let them impinge on a fluorescent screen. The interatomic distances in such a foil can be quite accurately measured by X rays. If the electrons are very small we can expect most of them to pass straight through the space between the atoms and produce a bright narrow spot on the screen. Some of the electrons will come close enough to an atom in the foil to be partly deflected (scattered) by the atom, producing a fuzziness around the spot on the screen. Very few may even come so close to atom centers as to be strongly scattered, still further broadening the spot on the screen. Careful measurements of such scattering could be used to estimate the size of the electron. However, the actual result of such experiments is not a broad fuzzy spot on the screen but a series of rings. Figure 23-7 is a photograph of the image produced in such an experiment. It is obviously different from what might be expected. The central spot is understandable but where do the concentric rings come from? In Chapter 15 we saw that a diffraction grating produces several discrete images (orders) of any color. The grating was a one-dimensional array of equally spaced lines. In the metal foil we deal with a three-dimensional array of regularly spaced atoms. This should produce a set of discrete images that are symmetrical around the center spot. In fact this is the case when X rays, which are short wavelength photons, pass through a crystal. When passing through a metal foil the pattern will appear very much like Fig. 23-7.

In other words, the attempt to measure the size of the electron has produced the unexpected evidence that the electron has wave properties! Now we are faced with the same duality question that was raised at the end of Chapter 1.

23.5 Size of the electron

Margot Bergmann – Polytechnic Institute of Brooklyn

23-7 An electron diffraction pattern made with an electron microscope, of a gold film about 40 Å thick. The pattern shows the rings characteristic of a crystalline substance with random orientation of the particles.

Further experiments with electron patterns have shown that they vary not only with the type of metal foil through which the electrons are fired but also with the momentum of the electron beam. If a description of the electron is given in terms of its wavelength, and if this wavelength is computed from the changing ring patterns, we must conclude that the size of the electron varies with its momentum.

In the measurements of Thomson and Millikan the electron behaved as a charged particle in an electric or magnetic field. Now we see that it behaves as a wave. Does this mean that an electron is sometimes a particle and sometimes a wave? No. An electron sometimes exhibits particle characteristics and sometimes wave characteristics, depending upon the nature of the experiment and the measuring instruments used. Thus it may sometimes be described as a wave and sometimes as a particle. Actually, it is not just like a particle nor just like a wave —it is an electron.

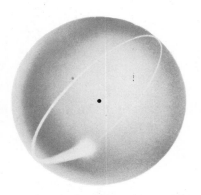

23-8   A hydrogen atom has a nucleus consisting of one proton. One electron moves about this nucleus in the K shell. Electron paths are not as definite as these diagrams show.

23.6 Motions of the electron

Figures 23-8 and 23-9 are typical representations of hydrogen and carbon atoms. The electrons are shown in a way that cannot definitely be called either a particle or a wave. The important thing, however, is that they are shown as being in rapid motion around the center of each atom. Electrons are negatively charged. Hence, a neutral atom must have an equal positive charge in its nucleus. If the electrons were not in motion, the force of attraction between these opposite charges would immediately produce a collapse of the atom. We will see later in this chapter that collapsed atoms could not account for known atomic and nuclear sizes, nor could they interact in chemical and nuclear reactions the way they do. The force of attraction between the electron and the nucleus provides a centripetal force sufficient to hold the electron in its orbit.

The wave-particle duality of the electron makes it difficult to describe its path around the nucleus. Each electron has a definite amount of energy which determines the *orbital* in which it moves. An orbital is not an orbit or path in the sense that the orbit of a spacecraft is. An orbital is a probable pattern of movement characteristic of the energy of the electron. Groups of orbitals in an atom are usually called *shells* and they are frequently designated by letters of the alphabet beginning with K and running sequentially to Q in the most complex elements. They also may be given numbers from 1 to 7. The number of orbitals in a shell is the square of the shell number (1st shell, 1 orbital; 2nd shell, 4 orbitals; 3rd shell, 9 orbitals, etc.) The maximum number of electrons which

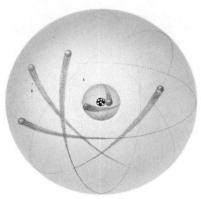

23-9   A carbon atom has a nucleus consisting of 6 protons and 6 neutrons. Two electrons are in the K shell and 4 electrons are in the L shell.

can occupy an orbital is 2; thus, the maximum number of electrons which can occupy a shell is two times the number of orbitals in the shell.

The aggregate of electrons is referred to as the *electron cloud*. It is the characteristics of the electron cloud about an atom which give it its volume and prevent the interpenetration of one atom by another under ordinary conditions.

Experiments have also shown that the electron not only revolves about the nucleus but spins on its own axis as well. The evidence and consequence of this motion, together with still other characteristics of electrons, were mentioned in Chapter 19 and will be further discussed in Chapter 25.

QUESTIONS

Group A

1. (a) Why are cathode rays so called? (b) What is the relationship between cathode rays and electrons?
2. (a) Who is credited with the discovery of the electron? (b) Why?
3. (a) What are two ways in which the mass of the electron can be determined? (b) Which way is more precise?
4. In what two ways was the charge placed on the oil drops in Millikan's experiment?
5. What difficulties are encountered in measuring the size of the electron?
6. Is an electron a particle or a wave?
7. What is the relationship between the orbital of an electron and an electron shell?
8. (a) How does the mass of an electron compare with the total mass of a hydrogen atom? (b) What does this signify?

THE NUCLEUS

23.7 Discovery of the atomic nucleus

It has already been noted that, in order to be electrically neutral, an atom must contain a positive charge of the same magnitude as the total negative charge of its electrons. But what is the exact location of the positive charge? At the time of the discovery of the electron, there were a number of theories about this. Some scientists suggested that the atom has a uniform structure in which the electrons are distributed evenly throughout a positively charged mass, something like the fruit in a fruit cake. Others thought that the positive charge was concentrated at the center and that the electrons surrounded the nucleus.

To test the validity of these theories, the English physicist Ernest Rutherford (1871–1937) conducted a series of experiments in 1911 with particles emitted by radioactive materials. As will be more fully explained in Chapter 24, certain elements

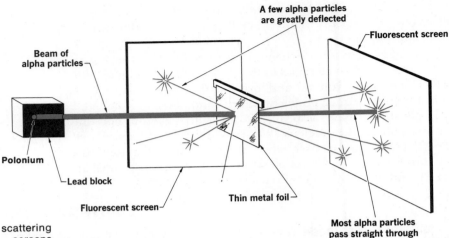

A few alpha particles
are greatly deflected

Fluorescent screen

Beam of
alpha particles

Polonium

Lead block

Fluorescent screen

Thin metal foil

Most alpha particles
pass straight through

23-10 Rutherford's alpha scattering experiment. Fluorescent screens show whether the alpha particles from a sample of polonium are deflected as they strike a metal foil.

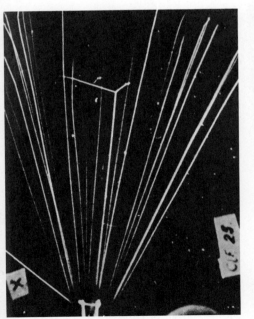

23-11 Alpha particle tracks in a sample of chlorine gas. Most of the particles are not scattered, but occasionally a particle is deflected through a large angle.

emit rays and particles that can be studied and identified as being subatomic in nature. One of these particles, called an *alpha particle*, was found to be the same as an atom of helium with its electrons missing. In other words, an alpha particle is a subatomic particle with a positive charge.

In his experiment, Rutherford used alpha particles that were emitted by a piece of radioactive polonium contained in a lead box (Fig. 23-10). These alpha particles have a velocity of 1.60×10^7 m/sec. This gave Rutherford subatomic "bullets" of known mass, charge, and velocity to explore the structure of other atoms.

Rutherford directed the alpha particles at thin metal foils of various kinds. First he used gold, because it can be hammered into extremely thin sheets. The thickness of the foil was about 10^{-7} m, equivalent to only a few hundred layers of gold atoms. Most of the alpha particles passed straight through the foil, which showed that the metal foil was very porous to them, even though the atoms were tightly packed into many layers. Some of the alpha particles were deflected from their paths, however, at angles ranging from a very slight deflection to a direct rebound. The large deflections were a surprise. How could a massive alpha particle be deflected up to 180° by electrons inside the atom that were known to have much smaller masses? See Fig. 23-11. In Rutherford's words: "It was about as credible as if you fired a 15-inch shell at a piece of tissue paper and it came back and hit you."

The answer must be that the positive charge within the atom is not uniformly distributed, as had been thought by some scientists. Instead, it is concentrated in a dense *atomic nucleus* that is able to deflect alpha particles the way a brick wall would deflect a tennis ball. Furthermore, the number of alpha particles rebounding compared with the number passing through the foil provided a clue to the size of the atomic nucleus in comparison with the size of the entire atom. Rutherford's students sat for hours in a darkened room to count and measure the deflections on a fluorescent screen. They found that about one out of every 8000 alpha particles was deflected by more than 90°.

From this and subsequent evidence, scientists have been able to determine the radius of the largest atomic nucleus at about 10^{-14} m or 10^{-4} Å. This is less than 1/10,000th of the diameter of the smallest atom, and less than 1/1,000,000,000,000th of its volume. No wonder that alpha particles, which are themselves atomic nuclei, are able to pass through the atomic structure of metal foils with only an occasional collision! This situation is like shooting at widely separated peas with an air rifle from the opposite side of a large football stadium.

Yet this tiny nucleus accounts for more than 99.95 percent of the mass of the entire atom. Thus the density of the atomic nucleus is extremely high, or about 10^{13} times the density of lead. One cubic centimeter of closely packed atomic nuclei would have a mass of 10,000,000 metric tons! Astrophysicists believe that some stars are made of such concentrated nuclei, the electrons having been forced into the nuclei by intense pressures.

The existence of positive charges in the atom was known even before the time of Rutherford's experiments. If a perforated disc is used as a cathode in a discharge tube, luminous rays are seen coming through the hole on the side opposite the anode (as in Fig. 23-1). In 1895, Perrin tested this radiation with magnets and with electrically charged plates and showed that it consists of particles with a positive charge. In 1907, Thomson named them *positive rays*.

It was found that the properties of the positive rays, unlike those of cathode rays, depend on the nature of the gas in the tube. The charge-to-mass ratio of the particles composing positive rays showed that they are charged particles formed from atoms of the gas in the tube. No positive particles with a charge-to-mass ratio similar to that of the electron were found. The lightest particle found in positive rays had the mass of a hydrogen atom, and carried a charge equal in magnitude but opposite in sign to that carried by the electron. This positive particle was assumed to be a hydrogen atom from which one electron had been removed.

The measurement of the amount of positive charge in the

23.8 The proton

nuclei of various elements was also the work of Rutherford and his colleagues. They developed equations stating that the scattering of alpha particles depends on three factors: the thickness of the metal foil, the velocity of the alpha particles, and the **amount of positive charge in the atomic nuclei.** Experiments soon showed that the first two of these relationships agreed remarkably with the results as predicted by the equations. So it could be assumed that the third relationship, scattering vs. **relative nuclear charge, is also true. Tests were made with many different elements, and it was found that** *the nuclear charge of the atoms of a given element is always the same and characteristic of that element.*

The smallest nuclear charge is that of the hydrogen nucleus. In 1920, the name ***proton*** was given to the nuclear particle carrying this unit positive charge. The number of protons, and therefore the amount of positive charge, measured in electron charge units, is called the ***atomic number***. They range from 1 for hydrogen to over 100 for the most massive elements. The positive charge of a proton has the same magnitude as the negative charge of an electron. Consequently. the atomic number of an element also gives the number of electrons surrounding the nucleus of neutral atoms.

The mass of the proton has been found to be 1.67252×10^{-27} kg, or 1.00727663 u on the atomic mass scale. This is $\frac{1836}{1837}$ of the mass of a hydrogen atom, and it shows that the mass of an atom is contained almost entirely in its nucleus.

23.9 The neutron

American Institute of Physics

James Chadwick (1891–1947), the English physicist who discovered the neutron.

If an atom consists entirely of electrons and protons, and if the mass of the atom is almost entirely contained in its protons, then it should be possible to predict the atomic mass of an element from its atomic number. For example, since the atomic number of oxygen is 8, the atomic mass of oxygen should be eight times the atomic mass of hydrogen which consists of a single proton and single electron. Similarly, the atomic mass of uranium ought to be 92. But this is not the case. The atomic mass of the most abundant form of oxygen is about 16 and that of the most common form of uranium is about 238. The same discrepancy shows up in all the elements except ordinary hydrogen. Why?

One possibility is that the excess mass is due to protons whose positive charge is neutralized by electrons located within the nucleus. However, such an arrangement presents a number of complex problems which rule it out as a possible solution. For instance, the spin of such nuclear electrons would produce effects that disagree with observed nuclear behavior.

The answer was provided by the English physicist, James

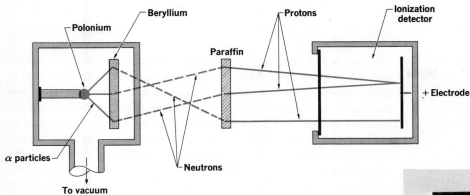

Beryllium — Protons — Ionization detector

Polonium

Paraffin

+ Electrode

α particles

Neutrons

To vacuum pump

23-12 Chadwick's neutron experiment. Particles ejected from beryllium were in turn able to knock protons out of a sample of paraffin. The intermediate particles were found to have no charge but a mass similar to that of the proton. Chadwick called them neutrons.

Chadwick. In 1930 physicists found that when certain elements, such as beryllium or boron, are bombarded with alpha particles from the radioactive element polonium, a radiation with very high penetrating power is obtained. Two years later Chadwick discovered that this radiation was able to knock protons out of a block of paraffin, a compound containing carbon and hydrogen atoms. Figure 23-12 is a schematic diagram of Chadwick's experiment. The radiation producing this proton emission was not a beam of X rays, because it can be shown that X rays would require unusually high energies to expel protons from paraffin. Chadwick reasoned that the radiation was a stream of neutral particles. Calculations showed that the particles had masses similar to that of the proton.

Additional experiments indicated that the same neutral particles can be expelled from a great variety of elements, which means that they are regular components of atomic nuclei. Chadwick called these particles **neutrons**. They have a mass of 1.67482×10^{-27} kg (very slightly higher than that of the proton), which is 1.0086654 on the atomic mass scale. The two particles are also quite similar in size.

Experiments have shown that the chemical properties of an element are related to its atomic number, Z. Thus, for hydrogen, $Z = 1$, for carbon, $Z = 6$, and for uranium, $Z = 92$. The total number of protons and neutrons in the nucleus of an atom is equal to the mass number, A (Section 7.3). Using the symbol N to represent the number of neutrons,

$$A = Z + N$$

Protons and neutrons are referred to collectively as *nucleons*. Thus, in the formula above, A equals the number of nucleons.

The number of neutrons in the atomic nucleus of a given

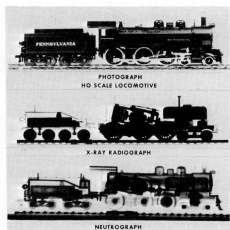

PHOTOGRAPH
HO SCALE LOCOMOTIVE

X-RAY RADIOGRAPH

NEUTROGRAPH

General Electric

Neutrons can be used to take pictures of opaque objects, revealing more inner detail than is obtainable with X rays. High-intensity neutrons that pass through the object strike a metallic converter, thereby releasing the rays that expose a photographic film.

23.10 Isotopes

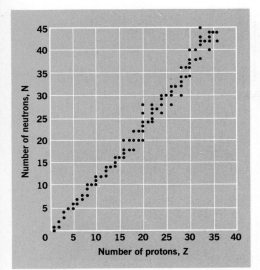

23-13 Nuclei of the stable isotopes of the light elements. Note that the lightest nuclides have equal numbers of neutrons and protons, but in the heavier nuclides there are more neutrons than protons.

element may vary. All atoms of an element have the same chemical properties, but their masses may be different. Atoms of a given element having different masses are called *isotopes*. *Isotopes of an element contain the same number of protons but different numbers of neutrons. Each different variety of atom as determined by the composition of its nucleus is called a **nuclide***. Nuclides having the same atomic number are isotopes. There are three nuclides of hydrogen: *protium* (ordinary hydrogen), 1 proton, no neutrons; *deuterium*, 1 proton, 1 neutron; and *tritium*, 1 proton, 2 neutrons. Isotopes of all chemical elements occur naturally or have been produced artificially.

In general, nuclei with odd atomic numbers exist naturally in only one or two isotopic forms. Those with even atomic numbers exist in several isotopic forms, some elements having as many as eleven variations. Figure 23-13 is a graph of the nuclei of the naturally occurring light nuclides in which Z is plotted on the horizontal axis and N on the vertical axis. Notice that Z and N are equal in many of the lightest nuclides, but that the neutrons outnumber the protons as the mass number increases. This fact is reflected in the properties of the elements, some of which will be discussed in the next chapter.

Naturally occurring elements are mixtures of isotopes in quite definite proportions. Hydrogen consists of 99.985% protium, 0.015% deuterium, and less than 0.001% tritium. *The **atomic weight** of an element is the average atomic mass of the atoms of the element, based on a large number of samples found in nature*. The atomic weight scale is based on the carbon isotope with mass number 12 u. This isotope is assigned the atomic mass of exactly 12 u. On this scale, naturally occurring carbon has an atomic weight of 12.01115 u, and hydrogen, an atomic weight of 1.00797 u. Similarly, the atomic weights of all naturally occurring elements are mixed numbers.

23.11 The mass spectrograph

The masses of ionized atoms can be measured with great precision in a device called a *mass spectrograph*. There are many different types of mass spectrographs, but their operation depends on the slight difference in mass between isotopes. One type of spectrograph is shown in Fig. 23-14.

A beam of ions enters from the bottom and passes into a region of crossed electric and magnetic fields which allows only the ions with a specific velocity to pass through the slit **S**. (Ions with other velocities are deflected and are blocked by the chamber wall around the slit.) As the ions enter the upper chamber they are influenced by another magnetic field perpendicular to the plane of the page. This magnetic field causes the ions to move in a circular path. If the ions have the same mass-charge ratio, they will all describe the same arc and will strike the photographic plate at the same place. However, if the beam entering the slit contains ions of various masses, the less massive ions will be deflected to a greater extent than the more massive ones and will strike the photographic plate at a different place.

If the photographic plate is replaced by collecting vessels, the mass spectrograph can be used to separate isotopes.

A very strong force holds protons and neutrons together in the nucleus. This force is not electrostatic because the similarly charged protons would then repel each other. The force cannot be gravitational either, because calculations show that it would be much too weak. It is a completely unique force that acts only within the extremely small distances between nucleons. Experiments have shown that this *nuclear binding force* is effective to a distance of 2.0×10^{-15} m or 2.0×10^{-5} Å, compared to the proton radius of 1.3×10^{-5} Å.

It has also been found that the nuclear binding force is the same for protons and neutrons. This again shows that the force is not electrostatic. The magnitude of the force has been investigated in several ways. One way is to study the scattering pattern when nucleons are fired at each other, very much like the scattering experiments of Rutherford and Chadwick. Another way is to compare the mass of a nucleus with the combined masses of the uncombined nucleons that make up the nucleus.

Careful measurements have shown that *the mass of a nucleus is always less than the sum of the uncombined masses of its constituent particles. This difference in mass is called the* **nuclear mass defect**. The reason for the nuclear mass defect is found in Einstein's equation $E = mc^2$. When a nucleus is formed, energy is released. This is similar to the energy release that occurs when atoms combine to form a molecule. Einstein's equation states that a decrease in energy must be accompanied by a corresponding decrease in mass, since the two quantities are directly proportional. This decrease in mass is the nuclear mass defect.

The nuclear mass defect can be used to compute the total *nuclear binding energy.* Binding energy is equivalent to the energy released during the formation of a nucleus, and is the energy that must be applied to the nucleus in order to break it apart. Take the formation of a helium nucleus (alpha particle), for example. It contains 2 protons and 2 neutrons. Each proton has a mass of 1.007277 u and each neutron has a mass of 1.008665 u. The mass of a helium nucleus is 4.001509 u. The nuclear mass defect can now be computed as follows:

23.12 Nuclear binding

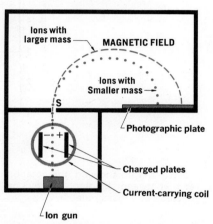

23-14 Diagram of a mass spectrograph. The magnetic field produced by the current-carrying coil and charged plates deflect the less massive ions more than the more massive ones.

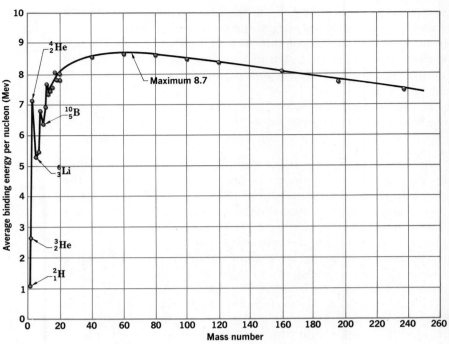

23-15 Graph showing the relationship between binding energy per
nucleon and mass number.

$$2 \text{ protons} = 2 \times 1.007277 \text{ u} = 2.014554 \text{ u}$$
$$2 \text{ neutrons} = 2 \times 1.008665 \text{ u} = \underline{2.017330 \text{ u}}$$
$$4.031884 \text{ u}$$
$$\text{helium nucleus} = \underline{4.001509 \text{ u}}$$
$$\text{nuclear mass defect} = \underline{0.030375 \text{ u}}$$

In nuclear physics, nuclear binding energy is expressed in
electron volts. *An **electron volt** is the energy required to move an
electron between two points which have a potential difference of one
volt.* The mega electron volt (Mev) is also used. A single atomic
mass unit is the equivalent of 931 Mev. Hence, the binding
energy of the helium nucleus is

$$0.030375 \text{ u} \times 931 \text{ Mev/u} = 28.3 \text{ Mev}$$

If the nuclear binding energy is divided by the number of
nucleons, the binding energy per nucleon is obtained. For
helium, this is 28.3 Mev/4 = 7.1 Mev/nucleon. The graph in
Fig. 23-15 shows the variation of binding energy per nucleon
with the mass number. Note that elements of low or high mass
number have lower binding energies per nucleon than those
of intermediate mass number. The binding energy per nucleon
is low for the lightest nuclei because the nucleons are all on

the surface of the nucleus and are not held on all sides by other nucleons. This geometry reduces the binding energy per nucleon. As the number of nucleons increases, more and more of them are completely surrounded, and the binding energy per nucleon also increases. Beyond the maximum of 8.7 Mev/nucleon; however, the repelling force between the protons begins to cancel the binding force. Finally, a point is reached where the nucleus begins to fall apart. This disintegration is a form of nuclear reaction, which will be studied in the next chapter.

QUESTIONS

Group A

1. Compare the relative masses, charges, and sizes of the following particles: molecule, atom, electron, proton, neutron, nucleus.
2. Distinguish between atomic mass and atomic weight.
3. (a) What do the isotopes of an element have in common? (b) How do they differ?
4. Define the following: (a) A, (b) Å, (c) Z, (d) N, (e) u, (f) Mev.
5. What is the standard for the system of atomic weights?
6. Copy and complete the following table on a separate sheet of paper.

Nuclide	Z	A	N	Binding energy/nucleon (Mev/A)
deuterium	1			
carbon-14	6			
oxygen-18	8			
sodium-23	11			
sulfur-32	16			
argon-40	18			
uranium-235	92			
uranium-238	92			

Group B

7. (a) How did Rutherford obtain alpha particles? (b) How did he detect them after they had passed through the metal foils?
8. (a) What did the experiments of Perrin and Rutherford have in common? (b) Of Rutherford and Chadwick?
9. How did Rutherford know that the alpha particles did not rebound from the electrons in the metal foils?
10. What is the general relationship between the atomic number of an atom and the number of its isotopes?
11. (a) What is meant by nuclear mass defect? (b) What is nuclear binding energy? (c) How are they related?
12. What element has the highest Mev/nucleon?

PROBLEMS

(Note: Consult Table 23 in the Appendix for the atomic masses of nuclides.)

Group A

1. (a) Calculate the mass in grams of an atom of an isotope of iron which has an atomic mass of 55.9349. (b) What is the mass number of this isotope?

2. The mass of an atom of an unstable isotope of neon is 3.818×10^{-23} g. (a) What is its atomic mass? (b) Its mass number?

3. A calcium ion has 20 protons, 20 neutrons, and 18 electrons. What is the magnitude of its charge in coulombs?

4. (a) What is the atomic number of a zinc atom composed of 30 protons, 34 neutrons, and 30 electrons? (b) What is the mass number of the atom?

5. What particles, and how many of each, make up an atom of silver (atomic number 47, mass number 109)?

Group B

6. Calculate the binding energy per nucleon in Mev for carbon-12. This nuclide consists of 6 protons, 6 neutrons, and 6 electrons. Its atomic mass is 12.00000.

7. Calculate the binding energy per nucleon in Mev for sulfur-32 which consists of 16 protons, 16 neutrons, and 16 electrons.

8. Calculate the atomic weight for chlorine if naturally occurring chlorine consists of 75.4% Cl-35 and 24.6% Cl-37.

9. Naturally occurring magnesium consists of 78.6% Mg-24, 10.1% Mg-25, and 11.3% Mg-26. Calculate the atomic weight.

10. An electron pair is produced from X rays with a total energy of 1.5 Mev. If the positron and electron each receive half of the extra energy, calculate what the resulting velocity of each particle would be if we could disregard relativity.

Chapter 24

Nuclear Reactions

TYPES OF NUCLEAR REACTIONS

At the same time that J. J. Thomson was conducting his experiments with cathode rays (Section 23.2) other scientists were accumulating additional evidence that the atom could be subdivided. In fact, this new evidence showed that some atoms disintegrate by themselves. In 1896, Henri Becquerel (1852–1908) discovered this phenomenon while investigating the properties of *fluorescent* minerals. Fluorescent minerals glow after they have been exposed to strong light. Becquerel used photographic plates to record this fluorescence.

One of the minerals Becquerel worked with was a uranium compound. During a day when it was too cloudy to expose his mineral samples to direct sunlight, he stored some of the compound in the same drawer with the photographic plates. Later, when he used these same plates in his experiments and developed them he discovered that they were fogged. What could have produced this fogging? They were wrapped tightly before being used, so the fogging was not due to stray light. Besides, only the plates that were in the drawer with the uranium compound were fogged. Becquerel reasoned that the uranium compound must be giving off a type of radiation that could penetrate heavy paper and affect photographic film.

Elements which emit such radiation are *radioactive* and they have the property called *radioactivity*. **Radioactivity** *is the spontaneous, uncontrollable decay of an atomic nucleus with the emission of particles and rays.* At the suggestion of Becquerel, the Curies, Pierre (1859–1906) and Marie (1867–1934) investigated uranium and its various ores quite thoroughly. They found that

24.1 Discovery of radioactivity

The Bettman Archive

Henri Becquerel, the French physicist who discovered radioactivity.

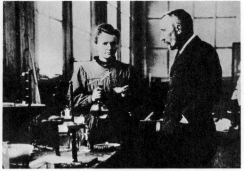

French Embassy Press and Information Division

Marie and Pierre Curie in their laboratory.

24.2 Nature of radioactivity

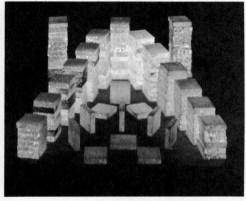

Oak Ridge National Laboratory

24-1 Rectangular blocks containing 70,000 curies of $^{137}CsCl$. The only source of illumination for this time-exposure, which was taken through a 3-foot-thick heavy-glass window, was the natural radioactivity of the cesium-137.

all uranium ores were radioactive but that one of them, pitch-blende, was four times as radioactive as might be expected from the amount of uranium in it. Further studies showed that this extra radiation was really due to the presence of two previously unknown elements, *polonium* and *radium*, both of which are intensely radioactive. Both of these elements were discovered and named by the Curies.

Several more radioactive elements have since been discovered and isolated. All of the naturally occurring elements with atomic numbers greater than 83 are radioactive. A few naturally radioactive isotopes of elements with atomic numbers smaller than 83 are also known. Many artificial radioactive nuclides have been produced and put to use in many different ways, as we shall see later in this chapter.

All radioactive nuclides have certain common characteristics.

1. Their radiations affect the emulsion on a photographic film. Even though photographic film is wapped in heavy black paper and kept in the dark, radiations from radioactive nuclides penetrate the wrapping and affect the film. When the film is developed, a black spot can be seen where the invisible radiations struck it. The radiations penetrate paper, wood, flesh, and *thin* sheets of metal (Fig. 24-1).

2. Their radiations ionize the surrounding air molecules. The radiations from radioactive nuclides knock electrons from the gas molecules in the air surrounding the radioactive material, leaving the gas molecules with a positive charge. This effect can be detected by special instruments such as the electroscope. (An atom or a group of atoms having an electric charge is called an ion. The production of ions is termed ionization.)

3. Their radiations make certain compounds fluoresce. Radiations from radioactive nuclides produce bright flashes of light when they strike certain compounds. The combined effect of these flashes is a glow or fluorescence given off by the affected material. For example, radium compounds added to zinc sulfide cause the zinc sulfide to glow. Since the glow is visible in the dark, the mixture is useful as an ingredient in luminous paint.

4. Their radiations have special physiological effects. Radiations from natural radioactive sources can destroy the germinating power of plant seeds, kill bacteria, and even injure and kill larger animals. Burns from radioactive materials heal with great difficulty and may sometimes be fatal.

5. They undergo radioactive decay. The atoms of all radioactive elements continually decay into simpler atoms and simultaneously emit radiations. However, it is not possible to predict when a specific atom will decay. The rate of decay may be described by a rule which states about how long it will take for half of the atoms in a given sample to decay. The accuracy of the rule is greater for larger samples. The time associated with radioactive decays of a certain type is called the *half-life* of the nuclide. *During one half-life, on the average, half of a large number of radioactive nuclides will decay.* For example the half-life of radium-226 is 1620 years, which means that one-half of a given sample of radium-226 atoms can be expected to decay into simpler atoms in 1620 years.

In the course of his alpha scattering experiments (Section 23.10), Rutherford discovered that the radiations from radioactive materials can be separated into three distinct types by means of a strong magnet (Fig. 24-2).

1. α (alpha) particles. These are composed of two protons and two neutrons, hence they are helium nuclei. This conclusion can be proved by collecting large quantities of alpha particles in a tube and passing an electric discharge through the tube. The resulting spectrum is the same as that for helium. Alpha particles have two positive electric charges, a mass about four times that of the hydrogen atom, and speeds about one-tenth the speed of light. Hence they are deflected only slightly by the field of a magnet as shown in Fig. 24-2. Their penetrating power is not very great. They can be stopped by a thin piece of aluminum foil or by a thin sheet of paper. Nevertheless they can strip electrons from gas molecules quite readily.

2. β (beta) particles. These are electrons just like cathode rays. They have single negative charges and may travel with nearly the speed of light. Their mass is only a small fraction of the mass of alpha particles. Hence they are deflected much more by a magnetic field, and in the opposite direction. The high speed of beta particles makes them much more penetrating than alpha particles. It was the beta particles from the uranium compound that fogged Becquerel's photographic plates.

3. γ (gamma) rays. These are high energy photons—the same kind of radiation as visible light, but of much shorter wavelength, thus higher frequency. Gamma rays are produced by energy transitions in the nucleus that do not change the composition of the nuclide. They are the most penetrating radiations given off by radioactive elements. They are not electrically charged and are not deflected by a magnetic field.

Changes in matter can be classified into three types: *physical, chemical,* and *nuclear.* When a physical change occurs, the identity of the substance is not lost. When water freezes and forms ice, the composition of its molecules is not changed; if we heat the ice, it changes back into water. When sugar dis-

24.3 Types of natural radioactivity

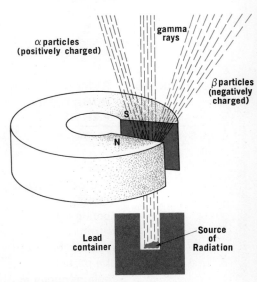

24-2 Types of radioactivity. Alpha and beta particles are deflected by a magnet, but gamma rays are not.

24.4 Nuclear symbols and equations

solves in water it undergoes a physical change; if the water evaporates, the sugar remains behind. *In a **physical change** the composition of the substance is not changed.* The substance consists of the same molecules, or atoms, or charged particles as it did before the change occurred.

When a chemical change occurs, new substances having their own distinct properties are formed, using the atoms or ions of the original substances. Ions are atoms or groups of atoms with an excess or deficiency of electrons. The rusting of iron produces a new material, iron oxide. Sour milk certainly has different properties from the sweet milk it was originally. *In a **chemical change** the composition of the substance is changed, and new substances with new properties are produced.* We still have the same atoms or ions, as well as the same number of atoms or ions, but they are rearranged to form new substances. A chemical change does not involve the nuclei of the interacting atoms.

A nuclear change is similar to a chemical change insofar as new substances with new properties are formed. However, *in a **nuclear change**, the new materials are formed by changes in the identity of the atoms themselves.* The radioactive decay of radium is a nuclear change, as are all forms of alpha, beta, and gamma emission.

Both chemical and nuclear changes are usually represented by equations. In such equations, symbols or formulas are used to stand for the particles that enter into a reaction and that are produced by it. You are probably already familiar with the symbols of many of the chemical elements. In working with nuclear equations, you must also know how to use the symbols for some of the subatomic particles and radiations. The most basic of these are given in Table 24-1. (A number of others will be discussed in Chapter 25.)

Except for the gamma-ray symbol, all the symbols in the table have subscripts and superscripts. The subscript designates the electric charge of the particle. The superscript stands for the number of nucleons in the particle. These charge and nucleon designations are also used with the symbols of all other atomic nuclei used in nuclear equations.

In a chemical equation, the same atoms appear on both sides of the equation in equal numbers. This is true because the identity of the atoms is not changed. In a nuclear equation, however, the same atomic symbols do not necessarily appear on both sides. Instead, the factors that remain constant in a nuclear equation are the total number of nucleons and the arithmetic sum of the electric charges on each side. An example will illustrate this.

Table 24-1   SYMBOLS FOR SUBATOMIC PARTICLES

Symbol	Particle
$_0^1n$	neutron
$_1^1H$	proton (hydrogen nucleus)
$_{-1}^0e$	electron (beta particle)
$_{+1}^0e$	positron (positive electron)
$_2^4He$	alpha particle (helium nucleus)
γ	gamma ray

Note: In the case of the proton and the alpha particle the atomic symbols for hydrogen and helium are used to designate the nuclei only.

$$^{14}_{7}\text{N} + ^{4}_{2}\text{He} \rightarrow ^{17}_{8}\text{O} + ^{1}_{1}\text{H}$$

In this equation, a nitrogen nucleus (charge, 7; nucleons, 14) reacts with an alpha particle (charge, 2; nucleons, 4) to form an oxygen nucleus (charge, 8; nucleons, 17) and a proton (charge, 1; nucleon, 1). There is a total of 9 electric charges and 18 nucleons on each side of the equation.

It has already been noted (Section 24.1) that the atoms of all naturally occurring elements with atomic numbers greater than 83 are unstable and decay spontaneously into lighter particles. This is also true of several naturally occurring nuclides and a great many artificially made nuclides with atomic numbers below 83. As a general rule, an atomic nucleus is stable only if the ratio of its neutrons to its protons is about 1 for the light elements and about $1\frac{1}{2}$ for the heavier ones. When there are more neutrons than this, a *nuclear transformation* will probably take place.

Figure 24-3 shows a series of nuclear transformations beginning with uranium-238 and ending with lead-206. Each step of the series can be represented by a nuclear equation in which nucleons and charge are conserved. For instance, the equation for the first step in the chart may be written as follows:

$$^{238}_{92}\text{U} \rightarrow ^{234}_{90}\text{Th} + ^{4}_{2}\text{He}$$

24.5 Radioactive decay

24-3 The uranium disintegration series.

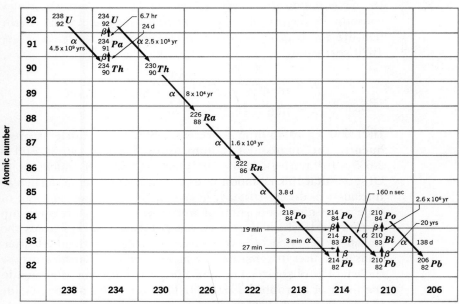

Atomic number / Mass number

Because an alpha particle is emitted in this reaction, it is called *alpha decay*.

The next two steps in the series are examples of *beta decay*. In the first step, a neutron in the thorium nucleus ejects a beta particle and becomes a proton. This transformation increases the nuclear charge by one, and the nucleus becomes a protactinium nucleus. The equation follows:

$$^{234}_{90}\text{Th} \rightarrow {}^{234}_{91}\text{Pa} + {}^{0}_{-1}\text{e}$$

The chart also shows the half-life of each nuclide in the decay series. You will notice that there is a wide variation in these values, from small fractions of a second to millions of years. The exact length of the half-life in each case is related to the energy change that accompanies the transformation. As a rule, the shorter the half-life of the nuclide, the greater is the kinetic energy of the alpha particle it emits.

From the definition of half-life, it is obvious that the radioactivity of a substance depends on the total number of nuclei present. Consequently, if the half-life of a nuclide is known, its *decay constant* (the ratio between the number of nuclei decaying per unit time and the total number of original nuclei) can be calculated. The equation that has been derived for this purpose follows:

$$\lambda = \frac{0.693}{T_{1/2}}$$

In this equation the Greek letter lambda designates the decay constant in reciprocal seconds written as 1/sec or sec^{-1} if the half-life $T_{1/2}$ is given in seconds. For example, for $^{226}_{88}\text{Ra}$, $T_{1/2} = 1620$ years and

$$\lambda = \frac{0.693}{1620 \text{ yr} \times 365 \text{ da/yr} \times 86{,}400 \text{ sec/da}}$$

$$\lambda = 1.36 \times 10^{-11} \text{ sec}^{-1}$$

In 1.000 kg of radium there are 2.665×10^{24} nuclei. Consequently, the number of radium nuclei decaying per second is 2.665×10^{24} nuclei $\times 1.36 \times 10^{-11}$ $\text{sec}^{-1} = 3.62 \times 10^{13}$ nuclei sec^{-1}. Observe that this equation does not indicate when a particular nucleus will decay. Instead, it says that in a certain amount of time a definite proportion of nuclei will decay. A relationship of this kind, which is very common in science, represents the statistical behavior of a very large number of individual situations and uses the mathematical methods of statistics or the theory of probability. The half-life probability law is shown in the form of a graph in Fig. 24-4. The *average life* of any nuclide is 1.44 times its half-life.

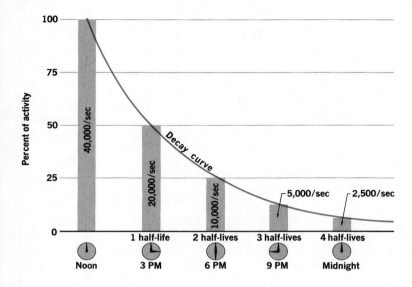

24-4 Half-life curve of a radioactive nuclide with a half-life of three hours and an original strength of 40,000 disintegrations per second.

The commonly used unit of radioactivity is the ***curie***, which is equal to *3.70 × 10¹⁰ disintegrations per second.* This rate of radioactivity is very close to that of one gram of radium. Since the curie is a very large unit, the millicurie (10^{-3} curie) and microcurie (10^{-6} curie) are frequently used. For example a source with a strength of 4 microcuries emits 1.48×10^5 particles per second.

The unit used to measure exposure to gamma rays and to determine their effects on living organisms is the *roentgen*. It is named after Wilhelm Roentgen (1845–1923), the German physicist who discovered X rays. *A **roentgen** is the amount of gamma radiation that will produce 1.61 × 10¹² pairs of ions when it is absorbed in one gram of air.* How much radiation a human being can tolerate depends on a number of factors, such as the rate at which the radiation is being absorbed and the region of the body being exposed. A dose of 700 roentgens, for example, would be fatal if it were absorbed by the entire body at one time. But the same dosage might not be harmful if it were accumulated over a period of many years or were given to only one part of the body, as when cancer is being treated by X rays or cobalt-60 radiation. Genetic effects, on the other hand, seem to be cumulative and depend only upon the total dosage received, regardless of rate.

The study of radioactive decay led scientists to the belief that human-made transformations might be produced by adding protons to the nucleus, thus producing a different element

24.6 Nuclear bombardment

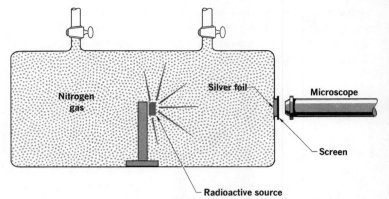

24-5 Rutherford's transformation experiment. Bombardments from the radioactive sample ejected protons from the nitrogen gas in the chamber. The protons produced scintillations on a fluorescent screen.

artificially. The first successful transformation of this kind was carried out by Rutherford in 1919. A diagram of the apparatus is shown in Fig. 24-5. The container was filled with nitrogen gas. A radioactive source emitted alpha particles. A silver foil thick enough to absorb any alpha particles not absorbed by the nitrogen gas was used. A zinc sulfide screen recorded the scintillations of any particles with enough energy to pass through the silver foil. These scintillations could be observed through the microscope.

Rutherford observed scintillations on the screen when the chamber was filled with nitrogen and other light gases. However, there were no scintillations when he used oxygen and other heavy gases such as carbon dioxide. He concluded that low density gases were changed by the alpha-particle bombardment, resulting in the emission of a high-energy particle such as a proton. The nuclear equation in Section 24.4 represents the transformation produced by the alpha bombardment of nitrogen. The detection of oxygen gas in the container after bombardment of pure nitrogen helps to verify the validity of the equation.

The alpha bombardment of nitrogen results in the emission of protons. Other bombardments produce other subatomic particles. In 1932, J. D. Cockcroft and E. T. S. Walton bombarded lithium with high-speed protons, with the following result:

$$^{7}_{3}\text{Li} + ^{1}_{1}\text{H} \rightarrow ^{4}_{2}\text{He} + ^{4}_{2}\text{He} + \text{energy}$$

In this case, all resulting products have lower mass numbers than the original target material. In addition, there is the release of a considerable amount of binding energy. Actually, adjustments in binding energy are involved in all nuclear reactions. (The method of computing this energy was described in Section 23.12.) Cockcroft and Walton found that the measured energy in their experiments agreed closely with the theoretical value as derived from Einstein's equation, $E = mc^2$.

Another nuclear bombardment, also carried out in 1932, led to the discovery of the neutron (Section 23.9). The nuclear equation for Chadwick's experiment is

$$^{9}_{4}\text{Be} + ^{4}_{2}\text{He} \rightarrow ^{12}_{6}\text{C} + ^{1}_{0}\text{n} + \textbf{energy}$$

Many similar bombardments have since been found to produce neutrons. Since the neutron is not electrically charged, it penetrates atomic nuclei more easily than do charged particles like the proton or the alpha particle. Hence the neutron has become an important nuclear "bullet." In fact, one of the main problems in neutron bombardment is to get the neutrons to move *slowly* enough to produce a transformation. The problem is quite the opposite with charged particles. The equation for a typical neutron absorption is

$$^{10}_{5}\text{B} + ^{1}_{0}\text{n} \rightarrow ^{7}_{3}\text{Li} + ^{4}_{2}\text{He} + \textbf{energy}$$

Bombardment reactions are usually designated by the symbols for the incident and emitted subatomic particles. For example, the preceding equation is called a (n, α) reaction. In bombardment reactions, the mass number of the target nucleus is increased or decreased by several units. Sometimes, however, a nucleus will split into two large segments when struck by a neutron moving at just the right speed. This reaction is extremely important in nuclear physics and will be the topic of the next section.

24.7 Fission

As has already been mentioned, fast moving neutrons are not effective for nuclear bombardment. Neutrons with energies of about 1 Mev will usually go right through an atom without causing much change in it. On the other hand, slow neutrons, with energies of the order of 10 ev, are frequently trapped by a nucleus, which then becomes unstable. Fast neutrons may be slowed down by passage through materials called *moderators*, composed of elements of low atomic weight. Deuterium oxide or graphite are useful moderators.

When a slow neutron is captured by $^{238}_{92}\text{U}$, the following reaction takes place:

$$^{238}_{92}\text{U} + ^{1}_{0}\text{n} \rightarrow ^{239}_{92}\text{U}$$

This new isotope of uranium is unstable, however, and it emits a beta particle:

$$^{239}_{92}\text{U} \rightarrow ^{239}_{93}\text{Np} + ^{0}_{-1}\text{e}$$

$^{239}_{93}\text{Np}$ has a half-life of 2.3 days and decays by emitting another beta particle:

$$^{239}_{93}\text{Np} \rightarrow ^{239}_{94}\text{Pu} + ^{0}_{-1}\text{e}$$

Neptunium and plutonium were the first two man-made *transuranium* elements. *A transuranium element is one with an atomic number greater than 92, the atomic number of uranium.* At the time of this printing, thirteen artificial transuranium elements have been confirmed. All of them are radioactive, and some of them exist only for a small fraction of a second.

Uranium-238 accounts for 99.3% of naturally occurring uranium. 0.7% consists of uranium-235, and there are also traces of uranium-234. When $^{235}_{92}U$ absorbs a slow neutron, the reaction is quite different from that described above for $^{238}_{92}U$. Instead of emitting alpha or beta particles, the $^{235}_{92}U$ may split into segments of intermediate mass. *The splitting of a heavy nucleus into nuclei of intermediate mass is called* **fission**. During the process of fission, neutrons are emitted and a large amount of energy is released. One equation for the fission of $^{235}_{92}U$ is

$$^{235}_{92}U + ^{1}_{0}n \rightarrow ^{138}_{56}Ba + ^{95}_{36}Kr + 3^{1}_{0}n + energy$$

The energy involved in this reaction can be computed from the atomic masses of the particles (See Appendix B, Table 23):

$$
\begin{aligned}
^{235}_{92}U &= 235.0439 \quad u \\
^{1}_{0}n &= \underline{1.008665 \; u} \\
& 236.0526 \quad u
\end{aligned}
$$

$$
\begin{aligned}
^{138}_{56}Ba &= 137.9050 \quad u \\
^{95}_{36}Kr &= 94.9 \qquad\;\; u \\
3 \times ^{1}_{0}n &= \underline{3.025995 \; u} \\
& 235.8 \qquad u
\end{aligned}
$$

nuclear mass defect = 236.0526 − 235.8 = 0.3 u

binding energy released = 0.3 u × 931 Mev/u = 300 Mev

The above calculation was simplified by using the masses of the neutral atoms given in the table, rather than the masses of the nuclei by themselves. No error is introduced in this case because the masses of the electrons cancel out. When a beta particle or a positron is emitted, however, the masses of the nuclides must be used in the calculation.

Note that the atomic mass of $^{95}_{36}Kr$ is not known with the same precision as the masses of the other particles in this reaction. This uncertainty is due to the fact that the atoms of the nuclide are so unstable that it is very difficult to measure their mass. Since the mass of krypton-95 is given in three significant figures, the mass defect and binding energy can be computed with a precision of only one significant figure.

The first successful fission reaction was carried out in 1939. Later it was discovered that the man-made element, plutonium, also undergoes fission and produces more neutrons when bombarded with slow neutrons.

24.8 Fusion

The graph of binding energy per nucleon in Section 23.11 suggests that a great deal of binding energy could be released by combining nuclei of the light elements into nuclei of medium mass. In fact, we could expect energies of about 7 Mev/nucleon as compared with about 1 Mev/nucleon for fission reactions. *A reaction in which light nuclei combine to form a nucleus with greater mass is called fusion.* Because fusion can take place only under extremely high temperature conditions, the process is also called a *thermonuclear reaction.*

One of the first fusion reactions to be accomplished was the combination of two deuterons (nuclei of the isotope of hydrogen, deuterium):

$$^{2}_{1}H + ^{2}_{1}H \rightarrow ^{3}_{2}He + ^{1}_{0}n + 3.3 \text{ Mev}$$

The total energy released in this reaction is less than that of uranium fission, but the energy per nucleon is much greater. In other words, less material is required to produce the energy. In 1938, the astrophysicist Hans Bethe (b. 1906) suggested that the tremendous and long-lasting rate of energy production of the sun and other stars is due to nuclear fusion. The high temperatures and pressures of a star are sufficient to bring about the fusion of hydrogen nuclei to form nuclei of helium, with the accompanying release of energy. The net result of such a reaction is the following:

$$4^{1}_{1}H \rightarrow ^{4}_{2}He + 2^{0}_{+1}e + 25.7 \text{ Mev}$$

The intermediate steps that take place in the thermonuclear reactions in the stars are not completely understood. Some scientists believe that the reaction is somewhat different in different parts of the interior of a star. But it is almost certain that several other atomic nuclei, especially those of oxygen and nitrogen, play an important role. Both elements have been identified in the sun and other stars.

Estimates of the sun's energy output indicate that about 6×10^{11} kg of hydrogen are converted into helium every second, with a mass defect of 4×10^9 kg *every second*. It is good to know, however, that the sun has a mass of 2×10^{30} kg, so that there is no immediate danger of its disappearance as a source of energy for the earth.

A thermonuclear bomb, sometimes called a hydrogen bomb or H-bomb, produces energy by a fusion reaction. One possible reaction in a hydrogen bomb is the formation of alpha particles and tremendous energy from a compound of lithium

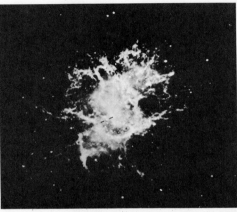

Steward Observatory, University of Arizona

The Crab Nebula was produced by an exploding star. The rapidly pulsating remnant (called a pulsar) is visible between the two short, dark marking lines near the center.

Atomic Industrial Forum, Inc.

24-6 Segment of a thermonuclear research device at Los Alamos Scientific Laboratory in New Mexico. Temperatures close to 10,000,000°C are produced in this apparatus as part of the effort to produce controlled nuclear fusion.

and deuterium, $_3^6\text{Li}_1^2\text{H}$. This reaction is started by subjecting the compound to extremely high temperatures and pressure, using a fission reaction as a detonator.

$$_3^6\text{Li}_1^2\text{H} \rightarrow 2_2^4\text{He} + 22.4 \text{ Mev}$$

This reaction then results in 22.4 Mev for 8 nucleons, or 2.80 Mev/nucleon, as compared with 186 Mev for 236 nucleons in uranium fission, or only 0.788 Mev/nucleon. In addition, a thermonuclear bomb is theoretically unlimited in possible size. As we shall see in the next section, this is not true of a fission bomb. Unfortunately, the problem of releasing fusion energy in controlled amounts has not yet been solved. But a great deal of research is presently being carried on to harness this promising source of energy. One approach that is being studied is the use of "magnetic bottles" to withstand the extremely high temperatures of fusion reactions (Fig. 24-6).

QUESTIONS

Group A

1. (a) How was radioactivity discovered? (b) By whom?
2. (a) Define radioactivity. (b) Which elements are naturally radioactive?
3. List four effects of radioactive radiation.
4. Give another name for (a) alpha particles, (b) beta particles, (c) gamma rays.
5. In a nuclear equation, (a) what do the letter symbols represent, (b) what do the subscripts indicate, (c) what do the superscripts indicate?
6. (a) What is a nuclear transformation? (b) Describe two ways in which it can occur.
7. (a) Define half-life. (b) How is half-life used to find the decay constant of a radioactive nuclide? (c) What is the unit of radioactivity?
8. What important conclusion was drawn from the experimental work of Cockcroft and Walton?
9. Why are neutrons more effective than other particles for bombarding nuclei?
10. (a) What is the purpose of a moderator? (b) List two substances that are used as moderators.
11. (a) How many chemical elements are known today? (b) How many of them occur naturally?
12. (a) Write the equation for the reaction that is believed to be responsible for the energy of the stars. (b) How is this reaction used on earth? (c) What problems are associated with its use?
13. List two quantities that are equal to each other on both sides of a balanced nuclear equation.

14. How can a magnet be used to identify the radiations from a radio-active substance?

15. List three differences between gamma rays and other radioactive emissions.

16. (a) What is the source of the energy released in a nuclear reaction? (b) Give a specific example.

17. How does the stability of a nucleus vary with (a) mass, (b) the proton-neutron ratio?

18. (a) What is the difference between the average life of a radioactive nuclide and its half-life? (b) What is the relationship between the average life of a nuclide and its half-life?

19. (a) Suggest a way in which $^{200}_{80}Hg$ (mercury) might be changed into $^{196}_{79}Au$ (gold). (b) Write nuclear equations for the reactions that are required.

20. Write the nuclear equations for the alpha decay of (a) $^{234}_{90}Th$, (b) $^{234}_{92}U$, (c) $^{214}_{83}Bi$, (d) $^{210}_{84}Po$.

21. Write nuclear equations showing the preparation of $^{239}_{94}Pu$ from $^{238}_{92}U$.

22. (a) Which nuclides have the smallest binding energy per nucleon? (b) Which have the largest binding energy per nucleon? (c) How does the binding energy per nucleon affect the stability of a nucleus?

23. Describe the difference in the results when $^{235}_{92}U$ and $^{238}_{92}U$ absorb neutrons.

24. (a) Does the half-life of an element tell when a specific nucleus will disintegrate? (b) Explain with a specific example.

25. When a radioactive nucleus disintegrates, the products have kinetic energy even though the original nucleus was at rest. What is the source of this energy?

PROBLEMS

Group A

(Note: Consult Table 23 in Appendix B for the atomic masses of nuclides.)

1. How much energy in Mev is evolved in the decay of a $^{222}_{86}Rn$ nucleus?

2. Calculate the energy evolved when a $^{214}_{82}Pb$ nucleus decays.

3. What is the decay constant of $^{222}_{86}Rn$ which has a half-life of 3.82 da?

4. Determine the decay constant of $^{238}_{92}U$ if its half-life is 4.49×10^9 years.

Group B

5. (a) What is the radioactivity in millicuries of $10\bar{0}$ g of pure $^{232}_{90}Th$? Half-life: 1.4×10^{10} yr. It decays to $^{228}_{88}Ra$. (b) What is the rate of energy evolution?

6. (a) Calculate the radioactivity of 5.00×10^{-3} g of $^{222}_{86}Rn$. (b) What is the rate of energy evolution?

7. Compare the energy evolved from equal masses of fuel elements in the following reactions: (a) fission: $^{239}_{94}Pu + ^{1}_{0}n \rightarrow ^{137}_{52}Te + ^{100}_{42}Mo + 3^{1}_{0}n + energy$, (b) fusion: $2^{2}_{1}H \rightarrow ^{4}_{2}He + energy$.

Group B

8. If the sun should continue producing energy at its present rate, what fraction of the sun's mass would disappear in the next 1000 years?

9. The earth receives 3×10^{22} joules of energy from the sun per day. If this energy is expressed as mass, what is the proportional increase in the earth's mass in one year? (The mass of the earth is presently 6×10^{24} kg.)

10. Compute the (a) mass defect and (b) binding energy per nucleon of $^{13}_{6}C$.

11. (a) Compute the mass defect and binding energy per nucleon of $^{12}_{7}N$. (b) Compare the stability of $^{13}_{6}C$ and $^{12}_{7}N$.

USES OF NUCLEAR ENERGY

24.9 Chain reactions

In a fission reaction, the target nucleus may break up in a great many different ways. The reaction involving uranium-235 in Section 24.7, for example, is only one of the ways in which this nucleus may react under neutron bombardment. In most cases, however, two or three neutrons are emitted in the process. This is an example of a *chain reaction*. *In a **chain reaction** the material or energy that starts a reaction is also one of the products and can cause similar reactions.* The neutrons emitted during fission are moving too fast to be absorbed by other fissionable nuclei. Hence the neutrons must be slowed down by a suitable moderator. The first controlled chain reaction was carried out at the University of Chicago in 1942 under the direction of the Italian physicist, Enrico Fermi (1901–1954).

If the material surrounding a fission reaction has the right dimensions and characteristics, the reaction is self-sustaning. *The amount of a particular fissionable material required to make a fission reaction self-sustaining is called the **critical mass**.* If the critical mass is exceeded, and if the emitted neutrons are not absorbed by nonfissionable material, the reaction runs out of control and

24-7 A chain reaction. Neutrons from the fission of a U-235 nucleus, when slowed down by a moderator, can cause fission in other U-235 nuclei. Fission products other than barium and krypton are also produced.

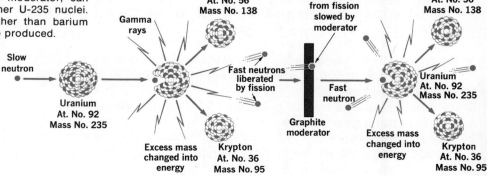

a nuclear explosion results. For example, suppose that two neutrons from each fission are able to produce further fission reactions, and that 10^{-8} second elapses between successive reactions. In one millionth of a second, 100 successive reactions can take place. The total energy released is 200 Mev/nucleus $\times$ 2^{100} reactions $= 2 \times 10^8$ ev/nucleus $\times$ 1.3×10^{30} reactions $\times$ 1.6×10^{-19} j/ev or an enormous 4×10^{19} j!

Actually, the chain reaction continues until all the fissionable nuclei have split or until the neutrons no longer strike the fissionable material. This is what happens in an uncontrolled chain reaction such as the explosion of a nuclear warhead. Two subcritical masses are placed a short distance from each other inside the warhead. To detonate it, the two masses are brought quickly together by means of explosive charges. The resulting mass exceeds the critical mass, and an uncontrolled chain reaction takes place.

24.10 Nuclear reactors

*A **nuclear reactor** is a device in which the controlled fission of certain substances is used to produce new substances and energy.* One of the earliest reactors using natural uranium as a fuel was built at Oak Ridge, Tennessee, in 1943. It had a lattice-type construction with blocks of graphite forming the framework and acting as a moderator. Rods of uranium were placed between the blocks of graphite. Control rods of neutron-absorbing boron steel were inserted in the lattice to regulate the number of free neutrons. The reactor contained a critical mass of uranium.

Two types of reactions occur in this kind of reactor. Neutrons cause $^{235}_{92}$U nuclei to undergo fission. Fast neutrons from this fission are slowed down by passage through the graphite. Some strike other $^{235}_{92}$U nuclei and continue the chain reaction while others strike $^{238}_{92}$U nuclei and initiate the changes which produce plutonium (Section 24.7). Great quantities of heat energy are liberated, so the reactor is cooled continuously by air blown through tubes in the lattice. The rate of the nuclear reactions is controlled by insertion or removal of the control rods.

A *materials testing reactor* is used for testing the behavior of various materials under high radioactivity. *A **breeder reactor** is one in which one fissionable material, such as plutonium-239, is produced at a greater rate than the fuel, mostly uranium 235, is consumed.* Breeder reactors use up to 60 per cent of the potential energy in uranium, compared with only one or two per cent for conventional reactors. Another advantage of breeder reactors is that they do not release dangerous combustion products into the atmosphere.

Brookhaven National Laboratory

A nuclear reactor. One workman is inserting a sample into the pile for neutron bombardment while the other is monitoring the level of radioactivity in the area.

24.11 Nuclear power

A kilogram of uranium has a volume of only about 52 cm³. Yet it has about the same fuel value, when it is completely utilized in fission reactions, as 3,000,000 kilograms of coal or 12,000,000 kilograms of oil burned in the conventional way (Fig. 24-8). Obviously, nuclear power is an important substitute for the world's dwindling supplies of fossil fuels, provided that it can be produced economically and safely.

There is not as much difference between a nuclear power plant and an ordinary power plant as many people imagine. As Fig. 24-9 shows, the only real difference is in the way in which the steam that turns the turbines is produced. In an ordinary plant, the steam comes from a boiler fired with coal, oil, or gas. In a nuclear plant, the steam is generated by the heat released during the fission process in the reactor.

The reactor in a nuclear power plant must be able to sustain a chain reaction. Whether a chain reaction will continue depends on several factors which may be expressed in an equation as follows:

$$k = \frac{P}{A + L}$$

In this equation k is called the *multiplication factor*, P is the rate of production of neutrons in the reactor, A is the rate of absorption, and L is the rate of leakage. When $k = 1$, the reactor is said to be *critical*, and the reaction is self-sustaining.

The power production of a nuclear reactor, obviously, depends largely on the rate of neutron production. Neutron production, in turn, reduces the amount of fissionable material in the reactor. Hence, to keep the reactor critical it is necessary to reduce the rate of absorption A, or to increase the production of neutrons P. The former is accomplished by gradually withdrawing the control rods, while the latter requires the addition of fissionable material.

Natural uranium contains only about 0.7 percent of the fissionable isotope U-235. Consequently, when natural uranium is used as a reactor fuel, the rate of neutron leakage L is so high that the reactor can never become critical. However, L can be reduced by using a moderator to slow down the neu-

Atomic Industrial Forum, Inc.

24-8 Bundles of uranium fuel elements being inspected before insertion in a nuclear power reactor.

24-9 A nuclear power plant differs from other power plants only in the way in which steam is generated for the turbines.

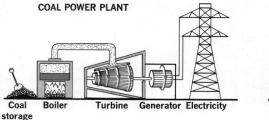

COAL POWER PLANT

Coal storage   Boiler   Turbine   Generator   Electricity

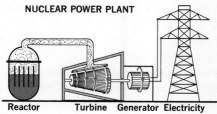

NUCLEAR POWER PLANT

Reactor   Turbine   Generator   Electricity

trons so that they are more likely to strike U-235 nuclei. Another way to make the reactor critical is to use fuel which has been processed to increase the concentration of U-235.

A typical "neutron history" in a nuclear reactor is given in Table 24-2. It shows the relative number of neutrons involved in other events for every 100 neutrons that produce new fissions.

Thus, of a total of 256 neutrons, only the two that are absorbed by the control rods are available for increasing the power of the reactor. When the control rods are withdrawn, of course, these two neutrons will raise the multiplication factor of the reactor.

The first non-explosive application of nuclear power was in the American submarine, *Nautilus*, which was launched in 1954. Two years later, the first large scale nuclear power plant was placed in operation in Shippingport, Pennsylvania, with an output of 60,000 kilowatts of electric power. Today there are many similar plants in operation or under construction throughout the country. The largest of these, in Alabama, has a rated capacity of nearly 3,500,000 kw (Fig. 24-10).

A proposed new type of nuclear fuel involves both fission and fusion. In the process, laser pulses are aimed at pellets of boron-11 containing cores of deuterium and tritium (isotopes of hydrogen). The deuterium and tritium then fuse, producing enough heat to split the boron nuclei. Almost no radioactive

Table 24-2 NEUTRONS IN A REACTOR

Number of Neutrons	History
100	Produce new fissions
90	Captured by U-238
20	Captured by U-235
30	Absorbed by moderator
5	Absorbed by housing
9	Escape from reactor
2	Absorbed by control rods
256	

Tennessee Valley Authority

24-10 Browns Ferry Nuclear Plant in northern Alabama. Research on the effect of heated water from the plant on aquatic life is carried out in the six long channels in the foreground.

wastes and very little thermal pollution would result from the reaction.

24.12   Radioisotopes

*A **radioisotope** is a radioactive isotope of an element.* Some radioisotopes are the products of natural radioactive decay, as in the case of the uranium disintegration series in Section 24.5. Since the advent of the nuclear reactor, however, a far greater number of radioisotopes has been prepared artificially. The reactor produces radioisotopes during the fission process. In addition, radioisotopes can be prepared by inserting elements into the reactor while it is operating. Radioisotopes of all the elements have been prepared in this way.

One way in which an element becomes radioactive in a reactor is by absorbing a neutron. For example, $^{13}_{6}C$ will turn into $^{14}_{6}C$, which is a radioisotope. In other cases, elements will absorb a neutron and immediately emit a proton. This process lowers the atomic number of the element but does not change its mass number. For example, natural sulfur may change into radiophosphorus in the following way:

$$^{32}_{16}S + ^{1}_{0}n \rightarrow ^{32}_{15}P + ^{1}_{1}H$$

A large reactor, such as the one at Oak Ridge (Section 24.10), can release neutrons at the rate of 10^{14} neutrons/cm² sec. When the reactor is used to produce radioisotopes, it must be run at a rate that is somewhat higher than is needed for a chain reaction by itself. The extra neutrons are then available for radioisotope production. Special control and shielding arrangements make it possible to insert and remove substances without shutting down the reactor.

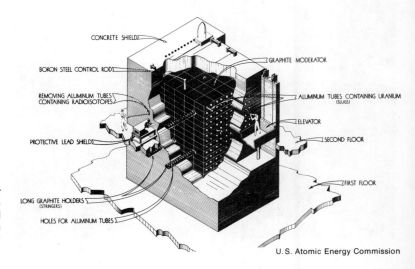

CONCRETE SHIELD

GRAPHITE MODERATOR

BORON STEEL CONTROL RODS

REMOVING ALUMINUM TUBES
CONTAINING RADIOISOTOPES

ALUMINUM TUBES CONTAINING URANIUM
(SLUGS)

ELEVATOR

PROTECTIVE LEAD SHIELD

SECOND FLOOR

FIRST FLOOR

LONG GRAPHITE HOLDERS
(STRINGERS)

HOLES FOR ALUMINUM TUBES

U.S. Atomic Energy Commission

Cutaway view of a uranium reactor used for the preparation of radioisotopes. Note the thick concrete shield used to protect the workmen from radiation.

Often it is desirable to incorporate radioisotopes into specific compounds before they are used. This can be done by combining the radioisotope chemically with other elements. The *radiocompound* that results is then said to be tagged, or *labeled*. Complex compounds that cannot be prepared in this way can sometimes be labeled through the biological processes of plants and animals. Radioisotopes are injected into or fed to an animal and then removed in the form of radiocompounds from the blood or tissue. Similar procedures can be used with plants.

The many uses of radioisotopes can be divided into three categories:

1. Effects of radioisotope radiations on materials.
2. Effects of materials on radioisotope radiations.
3. Tracing materials with radioisotope radiations.

In the first of these categories, the radioisotope is used as a source of radiation just as X rays and radium are used. The target material consists of the substance that is to be changed or destroyed by the radiation. Cancer can be treated in this way, food and drugs can be sterilized to prevent deterioration, plastic can be irradiated to change its properties, static electricity can be reduced or eliminated by irradiating the air surrounding the source of the static electricity, and special paints can be made to luminesce by incorporating radioisotopes. Radiations from radioisotopes are also used to form larger molecules from smaller ones by causing molecular bonds to form. In the case of food preservation by radioisotope irradiation, it is important to note that the food does not become radioactive in the process and is safe to eat.

In the second category of radioisotope utilization, the effect of the material on the radiation yields information about the material. Radiation is beamed at a target and the amount that is transmitted or reflected is recorded on photographic film or with some other detection device. Radiations from radioisotopes have been used instead of X rays, for example, for medical diagnosis purposes. This method can also be used to measure the thickness of a moving sheet of metal or other material, to analyze the internal structure of a metal casting, to measure the level of a liquid inside a closed container, and even to sort out materials on a moving conveyor.

The third category of radioisotope utilization is probably the most widely used. In this method, a carefully selected radioisotope acts as a *tracer* that makes it possible to follow the course of some complicated chemical or biological process. (See Fig. 24-11.) The target and the radioisotope are intimately mixed or combined. The radioisotope then serves as the label that indi-

Brookhaven National Laboratory

This scanning device is used in conjunction with radioisotopes that concentrate in tumors. The radioisotopes emit positrons that then combine with electrons to produce gamma rays. These are detected by crystals in the banks of scanners above and below the patient.

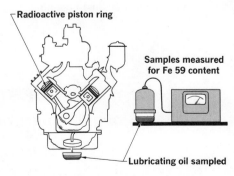

24-11 A tracer experiment. Radioactive iron (Fe-59) in the piston rings is transferred to the oil through friction while the motor is running. As little as 0.0003 gram of iron in the oil can be detected by the counter at the right.

24-12 Carbon-14 dating. The age of organic compounds can be determined by measuring the remaining amount of radioactive carbon. The relative error is between 5 percent and 10 percent.

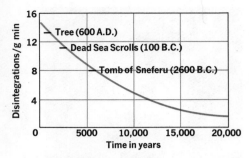

Willard F. Libby

The linen wrapping of one of the Dead Sea Scrolls, the age of which was established by carbon-14 dating.

cates the whereabouts of the successive compounds or materials with which the radioisotope becomes associated. Detection instruments or photographic film again serve as measuring devices. The material that is labeled and traced may be food that is consumed by a human being, feed that is converted into milk inside the body of a cow, water that is running out of an undiscovered underground leak, atoms that are rearranged to form a complex molecule, wax that is worn away from the hood of a polished car, or any one of a great many other research materials or industrial products.

An interesting use of a natural radioisotope is the process known as *carbon-14 dating*, which was developed by the American chemist, W. F. Libby (b. 1908), in 1952. $^{14}_{7}N$ atoms in the atmosphere are constantly being bombarded by radiations from outer space, converting them into the radioisotope $^{14}_{6}C$. Living plants absorb $^{14}_{6}C$ (as carbon dioxide) along with the more common and nonradioactive $^{12}_{6}C$ in the process of photosynthesis. When the plant dies it no longer replaces the carbon atoms in its cells with carbon atoms from the atmosphere, and the intake of $^{14}_{6}C$ stops. The amount of radioactivity in the plant gradually decreases due to the fact that the half-life of $^{14}_{6}C$ is 5600 years. Measurements show that a gram of carbon from a living plant has an activity of 16 disintegrations/min. Consequently, a sample showing an activity of 8 disintegrations/g min is assumed to be 5600 years old, a sample with 4 disintegrations/g min is 11,200 years old, etc. The precision of carbon-14 dating falls off rapidly after several half-life periods, although objects up to about 30,000 years old have been dated in this way. (See Fig. 24-12.)

Other nuclear dating methods are used to learn the age of rocks on the earth and the moon. Moon rocks as old as 4.5 billion years have been dated. It is believed that the solar system itself is not much older than this.

QUESTIONS

Group A

1. (a) What conditions are necessary for a chain reaction? (b) What is meant by critical mass?
2. (a) What are radioisotopes? (b) How are they made?
3. (a) How does a nuclear reaction produce electric power? (b) What is meant by a critical reactor? (c) How can natural uranium be used in a critical reactor?
4. How could radioisotopes be used to determine the effectiveness of a fertilizer?
5. Estimate the age of a carbon sample showing an activity of 3 decays/min g.

Chapter 25

Particle Physics

DETECTION INSTRUMENTS

Since subatomic particles are too small to observe and measure directly, their properties must be determined through the effects they produce. The development of devices that measure such effects has made the study of nuclear interactions one of the most important branches of modern physics.

The operation of detection instruments depends on three main characteristics of the particles and rays emitted in nuclear reactions:

1. They have the ability to ionize certain substances.
2. They cause certain substances to fluoresce.
3. They affect photographic emulsions.

Instruments that make use of the ionization effect are the electroscope, the Geiger counter, the cloud chamber, the bubble chamber, the spark chamber, the ionization chamber, and the solid-state detector. The scintillation counter and the spinthariscope are based on the principle of fluorescence. Photographic emulsions are used both as a direct means of detection and in conjunction with other instruments. Before we describe some of the recent discoveries of particle physics, it will be helpful to explain each of these detection instruments briefly.

1. The electroscope. One of the first instruments to be used in detecting and measuring radioactivity was the electroscope. The use of the electroscope in the identification of static charges has already been discussed in Chapter 16. In addition to charging and discharging the instrument by conduction and induction, however, one can also use it to detect and measure

25.1 Principles of particle detection

Jack Fletcher for USAEC Maritime Adm.

A technician monitors radioactivity with a Geiger counter during fuel-loading procedures aboard a nuclear ship.

25.2 Ionization devices

Welch Scientific Co.

25-1 A gold leaf electroscope. Radioactive materials are placed in the hinged drawer at the bottom.

the presence of ions in the surrounding air. A negatively charged electroscope becomes discharged when ions in the air take electrons from the electroscope disc. See Fig. 25-1. Similarly, a positively charged electroscope becomes discharged as it takes electrons from ions in the air. Thus, the rate at which an electroscope is discharged is a measure of the number of ions in the air near the electroscope.

Madame Curie used the electroscope to study the radioactivity of uranium ore. She found that some ores discharged the electroscope more rapidly than others. This finding suggested the presence of an undiscovered, highly radioactive element in some of the ores, and led to the isolation of radium.

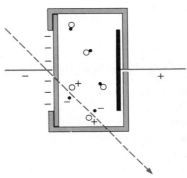

25-2 An ionization chamber. The passage of a subatomic particle (represented by the arrow) separates the gas in the chamber into charged particles. The negatively charged particles are then attracted to the anode on the right side of the chamber.

2. *The ionization chamber.* The ionization chamber contains fixed electrodes. See Fig. 25-2. When the gas in the chamber becomes ionized through the passage of a high-speed particle or ray, the electrons and ions drift to the electrodes. The electrons drift to the positive plate while the positively charged ions drift to the negative plate.

The charge produced by a single passing particle is much too small to activate the circuit in an ionization chamber, so an amplifier is used in conjunction with the instrument. The resulting impulse can then be used to trigger a light or some other recording device.

3. *The Geiger counter.* The principle of the ionization chamber is also used in the Geiger counter. See Fig. 25-3. A hollow cylinder acts as the negative electrode and a thin wire down the center is charged positively. The tube is filled with a gas at low pressure and a potential difference of about 1000 volts is applied to the electrodes. This potential difference is slightly less than the voltage required to ionize the gas and enable it to conduct an electric current between the electrodes.

When a charged particle or gamma ray enters the Geiger tube, it releases electrons from the atoms in its path and produces

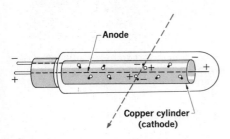

25-3 A Geiger tube. The ions produced by the subatomic particle (arrow) permit the passage of a flow of electrons between the cathode and anode.

ions. These electrons are then attracted to the positively charged wire. As they move in the direction of the wire, they collide with more gas atoms to produce additional free electrons and positive ions. Eventually, the surge of electrons toward the positive electrode is large enough to register as a detectable current flowing through the tube. Thus, the Geiger tube acts as its own amplifier for the detection of nuclear events. In addition, the instrument can be used in conjunction with external circuits to activate flashing lights, a loudspeaker, or a counting device.

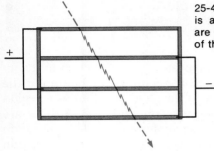

25-4 A spark chamber. When voltage is applied to the electrodes, sparks are produced along the ionized trail of the subatomic particle (arrow).

Educational Services Incorporated

25-5 A simple cloud chamber. The radioactive source is placed in the eye of the needle that is suspended from the cork.

4. Spark chamber. The migration of ions in an ionization chamber can also be made directly visible through an arrangement like the one shown in Fig. 25-4. The positive and negative electrodes are placed in series in this device. When a particle or ray triggers a current in such a spark chamber, its path becomes visible as a series of light flashes. These flashes can be easily photographed to provide permanent records. An image amplifier (Section 22.16) may be used to increase the visibility of the spark discharges. Computers are also being used with the chamber to analyze the resulting photos or to make only the desired tracks visible.

5. The cloud chamber. Another device that makes the paths of ionizing particles clearly visible is the cloud chamber. It was invented by the British physicist, C. T. R. Wilson (1869–1959), in 1911. Its principle of operation is quite simple, and an operating cloud chamber can be assembled with a minimum of material and efforts. Figure 25-5 shows a simple, homemade cloud chamber.

The chamber is a plastic or glass container. It is resting on a block of Dry Ice. A piece of dark cloth is saturated with alcohol and placed around the inside of the container near the top. A radioactive source is placed in the eye of a needle which is suspended from a cork placed on the lid of the container. A photo of alpha-particle tracks in such a cloud chamber is shown in Fig. 25-6.

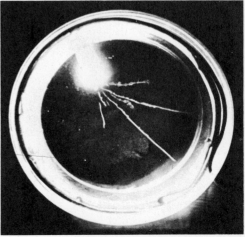

Educational Services Incorporated

25-6 Tracks of alpha particles in a simple cloud chamber.

25-7 This photograph shows nuclear interactions in a liquid hydrogen bubble chamber resulting from its bombardment by a beam of 2.85 Gev protons from the Cosmotron at Brookhaven National Laboratory, Upton, Long Island, New York. Two charged particles arise from the collision shown at the left. One of these undergoes an additional collision at lower left center. The straight tracks show that many protons travel through the hydrogen without interaction. Some protons collide with electrons of the hydrogen atoms in the chamber. These electrons move in spiral paths under the influence of the powerful magnetic field which is acting on the bubble chamber.

In the chamber, alcohol evaporates from the cloth and condenses again as it reaches the cold region at the bottom of the chamber. Just above the floor of the chamber there is a region where the alcohol vapor does not condense unless there are "seeds" around which drops of alcohol can form. (The situation is very much like that in a cloud which can be made to form rain by "seeding" it with a powdered chemical.) If there is no dust in the chamber, the only seeds available are ions produced by the passage of charged particles or rays. The resulting trail of alcohol droplets is then visible against the black bottom of the chamber and can be photographed.

The device we have just described is called a *diffusion cloud chamber*. Others, including the chamber developed by Wilson, rely on pressure changes instead of low temperatures to produce condensation. It is possible to use many other liquid-vapor arrangements to produce the tracks; but in all cloud chambers, it is the ionizing effect of high-speed particles that makes a visible trail possible.

6. The bubble chamber. In a cloud chamber, a substance like alcohol condenses from a gas to a liquid to make nuclear events visible. In a bubble chamber, exactly the opposite principle is used. A container is filled with a liquid and the tracks of particles become visible as a series of bubbles when the liquid boils.

One substance used in bubble chambers is liquid hydrogen. As long as the temperature and pressure conditions are right, the hydrogen stays in liquid form. But if the pressure is suddenly lowered, the hydrogen boils violently. If, at the same instant, high-speed charged particles are allowed to pass through the hydrogen, ions are formed. The hydrogen boils a few thousandths of a second sooner around these ions than in the rest of the chamber. Carefully timed photos are used to record the resulting bubble trails. See Fig. 25-7.

The advantage of the bubble chamber over the cloud chamber is that more nuclear collisions take place in the dense liquid of the bubble chamber. This difference makes it possible to study particles and rays having speeds that are much higher than those which produce recordable events in a cloud chamber.

7. Solid-state detectors. When certain nonconducting solids are exposed to charged nuclear particles, tracks are produced in the solids that can be seen with an electron microscope. The tracks are regions of distortion of the crystal lattices of the solids. Etching the solids with acid makes the tracks more permanent and more readily visible.

Cosmic rays and various radioactive decay products have left tracks in naturally occurring solids since the origin of the solar system. Through the etching technique just described, scientists are able to gather important clues about the history of the earth by examining these fossil tracks in rocks, in ancient human-made objects, in meteorites, and in lava from the ocean floor. The same technique is being used on lunar samples.

One of the first solid-state detectors made by human beings was a thin sheet of mica used by two British scientists in 1959 in connection with a fission experiment. Glass and certain plastics have also been used as detectors. Plastics are particularly sensitive to slow protons and alpha particles.

Each solid used as a solid-state detector has a threshold below which no tracks are produced. This property makes the detector particularly suited for the study of high-energy particles, since the dense background of light-particle tracks that is present in other types of detectors is eliminated by the threshold property of the solid-state detector. It was with the help of glass detectors that Russian scientists first studied the production of element No. 104, khurchatovium, from the bombardment of plutonium with high-energy neon atoms.

Another type of solid-state detector, the *junction detector*, is based on the transistor principle (Fig. 25-8). An applied bias removes all free carriers from the detector. When charged particles enter the device, ionization is produced in the base and an output signal results. In essence, the junction detector is a solid-state ionization chamber. However, the junction detector is smaller in size, requires less power, has a faster response, is completely insensitive to magnetic fields, and produces an output signal that is directly proportional to the energy of the incident particle.

1. The spinthariscope. The spinthariscope is another instrument which was used in early studies of radioactivity. In this device, alpha and beta particles from radioactive materials or nuclear

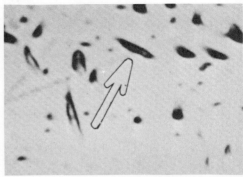

U.S. Atomic Energy Commission

By etching fragments of lunar material collected by Apollo astronauts, scientists have discovered that the rocks are marked with tracks left by cosmic rays. Studies of the tracks may provide clues to the origin of cosmic rays. The arrow points to a typical cosmic-ray track.

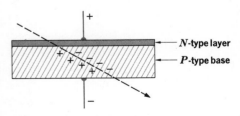

25-8 A junction detector. The passage of a charged particle (represented by the arrow) ionizes a region of the P-type base and produces an output signal.

25.3 Scintillation devices

collisions strike a zinc sulfide screen. Where they strike the screen they produce a momentary flash of light which can be observed through a magnifier. By counting the number of flashes in a given period of time, the intensity of the radiation can be determined. The principle of the spinthariscope was used in the early studies of alpha-particle scattering described in Chapter 23.

2. The scintillation counter. To make it possible to count the scintillations produced by subatomic particles hitting a fluorescent screen, the scintillation counter uses a *photomultiplier tube.* In effect, the photomultiplier complements the spinthariscope principle: the spinthariscope changes particle energy to light energy and the photomultiplier tube changes light energy to electric energy.

The electric current is then used to activate a counter. In many applications, the scintillation counter has been found superior to the Geiger counter.

25.4 Photographic emulsions

It has already been pointed out that cameras are used in conjunction with such detection devices as cloud and bubble chambers to provide permanent records of nuclear events. In addition, photographic film can be used to record the passage of subatomic particles and rays directly. In fact, it was the fogging of a photographic plate that led to the discovery of radioactivity by Becquerel. See Section 24.1.

When charged particles or gamma rays strike photographic film, they change the chemicals in the emulsion much the same

25-9 Tracks of nuclear particles on photographic film. An antiproton (p^-) entered from the left and produced a shower of eight other particles when it collided with a proton. This is the first photo of the reaction between a proton and its antiparticle.

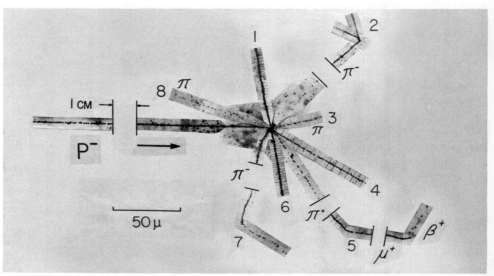

way that a ray of light changes them. When the film is developed, the passage of the particle or ray is recorded as a spot. If a stack of photographic film is exposed to a nuclear event, it is recorded as a series of streaks through the emulsions, as seen in Fig. 25-9. The proper development and alignment of these plates requires considerable skill, but it is one of the most direct and most useful detection techniques in particle physics.

QUESTIONS

1. Describe the construction of a simple cloud chamber.
2. List three effects of nuclear radiations that are used in detection instruments.
3. (a) List one similarity and one difference between a Geiger counter and an electroscope. (b) What is the relationship between a Geiger tube and a Geiger counter?
4. (a) What substance is commonly used in a bubble chamber? (b) Why?
5. (a) Which detection instrument was the first to record the effects of a nuclear radiation? (b) Describe the event.
6. (a) What does a photomultiplier tube multiply? (b) How is this accomplished?
7. Evaluate the statement: "It is possible to see subatomic particles with a bubble chamber."
8. What property of solid-state detectors makes them particularly suited for the study of high-energy nuclear particles?
9. (a) What is the derivation of the term "spinthariscope?" (b) How does this instrument detect subatomic particles?

PARTICLE ACCELERATORS

As we have seen in Chapter 24, nuclear reactions can be caused by certain radiations from naturally radioactive substances. But the nuclear research that can be conducted in this way is limited by the energy of the radioactive emissions. To provide nuclear "bullets" with greater penetrating power, it is necessary to accelerate them in some way. A brief description of several modern particle accelerators follows.

25.5 Van de Graaff generators

One of the earliest particle accelerators was developed by the American physicist, R. J. Van de Graaff (1901–1967), in 1931. From Fig. 25-10, we see that a Van de Graaff generator is a kind of escalator for electrons. Electrons are sprayed on an insulated moving belt by repulsion from a strongly negative

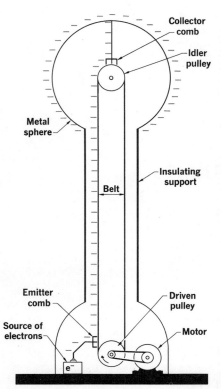

25-10 A simplified schematic diagram of a Van de Graaff generator.

electrode. They ride up on the belt to the top of the generator, where they are picked off by a collector and transferred to the top terminal. Since the charge always resides on the *outside* of a hollow conductor, the inside of the top terminal is able to receive more charges. Thus a large negative charge is built up on the top terminal.

Conversely, a large positive charge may be built up on the top terminal by removing electrons from the belt at the bottom by using a strongly positive electrode. The large difference of electric potential thus obtained can be used to accelerate electrons or ions. Since the high charge on a Van de Graaff generator leaks off into the atmosphere if the air is humid, such generators are sometimes built under a large, pear-shaped shell which is filled with dry air under pressure to keep the charge on the top terminal. Also, to avoid the necessity of tall buildings, many large Van de Graaff generators are now being installed horizontally.

To provide maximum energy to particles, Van de Graaff generators are sometimes used in series with linear accelerators (which will be explained in Section 25.7). Modern Van de Graaff generators provide energies ranging up to about 20 Mev, depending on the charge of the "bullets" being accelerated. The world's most powerful Van de Graaff installation is a pair of generators in series at the Brookhaven National Laboratory in New York, which is capable of accelerating hydrogen ions to an energy of 30 Mev. This is not as high as the energies produced in other types of large accelerators, but Van de Graaff machines have certain other advantages. For example, the particle beam can be more precisely focused, energy variations are more easily controlled, and a wide range of particles can be employed.

25.6 Circular accelerators

Shortly after the development of the Van de Graaff generator, it was found that charged particles can be accelerated to very high velocities by driving them in a circular path by means of electromagnets. A variety of such accelerators has since been built, some of which are briefly described below.

1. The betatron. As its name implies, the betatron is used to accelerate beta particles (electrons). It uses the principle of the transformer, in which the primary is a huge electromagnet and the secondary is the stream of electrons being accelerated. The electrons are enclosed in a circular, evacuated tube called the *doughnut*. After the electrons have acquired maximum energy, they are directed to a metal plate. The impact produces high-energy X rays for nuclear studies and for applications in industry and medicine. In effect, the betatron is a large X-ray

University of Illinois

25-11 The inventor of the betatron, Donald Kerst, is shown with his original accelerator, a 2.5-Mev model built in 1940. At the rear is the world's biggest betatron, a 340-Mev instrument used at the University of Illinois.

machine, producing energies up to about 300 Mev (Fig. 25-11). Beyond this range, electrons rapidly lose energy by electromagnetic radiation.

2. Cyclotrons. In 1932, the American physicist E. O. Lawrence (1901–1958) developed a circular accelerator in which various kinds of charged particles could be used. He called it a *cyclotron.* It consists of a large cylindrical box placed between the poles of an electromagnet. The box is exhausted until a very high vacuum exists inside. Charged particles, such as protons or deuterons, are fed into the center of the box. Inside the box are two hollow, D-shaped electrodes, called *dees,* which are connected to a source of high-voltage electricity (Fig. 25-12).

When the cyclotron is in operation, the electric charge on the dees is reversed very rapidly by an oscillator. The action of the field of the electromagnet causes the charged particles inside the cylindrical box to move in a semicircle in a fixed period of time. The potential applied to the dees is adjusted to reverse itself in the same time period. Thus at each transit across the gap between the dees the ions gain energy from the electric field. They move faster and faster as they approach the outside of the box. When they reach the outer rim of the box, they are deflected toward the target.

The energy of particles accelerated in a conventional cyclotron may reach 15 Mev. To obtain higher values, it is necessary

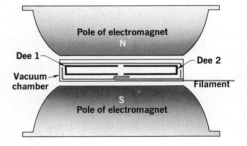

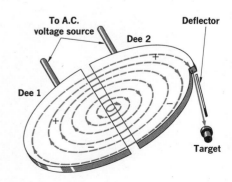

25-12 Schematic diagram of a cyclotron.

25-13 Sequential progress of protons through the world's most powerful accelerator. The voltage multiplier at the far left supplies an initial acceleration to 750 kev. Second from left is a view of the linear accelerator that drives the protons up to 200 Mev. At the top right is part of the magnet ring of the booster accelerator that raises the energy to 8 Gev. The main accelerator tunnel, a section of which is shown at the bottom right, is four miles long. Protons emerge from this final stage of the accelerator with energies of more than 500 Gev.

to modify the accelerator to deal with the relativistic increase in mass of the particles as their velocity increases. (See Section 1.12.) This increased mass keeps the particles from gaining enough speed to reach the dees by the time the oscillating voltage reverses. To overcome this difficulty, it is necessary to vary the oscillating frequency. Then, as the mass of the particles increases and their acceleration decreases, the frequency of the oscillator can be reduced. The changes in voltage of the field are timed to coincide with the slower acceleration of the more massive particles. This type of accelerator is called a *synchrocyclotron*. It can boost the energy of particles to about 800 Mev.

3. Synchrotrons. A newer type of particle accelerator is the *synchrotron.* Like the cyclotron, it operates on the principle of accelerating particles by making them move in a circular path with increasing velocity. However, the path of the particles is confined to a doughnut (as in the betatron) by varying both the oscillating voltage and the magnetic field.

The energies attainable in a synchrotron are theoretically unlimited. At the present time, the installation recently completed at the Fermi National Accelerator Laboratory in Illinois is the world's most powerful accelerator (Fig. 25-13). The circular path provided for subatomic particles in the accelerator is four miles long. Scientists plan to use superconducting magnets in conjunction with this synchrotron and to obtain eventual proton energies of 1000 Gev (1 Tev) and velocities greater than 99.999 percent of the velocity of light. High energy synchrotrons are sometimes called *bevatrons* or *cosmotrons*.

25.7 Linear accelerators

A linear accelerator is a device that moves charged particles to high velocities along a straight path, in contrast to the circular arrangements in cyclotrons and synchrotrons. Linear accelerators are used both individually and in conjunction with other accelerators.

A simplified diagram of a linear accelerator is shown in Fig. 25-14. A series of hollow *drift tubes* is mounted in a long, evacuated chamber. Charged particles are fed into one end of this arrangement and are accelerated by means of a high-frequency alternating voltage applied to the drift tubes. At any given instant alternate tubes have opposite charges. The alternating voltage is timed in such a way that the particle is repelled by the tube it is leaving and attracted by the tube it is approaching. In this way, the particle is accelerated every time it crosses the gap between two tubes. Because of this acceleration, the drift tubes are successively longer so the particles will always be in a gap when the voltage is reversed.

A two-mile-long linear accelerator is operated near Palo Alto, California, by Stanford University (Fig. 25-15). Inside a copper tube in a concrete tunnel buried 25 feet underground, electrons are accelerated to 40 Gev. As mentioned previously, some circu-

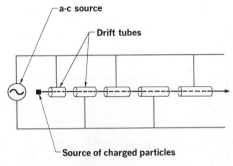

25-14 Schematic diagram of a linear accelerator. Charged particles accelerate as they are attracted by the alternately charged drift tubes.

Roland Quintero

25-15 The world's largest linear accelerator. Electrons are injected at the far end of the two-mile-long structure (upper right). Particle production and analysis take place in the two buildings at the lower left.

lar accelerators are limited in their ability to accelerate electrons because of electromagnetic radiation losses. This difficulty is not encountered in linear accelerators. In addition, the beam of particles can be more easily controlled in a linear accelerator than in a circular one. A linear accelerator is more accessible, and it can provide a higher frequency of impacts on the target material.

25.8 Cosmic rays

When a charged electroscope is exposed to the air, it will slowly discharge. A Geiger counter will continue to click slowly even though no radioactive material is present. These effects indicate that there are always some ions in the atmosphere. Experiments have shown that most of this ionization is caused by particles coming into the atmosphere at great speeds from outer space. The source of these particles is not definitely known, but their high energy suggests that they come from beyond the solar system. They are called *cosmic rays*.

Cosmic rays have great penetrating power (Fig. 25-16), far exceeding that of particles in the most powerful human-made accelerator. The intensity of cosmic rays varies with latitude, indicating that they are charged and are affected by the earth's magnetic field. Scientists believe that cosmic rays consist largely of the nuclei of elements of low atomic weight, protons (hydrogen nuclei) being the most abundant type. Other nuclei, ranging up to those as heavy as iron and beyond, have also been detected in the upper atmosphere. A few of these particles from outer space reach the surface of the earth, but most of them collide with the gas particles in the upper atmosphere and produce showers of secondary particles. In effect, cosmic rays are furnishing the nuclear physicist with a constant supply of bombarding nuclei which would otherwise not be available for study.

Scientists believe that gigantic magnetic fields in space, in galaxies, and near certain stars may be influential in producing cosmic rays. Some cosmic radiation is also thought to originate from highly energetic explosions on certain stars, including the flares that erupt from our own sun.

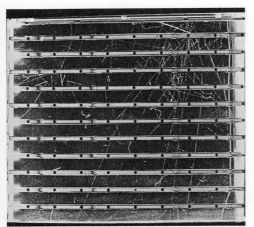

Massachusetts Institute of Technology

25-16 Cosmic-ray tracks in a cloud chamber. The tracks are visible in the spaces between one-half inch brass plates. Showers of particles are produced by collisions with atomic nuclei in the chamber.

QUESTIONS

Group A

1. (a) How does a Van de Graaff generator accelerate particles? (b) What type of particles can it *not* accelerate? (c) Why not?
2. (a) In what units is a particle accelerator rated? (b) Define the unit. (c) Give the ratings of a large Van de Graaff generator, a large cyclotron, and a large synchrotron.

3. Distinguish between a cyclotron and a synchrotron.
4. (a) What is the function of a drift tube in a linear accelerator? (b) Why are drift tubes made successively longer inside the accelerator?
5. One particle accelerator can accelerate electrons to a speed of 99.9 percent of the speed of light. Another machine can bring protons up to a speed of 10 percent of the speed of light. In terms of particle mass, which machine requires more energy?
6. (a) What are the advantages of cosmic rays over particles accelerated in human-made devices? (b) Name a disadvantage of using cosmic rays in nuclear research.
7. (a) How does a cyclotron accelerate a proton? (b) How does it keep the proton inside the machine? (c) Why is it impossible for a cyclotron to accelerate neutrons?
8. Why are magnets unnecessary in a linear accelerator?

REACTIONS BETWEEN FUNDAMENTAL PARTICLES

25.9 Classification of the fundamental particles

Through the use of the detection devices and particle accelerators just described, physicists have observed and identified more than 200 subatomic particles. Almost all of these particles are unstable, and many of them have extremely short half-lives. Nevertheless, these fleeting fragments of matter are essential pieces in the puzzle of nuclear structure. The puzzle is a long way from being completely solved, but great strides have been made during the past 30 years. In the remainder of this chapter, we shall take a look at the picture of the atom that is emerging from these investigations.

More than 100 years ago, scientists recognized relationships among the chemical elements that made it possible to arrange them in groups according to their properties. This listing is called the *periodic chart of the elements*. As more and more subatomic particles were discovered, it became evident that a similar grouping of fundamental particles could be made. In 1957, such a chart was proposed by the American physicist M. Gell-Mann and independently by the Japanese scientist K. Nishijima.

Table 25-1 shows the main features of the Gell-Mann/Nishijima chart of subatomic particles. Not all known particles in each category are listed, however enough of them are shown so that the purpose of the classification is clear.

The names and symbols of subatomic particles are taken from Greek words and letters. The names refer to the masses: *baryon* (berry-on) means heavy, *meson* (mez-on) means medium, and *lepton* (lep-ton) means small. Baryons and mesons are

Table 25-1   FUNDAMENTAL PARTICLES

Category	Name	Symbol	Antiparticle	Rest mass	Baryon number	Lepton number	Strangeness number	Half-life (sec)
baryons	omega hyperon	Ω^-	Ω^+	3280	+1	0	-3	1.3×10^{-10}
	xi hyperon	Ξ^-	$\overline{\Xi}^-$	2584	+1	0	-2	1.2×10^{-10}
		Ξ^0	$\overline{\Xi}^0$	2572	+1	0	-2	2.1×10^{-10}
	sigma hyperon	Σ^-	$\overline{\Sigma}^-$	2343	+1	0	-1	1.0×10^{-10}
		Σ^0	$\overline{\Sigma}^0$	2333	+1	0	-1	$\sim 10^{-20}$
		Σ^+	$\overline{\Sigma}^+$	2327	+1	0	-1	5.5×10^{-11}
	lambda hyperon	Λ^0	$\overline{\Lambda}^0$	2183	+1	0	-1	1.8×10^{-10}
	neutron	n	$\overline{n}$	1839	+1	0	0	700
	proton	p	$\overline{p}$	1836	+1	0	0	stable
mesons	eta meson	η^0	$\overline{\eta}^0$	1074	0	0	0	$\sim 10^{-20}$
	kappa meson (kaon)	K^+	K^-	966	0	0	+1	8.5×10^{-7}
		K^0	$\overline{K}^0$	975	0	0	+1	6.4×10^{-9} 3.5×10^{-8}
	pi meson (pion)	π^+	π^-	273	0	0	0	1.0×10^{-8}
		π^0	$\overline{\pi}^0$	264	0	0	0	0.6×10^{-16}
	mu meson (muon)	μ^-	μ^+	207	0	+1	-1	1.5×10^{-6}
leptons	electron	e^-	e^+	1	0	+1	0	stable
	neutrino$_\mu$	ν_μ	$\overline{\nu}_\mu$	0	0	+1	0	stable
	neutrino$_e$	ν_e	$\overline{\nu}_e$	0	0	+1	0	stable
bosons	photon	γ	γ	0	0	0	0	stable
	graviton	g	g	0	0	0	0	stable

Note: The baryon, lepton, and strangeness numbers are those of the particle named at the left. In each case, the antiparticle has numbers with the same magnitude but with opposite sign. The half-life is that of the particle at the left.

sometimes also called *hadrons* (had-rons) which comes from a Greek word meaning bulky. The four major divisions of the chart are based largely on masses. There is a sharp distinction between the masses of the baryons and the mesons and between the mesons and the leptons. The one exception is the mu-meson, which seemingly should be classified with the mesons. The reason for this seeming discrepancy will be explained in Section 25.11. In many ways this particle is a mystery to scientists, which led one leading nuclear physicist to remark: "Who ever ordered the mu-meson?"

With a few exceptions, each of the fundamental particles has a corresponding antiparticle. In some cases, a particle is its own antiparticle. Antiparticles are more fully discussed in Section 25.12.

The masses of the particles are based on a rest mass of 1 for the electron. Neutrinos and photons are given a mass of zero because they do not exist as stationary entities.

Baryon, lepton, and strangeness numbers will be explained in Section 25.11.

The main reasons for the construction of ever-larger particle accelerators is to study the interrelationships between nuclear particles and to see if they are, in turn, composed of still simpler particles. As we shall see in the remainder of this chapter, discoveries made with high-energy accelerators often require the revision of existing theories on the structure of matter. These studies of the building blocks of the universe are appropriately entitled "modern physics."

25.10 Particle interactions

All reactions between substances are governed by forces in the region where they are located. In our study, we have already recognized the nature of the *gravitational force*, the *electromagnetic force*, and the *nuclear force*. We shall now see how these forces affect interactions between subatomic particles. We will also learn about still another force in atomic nuclei, the so-called *weak force*.

Arranged in the order of decreasing strength of the forces involved, particle interactions are classified as follows:

1. Strong (nuclear) interactions. The nature of the nuclear force was discussed in Chapter 23. It holds the particles of the nucleus together against the electromagnetic repulsion of its similarly charged particles. The nuclear force is independent of charge. In other words, the attraction between two neutrons is the same as that between a proton and a neutron or between two protons.

Although the nuclear force is the strongest of all forces, it has a very limited range. It is not effective beyond a distance

University of Maryland

25-17 Joseph Weber with one of his gravity wave receivers (top). Small changes in the surface of the aluminum cylinder are thought to be the result of gravity radiations from certain stars. In the lower photo, Dr. Weber adjusts an aluminum disc inside a receiver that is used to determine the direction of the source of gravity waves.

of 2.0×10^{-5} Å. The carrier of the nuclear force is believed to be the meson; there is a constant exchange of mesons among the baryons of a stable nucleus. When the baryons are separated through the intervention of a high-energy particle from an accelerator, the carrier mesons are released.

The theory of the existence of energy-carrying mesons to explain the nuclear force was proposed by the Japanese physicist, Hideki Yukawa in 1935. But mesons were not actually detected until 1947.

2. Electromagnetic interactions. The nature of electromagnetic forces was discussed in Chapter 19. They differ from all other forces in several ways. (*1*) Electromagnetic forces can either attract or repel the objects on which they are acting. The other three forces are attractive forces only. (*2*) Electromagnetic forces can act in directions other than along a straight line between objects. (*3*) The electromagnetic forces depend on the relative velocities of particles. This is not true of other forces. The carrier of the electromagnetic force is the photon.

Electromagnetism keeps electrons in orbit around the nucleus. The same force is responsible for the bonding between atoms to form molecules and between molecules to form larger substances. Nevertheless, the electromagnetic force is less than 1/100th as strong as the nuclear force.

3. Weak interactions. This is the most mysterious of the known interactions between particles. As the study of the nucleus progressed and the number of subatomic particles grew, a "strange" principle was discovered. Some of the particles were always produced in pairs (such as a lambda hyperon and K meson), and these particles had much longer half-lives than was expected.

To explain the behavior of these so-called "strange particles," the "weak force" was postulated. Its ratio to the nuclear force is only about 10^{-13} to 1, so it affects only leptons. Beta decay is an example of a weak interaction.

The proposed carrier for weak interactions is the so-called *W-meson*, but this particle has not yet been detected. Some scientists believe that, as in the case of the mesons, the carrier may turn out to be a whole family of particles.

4. Gravitational interactions. Gravitation was the first of the fundamental forces to be studied in the history of science, yet it is the weakest of them all. (Its ratio to the nuclear force is only 10^{-38} to 1.) Gravitation has no known distance limitations, so that its effects are easily observed in the behavior of large objects on the earth and in the motions of celestial bodies. Within the atomic nucleus, the effect of gravitational forces is negligible in comparison with the other forces that are present.

The carrier for the gravitational force has been named the *graviton*. Like the photon, its rest mass is thought to be zero. After a ten-year effort, Joseph Weber of the University of Maryland announced that he had detected gravity waves from certain stars using one-ton aluminum cylinders as receivers (Fig. 25-17). Although the validity of these findings has been challenged, other searches for gravity waves are presently being made.

Repeatedly in your study of physics, the importance of the conservation principles has been emphasized. The conservation of mass-energy, the conservation of linear and angular momentum, the conservation of electric charge—these laws are basic to an understanding of all interactions above the atomic scale. The same laws hold true in the subatomic world. We have already seen in Chapter 24, for example, that both mass-energy and electric charge are conserved in nuclear reactions. As other subatomic particles were discovered, additional conservation laws were formulated.

25.11 Nuclear conservation laws

1. Conservation of baryons. When a baryon decays or reacts with another particle, the number of baryons is the same on both sides of the equation. For example, if a neutron is left by itself it will decay as follows:

$$n^0 \rightarrow p + e^- + \bar{\nu}$$

The neutron and proton are both baryons, while the electron and antineutrino have baryon numbers of zero. Consequently, the baryon number of the equation is 1 on each side.

The conservation of baryons keeps the universe from deteriorating into mesons and leptons. If this would happen, atoms as we know them would no longer exist, and matter would become a rather homogeneous mixture of a few kinds of low-mass particles.

2. Lepton conservation. The decay of the neutron illustrates another nuclear conservation principle. The lepton number of the neutron and proton is zero. The lepton number of the electron is $+1$. The lepton number of the antineutrino is -1 (since it is an antiparticle). Consequently, the arithmetic sum of the lepton numbers is the same on each side of the equation. This principle holds true for every interaction in which leptons are involved.

Lepton conservation explains the necessity of pair production, which was considered "strange" when it was first discovered (Section 25.10, Part 3). When a lepton is created in an interaction, a particle with the opposite lepton number must also be created in order to conserve the lepton value of the reaction. Similarly, a lepton can be annihilated only by interacting with a particle of opposite lepton value.

The conservation of baryons and leptons does not prevent the change of a particle to another particle within the same category, however. In neutron decay, one kind of baryon (the neutron) changed into another kind (the proton). The decay of the antimuon is another example:

$$\mu^+ \to e^+ + \nu - \bar{\nu}$$

Lepton No. $= -1 = -1 \quad +1 \quad -1$

3. Conservation of strangeness. It has already been noted that many of the particles that are produced in pairs and that have relatively long half-lives are called "strange particles." In the chart of particles on page 636, a "strangeness number" is assigned to each of these unusual particles. The sign and value of the strangeness numbers is derived from the observation of their creation and interactions.

Consider the following interaction involving strange particles:

$$\overline{K^+} + p \to \Xi^0 + K^0$$

Strangeness No. $= -1 + 0 = -2 \quad +1$

The identity of the original particles has changed completely, but the sum of the strangeness numbers is -1 on each side of the equation.

The principle of strangeness was devised by Gell-Mann and led directly to the formulation of the chart of particles. He assigned strangeness numbers of zero to some of the particles because they did not exhibit the same properties of strangeness that the numbered particles did. Gell-Mann also noticed another aspect of the strangeness scheme: when strange particles are involved in slow-decay reactions, strangeness changes up or down by one unit. Slow decays are usually cases of weak interactions (Section 25.10), the mechanism of which is not well understood. Perhaps when the carrier of the weak force is finally identified, it will be found that strangeness is conserved in weak interactions after all.

25.12 Antimatter   For many years, nuclear physicists have speculated on the interesting idea that every particle in the universe has a mirror-image counterpart. The chart of fundamental particles suggests this idea by listing an antiparticle for each particle. (The electron-positron pair discussed in Section 23.5 is an example of antiparticles.)

In all respects except in the accounting of the amount of energy, adding an antiparticle to a physical system is equivalent to removing a particle, and removing an antiparticle is equivalent to adding a particle. Thus, when putting a particle and its antiparticle together, all physical quantities associated with the particle or antiparticle (mass, charge, etc.) disappear and pure energy is left.

A substance composed of antiparticles is called antimatter. The collision of a particle with its antiparticle, or of matter with antimatter, results in the annihilation of matter and illustrates the interchangeability of matter and energy (Section 1.12). Scientists believe that large quantities of antimatter may exist in the universe in the form of stars or even entire galaxies (or antistars and antigalaxies, to be more exact).

In nuclear physics, the distribution of matter in space is often described in terms of *parity*. *The **law of parity** states that for every process in nature there is a mirror-image process which is indistinguishable from the original process.* Another way to state this law is to say that there is no absolute and independent way of describing right and left, clockwise and counterclockwise in the universe. Any experiment devised to establish one of these directions is matched by an equally probable event in the opposite direction.

Parity experiments deal largely with the spin of nuclear particles. Spin is also responsible for the direction in which particles are emitted in nuclear interactions. The conservation of parity stipulates that particles will be emitted in opposite directions in equal numbers since nature shows no preference for spin direction. But in 1956 a series of experiments based on predictions by T. D. Lee and C. N. Yang showed that this was not the case. In the case of weak interactions involving beta decay, parity was not conserved!

Experiments were now specifically designed to test the conservation of parity in other interactions. Specifically, the question was whether parity is still conserved in a larger sense when particles are replaced by their antiparticles in nuclear interactions. In 1966, physicists at the Brookhaven National Laboratory discovered a violation of parity with antiparticles as well. So perhaps there is an absolute sense of direction in the universe after all.

On the other hand, it may well be that the so-called fundamental particles are not really fundamental at all. Perhaps each of them is composed of more elementary bits of matter-energy.

In 1974, evidence was found that the three nuclear conservation laws are not completely inviolate at high energies. At 300 Gev, collisions of electrons and positrons were found to produce hadrons, and vice versa. This suggests that the weak force is not a constant and that under certain conditions it may become stronger than the electromagnetic force.

California Institute of Technology, Lauristen Laboratory of Physics

25-18 The quark theory was proposed by the American physicists Murray Gell-Mann (top) and Richard Feynman. Both have received the Nobel Prize for their work in physics.

One explanation of this phenomenon suggests that colliding leptons exchange a so-called Z particle. This interaction is known as a *neutral weak current* (since there is no change in the charges of the colliding particles). The discovery of neutral weak currents is an important step toward a *unified field theory,* in which all forces in the universe are part of a single concept.

Also in 1974, two subnuclear particles were discovered that do not fit into present classifications. Both particles have unusually large masses and half-lives. They have been named psi 3100 and psi 3700 (representing their masses in Mev units) by scientists at the Stanford Linear Accelerator Center. Scientists at Brookhaven National Laboratory have called the particles J-1 and J-2 (since J is one of the few remaining unused letters in nuclear terminology). It has been proposed that these newly discovered particles consist of quarks with "charm" and "color" different from those of the quarks of other subatomic particles. (Charm and color are quantum designations analogous to those used with electrons in Section 25.14.)

QUESTIONS

Group A

1. (a) Who proposed the chart of subatomic particles? (b) How many such particles are known today?
2. Define: (a) baryon, (b) meson, (c) lepton.
3. (a) List three conservation laws that apply to all interactions of matter. (b) List three conservation laws that apply only to nuclear interactions.
4. (a) List the four types of forces in the universe in order of their increasing magnitude. (b) Name the carrier of each force. (c) Which of these forces is effective only within the size range of the atomic nucleus?
5. (a) What is a quark? (b) Describe a possible alternative to the quark theory.
6. (a) Why are some subatomic particles called "strange"? (b) Name three of them.
7. How does the conservation of baryons prevent the collapse of matter?
8. (a) What is the connection between symmetry and parity? (b) What is meant by the conservation of parity?
9. Why did it take twelve years to discover the meson after its existence was predicted by Yukawa in 1935?

ATOMIC MODELS

Now that we have followed the efforts of scientists as they "dissect" the atom with powerful accelerators and sensitive recording devices, it will be helpful to take a look at the picture of atomic structure that is emerging from these studies. In Chapter 23, where the discovery of the first subatomic particles was discussed, it was mentioned that several theories of atomic structure were proposed when the electron was discovered, only to be discarded when more information about the atom was obtained. Let us now study the deficiencies of these early atomic models. This study can serve as a review of some of the important physical principles emphasized in your study of physics.

Thomson, who discovered the electron, proposed that the positive charge of an atom permeated the whole atom and that the electrons were imbedded uniformly in this positive continuum. This picture of the atom was discredited by the alpha-scattering experiments of Rutherford (Chapter 23) which showed that the positive charge of the atom was concentrated in a small nucleus.

There were other reasons for discarding the Thomson model, however. As we learned in Chapter 12, even the simplest atom (hydrogen) produces a number of different spectral lines when it is energized. It is difficult to explain how a single electron in the Thomson model could vibrate in a way that would give rise to the various spectral series of hydrogen. The situation becomes even more difficult with more complex atoms. Furthermore, it is impossible to arrange the electrons in a Thomson atom in a geometric pattern which will explain the chemical properties of the atoms. (This behavior of atoms will be discussed more fully in the section on bonding, Section 25.15, at the end of this chapter.)

Rutherford succeeded in showing that the atom has a positively charged nucleus and that the rest of the atom is mostly empty space. In other words, the negatively charged electrons are separated from the nucleus by comparatively large distances (in terms of the dimensions of the nucleus). But the electrons are still well within the field of electromagnetic forces which would instantly draw the electrons into the oppositely charged nucleus.

To overcome this difficulty in his model, Rutherford proposed that the electrons revolved around the nucleus with sufficient velocity to overcome the attraction of the nucleus but with less than escape velocity. This picture of the atom was analogous to the Copernican system, in which the planets revolve around a central sun. There was one important difference between the

25.13 Deficiencies of early models

two pictures, however, and it was this difference that made the Rutherford model unsatisfactory. An orbiting planet is held in the solar system by gravitation, whereas the attractive force in the atom is electromagnetic. It was stated in Chapter 21 that when an electric charge accelerates (which the electron is doing as it orbits the nucleus in a constantly changing direction), energy is radiated away from the charge. If this were the case, the electron would quickly lose the energy it needs to stay in orbit and would collapse into the nucleus. The situation would be very much like the decay of the orbit of an earth satellite as it loses energy to the earth's atmosphere during reentry, except that the elapsed time of the decay is vastly different in the two cases.

Bohr suggested a solution to the difficulties of the Rutherford model. As we saw in Chapter 12, the quantum theory states that light exhibits particle-like properties in certain experiments, which means that light energy is transferred in discrete quantities or photons. Applying this idea to the atom, Bohr said that the electron is not free to assume any orbit whatever, but rather that the size and shape of the orbit are governed by the quantum theory. An electron cannot move into a lower orbit unless it loses enough momentum to emit a photon. An electron must stay in its orbit unless enough momentum is gained or lost to enable it to jump abruptly into a different orbit. This process can occur spontaneously.

Bohr's model was remarkably successful in explaining the spectral lines of low-atomic-numbered elements as well as a number of experiments (known as the Franck-Hertz experiments) especially designed to test the validity of the quantized-momentum idea. But the model ran into trouble in trying to explain the behavior of helium atoms or atoms with large atomic numbers. Then, too, small but important differences were found between the predictions of the Bohr model and the results of experiments based on the predictions. Attempts were made to account for these differences by suggesting that electron orbits are elliptical rather than circular and by using relativistic mass (a method which was successful in solving a similar problem with the orbit of the planet Mercury), but this took care of only some of the discrepancies.

There were other problems with the Bohr atom as well. It did not at first take into account the effect of the spin of the electron (Chapter 23) on its orbital motion. Such spinning would set up electromagnetic forces that must be taken into account in computing the total energy of the orbiting electron.

Perhaps the most serious blow to the Bohr model came with the announcement of the *uncertainty principle* by Werner Heisen-

Niels Bohr Library

Three pioneers of particle physics: Robert A. Milikan (left), Marie Curie, and Werner Heisenberg.

berg in 1927: *it is impossible to specify simultaneously the exact position of an object and its momentum*—or any similar pair of physical quantities related to its motion such as energy and time. For bodies of ordinary mass, the mathematical error in any such simultaneous determination is smaller than errors in measurement, and the uncertainty effect is not observable. With electrons, however, the effect is pronounced. This principle means that it may be possible to determine where an electron is, but it is not possible at the same time to determine its exact speed or direction. The reason is that the method (short wavelength radiation) which is used to determine the position of the electron changes its momentum. Likewise, to determine an electron's momentum, an instrument must be used that changes the electron's direction of motion, thus preventing the determination of the electron's position.

In view of the uncertainty principle, it is really meaningless to talk about specific electron orbits at all. Since the orbits can never be pinpointed, it is only possible to predict the probability of the position and motion of an electron for a given instant of time. The mathematics of these predictions leads to still another atom model which we shall now investigate.

25.14 Quantum mechanics

In Section 12.11 we saw that the quantum theory was quite successful in explaining the spectral lines of the energized hydrogen atom. A model of the atom based on the principles of the quantum theory avoids many of the difficulties of the Bohr model. To understand the description of the atom according to the quantum theory, it is necessary to be familiar with the idea of *quantum numbers*. As used in atomic physics, a **quantum number** *is a number that is used to describe the allowable value of certain physical quantities.* For example, quantum numbers are used in special equations to compute the energy of a particle, such as the electron. *The branch of physics that deals with the behavior of particles whose specific properties are given by quantum numbers is called* **quantum mechanics**. One of its developers was the German physicist, Max Born (1882–1970) (Fig. 25-19), for which he was awarded the Nobel Prize.

The quantum-theory model of the atom is a three-dimensional one. The motion of the electron is not restricted to a single plane, as in the Bohr atom. Within the limits prescribed by its quantum numbers, the electron describes an orbit which completely encloses the nucleus.

The first quantum number for the electron is the one that describes the radius of its orbit. It is called the *principal quantum number* and is designated by the letter n. The principal quantum number may have the integral values 1, 2, 3, 4, etc., which

Niels Bohr Library

25-19 Max Born, the German physicist who helped to pioneer the quantum-mechanical view of the atom.

correspond to the similarly numbered energy levels of the Bohr atom. For example, an electron with a principal quantum number 1 is in the first energy level, an electron with the number 2 is in the second level, and so on.

The equation for finding the energy of an electron from its principal quantum number is

$$E = -\frac{me^4}{8\,\epsilon_0^2 h^2 n^2}$$

where E is the energy of the electron, m is its mass, e is the electronic charge, ϵ_0 is a constant with the value 8.854×10^{-12} c²/n m², h is Planck's constant, and n is the principal quantum number. The energy is expressed as a negative quantity to show that the electron is held by the nucleus.

Thus far, the use of the principal quantum number yields exactly the same quantitative results that Bohr obtained for his atomic model. But here the similarity stops. A second quantum number, called the *angular momentum quantum number* or *secondary quantum number*, describes the magnitude of the angular momentum of the orbiting electron. Unlike energy, which is a scalar quantity, angular momentum is a vector with both magnitude and direction. The equation for the magnitude of the angular momentum is

$$L = \sqrt{l(l+1)}\,\frac{h}{2\pi}$$

where L is the angular momentum, l is the angular momentum quantum number, and h is Planck's constant. l may have integral values ranging from zero to $n-1$ and is therefore limited by the principal quantum number. In effect, a high value of l means that the electron's orbit is circular. The lower the value of l, the more elliptical the orbit is.

The magnitude of the angular momentum in a specific direction is described by a third quantum number, the *magnetic quantum number*. It is designated as m_l and can have integral values ranging from $-l$ through zero to $+l$. The equation using m_l is

$$L_z = m_l\,\frac{h}{2\pi}$$

in which L_z is the component of the angular momentum that is parallel to a magnetic field.

Since m_l can have several values for all values of n except $n = 1$, the energy levels of an atom are split into two or more sublevels when the atom is subjected to a magnetic field. This effect can be detected in the spectra of excited atoms and is called the *Zeeman effect* (Fig. 25-20).

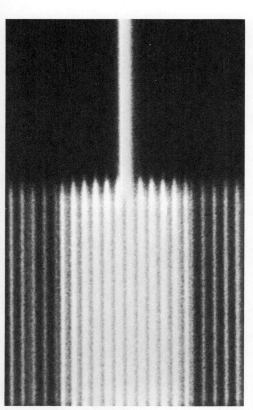

University of California Lawrence Radiation Laboratories

25-20 The Zeeman effect. The single line at the top is the 3779-Å line of the element curium. At the bottom is the spectrum of the same line in a powerful magnetic field.

Not all cases of the Zeeman effect can be explained in terms of L_z, however. In the 1920's it was discovered that many pairs of spectral lines could be the result of electrons spinning on their axes and that this electron spin also harmonizes with the relativistic explanation of the behavior of matter. The spin of the electron is designated by the *spin quantum number, m_s*, which may have the values $+\frac{1}{2}$ and $-\frac{1}{2}$. The equation using m_s is:

$$L_s = m_s \frac{h}{2\pi}$$

in which L_s is the component of angular momentum which is parallel to a magnetic field and which is due to electron spin. The values of L_s are, therefore, $+\frac{1}{2}h/2\pi$ and $-\frac{1}{2}h/2\pi$. The $+$ and $-$ signs in front of these ratios indicate that the electrons are spinning in opposite directions.

The assignment of four quantum numbers to each electron leads to the logical question of how the quantum numbers of any one electron compare with the numbers of other electrons. Does it ever happen that two electrons have the same set of numbers? The answer to this question is provided by the *Exclusion Principle* of Wolfgang Pauli (1900–1958), which states that *no two electrons in an atom can have the same set of quantum numbers*. The number of different energy levels that could be computed if there were no restrictions on the quantum numbers associated with each electron is far greater than those revealed by spectral evidence.

With the help of the four quantum numbers and the Exclusion Principle it is possible to determine the electron configuration of any particular atom. A table of such configurations is shown in Table 25-2. In each case, the number of electrons in a particular sublevel is found by using the permissible values of each quantum number. For example, aluminum has 13 electrons. When $n = 1$, $l = 0$, $m_l = 0$, and m_s can have values of $+\frac{1}{2}$ and $-\frac{1}{2}$. In other words, two electrons can be listed in the column headed $n = 1$. When $n = 2$, l can be 0 or 1. When $l = 0$, $m_l = 0$, and m_s can be $+\frac{1}{2}$ and $-\frac{1}{2}$, as before. Hence two electrons are listed under $l = 0$ in this column. When $l = 1$, m_l can be $+1$ or 0 or -1. For each of these three values of m_l there are again two values of m_s. In other words, there are six possible combinations of quantum numbers when $l = 1$. When $n = 3$ and $l = 0$, two values of m_s are again possible. This tally leaves only one more electron to account for in the aluminum atom, and this final electron is listed under $l = 1$. All atoms can be analyzed in this manner.

A final word of explanation concerning the equations of the quantum theory is necessary at this point. You will notice that

Table 25-2 ELECTRON CONFIGURATION OF THE LIGHT ELEMENTS

Atomic number	Symbol	Element	Electron configuration of atom							
			$n=1$	$n=2$		$n=3$			$n=4$	
			$l=0$	$l=0, l=1$		$l=0, l=1, l=2$			$l=0, l=1$	
1	H	hydrogen	1							
2	He	helium	2							
3	Li	lithium	2	1						
4	Be	beryllium	2	2						
5	B	boron	2	2	1					
6	C	carbon	2	2	2					
7	N	nitrogen	2	2	3					
8	O	oxygen	2	2	4					
9	F	fluorine	2	2	5					
10	Ne	neon	2	2	6					
11	Na	sodium	2	2	6	1				
12	Mg	magnesium	2	2	6	2				
13	Al	aluminum	2	2	6	2	1			
14	Si	silicon	2	2	6	2	2			
15	P	phosphorus	2	2	6	2	3			
16	S	sulfur	2	2	6	2	4			
17	Cl	chlorine	2	2	6	2	5			
18	Ar	argon	2	2	6	2	6			
19	K	potassium	2	2	6	2	6		1	
20	Ca	calcium	2	2	6	2	6		2	
21	Sc	scandium	2	2	6	2	6	1	2	
22	Ti	titanium	2	2	6	2	6	2	2	
23	V	vanadium	2	2	6	2	6	3	2	
24	Cr	chromium	2	2	6	2	6	5	1	
25	Mn	manganese	2	2	6	2	6	5	2	
26	Fe	iron	2	2	6	2	6	6	2	
27	Co	cobalt	2	2	6	2	6	7	2	
28	Ni	nickel	2	2	6	2	6	8	2	
29	Cu	copper	2	2	6	2	6	10	1	
30	Zn	zinc	2	2	6	2	6	10	2	
31	Ga	gallium	2	2	6	2	6	10	2	1
32	Ge	germanium	2	2	6	2	6	10	2	2
33	As	arsenic	2	2	6	2	6	10	2	3
34	Se	selenium	2	2	6	2	6	10	2	4
35	Br	bromine	2	2	6	2	6	10	2	5
36	Kr	krypton	2	2	6	2	6	10	2	6

Planck's constant, *h*, is used in each of the equations. In Section 12.11, we saw that *h* is associated with wave motion. The use of this same constant in describing the behavior of subatomic particles suggests that the particles have wave-like characteristics. This wave-particle duality was mentioned in the very first chapter and in the discussion of light. Now it is important to emphasize it once more. About 1924, the French physicist Louis de Broglie (Fig. 25-21) suggested that *all* matter possesses wave characteristics and that these matter waves become more pronounced as the momentum of a particle of matter decreases.

In Section 12.11, the wavelength of a matter wave was given by the equation

$$\lambda = \frac{h}{mv}$$

where λ is the wavelength, *h* is Planck's constant, *m* is the mass of the particle, and *v* is its velocity. Since *h* has a very small value (6.62×10^{-34} joule sec), it can be seen from the equation that *m* must likewise be extremely small before λ can become large enough to be detectable. This is why the wave properties of, let us say, a moving baseball are completely undetectable, while the wavelength of the electron is long enough to consider in the modern view of the atom.

It must not be assumed, however, that a de Broglie wave is like the physical disturbance of the water in a ripple tank. A de Broglie wave is not a motion of matter, but rather a property. Matter waves can exist in a vacuum in the same way that light waves can. They permeate space in the way a gravitational or magnetic field influences the area surrounding a mass or a magnet. In the final analysis, it is not possible to construct an analogy for matter waves. Furthermore, it should be recognized that de Broglie waves, like so many other descriptions in science, represent a particular model of the universe. As with all models in the history of science, this one can also be modified and improved as our understanding of the universe keeps growing.

A successful model of the atom must explain not only the behavior of such subatomic particles as the electron but also the properties of substances on a larger scale. The mechanisms that hold the parts of the atom together should also be able to bind atoms together. Two types of atomic bonding are *ionic bonding* and *covalent bonding*.

1. Ionic bonding. Quantum mechanics allows only a definite number of orbiting electrons for each value of the principal quantum number. For $n = 1$, it is 2 electrons, for $n = 2$, it is 8 electrons, and so on. When an atom has the maximum number of electrons for a particular electron shell (or subshell for heavy

25-21 Louis de Broglie, the French physicist who proposed the wave nature of matter.

25.15 Bonds between atoms

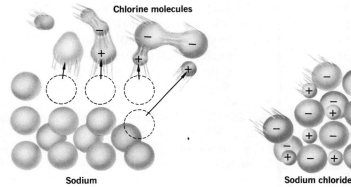

25-22 When sodium reacts with chlorine to form common salt, an electron is transferred from the outer shell of each sodium atom to the outer shell of each chlorine atom. The particles composing the salt are sodium ions and chloride ions.

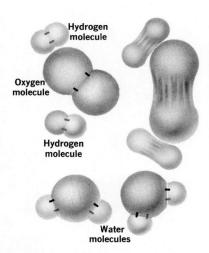

25-23 In the water molecules which result from the reaction of hydrogen and oxygen, the oxygen atom shares an outer-shell electron with each of two hydrogen atoms, while each of the hydrogen atoms shares its single electron with the oxygen atom. This is an example of covalent bonding.

atoms), it is said to have a *closed shell.* In most cases, atoms are stable when they have closed shells.

The stability of an electron is described in terms of *ionization energy.* **Ionization energy** *is the energy required to remove an electron from an atom.* Obviously, the ionization energy must be equal to the energy of the electron as described by its quantum numbers and must also have the same sign. As n increases, the energy of the electron decreases. Consequently, the outermost electrons are usually the easiest to remove from an atom.

Whether an atom will lose electrons or take electrons from another atom, however, depends on another factor called *electron affinity.* **Electron affinity** *is the measure of the energy that is released when an electron is added to a neutral atom.* An atom with a high electron affinity holds its electrons tightly. In other words, it also has a high ionization energy. Similarly, atoms with low electron affinities also have low ionization energies.

An atom with a low ionization energy is likely to lose an electron to an atom with high electron affinity. When this happens, the first atom becomes a positively charged ion and the second one becomes a negatively charged ion. These two oppositely charged ions are held together by electrostatic forces in an *ionic bond* (Fig. 25-22).

2. Covalent bonding. Atoms that do not meet the requirements for ionic bonding can still form compounds by sharing one or more electrons instead of transferring them from one atom to the other. The sharing of electrons by two or more atoms is called *covalent bonding* (Fig. 25-23). A good example of covalent bonding is the formation of a hydrogen molecule from two atoms of hydrogen. Since the two hydrogen atoms have identical ionization energies and electron affinities, there can be no ionic bonding. But each atom can share its lone electron with the other atom, thus giving each of them a closed outer shell of two electrons (at least on a part-time basis).

There is an important requirement in covalent bonding, however, and that is that the shared electrons forming a given bond must not have the same set of quantum numbers. Such a situation would violate the Exclusion Principle. In the hydrogen molecule, for instance, the electrons can be shared only if the two electrons have opposite spins (and therefore different magnetic spin quantum numbers).

Some atoms have a much greater tendency to form covalent bonds than do other atoms. Carbon, for example, has four electrons in its outer shell and is able to form several covalent bonds simultaneously. More than three million compounds of carbon are known. However, as might be expected from the nature of the covalent bond, covalent compounds generally are not as stable as are the compounds that are held together by the electrostatic forces of ionic bonds. The stability of a compound is also affected by the fact that bonds may be intermediate—that is, partly ionic and partly covalent. When two identical atoms form a bond such as the one in the hydrogen molecule, the bond is purely covalent. However, when unlike atoms combine, electron sharing and transfer will vary according to the energy requirements of the individual atoms. In these intermediate cases, an electron can be thought of as spending proportionately more time around one atom than around the other. When a bond is more than 50 percent ionic, it is referred to as an ionic bond even though some electron sharing is still involved.

A type of bonding which cannot be completely explained as either ionic or covalent is the one that exists in the structure of metals. As we know, metals are good conductors of electricity, yet the electrons in ionic and covalent bonds are restricted to the region around specific atoms. Furthermore, metals are malleable and ductile, while nonmetallic crystals like sodium chloride do not have these properties. Also, the luster of metals cannot be accounted for as either an ionic or a covalent phenomenon.

The properties of metals can be explained, however, if it is assumed that metals contain a "gas" of freely moving electrons that are not bound to any specific atoms within the metal. Such freely moving electrons could then easily conduct electricity (a stream of electrons) through the metal. Also, the free electrons can be set in vibration by incident light rays and then reradiate them as "reflected" light. This process explains the luster of metals.

QUESTIONS

Group A
1. (a) Why is it impossible to determine simultaneously the position and velocity of an electron? (b) What is the name of this principle? (c) Who first postulated it?
2. (a) What is quantum mechanics? (b) How is it used to explain atomic structure?
3. (a) Define the four quantum numbers of an electron. (b) What quantum number can always have only two values? (c) Why?
4. What experiment showed flaws in the Thomson model of the atom?
5. (a) Why are ionic bonds stronger than covalent bonds? (b) Why is it impossible for two hydrogen atoms to form an ionic bond?
6. (a) What is the relationship between ionization energy and the activity of elements? (b) Between ionization energy and electron affinity?
7. (a) Why did Rutherford propose that electrons move in orbits around the nucleus? (b) What was wrong with his atomic model?
8. (a) What is the Zeeman effect? (b) How can spectra be used to tell whether a specific example of the Zeeman effect is the result of the angular momentum of an electron or of electron spin?
9. (a) What is meant by the Exclusion Principle? (b) Who postulated it? (c) What led him to this conclusion?
10. Why is the wavelength of a moving baseball undetectable, while that of a much smaller and less massive electron is noticeable?
11. (a) What is it that waves in a matter wave? (b) Describe an analogy for de Broglie waves.
12. (a) List three properties of metals that cannot be adequately explained in terms of ionic or covalent bonding. (b) Tell how these properties *can* be explained.

PROBLEMS

Group A
1. List the quantum numbers for each electron in the following atoms: (a) helium, (b) sodium, (c) argon, (d) magnesium.
2. (a) Compute the energy of an electron with a principal quantum number of 3. Use MKS units. The mass and charge of the electron and the value of Planck's constant are given in Table 4, Appendix B. (b) Convert this energy to electron volts and compare it with the ionization energy of the outer electron of the neutral sodium atom.

Group B
3. (a) Find the wavelength of a baseball with a mass of 0.15 kg and a velocity of 26 m/sec. (b) Compare this wavelength with that of an electron moving at 5.5×10^6 m/sec.
4. Show that the number of electrons that can exist in a particular shell is given by the expression $2n^2$, in which n is the principal quantum number.

Mathematics Refresher

1. Introduction.

The topics selected for this Mathematics Refresher are those which sometimes trouble physics students. You may want to study this section before working on certain types of physics problems. The presentation here is not so detailed as that given in mathematics textbooks, but there is sufficient review to help you perform certain types of mathematical operations.

The following references are given for your convenience in reviewing these topics also:

Section 2.5 defines *significant figures* and gives rules for their notation.

Section 2.6 explains the *exponential notation* system.

Section 2.9 explains the *orderly procedure* you should use *in problem solving*, and the proper method of handling units in computations.

2. The slide rule.

With the slide rule, you can perform many mathematical operations in a fraction of the time that it would take you to do them on paper.

1. *Locating numbers.* The numbers on a slide rule are not evenly spaced. The upper figure (below) shows the location of the number 246 on the *C* and *D* scales. The lower figure shows the location of 1865.

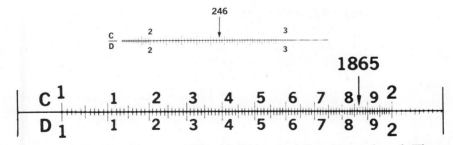

2. *Multiplication.* The scales on a slide rule have a number 1 at each end. These end numbers are called *indices*. To multiply, set an index of the *C* scale above one of the factors on the *D* scale. Then slide the cursor (the transparent window containing a hairline) to the other factor on the *C* scale. The product will be under the hairline on the *D* scale. The figure on the next page shows the setting for the problem $18 \times 26 = 468$.

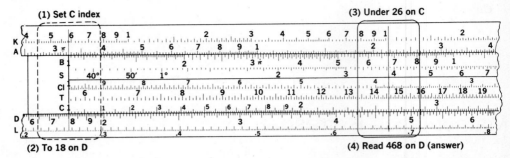

(1) Set C index   (3) Under 26 on C

(2) To 18 on D   (4) Read 468 on D (answer)

3. *Division.* The process for division is the reverse of the multiplication process. Hence, the figure above also shows the setting for the problem $468 \div 26 = 18$. When problems involve numbers with decimal points, disregard the decimal points when making the settings and place the decimal point in the answer by inspection.

4. *Squares and square roots.* Only the **A** and **D** scales are needed for these problems. To find the square of a number, move the hairline to that number on the **D** scale and read the answer under the hairline on the **A** scale. To find the square root of a number, locate the number on the **A** scale and read the square root on the **D** scale. If the number is greater than 1 and contains an odd number of digits to the left of the decimal point, use the left half of the **A** scale. If it has an even number of digits to the left of the decimal point, use the right half of the **A** scale. If the number is less than 1, count the number of zeros between the decimal point and the first significant figure. If the number of zeros is *odd*, use the left half of the **A** scale. If the number of zeros is even (or if there are no zeros), use the right half of the **A** scale.

5. *Porportions.* With any setting of the **C** and **D** scales, all readings opposite each other on the two scales are in the same ratio. For example, in the previous figure, $1:18 = 26:468 = 30:540$, etc.

3. Conversion of a fraction to a decimal.

Divide the numerator by the denominator, carrying the answer to the required number of significant figures.

Example

Convert $\dfrac{45}{85}$ to a decimal.

Solution

Dividing 45 by 85, we find the equivalent decimal to be 0.53, rounded to two significant figures.

```
     0.529
85 ) 45.000
     42 5
      2 50
      1 70
        800
        765
```

4. Calculation of percentage.

Uncertainty always exists in measurements of physical phenomena. Uncertainty exists because measuring instruments have limited precision. The instruments you use in laboratory experiments generally have less precision than those used by the physicists who obtained the "best known values" you find in tables. *The precision of any measurement is limited to the measurement detail which the instrument used is capable of providing.* In physics, an error is defined as the difference between experimentally obtained data and the accepted values for these data. In experimental work, the *relative error* (percentage error) is usually more significant than the *absolute error* (the actual difference between an observed value and its accepted value). Hence, as a physics student you must be able to calculate percentages and percentage errors, and convert fractions to percentages and percentages to decimals.

Example
What percentage of 19 is 13?

Solution
We divide 13 by 19, and multiply the quotient by 100%. A multiplication by 100% does not change the value of the quotient, since 100% actually has a value of 1. When we multiply by 100%, we multiply the number by 100, and affix the % sign to the product: $\frac{13}{19} \times 100\% = 68\%$ rounded to two significant figures.

5. Calculation of relative error.

$$\text{Relative Error} = \frac{\text{Absolute Error}}{\text{Accepted Value}} \times 100\%$$

where the *absolute error* is the difference between the *observed value* and the *accepted value*.

Example
In a laboratory experiment carried out at 20.0° C, a student found the speed of sound in air to be 329.8 m/sec. The accepted value at this temperature is 343.5 m/sec. What was his relative error?

Solution
$$\text{Absolute Error} = 343.5 \text{ m/sec} - 329.5 \text{ m/sec}$$
$$= 13.7 \text{ m/sec}$$
$$\text{Relative Error} = \frac{13.7 \text{ m/sec}}{343.5 \text{ m/sec}} \times 100\% = 3.99\%$$

6. Conversion of fractions to percentages.

To convert a fraction to a percentage, divide the numerator by the denominator, and multiply the quotient by 100%.

Example
Express $\frac{11}{13}$ as a percentage.

Solution
$\frac{11}{13} \times 100\% = 85\%$, rounded to two significant figures.

7. *Conversion of percentages to decimals.*

To convert a percentage to a decimal, move the decimal point two places to the left, and remove the percent sign.

Example
Convert 62.5% to a decimal.

Solution
If we express 62.5% as a fraction, it becomes 62.5/100. If we actually perform the indicated division, we obtain 0.625 as the decimal equivalent. Observe that the only changes have been to move the decimal point two places to the left, and remove the percent sign.

8. *Proportions.*

Many physics problems involving the temperature, pressure, and volume relationships of gases may be solved by using proportions.

Example
Solve the proportion $\dfrac{x}{225 \text{ ml}} = \dfrac{273°}{298°}$ for x.

Solution
Multiply both sides of the equation by 225 ml, the denominator of x, giving $x = \dfrac{225 \text{ ml} \times 273°}{298°}$. Solving, $x = 206$ ml.

9. *Fractional Equations.*

The equations for certain problems involving lenses, mirrors, and electric resistances produce fractional equations where the unknown is in the denominator. To solve such equations, clear them of fractions by multiplying each term by the lowest common denominator. Then isolate the unknown, and complete the solution.

Example
Solve $\dfrac{1}{s_o} + \dfrac{1}{s_i} = \dfrac{1}{f}$ for f.

Solution
The lowest common denominator of s_o, s_i, and f is $s_o s_i f$. Multiplying the fractional equation by this product, we obtain

$$\frac{s_o s_i f}{s_o} + \frac{s_o s_i f}{s_i} = \frac{s_o s_i f}{f} \qquad \text{or} \qquad s_i f + s_o f = s_o s_i$$

Thus, $f(s_o + s_i) = s_o s_i$ $\qquad$ and $\qquad$ $f = \dfrac{s_o s_i}{s_o + s_i}$

10. *Equations.*

When a known equation is employed in solving a problem and the unknown quantity is not the one usually isolated, the equation should be solved algebraically to isolate the unknown quantity of the particular problem. Then the values (with units) of the known quantities can be substituted and the indicated operations performed.

Example

From the equation for potential energy, $E_p = mgh$, we are to calculate h.

Solution

Before substituting known values for E_p, m, and g, the unknown term h is isolated and expressed in terms of E_p, m, and g. This is accomplished by dividing both sides of the basic equation by mg.

$$\frac{E_p}{mg} = \frac{mgh}{mg} \quad \text{or} \quad h = \frac{E_p}{mg}$$

If E_p is given in joules, m in kilograms, and g in meters/second^2, the unit of h is

$$h = \frac{j}{\text{kg m/sec}^2} = \frac{\text{kg m}^2/\text{sec}^2}{\text{kg m/sec}^2} = m \quad \text{Thus, } h \text{ is expressed in meters.}$$

11. Laws of exponents.

Operations involving exponents may be expressed in general fashion as $a^m \times a^n = a^{m+n}$; $a^m \div a^n = a^{m-n}$; $(a^m)^n = a^{mn}$; $\sqrt[n]{a^m} = a^{m/n}$. For example:

$$x^2 \times x^3 = x^5 \quad 10^5 \div 10^{-3} = 10^8 \qquad (t^2)^3 = t^6 \quad \sqrt[4]{4^2} = 4^{2/4} = 4^{1/2} = 2$$

12. Quadratic formula.

The two roots of the quadratic equation $ax^2 + bx + c = 0$ in which a does not equal zero, are given by the quadratic formula

$$x = \frac{-b \pm \sqrt{b^2 - 4ac}}{2a}$$

13. Triangles.

In physics some facts about triangles are used to solve problems about forces and velocities.

1. *30°—60°—90° right triangle.* It is useful to remember that the hypotenuse of such a triangle is twice as long as the side opposite the 30° angle. The length of the side opposite the 60° angle is $\mathbf{s}\sqrt{3}$, where $\mathbf{s}$ is the length of the side opposite the 30° angle.

2. *45°—45°—90° right triangle.* The sides opposite the 45° angles are equal. The length of the hypotenuse is $\mathbf{s}\sqrt{2}$, where $\mathbf{s}$ is the length of a side.

3. *Trigonometric functions.* Trigonometric functions are ratios of the lengths of sides of a right triangle and depend on the magnitude of one of its acute angles. Using right triangle **ABC**, below, we define the following trigonometric functions of $\angle \mathbf{A}$:

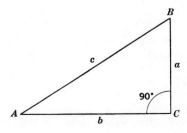

$$\text{sine } \angle \mathbf{A} = \frac{\mathbf{a}}{\mathbf{c}}$$

$$\text{cosine } \angle \mathbf{A} = \frac{\mathbf{b}}{\mathbf{c}}$$

$$\text{tangent } \angle \mathbf{A} = \frac{\mathbf{a}}{\mathbf{b}}$$

These functions are usually abbreviated as sin **A**, cos **A**, and tan **A**. Table 6, Appendix B, gives values of trigonometric functions.

Example

In a right triangle, one side is 25.3 and the hypotenuse is 37.6. Find the angle between these two sides.

Solution

Using the designations in the triangle shown above, $b = 25.3$ and $c = 37.6$. You are to find $\angle A$. Hence you will use the trigonometric function $\cos A = b/c$, or $\cos A = 25.3/37.6 = 0.673$. From Table 6, Appendix B, the cosine of 47.5° is 0.676 and the cosine of 48.0° is 0.669. The required angle is $3/7 \times 0.5°$, or 0.2°, greater than 47.5°. Thus, $\angle A = 47.7°$.

Example

In a right triangle, one angle is 23.8° and the adjacent side (not the hypotenuse) is 43.2. Find the other side.

Solution

Again using the designations in the above triangle, $\angle A = 23.8°$ and $b = 43.2$. The function involving these values and the unknown side, a, is $\tan A = a/b$. Solving for a: $a = b \tan A$. From Table 6, Appendix B, $\tan 23.8° = 0.441$. Thus, $a = 43.2 \times 0.441 = 19.1$.

4. Sine law and cosine law. For any triangle **ABC**, below, the sine law and the cosine law enable us to calculate the magnitudes of the remaining sides and angles if the magnitudes of one side and of any other two parts are given.

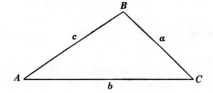

Sine law: $\dfrac{a}{\sin A} = \dfrac{b}{\sin B} = \dfrac{c}{\sin C}$

Cosine law: $a = \sqrt{b^2 + c^2 - 2bc \cos A}$
$b = \sqrt{c^2 + a^2 - 2ca \cos B}$
$c = \sqrt{a^2 + b^2 - 2ab \cos C}$

14. Circles.

The circumference of a circle is $c = \pi d$, where d is the diameter.
The area of a circle is $A = \pi r^2$, where r is the radius.

15. Cylinders.

The volume of a right circular cylinder is $V = \pi r^2 h$, where r is the radius of the base and h is the height.

16. Spheres.

The surface area of a sphere is $A = 4\pi r^2$, where r is the radius.
The volume of a sphere is $V = \frac{4}{3}\pi r^3$, where r is the radius.

17. Logarithms.

The common logarithm of a number is the exponent or the power to which 10 must be raised in order to obtain the given number. A logarithm is composed of two parts: the *characteristic*, or integral part; and the *mantissa*, or decimal part. The characteristic of the logarithm *of any whole or mixed number* is one less than the number of digits to the left of its decimal point. The characteristic of the logarithm *of a decimal fraction* is always negative and is numerically one greater than the number of zeros immediately to the right of the decimal point. Mantissas are always positive and are read from tables such as Table 24 in Appendix B. Proportional parts are used when numbers having four significant figures are involved. In determining the mantissa the decimal point in the original number is ignored since its position is indicated by the characteristic.

Logarithms are exponents and follow the laws of exponents:

Logarithm of a product = sum of the logarithms of the factors

Logarithm of a quotient = logarithm of the dividend minus logarithm of the divisor

To find the number whose logarithm is given, determine the digits in the number from the table of mantissas. The characteristic indicates the position of the decimal point.

Example

Find the logarithm of 35.76.

Solution

There are two digits to the left of the decimal point. Therefore the characteristic of the logarithm of 35.76 is one less than two, or 1. To find the mantissa, ignore the decimal point and look up 3576 in Table 24, Appendix B. Read down the *n* column to 35. Follow this row across to the 7 column, where you will find 5527. This is the mantissa of 3570. Similarly, the mantissa for 3580 is 5539. To calculate the mantissa for 3576, take 6/10 of the difference between 5527 and 5539, or 7, and add it to 5527. Thus, the required mantissa is 5534, and the complete logarithm of 35.76 is 1.5534.

Example

Find the logarithm of 0.4692.

Solution

There are no zeros immediately to the right of the decimal point, hence the characteristic of the logarithm of 0.4692 is -1. However, only the characteristic is negative; the mantissa is positive and is found from Table 24, Appendix B, to be 6714. The complete logarithm of 0.4692 may be written as $\bar{1}.6714$, or $0.6714 - 1$, or $9.6714 - 10$.

Example

Find the logarithm of (1) 357,600,000   (2) 0.0000003576

Solution

(1) $357,600,000 = 3.576 \times 10^8$ log = 8.5534

(2) $0.0000003576 = 3.576 \times 10^{-7}$ log = $\bar{7}.5534$, or $0.5534 - 7$, or $3.5534 - 10$

Appendix A—Equations

(The number indicates the section in which the equation is introduced.)

1.9 Mass Density

$$\text{mass density} = \frac{\text{mass}}{\text{volume}}$$

1.14 Mass-Energy Relationship

$$E = mc^2$$

E is energy; *m* is mass; *c* is speed of light.

3.2 Speed

$$\text{Average Speed} = \frac{\text{total path length}}{\text{elapsed time}}$$

3.3 Velocity

$$v_{av} = \frac{s_f - s_i}{t_f - t_i} = \frac{s}{t}$$

v_{av} is average velocity; s_i is initial position at time t_i; s_f is final position at time t_f; *s* is displacement; *t* is time interval.

3.5 Acceleration

$$a_{av} = \frac{v_f - v_i}{t_f - t_i} = \frac{v}{t}$$

a_{av} is average acceleration; v_i is initial velocity at time t_i; v_f is final velocity at time t_f; *v* is change in velocity; *t* is time interval.

3.6 Uniformly Accelerated Motion

$$v_f = v_i + at \quad \text{or} \quad v_f = v_i + gt$$

v_f is final velocity; v_i is initial velocity; *a* is acceleration or *g* is free fall acceleration; *t* is elapsed time.

3.6 Accelerated Motion

$$s = v_i t + \tfrac{1}{2}a(t)^2 \quad \text{or} \quad s = v_i t + \tfrac{1}{2}g(t)^2$$

s is displacement; v_i is initial velocity; *t* is elapsed time; *a* is acceleration or *g* is free fall acceleration.

3.6 Accelerated Motion

$$v_f = \sqrt{v_i^2 + 2as} \quad \text{or} \quad v_f = \sqrt{v_i^2 + 2gs}$$

v_f is final velocity; v_i is initial velocity; *a* is acceleration or *g* is free fall acceleration; *s* is displacement.

3.9 Newton's Second Law of Motion

$$F = ma$$

F is force; *m* is mass; *a* is acceleration.

3.9 Force and Acceleration on Bodies of Known Weight

$$F = \frac{F_w a}{g}$$

F is force; F_w is weight; *a* is acceleration; *g* is free fall acceleration.

3.9 Weight and Mass

$$F_w = mg$$

F_w is weight; *m* is mass; *g* is free fall acceleration.

3.11 Law of Universal Gravitation

$$F = \frac{G\, m_1 m_2}{s^2}$$

F is force of attraction; *G* is gravitational constant; m_1 and m_2 are masses of bodies; *s* is distance between their centers of mass.

$$s^2 = \frac{Gm_e}{g}$$

3.12 Acceleration of Gravity

$$g = \frac{Gm_e}{s^2}$$

g is free fall acceleration; G is gravitational constant; m_e is mass of earth; s is distance from center of earth.

4.5 Composition of Forces – The resultant of two forces acting at an angle of between 0° and 180° upon a given point is equal to the diagonal of a parallelogram of which the two force vectors are sides. The equilibrant force has a magnitude equal to that of the resultant of the separate forces, but it acts in the opposite direction.

4.9 Coefficient of Friction

$$\mu = \frac{F_f}{F_N}$$

μ is coefficient of friction; F_f is force needed to overcome friction; F_N is force normal to surface.

5.2 Centripetal Force

$$\text{Centripetal Force} = \frac{mv^2}{r}$$

m is mass; v is velocity; r is radius of path.

5.3 Motion in Vertical Circle

$$v_{min} = \sqrt{rg}$$

v_{min} is critical velocity; r is radius of vertical circle; g is free fall acceleration.

5.6 Angular Velocity

$$\omega = \frac{\theta}{t}$$

ω is angular velocity; θ is angular displacement; t is time.

5.7 Angular Acceleration

$$\alpha = \frac{\omega}{t}$$

α is angular acceleration; ω is angular velocity; t is time.

5.7 Accelerated Rotary Motion

$$\omega_f = \omega_i + \alpha t$$
$$\theta = \omega_i t + \tfrac{1}{2}\alpha t^2$$
$$\omega_f = \sqrt{\omega_i^2 + 2\alpha\theta}$$

ω_f is final angular velocity; ω_i is initial angular velocity; α is angular acceleration; t is time; θ is angular displacement.

5.8 Rotational Inertia

$$T = I\alpha$$

T is torque; I is rotational inertia; α is angular acceleration.

5.8 Torque

$$T = Fr$$

T is torque; F is tangential force; r is distance from pivot point to point of application of force.

5.12 Pendulum

$$T:T' = \sqrt{l}:\sqrt{l'}$$

T is period of first pendulum; T' is period of second pendulum; l is length of first pendulum; l' is length of second pendulum.

5.12 Pendulum

$$T = 2\pi\sqrt{\frac{l}{g}}$$

T is period; l is length; g is free fall acceleration.

6.1 Work

$$W = Fs$$

W is work; F is force; s is displacement.

6.3 Work (Rotary Motion)

$$W = T\theta$$

W is work; T is torque; θ is angular displacement.

6.4 Power

$$P = \frac{Fs}{t}$$

P is power; F is force; s is displacement; t is time.

6.5 Power (Rotary Motion)

$$P = T\omega$$

P is power; T is torque; ω is angular velocity.

6.6 Gravitational Potential Energy

$$E_p = mgh$$

E_p is gravitational potential energy; m is mass; g is free fall acceleration; h is vertical distance.

6.7 Kinetic Energy

$$E_K = \tfrac{1}{2}mv^2$$

E_K is kinetic energy; m is mass; v is velocity.

6.7 Kinetic Energy (Rotary Motion)

$$E_K = \tfrac{1}{2}I\omega^2$$

E_K is kinetic energy; I is rotational inertia; ω is angular velocity.

6.9 Potential Energy (Elastic)

$$E_p = \tfrac{1}{2}ks^2$$

E_p is potential energy; k is elastic constant; s is displacement.

6.12 Efficiency

$$\text{Efficiency} = \frac{W_{out}}{W_{in}}$$

W_{out} is work output; W_{in} is work input.

6.13 Impulse and Change of Momentum

$$Ft = mv$$

F is force; t is elapsed time; the product Ft is impulse; m is mass; v is change of velocity; the product mv is the change of momentum.

6.15 Elastic Collisions in One Dimension

$$mv_i + m'v_i' = mv_f + m'v_f'$$

m is mass of first body, v_i its initial velocity, v_f its final velocity; m' is mass of second body, v_i' its initial velocity, v_f' its final velocity.

6.16 Angular Impulse and Change of Angular Momentum

$$Tt = I\omega_f - I\omega_i$$

T is torque; t is elapsed time; the product Tt is angular impulse; I is moment of inertia; ω_f is final angular velocity; ω_i is initial angular velocity; the product $I\omega$ is angular momentum.

7.9 Hooke's Law

$$Y = \frac{Fl}{lA}$$

Y is Young's modulus; F is distorting force; l is original length; l is change in length; A is cross-sectional area.

8.3 Kelvin Temperature

$$°K = °C + 273°$$

$°K$ is Kelvin temperature; $°C$ is Celsius temperature.

8.5 Heat Capacity

$$\text{heat capacity} = Q/\Delta T$$

Q is quantity of heat; ΔT is change in temperature.

8.6 Specific Heat

$$c = \frac{Q}{m\,\Delta T}$$

c is specific heat; Q is quantity of heat; m is mass of material; ΔT is change in temperature.

8.7 Heat Exchange

$$Q_1 = Q_g$$

Q_1 is heat lost; Q_g is heat gained.

8.8 Linear Expansion

$$\Delta l = \alpha l\,\Delta T$$

Δl is change in length; α is coefficient of linear expansion; l is original length; ΔT is change in temperature.

8.9 Volume Expansion

$$\Delta V = \beta V\,\Delta T$$

ΔV is change in volume; β is coefficient of volume expansion; V is original volume; ΔT is change in temperature.

8.11 Charles' Law

$$\frac{V}{T_K} = \frac{V'}{T_K'}$$

V is original volume; T_K is original Kelvin temperature; V' is new volume; T_K' is new Kelvin temperature; provided pressure is constant.

8.12 Boyle's Law

$$pV = p'V'$$

p is original pressure; V is original volume; p' is new pressure; V' is new volume; provided pressure is constant.

8.12 Variation of Gas Density with Pressure

$$\frac{D}{D'} = \frac{p}{p'}$$

D is gas density at pressure p; D' is gas density at pressure p'.

8.13 Boyle's and Charles' Laws Combined

$$\frac{PV}{T_K} = \frac{p'V'}{T_K'}$$

p, V, and T_K are original pressure, volume, and Kelvin temperature, respectively; p', V', and T_K' are new pressure, volume, and Kelvin temperature, respectively.

9.1 Mechanical Equivalent of Heat

$$W = JQ$$

W is work; J is mechanical equivalent of heat; Q is heat.

9.6 Ideal Heat Engine Efficiency

$$\text{Efficiency} = \frac{T_1 - T_2}{T_1} \times 100\%$$

T_1 is input Kelvin temperature; T_2 is exhaust Kelvin temperature.

9.7 Change in Entropy

$$\Delta S = \Delta Q / T$$

ΔS is change in entropy; ΔQ is heat added or removed; T is absolute temperature.

10.6 Wave Formula

$$v = f\lambda$$

v is wave speed; f is frequency; λ is wavelength.

11.7 Intensity Level

$$\beta = 10 \log\frac{I}{I_0}$$

β is intensity level in db; I is intensity of sound; I_0 is intensity of threshold of hearing.

11.9 Doppler effect

1. Source moving toward stationary listener.

$$f_{LF} = f_s\frac{v}{v - v_s}$$

2. Source moving away from stationary listener.

$$f_{LB} = f_s\frac{v}{v + v_s}$$

3. Listener moving toward stationary source.

$$f_{LC} = f_s\frac{v + v_{LC}}{v}$$

4. Listener moving away from stationary source.

$$f_{LO} = f_s\frac{v - v_{LO}}{v}$$

f_{LF}, f_{LB}, f_{LC}, f_{LO} represent frequency of sound reaching the listener in the different listener-source conditions stated; f_s is the frequency of the source; v is the velocity of sound in the medium; v_s is the velocity of the source; v_{LC} is the closing velocity of the listener; v_{LO} is the opening velocity of the listener.

11.13 Laws of Strings

1. Law of Lengths

$$\frac{f}{f'} = \frac{l'}{l}$$

f and f' are frequencies corresponding to lengths l and l'.

2. Law of Diameters

$$\frac{f}{f'} = \frac{d'}{d}$$

f and f' are frequencies corresponding to diameters d and d'.

3. Law of Tensions

$$\frac{f}{f'} = \frac{\sqrt{F}}{\sqrt{F'}}$$

f and f' are frequencies corresponding to tensions F and F'.

4. Law of Densities

$$\frac{f}{f'} = \frac{\sqrt{D'}}{\sqrt{D}}$$

f and f' are frequencies corresponding to densities D and D'.

11.15 Resonance in Tubes

1. Closed Tube

$$\lambda = 4(l + 0.4d)$$

λ is wavelength; l is length of tube; d is diameter of tube.

2. Open Tube

$$\lambda = 2(l + 0.8d)$$

λ is wavelength; l is length of tube; d is diameter of tube.

11.16 Beats

$$f_{av} = \tfrac{1}{2}(f_1 + f_h)$$

f_{av} is difference frequency; f_1 is lower frequency; f_h is higher frequency.

12.9 Photon Energy

1. Energy of Photon

$$E = hf$$

E is energy; h is Planck's constant (6.63×10^{-34} joule sec); f is frequency.

12.10   Photoelectric Equation

$$\tfrac{1}{2}mv^2_{max} = hf - w$$

$\tfrac{1}{2}mv^2_{max}$ is maximum kinetic energy of photoelectrons; h is Planck's constant; f is frequency of im-

pinging radiation; w is work function of emitting material.

12.11 Photon Wavelength

$$\lambda = \frac{h}{mc}$$

λ is photon wavelength; h is Planck's constant; c is velocity of light; mc is photon momentum.

12.11 Wavelength of Particle Having a Velocity v

$$\lambda = \frac{h}{mv}$$

λ is particle wavelength; h is Planck's constant; m is mass of particle; v is velocity; (mv is particle momentum).

12.16 Illumination

1. Uniformly Illuminated Surface

$$E = \frac{\Phi}{A}$$

E is illumination; Φ is luminous flux; A is area uniformly illuminated.

2. Surface Perpendicular to Luminous Flux

$$E = \frac{I}{r^2}$$

E is illumination; I is intensity of source; r is the distance from source to surface perpendicular to the beam.

3. Surface at Any Angle to Luminous Flux

$$E = \frac{I \cos \theta}{r^2}$$

E is illumination; I is intensity of source; θ is the angle which the light beam makes with the normal to the illuminated surface; r is the distance from source to surface.

13.12 Images in Mirrors and Lenses

$$\frac{h_i}{h_o} = \frac{s_i}{s_o}$$

h_o is object size; h_i is image size; s_o is object distance; s_i is image distance.

13.12 Focal Length of Mirrors and Lenses

$$\frac{1}{f} = \frac{1}{s_o} + \frac{1}{s_i}$$

f is focal length; s_o is object distance; s_i is image distance.

14.3 Snell's Law

$$n = \frac{\sin i}{\sin r}$$

n is index of refraction; i is the angle of incidence; r is the angle of refraction.

14.12 Simple Magnifier

$$M = \frac{25 \text{ cm}}{f} \text{ (approx.)}$$

f is focal length of lens in cm.

14.13 Compound Microscope

$$M = \frac{25 \text{ cm} \times l}{f_e \times f_o} \text{ (approx.)}$$

l is length of tube; f_e is focal length of eyepiece lens; f_o is focal length of objective lens in cm.

14.14 Refracting Telescope

$$M = \frac{f_o}{f_e}$$

f_o is focal length of objective lens; f_e is focal length of eyepiece lens.

15.4 Diffraction Grating Equation

$$\lambda = \frac{d \sin \theta_n}{n}$$

λ is wavelength; d is grating constant; θ is diffraction angle; n is the order of image.

16.8 Coulomb's Law of Electrostatics

$$F = k\frac{Q_1 Q_2}{s^2}$$

F is force between two point charges; k is a proportionality constant; Q_1 and Q_2 are the two charges; s is distance separating the charges.

16.10 Potential Difference

$$V = \frac{W}{q}$$

V is potential difference; W is work done in moving a charge; q is quantity of charge moved.

16.14 Capacitance of a Capacitor

$$C = \frac{Q}{V}$$

C is capacitance of a capacitor; Q is charge on either plate; V is potential difference between the plates.

16.17 Capacitors in Parallel

$$C_T = C_1 + C_2 + C_3 + \text{ etc.}$$

C_T is total capacitance; C_1, C_2, C_3, etc. are separate capacitances connected in parallel.

16.17 Capacitors in Series

$$\frac{1}{C_T} = \frac{1}{C_1} + \frac{1}{C_2} + \frac{1}{C_3} + \text{ etc.}$$

C_T is total capacitance; C_1, C_2, C_3, etc. are separate capacitances connected in series.

17.1 Electric Current

$$I = \frac{Q}{t}$$

I is current; Q is quantity of charge; t is time.

17.6 Ohm's Law of Resistance

1. Entire Circuit Including a Source of emf

$$E = IR \quad \text{or} \quad E = IZ$$

E is emf of source; I is current in the circuit; R is resistance of the circuit; Z is impedance of a-c circuit.

2. Any Part of a Circuit That Does Not Include a Source of emf

$$V = IR \quad \text{or} \quad V = IZ$$

V is potential difference across a part of the circuit; I is the current in that part of the circuit; R is the resistance of that part of the circuit; Z is the impedance of that part of an a-c circuit.

17.8 Resistances in Series

$$R_T = R_1 + R_2 + R_3 + \text{etc.}$$

R_T is the total resistance; R_1, R_2, R_3, etc. are separate resistances connected in series.

17.9 Resistances in Parallel

$$\frac{1}{R_{eq}} = \frac{1}{R_1} + \frac{1}{R_2} + \frac{1}{R_3} + \text{etc.}$$

R_{eq} is equivalent resistance; R_1, R_2, R_3, etc. are separate resistances connected in parallel.

17.11 Law of Resistance

$$R = \rho\,\frac{l}{A}$$

R is resistance; ρ is resistivity, a proportionality constant; l is length; A is cross-sectional area.

18.3 Joule's Law

$$Q = \frac{I^2 R t}{J}$$

Q is heat energy; I is current; R is resistance; t is time; J is the mechanical equivalent of heat.

18.4 Electric Power

1. Total Power Consumed in a Circuit

$$P_T = I_T^2 R_T \quad \text{or} \quad P_T = EI \cos \phi$$

P_T is total power; I_T is total current; R_T is total resistance; E is emf; ϕ is phase angle between current and voltage in an a-c circuit.

2. Power Expended in the Circuit Load

$$P_L = I^2 R_L \quad \text{or} \quad P_L = I^2 Z_L$$

P_L is load power; I is current; R_L is load resistance; Z_L is load impedance of an a-c circuit.

3. Power Dissipated in a Source of emf

$$P_r = I^2 r$$

P_r is power dissipated in the internal resistance of source; I is current; r is internal resistance of source.

18.9 Faraday's Laws of Electrolysis

$$m = zIt$$

m is mass; z is the electrochemical equivalent; I is current; t is time.

20.3 Induced emf *(Coil in a Magnetic Field)*

$$E = -N\frac{\Delta\Phi}{\Delta t}$$

E is induced emf; N is number of turns; $\Delta\Phi/\Delta t$ is the change in flux linkage in a given interval of time.

20.4 Induced emf *(Conductor in a Magnetic Field)*

$$E = Blv$$

E is induced emf; B is flux density of the magnetic field; l is length of conductor; v is velocity of conductor across magnetic field.

20.9 Instantaneous Voltage

$$e = E_{max} \sin \theta$$

e is instantaneous voltage; E_{max} is maximum voltage; θ is displacement angle, the angle between the plane of the conducting loop and the perpendicular to the magnetic flux.

20.9 Instantaneous Current

$$i = I_{max} \sin \theta$$

i is instantaneous current; I_{max} is maximum current; θ is displacement angle, the angle between the plane of the conducting loop and the perpendicular to the magnetic flux.

20.14 The Motor Effect

$$\text{Torque} = Fw \cos \alpha$$

F is magnetic force acting on either conductor of loop; w is width of conducting loop; α is the angle between the plane of the loop and the magnetic flux.

20.18 Mutual Inductance

$$M = \frac{-E_S}{\Delta I_P/\Delta t}$$

M is mutual inductance; E_S is average induced emf across the secondary; $\Delta I_P/\Delta t$ is time rate of change of current in the primary.

20.19 Self-inductance

$$L = \frac{-E}{\Delta I / \Delta t}$$

L is self-inductance; E is the average emf induced across the coil; $\Delta I / \Delta t$ is time rate of change of current in the coil.

20.20 Inductors in Series

1. No Mutual Inductance Between Inductors

$$L_T = L_1 + L_2 \pm 2M$$

L_T is total inductance; L_1, L_2, L_3, etc. are separate inductances connected in series.

2. Mutual Inductance Between Two Inductors

$$L_T = L_1 + L_2 + 2M$$

L_T is total inductance; L_1 and L_2 are inductances connected in series; M is mutual inductance between them.

20.20 Inductors in Parallel

$$\frac{1}{L_T} = \frac{1}{L_1} + \frac{1}{L_2} + \frac{1}{L_3} + \text{etc.}$$

L_T is total inductance; L_1, L_2, L_3, etc. are separate inductances connected in parallel so that each is unaffected by the magnetic field of the other.

20.21 Transformer

1. Voltage Ratio

$$\frac{V_S}{V_P} = \frac{N_S}{N_P}$$

V_S and V_P are secondary and primary terminal voltages; N_S/N_P is the turns ratio, secondary to primary.

2. Current Ratio

$$\frac{I_P}{I_S} = \frac{N_S}{N_P}$$

I_P and I_S are primary and secondary currents; N_S/N_P is the turns ratio, secondary to primary.

21.5 Power Factor

$$\text{pf} = \cos\phi$$

pf is power factor; ϕ is phase angle between voltage and current.

21.6 Inductive Reactance

$$X_L = 2\pi f L$$

X_L is inductive reactance; f is frequency; L is inductance.

21.8 Capacitive Reactance

$$X_C = \frac{1}{2\pi f C}$$

X_C is capacitive reactance; f is frequency; C is capacitance.

21.9 Impedance

$$Z = \sqrt{R^2 + X^2} \; \underline{|\arctan X/R}$$

Z is impedance; R is resistance; X is reactance $(X_L - X_C)$.

21.11 Transformer Impedance Ratio

$$\frac{Z_S}{Z_P} = \left(\frac{N_S}{N_P}\right)^2$$

Z_S and Z_P are secondary and primary impedances; N_S/N_P is the turns ratio, secondary to primary.

21.14 Resonance

$$f_r = \frac{1}{2\pi\sqrt{LC}}$$

f_r is resonant frequency; L is inductance; C is capacitance.

22.9 Triode Characteristics

1. Amplification Factor

$$\mu = -\frac{\Delta e_P}{\Delta e_G} \; (i_P \text{ constant})$$

μ is amplification factor; Δe_P is small change in plate voltage; Δe_G is small change in grid voltage.

2. Dynamic Plate Resistance

$$r_P = \frac{\Delta e_P}{\Delta i_P} \; (e_G \text{ constant})$$

r_P is plate resistance; Δe_P is small change in plate voltage; Δi_P is small change in plate current.

3. Transconductance

$$g_m = \frac{\Delta i_P}{\Delta e_G} \quad (e_P \text{ constant})$$

g_m is transconductance; Δi_P is small change in plate current; Δe_G is small change in grid voltage.

22.23 Transistor Characteristics

1. Current gain, common-base circuit

$$\alpha = \frac{\Delta I_C}{\Delta I_E} \quad (V_{CB} \text{ constant})$$

α is current gain; ΔI_C is change in collector current; ΔI_E is change in emitter current.

2. Current gain, common-emitter circuit

$$\beta = \frac{\Delta I_C}{\Delta I_B} \quad (V_{CE} \text{ constant})$$

β is current gain; ΔI_C is change in collector current; ΔI_B is change in base current.

23.13 Mass Number

$$A = Z + N$$

A is mass number of an atom; Z is atomic number; N is number of neutrons.

24.5 Decay Constant

$$\lambda = \frac{0.693}{T_{1/2}}$$

λ is decay constant; $T_{1/2}$ is half-life.

25.14 Quantum Mechanics

1. Energy of Electron

$$E = -\frac{me^4}{8\epsilon_0^2 h^2 n^2}$$

E is energy; m is mass; e is electronic charge; ϵ_0 is a constant; h is Planck's constant; n is principal quantum number.

2. Angular Momentum of Electron

$$L = l(l + 1)\frac{h}{2\pi}$$

L is angular momentum; l is angular momentum quantum number; h is Planck's constant.

Appendix B—Tables

Contents

Table 1 PREFIXES OF THE METRIC SYSTEM

Factor	Prefix	Symbol
10^{12}	tera	T
10^{9}	giga	G
10^{6}	mega	M
10^{3}	kilo	k
10^{2}	hecto	h
10	deka	da
10^{-1}	deci	d
10^{-2}	centi	c
10^{-3}	milli	m
10^{-6}	micro	μ
10^{-9}	nano	n
10^{-12}	pico	p
10^{-15}	femto	f
10^{-18}	atto	a

Table 2 GREEK ALPHABET

Greek letter		Greek name	English equivalent	Greek letter		Greek name	English equivalent
A	α	alpha	ä	N	ν	nu	n
B	β	beta	b	Ξ	ξ	xi	ks
Γ	γ	gamma	g	O	o	omicron	o
Δ	δ	delta	d	Π	π	pi	p
E	ϵ	epsilon	e	P	ρ	rho	r
Z	ζ	zeta	z	Σ	σ	sigma	s
H	η	eta	ā	T	τ	tau	t
Θ	θ	theta	th	Υ	υ	upsilon	ü, ōō
I	ι	iota	ē	Φ	ϕ	phi	f
K	κ	kappa	k	X	χ	chi	h
Λ	λ	lambda	l	Ψ	ψ	psi	ps
M	μ	mu	m	Ω	ω	omega	ō

Table 3 SELECTED PHYSICAL QUANTITIES AND MEASUREMENT UNITS

Physical quantity	Quantity symbol	Measurement unit	Unit symbol	Unit dimensions
		Fundamental Units		
length	l	meter	m	m
mass	m	kilogram	kg	kg
time	t	second	sec	sec
electric charge	Q	coulomb	c	c
temperature	T	degree Kelvin	°K	°K
luminous intensity	I	candle	cd	cd
		Derived Units		
acceleration	a	meter per second per second	m/sec²	m/sec²
area	A	square meter	m²	m²
capacitance	C	farad	f	c² sec²/kg m²
density	D	kilogram per cubic meter	kg/m³	kg/m³
electric current	I	ampere	a	c/sec
electric field intensity	$\mathscr{E}$	newton per coulomb	n/c	kg m/c sec²
electric resistance	R	ohm	Ω	kg m²/c²sec
emf	E	volt	v	kg m²/c sec²
energy	E	joule	j	kg m²/sec²
force	F	newton	n	kg m/sec²
frequency	f	hertz	hz	sec⁻¹
heat	Q	joule	j	kg m²/sec²
illumination	E	lumen per square meter	lm/m²	cd sr/m²
inductance	L	henry	h	kg m²/c²

Table 3   SELECTED PHYSICAL QUANTITIES AND MEASUREMENT UNITS (cont'd)

Physical quantity	Quantity symbol	Measurement unit	Unit symbol	Unit dimensions
luminous flux	Φ	lumen	lm	cd sr
magnetic flux	Φ	weber	wb	kg m²/c sec
magnetic flux density	B	weber per square meter	wb/m²	kg/c sec
potential difference	V	volt	v	kg m²/c sec²
power	P	watt	w	kg m²/sec³
pressure	p	newton per square meter	n/m²	kg/m sec²
velocity	v	meter per second	m/sec	m/sec
volume	V	cubic meter	m³	m³
work	W	joule	j	kg m²/sec²

Table 4   PHYSICAL CONSTANTS

Quantity	Symbol	Value
atmospheric pressure, normal	atm	1.01325×10^5 n/m²
atomic mass unit, unified	u	$1.6605655 \times 10^{-27}$ kg
avogadro number	N_A	6.022045×10^{23}/mole
charge to mass ratio for electron	e/m_e	1.7588047×10^{11} c/kg
electron rest mass	m_e	9.109534×10^{-31} kg
		5.4858026×10^{-4} u
electron volt	ev	1.60210×10^{-19} j
electrostatic constant	k	8.987×10^9 n m²/c²
elementary charge	e	$1.6021892 \times 10^{-19}$ c
faraday	f	9.648456×10^4 c/mole
gas constant, universal	R	6.236×10^4 mm cm³/mole °K
		8.2057×10^{-2} l atm/mole °K
		8.3143×10^0 j/mole °K
gravitational acceleration, standard	g	9.80665×10^0 m/sec²
mechanical equivalent of heat	J	4.1868×10^0 j/cal
molar volume of ideal gas at STP	V_m	2.241383×10^1 l/mole
neutron rest mass	m_n	$1.6749543 \times 10^{-27}$ kg
		1.008665012×10^0 u
Planck's constant	h	6.626176×10^{-34} j sec
proton rest mass	m_p	$1.6726485 \times 10^{-27}$ kg
		1.007276470×10^0 u
speed of light in a vacuum	c	2.99792458×10^8 m/sec
speed of sound in air at S.T.P.	v	3.3145×10^2 m/sec
universal gravitational constant	G	6.6720×10^{-11} n m²/kg²

Table 5   CONVERSION FACTORS

LENGTH

$1 \text{ m} = 10^{-3} \text{ km} = 10^2 \text{ cm} = 10^3 \text{ mm} = 10^6 \ \mu\text{m} = 10^9 \text{ nm} = 10^{10} \ \mathring{\text{A}}$

$1 \ \mu = 1 \ \mu\text{m} = 10^{-6} \text{ m} = 10^{-4} \text{ cm} = 10^{-3} \text{ mm} = 10^3 \text{ m}\mu = 10^3 \text{ nm} = 10^4 \ \mathring{\text{A}}$

$1 \text{ m}\mu = 1 \text{ nm} = 10^{-9} \text{ m} = 10^{-7} \text{ cm} = 10^{-6} \text{ mm} = 10 \ \mathring{\text{A}}$

$1 \ \mathring{\text{A}} = 10^{-10} \text{ m} = 10^{-8} \text{ cm} = 10^{-4} \ \mu = 10^{-1} \text{ m}\mu = 10^{-1} \text{ nm}$

AREA

$1 \text{ m}^2 = 10^{-6} \text{ km}^2 = 10^4 \text{ cm}^2 = 10^6 \text{ mm}^2$

VOLUME

$1 \text{ m}^3 = 10^{-9} \text{ km}^3 = 10^3 \text{ l} = 10^6 \text{ cm}^3$

$1 \text{ l} = 10^3 \text{ ml} = 10^3 \text{ cm}^3 = 10^{-3} \text{ m}^3$

ANGULAR

$1° = 1.74 \times 10^{-2} \text{ radian} = 2.78 \times 10^{-3} \text{ revolution}$

$1 \text{ radian} = 57.3° = 1.59 \times 10^{-1} \text{ revolution}$

$1 \text{ revolution} = 360° = 6.28 \text{ radians}$

MASS

$1 \text{ kg} = 10^3 \text{ g} = 10^6 \text{ mg} = 6.02 \times 10^{26} \text{ u}$

$1 \text{ g} = 10^{-3} \text{ kg} = 10^3 \text{ mg} = 6.02 \times 10^{23} \text{ u}$

$1 \text{ u} = 1.66 \times 10^{-24} \text{ g} = 1.66 \times 10^{-21} \text{ mg} = 1.66 \times 10^{-27} \text{ kg}$

TIME

$1 \text{ hr} = 60 \text{ min} = 3.6 \times 10^3 \text{ sec}$

$1 \text{ min} = 60 \text{ sec} = 1.67 \times 10^{-2} \text{ hr}$

$1 \text{ sec} = 1.67 \times 10^{-2} \text{ min} = 2.78 \times 10^{-4} \text{ hr}$

VELOCITY

$1 \text{ km/hr} = 10^3 \text{ m/hr} = 16.7 \text{ m/min} = 2.78 \times 10^{-1} \text{ m/sec}$

$1 \text{ m/min} = 10^2 \text{ cm/min} = 1.67 \times 10^{-2} \text{ m/sec} = 1.67 \text{ cm/sec}$

$1 \text{ m/sec} = 10^{-3} \text{ km/sec} = 3.6 \text{ km/hr} = 10^2 \text{ cm/sec}$

ACCELERATION

$1 \text{ cm/sec}^2 = 10^{-2} \text{ m/sec}^2 = 10^{-5} \text{ km/sec}^2$

$1 \text{ m/sec}^2 = 10^2 \text{ cm/sec}^2 = 10^{-3} \text{ km/sec}^2$

$1 \text{ km/hr/sec} = 10^3 \text{ m/hr/sec} = 2.78 \times 10^{-1} \text{ m/sec}^2 = 2.78 \times 10^1 \text{ cm/sec}^2 = 2.78 \times 10^2 \text{ mm/sec}^2$

FORCE

$1 \text{ n} = 10^5 \text{ dynes}$

$1 \text{ dyne} = 10^{-5} \text{ n}$

PRESSURE

$1 \text{ atm} = 760.00 \text{ mm Hg} = 1.013 \times 10^5 \text{ n/m}^2 = 1.013 \times 10^6 \text{ dynes/cm}^2$

$1 \text{ n/m}^2 = 10 \text{ dynes/cm}^2 = 9.87 \times 10^{-6} \text{ atm}$

ENERGY

$1 \text{ j} = 10^7 \text{ ergs} = 2.39 \times 10^{-1} \text{ cal} = 2.39 \times 10^{-4} \text{ kcal} = 2.78 \times 10^{-7} \text{ kw hr} = 6.25 \times 10^{18} \text{ ev}$

$1 \text{ cal} = 10^{-3} \text{ kcal} = 4.19 \text{ j} = 1.16 \times 10^{-6} \text{ kw hr}$

$1 \text{ kcal} = 10^3 \text{ cal} = 4.19 \times 10^3 \text{ j} = 1.16 \times 10^{-3} \text{ kw hr}$

$1 \text{ ev} = 10^{-6} \text{ Mev} = 1.60 \times 10^{-12} \text{ erg} = 1.60 \times 10^{-19} \text{ j}$

$1 \text{ kw hr} = 10^3 \text{ w hr} = 3.6 \times 10^3 \text{ kw sec} = 3.6 \times 10^6 \text{ w sec} = 8.6 \times 10^5 \text{ cal}$

$1 \text{ w sec} = 2.78 \times 10^{-4} \text{ w hr} = 2.78 \times 10^{-7} \text{ kw hr}$

MASS-ENERGY

$1 \text{ j} = 1.11 \times 10^{-17} \text{ kg} = 1.11 \times 10^{-14} \text{ g} = 6.69 \times 10^9 \text{ u}$

$1 \text{ ev} = 1.07 \times 10^{-9} \text{ u} = 1.78 \times 10^{-33} \text{ g}$

$1 \text{ u} = 1.49 \times 10^{-3} \text{ erg} = 1.49 \times 10^{-10} \text{ j} = 931 \text{ Mev} = 9.31 \times 10^8 \text{ ev}$

$1 \text{ kg} = 9.00 \times 10^{16} \text{ j} = 9.00 \times 10^{23} \text{ ergs}$

Table 6 NATURAL TRIGONOMETRIC FUNCTIONS

Angle (°)	Sine	Cosine	Tangent	Angle (°)	Sine	Cosine	Tangent
0.0	0.000	1.000	0.000				
0.5	0.009	1.000	0.009	23.0	0.391	0.921	0.424
1.0	0.017	1.000	0.017	23.5	0.399	0.917	0.435
1.5	0.026	1.000	0.026	24.0	0.407	0.914	0.445
2.0	0.035	0.999	0.035	24.5	0.415	0.910	0.456
2.5	0.044	0.999	0.044	25.0	0.423	0.906	0.466
3.0	0.052	0.999	0.052	25.5	0.431	0.903	0.477
3.5	0.061	0.998	0.061	26.0	0.438	0.899	0.488
4.0	0.070	0.998	0.070	26.5	0.446	0.895	0.499
4.5	0.078	0.997	0.079	27.0	0.454	0.891	0.510
5.0	0.087	0.996	0.087	27.5	0.462	0.887	0.521
5.5	0.096	0.995	0.096	28.0	0.470	0.883	0.532
6.0	0.104	0.995	0.105	28.5	0.477	0.879	0.543
6.5	0.113	0.994	0.114	29.0	0.485	0.875	0.554
7.0	0.122	0.992	0.123	29.5	0.492	0.870	0.566
7.5	0.131	0.991	0.132	30.0	0.500	0.866	0.577
8.0	0.139	0.990	0.141	30.5	0.508	0.862	0.589
8.5	0.148	0.989	0.149	31.0	0.515	0.857	0.601
9.0	0.156	0.988	0.158	31.5	0.522	0.853	0.613
9.5	0.165	0.986	0.167	32.0	0.530	0.848	0.625
10.0	0.174	0.985	0.176	32.5	0.537	0.843	0.637
10.5	0.182	0.983	0.185	33.0	0.545	0.839	0.649
11.0	0.191	0.982	0.194	33.5	0.552	0.834	0.662
11.5	0.199	0.980	0.204	34.0	0.559	0.829	0.674
12.0	0.208	0.978	0.213	34.5	0.566	0.824	0.687
12.5	0.216	0.976	0.222	35.0	0.574	0.819	0.700
13.0	0.225	0.974	0.231	35.5	0.581	0.814	0.713
13.5	0.233	0.972	0.240	36.0	0.588	0.809	0.726
14.0	0.242	0.970	0.249	36.5	0.595	0.804	0.740
14.5	0.250	0.968	0.259	37.0	0.602	0.799	0.754
15.0	0.259	0.966	0.268	37.5	0.609	0.793	0.767
15.5	0.267	0.964	0.277	38.0	0.616	0.788	0.781
16.0	0.276	0.961	0.287	38.5	0.622	0.783	0.795
16.5	0.284	0.959	0.296	39.0	0.629	0.777	0.810
17.0	0.292	0.956	0.306	39.5	0.636	0.772	0.824
17.5	0.301	0.954	0.315	40.0	0.643	0.766	0.839
18.0	0.309	0.951	0.325	40.5	0.649	0.760	0.854
18.5	0.317	0.948	0.335	41.0	0.656	0.755	0.869
19.0	0.326	0.946	0.344	41.5	0.663	0.749	0.885
19.5	0.334	0.943	0.354	42.0	0.669	0.743	0.900
20.0	0.342	0.940	0.364	42.5	0.676	0.737	0.916
20.5	0.350	0.937	0.374	43.0	0.682	0.731	0.932
21.0	0.358	0.934	0.384	43.5	0.688	0.725	0.949
21.5	0.366	0.930	0.394	44.0	0.695	0.719	0.966
22.0	0.375	0.927	0.404	44.5	0.701	0.713	0.983
22.5	0.383	0.924	0.414	45.0	0.707	0.707	1.000

Table 6   NATURAL TRIGONOMETRIC FUNCTIONS (cont'd)

Angle (°)	Sine	Cosine	Tangent	Angle (°)	Sine	Cosine	Tangent
45.5	0.713	0.701	1.018	68.0	0.927	0.375	2.475
46.0	0.719	0.695	1.036	68.5	0.930	0.366	2.539
46.5	0.725	0.688	1.054	69.0	0.934	0.358	2.605
47.0	0.731	0.682	1.072	69.5	0.937	0.350	2.675
47.5	0.737	0.676	1.091	70.0	0.940	0.342	2.747
48.0	0.743	0.669	1.111	70.5	0.943	0.334	2.824
48.5	0.749	0.663	1.130	71.0	0.946	0.326	2.904
49.0	0.755	0.656	1.150	71.5	0.948	0.317	2.983
49.5	0.760	0.649	1.171	72.0	0.951	0.309	3.078
50.0	0.766	0.643	1.192	72.5	0.954	0.301	3.172
50.5	0.772	0.636	1.213	73.0	0.956	0.292	3.271
51.0	0.777	0.629	1.235	73.5	0.959	0.284	3.376
51.5	0.783	0.622	1.257	74.0	0.961	0.276	3.487
52.0	0.788	0.616	1.280	74.5	0.964	0.267	3.606
52.5	0.793	0.609	1.303	75.0	0.966	0.259	3.732
53.0	0.799	0.602	1.327	75.5	0.968	0.250	3.867
53.5	0.804	0.595	1.351	76.0	0.970	0.242	4.011
54.0	0.809	0.588	1.376	76.5	0.972	0.233	4.165
54.5	0.814	0.581	1.402	77.0	0.974	0.225	4.331
55.0	0.819	0.574	1.428	77.5	0.976	0.216	4.511
55.5	0.824	0.566	1.455	78.0	0.978	0.208	4.705
56.0	0.829	0.559	1.483	78.5	0.980	0.199	4.915
56.5	0.834	0.552	1.511	79.0	0.982	0.191	5.145
57.0	0.839	0.545	1.540	79.5	0.983	0.182	5.396
57.5	0.843	0.537	1.570	80.0	0.985	0.174	5.671
58.0	0.848	0.530	1.600	80.5	0.986	0.165	5.976
58.5	0.853	0.522	1.632	81.0	0.988	0.156	6.314
59.0	0.857	0.515	1.664	81.5	0.989	0.148	6.691
59.5	0.862	0.508	1.698	82.0	0.990	0.139	7.115
60.0	0.866	0.500	1.732	82.5	0.991	0.131	7.596
60.5	0.870	0.492	1.767	83.0	0.992	0.122	8.144
61.0	0.875	0.485	1.804	83.5	0.994	0.113	8.777
61.5	0.879	0.477	1.842	84.0	0.994	0.104	9.514
62.0	0.883	0.470	1.881	84.5	0.995	0.096	10.38
62.5	0.887	0.462	1.921	85.0	0.996	0.087	11.43
63.0	0.891	0.454	1.963	85.5	0.997	0.078	12.71
63.5	0.895	0.446	2.006	86.0	0.998	0.070	14.30
64.0	0.899	0.438	2.050	86.5	0.998	0.061	16.35
64.5	0.903	0.431	2.097	87.0	0.999	0.052	19.08
65.0	0.906	0.423	2.145	87.5	0.999	0.044	22.90
65.5	0.910	0.415	2.194	88.0	0.999	0.035	28.64
66.0	0.914	0.407	2.246	88.5	1.000	0.026	38.19
66.5	0.917	0.399	2.300	89.0	1.000	0.017	57.29
67.0	0.921	0.391	2.356	89.5	1.000	0.009	114.1
67.5	0.924	0.383	2.414	90.0	1.000	0.000	. . .

Table 7   TENSILE STRENGTH OF METALS

Metal	Tensile strength (n/m²)
aluminum wire	2.4×10^8
copper wire, hard drawn	4.8×10^8
iron wire, annealed	3.8×10^8
iron wire, hard drawn	6.9×10^8
lead, cast or drawn	2.1×10^8
plantinum wire	3.5×10^8
silver wire	2.9×10^8
steel (minimum)	2.8×10^8
steel wire (maximum)	$32 \ \ \times 10^8$

Table 8   YOUNG'S MODULUS

Metal	Elastic modulus (n/m²)
aluminum, 99.3%, rolled	6.96×10^{10}
brass	9.02×10^{10}
copper, wire, hard drawn	11.6×10^{10}
gold, pure, hard drawn	7.85×10^{10}
iron, cast	$9.1 \ \times 10^{10}$
iron, wrought	$19.3 \ \times 10^{10}$
lead, rolled	1.57×10^{10}
platinum, pure, drawn	$16.7 \ \times 10^{10}$
silver, hard drawn	7.75×10^{10}
steel, 0.38% C, annealed	$20.0 \ \times 10^{10}$
tungsten, drawn	$35.5 \ \times 10^{10}$

Table 9   RELATIVE DENSITY AND VOLUME OF WATER

The mass of one cm³ of water at 4°C is taken as unity.
The values given are numerically equal to the absolute density in g/ml.

T (°C)	D (g/cm³)	V (cm³/g)	T (°C)	D (g/cm³)	V (cm³/g)
−10	0.99815	1.00186	45	0.99025	1.00985
−5	0.99930	1.00070	50	0.98807	1.01207
0	0.99987	1.00013	55	0.98573	1.01448
+1	0.99993	1.00007	60	0.98324	1.01705
2	0.99997	1.00003	65	0.98059	1.01979
3	0.99999	1.00001	70	0.97781	1.02270
4	1.00000	1.00000	75	0.97489	1.02576
5	0.99999	1.00001	80	0.97183	1.02899
+10	0.99973	1.00027	85	0.96865	1.03237
15	0.99913	1.00087	90	0.96534	1.03590
20	0.99823	1.00177	95	0.96192	1.03959
25	0.99707	1.00294	100	0.95838	1.04343
30	0.99567	1.00435	110	0.9510	1.0515
35	0.99406	1.00598	120	0.9434	1.0601
40	0.99224	1.00782	150	0.9173	1.0902

Table 10   SURFACE TENSION OF VARIOUS LIQUIDS

Liquid	In contact with	Temp. (°C)	Surface tension (n/m)
carbon disulfide	vapor	20	3.233×10^{-2}
carbon tetrachloride	vapor	20	2.695×10^{-2}
ethyl alcohol	air	0	2.405×10^{-2}
ethyl alcohol	vapor	20	2.275×10^{-2}
water	air	20	7.275×10^{-2}

Table 11   MASS DENSITY OF GASES

($T = 0°C$; $p = 760$ mm Hg)

Gas	Formula	Density (g/l)
acetylene	C_2H_2	1.17910
air, dry, CO_2 free		1.29284
ammonia	NH_3	0.77126
argon	Ar	1.78364
chlorine	Cl_2	3.214
carbon dioxide	CO_2	1.9769
carbon monoxide	CO	1.25004
ethane	C_2H_6	1.3562
helium	He	0.17846
hydrogen	H_2	0.08988
hydrogen chloride	HCl	1.6392
methane	CH_4	0.7168
neon	Ne	0.89990
nitrogen	N_2	1.25036
oxygen	O_2	1.42896
sulfur dioxide	SO_2	2.9262

Table 12   EQUILIBRIUM VAPOR PRESSURE OF WATER

Temp. (°C)	Pressure (mm Hg)	Temp. (°C)	Pressure (mm Hg)	Temp. (°C)	Pressure (mm Hg)
0	4.6	25	23.8	90	525.8
5	6.5	26	25.2	95	633.9
10	9.2	27	26.7	96	657.6
15	12.8	28	28.3	97	682.1
16	13.6	29	30.0	98	707.3
17	14.5	30	31.8	99	733.2
18	15.5	35	42.2	100	760.0
19	16.5	40	55.3	101	787.5
20	17.5	50	92.5	103	845.1
21	18.7	60	149.4	105	906.1
22	19.8	70	233.7	110	1074.6
23	21.1	80	355.1	120	1489.1
24	22.4	85	433.6	150	3570.5

Table 13 HEAT CONSTANTS

Material	Specific heat (cal/g C°)	Melting point (°C)	Boiling point (°C)	Heat of fusion (cal/g)	Heat of vaporization (cal/g)
alcohol, ethyl	0.581 (25°)	−115	78.5	24.9	204
aluminum	0.214 (20°)	660.2	2467	94	2520
	0.217 (0–100°)				
	0.220 (20–100°)				
	0.225 (100°)				
ammonia, liquid	1.047 (−60°)	−77.7	−33.35	108.1	327.1
liquid	1.125 (20°)				
gas	0.523 (20°)				
brass (40% Zn)	0.0917	900			
copper	0.0924	1083	2595	49.0	1150
glass, crown	0.161				
iron	0.1075	1535	3000	7.89	1600
lead	0.0305	327.5	1744	5.47	207
mercury	0.0333	−38.87	356.58	2.82	70.613
platinum	0.0317	1769	3827 ± 100	27.2	
silver	0.0562	960.8	2212	26.0	565
tungsten	0.0322	3410 ± 10	5927	43	
water	1.00		100.00		538.7
ice	0.530	0.00		79.71	
steam	0.481				
zinc	0.0922	419.4	907	23.0	420

Table 14 COEFFICIENT OF LINEAR EXPANSION

(Increase in length per unit length per Celsius degree)

Material	Coefficient ($\Delta l/l$ C°)	Temperature (°C)	Material	Coefficient ($\Delta l/l$ C°)	Temperature (°C)
aluminum	23.8 × 10⁻⁶	20–100	invar (nickel steel)	0.9 × 10⁻⁶	20
brass	19.30 × 10⁻⁶	0–100	lead	29.40 × 10⁻⁶	18–100
copper	16.8 × 10⁻⁶	25–100	magnesium	26.08 × 10⁻⁶	18–100
glass, tube	8.33 × 10⁻⁶	0–100	platinum	8.99 × 10⁻⁶	40
crown	8.97 × 10⁻⁶	0–100	rubber hard	8̄0 × 10⁻⁶	20–60
pyrex	3.3 × 10⁻⁶	20–300	quartz, fused	0.546 × 10⁻⁶	0–800
gold	14.3 × 10⁻⁶	16–100	silver	18.8 × 10⁻⁶	20
ice	50.7 × 10⁻⁶	−10–0	tin	26.92 × 10⁻⁶	18–100
iron, soft	12.10 × 10⁻⁶	40	zinc	26.28 × 10⁻⁶	10–100
steel	10.5 × 10⁻⁶	0–100			

The coefficient of cubical expansion may be taken as three times the linear coefficient.

Table 15   COEFFICIENT OF VOLUME EXPANSION

(Increase in volume per unit volume per C° at 20° C)

Liquid	Coefficient ($\Delta V/V$ C°)
acetone	14.87×10^{-4}
alcohol, ethyl	11.2×10^{-4}
benzene	12.37×10^{-4}
carbon disulfide	12.18×10^{-4}
carbon tetrachloride	12.36×10^{-4}
chloroform	12.73×10^{-4}
ether	16.56×10^{-4}
glycerol	5.05×10^{-4}
mercury	1.82×10^{-4}
petroleum	9.55×10^{-4}
turpentine	9.73×10^{-4}
water	2.07×10^{-4}

Table 16   HEAT OF VAPORIZATION OF SATURATED STEAM

Temp. (°C)	Pressure (mm Hg)	Heat of vaporization (cal/g)
95	634.0	541.9
96	657.7	541.2
97	682.1	540.6
98	707.3	539.9
99	733.3	539.3
100	760.0	538.7
101	787.5	538.1
102	815.9	537.4
103	845.1	536.8
104	875.1	536.2
105	906.1	535.6
106	937.9	534.9

Table 17   SPEED OF SOUND

Substance	Density (g/l)	Velocity (m/sec)	$\Delta v/\Delta t$ (m/sec C°)
GASES (S.T.P.)			
air, dry	1.293	331.45	0.59
carbon dioxide	1.977	259	0.4
helium	0.178	965	0.8
hydrogen	0.0899	1284	2.2
nitrogen	1.250	334	0.6
oxygen	1.429	316	0.56
LIQUIDS (25°C)	(g/cm³)		
acetone	0.79	1174	
alcohol, ethyl	0.79	1207	
carbon tetrachloride	1.595	926	
glycerol	1.26	1904	
kerosene	0.81	1324	
water, distilled	0.998	1498	
water, sea	1.025	1531	
SOLIDS (thin rods)			
aluminum	2.7	5000	
brass	8.6	3480	
brick	1.8	3650	
copper	8.93	3810	
cork	0.25	500	
glass, crown	2.24	4540	
iron	7.85	5200	
lucite	1.18	1840	
maple (along grain)	0.69	4110	
pine (along grain)	0.43	3320	
steel	7.85	5200	

Table 18 INDEX OF REFRACTION

($\lambda = 5893$ Å; *Temperature* $= 20°C$ *except as noted*)

Material	Refractive index
air, dry (S.T.P.)	1.00029
alcohol, ethyl	1.360
benzene	1.501
calcite	1.6583
	1.4864
canada balsam	1.530
carbon dioxide (S.T.P.)	1.00045
carbon disulfide	1.625
carbon tetrachloride	1.459
diamond	2.4195
glass, crown	1.5172
flint	1.6270
glycerol	1.475
ice	1.310
lucite	1.50
quartz	1.544
	1.553
quartz, fused	1.45845
sapphire (Al_2O_3)	1.7686
	1.7604
water, distilled	1.333
water vapor (S.T.P.)	1.00025

Table 19 ELECTROCHEMICAL EQUIVALENTS

Element	g-at wt (g)	Valence (+ ionic charge)	z (g/c)
aluminum	27.0	3	0.0000932
cadmium	112	2	0.0005824
calcium	40.1	2	0.0002077
chlorine	35.5	1	0.0003674
chromium	52.0	6	0.0000898
chromium	52.0·	3	0.0001797
copper	63.5	2	0.0003294
copper	63.5	1	0.0006558
gold	197	3	0.0006812
gold	197	1	0.0020435
hydrogen	1.01	1	0.0000104
lead	207	4	0.0005368
lead	207	2	0.0006150
magnesium	24.3	2	0.0001260
nickel	58.7	2	0.0003041
oxygen	16.0	2	0.0000829
potassium	39.1	1	0.0004051
silver	108	1	0.0011179
sodium	23.0	1	0.0002383
tin	119	4	0.0003075
tin	119	2	0.0006150
zinc	65.4	2	0.0003388

Table 20 RESISTIVITY

(*Temperature* $= 20°$ C)

Material	Resistivity (Ω cm)	Melting point (°C)
advance	48×10^{-6}	1190
aluminum	2.824×10^{-6}	660
brass	7.00×10^{-6}	900
climax	87×10^{-6}	1250
constantan (Cu 60, Ni 40)	49×10^{-6}	1190
copper	1.724×10^{-6}	1083
german silver (Cu 55, Zn 25, Ni 20)	33×10^{-6}	1100
gold	2.44×10^{-6}	1063
iron	$1\bar{0} \times 10^{-6}$	1535
magnesium	4.6×10^{-6}	651
manganin (Cu 84, Mn 12, Ni 4)	44×10^{-6}	910
mercury	95.783×10^{-6}	−39
monel metal	42×10^{-6}	1300
nichrome	115×10^{-6}	1500
nickel	7.8×10^{-6}	1452
nickel silver (Cu 57, Ni 43)	49×10^{-6}	1190
plantinum	$1\bar{0} \times 10^{-6}$	1769
silver	1.59×10^{-6}	961
tungsten	5.6×10^{-6}	3410

Table 21 PROPERTIES OF COPPER WIRE

(*Temperature*, 20°C)

Gauge number	Diameter (mm)	Cross section (mm²)	Resistance (Ω/km)	(m/Ω)
	American Wire Gauge (B&S)—for any metal		for copper only	
			Resistance	
0000	11.68	107.2	0.1608	6219
000	10.40	85.03	0.2028	4932
00	9.266	67.43	0.2557	3911
0	8.252	53.48	0.3224	3102
1	7.348	42.41	0.4066	2460
2	6.544	33.63	0.5027	1951
3	5.827	26.67	0.6465	1547
4	5.189	21.15	0.8152	1227
5	4.621	16.77	1.028	972.9
6	4.115	13.30	1.296	771.5
7	3.665	10.55	1.634	611.8
8	3.264	8.366	2.061	485.2
9	2.906	6.634	2.599	384.8
10	2.588	5.261	3.277	305.1
11	2.305	4.172	4.132	242.0
12	2.053	3.309	5.211	191.9
13	1.828	2.624	6.571	152.2
14	1.628	2.081	8.258	120.7
15	1.450	1.650	10.45	95.71
16	1.291	1.309	13.17	75.90
17	1.150	1.038	16.61	60.20
18	1.024	0.8231	20.95	47.74
19	0.9116	0.6527	26.42	37.86
20	0.8118	0.5176	33.31	30.02
21	0.7230	0.4105	42.00	23.81
22	0.6438	0.3255	52.96	18.88
23	0.5733	0.2582	66.79	14.97
24	0.5106	0.2047	84.21	11.87
25	0.4547	0.1624	106.2	9.415
26	0.4049	0.1288	133.9	7.486
27	0.3606	0.1021	168.9	5.922
28	0.3211	0.08098	212.9	4.697
29	0.2859	0.06422	268.5	3.725
30	0.2546	0.05093	338.6	2.954
31	0.2268	0.04039	426.9	2.342
32	0.2019	0.03203	538.3	1.858
33	0.1798	0.02540	678.8	1.473
34	0.1601	0.02014	856.0	1.168
35	0.1426	0.01597	1079	0.9265
36	0.1270	0.01267	1361	0.7347
37	0.1131	0.01005	1716	0.5827
38	0.1007	0.007967	2164	0.4621
39	0.08969	0.006318	2729	0.3664
40	0.07987	0.005010	3441	0.2906

Table 22   THE CHEMICAL ELEMENTS

Name of element	Sym-bol	Atomic number	Atomic weight g/mole	Name of element	Sym-bol	Atomic number	Atomic weight
actinium	Ac	89	[227]	lawrencium	Lr	103	[257]
aluminum	Al	13	26.9815	lead	Pb	82	207.19
americium	Am	95	[243]	lithium	Li	3	6.939
antimony	Sb	51	121.75	lutetium	Lu	71	174.97
argon	Ar	18	39.948	magnesium	Mg	12	24.312
arsenic	As	33	74.9216	manganese	Mn	25	54.9380
astatine	At	85	[210]	mendelevium	Md	101	[256]
barium	Ba	56	137.34	mercury	Hg	80	200.59
berkelium	Bk	97	[249*]	molybdenum	Mo	42	95.94
beryllium	Be	4	9.0122	neodymium	Nd	60	144.24
bismuth	Bi	83	208.980	neon	Ne	10	20.183
boron	B	5	10.811	neptunium	Np	93	[237]
bromine	Br	35	79.904	nickel	Ni	28	58.71
cadmium	Cd	48	112.40	niobium	Nb	41	92.906
calcium	Ca	20	40.08	nitrogen	N	7	14.0067
californium	Cf	98	[251]	nobelium	No	102	[254]
carbon	C	6	12.01115	osmium	Os	76	190.2
cerium	Ce	58	140.12	oxygen	O	8	15.9994
cesium	Cs	55	132.905	palladium	Pd	46	106.4
chlorine	Cl	17	35.453	phosphorus	P	15	30.9738
chromium	Cr	24	51.996	platinum	Pt	78	195.09
cobalt	Co	27	58.9332	plutonium	Pu	94	[242]
copper	Cu	29	63.546	polonium	Po	84	[210*]
curium	Cm	96	[247]	potassium	K	19	39.102
dysprosium	Dy	66	162.50	praseodymium	Pr	59	140.097
einsteinium	Es	99	[254]	promethium	Pm	61	[147*]
erbium	Er	68	167.26	protactinium	Pa	91	[231]
europium	Eu	63	151.96	radium	Ra	88	[226]
fermium	Fm	100	[253]	radon	Rn	86	[222]
fluorine	F	9	18.9984	rhenium	Re	75	186.2
francium	Fr	87	[223]	rhodium	Rh	45	102.905
gadolinium	Gd	64	157.25	rubidium	Rb	37	85.47
gallium	Ga	31	69.72	ruthenium	Ru	44	101.07
germanium	Ge	32	72.59	samarium	Sm	62	150.35
gold	Au	79	196.967	scandium	Sc	21	44.956
hafnium	Hf	72	178.49	selenium	Se	34	78.96
hahnium	Ha	105	[260]	silicon	Si	14	28.086
helium	He	2	4.0026	silver	Ag	47	107.868
holmium	Ho	67	164.930	sodium	Na	11	22.9898
hydrogen	H	1	1.00797	strontium	Sr	38	87.62
indium	In	49	114.82	sulfur	S	16	32.064
iodine	I	53	126.9044	tantalum	Ta	73	180.948
iridium	Ir	77	192.2	technetium	Tc	43	[99*]
iron	Fe	26	55.847	tellurium	Te	52	127.60
krypton	Kr	36	83.80	terbium	Tb	65	158.924
kurchatovium	Ku	104	[257]	thallium	Tl	81	204.37
lanthanum	La	57	138.91				

Table 22 THE CHEMICAL ELEMENTS (cont'd)

Name of element	Sym-bol	Atomic number	Atomic weight	Name of element	Sym-bol	Atomic number	Atomic weight
thorium	Th	90	232.038	vanadium	V	23	50.942
thulium	Tm	69	168.934	xenon	Xe	54	131.30
tin	Sn	50	118.69	ytterbium	Yb	70	173.04
titanium	Ti	22	47.90	yttrium	Y	39	88.905
tungsten	W	74	183.85	zinc	Zn	30	65.37
uranium	U	92	238.03	zirconium	Zr	40	91.22

A value given in brackets denotes the mass number of the isotope of longest known half-life, or for those marked with an asterisk, a better known one. The atomic weights of most of these elements are believed to have no error greater than ±0.5 of the last digit given.

Table 23 MASSES OF SOME NUCLIDES

Element	Symbol	Atomic mass* (u)**	Element	Symbol	Atomic mass* (u)**
hydrogen	$^{1}_{1}$H	1.007825	sodium	$^{23}_{11}$Na	22.98977
deuterium	$^{2}_{1}$H	2.01410	magnesium	$^{24}_{12}$Mg	23.98504
helium	$^{3}_{2}$He	3.01603		$^{25}_{12}$Mg	24.98584
	$^{4}_{2}$He	4.00260		$^{26}_{12}$Mg	25.98259
lithium	$^{6}_{3}$Li	6.01513	chlorine	$^{35}_{17}$Cl	34.96885
	$^{7}_{3}$Li	7.01601		$^{37}_{17}$Cl	36.96590
beryllium	$^{6}_{4}$Be	6.0198	potassium	$^{39}_{19}$K	38.96371
	$^{8}_{4}$Be	8.00531		$^{41}_{19}$K	40.96184
	$^{9}_{4}$Be	9.01219	krypton	$^{95}_{36}$Kr	94.9
boron	$^{10}_{5}$B	10.01294	molybdenum	$^{100}_{42}$Mo	99.9076
	$^{11}_{5}$B	11.00931	silver	$^{107}_{47}$Ag	106.9041
carbon	$^{12}_{6}$C	12.00000		$^{109}_{47}$Ag	108.9047
	$^{13}_{6}$C	13.00335	technetium	$^{137}_{52}$Te	137.0000***
nitrogen	$^{12}_{7}$N	12.0188	barium	$^{138}_{56}$Ba	137.9050
	$^{14}_{7}$N	14.00307	lead	$^{214}_{82}$Pb	213.9982
	$^{15}_{7}$N	15.00011	bismuth	$^{214}_{83}$Bi	213.9972
oxygen	$^{16}_{8}$O	15.99491	polonium	$^{218}_{84}$Po	218.0089
	$^{17}_{8}$O	16.99914	radon	$^{222}_{86}$Rn	222.0175
	$^{18}_{8}$O	17.99916	radium	$^{228}_{88}$Ra	228.0303
fluorine	$^{19}_{9}$F	18.99840	uranium	$^{235}_{92}$U	235.0439
neon	$^{20}_{10}$Ne	19.99244		$^{238}_{92}$U	238.0508
	$^{22}_{10}$Ne	21.99138	plutonium	$^{239}_{94}$Pu	239.0522

*Atomic mass of neutral atom is given.
**1 atomic mass unit (u) = 1.66043×10^{-27} kg.
***Mass not accurately known. Maximum possible value is given.

Table 24 FOUR-PLACE LOGARITHMS

n	0	1	2	3	4	5	6	7	8	9
10	0000	0043	0086	0128	0170	0212	0253	0294	0334	0374
11	0414	0453	0492	0531	0569	0607	0645	0682	0719	0755
12	0792	0828	0864	0899	0934	0969	1004	1038	1072	1106
13	1139	1173	1206	1239	1271	1303	1335	1367	1399	1430
14	1461	1492	1523	1553	1584	1614	1644	1673	1703	1732
15	1761	1790	1818	1847	1875	1903	1931	1959	1987	2014
16	2041	2068	2095	2122	2148	2175	2201	2227	2253	2279
17	2304	2330	2355	2380	2405	2430	2455.	2480	2504	2529
18	2553	2577	2601	2625	2648	2672	2695	2718	2742	2765
19	2788	2810	2833	2856	2878	2900	2923	2945	2967	2989
20	3010	3032	3054	3075	3096	3118	3139	3160	3181	3201
21	3222	3243	3263	3284	3304	3324	3345	3365	3385	3404
22	3424	3444	3464	3483	3502	3522	3541	3560	3579	3598
23	3617	3636	3655	3674	3692	3711	3729	3747	3766	3784
24	3802	3820	3838	3856	3874	3892	3909	3927	3945	3962
25	3979	3997	4014	4031	4048	4065	4082	4099	4116	4133
26	4150	4166	4183	4200	4216	4232	4249	4265	4281	4298
27	4314	4330	4346	4362	4378	4393	4409	4425	4440	4456
28	4472	4487	4502	4518	4533	4548	4564	4579	4594	4609
29	4624	4639	4654	4669	4683	4698	4713	4728	4742	4757
30	4771	4786	4800	4814	4829	4843	4857	4871	4886	4900
31	4914	4928	4942	4955	4969	4983	4997	5011	5024	5038
32	5051	5065	5079	5092	5105	5119	5132	5145	5159	5172
33	5185	5198	5211	5224	5237	5250	5263	5276	5289	5302
34	5315	5328	5340	5353	5366	5378	5391	5403	5416	5428
35	5441	5453	5465	5478	5490	5502	5514	5527	5539	5551
36	5563	5575	5587	5599	5611	5623	5635	5647	5658	5670
37	5682	5694	5705	5717	5729	5740	5752	5763	5775	5786
38	5798	5809	5821	5832	5843	5855	5866	5877	5888	5899
39	5911	5922	5933	5944	5955	5966	5977	5988	5999	6010
40	6021	6031	6042	6053	6064	6075	6085	6096	6107	6117
41	6128	6138	6149	6160	6170	6180	6191	6201	6212	6222
42	6232	6243	6253	6263	6274	6284	6294	6304	6314	6325
43	6335	6345	6355	6365	6375	6385	6395	6405	6415	6425
44	6435	6444	6454	6464	6474	6484	6493	6503	6513	6522
45	6532	6542	6551	6561	6571	6580	6590	6599	6609	6618
46	6628	6637	6646	6656	6665	6675	6684	6693	6702	6712
47	6721	6730	6739	6749	6758	6767	6776	6785	6794	6803
48	6812	6821	6830	6839	6848	6857	6866	6875	6884	6893
49	6902	6911	6920	6928	6937	6946	6955	6964	6972	6981
50	6990	6998	7007	7016	7024	7033	7042	7050	7059	7067
51	7076	7084	7093	7101	7110	7118	7126	7135	7143	7152
52	7160	7168	7177	7185	7193	7202	7210	7218	7226	7235
53	7243	7251	7259	7267	7275	7284	7292	7300	7308	7316
54	7324	7332	7340	7348	7356	7364	7372	7380	7388	7396

Table 24 FOUR-PLACE LOGARITHMS (cont'd)

n	0	1	2	3	4	5	6	7	8	9
55	7404	7412	7419	7427	7435	7443	7451	7459	7466	7474
56	7482	7490	7497	7505	7513	7520	7528	7536	7543	7551
57	7559	7566	7574	7582	7589	7597	7604	7612	7619	7627
58	7634	7642	7649	7657	7664	7672	7679	7686	7694	7701
59	7709	7716	7723	7731	7738	7745	7752	7760	7767	7774
60	7782	7789	7796	7803	7810	7818	7825	7832	7839	7846
61	7853	7860	7868	7875	7882	7889	7896	7903	7910	7917
62	7924	7931	7938	7945	7952	7959	7966	7973	7980	7987
63	7993	8000	8007	8014	8021	8028	8035	8041	8048	8055
64	8062	8069	8075	8082	8089	8096	8102	8109	8116	8122
65	8129	8136	8142	8149	8156	8162	8169	8176	8182	8189
66	8195	8202	8209	8215	8222	8228	8235	8241	8248	8254
67	8261	8267	8274	8280	8287	8293	8299	8306	8312	8319
68	8325	8331	8338	8344	8351	8357	8363	8370	8376	8382
69	8388	8395	8401	8407	8414	8420	8426	8432	8439	8445
70	8451	8457	8463	8470	8476	8482	8488	8494	8500	8506
71	8513	8519	8525	8531	8537	8543	8549	8555	8561	8567
72	8573	8579	8585	8591	8597	8603	8609	8615	8621	8627
73	8633	8639	8645	8651	8657	8663	8669	8675	8681	8686
74	8692	8698	8704	8710	8716	8722	8727	8733	8739	8745
75	8751	8756	8762	8768	8774	8779	8785	8791	8797	8802
76	8808	8814	8820	8825	8831	8837	8842	8848	8854	8859
77	8865	8871	8876	8882	8887	8893	8899	8904	8910	8915
78	8921	8927	8932	8938	8943	8949	8954	8960	8965	8971
79	8976	8982	8987	8993	8998	9004	9009	9015	9020	9025
80	9031	9036	9042	9047	9053	9058	9063	9069	9074	9079
81	9085	9090	9096	9101	9106	9112	9117	9122	9128	9133
82	9138	9143	9149	9154	9159	9165	9170	9175	9180	9186
83	9191	9196	9201	9206	9212	9217	9222	9227	9232	9238
84	9243	9248	9253	9258	9263	9269	9274	9279	9284	9289
85	9294	9299	9304	9309	9315	9320	9325	9330	9335	9340
86	9345	9350	9355	9360	9365	9370	9375	9380	9385	9390
87	9395	9400	9405	9410	9415	9420	9425	9430	9435	9440
88	9445	9450	9455	9460	9465	9469	9474	9479	9484	9489
89	9494	9499	9504	9509	9513	9518	9523	9528	9533	9538
90	9542	9547	9552	9557	9562	9566	9571	9576	9581	9586
91	9590	9595	9600	9605	9609	9614	9619	9624	9628	9633
92	9638	9643	9647	9652	9657	9661	9666	9671	9675	9680
93	9685	9689	9694	9699	9703	9708	9713	9717	9722	9727
94	9731	9736	9741	9745	9750	9754	9759	9763	9768	9773
95	9777	9782	9786	9791	9795	9800	9805	9809	9814	9818
96	9823	9827	9832	9836	9841	9845	9850	9854	9859	9863
97	9868	9872	9877	9881	9886	9890	9894	9899	9903	9908
98	9912	9917	9921	9926	9930	9934	9939	9943	9948	9952
99	9956	9961	9965	9969	9974	9978	9983	9987	9991	9996

Glossary

abscissa. The value corresponding to the horizontal distance of a point on a graph from the Y axis. The X coordinate.

absolute zero. The temperature of a body that is incapable of giving up any thermal energy; $0°K$ or $-273.15°C$.

absorption spectrum. A continuous spectrum interrupted by dark lines or bands which are characteristic of the medium through which the radiation has passed.

acceleration. Time rate of change of velocity.

acceleration, angular. Time rate of change of angular velocity.

acceleration, centripetal. Acceleration directed toward the center of a circular path.

acceptor. An element with three valence electrons per atom which when added to a semiconductor crystal, provides electron "holes" in the lattice structure of the crystal.

accuracy. Closeness of a measurement to the accepted value for a specific physical quantity; expressed as absolute or relative error.

adhesion. The force of attraction between unlike molecules.

adiabatic process. A thermal process in which no heat is added to or removed from a system.

alpha (α) particle. A helium-4 nucleus, especially when emitted from the nucleus of a radioactive atom.

alternating current. An electric current which has one direction during one part of a generating cycle and the opposite direction during the remainder of the cycle.

ammeter. An electric meter designed to measure current.

amorphous. Having a random arrangement of particles; noncrystalline.

ampere. The unit of current in the MKS system, one coulomb per second.

amplification factor. A vacuum-tube constant equal to the ratio of a small change in plate voltage to a small change in grid voltage of the opposite sense, which maintains a constant plate current.

amplifier. A device consisting of one or more vacuum tubes (or transistors) and associated circuits, used to increase the strength of a signal.

amplitude. The maximum displacement of a vibrating particle from its equilibrium position.

angle of incidence. The angle between the incident ray and the normal drawn to the point of incidence.

angle of reflection. See *reflection, angle of.*

angle of refraction. See *refraction, angle of.*

Ångström. A unit of linear measure equal to 10^{-10} m.

angular acceleration. See *acceleration, angular.*

angular impulse. See *impulse, angular.*

angular momentum. See *momentum, angular.*

angular velocity. See *velocity, angular.*

anode. (1) The positive electrode of an electric cell. (2) The positive electrode or plate of an electronic tube. (3) The electron-poor electrode.

antimatter. A substance composed of anti-particles.

antiparticle. A counterpart of a subatomic particle having opposite properties (except for equal masses).

aperture. Any opening through which radiation may pass. The diameter of an opening that admits light to a lens or mirror.

apparent power. See *power, apparent.*

armature. A coil of wire formed around an iron or steel core which rotates in the magnetic field of a generator or motor.

atom. The smallest particle of an element that can exist either alone or in combination with others of the same or other elements.

atomic mass unit. One-twelfth of the mass of carbon-12, or $1.6605655 \times 10^{-27}$ kg.

atomic number. The number of protons in the nucleus of an atom.

atomic weight. See *weight, atomic.*

atto-. Metric system prefix, 10^{-18}.

audio signal. The alternating voltage proportional to the sound pressure produced in an electric circuit.

back emf. An induced emf in the armature of a motor which opposes the applied voltage.

band spectrum. An emission spectrum consisting of fluted bands of color. The spectrum of a substance in the molecular state.

barometer. A device used to measure the pressure of the atmosphere.

baryon. A subatomic particle with a large rest mass, e.g., the proton.

beam. Several parallel rays of light considered collectively.

beat. The interference effect resulting from the superposition of two waves of slightly different frequencies propagating in the same direction. The resultant wave is characterized by an amplitude which varies with time.

beta (β) particle. An electron emitted from the nucleus of a radioactive atom.

betatron. A device which accelerates electrons by means of the transformer principle.

binding energy. See *energy, binding.*

boiling. Rapid vaporization which disturbs a liquid and which occurs when the vapor pressure of the liquid equals the pressure on its surface.

boiling point. The temperature at which the vapor pressure of a liquid equals the pressure of the atmosphere. If the pressure on the liquid varies, the boiling point varies.

boson. A subatomic particle with zero charge and rest mass, e.g., the photon.

Boyle's law. See *law, Boyle's.*

breeder reactor. A nuclear reactor in which one fissionable material is produced at a greater rate than the fuel is consumed.

Brownian movement. The irregular and random movement of small particles suspended in a fluid, known to be a consequence of the thermal motion of fluid molecules.

bubble chamber. Instrument used for making the paths of ionizing particles visible as a trail of tiny bubbles in a liquid.

calorie. The quantity of heat equal to 4.19 joules.

candle. The unit of luminous intensity of a light source.

capacitance. The ratio of the charge on either plate of a capacitor to the potential difference between the plates.

capacitive reactance. See *reactance, capacitive.*

capacitor. A combination of conducting plates separated by layers of a dielectric and used to store an electric charge.

capillarity. The elevation or depression of liquids in small diameter tubes.

cathode. (1) The negative electrode of an electric cell. (2) The electron-emitting electrode of an electronic tube. (3) The electron-rich electrode.

cathode rays. Particles emanating from a cathode; electrons.

Celsius scale. The temperature scale using the ice point as 0 and the steam point as

100, with 100 equal divisions or degrees between.

center of curvature. The center of the sphere of which the mirror or lens surface forms a part.

center of gravity. That point at which all of the weight of a body may be considered to be concentrated.

centi-. Metric system prefix, 10^{-2}.

centigrade scale. The Celsius scale.

centripetal acceleration. See *acceleration, centripetal.*

centripetal force. See *force, centripetal.*

chain reaction. A reaction in which the material or energy which starts the reaction is also one of the products and can cause similar reactions.

Charles' law. See *law, Charles'.*

chemical change. A change in which new substances with new properties are formed.

chemical element. One of the simple substances of which matter is composed; a substance which cannot be simplified by chemical means.

chemical equivalent. The quantity of an element expressed in grams, equal to the ratio of its atomic weight to its valence.

chromatic aberration. The nonfocusing of light of different colors.

circular motion. See *motion, circular.*

cloud chamber. A device used to detect the passage of charged subatomic particles by the trails of liquid droplets they form in a special chamber.

coefficient of area expansion. The change in area per unit area of a solid when its temperature is changed one degree.

coefficient of cubic expansion. The change in volume per unit volume of a solid or liquid when its temperature is changed one degree.

coefficient of friction. See *friction, coefficient of.*

coefficient of linear expansion. The change in length per unit length of a solid when its temperature is changed one degree.

cohesion. The force of attraction between like molecules.

color. A description of a sensation received through our eyes.

commutator. A split ring in a d-c generator, each segment of which is connected to an end of a corresponding armature loop.

complementary colors. Two colors which combine to form white light.

component. One of the several vectors which can be combined geometrically to yield a resultant vector.

composition of forces. The combining of two or more component forces into a single resultant force.

compression. The region of a longitudinal wave in which the vibrating particles are closer than their equilibrium distance.

concave. Curved inward away from the observer.

concave lens. A lens which diverges parallel light rays (assuming the outside refractive index to be smaller).

concave mirror. A mirror which converges parallel light rays incident on its surface.

concurrent forces. See *forces, concurrent.*

condensation. The change of phase from a gas or vapor to a liquid.

condition. A description of the environment of matter.

conductance. The reciprocal of the ohmic resistance.

conductor. A material through which an electric charge is readily transferred.

conservation of baryons, law of. When a baryon decays or reacts with another particle, the number of baryons is the same on both sides of the equation.

conservation of energy, law of. The total amount of energy of all kinds in a given situation is a constant.

conservation of leptons, law of. In a nuclear reaction involving leptons, the arithmetic sum of the lepton numbers is the same on each side of the equation.

continuous spectrum. A spectrum without

dark lines or bands, or in which there is an uninterrupted change from one color to another.

converging lens. A lens that is thicker in the middle than it is at the edge, and bends incident parallel rays toward a common point.

conversion factor. The ratio between two different units used to describe the same physical quantity.

convex. Curved outward towards the observer.

convex lens. A lens which converges parallel light rays (assuming the outside refractive index to be smaller).

convex mirror. A mirror which diverges parallel light rays incident on its surface.

cosmic rays. High energy particles, apparently originating from beyond our solar system.

coulomb. The quantity of electricity equal to the charge on 6.25×10^{18} electrons.

Coulomb's law for magnetism. The force between two magnetic poles is directly proportional to the strengths of the poles and inversely proportional to the square of their distance apart.

Coulomb's law of electrostatics. See *electrostatics, Coulomb's law of.*

couple. Two forces of equal magnitude acting in opposite directions in the same plane, but not along the same line.

covalent bonding. Bonding between atoms produced by electron sharing.

crest. A region of upward displacement in a transverse wave.

critical angle. That limiting angle of incidence in the optically denser medium which results in an angle of refraction of 90°.

critical mass. The amount of a particular fissionable material required to make a fission reaction self-sustaining.

critical pressure. See *pressure, critical.*

critical temperature. See *temperature, critical.*

crystalline. Having a regular arrangement of particles.

curie. A unit of radioactivity; 3.70×10^{10} nuclear disintegrations per second.

current sensitivity. Current per unit scale division of an electric meter.

curvilinear motion. See *motion, curvilinear.*

cut-off bias. The smallest negative grid voltage, for a given plate voltage, which causes a vacuum tube to cease to conduct.

cut-off frequency. See *frequency, cut-off.*

cut-off potential. A negative potential on the collector of a photoelectric cell which reduces the photoelectric current to zero.

cycle. A series of changes produced in sequence resulting in the system returning periodically to its initial condition.

cyclotron. A device for accelerating charged atomic particles by means of D-shaped electrodes.

damping. The reduction in amplitude of a wave due to the dissipation of wave energy.

decay constant. The ratio between the number of nuclei decaying per second and the total number of nuclei.

deci-. Metric system prefix, 10^{-1}.

decibel. A unit of sound intensity level. The smallest change of sound intensity that the normal human ear can detect.

deka-. Metric system prefix, 10^1.

diamagnetism. The property of a substance whereby it is feebly repelled by a strong magnet.

dichroism. A property of certain crystalline substances in which one polarized component of incident light is absorbed and the other is transmitted.

dielectric. An electric insulator. A nonconducting medium.

dielectric constant. The ratio of the capacitance with a particular material separating the plates of a capacitor to the capacitance with a vacuum between the plates.

diffraction. The spreading of a wave disturbance into a region behind an obstruction.

diffraction angle. The angle that a diffracted wave front forms with the grating plane.

diffraction grating. An optical surface, either transmitting or reflecting, with several thousand equally spaced and parallel grooves ruled in it.

diffusion. (1) The penetration of one type of particle into a mass of a second type of particle. (2) The scattering of light by irregular reflection.

diode. A two-terminal device which will conduct electric current more easily in one direction than in the other.

direct current. An essentially constant-value current in which the movement of charge is in only one direction.

direct proportion. The relation between two quantities whose ratio is a constant.

dispersion. The process of separating polychromatic light into its component wavelengths.

displacement. A change of position in a particular direction.

distillation. The evaporation of volatile materials from a liquid or solid mixture and their condensation in a separate vessel.

distillation, fractional. The process of separating the components of a liquid mixture through differences in their respective boiling points.

distortion. The production of an output wave that is not a true reproduction of the input wave.

disturbance. A displacement of some sort in matter.

diverging lens. A lens that is thicker at the edge than it is in the middle, and bends incident parallel rays so they appear to come from a common point.

domain. A microscopic magnetic region composed of a group of atoms whose magnetic fields are aligned in a common direction.

donor. A substance with five valence electrons per atom which, when added to a semiconductor crystal, provides free electrons in the lattice structure of the crystal.

Doppler effect. The change observed in the frequency with which a wave from a given source reaches an observer when the source and the observer are in relative motion.

double refraction. See *refraction, double*.

drift tubes. Charged cylinders used to accelerate charged subatomic particles in a linear accelerator.

ductility. The property of a metal that enables it to be drawn through a die to produce a wire.

dynamic plate resistance. See *resistance, dynamic plate*.

dyne. A unit of force; the force required to accelerate one gram of mass at the rate of one centimeter per second^2; 10^{-5} newton.

eddy currents. Closed loops of induced current set up in a piece of metal when there is relative motion between the metal and a magnetic field. Eddy currents are in such direction that the resulting magnetic forces tend to stop the relative motion.

Edison effect. The emission of electrons from a heated metal in a vacuum.

effective value of current. The magnitude of an alternating current which, in a given resistance, produces heat at the same average rate as that magnitude of steady direct current.

efficiency. The ratio of the useful work output of a machine to total work input.

elastic limit. The condition in which a substance is on the verge of becoming permanently deformed.

elastic modulus. The ratio of stress to strain.

elasticity. The ability of an object to return to its original size or shape, when the external forces producing distortion are removed.

electric current. The rate of flow of charge past a given point in an electric circuit.

electric field. The region in which a force acts on an electric charge brought into the region.

electric field intensity. See *intensity, electric field.*

electrification. The process of charging a body by adding or removing electrons.

electrochemical cell. A cell in which chemical energy is converted to electric energy by a spontaneous electron-transfer reaction.

electrochemical equivalent. The mass of an element, in grams, deposited by one coulomb of electricity.

electrode. A conducting element in an electric cell, electronic tube, or semiconductor device.

electrodynamometer. A device, similar to a galvanometer movement, in which a moving coil rotates in a magnetic field created by a pair of fixed coils carrying a magnetizing current.

electrolysis. The conduction of electricity through a solution of an electrolyte or through a fused ionic compound, together with the resulting chemical changes.

electrolyte. A substance whose solution conducts an electric current.

electrolytic cell. A cell in which electric energy is converted to chemical energy by means of an electron-transfer reaction.

electromagnetic force. See *force, electromagnetic.*

electromagnetic induction. See *induction, electromagnetic.*

electromagnetic waves. Transverse waves having an electric component and a magnetic component, each being perpendicular to the other and both perpendicular to the direction of propagation.

electromotive force. See *emf.*

electron. A negatively charged subatomic particle, having a rest mass of 9.109534×10^{-31} kg.

electron affinity. The measure of the energy released when an electron is added to a neutral atom.

electron cloud. The aggregate of electrons about the nucleus of an atom.

electron shell. A region about the nucleus of an atom in which electrons move; made up of electron orbitals.

electron volt. See *volt, electron.*

electronics. The branch of physics which is concerned with the emission, behavior, and effects of electrons.

electroscope. A device used to observe the presence of an electrostatic charge.

electrostatics, Coulomb's law of. The force between two point charges is directly proportional to the product of their magnitudes and inversely proportional to the square of the distance between them.

electrostatics, basic law of. Objects that are similarly charged repel each other; those with unlike charges attract each other.

elementary colors. The six regions of color in the solar spectrum observed by the dispersion of sunlight: red, orange, yellow, green, blue, and violet.

elongation strain. The ratio of the increase in length to the unstretched length.

emf. The energy per unit charge supplied by a source of electric current.

emission spectrum. A spectrum formed by the dispersion of light from an incandescent solid, liquid, and gas.

energy. A physical quantity that has the capacity for doing work.

energy, kinetic. The energy due to the motion of an object.

energy level. One of a series of discrete energy values which characterize a physical system governed by quantum rules.

energy, nuclear binding. The energy that must be applied to a nucleus to break it apart.

energy, potential. Energy that is due to the position of a mass.

energy, thermal. The total potential and kinetic energy associated with the random motions of the particles of a material.

entropy. (1) The physical quantity which describes the ability of a system to do work.

(2) That property which describes the disorder of a system.

equilibrant force. See *force, equilibrant.*

equilibrium, rotational. The state of a body in which the sum of all the clockwise torques in a given plane equals the sum of all the counterclockwise torques about a pivot point.

equilibrium, translational. The state of a body in which there are no unbalanced forces acting on it.

equilibrium vapor pressure. See *pressure, equilibrium vapor.*

erg. A unit of work; a force of one dyne acting through a distance of one centimeter; 10^{-7} joule.

evaporation. The change of phase from a liquid to a gas or vapor.

exclusion principle. No two electrons in an atom can have the same set of quantum numbers.

expansion, linear, coefficient of. See *coefficient of linear expansion.*

expansion, cubic, coefficient of. See *coefficient of cubic expansion.*

exponential notation. The use of powers of ten in writing a number; $M \times 10^n$.

"f" number. The ratio of the focal length of a lens to the effective aperture.

farad. The MKS unit of capacitance; one coulomb per volt.

faraday. The quantity of electricity (96,500 coulombs) required to deposit one chemical equivalent of an element.

Faraday's first law. See *law, Faraday's first.*

Faraday's second law. See *law, Faraday's second.*

femto-. Metric system prefix; 10^{-15}.

ferromagnetism. The property of a substance by which it is strongly attracted by a magnet.

field. A region in which certain objects are subject to a force.

field intensity. See *intensity, field.*

fission. The splitting of a heavy nucleus into nuclei of medium mass.

flash tube. The ionization tube that emits the light in a chemical laser.

Fleming valve. First vacuum tube diode.

fluid. A liquid or a gas.

flux. Flow.

focal length. The distance between the principal focus of a lens or mirror and its optical center or vertex.

focus. A point at which light rays meet or from which rays of light diverge.

focus, principal. A point to which rays parallel to the principal axis converge, or from which they diverge, after reflection or refraction.

force. A measure of the momentum gained per second by an accelerating body.

force, centripetal. The force that produces centripetal acceleration.

force, equilibrant. The force which produces equilibrium.

force, gravitational. The mutual force of attraction between particles of matter.

force, line of. A line so drawn that a tangent to it at any point indicates the orientation of the field at that point.

force, magnetic. A force associated with the motion of electric charges.

force, nuclear. The binding force that acts within the small distances between nucleons.

force, resultant. The single force which has the same effect as two or more forces applied simultaneously at the same point.

force, weak. A nuclear force which is responsible for the emission of leptons.

forced vibration. Vibration which is due to the application of a periodic force, and not to the natural vibrations of the system.

forces, concurrent. Forces with lines of action that pass through the same point.

fractional distillation. See *distillation, fractional.*

frame of reference. Any system for specifying the precise location of objects in space.

frame of reference, inertial. A nonaccelerating frame of reference, in which Newton's first law holds true.

freezing point. The temperature at which a liquid changes into a solid.

frequency. Number of vibrations, oscillations, or cycles per unit time.

frequency, cut-off. A characteristic threshold frequency of incident light below which, for a given material, the photoelectric emission of electrons ceases.

friction. A force that resists the relative motion of objects which are in contact with each other.

friction, coefficient of. The ratio of the force needed to overcome friction to the normal force pressing the surfaces together.

fuel cell. An electrochemical cell in which the chemical energy of continuously supplied fuel is converted into electric energy.

fundamental. The lowest frequency produced by a musical tone source. The harmonic component of a wave that has the lowest frequency.

fuse. A safety device consisting of a strip of low-melting-point alloy inserted in an electric circuit to melt and thus open the circuit under an overload condition.

fusion. (1) The change of phase from a solid to a liquid. (2) A reaction in which light nuclei combine to form a nucleus with greater mass.

fusion, heat of. The heat required per unit mass to change a substance from solid to liquid at constant temperature and pressure.

galvanometer. An instrument used to measure minute electric currents.

gamma (γ) ray. See *ray, gamma (γ)*.

gas. The phase of matter in which the average separation of the molecules is comparatively large; it has neither definite volume nor shape.

gas, ideal. A theoretical gas consisting of infinitely small molecules which exert no forces on each other.

Geiger counter. Instrument used for the detection and measurement of radioactivity.

giga-. Metric system prefix, 10^9.

gram. A unit of mass in the metric system; 10^{-3} standard kilogram.

gravitational force. See *force, gravitational*.

graviton. The carrier for the gravitational force.

gravity, force of. The force of gravitational attraction on or near the surface of a celestial body.

grid. An element of an electronic tube; an electrode used to control the flow of electrons from the cathode to the plate.

grid bias. The grid to cathode voltage.

half-life. The length of time during which, on the average, half of a large number of radioactive nuclides decay.

harmonics. The fundamental and the tones whose frequencies are whole number multiples of the fundamental.

harmony. A combination of musical tones which is pleasant to the ears.

heat. Thermal energy in the process of being added to, or removed from, a substance.

heat capacity. The quantity of heat needed to raise the temperature of a body one degree.

heat exchange, law of. In any heat transfer system, the heat lost by hot materials equals the heat gained by cold materials.

heat, mechanical equivalent of. The conversion factor which relates heat units to work units. 4.19 j/cal; 4.19×10^7 erg/cal; 4.19×10^3 j/kcal.

heat of fusion. See *fusion, heat of*.

heat of vaporization. See *vaporization, heat of*.

heat, specific. The heat capacity of a material per unit mass.

hecto-. Metric system prefix, 10^2.

henry. The MKS unit of inductance; one henry of inductance is present in a circuit when a change in the current of 1 ampere per second induces an emf of 1 volt.

Hooke's law. See *law, Hooke's.*

hypothesis. A plausible solution to a problem.

hysteresis. The lagging of the magnetization of ferromagnetic material behind the magnetizing force.

ice point. The temperature of a mixture of pure ice and water exposed to the air at standard atmospheric pressure.

ideal gas. See *gas, ideal.*

illumination. The luminous flux per unit area of a surface.

image. The optical counterpart of an object formed by lenses or mirrors.

image, real. An image which is formed by actual rays of light.

image, virtual. An image which only appears to be formed by rays of light.

impedance. (1) The ratio of applied wave-producing force to resulting displacement velocity of a wave-transmitting medium. (2) The ratio of sound pressure to volume displacement at a given surface in a sound-transmitting medium. (3) The ratio of the effective voltage to the effective current in an a-c circuit.

impedance matching. A technique used to insure maximum transfer of energy from the output of one circuit to the input of another.

impenetrability. The property of matter that prevents two bodies from occupying the same space at the same time.

impulse. The product of a force and the time interval during which it acts.

impulse, angular. The product of a torque and the time interval during which it acts.

index of refraction. See *refraction, index of.*

induced magnetism. Magnetism produced in a ferromagnetic substance by the influence of a magnetic field. Magnetization.

inductance. The property of an electric circuit by which a varying current induces an emf in that circuit or a neighboring circuit.

inductance, mutual. The ratio of the induced emf in one circuit to the rate of change of current in the other.

inductance, self. The ratio of the induced emf across a coil to the rate of change of current in the coil.

induction. The process of charging one body by bringing it into the electric field of another charged body.

induction, electromagnetic. The process by which an emf is set up in a conducting circuit by a changing magnetic flux linked by the circuit.

inductive reactance. See *reactance, inductive.*

inertia. The property of matter that opposes any change in its state of motion.

inertia, rotational. The property of an object that resists changes in its angular momentum when the object is rotating.

inertial frame of reference. See *frame of reference, inertial.*

infrared light. See *light, infrared.*

infrasonic range. Vibrations in matter below 20 cycles/second.

instantaneous current. The magnitude of a varying current at any instant of time.

instantaneous voltage. The magnitude of a varying voltage at any instant of time.

insulator. A material through which an electric charge is not readily transferred.

intensity, sound. The rate at which sound energy flows through a unit area.

intensity, electric field. The force per unit positive charge at a given point in an electric field.

intensity, magnetic field. The force exerted by a magnetic field on a unit N pole situated in the field.

intensity level. The logarithm of the ratio of the intensity of a sound to the intensity of the threshold of hearing.

interference. (1) The superposing of one

wave on another. (2) The mutual effect of two beams of light, resulting in a reduction of energy in certain areas and an increase of energy in others.

inverse photoelectric effect. See *photoelectric effect, inverse.*

inverse proportion. The relation between two quantities whose product is a constant.

ion. An atom or a group of atoms having an electric charge.

ionic bonding. Bonding between atoms produced by electron transfer.

ionization chamber. A device used to detect the passage of charged rays or particles by their ionizing effect on a gas.

ionization energy. The energy required to remove an electron from an atom.

isothermal process. A thermal process which occurs without a change in temperature.

isotopes. Atoms whose nuclei contain the same number of protons but different numbers of neutrons.

joule. The MKS unit of work; the product of a force of one newton acting through a distance of one meter.

Joule's law. See *law, Joule's.*

Kelvin scale. The absolute thermodynamic scale of temperature having a single fixed point, the temperature of the triple point of water, which is assigned the value 273.16° K.

kilo-. Metric system prefix, 10^3.

kilocalorie. Heat energy equal to 4.19×10^3 joules.

kilowatt hour. A unit of electric energy; equal to 3.6×10^6 w sec.

kinetic energy. See *energy, kinetic.*

kinetic theory. See *theory, kinetic.*

Kirchhoff's first law. See *law, Kirchhoff's first.*

Kirchhoff's second law. See *law, Kirchhoff's second.*

law. A statement that describes a natural phenomenon; a principle.

law, Boyle's. The volume of a dry gas varies inversely with the pressure exerted upon it, provided the temperature is constant.

law, Charles'. The volume of a dry gas is directly proportional to its Kelvin temperature, providing the pressure is constant.

law, Faraday's first. The mass of an element deposited during electrolysis is proportional to the quantity of charge that passes through the electrolytic cell.

law, Faraday's second. The mass of an element deposited during electrolysis is proportional to the chemical equivalent of the element.

law for magnetism, Coulomb's. See *Coulomb's law for magnetism.*

law, Hooke's. Within the limits of perfect elasticity, strain is directly proportional to stress.

law, Joule's. The heat developed in a conductor is directly proportional to the resistance of the conductor, the square of the current, and the time the current is maintained.

law, Kirchhoff's first. The algebraic sum of the currents at any circuit junction is equal to zero.

law, Kirchhoff's second. The algebraic sum of all the changes in potential occurring around any loop in a circuit is equal to zero.

law, Lenz's. An induced current is in such direction that its magnetic property opposes the change by which the current is induced.

law of conservation of energy. See *conservation of energy, law of.*

law of electrostatics, Coulomb's. See *electrostatics, Coulomb's law of.*

law of electrostatics, basic. See *electrostatics, basic law of.*

law of heat exchange. See *heat exchange, law of.*

law of parity. See *parity, law of.*

law of universal gravitation, Newton's. See *universal gravitation, Newton's law of.*

law, Ohm's. The ratio of the emf applied to a closed circuit to the current in the circuit is a constant.

laws of motion, Netwon's. See *motion, Newton's laws of.*

laws of photoelectric emission. See *photoelectric emission, laws of.*

laws of thermodynamics. See *thermodynamics, laws of.*

lepton. A subatomic particle with a small rest mass, e.g., the electron.

light. Radiant energy which an observer can see.

light, infrared. Electromagnetic waves longer than visible light but shorter than radio waves.

light, monochromatic. Light consisting of only one color.

light, polarized. Light in which vibrations occur in a single plane perpendicular to the ray.

light, polychromatic. Light composed of several colors.

light, ultraviolet. Electromagnetic radiations of shorter wavelength than visible light but longer than X rays.

line of flux. A line so drawn that a tangent to it at any point indicates the direction of the magnetic field.

line of force. See *force, line of.*

line spectrum. A spectrum consisting of monochromatic slit images having wavelengths characteristic of the atoms present in the source.

linear accelerator. A device for accelerating particles in a straight line through many stages of small potential difference.

liquefaction. The production of a liquid from matter in another physical state.

liquid. The phase of matter in which the molecules move over each other easily; it has definite volume, but takes the shape of its container.

liter. A unit of capacity in the metric system; the volume equal to one cubic decimeter.

longitudinal wave. A wave in which the vibrations are parallel to the direction of propagation of the wave.

loop. A midpoint of a vibrating segment of a standing wave.

loudness. The sensation which depends principally on the intensity of sound waves reaching the ear.

lumen. The unit of luminous flux; the luminous flux on a unit surface all points of which are unit distance from a point source of one candle.

luminous. Visible because of the light emitted by its oscillating particles.

luminous flux. The part of the total energy radiated per unit of time from a luminous source which is capable of producing the sensation of sight.

magnetic field. A region in which a magnetic force can be detected.

magnetic flux. Lines of flux through a region of a magnetic field, considered collectively.

magnetic flux density. The magnetic flux through a unit area normal to the magnetic field.

magnetic force. See *force, magnetic.*

magnetosphere. A region of the upper atmosphere in which the motion of charged particles is governed primarily by the magnetic field of the earth.

magnification. The ratio of the image distance to the object distance; the ratio of the image size to the object size.

malleability. The property of a metal that enables it to be hammered or rolled into sheets.

mass. A measure of the quantity of matter.

mass, relativistic. The mass of an object in motion with respect to the observer.

mass, rest. The mass of an object at rest with respect to the observer.

mass defect, nuclear. The arithmetic difference between the mass of a nucleus and the larger sum of its uncombined constituent particles.

mass density. Mass per unit volume of a substance.

mass number. (1) The sum of the number of protons and neutrons in the nucleus of an atom. (2) The integer nearest to the atomic mass.

mass spectrograph. Instrument used to determine the mass of ionized particles.

mass unit, atomic. See *atomic mass unit.*

matter. Anything that has the properties of mass and inertia.

mechanical equivalent of heat. See *heat, mechanical equivalent of.*

mechanical wave. A wave that originates in the displacement of a portion of an elastic medium from its normal position, causing it to oscillate about an equilibrium position.

medium. Any region through which a wave disturbance propagates. Mechanical waves require a matter medium. Electromagnetic waves propagate through a vacuum and various matter media.

mega-. Metric system prefix, 10^6.

melting. The change of phase from a solid to a liquid.

melting point. The temperature at which a solid changes to a liquid.

meniscus. The crescent-shaped surface of a liquid column.

meson. A subatomic particle with a rest mass intermediate between that of a lepton and a baryon.

metallic bonding. Bonding between atoms produced by a "gas" of freely moving electrons.

meter. A unit of length in the metric system: equivalent to 1,650,763.73 wavelengths of the orange-red light emitted by krypton-86.

mho. The unit of conductance; the reciprocal of the ohm.

micro-. Metric system prefix, 10^{-6}.

micron. A metric unit of length; 10^{-6} meter.

milli-. Metric system prefix, 10^{-3}.

MKS system. The metric system of measurement using the meter, kilogram, and second as basic units.

moderator. A material which slows neutrons.

molecule. The smallest particle of an element or compound capable of stable independent existence.

momentum. The product of the mass and velocity of a moving body.

momentum, angular. For a rigid body rotating about a fixed axis, the product of the rotational inertia of the body and its angular velocity.

monochromatic light. See *light, monochromatic.*

motion. Change of position of an object in relation to objects that are considered to be stationary.

motion, circular. Motion of a body along a circular path.

motion, curvilinear. Motion of a body along a curved path.

motion, Newton's first law of. If there is no net force acting on a body, it will continue in its state of rest, or will continue moving along a straight line with uniform velocity.

motion, Newton's second law of. The acceleration of a body is directly proportional to the net force exerted on the body, is inversely proportional to the mass of the body, and is in the same direction as the force.

motion, Newton's third law of. Whenever one body exerts a force on another, the second body exerts on the first a force of equal magnitude in the opposite direction.

motion, periodic. Any motion that repeats itself at regular intervals of time.

motion, rotary. Motion of a body about an axis.

motion, simple harmonic. Motion in which the force exerted on the particle and the resulting acceleration are directly proportional to the displacement from the equilibrium position, and in which the force and acceleration are directed toward the equilibrium position.

musical tone. Sound produced by regular vibrations in matter and which is pleasant to the listener.

mutual inductance. See *inductance, mutual.*

nano-. Metric system prefix, 10^{-9}.

neutral weak current. A nuclear reaction in which leptons collide without a change in the charges of the colliding particles.

neutron. A neutral subatomic particle having a mass of 1.674943×10^{-27} kg.

newton. The unit of force in the MKS system; the force required to accelerate one kilogram of mass at the rate of one meter per second each second.

Newton's law of universal gravitation. See *universal gravitation, Newton's law of.*

Newton's laws of motion. See *motion, Newton's laws of.*

node. A point of no disturbance of a standing wave.

noise. Sound produced by irregular vibrations in matter and which is unpleasant to the listener.

normal. A line drawn perpendicular to a line or surface.

notation, exponential. See *exponential notation.*

N-type germanium. "Electron rich" germanium consisting of equal numbers of free electrons and bound positive charges so that the net charge is zero.

nuclear change. A change in the identity of atomic nuclei.

nuclear force. See *force, nuclear.*

nuclear reactor. A device in which the controlled fission of certain substances is used to produce new substances and energy.

nucleon. A proton or neutron in the nucleus of an atom.

nucleus. The positively charged dense central part of an atom.

nuclide. An atom of a particular mass and of a particular element.

octave. The interval between a given musical tone and one with double or half the frequency.

ohm. The unit of electric resistance in the MKS system, one volt per ampere.

Ohm's law. See *law, Ohm's.*

optical center. The point in a thin lens through which the secondary axes pass.

optical density. A property of a transparent material which is a measure of the speed of light through it.

orbital. The probability pattern of position of an electron about the nucleus of an atom.

order of magnitude. A numerical approximation to the nearest power of ten.

ordinate. The value corresponding to the vertical distance of a point on a graph from the X axis. The Y coordinate.

oscilloscope. A cathode-ray tube with associated electronic circuits which enable external voltages to deflect the electron beam of the cathode-ray tube simultaneously along both horizontal and vertical axes.

parallel circuit. An electric circuit in which two or more components are connected across two common points in the circuit so as to provide separate conducting paths for the current.

parallel forces. Forces acting along parallel lines.

paramagnetism. The property of a substance by which it is feebly attracted by a strong magnet.

parity, law of. The principle that for every process in nature there is a mirror-image process which is indistinguishable from the original process.

pendulum. A body suspended so that it can swing back and forth about an axis.

pentode. Electronic tube having five elements: suppressor grid; control grid; screen grid; plate; cathode.

penumbra. The partly illuminated part of a shadow.

period. (1) The time for one complete cycle, vibration, revolution, or oscillation. (2) The time required for a single wavelength to pass a given point.

periodic motion. See *motion, periodic.*

permeability. The property of a material by which it changes the flux density in a magnetic field from the value in air.

phase. (1) A condition of matter. (2) In any periodic phenomenon, a number which describes a specific stage within each oscillation. (3) The angular relationship between current and voltage in an a-c circuit. (4) The number of separate voltage waves in a commercial a-c supply.

phase angle. (1) Of any periodic function, the angle obtained by multiplying the phase by 360 if the angle is to be expressed in degrees, or by 2π if in radians. (2) The angle between the voltage and current vectors.

photoelastic. Pertaining to certain materials that become double refracting when strained.

photoelectric effect. The emission of electrons by a substance when illuminated by electromagnetic radiation of sufficiently short wavelength.

photoelectric effect, inverse. The emission of photons of radiation due to the bombardment of a material with high-speed electrons.

photoelectric emission, first law of. The rate of emission of photoelectrons is directly proportional to the intensity of the incident light.

photoelectric emission, second law of. The kinetic energy of photoelectrons is independent of the intensity of the incident light.

photoelectric emission, third law of. Within the region of effective frequencies, the maximum kinetic energy of photoelectrons varies directly with the difference between the frequency of the incident light and the cut-off frequency.

photoelectrons. Electrons emitted from a light-sensitive material when it is illuminated with light of sufficiently short wavelength.

photometer. An instrument used for comparing the intensity of a light source with that of a standard source.

photometry. The quantitative measurement of visible radiation from light sources.

photon. A quantum of light energy.

physical change. A change in which the composition and identifying properties of a substance remain unchanged.

pico-. Metric system prefix, 10^{-12}.

piezoelectric effect. The property of certain natural and synthetic crystals to develop a potential difference between opposite surfaces when subjected to a mechanical stress, and conversely.

pitch. (1) The distance between the threads of a screw. (2) The identification of a certain sound with a definite tone; depends on the frequency which the ear receives.

pivot point. The point from which the lengths of all torque arms are measured.

Planck's constant. A fundamental constant in nature that determines what values are allowed for physical quantities in quantum mechanics; $h = 6.63 \times 10^{-34}$ j sec.

plate. The anode of an electronic tube.

***P-N* junction.** The plane at which a *P*-type semiconductor crystal joins an *N*-type semiconductor crystal.

polarization (cell). The formation of a gas at the anode of a primary cell.

polarized light. See *light, polarized.*

polarizing angle. A particular angle of incidence at which polarization of reflected light is complete.

polychromatic light. See *light, polychromatic.*

positive rays. Rays coming through holes in

a cathode on the side opposite the anode in a discharge tube; positively charged ions.

potential difference. The work done per unit charge as a charge is moved between two points in an electric field.

potential energy. See *energy, potential.*

potential gradient. The change in potential per unit distance.

power. The time rate of doing work.

power, apparent. The product of the effective values of alternating voltage and current.

power factor. The cosine of the phase angle between current and voltage in an a-c circuit.

precession. The motion that results from the application of a torque that tends to displace the axis of rotation of a rotating object.

precision. Agreement among several measurements made in the same way; expressed in terms of deviation.

pressure. Force per unit area.

pressure, critical. The pressure needed to liquefy a gas at its critical temperature.

pressure, equilibrium vapor. The pressure exerted by vapor molecules in equilibrium with liquid.

pressure, standard. The pressure exerted by exactly 760 mm of mercury at 0° C under standard gravitational acceleration *g*.

primary. A transformer winding that carries current and normally induces a current in one or more secondary windings.

primary cell. An electrochemical cell in which the reacting materials must be replaced after a given amount of energy has been supplied to the external circuit.

primary colors. Colors in terms of which all other colors may be described, or from which all other colors may be evolved by mixtures.

primary pigments. The complements of the primary colors.

principal axis. (1) A line drawn through the center of curvature and the vertex of a curved mirror. (2) A line drawn through the center of curvature and the optical center of a lens.

principal focus. See *focus, principal.*

principle. See *law.*

property. A measurable aspect of matter, e.g., mass and inertia.

proton. A positively charged subatomic particle, having a mass of $1.6726485 \times 10^{-27}$ kg.

P-type germanium. "Hole-rich" germanium consisting of equal numbers of free positive holes and bound negative charges so that the net charge is zero.

pulse. A single nonrepeated disturbance.

quality. The property of sound waves which depends on the number of harmonics and their prominence.

quantum. An elemental unit of energy; a photon of energy *hf*.

quantum mechanics. The branch of physics that deals with the behavior of particles whose specific properties are given by quantum numbers.

quantum number. One of a set of notations used to characterize a discrete value that a quantized variable is allowed to assume.

quantum theory. See *theory, quantum.*

quark. A hypothetical subatomic particle of which all other subatomic particles are composed.

radian. A unit of angular measurement; that angle which, when placed with its vertex at the center of a circle, subtends on the circumference an arc equal in length to the radius of the circle; 57.3° approximately.

radio waves. Also called Hertzian waves. Electromagnetic radiations produced by rapid reverses of current in a conductor.

radioactivity. The spontaneous, uncontrollable decay of an atomic nucleus with the emission of particles and photons.

radioisotope. An isotope of an element that is radioactive.

rarefaction. The region of a longitudinal wave in which the vibrating particles are farther apart than their equilibrium distance.

ray, light. A directed line showing the direction of propagation of light.

ray, gamma (γ). High energy photon emitted from the nucleus of a radioactive atom.

reactance. The nonresistive opposition to current in an a-c circuit.

reactance, capacitive. Reactance in an a-c circuit, due to capacitance, which produces a lagging voltage.

reactance, inductive. Reactance in an a-c circuit, due to inductance, which produces a lagging current.

reaction motor. A heat engine whose acceleration is produced by the thrust of exhaust gases.

real image. See *image, real*.

rectifier. A device for changing alternating current to direct current.

rectilinear propagation. Traveling in a straight line.

reflectance. The ratio of the light reflected from a surface to the light falling on it, expressed in percentage.

reflection. The return of a wave from the boundary of a medium.

reflection, angle of. The angle between the refracted ray and the normal drawn to the point of incidence.

reflection, irregular. Scattering. Reflection in many different directions from an irregular surface.

reflection, regular. Reflection from a polished surface in which scattering effects are negligible.

reflection, total. The reflection of light at the boundary of two transparent media when the angle of incidence exceeds the critical angle.

refraction. The bending of a wave disturbance as it passes obliquely from one medium into another in which the disturbance has a different velocity.

refraction, angle of. The angle between the refracted ray and the normal drawn to the point of refraction.

refraction, double. The separation of a beam of unpolarized light into two refracted plane-polarized beams by certain crystals such as quartz and calcite.

refraction, index of. The ratio of the speed of light in a vacuum to its speed in a given substance.

regelation. The melting of a substance under pressure and the refreezing after the pressure is released.

residual magnetism. Magnetism retained in magnet after the magnetizing field has been removed.

resistance. The ratio of the potential difference across a conductor to the magnitude of current in it.

resistance, dynamic plate. A vacuum tube constant; the ratio of a small change in plate voltage to the small change in plate current when the grid voltage remains constant.

resistivity. A proportionality constant that relates the length and cross-sectional area of a given electric conductor to its resistance, at a given temperature.

resolution of forces. The resolving of a single force into component forces acting in given directions on the same point.

resonance. (1) The inducing of vibrations of a natural rate by a vibrating source having the same frequency. (2) The condition in an a-c circuit in which the inductive reactance and capacitive reactance are equal.

resonance, series. A condition in which the impedance of a series circuit containing resistance, inductance, and capacitance is equal to the resistance of the circuit, and the voltage across the circuit is in phase with the current.

resultant. A vector representing the geometric sum of several components.

resultant force. See *force, resultant.*

rheostat. A variable resistance.

roentgen. A unit of measurement of exposure to radioactivity; the amount of gamma radiation that will produce 1.61×10^{12} pairs of ions when absorbed in one gram of air.

root-mean-square (rms) current. The effective value of an alternating current; the square root of the mean of the instantaneous values squared.

rotary motion. See *motion, rotary.*

rotational inertia. See *inertia, rotational.*

scalar quantity. A quantity that is completely specified by a numeral and a unit. It has magnitude only.

scintillation counter. A device that counts the impacts of charged subatomic particles on a fluorescent screen by means of a photomultiplier tube.

second. A unit of time; equivalent to 9,192, 631,770 vibrations of cesium-133.

secondary. A transformer output winding in which the current is due to inductive coupling with another winding called the primary.

secondary axis. Any line other than the principal axis drawn through the center of curvature of a mirror or the optical center of a lens.

secondary emission. Emission of electrons as a result of the bombardment of an electrode by high velocity electrons.

selectivity. The property of a tuned circuit which discriminates between signal voltages of different frequencies.

self-inductance. See *inductance, self.*

series circuit. An electric circuit in which the components are arranged to provide a single conducting path for current.

series resonance. See *resonance, series.*

short circuit. An electric circuit through a negligible resistance which usually shunts a normal load and overloads the circuit.

significant figures. Those digits in a number that are known with certainty plus the first digit that is uncertain.

simple harmonic motion. See *motion, simple harmonic.*

solar spectrum. The band of colors produced when sunlight is dispersed by a prism.

solenoid. A long helically wound coil of insulated wire.

solid. The phase of matter in which the molecules are held in a relatively fixed pattern; it has definite volume and definite shape.

solid state detector. A device used to detect the passage of charged subatomic particles by their crystal distorting or ionizing effects on a nonconducting or semiconducting solid.

solidification. The change of phase from a liquid to a solid.

sonometer. A device, consisting of two or more wires or strings stretched over a sounding board, used for testing the frequency of strings and for showing how they vibrate.

sound. The series of disturbances in matter to which the human ear is sensitive. Also similar disturbances in matter above and below the normal range of human hearing.

space charge. The negative charge in the interelectrode space between the cathode and plate of a vacuum tube.

spark chamber. A device used to detect the passage of charged subatomic particles by the light flashes they trigger.

specific heat. See *heat, specific.*

spectroscope. Optical instrument used for the study of spectra.

speed. Time rate of motion.

spherical aberration. The failure of parallel rays to meet at a single point after reflection or refraction on a spherical surface.

spinthariscope. A device used to detect subatomic particles by the light flashes they produce on a zinc sulfide screen.

standard pressure. See *pressure, standard.*

standard temperature. See *temperature, standard.*

standing wave. The resultant of two wave trains of the same wavelength, frequency, and amplitude traveling in opposite directions through the same medium.

static electricity. Electricity at rest.

steam point. The temperature of steam from pure water boiling at standard atmospheric pressure.

steradian. The ratio of the intercepted surface area of a sphere to the square of the radius. A unit of solid angle.

storage cell. An electrochemical cell in which the reacting materials are renewed by the use of a reverse current from an external source.

strain. The relative amount of distortion produced in a body under stress.

strange particle. A subatomic particle that is produced in pairs and has a relatively long half-life, e.g., the mu meson.

stress. The distorting force per unit area.

strong nuclear interaction. A nuclear reaction in which a meson acts as the carrier of the nuclear force between two baryons.

sublimation. The transformation of a solid directly to a gas followed by condensation directly to the solid phase.

superconductivity. The condition of zero resistivity below the transition temperature of a substance.

supercooling. The process of cooling a substance below its normal phase-change point without a change of phase.

superposition. Combining the displacements of two or more waves vectorially to produce a resultant displacement.

surface tension. The tendency of a liquid surface to contract; the measure of this tendency in newtons per meter.

symmetry, principle of. The concept that the distribution of particles and anti-particles in the universe is a completely random one.

sympathetic vibration. See *resonance.*

synchrotron. A particle accelerator in which the oscillating frequency varies.

technology. Applied science.

temperature. The physical quantity that is proportional to the average kinetic energy of translation of particles in matter.

temperature, critical. The temperature to which a gas must be cooled before it can be liquefied by pressure.

temperature, standard. $0°$ C; $273.15°$ K.

temporary magnet. A magnet produced by induction.

tensile strength. The force required to break a rod or wire of unit cross-sectional area.

tera-. Metric system prefix, 10^{12}.

theory. A plausible explanation for observed phenomena in terms of a simple model which has familiar properties.

theory, kinetic. A theory which assumes that the molecules of matter are in constant motion and that collisions between molecules are perfectly elastic.

theory, quantum. A unifying theory based on the concept of the subdivision of radiant energy into discrete quanta (photons) and applied in the studies of structure at the atomic and molecular levels.

theory, Young-Helmholtz color vision. The theory that the retina of the eye is provided with three sets of receptors, each of which is sensitive to one of the three primary colors.

thermal energy. See *energy, thermal.*

thermionic emission. The liberation of electrons from the surface of a hot body.

thermocouple. An electric circuit composed of two dissimilar metals whose junctions are maintained at different temperatures.

thermodynamics. Study of quantitative relationships between heat and other forms of energy.

thermodynamics, first law of. When heat is converted to another form of energy, or when other forms of energy are converted into heat, there is no loss of energy.

thermodynamics, second law of. It is impossible for an engine to transfer heat from one body to another at a higher temperature unless work is done on the engine.

thermoelectric effect. The production of an electron current in a closed circuit consisting of two dissimilar metals as a result of the emf developed when the two junctions are maintained at different temperatures.

threshold of hearing. The intensity of the faintest sound audible to the average human ear, 10^{-16} w/cm² at 10^3 hz.

threshold of pain. For audible frequencies of sound, an intensity level above which pain results in the average human ear.

torque. Product of a force and the effective length of its torque arm.

total reflection. See *reflection, total.*

transconductance. A vacuum tube constant equal to the ratio of a small change in plate current to the small change in grid voltage producing it, when plate voltage is constant.

transducer. Any device actuated by power from one system and supplying power to another system.

transformer. A device for changing an alternating voltage from one potential to another.

transistor. A semiconductor device used as a substitute for vacuum tubes in electronic applications.

translucent. Transmitting light waves but diffusing them so that objects cannot be distinguished.

transuranium elements. Elements with atomic number greater than 92.

transverse wave. A wave in which the vibrations are at right angles to the direction of propagation of the wave.

triode. Vacuum tube consisting of a plate, grid, and cathode.

triple point. The single condition of temperature and pressure at which the solid, liquid, and vapor phases of a substance can coexist in stable equilibrium.

trough. A region of downward displacement in a transverse wave.

tuning fork. A metal two-prong fork which produces a sound of a definite pitch.

ultrasonic range. Vibrations in matter above 20,000 vibrations/second.

ultraviolet light. See *light, ultraviolet.*

umbra. The part of a shadow from which all light rays are excluded.

uncertainty principle. It is impossible simultaneously to determine exactly both the position of an object and its momentum.

unit magnetic pole. One which repels an exactly similar pole placed one centimeter away with a force of one dyne.

universal gravitation, Newton's law of. The force of attraction between two objects is directly proportional to the product of their masses and inversely proportional to the square of the distance between their centers of gravity.

Van de Graaff generator. A particle accelerator that transfers a charge from an electron source to an insulated sphere by means of a moving belt composed of an insulating material.

vapor. The gaseous phase of a substance which exists as a liquid or solid under normal conditions.

vaporization. The change in phase from a liquid to a gas.

vaporization, heat of. The heat required per unit mass to change a substance from liquid to vapor at constant temperature and pressure.

vector. An arrow whose length indicates the magnitude of a quantity and whose direction indicates the direction of this quantity.

vector quantity. A quantity that is completely specified by a numeral, a unit, and a direction. It has both magnitude and direction.

velocity. Speed in a particular direction.

velocity, angular. The rate of angular displacement.

vertex. The center of a curved mirror.

virtual image. See *image, virtual.*

viscosity. The internal friction of a fluid.

volt. The MKS unit of potential difference; the potential difference between two points in an electric field such that one joule of work moves a charge of one coulomb between these points.

volt, electron. The energy required to move an electron between two points which have a potential difference of one volt.

voltage sensitivity. Voltage per unit scale division of an electric instrument.

voltaic cell. A device which changes chemical into electric energy by the action of two dissimilar metals immersed in an electrolyte.

voltmeter. An instrument used to measure the difference of potential between two points in an electric circuit.

watt. The MKS unit of power; one joule per second.

wave mechanics. An extension of the quantum theory whereby elementary particles are endowed with wave properties and the structure of matter is interpreted on the basis of these properties.

wavelength. In a periodic wave, the distance between consecutive points of corresponding phase.

weak force. See *force, weak.*

weak nuclear interactions. A nuclear reaction in which leptons are emitted.

weber. The unit of magnetic flux in the MKS system.

weight. The measure of the gravitational force acting on a substance.

weight, atomic. The weighted average of the atomic masses of isotopes based on their relative abundance.

Wheatstone bridge. Instrument used for the measurement of electric resistance.

work. The product of a displacement and the force in the direction of the displacement.

work function. The minimum energy required to remove an electron from the surface of a material and send it into field-free space.

X rays. Invisible electromagnetic radiations of great penetrating power.

Young-Helmholtz color vision theory. See *theory, Young-Helmholtz color vision.*

Young's modulus. (For a rod or wire.) The ratio of the tensile stress to the associated linear strain.

Zeeman effect. The splitting of atomic energy levels into two or more sublevels by means of a magnetic field as seen in spectral lines under these conditions.

Index